THE IRVING YOUNGER COLLECTION

Cover design by ABA Publishing.

Printed in the United States of America.

14 13 12 11 10 5 4 3 2

Library of Congress Cataloging-in-Publication Data

Younger, Irving.
The Irving Younger collection : wisdom and wit from the master of trial advocacy / Stephen D. Easton, Editor.
p. cm.
Includes index.
ISBN 978-1-60442-600-7
1. Law—United States. 2. Trial practice—United States. 3. Evidence (Law)—United States. I. Easton, Stephen D., 1958– II. Title.
KF213.Y68E17 2010
347.73'7—dc22
2010011167

Discounts are available for books ordered in bulk. Special consideration is given to state bars, CLE programs, and other bar-related organizations. Inquire at Book Publishing ABA Publishing, American Bar Association, 321 North Clark Street, Chicago, Illinois 60654-7598.

www.ababooks.org

THE IRVING YOUNGER COLLECTION

WISDOM & WIT FROM THE MASTER OF TRIAL ADVOCACY

AMERICAN BAR ASSOCIATION
Section of Litigation

The Irving Younger Collection, *Wisdom & Wit from the Master of Trial Advocacy,* consists of literal transcripts from audio recordings of ten of Younger's timeless, classic lectures on the art of advocacy and law.

The ABA has partnered with the organization that originally sponsored those lectures, The Professional Education Group, to make them available in this new format.

Video DVDs and Audio CDs of Younger's original lectures (with recent updates by Dean Stephen D. Easton) remain tremendously popular and are available exclusively from The Professional Education Group, www.proedgroup.com, 800.229.CLE1 (2531), 12401 Minnetonka Boulevard, Minnetonka MN 55305-3994.

The Professional Education Group
Ignite the Passion

With Special Appreciation to Professor Judith T. Younger

The Publisher and Editors extend their gratitude and deep appreciation to Professor Judith T. Younger, University of Minnesota Law School, Minneapolis, MN, for her tireless and devoted assistance in the publication of this collection of her husband's extraordinary work.

Professor Younger is a highly regarded professor and authority in her own right, and has been an invaluable resource in the publication of this collection.

Contents

PAGE

Foreword ix
Preface xiii

PART I

Chapter 1. Discovery: Practice and Procedure 3

Chapter 2. Expert Witnesses 95

Chapter 3. Scientific Evidence 159

Chapter 4. Hearsay 231

Chapter 5. Jury Selection 311

Chapter 6. Credibility and Cross-Examination 395

PART II

Chapter 7. *Ulysses* in Court 477

Chapter 8. The Trial of Alger Hiss 511

Chapter 9. What Happened in Erie? A Probing Examination of *Erie v. Tompkins* 579

Chapter 10. In Praise of Simplicity 609

Curriculum Vitae 617
Index 627

Foreword

Irving Younger was famous. Indeed, he was the closest thing to a rock star our profession has ever seen. We lawyers flocked to his seminars and watched his videotapes (now DVDs and CDs) as avid fans, hungry for the entertaining, enlightening wisdom he was sure to dispense. Despite his enormous celebrity and erudition, though, Irving had the ability to appeal to the interests and sensibilities of ordinary lawyers who tried cases. He was one of us, just another hard-working trial lawyer trying to do his best. We accepted him in that role, and in that role he touched our lives in a rich and meaningful way. We felt like colleagues; we knew him.

Many did know him, literally. Tens of thousands of trial lawyers "met" him at his trial seminars. Thousands more were students in his law school classes. All of these saw him perform—and his performances were eloquent, exquisitely crafted, memorable in every way. Many of those who saw him also talked with him, one-on-one, about their lives and trials, trading stories. Irving loved a good story, especially a trial story, whether he was telling it or listening to it.

Many more of us, especially those who came to the practice after Irving's untimely death, know him only via The Professional Education Group's recordings of his popular and timeless seminars. Even now, he reaches out from the screen and somehow tells us that we are special because we are trial lawyers.

Irving loved us. He loved life, as well. He had an amazing appetite for it all—art, theater, sports, history, science, mathematics, music, and, of course, law. His enthusiasm filled his life and lectures. We watched him and listened to him, and his excitement became our own.

With the exception of his family, the one thing that interested him above all others was The Law. Not just the law . . . Lawyers. And not just any lawyers. Trial Lawyers—those who had the courage to walk into court to try cases to juries. Irving Younger believed, as most of us in the trial business do, that *"there is no enterprise a human being can engage in that is more complicated than trying a case"* to a jury. He relished the challenge of attempting to manage all of the unmanageable variables trial lawyers face in the courtroom, and he loved those willing to take on that challenge. Irving loved the theater, but his first love was the theater of the courtroom. He built his career around the courtroom and teaching us lawyers to be effective players in the dramas that played out in it.

I had the good fortune to see him once in a courtroom, but I did not have the chance to attend one of his live seminars. Still, he is my partner to this day. Professor Judith T. Younger and The Professional Education Group have granted me the honor of presenting professional development seminars "with" Professor Irving Younger. Although Irving appears at these seminars via video, while I am there in the flesh, we are partners in the continuing endeavor of educating trial lawyers about the complex tools of our trade.

I am humbled by this privilege, and I am grateful it came my way. There is special pleasure in clicking a key on my computer to start a video of a classic Irving Younger clip, thinking "they are going to love this," then watching the faces of fellow trial lawyers broaden into smiles and often laughter as Professor Younger unleashes one of his "commandments" of trial attorney wisdom.

All of us who have followed in the considerable wake of Irving Younger's teaching pale in comparison to the master. Younger was captivating packed audiences of hundreds of trial attorneys before anyone even invented the term "continuing legal education." Irving Younger was the contemporary father of the legal profession's professional development movement. He was the pioneer who first saw the value of gathering practicing lawyers together to educate us about the real world skills we needed to represent our clients successfully. He was more than just a pioneer. He was also a master of the art form. As Bill Barton of Newport, Oregon, also a legend of the trial bar and the continuing legal education circuit, likes to put it, *"There will never again be a lawyer who can master the platform like Irving did."*

As a fan of theater, movies, and opera, Irving Younger knew the importance of the well-turned phrase, the value of the well-timed pause, and the suspense of a story well told. He used all of them to hold his audiences of trial lawyers in the palm of his hand. As one who has seen his videos and taught beside him at seminars across the country, I can report that he still does.

Irving Younger never told a story without a reason. He used stories as vehicles to teach us how to be effective in court, to help drive home a point. Like other master teachers, Professor Younger knew that a story well told made a lesson memorable.

This book has been compiled by the ABA Section of Litigation from The Professional Education Group's recordings of Professor Irving Younger's classic continuing legal education programs. In these pages, we are entertained, but also taught. No one taught Irving Younger. He learned in the school of hard knocks and translated his experiences there into his classic lectures. In them, Younger brilliantly passes his wisdom to others.

Those who have never heard of Irving Younger, or whose knowledge of him is only slight and have been educated in the ways of the courtroom by others, will find some of this book familiar. As many younger attorneys have told me at The Professional Education Group seminars where Professor Younger and I teach together, some of Younger's suggestions have been taught to them without attribution. Thus, they did not know they came originally from Younger. As Molière's "bourgeois gentleman" learned to his delight, these young lawyers have been speaking Irving Younger's prose without realizing it.

These lawyers do not realize either that their teachers are themselves disciples of Irving Younger. It was Younger who invented and articulated the Ten Commandments of Cross-Examination that became legend. It was Younger who found a way to explain the labyrinth of hearsay so that we came to understand and internalize it. It was Younger who found ways to make the concepts of judicial notice and even the

Best Evidence Rule (topics most lawyers would rather avoid) valuable tools in our courtroom tool belts. All of these lessons, and many, many others, are contained in this timeless anthology.

In this new collection, the ABA Section on Litigation provides yet another means for lawyers to learn directly from the incomparable Irving Younger. That alone would be enough to justify its long overdue publication. There is another benefit, however. We who knew Irving when he was alive know very well that the world of trials will never be the same without him. This book will help us now that our hair has gone gray (or left us entirely). It will reinforce the lessons we learned from Younger long ago. We were younger lawyers then. This book reminds us that we are still Younger lawyers now. That is a wonderful thing!

STEPHEN D. EASTON

* * *

STEPHEN EASTON is the Dean at the University of Wyoming College of Law. He is a former award-winning Professor at the University of Missouri School of Law. A graduate of Stanford Law School, he has clerked for the Ninth Circuit, worked with a civil litigation firm before and after serving as a United States Attorney, and written extensively on the art of the courtroom. In each capacity after clerking, he has tried cases, in both the civil and criminal arenas. For more than a decade, he has also been a principal professional development lecturer throughout the United States and Canada for The Professional Education Group, "team-teaching" CLE programs with the assistance (via video) of Professor Irving Younger.

Preface

It is difficult to believe Irving Younger has been gone twenty years. He was too immediate to be gone, and certainly not so long.

Spending time with Irving was a delight. It was verbal champagne. Ideas bubbled, and popped. Some floated again, or were replaced by better. A chat became a free-association symphony.

Some of the effervescence must have come from his protean nature. He'd been valedictorian of New York City's leading science high school, starting college as a pre-med; thereafter it was all arts, theater, music, and English. With that background, it had to be Law—the only field encompassing the full range of his interest.

Irving's law was not a mere academic or society-regulating exercise. It was one of the lively arts. Like music, or painting, or theater, or dance, it enlightened our humanity. The law was a theme, embodying the things making us human and life worth living.

Oh, I suspect, like many of us, he'd struggled to find romance in the IRS code, or a traffic fine table. But then, he'd think about how society regulated behaviors using tax incentives, or how a family might have to hurry to get to a favorite vacation site. Under those conditions, even the most mundane rules might enlighten the human spirit.

I first saw him in the early 1970s. The Federal Rules of Evidence were newly adopted and Irving came to Chicago to teach them. I'd heard of a person who could make evidence—*evidence!*—fun and interesting. One who could do that could certainly spin straw into gold.

The lectures (two of them, two and a half hours apiece) flew by. This was law as I'd never learned it, heard it, or seen it. The Rules were there, but funny, enlightening, and stunningly lucid. What in the world had I studied when I took that course? This was evidence as people, how they lived, and how they worked.

Many years later, Irving and his beloved Judith—herself a distinguished law professor and former law school dean—moved to Minnesota. There, I was lucky enough to get to know them, and there I heard him deliver his astounding lectures on "The Trial of Alger Hiss" and "What Happened in *Erie*?"

Irving brought Alger Hiss's times and trial to life, illuminating the Cold War and the 1950's "Red Scare." This was a spy novel, careening from the State Department, to Wisconsin's Joe McCarthy, to Richard Nixon and the "Pumpkin Papers," with a terrifying inevitability. This was no history lesson. It was a tale of real people, under pressure, culminating in a pivotal trial, which would pave the way for Richard Nixon's elections and, ultimately, to Watergate.

In the same way, we all know how every law student chews through *Erie v. Tompkins*. This story, however, is far different from the one we learned in law school. We visit the accident site, agonize with the trial judge, and find that the ultimate appeal hangs as much on the personalities of the lawyer who pursued it and on the Justice who accepted it as it does on the facts. This is a human drama, not simply the most cited case in Supreme Court history.

Irving unfolds the mysteries of hearsay, peopled with gangsters and hucksters and fools and knaves. The Rule is no longer a collection of slogans and exceptions, but a sensible set of principles making logical sense, fit into a human drama.

This book reminds us of Irving Younger's mastery of the courtroom. He knew its techniques and its foibles. But he deeply understood the practice of law is first and foremost a tale of people and those they touch.

These technical lessons and personal tales show us why the law is a subject of value. Irving Younger was timeless, much as Shakespeare and Dickens were timeless. For each, the stories that last illuminate our common humanity and experiences. These stories are enlightening as well as educational. Reading this book, we spend a few hours with a master. It's time well spent.

James M. Rosenbaum
Senior United States District Judge
District of Minnesota
Minneapolis, MN
2010

Part I

Chapter 1

Discovery
Practice and Procedure

DEAN STEVE EASTON: It is my honor to assist The Professional Education Group in bringing Irving Younger's presentations on trial advocacy to a new generation of lawyers. The following chapter covers discovery. In this seminar Professor Younger challenges us to think about why we use certain discovery devices and how to use them effectively. He tells us that we should keep in mind the goal we are attempting to achieve when we use the discovery process. Everything he says in that regard is just as valid today as it was when he recorded this seminar in 1986.

Of course, we've changed some of the discovery rules in the time since 1986 because, quite frankly, we are always changing the discovery rules. So there have been several changes to Rules 26 to 37 of the Federal Rules of Civil Procedure. Also, keep in mind that every time the Federal Rules of Civil Procedure are changed, some of the states adopt some of those changes and some of the states do not adopt those changes. Therefore, if you are litigating a case in state court, you are going to want to make reference to the state discovery rules to determine what the status of those rules is and what your discovery options are.

We will focus on the federal rules, as Professor Younger does. I will not mention in this preview every single change in Rules 26 to 37, i.e., the discovery rules of the Federal Rules of Civil Procedure. But I do want to mention changes in those discovery provisions that Professor Younger mentions in the seminar that you are about to see. We will take them in the order that Professor Younger will mention them.

First, the scope of discovery language in Rule 26(b) was changed so that the rule now says that we are allowed to discover unprivileged matters "relevant to any party's claim or defense." With regard to the timing of discovery issues that Professor Younger discusses—i.e., who gets to do discovery first and whether both parties are allowed to conduct simultaneous discovery—there have been a couple of pretty significant changes. In 1993 the automatic disclosure provisions of Rule 26(a) were added to the Federal Rules of Civil Procedure so that now, as you know if you litigate federal cases, you have an obligation to provide certain information even before your opponent issues a discovery request. Rule 26(d) has also been amended to provide that in most cases there is a moratorium on discovery until the initial automatic disclosure period is complete.

Professor Younger mentions that depositions, while a very valuable discovery device, have the disadvantage of being a very time-consuming discovery device. There has been a change in the Federal Rules that is significant with regard to the consumption of time. Rule 30(d)(1) now provides a time limit of one day of seven hours and, of course, provides that that time limit can be extended by a court order or by a stipulation between the parties.

With regard to expert witnesses, there has been a significant expansion of the discovery beyond that which existed before 1993 with the standard expert witness interrogatory and the response to that interrogatory. After 1993's adoption of the automatic disclosure provisions, we are now required in civil cases to identify individuals who will present expert testimony at trial. Also, under Rule 26(a)(2) those expert witnesses, in most instances, are required to file a report that includes a notation of the data or other information considered by the witness in forming her opinions.

Professor Younger also discusses protective orders. For the current law regarding protective orders, refer to subsections (b)(2) and (c) of Rule 26. With regard to discovery conferences, Rule 26(f) now usually requires the opposing parties to meet to attempt to identify whether this is a case that can be settled and to set a discovery schedule early in the discovery process.

Professor Younger notes that, at the time of his presentation, several courts were adopting limits on the numbers of interrogatories. Now, Rule 33(a) has been amended to provide a standard limit to the number of interrogatories of 25, "including all discreet subparts." That limit applies in the absence of a written stipulation of the parties or a court order to the contrary. The insurance information that Professor Younger suggests that we attempt to acquire through interrogatories is now part of that automatically disclosed information under Rule 26(a)(1)(A). Finally, the option to produce business records in response to an interrogatory is now found in Rule 33(d).

IRVING YOUNGER: Well, the subject, ladies and gentlemen, is discovery. And whenever one talks about discovery, it is important to know the viewpoint of the person doing the talking. And so I'd better begin by telling you what mine is. Now, you're all familiar with the phenomenon of the litigating lawyer. That is the lawyer who undertakes to represent clients in litigation business, but always sublimely confident that no lawsuit handled by that lawyer will ever go to trial. There will be a settlement or some other disposition short of a trial. And for that lawyer, I think it's fair to say, discovery is the objective. Discovery is what the enterprise is all about because that lawyer, at least in my experience and as I have observed the phenomenon, will engage in discovery virtually in a mindless manner, taking depositions of everybody on the landscape simply for the sake of taking those depositions, serving interrogatories, conducting discovery and inspection. Every once in a while, simply for a change of pace, making a motion or two, to the end that ultimately the other side has had enough, throws in the towel, and the case will be settled.

Well, that's the litigating lawyer. More power to him or her, but that's not yours truly. Yours truly, ladies and gentlemen, regards himself as a trial lawyer and for a trial lawyer, the objective is the actual trial of the lawsuit, be it state, federal, civil, criminal, protracted and complicated, or fairly short and relatively simple. The trial is the end and everything else is a means calculated to achieve that end or to make the end occur in a more efficient and aesthetically satisfactory way. From the viewpoint of a trial lawyer then, which I now trust is clear, is my viewpoint, discovery is not something to be engaged in automatically or unthinkingly. Discovery is a means to achieving an objective. And so as with everything else, you first must know your objective and then you can calculate the means to see whether the means is reasonably likely to achieve the objective that you have in mind. Well, there is the viewpoint. Let me leave it at that. I trust it will be reasonably clear, albeit implicit, in everything else that I have to say in the course of the day.

Let's begin with the scope of discovery under the Federal Rules of Civil Procedure and their analogues in the states and essentially that means all of the states. And there's really very little to be said about it, precisely because, unlike what you would gather from simply looking at the language of Rule 26(b)(1) of the Rules of Civil Procedure, the scope of discovery as that language has been construed by the courts is wide open. We all remember from law school, and in this instance, what we were taught in law school is quite true. You may discover anything that would be evidence at the trial or that is likely to lead to evidence, which means that so long as you're pretty good at making arguments and showing the judge how things are connected with other things, anything is discoverable, with exceptions to be sure. Exceptions with respect to the evidentiary privileges, to work product and the like, which we will come to in due course.

But I think from the standpoint of the working lawyer the scope of discovery is an issue not worth thinking about. Discovery is wide open. Anything can be discovered, with exceptional situations, of course, where you've got a kind of immunity from discovery, and beyond that the working lawyer will say to himself or herself, "What is the purpose of discovery?" Granted that you can discover virtually anything that's out there. What is the purpose of discovery? And it seems to me in reflecting on this question, ladies and gentlemen, that there are three big purposes to discovery. Now, obviously, the purpose that will be involved at any particular moment will depend upon the circumstances of the case, what stage of your discovery program you are at, and the like.

But looking at the picture as a whole, you've got three big purposes. And let me identify what they are. First, classically, stated most frequently, the purpose of discovery is to discover, to get information about the case and, most importantly, information that you do not already have, to find out things about this case that are not already known to you. And far be it from me to dispute the proposition that that is one of the purposes of discovery. But in my experience as a trial lawyer, that is one of the less important purposes of discovery. In my experience as a trial lawyer, more important than that purpose is the one I will mention now—a second purpose of discovery. It's not normal to talk about this, but any lawyer who has engaged in civil litigation is aware that this is one of the aims that you seek to accomplish when you indulge in discovery—not to find out what you don't already know, but to find out what the other side already knows so that you are prepared to deal with it when the case is reached for trial.

So first you want to find out about the case, find out what you don't already know. Second, you want to find out what the other side knows. And now, third, you use discovery to prepare for trial, to streamline the case, to marshal the proof, so that when finally you do try the case it goes in smoothly, efficiently, with minimum effort, and with maximum persuasiveness.

And it seems to me that under the general heading of preparing for trial there are three principal goals that you will seek to achieve. First, you will want to pin the other side down to its position. The other side has a position on any one of the issues in the case. The other side's position is not necessarily favorable to you, but you want to be sure that it doesn't change between now and then so that whatever you are presently told their position will be is exactly the position that you will need to attack at the time of trial. Call that pinning down or freezing the other side.

Second, you will engage in discovery so as to preserve testimony, having in mind that people die, leave the jurisdiction, or otherwise become unavailable for testimony at trial. Well, it's now, time present. The trial will take place in time future, months or years away. Let's take the testimony now, in such a form that we can use it at the time of trial.

And, finally, under the general heading of preparing for trial, increasingly important in these days when so much civil litigation will involve large amounts of documentary evidence. As you all know, the manipulation of documents in the courtroom is not intellectually difficult. It does not challenge the rational faculties, but it requires a certain choreography which every trial lawyer fairly quickly masters. But that choreography is very boring to a jury. There is nobody listening to me who does not know the footsteps necessary to bring it about, for example, that a document is received in evidence under the business entries or business records exception to the rule against hearsay. But to lay that particular foundation time and time again in the course of a trial is to drive a jury insane with tedium and generally it is to your disadvantage to drive a jury insane with tedium. You want to keep a jury just as entertained as you possibly can in the course of a trial. Granted, that's difficult in most civil lawsuits, but for heaven sakes, don't make it harder than it has to be. And it's harder than it has to be when you go through this choreography involving documents in front of the jury. Most of it can be finessed and it can be finessed by adept use of discovery. So under the general heading of preparation for trial, in addition to pinning down or freezing the other side, in addition to perpetuating testimony that may otherwise become unavailable when the case is reached for trial, you've got the authentication of documents and the marshaling of the evidence generally to the end that your presentation in front of that jury be as smooth and as entertaining as you can possibly make it.

Now, no matter what the nature of the case, no discovery ought to be indulged in a haphazard or miscellaneous fashion. Just as you try a case in accordance with a plan, so you must conduct discovery in accordance with a plan. And all too many lawyers, in my experience, do not. They conduct discovery with a plan that's nothing more focused than sort of pulling the trigger on a shotgun and hoping that the pellets hit a target out there. To continue the analogy to weapons, I think that discovery ought to be a rifle, not a shotgun, and you take careful aim at your target and you hit that target right in the bull's eye. You can't hit the target in the bull's eye if you don't know what the target is and you won't know what the target is unless you have devised a plan for the conduct of discovery in this case.

In devising that plan, the following factors are to be considered. Now, obviously, I can't tell you what the plan ought to be. There's no recipe that's going to give you the plan of discovery in the next lawsuit for which you become responsible. Everything will depend upon the circumstances of the case and the issues presented. But in working out your plan for discovery, these five factors will play a part.

First, expense. Now, for a very few lawyers that is an unimportant factor. Indeed, it's a factor that may not need to be considered at all.

And that applies to the fortunate few who have clients with bottomless pocketbooks, who are involved in lawsuits where, as the saying goes, the company is on the line. I suppose in those rare cases you don't have to consider expense. One thinks of the statement of the chairman of the board of IBM some years ago when IBM was engaged in all kinds of company-threatening litigation and he announced at the annual meeting of stockholders that the budget for legal affairs this year has been without limit and it has already been exceeded. Well, if you have the good fortune to represent that kind of client in that kind of lawsuit, I guess you needn't consider expense. But for the rest of us, the great unwashed, expense is a factor and an important one. Discovery is always expensive in that it's never free and then within discovery there are the less expensive discovery devices, the more expensive discovery devices and, surely, expense is a factor to be considered.

Second—delay. Meaning for the most part, the delay that is the inevitable consequence of the discovery that you conduct. Now, we all understand that it's possible for the other side to conduct discovery for the illegitimate purpose of frustrating and delaying you. And we'll talk about that at the very end and there are things that you may be able to do to prevent that from happening. Assuming good faith all around, remember that all discovery takes time. And so if you decide to conduct ten depositions, it's going to take at least whatever, 90 days, 120 days, six months to conduct those depositions. And those are 90 days, 120 days, or six months when you're not in line waiting to be tried, when the case cannot be tried because you're still in the discovery phase. That factor of delay may be very important in some cases and, as a matter of fact, it may be that the factor of delay can be turned to your advantage in that if you've got an opponent who is a litigating lawyer, who assumes that in civil litigation what you do is engage in discovery and you keep engaging in discovery until finally the case is settled, maybe the thing to do the instant the pleadings are complete is to say to your opponent, "I'm ready for trial. I don't need a single deposition. I have no interrogatories for you whatsoever. What I want is a trial. I am ready to pick the jury at

2 o'clock this afternoon." Your opponent will be prostrate, absolutely prostrate, because what is now looming before your opponent is the possibility that he or she may have to try a case. He's never done that. He doesn't know how to do it. And it's at that point that you may discover that you suddenly have a settlement on favorable terms offered to you.

Next, and here it gets to be a little bit subtler. But the fact that it's subtle doesn't mean that it should be overlooked. In addition to expense, in addition to delay, remember that just about every single time you conduct discovery, no matter the nature of the discovery you conduct, you may be finding out about the case, but simultaneously you are telling the other side something about your case. You are tipping your hand. To some extent you are showing the cards that you are holding. At a deposition, for example, a deposition on all questions, one out of every two questions will communicate something about your familiarity with the case to the other side. Well, you want to take that into account. Is that a risk that's worth running? There's got to be a way to quantify it, to put a value on it. You put a value on it and you throw it into the balance along with the other factors that we've mentioned.

Next, and this is one that litigating lawyers almost never consider, though it's really a matter of common sense. You've got a purpose in conducting this particular piece of discovery, there's something you want to accomplish in this deposition, there's something you want to accomplish by serving this set of interrogatories. Ask yourself, what is the likelihood of accomplishing that purpose? And if the likelihood of accomplishing that purpose is very low, well, of course, that becomes a very important factor militating against conducting this particular piece of discovery. So what is the likelihood of success, of achieving what it is that you want to achieve with this item of discovery?

I've given you four factors—and now the fifth. And the fifth is one that, as competent and effective counsel for your client, you owe it to your client to think about and, if need be, discuss with the client. Remember that there will be occasions—not always—but there will be occasions when the conduct of discovery will have consequences for the client apart from this lawsuit. What I called in the outline non-litigation consequences. Ask yourself whether there will be any such consequences. If so, what will they be? And discuss them with your client and that becomes a factor to be weighed along with the others, with all of the others. For example, taking discovery may elicit the interest of governmental agencies. It may end up in the newspapers. It may raise the likelihood of a stockholder suit against the corporation. That's what I mean by non-litigation consequences—consequences apart from having an impact upon this particular lawsuit. All of those are factors to be weighed. Let me end where I began. The way in which you weigh them I cannot lay down in general. Obviously, there's no recipe that gives you a pat answer in any particular case.

Let's move along to a subject which is no longer center burner, but if you will forgive the autobiographic note, when I began to learn the business of litigation, the business of trying cases, a fairly long time ago, this was a very controversial subject. It is no longer controversial because the Federal Rules have been amended since then to resolve the problem. But there are many states in which the statute or the rule is in the form in which you would have found it in the Federal Rules 30 some odd years ago and in those states this is a live matter and so let me spend no more than, let's say, five minutes on it.

This is the subject of priority. That is a term lawyers and judges have applied to an issue that does not appear anywhere in the Federal Rules explicitly and it never appeared in the Federal Rules explicitly. This was something invented by lawyers and ultimately approved by judges. The word priority connoted the question "Who goes first with respect to discovery?" And as it came to be construed in the federal cases before the amendment to the Federal Rules of Civil Procedure, the answer to the question "Who goes first?" included the idea that whoever went first continued discovery to a conclusion before the other side could start. So that priority was a very substantial factor in the pretrial maneuvering that's part of every piece of civil litigation. Because if the plaintiff or the defendant had priority, it meant that the plaintiff or the defendant could start his discovery and continue it to a conclusion before the opposing litigant, the defendant or the plaintiff, could start his discovery.

Now it worked this way under the rules before they were amended, the Federal Rules before they were amended. And I talk about it, I repeat, because in many states this will be the practice still, to this very day. The judges engrafted on to the Rules of Civil Procedure a judge-made rule as follows. Priority went to that litigant who first demanded discovery and since typically you demanded discovery by serving a notice of oral deposition, in most cases the rule meant whoever serves the first notice of deposition establishes priority. Observe that the trigger event is not taking the deposition, it is serving a notice of deposition before the other side serves a notice of deposition. So first in time meant first in right.

You will recall, if you're old enough to have practiced in those days, and as a matter of fact, it is still part of the Federal Rules, though it no longer gives you priority, that the rules with respect to depositions and notices of deposition are so devised so as to give a defendant an automatic head start. Remember, a defendant may serve a notice of deposition immediately upon being served with the summons and complaint. Whereas a plaintiff may not serve a notice of deposition for a period of time set forth in the rule unless you get leave of the court and that leave is not very easy to get. The defendant has no requirement of getting leave of the court, the defendant can go at once. So that under the old practice it used to be said that it was malpractice for a lawyer representing the defendant in a piece of civil litigation not to have priority. Because to have priority, all you needed to do was serve the first notice of deposition. You could schedule a deposition for two years away, so long as the notice went out right now. That established your priority and it meant that you could keep at it and keep at it until you were finished and the other side couldn't even get started.

Well, the ways in which tough and imaginative counsel could use priority need not be spread upon the record by me. They're clear, I'm sure, to your imagination. This was an enormous advantage. But remember, it was an advantage that derived from a rule that was invented by judges. There was nothing in the Federal Rules of Civil Procedure that said first in time, first in right. Federal judges said first in time, first in right.

Along about 1960 or '61 this matter came to the attention of the Advisory Committee that keeps continuing oversight on the Federal Rules of Civil Procedure. And then along about the mid- or late-1960s, the Advisory Committee saw to it that the Federal Rules of Civil Procedure were amended in the way that you will read today in Rule 26(d). Now, I'm not going to read it to you, but in summary and paraphrase, this is what it says. There is no rule of priority. Nobody gets to go first in the sense of starting and continuing until you're all complete and only then may the other side begin. Instead, the rule under 26(d) is that either side may go first and you proceed alternately. And if there's a dispute about what that means, the judge will specify two weeks for you, two weeks for you or three weeks for you, three weeks for you—whatever makes sense in the circumstances—so that each side gets to conduct its discovery essentially simultaneously with the discovery conducted by the other side. So under the Federal Rules of Civil Procedure, the concept of priority is no longer important. But, I repeat, in many states it still is and we can move along.

We can move along, ladies and gentlemen, to an aspect of discovery that, in my experience, many lawyers pay no attention to whatsoever. And in ignoring this aspect of discovery, it seems to me that these lawyers do themselves and their clients a disservice because this is an aspect of discovery that is potentially enormously fruitful. It is always fairly inexpensive, requiring only an expenditure on the part of the lawyer of that rarest of commodities, energy, and perhaps a little bit of imagination. And, best of all, you indulge in this kind of discovery without telling the other side. And ex parte or private discovery is, of course, enormously advantageous. This is what I call in the outline informal discovery. And by informal discovery, I mean discovery apart from what is available under the Federal Rules of Civil Procedure. Discovery that you carry out on your own. Now, you may not be able to perpetuate testimony by informal discovery, but it's a wonderful way to find out about the case, absolutely wonderful. Far better than anything you can do under the Federal Rules of Civil Procedure. It's far better than anything you can do using the formal discovery devices.

So let me spend a fair amount of time discussing these informal modes of discovery and if any of this is new to you, if it proves useful to you in your practice, please use it. I will be delighted and chances are you will be that much ahead of your opponent because chances are that your opponent is doing nothing with respect to informal discovery.

To begin with, there is the kind of investigation that a lawyer conducts on his or her own. And if not necessarily with the lawyer out there walking the sidewalks, the investigation is being conducted by investigative types working on behalf of the lawyer. Investigation. And investigation may involve a number of things. First, and I suppose most importantly, it will involve interviewing potential witnesses. Now, that's kind of self-evident. Many of you who are listening or looking will say, well, obviously, you go out and you try to interview potential witnesses. We didn't need to be told that, I grant you. Most lawyers don't need to be told that it's important to interview potential witnesses, but I have found that many lawyers seem to be unaware that there is a technique to the interviewing of potential witnesses. There is a right way to do it and because the right way to do it has much to commend it, I urge you, if you don't already find yourself a master of the right way of interviewing witnesses, to make yourself a master of this technique. Here's how I would state that technique.

First, you've got to move fast. Immediately after the occurrence of the event which is probably going to engender the lawsuit, you've got to move fast to talk to potential witnesses. And if you can't move fast enough to talk to everybody, talk to the witnesses in approximately the order of their importance, so that you make sure you reach the important potential witnesses early. Get to them on the first day. Then the next most important witnesses on the next day, et cetera, so that if there's any potential witness you don't get to talk to, it is a potential witness whose importance is fairly low down in the scale. And the reason for that is this and this is just one of the truths of human nature that you've got to be aware of if you're going to try lawsuits. Even though the witness is, in the eyes of the law, a disinterested person, a third person, a mere bystander who has no involvement, no personal involvement in this lawsuit whatsoever, it is in the nature of that form of human nature that manifests itself among Americans to want to root for one side or another.

Every one of us has run into that in our own lives. You know, you're off in a strange city and you have business tomorrow morning, but this evening you're free. What are you going to do? Sometimes you go to the movies, sometimes you watch television, sometimes you go to bed early, but sometimes you may go to the ballpark to watch a ball game. And even though the two teams are totally unrelated to the team you normally root for, you will recall that, as you sit there watching the game, you choose one side or the other and you root for that team. It just adds to the enjoyment with which you watch the athletic contest. It's part of what I've said is human nature as it manifests itself in Americans.

You want the witnesses to root for your side because, even though I do not for one moment suggest that witnesses deliberately alter their testimony to help one side or the other, there's so much that's beneath the level of consciousness that will work in your favor if the witness is rooting for you. And you know for whom the witness will root? The witness will root for the side that first talks to him or her because the witness has no reason to root for one side or the other, so automatically the witness will come out on the side whose representative first talks to him. And that is why you do your best to speak to potential witnesses early and, if you have to make a choice, talk to the important witnesses. Leave the unimportant ones alone because in talking to the important ones, chances are you enlist their sympathies, they are rooting for you from the beginning.

Next, if you're going to go to the trouble of talking to anyone, get some kind of record of the conversation. Now, the nature of the record will depend upon how you like to do it and who the person is you're talking to. The person may be willing to give you a written statement. Get it. The person may be willing to look over and initial a statement that you write out based upon what the witness has told you. Do it that way. Some people are willing to talk into the microphone of a tape recorder. Do it that way. But make sure that there is a record of what was said. The reasons for that are perfectly obvious. People being what they are and litigation being the high pressure process that it is, people may change their minds about things, their recollections may fail, all kinds of things may go wrong. You want that statement.

Next, do not neglect, when you talk to a potential witness, to ask a question, in essence, as follows: "Do you know of anybody else who knows about this matter?" Use the witness to lead you to other witnesses.

Next—this may prove invaluable to some of you. It has proved invaluable to me from time to time and I'm much in the debt of the lawyer, whose name I cannot remember, who taught it to me when I was a youngster, just starting out. Remembering that you're talking to people who will be witnesses in a civil trial, that trial is going to take place years from now, literally, assuming that the case is going to be tried in any urban jurisdiction these days. The state of the calendars is such that you've got to count on a delay that is measured in years, not months or weeks. That being so, you've got to concern yourself with the problem of the witness who moves. Never mind the witness who dies or who otherwise disappears from off the face of the earth, but the witness who simply moves. How do you track him down? Here's how to track him down. Sometime in the course of your conversation with that witness, ask the witness—of course, you've asked for the witness' address and telephone number, but if the witness has moved that may not help you. Ask the witness for the name, address, and telephone number of somebody close to the witness. If it's a young person with living parents, get the name, address, and phone number of his parents. If it's an older person with children who are living independently, get the name, address, and phone number of the children. And do you see how you use it? If five years from now you need that witness and it turns out that the witness has moved away, you have the name, address, and phone number of someone else whom you can get hold of who will, in all probability, know where the witness now is to be found. Right? So much for interviewing witnesses. Not that we've exhausted that little subject, but we've got so much to talk about, we must move along.

Next, in addition to examining witnesses, remember that many lawsuits, perhaps more than half, involve some particular physical location. I present it to you as an axiom of trial practice. You will never try a case involving a physical location where you have not, yourself, examined the location. Go and look at the intersection where the cars collided. Go and look at the branch bank where something took place that is the subject matter of the lawsuit. Whatever the physical location, go and examine it yourself.

Apart from examining it, I suggest that you do the following. The first couple of times you do it, you feel a little silly, but then you kind of get into the swing of it and you feel kind of professional doing it. First, where there is any question involving distances and angles, measure those distances and angles yourself. Now, you may have a professional investigator do it in addition, but do it yourself to make it part of you so that you understand in way that you can never lose how the dimensions work out and how things are related physically to other things.

Next, consider the possibility of taking photographs. Given the ease of use, the cheapness of Polaroid photography these days, you can always have a Polaroid camera in your briefcase when you go out to look at a scene and do not hesitate to take photographs. But if you are measuring or if you are taking photographs in circumstances where there is any possibility at all that your measurements or your photographs may actually function as evidence when the case is tried, in short, you're not doing this just to educate yourself, but you're out there a day or two after the accident happened and your photographs may be important as demonstrating how the foliage obscured the sidelines at this intersection or something of that kind. You must anticipate that possibility and, if there is that possibility, take someone with you so that if it does become necessary to prove the measurements or the photographs at the time of trial, there is a foundation witness other than yourself. If you have to be the foundation witness, first, there's a chance that it may be improper for you to try the case and that, of course, is a tragedy. And, second, even if it's technically proper for you to try the case, it is awkward to be a witness to however inconsequential a thing as taking measurements or a photograph and then having to be counsel in the case. You're a witness or you're a counsel and my advice is don't let the two categories overlap and you'll prevent it from overlapping if you take somebody with you so that person is in a position to testify to the measurements or to the photographs.

And, finally, if you pick up anything at the scene, you know, a loose nail, a fragment of something, bear in mind that that may have to be offered in evidence at the trial and to offer it in evidence, you're probably going to have to prove the chain of custody. This is something that all policemen and FBI agents learn in the course of their training. You have to teach it to yourself and it's not very difficult. If you pick up a fragment, a nail or the like, let me give you the following suggestion. It is not the only way to do it, but it's a neat and efficient way to do it.

Assuming you have somebody with you, reach into your briefcase and out of it take a blank envelope. A supply of blank envelopes should always be in a lawyer's briefcase. Put the nail, the fragment of wood, whatever it may be, into that envelope and seal it. Then have your potential foundation witness sign it and date it by writing across the sealed flap, his name and the date. Two or three questions at the time of trial will then be enough to get this object into evidence, because actually you don't really need the chain of custody. It's in the sealed envelope, that makes it unique in the sense that there's only one such envelope in the world containing such a fragment and in it will go. It's a little bit beyond our jurisdiction to run through the questions that you would ask of the witness at the trial. Leave it that you have done the necessary to set that witness up so that the witness will be able to answer those simple questions and the object that you found upon investigating the scene will be received in evidence.

Now, that's not the end of investigation. Investigation includes talking to witnesses, it includes examining the scene and, third, though this need not be done at the very beginning, it involves exploring the literature or the clerk's offices for other cases in point. And by other cases in point, I mean your client is being sued by Mr. Plaintiff. Has Mr. Plaintiff ever sued anybody else? Especially has he ever sued anybody on a claim similar to this one? You represent the plaintiff and you're suing the defendant. Has the defendant ever been sued on claims similar to this one? Don't stop there. You have an opposing counsel. Has counsel made a specialty of cases of this kind? Chances are there will be an expert on the other side. Can you find any cases in which the other side's expert has testified?

Now, finding other cases is sometimes very difficult. Finding them may ultimately turn out to be a matter of luck more than anything else, but make the effort. Go to the clerk's office, look at the index of plaintiffs and defendants. Talk to other lawyers, pick up whatever information is on the grapevine. Get all of the information that you possibly can on other cases in point. And you see that in point means a number of things and let's move along. An aspect of investigation which I tell you, even though it's unduly personal, perhaps, I've found to be enormously useful and I made it an invariable part of my discovery program, because my discovery programs always included informal discovery and that's what we're considering now. As soon as the other side is represented, I made it my business to talk to opposing counsel, early in the game. This is not talking to opposing counsel on the morning of the trial. I mean, talk to opposing counsel a couple of days after the complaint and answer have been served on the defendant. Opposing counsel will give you a call. He says, "I'm going to be representing the defendant. How about giving me an extra two weeks to answer?" "Sure," say you. I mean, you always say yes. But I will also add, if it's somebody I don't know, "Why don't we have lunch one of these days? Let's talk things over." The answer from opposing counsel is always, "Yeah, let's have lunch," because he thinks I want to settle it. I don't want to settle it, I want to engage in informal discovery.

And it is amazing how frequently you will get all kinds of information about the case by talking to opposing counsel. If you talk to him in a special way—and it's not to go beyond these four walls because this is highly confidential information. You know how you talk to opposing counsel? Don't say anything. Just sit there with your mouth shut, right? Most of us have been brought up by our mothers to be made very uncomfortable by silence. You know, at the Thanksgiving dinner table, you've got eight or twelve people and everybody's buzz, buzz, buzzing, and then suddenly, by accident, there's a moment where nobody's talking? You know, there's that second of silence and you know what happens. After one or two seconds, all twelve people at the table start to talk at once. Everybody is anxious to cover that silence; it's just part of the way we've been brought up. Silence is embarrassing.

I've made most use of this business of talking to opposing counsel in the days when I was primarily a criminal lawyer, not a civil lawyer. That means you have no discovery whatsoever. I discovered the best discovery you can have as defense counsel was to call the prosecutor up and go to his office. And you walk in and you introduce yourself and he's sitting there thinking, oh boy, here it comes, guilty plea, my name's going to be in the newspapers, et cetera. And after you shake his hand and introduce yourself and give him your card and your telephone number, sit down and look at him. And within five seconds he's going to start to talk because he can't stand the silence. And what's he going to talk about except the case? And it's amazing what he will tell you about the case, usually unaware that he's telling you. And if that kind of thing doesn't work, well, then you draw him out a little bit. If it's a civil lawsuit, you're not going to go to his office. You know, one side is not going to want to go to the other side's office, so you meet on neutral ground. You meet at a local coffee shop or restaurant and you get the conversation going and, after a while, turn it to this case and you say nothing. Let the other fellow do the talking and I guarantee it will be absolutely extraordinary to you how much information you pick up about that case. So much for the kind of investigation that you, the lawyer, may conduct. By no means is it so much for other types of informal discovery.

Let me run through a kind of a checklist of the possibilities with respect to informal discovery and remember, ladies and gentlemen, the utility of a checklist. You don't have to invent the wheel every time you go out. The checklist gives you the universe of possibilities. Well, accept it as such and from this universe of possibilities, select those one or more items which make sense given the circumstances of your case. So you don't do any of these things unthinkingly, but whatever you do, you draw from this list, right? The checklist of possibilities for informal investigation.

Assume that your opponent in this lawsuit is a corporation. If it is a corporation of any size, it will have a public relations department. And when you call that public relations department and say, "Will you please send me all the press releases you've issued for the last year and put me on your mailing list to get all press releases still to be issued," they will fall all over themselves to send you the press releases. Remember, they're not confidential documents by definition, they're documents issued to the outside world. There's nothing improper in asking for them. There may be something a little unintelligent in the corporation blithely sending them out in that matter, but it's hardly improper. And in those press releases, you may discover useful information.

Next, the opposing litigant may be a business or a businessman involved in a particular kind of activity and those involved in that activity may have a trade association. One of the purposes of trade associations is to issue literature about the trade. It's all available to the public. You are a member of the public. Get that literature. Just ask the trade association for it. It will give you a picture of the trade, which will be useful as background and it may also supply information that is specifically relevant to your lawsuit.

Next, especially if you work in the product liability field, pay careful attention because this may prove to be a gold mine and most lawyers in product liability work or otherwise don't use it. If you're in the product liability field your lawsuit, by definition, involves a product that allegedly miscarried in some way. More often than not, by which I mean more than one time out of two, that product is the subject of a patent or a patent application. Get it. Get the patent or the patent application. Remember, the patent or the patent application contains the inventor's claims for the product and those claims may turn out to be marvelous admissions, helpful to you in your suit against the product, the inventor of the product, the distributor of the product.

Item D. If opposing litigant is in a particular business and you can find other people in that business, find those people and talk to them simply about the gossip in the trade. Gossip about the trade in general, gossip about your opposing litigant in particular. It's only gossip, but remember, this is discovery and it may lead to other things which will prove to be admissible in evidence.

Next—this is something that lawyers who are not familiar with the workings of the world of academia need to be reminded of. From time to time I find myself in that world and let me remind you that there are an enormous number of graduate students at universities scattered all across the country. They are desperate for topics for theses. And those topics sometimes are very arcane, abstruse, kind of out of the way. And sometimes those topics touch directly upon issues in your case. There are indices to unpublished academic theses. Every time a thesis is presented for a master's degree or a doctor's degree at any American university, that thesis will be added to the index. The librarian at the general library at your state university library or your local public library in a large city, will be able to show you how to use that index. And, often enough, to make it worth the expenditure of an hour that it takes to go through the index, you will discover that someone somewhere has written a thesis on a topic that overlaps the issue in your case. And that thesis can then be obtained for you by your librarian friend on inter-library loan. You read the thesis and you may find it to be a compendium of marvelous information about your lawsuit, the issues presented in the lawsuit and the like.

Next—remember that newspapers and magazines, not always but frequently, put out an index to themselves. Most of us are familiar with the index to the *New York Times,* a basic tool of historical research. Many other newspapers and magazines publish such an index. A large number of newspapers and magazines do not publish such an index, but maintain it for internal use. And if you ask in a nice way, you will be given access to that index, which is maintained for internal use. And in that index, you may find news items that otherwise would slip right by and those news items may prove to be useful. Related to the use of indices, remember that journalists are an enormous fund of information. Some of it is little above the level of gossip, some of it is absolutely gold.

Remember that in large cities major newspapers assign reporters to a particular beat for a lengthy period of time. A paper like *The New York Times,* for example, has reporters or one reporter, at least, who spends all of his or her time covering the advertising business, another reporter who spends all of his or her time covering the automobile business, and the like. If you can establish friendly relations with such a reporter, that reporter may prove to be a wonderful source of information.

Next, remember that many trades have a specialized newspaper or magazine—what in the outline I call the trade press. And the trade press will print items that do not appear in *The New York Times* or the *Wall Street Journal*—items of very specialized interest within that trade, but it may be of more than specialized interest in your lawsuit. So go through the trade press and see what you can discover.

Next, if your opponent is a firm of very substantial dimensions, chances are it has an in-house publication—a newspaper or magazine put out solely for employees of the firm. It's solely for employees of the firm in the sense that you can't subscribe to it or buy it on a newsstand, but if you ask for it, you may be given copies of it. There may be copies of it on file at the Securities and Exchange Commission, along with 8-Ks and 10-Ks. Do what you can to get access to the in-house magazine and go through it. Once again, you may find useful information there.

I've mentioned the 8-Ks and the 10-Ks. I'll expand that. Any corporation whose stock is publicly held is under a legal obligation to disseminate all kinds of information to that public—annual reports, 8-Ks, 10-Ks, press releases, and the like. Remember that all of those documents are public records. You need only make your way to the nearest library maintained by a regional office of the Securities and Exchange Commission. You ask for the materials for the ABC Corporation and you are given it. And you go through it and who knows what you're going to find in there.

In a product liability case or any other case involving a particular product, I think it is essential that you buy the product and play with it until you have become as adept at using it as you possibly can be. This is the equivalent of examining with your own eyes the physical location of any lawsuit which involves a physical location. If the product involves a particular child's doll, buy such a doll and play with it. Take it apart, put it back together. Just see what happens to it when you do play with it. Make yourself just as familiar with it as its manufacturer is going to be.

Next, many of you know more about it than I do, but I know enough to be aware that there are now enormous databases in the computer, databases which you get access to simply for the asking and upon paying a fee, of course. Those databases may prove to be a productive source of information. We all know about WestLaw and Lexis databases of legal materials. But, remember, there is Nexis. Essentially, everything that's happening in the world is in the computer and if you ask the right questions, you'll come up with the answers and you may come up with things that you didn't know and that you might not otherwise have been able to find out about.

Now, remember the various reports that are filed with government agencies. Many of those reports are not available to you because, by statute, they are confidential. But other such reports are not confidential and if the opposing litigant has been under a legal duty to file such reports, get hold of them.

The next item may be peculiar to someone with my background. Let me indulge in the luxury of taking a couple of minutes to tell you what I mean by buffs and the like. The outline says cultivate court clerks, buffs and the like. I began as a law student and as a lawyer in New York City and, while New York City is sui generis, absolutely unique, there's no place in the world like it, it has many of the characteristics of other large cities. And so what I'm about to describe to you may well be true of your city, even though it is not New York City.

New York City has a substantial population of sober, retired, respectable people who live on their Social Security checks. And those checks are not very large, as you know. It will pay the rent and it will buy groceries, but there isn't much left over for entertainment. These people have discovered that the best entertainment in New York City and I mean New York City, including Broadway and Lincoln Center and all the rest of it—the best entertainment in New York City is available for nothing. It is available in the courthouses of New York City. And what these people do is assemble every morning when the courts are open in a little park outside the Federal and State Courthouse in downtown Manhattan, for example, and they decide what trial to go watch that day. If there is a particularly glamorous trial underway, they'll go to that trial. If there is no particularly glamorous trial, they will follow interesting lawyers. And if there are no interesting lawyers around that day, they will go to good judges. We call them in New York the "buffs," and they are invaluable people to be friends with because they're in court every day and they accumulate all kinds of information about what's going on in the courthouse. Do you want to know whether the lawyer opposing you in this case has ever had a similar case before and you can't find it out in the clerk's office? Go ask the buffs. They will know. The other side is calling as an expert Dr. Jones and you wonder whether Dr. Jones has ever testified as an expert in this kind of case before and you can't find out in any other way, go ask the buffs. They will know. You wonder whether this judge is inclined to sustain objections on the ground of leading questions. You know, that's a ruling that depends on the judge's basal metabolism. Let me take the judge's basal metabolism and I'll tell you how he's going to rule on a leading question objection. But the judge won't let me take his basal metabolism. I don't have to—go talk to the buffs. They will know. And if you're nice about it, they will tell you how this judge is inclined to rule on matters of this kind. So I regard that as discovery, informal discovery to be sure.

I suppose everybody in this audience has reached that level of sophistication where you know about FOIA, the Freedom of Information Act and its state analogues, and you will take advantage of it. And I don't suppose there's any firm in the country that handles civil litigation that does not use FOIA. The Federal FOIA is Section 552 of Title 5 of the United States Code, the Freedom of Information Act. Subject to exceptions, governmental files are available to the public. And chances are—by that I mean I suppose 7 or 8 times out of 10—there will be governmental files directly bearing on the issues to be tried in your case. Get hold of those files by making a FOIA request. Do it early because the bureaucratic wheels turn kind of slowly and it takes a long time 'til you get the information, but ultimately you will get the information and you may find a treasure trove in those files. And, by the way, all you do is pay the cost of Xeroxing. Ten cents a page and it's yours. There's no fee beyond that.

Finally, on this checklist of loads of informal discovery, ladies and gentlemen, is the use of credit reports and the like. It's moderately expensive to pull a Dun & Bradstreet or a profit report or something of that kind. Remember, though, that your client may be a repository of information about people in the community and the opposing litigant may be a person in the community. In using a credit report or information in your client's file, you must be aware of the restrictions imposed by the Fair Credit Reporting Act and similar statutes—statutes which guarantee the privacy of people who are the subject[1] of credit information of one sort or another. The *Houghton* case, decided by the Third Circuit a year and a half or so ago, holds in essence that when you use credit information in connection with discovery in a lawsuit, that does not raise issues under the Fair Credit Reporting Act. You are not subject to the restrictions of the Fair Credit Reporting Act. Well, that's one circuit and perhaps other circuits won't follow it. In any event, act in a dignified and professional, gentlemanly and civilized manner and, at a minimum, you will not be subject to criticism and let's move along.

Having spent as much time as we have on the informal discovery devices, it's only fair that we spend an equal or greater period of time on the formal discovery devices, the devices given us by the Rules of Civil Procedure for conducting discovery. Let's talk about them. For oral depositions, take a look at Rule 30 of the Federal Rules of Civil

---

1. *Houghton v. New Jersey Manufacturers Insurance Co.*, 795 F.2d 1144 (3d Cir. 1986).

Procedure and let me devote our precious time together to a consideration of tactics and strategy and the kinds of purposes that a trial lawyer will seek to achieve when he considers the question, "Should a deposition be taken?"

In the outline, I raise the question, "Who should be deposed?" Now, a litigating lawyer would say that the answer to that question is obvious—you depose everybody, everybody and his brother-in-law—and then you're certain to have deposed the few people whose depositions you really need in this case. The trial lawyer would say no, at a minimum, that's too expensive. It also is going to take an awful lot of time. You're also going to tip your hand unduly and various other considerations may leave you to carve out a program for taking depositions that involves taking the deposition of many fewer people than are out there as potential candidates.

Here are my rules of thumb for determining whose deposition should be taken. First, always take the opposing party's deposition, always. That's self-evident, I suppose. Second, if the person to be deposed is a mere witness, a bystander, and you have every reason to believe that that mere witness or bystander is friendly to your side, is rooting for you, and that person is in reasonably good health, don't take his deposition. Why? You don't need it. You already know that he's on your side. Remember, you interviewed him. You took a statement from him as part of informal discovery. If you do take his deposition, you simply tell the other side what he's going to say, you tip your hand, and you perpetuate his testimony. Since he's in good health, there's really not much of a factor in perpetuating his testimony, that's not something to be concerned with. So mainly what you've done is tip your hand as well as run up the bills, spend money needlessly, and the like. So I say don't take that person's deposition.

Next, you've got a witness whom you have every reason to believe is adverse to you, is against you for whatever reason, and that witness is in bad health or advanced years. This may strike you as harsh, cynical, or even comical, but I intend it to be taken in all seriousness because that's the spirit in which I give it to you. I would not take his deposition.

I know he's against me. So be it. In a general way I know what he's going to say. But if I take his deposition, I will have perpetuated his testimony and since by definition he is in bad health or advanced years, I don't want to do that. If the other side is going to do it, let them do it. Let them spend the money, not me.

Next, if you've got a witness who is adverse to you and who is in good health and relatively young in years, take his deposition. You don't have to worry too much about perpetuating his testimony because chances are he's going to survive 'til the time of trial and now the advantage tips in favor of knowing exactly what he's going to say. Pin him down so that you deal with it, but only with that at the time of trial.

Next—and then this gets to be a little bit rough. It's kind of close to the bone. It touches the nerve. But civil litigation is frequently that way. Of course, criminal litigation is almost always that way. Suppose there's a witness out there whom you have every reason to believe is dishonest. The other side is going to call that witness. Take his deposition and take it early in the game, preferably before the depositions of all of the other potential witnesses are taken. Do you see why? If he is, indeed, the dishonest person that you think he is, if he understands what other people have been saying in their depositions, he will temper his testimony to accord with their version. But if you take his deposition first, he has nothing against which to measure his own testimony, he kind of gives it to you on the wing. He is flying blind and I guarantee that the inconsistencies will be large in number and considerable in extent—inconsistencies between his testimony and the testimony you get from the other witnesses, all of whom are more or less honest. But suppose this person, whom you have every reason to believe is dishonest, is so situated that you must call him to the stand? You wish you didn't have to. You don't want to sponsor his testimony to the jury, but you have no choice. You've got to call him to the stand. This may strike you as approaching even the cynical, but it's true. If you're going to take that person's deposition, take it at the end. Let everybody else have been deposed so that this person has heard what their testimony is and he will temper his testimony to meet theirs. And since, by definition, they are testifying essentially to the truth, they are honest people, you will end up getting a more or less honest version from this potentially dishonest witness.

Now, there are four or five rules of thumb for determining whose deposition should be taken. But there are still factors to be worked into the calculus before you can answer the question, let's go ahead with the deposition or let's not go ahead with the deposition. There are advantages and there are disadvantages to the taking of a deposition. Let me tick off what seems to me to be the list of the six principal advantages to the taking of a deposition.

First, and at least to my taste, to my way of thinking, this is probably the most important. When you take an oral deposition, you get to observe the person being deposed—what in law school we called demeanor. And I find that enormously important because it is a kind of preview of the coming attraction that will play itself out when the case is tried.

Next, an oral deposition is flexible, it is easy to follow things up. You ask a question, you get an answer. That answer suggests other questions. You ask them right then and there.

Next, and here we begin to get a little bit subtle, I suppose. Remember my concern with tipping your hand, telling the other side something about what you know about the case that you'd rather not? If you conduct an oral deposition it is easier than it is in connection with the other discovery devices to conceal revealing questions. If you've got a question that gives a great deal away, you conceal it or you do your best to conceal it. You put it in with a lot of inconsequential questions. You ask it in such a way so that you don't flag its importance. You can't do that with any of the other discovery devices, but you can do it with an oral deposition.

Next—I guess we're up to number four. On an oral deposition, the style, the tone, the substance of the questions can be adapted to the witness. If the witness is a tough cookie who's belligerent and who's against you, you can let him feel your steel at the deposition and he continues to feel it until the time of trial, so that he's in a considerably better temper when you get to the trial. On the other hand, if the witness is kind of hesitant, immature, perhaps lacking in emotional or intellectual wherewithal, you can frame the question softly. Your tone can be hospitable. You can adapt your style to the needs of the occasion. You can't do that with any of the other discovery devices.

Next—this is just an aspect of what I just said. With the oral deposition, the length can be adjusted. You strike gold right at the start, you had planned to spend all day on this deposition, maybe the thing to do is to stop it right then and there. You've spent an hour on it, but that hour has been enormously productive, call it quits. Make a decision on the spot to end the deposition. You can only do that with the oral deposition. On the other hand, you're taking the deposition of the chairman of the board of the opposing company, a man who has risen to this eminence for very good reason. He's smart and he's tough and he doesn't like you and your client. Take his deposition all day, you accomplish nothing. Take his deposition for five or six days in a row and by the fifth or sixth day you are accomplishing something because fatigue is working in your favor. So you can adjust the length in either direction.

And, finally, and again this may strike you as approaching the cynical, but it's important. In the oral deposition the participation of opposing counsel is minimized. Opposing counsel is there and will play a part, there's no doubt about that. But opposing counsel does not answer the questions. The witness answers the questions and that is an enormous benefit. Draw the contrast—in case I forget to do it when we arrived at the interrogatory—draw the contrast with the interrogatory. Who drafts answers to interrogatories? Counsel drafts answers to interrogatories, hence the possibilities for obfuscation, frustration, and delay are virtually infinite. But at the deposition it's possible to accomplish something because counsel can do only so much to obfuscate, frustrate, or delay.

Now, there are the advantages. Let me give you what, to my mind, are the four principal disadvantages of the oral deposition and how you balance them out will vary from case to case, of course. There's no way to say in advance how the balance ultimately will be stricken. First, and at least in my mind, maybe most important, the oral deposition is incredibly expensive. It is expensive in the direct cost of what you have to pay the stenographer and in the indirect cost of lawyer's time, facilities, witnesses' time, and the rest. Second, an oral deposition is time consuming. I don't think I have ever heard of an oral deposition, even of the most ordinary witness in the most straightforward kind of case, that took less than half a day. That's a lot of time. And the longest oral deposition I know of—you're not going to believe me, ladies and gentlemen, but it is recorded in the Federal Reporters. The longest deposition I know of took place in an antitrust case that was ultimately disposed of in the Southern District of New York. The plaintiff was deposed for nine-and-a-half years. Nine-and-a-half years. Mmm hmm. And perhaps we'll talk a little bit about that when we get to discovery as a device for frustration and delay. You will wonder what, in heaven's name, they were asking him for nine-and-a-half years. Remember, the scope of discovery is wide open—anything that might lead to evidence. So, did you have a conversation with X? Yes. When? Where? Was he wearing clothes? Well, of course he was wearing clothes. Was he wearing a tie? Yeah, I guess so. Was it a blue tie? I don't remember. Let me try to help you. Was it a blue tie with red dots? Was it a blue tie with yellow dots? You notice you can spend all day on the tie and then tomorrow on the shirt. And before you know it, it adds up to nine-and-a-half years and then the plaintiff died. Which I'm sure is what the defendants wanted to accomplish from the beginning, because at that point the case kind of went away. But that's a story for another occasion and perhaps not in circumstances so formal or august as these. So, remember, a deposition is time consuming.

Third, a deposition by its nature preserves testimony. So that if you take somebody's deposition and that person dies or otherwise becomes unavailable to testify at trial, the other side can put the transcript of that deposition into evidence. And that may hurt you. And if you took the deposition, you, in fact, may have shot yourself in the foot. You're the one who injured yourself.

And, fourth, this is simply the other side of the coin of the first advantage. You take a deposition of a witness who's in your corner, you give the other side an opportunity to see that witness under fire. You give the other side the advantage of observing the witness's demeanor. And I repeat that I think that that is a major advantage, therefore it is a major disadvantage to give the other side that advantage.

All right, now we will assume that you've got a situation in which you have considered these various factors, you have weighed them just as carefully as you possibly can, and the balance is struck in favor of taking the deposition. So be it. Let us turn now to the consideration of technique—how to take a deposition. All right. Now, remember, we assume you're taking the deposition, not defending the deposition. First and foremost, this is not just a clerical convenience that it's number one, it is number one in importance. You must know your purpose at every moment of the deposition. You must know exactly what you're trying to accomplish and that purpose may change from moment to moment. But if I or somebody like me were to appear at your next deposition and kind of stop the clock and tap you on the shoulder and say, "Counselor, what are you trying to accomplish right now?" you should be able to tell me. You should know what it is that you're trying to accomplish. And what you then do is adapt the means that you're going to use in view of the purpose that you seek to accomplish. Select a means, calculate it to achieving that purpose. And in a while we'll talk about the way in which you actually couch questions in accordance with the purpose that you seek to accomplish.

But second, under the general heading of preparation, you must know the case. You can't take depositions and only then figure out what the case is all about, you've got to know pretty well what the case is about because you can't know what's important at the deposition unless you already know what the issues in this case are. And then, finally, adapt your tone, your style, your pace, the substance, to what it is you're trying to accomplish to the personality of the witness and to your feel of that particular moment. Some particular suggestions by way of the technique of answering questions will be what we will talk about in 10 or 15 minutes. But let's move along and consider some other matters that have to be considered right at the beginning.

Starting the deposition is a challenge to craft insufficiently appreciated by all too many lawyers. And, as a matter of fact, for the youngster—and remember, to be young or inexperienced is not a criticism, that is a condition that all of us once were in. If you have yet to take a deposition or have yet to take a large number of depositions, this problem of beginning the deposition is a very considerable one. Let me talk about some aspects of this problem. Now, obviously, the United States consists of a lot of space. And no lawyer and certainly not yours truly has taken a deposition in every part of the country. But in every part of the country where I have taken a deposition, it has always begun as follows. Whether I was deposing the defendant, the plaintiff, or a third person, almost always opposing counsel would begin by saying to me something like, "Mr. Younger, the usual stipulations?" And I dare say that that is how depositions start in your neck of the woods as well. Young lawyers and sometimes not-so-young lawyers will unthinkingly reply yes or of course or certainly or something to that effect. That's unthinking and, therefore, to be criticized. It may be that it's prudent to consent to the usual stipulations, but for heaven's sakes, think about it first.

Now, here are some things that you want to think about. To begin with, what are the usual stipulations? Now, I'm glad to hear you laugh, because I'm positive that if I were to ask three out of five lawyers who blithely say, "Of course, the usual stipulations," if I were to say to them, "What are the usual stipulations?" they won't know. I'm sure that if I were to ask the lawyer who says, "Shall we have the usual stipulations?" what are they, he won't know. Try it the next time you're out there. When opposing counsel says, "Counselor, the usual stipulations?" you can reply, "Well, probably, but first why don't you tick them off?" Suppose you're on the receiving end of that? Your opponent says to you, "Why don't you mention the usual stipulations?" you don't know what they are. Shall I give you an easy way out? Turn to the court reporter. Turn to the court reporter and say, "Perhaps you would state the stipulations," and the court reporter always knows them, see. So it gets you out of this little problem gracefully.

Now, let me just give you some of the considerations. I don't know what's right in your case, obviously not. But this is what I mean when I say don't do it unthinkingly. Let me take just two of these considerations. First, the laws provide that after the deposition is concluded, the court reporter, the stenographer, will type up a transcript. The transcript is sent to the witness or the litigant who's been deposed. The witness or the litigant can review the transcript, can change any answer he wants. You can fix grammatical errors or you can change answers of substance. You can change yes to no or no to yes. You're supposed to attach a statement explaining why you've made those changes and then you sign it and swear to it before a notary public, even though, of course, you were under oath when you answered the questions. And the deposition then becomes the corrected, signed transcript. Usual stipulation, at least in the areas where I've taken depositions, is that the signing and swearing and filing are waived. I don't care about filing, but does it really make sense to waive the signing of it? Now do you see, if you don't have it signed, your cross-examination at trial is going to be something like, "Do you remember coming to my office? Now it was four years ago, but do you remember I was there, your lawyer was there. Do you remember the court reporter was there? Do you remember the court reporter asked you to raise your right hand and swear to tell the truth and you took that oath?"

"Yes."

"And then you were asked this question, you gave this answer." And it's pretty powerful, but it's not a bomb. That's what you're going to have to do if you have waived the signing. If you don't waive the signing, what you will have at trial is a document that the jury can look at and it's signed and sworn to right on the document by the witness. And now, assuming that this is consistent with your style, you can say something like, "Mr. Witness, after you came to my office four years ago, remember about a month later you received a copy of the transcript, what the court reporter typed up from the court reporter's notes?"

"Yes."

"And you took that to a notary public, didn't you?"

"Yes."

"And you raised your right hand before the notary public, just the way you raised your right hand before the court reporter."

"Yes."

"And you swore to the notary public that you'd tell the truth, the whole truth and nothing but the truth, didn't you?"

"Yes."

"Just the way you'd sworn to the court reporter?"

"Yes."

"Just the way you swore to this jury yesterday morning that you would tell the truth, the whole truth and nothing but the truth, isn't that right?"

"Yes."

"And then did you sign it and is that your signature?"

And you see, the thing becomes much bigger. You've got it, not speaking precisely, but speaking loosely, you've got it in writing and in writing gives it a greater impact. On the other hand, if everybody agrees to waive the signing, the person being deposed does not have an opportunity to change an answer. You know, you have to weigh these factors.

Second, anybody who's been involved in the taking of depositions knows that evidentiary objections can get to be very complicated. They get to be very complicated because of this problem of the relationship between what you do at the deposition and what happens at trial. Now, do you recall what the Federal Rules of Civil Procedure say about evidentiary objections? It says that you don't have to make an objection. It's preserved for the time of trial. The witness can answer the question, you don't have to object to the question. You can object to it at the time of trial when the deposition is read into evidence except as to those evidentiary problems that could be obviated—that's the phrase—that could be obviated were objection to be made at the deposition. What in heaven's name does that mean, "could be obviated"? As a matter of English vocabulary, it means where the problem could be solved, where the objection could be somehow finessed, where the difficultly that objecting counsel is raising could be resolved. And I don't know of any problem in the law of evidence that can't be resolved if you know how to do it. So that if you operate under the rules as they stand, with no preliminary stipulation whatsoever, there is a good argument that any objection that was not made at the time of the deposition has, in fact, been waived because it could have been obviated at the time of the deposition, so that within the terms of the rules themselves there has been a waiver. If you are pretty good at evidence and your opponent is not so good at evidence, maybe that's the way to do it. Don't stipulate.

If you do stipulate, what do you stipulate to? The usual stipulation on evidence is that all objections, whether or not they could be obviated at the deposition, are reserved to the time of trial. You don't have to make any objection whatsoever, which takes a load off the mind of opposing counsel if opposing counsel is nervous about evidentiary objections. And maybe you don't want to relieve him of that burden of worry. Maybe you want him to be concerned about making objections. So these are some of the things that you think about.

Next, especially if you're young and are taking your first or any deposition up to about the tenth or the fifteenth, carefully work out in your mind and maybe even have on paper in front of you what you will say at the outset. What I call in the outline a preliminary statement. Have a preliminary statement prepared. It doesn't require any enormous brilliance. But especially if you're young and are obviously young, you know—clearly you're under the age of 40, that's young as trial lawyers go—you want the witness to get the impression that you know your stuff. And you convey that impression right at the beginning. You know, first impressions are the strongest impressions. Don't fumble around at the start. And you will not fumble around if you have prepared something to get you going.

Now, let me give you some possibilities. By no means do I suggest that these are the only possibilities and I don't even want to be understood as saying that these are the best. But they are possibilities and maybe you can improve upon them. Maybe you want to begin with a line of questions, something as follows, right? The witness has now been sworn, so here we go from the top. "Mr. Witness, do you understand that you are now under oath?" That's kind of a formidable question for someone who's not a lawyer and you're in there with that formidable impact right at the start. "Do you understand that you're now under oath? Do you understand what it means to be under oath? Do you understand that it means that you are under a moral and a legal obligation to do your best to tell the truth and that if you don't, there may well be trouble?"

Don't stop there, especially if you are young and the witness is old or older than you, especially if the witness is the chairman of the board of the opposing corporation, or something of that kind and you want that witness to feel your elbows and knees. After a line of questions about do you understand the oath and everything that goes through the oath, try this one. I guarantee it's going to annoy the hell out of them, right—and be ready for it. Call him Mr. Witness. I like to do that. Mr. Witness . . . then you depersonalize it. "Mr. Witness, is there anything that might prevent you from testifying truthfully this morning?" And he's going to lean back and look at you and say, "What do you mean?" And you might say, "Fair enough. Have you had anything to drink this morning? Have you had any drug of any kind this morning? Any Valium? Any tranquilizer? Any analgesic? Anything that might make you drowsy?" and so forth. And then you play it by ear. I mean, if you really want to drive him up the wall, you know, "Have you snorted cocaine this morning?" "No." "Well, when's the last time you did?" And, of course, at that point it all gets out of control, but that's what you wanted to happen. Remember, you do it deliberately.

Possibly continuing with the following or perhaps using the following as your preliminary statement, "Mr. Witness, I want you to listen carefully to my questions and I want you to answer my questions only if you have heard the question and understand it perfectly. If you didn't hear me, say so, don't answer the question. And if you don't understand the question, say so, don't answer it. All right, all right? Right." But now wrap it up with something like this because this is going to put him under pressure, this is going to keep him nervous. So that, "Mr. Witness, if you answer my question, everybody in the room is going to take it for granted that you heard it and you understood it." You've also done a little bit to minimize the possibility of changing answers on the ground of I didn't hear it or didn't understand it. He still can do it, can make the change, but it's more embarrassing. Other possibilities may occur to you. Let's just leave it at that in view of the passage of time.

Now let's talk a little bit about the actual conduct of the deposition. Remember, I said you must always know what it is that you are trying to accomplish. Let me try to make that clear to you by pointing out that the way in which you conduct the deposition will vary from moment to moment, from hour to hour, from day to day, depending upon your purpose. For example, suppose what you want to do is find out about the case. This is classic discovery. You want to find out what this witness can tell you about the transaction that constitutes the subject matter of the lawsuit. I think that the best way to do that is to ask the open-ended kind of question that you would never ask on cross-examination at a trial. The question that is on the order of, "What happened? What did you see? What did you do?" And you draw the witness out. You will frequently deliberately adopt a kind of warm and friendly manner to get the witness to ramble. Now, rambling is the kiss of death in the courtroom in front of the jury, but at a deposition session, it may be the best thing that can happen. Get the witness to ramble and, once the witness is rambling, don't interrupt. That's where you're going to strike gold. Don't cut it off. Let the witness keep talking and you listen. You listen with a concentration unknown to our colleagues in other branches of the profession and you're listening for that key bit of testimony or what will become the key bit of testimony that is embedded in this long and rambling answer.

Having completed his long ramble, the witness will now be taken back by you with a different purpose—not to find out what the witness can tell you about the case, but now your purpose may be to freeze it or to marshal it for use at the trial so that at trial it can be read to the jury in a crisp and forthright fashion. Let me give you an example, something like this. Assume you've got a two-car collision and it takes place at an intersection where one of the cars had no traffic control and the other car had a stop sign. Right? You represent the car that had no traffic control. You are deposing the opposing litigant who had the stop sign. What I would do was say, "Well, now, there was an accident, right? Everybody knows there was an accident. Yeah. A terrible thing." You know, try to get them relaxed and friendly. "So what happened? You know, tell me what happened?" Get him to ramble and, as he rambles on, he may say, along with lots of other things that are actually irrelevant, that he came to the stop sign and he stopped and he looked and he didn't see anything, so he kept going and then, bang, there was the collision. Now, that's embedded, as I say, in a lot of connective tissue that's unimportant. Don't stop him, let him go to the end. Now, when he goes to the end, go back.

And it's something like, "Let me understand you. You've told us that you came to the intersection and saw the stop sign."

"Yes."

"You stopped for the stop sign."

"Yes."

"And while you stopped, you looked to the right."

"Yes."

"And you looked to the left."

"Yes."

"You saw nothing on the right."

"Right."

"You saw nothing on the left."

"Correct."

"And then you proceeded."

"Yes."

"And maybe a half a second later there was the collision with my client's car."

"Yes."

You've probably won the case on summary judgment right there. Because there will be appellate decisions in your jurisdiction holding that one of the obligations of a reasonably careful motorist is not only to look but to see what is there to be seen. And, obviously, your client's car was there to be seen, otherwise there couldn't have been a collision. And you now have it in that very concise form that will give it its impact when you read it to the jury or when you quote it to the judge in support of a motion for summary judgment. And observe that the difference is in your objective. He rambles because you invite him to ramble when your objective is to find out what he knows. But when your objective is to pin it down and to get it in such a form that you can use it efficiently at the trial or in connection with summary judgment, you're going to ask those leading questions and just have him answer it, "yes, yes, yes."

As a kind of footnote to this, no representation from me as to whether if you're challenged on this a judge will allow it, but let me tell you where the suggestion comes from. A very able and well-known federal judge who sits in Los Angeles named William Matthew Byrne, Jr., just mentioned to me within the year that he will allow lawyers to depose a given witness twice. Once they ask open-ended questions. Just have the witness ramble. You end up with 120 pages of ramble of which 119 are absolutely worthless. But now you take the transcript and you examine it with a magnifying glass to figure out which of the pages are worthless and which are the one or two that are valuable. Now you go back and you take his deposition a second time. Two pages worth, with each question carefully formulated simply to put the spotlight on the fact that the witness can tell you that's important in the case. So that the first deposition is entirely exploratory, the second deposition is entirely for the purpose of marshaling the evidence for use at the trial.

Suppose you're taking the deposition of someone whose age or condition of health is such as to make it likely that he or she will not survive to the time of trial. Now you're perpetuating the testimony, you're probably going to have to read it to the jury, and you ought to conduct that deposition as if you were in front of the jury. There is an aspect of taking a deposition which I think warrants a somewhat more extended consideration and it's this. You are taking the deposition of someone who is not in your corner. This is an unfriendly witness. I'm not suggesting a dishonest witness, but I do have in mind the realities of human nature. You want to pin that witness down. You want to establish what it is the witness can say. Granted, it is adverse to your position in the lawsuit, but you want to know that this is it, it can't change, and it's not going to get any worse between now and the time of trial.

Technically, do you see what your problem is? Your problem is the problem of exhausting the witness's recollection. And there is a technique to doing it and let me run through that technique. Obviously, these are not the exact words in which you have to put questions to the witness, but it must add up to this kind of thing. Suppose the witness has testified to a conversation. Even if the witness appears to have given you the entire conversation and the sequence of questioning with the following subsequence, the purpose of which is to exhaust the witness's recollection, ask, "Is that the entire conversation?" And keep at it until you get a yes answer. If you haven't already asked it, "Who else was present?" If you haven't already asked it, "Were any notes or other documents available to you to help you to remember this conversation?"

Next, don't forget this one. It's perfectly proper so long as you do it in the right way. "Now, before coming to this deposition, you discussed the case with your lawyer, didn't you? Just tell me yes or no." And, of course, the answer is going to be yes. "Now, I don't want to know anything about what you and your lawyer said to each other," attorney-client privilege, et cetera, et cetera, "but did you discuss with your lawyer the conversation that you've now told me about?" And keep at it 'til you get a yes answer. And you see what you've done, you've closed that door. He can't later on say, "Well, I remember more because I talked with my lawyer." He's already talked with his lawyer. And then always end up with the kind of blunderbuss question, "Is there anything that might help you to remember anything more about this conversation?" He's going to say no and you've closed every possible door at this stage of the game.

Now, fairly quickly, let me run through a fair number of items dealing with the conduct of the deposition. And I'm just running through them in a kind of miscellaneous order. Some of them are fairly important, some of them are not so important. Right? First, do not act as if you're in front of the jury. Remember, you're not in front of the jury. If you begin to act in the melodramatic fashion that some lawyers, I think, foolishly permit to themselves when they're in front of a jury, it will work against your interests at the deposition.

Next, if the witness is at all forthcoming, I think the best manner for you to adopt is a warm and friendly one. Simply invite the witness to tell you more and you do that by your manner.

Next, this is worth doing simply to remind the witness that you really know your stuff and that you are a formidable customer. Every time there is a recess or an adjournment—you break for coffee in the morning, you go to lunch, or whatever—when you resume the deposition, the first question after you resume it should be, "Now, Mr. Witness, over the luncheon recess, did you discuss your testimony with anyone?" And it always takes them aback. And the answer may be yes. "With whom did you discuss it?" "My lawyer." Fine. On we go. Obviously, you don't ask about the content of a conversation, just establish that there was a conversation.

Next, for the same reason, if the witness consults with counsel, you know, Brendan Sullivan/Oliver North style, whispering in his ear, note it on the record. And it accomplishes only a psychological purpose. It establishes your presence in that room. Obviously, counsel has a perfect right to whisper in his client's ear, there's nothing you can do about it. But note it for the record and, after a while, counsel starts to get nervous about it.

Next, in a case such as a typical contemporary commercial case where there are lots and lots of documents, the first deposition might well be taken of the office manager or someone like the office manager and the purpose of the deposition is to find out how documents are prepared and filed. Just get the office routine down. And that two-hour deposition may save you an awful lot of fumbling around later in the trial.

Next, on the same principle that you always go to visit the physical location, if you're deposing the plaintiff in a personal injury case, so long as it's seemly and will not cause hysteria, ask to look at the injuries yourself. You're not a doctor and you're not going to poke them. Ask to see the scar or whatever it may be and then just make it part of your preparation. You now know what it looks like because you can bet your bottom dollar that the jury is going to get to see that scar at the time of the trial. So you see it, too. It's part of the deposition.

Next, this seems silly, but I have run into cases in which, after a two-day deposition, the witness did not know who is the person asking the questions. I don't mean that the witness has to know your name, but he'd better know who you are functionally. And so you might consider introducing yourself on the record. "Mr. Witness, my name is Younger. I am a lawyer here in town and in this case, the client I speak for is the ABC Corporation. Understood?" Understood. He now knows who you are. Do not take it for granted that without that kind of identification he will know who you are.

Next, where I am taking the deposition, after whatever other preliminaries I'm going to do, I will identify or have the witness identify every person in the room so that it will go something like, "Now, Mr. Witness, there's a gentleman seated to your right. Tell us who that is." And you know who that is. "Please just tell us who that is so that we have it on the record." That always scares them a little bit. "Well, that's William Smith, that's my lawyer." "And who is that sitting next to Mr. Smith?" And so on and so on until everybody has been identified.

Next, where the witness being deposed has information on more than one topic, I think it is almost always wise to mix up the questions. Do not pursue one topic to a conclusion, then the next, and then the next. That's too easy for the witness. You want to keep the witness off balance. You want to keep the witness in a state of moderate anxiety. And the way to do it is to mix the questions up. And here is a handy way to keep your notes so as to make it easy. Suppose you're going to depose this witness on three different topics. Prepare an outline of each topic. Each of those outlines is on a separate sheet or sheets of yellow paper. You have those sheets in front of you. You can shuffle them in any way you want. You're now asking questions, working off the outline on sheet two. After a half an hour, put a little mark so you remember where you stopped, and simply go to the top of sheet one and begin there. Put a little mark when you quit sheet one and now go to sheet three and start at the top. Now to back to sheet two and pick up where the check mark reminds you you left off, and so on. And this simple shuffling of the yellow pages that we're all familiar with will permit you to keep track of what you're doing, but will keep the witness in that desirable state of being somewhat off balance.

Next, watch for the non-verbal response. Anybody who's tried cases has run into that. After a while the witness gets tired or gets nervous and starts to respond this way, if I may have your attention for just a moment. "Now, Mr. Witness, did you then go home?" That's what you get. And there's nothing on the record, assuming it's not a videotaped deposition. Be alert to that and you be the one to pick it up. Say, "Mr. Witness, the nod of the head will not appear in the stenographic transcript. Will you say it in a word?" And the witness kind of gets the feeling that you are crowding him a little bit, and that's exactly the feeling that you want him to have.

Next, be alert to the ambiguous answer. And, you know, the ambiguous answer is easy. That is, it is easy to elicit when we, the lawyers, are nervous and are asking ambiguous or syntactically complicated questions. And when we're nervous we ask questions of that kind because we don't have the clarity of mind and the composure it takes to put a question directly, something like this: "You then went outside, did you not?" The "did you not" just makes it ambiguous. When he says yes, what does he mean—I did not or I did? It really is hard to tell. And the "did you not" is a nervous manifestation on the lawyer's part, I assure you. In any event, be alert to it and where you get that kind of ambiguous answer, clear it up at once by turning the question into an unambiguous question. Remember that the virtue of the oral definition is flexibility. You can follow up all kinds of things. If there's something to be followed up, follow it up.

Next, this verges on rough stuff, but you've got to be ready for it. Watch for the signs that show that the witness is being signaled by somebody in the room, typically his lawyer. Now, I'm glad you laugh. Has it ever happened? It has happened to me. And, for heaven's sakes, if it's going to happen to you, don't be the victim of it. Do something about it. And typically all you have to do is say, "Now, will you please keep your eyes on me when you answer the question? Don't look at Mr. Smith, your lawyer." At that point, Mr. Smith, of course, says, "I take offense at the suggestion that I have been signaling answers," et cetera, et cetera. And you say something like, "I make no such suggestion, I simply asked the witness to keep his eyes on me, not you." And on we go.

Do not let the witness argue with you. Do not let the witness ask you questions. And after a while you'll get to be pretty good at this. You turn the witness off, "Mr. Witness, I'm not here to answer questions," or "Mr. Witness, it is my job to ask the questions and your job to answer them," something of that kind. And you'll cut it short.

Next, I think that it is always to your advantage to insist upon the proper decorum. Call witnesses by last names with mister, miss, missus, whatever may be appropriate, and insist that you be called by last name with whatever title is appropriate.

Next, do not allow anything to be expunged from the record. A good court reporter will not allow that. Now, you can have a lawyer carry on and say, "I move to strike that from the record." Yeah, and that's what the record shows, "I move to strike it from the record." But if a lawyer says to the court reporter, "Physically expunge the last answer," don't let it happen. And if the lawyers are not in agreement, the court reporter will not expunge it. It will stand the way it is and don't let the record be tampered with in that manner.

Next, let me give you a checklist within a checklist. When an event is referred to in a deposition, I suggest questions as follows. I'm not going to give you the exact questions, not the wording of the questions, but the topics. You want to know first, when; second, where; third, who was present; fourth, how did it all happen; next, does anybody else know about it; next, are there photographs; and finally, are there any other notes of any sort? Where what is referred to is a conversation, here is a mini-checklist. When, where, who was present, was it recorded, were notes taken, and only then, what was the conversation, what did people say? A third mini-checklist with respect to a document. You want to know first, when was it prepared; next, by whom; next, are there underlying notes or earlier drafts; next, what is the location of the original of this document; next, what was the distribution of the document, who received copies; next, is the document complete, is this the entire document? And I'll give you a hint. Invariably, you will have been shown a Xerox copy. Look at the upper left-hand corner. If a staple has been removed, it leaves two dots that always show up very clearly on the Xerox machine. If you see those two dots, bring it to the witness's attention. This document in its original form had something stapled to it. What was the something? Because the document is not complete without the attachment. And only after you have gone through all of that, explain the document—what is its significance, what does it do.

And finally, on this checklist—it doesn't happen too often, but it happens. It's happened to me in my work as a lawyer, such as it is, more than once—if anything out of the ordinary occurs at the deposition, make a little statement so that the record shows that it happened. If a witness cries, show that. If a witness has some violent episode, show it. Just make a little statement, you know, the witness just . . . this actually happened to me. The witness just picked up the pack of cigarettes that he's had in front of him for the past two hours and threw it at me. He just reached his limit and over it went. As an aspect of this, remembering that there are some lawyers whose stock in trade is to misbehave, if you get involved in a kind of cat fight with opposing counsel, make sure it's on the record. Make sure it's on the record and I give you that advice under the assumption that if there is going to be a cat fight, you're the party in the right or more nearly in the right and opposing counsel is the party most nearly in the wrong. On that score, my favorite example is the transcript of the deposition I once saw. The deposition took place in New York City and, I'll grant you, in New York City things may get to be a little bit more extreme. The deposition begins, line one, page one, with one of the lawyers saying to the other, "What did you call me?" That's the beginning of the deposition. And he then tells him what he called him and it would have been well to have that on the record to begin with. I think the court reporter just decided to stay out of this until he had to get involved and then he was involved, so much simply because of the constraints of time, ladies and gentlemen, for taking a deposition.

The other side of that particular coin is defending a deposition. More specifically, preparing your client or witness for the taking of the client's or the witness's deposition. Let me talk to the extent that time will allow about defending a deposition. The most important thing to get across to your client, and by client I include a witness who is friendly to your side, but is technically a disinterested person. The most important thing to get across to the client, at least in my experience, is the following. And you don't have to get it across in these words, but this is the substance of it: "It is not your job at the deposition to persuade opposing counsel that he has no case. Opposing counsel cannot be persuaded to go away. It is for the jury or the judge to tell opposing counsel that opposing counsel has no case. So don't try to argue, don't try to persuade opposing counsel, don't try to talk him into seeing things your way. Your responsibility is really just one thing, though it has many parts. Your responsibility is to listen to the question, be sure you've heard it, be sure you understand it, and when you have heard it and understood it, answer it with the truth. And the truth in a trial, in a deposition no less than in a courtroom, means what you, yourself, know. "You've got to hammer that into the witness." It doesn't mean what you believe to be true. In ordinary parlance, sincerity equals truth. If you believe it, it's true. Not in a courtroom. It is true only if you know it and you know it because you saw it, heard it, smelled it, touched it or tasted it. That somebody else told it to you, that you have figured it out—that doesn't count, you don't know it. You know it only if you, yourself perceived it. And if you didn't perceive it, your answer is, 'I don't know,' because that is a truthful answer.

"If you once knew it, but you don't remember it, don't guess because then you're not telling the truth. The answer is, 'I don't remember,' because that is the truth."

And you're going to have to rehearse and rehearse and rehearse, because it takes an awful lot of browbeating before your typical client understands those important matters.

Next, what is there to say about protecting your expert in the context of an oral deposition? Well, there's a great deal—let me hit the highlights. First, we understand that under the Federal Rules of Civil Procedure and their equivalent in many states, the only discovery that is available of right with respect to your expert is under Rule 26(b)(4). And it's the identity of the expert. It is his background, credentials, if you will, and a statement of the substance of his testimony. Beyond that, a deposition is available only upon court order or upon consent. I put it to you that in some cases consent is the shrewdest thing to do. Remember, I'm talking about the other side taking your expert's deposition. Why should you consent? Because the experience of having his deposition taken will be enormously valuable to your expert. It is a kind of dry run for the trial. And where your expert does not have a vast amount of courtroom experience, maybe it is a good idea to give him that experience in the guise of a deposition.

We said that because of the utility of the experience of being under fire for your expert, sometimes you want to give serious consideration to the possibility of consenting to the deposition of your expert. On the other side of the ledger, remember that as your expert testifies at the deposition, you are tipping your hand to an extraordinary degree. Your expert's views of the matter, the way in which he analyzes the issues, et cetera, will be laid before opposing counsel and, hence, if nothing else, the element of surprise will be out of the case. But you conceivably may conclude that the element of surprise is unimportant and that the possibility of a favorable settlement will be enhanced if opposing counsel is aware of the strength of your expert's opinion. In that situation, it may be that the shrewd thing to do is to encourage your expert to volunteer, to go beyond the question that is asked at the deposition, even though normally you tell a witness never volunteer anything, just answer the question that is asked. But you want your expert to go beyond the question that is asked simply so that the full strength of the expert's presentation is made apparent to opposing counsel, hence, enhancing the likelihood of a favorable settlement.

Next, with respect to experts, if the deposition is being conducted not on your consent, but on the basis of a judge's order, remember that the order may contain limitations or conditions. And if there are limitations or conditions in the order authorizing the deposition, insist upon strict compliance with those limitations or conditions. Do not waive them.

Next, especially dangerous and, hence, an especially important booby trap for you to be aware of when you prepare the expert for deposition. While some qualifications may be out there in the cases, the following is an accurate enough statement for the purposes of a trial lawyer. Anything you show your expert to help get him ready for this deposition will be disclosable to counsel for the other side. All counsel for the other side has to say to your expert is, "Doctor, in the course of getting ready to give this deposition, did Mr. Younger show you certain documents?" "Yes." "What documents did he show you?" "Well, he showed me documents A, B, and C." "Mr. Younger, may I see them?"

Give it a more realistic air. The expert says, "Well, Mr. Younger showed me a looseleaf notebook in which he had organized what he thinks are the most important documents in this case with blue liner indicating the key language." Counsel: "Mr. Younger, may I have that notebook?" And the cases teach that counsel is entitled to the notebook. Listen, be very careful what you show the expert in the course of getting the expert ready to give his deposition. Or, for the matter of fact, in the course of getting the expert ready to testify at trial. The same thing can happen at trial.

Here's the rule to be aware of. Anything you show the expert, assume you're going to have to show opposing counsel. So if you do show it to the expert, make sure that you will not be embarrassed or disadvantaged by being obliged to show it to opposing counsel. If there's something you don't want to show to opposing counsel, such as your personal trial notebook, such as your selection of the key documents with underlining as to what is the important language, don't show it to the expert. Maybe you read it to him. I don't know, maybe you tell him about it. You do something to give him the benefit of it, but don't show it to him because that's going to make it disclosable to the other side.

And, finally, I'll mention this simply in summary form. When, as is not uncommon, the deposition of the expert is being videotaped, be sure that you have gone over with your expert the importance of the acting part of it. It's going to be on videotape. People are going to see you. Keep smirks to a minimum. Do not giggle. Do not do anything unpleasant with your body. In short, your demeanor should be as presentable and likable as possible and remember that the movies are different from the legitimate theater. It looks different on the screen and it may be that you're going to have to rehearse and rehearse and rehearse, letting your expert see himself on the video monitor, so that he understands how he must behave when the deposition is actually taken. I'll talk a little bit more about those matters when we get to a checklist of things to discuss with your client—things that apply to the client, to the expert, to anybody.

But let us turn now to what I call protecting the CEO, the chief executive officer—protecting the businessman who is one who occupies a high position with the firm that you are representing. And the reason we've got to talk about it specially is that it is a well-known tactic for the other side to demand to take the deposition of the chairman of the board because the chairman of the board has better things to do than sit here answering questions about things, in fact, he knows nothing of. You know, the lady slipped and fell at the supermarket. She broke her hip. That's a terrible thing and we're going to have to pay her a lot of damages. But the chairman of the board does not sweep up the lettuce leaves. He doesn't know about this matter. Still and all, you put the chairman of the board in the witness seat and you keep him there for a couple of days and before long he's ready to settle the case at any cost because he wants to get out of the deposition room. This was a tactic that was so common and so oppressive that it became a scandal in the administration of justice.

And not too many years ago the Federal Rules of Civil Procedure were amended so as to provide you with a device the purpose of which is expressly to permit you to protect the chief executive officer or the high-level businessman. You will find it in Federal Rule 26(b)(1). It is a special provision for a special kind of protective order. Now, you can read it for yourself as well as I can read it to you, so let me paraphrase and give you some idea of how you use it. You will invoke 26(b)(1) by making a motion asking that a deposition be canceled or limited on the ground that the person being deposed is not the person who has personal knowledge. That his deposition is being taken primarily for purposes of frustration and oppression. And you can make that argument because the legislative history makes it crystal clear that the purpose of the enactors in enacting 26(b)(1) was to permit you to protect your CEO or other high-placed businessman.

As a supplement to 26(b)(1), be aware of something that's not quite as new as 26(b)(1), but is relatively new and may post-date the time in law school of most of you in the audience and that is 26(f). You make not a motion for a protective order, but you make a motion for a discovery conference. If you make the motion, you are entitled to the conference. It gets you before the judge and you can then tell the judge what's being done that you regard as unfair, oppressive, frustrating, and improper use of discovery or the like, and the judge will make whatever regulatory order common sense and justice may require. Now, let's proceed now to talk about preparing your client and also your expert or your chief executive officer for deposition—a kind of checklist of things that you will discuss with your client.

All right. I'm going to move fairly quickly and I'm going to leave out some of the detail, confident that you understand that detail quite as well as I do and there's no need for me to recite it to you. First, make sure that the . . . I'm going to say the client, meaning the expert, the client or the witness who is allied with you. Make sure that that client is aware of the purpose and nature of a deposition. Remember that the client is not a lawyer. This is foreign territory to the client. Be sure that the client understands that the other side is finding out about the case, that the other side is pinning us down, and the like. If I may repeat myself, make sure that the client understands that it's pointless to try to persuade opposing counsel to go away. That's not going to happen. That's not the office or purpose of a deposition.

Next, make sure that the client understands the importance of the deposition—that whatever is said becomes a permanent part of the record of this case and can be used against us at trial. Hence, the importance of listening and being sure that you understand and of responding to each question with the truth, meaning what you, yourself, know.

Next, demeanor is important. Make sure the client knows that. And, to the extent necessary, discuss it with the client and even rehearse it. The other side is going to see you in action. Make sure that the other side sees you at your best. Dress properly. Minimal jewelry. Don't chew gum. Don't smoke during the deposition. And, of course, you put this just as delicately as you can—nothing to drink for 24 hours before. No medicine of any kind that morning and if you have to take medicine, tell me about it first—and so forth and so on.

Next, this is a sort of peculiar one, but you've got to watch for it. People have very strange streaks of vanity. If your client wears glasses, make sure that he wears glasses at the deposition. Don't let him sit there half-blind. And if he uses a hearing aid normally make sure he has the hearing aid in and on at the time of the deposition. Don't let vanity take over, that the client wants to appear youthful with uncorrected 20/20 vision, no hearing aid, and the like. He will be at a disadvantage if he is accustomed to those aids to perception, so he should be wearing them at the deposition.

Next, do not hesitate to ask for a break. If you just want to go out for a cigarette, remember, no smoking during the deposition. If you want to get a glass of water, if you want to go to the bathroom, or something of that kind, simply say that you want to take a recess and a recess will be taken.

Next, this is dirty pool. I think that these are dirty tactics, but I've run into these tactics and maybe you have, too. Your client is a nonsmoker. Any nonsmoker is aware that if somebody blows smoke at you—cigarette or cigar smoke or the like—it can be sickening. Watch out for opposing counsel laying down a smoke screen at your client to put him under pressure, to get him feeling sick to his stomach, or at least to get him feeling uneasy. I'm a nonsmoker and I get very uneasy sitting in an airplane when the people who are smoking have their stuff circulated around. I'd be very uncomfortable doing something as difficult as answering questions at a deposition and, at the same time, having smoke blown at me. If you see that that's happening, stop it. And if opposing counsel will not stop it, my advice is get up and walk out because the judge is going to be on your side.

Next, in whatever manner is appropriate to the client, help him maintain his poise. Don't get excited, don't laugh, don't cry—just treat it in a dignified and businesslike manner.

Next, as an aspect of this, don't quarrel with opposing counsel. If he asks a question that you think is foolish, the best way to answer is, "I really don't understand that," but don't quarrel with him over the foolishness of his question. Be courteous. Address opposing counsel as mister. If you can't remember the name, sir or madam is an all-purpose honorific and it'll get you by.

We've already said twice, let me say a third time, make sure the client understands that he must listen to the question, hear it, and understand it before answering it. And he answers it with the truth and the truth means exactly what the question calls for—nothing more and nothing less. Especially if you've got a high IQ client, what he is going to be inclined to do is to think ahead. Well, here's a question. What's counsel getting at? What's the next question going to be and the next question after that? That's the kiss of death. Do your best to persuade him not to do that. Focus on this question, answer this question, and then focus on the next question. But do not engage in a mental fencing match with opposing counsel. If the question is answerable, yes or no, that's the answer. Don't go beyond it. If the answer is "I don't know" or "I don't remember," that's the answer. Don't go beyond it.

Explain to opposing counsel what will happen if you make an objection. Give him some sense of why you make an objection and, most importantly, be sure that he understands that he's to wait until the lawyers finish their colloquy before answering the question.

Next, in a case involving distances, dimensions, and times, rehearse your client very carefully. Rehearse him so that he understands the importance of not being pinned down to a specific distance or a specific time. Rehearse him so that he prefaces whatever answer he makes with words to the effect of "This is only a rough estimate but it's the best I can give you."

Next, make sure your client understands that there's nothing wrong about his having discussed his testimony with you. And if he is asked that question, a truthful answer is, "Yes, I did discuss it with my lawyer, Mr. Younger," or whatever it may be. If the truthful answer is, yes, I did discuss it with anybody else, member of the family, or the like, that's the answer he must give. If he is asked what did your lawyer tell you to say, the answer is, "He told me to tell the truth," just that. Make sure that the client is set up with that answer just in case that old formula question comes.

Consider what poets call diction. When a poet uses the word diction, the poet does not mean how you pronounce your words, he means how you select your vocabulary, recalling that English has an enormously rich vocabulary, with many synonyms for virtually everything. To the ear of a poet, words that may mean the same thing in a dictionary sense do not mean the same thing in a poem. To the ear of a trial lawyer, words that may mean the same thing in a dictionary sense do not mean the same thing at a trial and, to the extent that you can, you want to consider with your client the use of one word as opposed to another word. For example, if your client is the defendant in a personal injury case arising out of an accident of some kind, I should think that your client should always use the word accident. If you are the plaintiff in that case, your client should always use the word crash, disaster, something of that kind. The words have different emotional overtones, though in a dictionary sense they mean the same thing. You can do even better than accident if you're the defendant. How about incident? Just as a personal footnote, how often I've heard plaintiff's lawyers put plaintiff on the stand at a trial and say, "Now, did an incident occur? Tell us about it." Mmm mmm. If you're the defendant, it's an incident. If you're the plaintiff, it's an appalling tragedy.

Now, a few remarks zeroed into the particular situation of the expert who is going to be deposed. And simply so that you understand and I'm not trying to be a comedian, my experience is that experts tend to be very difficult people. Actually, more often than not they tend to be just asses. There's no other way to describe it. And this is your expert as much as the other side's expert. And you have to work with them and work with them and work with them to minimize the asinine impression that inevitably they're going to make at the deposition. Right? Number one, don't engage in private conversation with opposing counsel. Experts love to do that. You know, they think they're going to explain to opposing counsel why opposing counsel is all wrong and he, the expert, is all right. Don't do that.

Next, if the deposition, as is not uncommon, is being taken at a place convenient to the expert, that place may well be the expert's office. Have you ever tried to take an expert's deposition while he responds to telephone calls and talks to people and answers letters and so forth? Make sure that he cuts off all of those distractions so that you've got the half a day or whatever it is uninterrupted in his office for the purpose of taking his deposition.

Next, review with your expert something that you know is going to come up on the deposition and that is his qualifications. Review them so that they're fresh in the expert's mind and that what he will testify to is what you want him to testify to—nothing more and nothing less. Most experts err on the side of too much. You know, they want to go on and on and on. And you may not want to do that, so you can rehearse with him so that he hits the highlights and then says something like, "For everything else, here's my resume," or something of that kind.

Next, don't volunteer. That applies to all witnesses, but it's especially important with respect to the expert. Answer only the question that is asked of you.

Next, try to answer in plain English. Avoid professional jargon or technical terms. That will prove to be close to impossible for the expert, but work on him, nevertheless.

Next, this, too, will prove to be close to impossible. Behave like an ordinary human being. Do not be condescending. Do not be patronizing. Maintain an appropriate professional dignity. You don't say things to your expert like, "Behave like a human being," because your expert will take it amiss. You rehearse it with him. You rehearse it and ideally you do it in front of the office video camera and let him see himself. And usually that's the most effective way of making clear that he's acting like an obnoxious stuffed shirt, when he actually sees it up there on the monitor.

Be sure the expert understands what objections are all about. Make sure that your expert understands the rule on impeaching an expert out of a treatise. You can't avoid that rule. It's 803(18) of the Federal Rules of Evidence, but make sure that your expert knows about it what he ought to know in order to be able to handle that kind of impeachment. Remember the old question about are you being paid for your testimony? Make sure that he knows that the answer is, "No, I'm not being paid for my testimony, I am being paid for my time." There is a difference and make sure that he knows that difference.

Let me talk about what I should have discussed before going into that fairly brief checklist. Remember, we assume that you're defending a deposition. When the other side finishes, you will have a right to cross-examine, to ask questions yourself. Should you cross-examine? My own view is that, unless there is compelling reason to do so, don't cross-examine. What you do primarily is tip your hand to such an extent that I think it's the decisive factor. If there's anything that desperately needs to be cleared up, all right, ask a question or two to clear it up. But unless it desperately needs clearing up, save it for the time of trial when the explanation will come as a surprise to opposing counsel. And as to handling the question, "Why didn't you give that explanation at the time of the deposition?" there's a wonderful answer, a wonderful answer that any witness can be prepared to give and it always works with the jury, and the answer is, "I wasn't asked that question." That's an end to it. Remember, the jury is on the witness's side. They're not thinking about lawyers maneuvering. And if he wasn't asked this question, that's why he didn't give this answer and he's giving it now for the first time at trial.

Which brings us, ladies and gentlemen, to something I was rather looking forward to because I don't know whether it's fair to call this precious knowledge, but it's unusual knowledge. I don't know that anybody has ever gone through the cases to pull this out. Remember the rule with respect to objections that must be made at the deposition or else you have waived them? Now, remember, we assume that you're defending a deposition, so it's your job to make objections at the risk of being deemed to have waived them. The rule says that you've got to object to anything that could be obviated at the time of the deposition and what that exactly means, nobody knows. At a minimum, however, it covers whatever we mean to include in that much used phrase, an objection as to form. As a matter of fact, many of us know as a matter of kind of lawyer's law that if your objection goes to the form of a question at a deposition, you must object at the time of the deposition or you will not be heard to object at the time of trial. Because an objection as to form is obviously an objection that could be obviated. Counsel asking the question simply reframes the question and the problem is resolved.

What is an objection to form? I dare say any experienced lawyer kind of recognizes it when he sees it, but the experienced lawyer would be hard put to make a list. I have made a list for you. There are nine different kinds of questions that are objectionable as to form. And while no one of these nine will come as a surprise to you, it will be handy, I trust, for you to have this list. So you might want to jot it down on the margin of your outline. In no particular order, first, a question which includes a quotation or summary of what this witness or another witness has earlier said and it's inaccurate is an objection as to form. Objection, you are misquoting the testimony of witness A. Or objection, that is not an accurate summary of what witness Z said. That is an objection as to form.

Next, a question that asks the witness to assume facts to be true, which facts are not in evidence. That's an objection as to form. And you've got to make it at the deposition or else you have waived it.

Next, in the course of deposing an expert, opposing counsel may ask a hypothetical question. If the hypothetical question is improper and it will be improper if at all because it includes a fact which may not be included. It may not be included because that fact is not in evidence and it's not the kind of thing on which experts in this field customarily rely. That is an objection as to form and you must make it at the deposition.

Next, a question that quarrels with the witness. The "how dare you say that" kind of question is a question that is bad as to form and you must object at the time.

Next, I think we're up to number five, a bullying question. Are you aware that I'm going to bring this testimony of yours to the attention of the district attorney? That's a bullying question. Object to it and it's deemed to be an objection as to form.

Next—now at this point, I'll grant you that there's a lot of give in the system, that these things don't have the arithmetic precision of 2 + 2 = 4. And, as a matter of fact, this and the next objection as to form are frequently used. They can be used and frequently are used to drive opposing counsel right up the wall. All right? Next objection, number six. The question calls for a narrative answer. See? "Well, what happened next?" Objection, that calls for a narrative. You've got to ask more pointed questions than that. Very good. He now changes it. "Well, the next thing that happened is that you got behind the wheel of your car, isn't that right?" And now you make the seventh objection, which is that it's leading. Right? So it calls for a narrative or it's leading and between those two, you can whipsaw opposing counsel to the point where he just is impotent, he doesn't know what to do. Now, of course, that's dirty pool and that's not the kind of behavior any of you would ever indulge in, but at least be aware that it's a possibility for opposing counsel. You may be on the receiving end of it and be aware of it.

Next, this is particularly common among young or inexperienced lawyers because it's a manifestation of nervousness. Two questions in one. "Well, what happened next? You got behind the wheel of your car, isn't that right?" Right, that's two questions in one. You should object to it. Objection as to form. "Counselor, you've asked two questions in one. Which question do you want the witness to answer?"

The ninth objection is my favorite because it permits not unpleasant teasing of opposing counsel. Have you ever heard the objection, "Objection, I don't understand the question," coming from opposing counsel? Never say that because if you say that to somebody like me, that is if somebody like me is your opponent, I'm going to say, "Counselor, your weakness of intellect is a ground of objection unknown to the law. The question is, does your client understand it." And, you know, every once in a while the client says, "I understand it," and the lawyer looks like a fool, right? The objection that should be made is not, "Objection, I don't understand it," it's just a matter of how you put it so that you deprive opposing counsel of the chance to one-up you. Say, "Objection, the question is unintelligible," which means nobody can understand it. That is a proper objection as to form and what counsel must now do is reframe the question, which does not say everything there is to say about the deposition on oral questions, ladies and gentlemen, but it does say what time permits us to say. And let us move on to the other formal discovery devices and, as you know, there is quite a handful of them.

The next formal discovery device, the mechanics of which are set forth in Rule 31 of the Federal Rules of Civil Procedure, is very rarely used. As a matter of fact, I know about it because I'm a student of and sometime teacher of civil procedure. But in my own practice and in my time on the bench, I cannot recall ever once using the deposition on written questions or seeing it used. It is exactly what you would think. It is a deposition, much as an oral deposition is a deposition. But instead of being done orally, the questions are written out in advance and submitted to the witness who responds to the questions in writing and, of course, under oath. The advantages of the deposition on written questions are, first, that by contrast with the oral deposition, it's cost free. I mean, there are some incidental costs, papers, postage, some stenographic expense. But it will rarely exceed $100 and you've got it. Whereas no oral deposition is ever going to cost as little as $100.

Next and final advantage, the only other advantage I can think of. Since both the direct and the cross-examination questions must be written in advance, when the adversary frames his cross-examination questions, invariably he tips his hand. He shows you a good deal about his case. And if he doesn't want to tip his hand, what he's got to do is forego cross-questions. Maybe that's the smart thing to do.

The disadvantages of the deposition on written question are weighty and probably account for what I said a moment ago, that you just never see this particular discovery device being used. First, it is totally inflexible. You realize that you've got to frame question two before you know the answer to question one. So you can go in a particular direction, but you can't change that direction in view of the answers the witness gives you because you don't know what those answers are at the time you write the questions. Next, there is no observation of the witness's demeanor. You don't get to see the witness in action. And, third—I guess it's really covered under the first—it's just inflexible, inflexible. You can't follow things up.

The one situation I can think of in which you might want to use a deposition on written questions is when you want to have something from the other side that you can offer in evidence as an admission. It is a matter on which you know you're going to get a helpful answer. They can't possibly change the fact. And you don't want to spend a lot of money. You know, sort of "Was there an accident on October 10, 1985?" That's not a very good example—here's a better example, "On the day the contract in issue was signed, how old were you?" Just that, that's all you want to know. How old was he? Was he above the age of infancy or below the age of infancy? One question using the device of the deposition on written questions will give you the answer in a form that you can read to the jury, put into evidence as an admission and you do it at minimal expense.

If you want to go beyond that, it seems to me that the deposition on written questions is not for you. What you will then consider is the discovery device that all of us are familiar with because anybody who's engaged in civil litigation has used this device. This is the device of the interrogatory. And since it always comes in numbers, it will be interrogatories. The mechanics governed by Rule 33 of the Federal Rules of Civil Procedure. Considerations that bear upon the tactical determination whether or not to use interrogatories? Well, let me mention five advantages. Five things you can do and do efficiently with an interrogatory. First, there is some kind of information and it's fairly frequent, it's not peculiar, it's not one in a million. It's almost an everyday occurrence. There is some kind of information that you could not possibly get on an oral deposition. For example, you're suing IBM, you are deposing the manager of the division of IBM that manufactures electric typewriters. And what you want to know is what you ask him in this question. "In 1978 how many electric typewriters did IBM sell in the United Kingdom and how many in 1979 and how many in 1980 . . ." and so forth. And the nature of the information is such that he's not going to be able to answer. You see, if anybody knows, this is the man who knows. But he doesn't know because nobody knows. This is not the kind of information that any one person carries in his or her head. This is information that rests in the files or, to use the lingo of the day, in the memory bank of the computer which serves as the files of the division of the company that manufactures electrical typewriters. So you use an interrogatory where what you want is detailed information or information in the form of a compilation that you could not possibly get in the course of an oral deposition.

Next, and this is a separate category, though of course it overlaps with the first. You may be looking for information that is not within the personal knowledge of any witness. Example: When was General Electric organized? What is the date of incorporation? I happen to know that the answer to that question is so long ago that there is no living person who can tell you of my own knowledge the date of incorporation was thus and so. So why bother with a deposition? An interrogatory is well calculated to give you that kind of information.

Next, remember that the interrogatory is the device intended by the draftsmen of the Federal Rules of Civil Procedure to be used when what you want is the other side's legal theory. It's right there in the rule. You may ask by way of an interrogatory how the facts are related to the law, which is simply a way of saying you can ask in an interrogatory, "What is your legal theory?"

Next, remember that interrogatories are available only from the opposing party. Plaintiff serves interrogatories upon defendant, defendant serves interrogatories upon plaintiff, which means, as you all understand—and if you don't, we'll have time to talk about it in the next hour—which means that the answers are admissible as an admission. The answers are themselves admissible as substantive evidence. And the fifth advantage is that it's relatively inexpensive. At least by contrast with the oral deposition it is inexpensive.

To go with those five advantages, there are four disadvantages. They are weighty and only you can decide how to strike the balance on the circumstances of any particular case. Disadvantage number one: No demeanor. You don't get to see anybody in action. Second, I personally regard this as an important aspect of the oral deposition: There is no possibility of the casual remark or the slip of the tongue. There is no possibility of the witness saying something unconsidered, saying something by mistake which then becomes the basis of a line of questioning. That possibility exists in an oral deposition, but not with interrogatories.

Next, because it's all done on papers back and forth between the lawyers, there is no follow-up. Or put it this way. There's no instant follow-up. You can follow up instantly at an oral deposition. Those of you who have engaged in heavy civil litigation will know that for interrogatories, what you do is send out interrogatories, you commonly call it set 1, and now when you get the answers back, some of the answers will suggest additional interrogatories. They go out as set two. So, yes, there's a follow-up, but it's cumbersome, it's disconnected in time, and it's not terribly efficient.

The fourth disadvantage is the principal one. The answers to interrogatories will ultimately be drafted by opposing counsel. The information may come from the opposing litigant, but it's the lawyer who writes the answers. Which means that if you want to be cute, if you want to obstruct, if you want to delay, if you want to engage in obfuscation, it can be done. Those possibilities are minimized at an oral deposition. But there are certain situations in which the interrogatory is, above all else, the device to use. And when you've got this kind of situation, I think you don't have to ponder it. Use the interrogatory, it's better than anything else.

First, when you want the names of witnesses, you use the interrogatory. Next, a little bit different from the names of witnesses, when you want the names of those the other side has interviewed, use the interrogatory. Next, when you want to know whether the other side has insurance and the amount of the insurance. The older hands in the room are aware that that is sometimes a key fact because that is the fact on which settlement depends. Younger lawyers sometimes need to be reminded that you bring civil lawsuits for a particular remedy. The remedy is money. That's what you want. And if the other side doesn't have money, it is pointless to pursue the lawsuit. Because we don't put people in jail for debt and it doesn't serve anybody's purpose to put him in jail anyway. You want the money. Frequently the only asset on the defendant's side is that insurance policy. If the limit of the insurance policy is $10,000, why try to get more if there are no other assets? And that is why knowing about the insurance will frequently lead to a settlement.

The other side tells you there is insurance and the policy limit is $10,000. Well, that's it, case settled. $9,500. Give the other side $500 sort of to show they did a job. Right? But if the insurance policy is $100,000, the case is settled for $99,000. And, you know, there was a time when you weren't allowed to know about insurance. Now, I'm not talking about telling the jury of insurance, I'm talking about information between counsel. And it's what, maybe 10 or 11 years ago that the Federal Rules were amended to provide that the fact of insurance and the amount of coverage must be disclosed and the best way to get it is by an interrogatory.

Next, the only discovery that under the Federal Rules you get of right with respect to experts is discovery by way of interrogatories—the identity, qualifications, and the summary of what the expert is going to say.

Next, information about documents is best obtained by way of interrogatories. Where are they? Who is in charge of them? How are the files arranged and the like? Technical data, statistics. Let me just run down the list here. Where I have nothing to add, I will not take the time to add anything. Other claims of this sort brought against the litigant—important in product liability litigation, obviously. A litigant's medical history. A litigant's work history. Legal theories we've already mentioned. Admissions that you know will be made, damages, the way in which the business organization is set up. And finally, and don't ever forget it—it should always be your final interrogatory. Who is the person who prepared the answers to these interrogatories? If more than one, who are they? Find out who they are and you might consider following up your interrogatories with an oral deposition of the person or persons on the other side who prepared the answers to the interrogatories.

We've already mentioned an aspect of contemporary legal practice that is commonplace. You're not limited to one interrogatory or one document containing a number of interrogatories. It is quite common for interrogatories to come in waves and lawyers commonly describe it not as a first wave, but as a first set of interrogatories, followed three months later by a second set, and so on. Sometimes you use the word series instead of the word set, but it means the same thing. Remember that interrogatories work very efficiently when you use them before you take the deposition of somebody. Get the basic information in the form of answers to interrogatories, then take your deposition.

Next, and I'm moving quickly because everybody, I dare say, is familiar with these aspects of interrogatory practice. It is unusual these days to see interrogatories that do not begin with a set of instructions and definitions. To the other side, in answering these interrogatories, proceed as follows. The following words shall be deemed to mean the following, and it's almost as if you are drafting the definitions section of a statute. What you're doing is trying to avoid skirmishing between the lawyers as to syntactical ambiguity or ambiguity in the vocabulary in which the interrogatories are couched. Be sure to include in the instructions or definitions or perhaps as a sort of second interrogatory after each main interrogatory if you have responded in words or in substance with, "I cannot answer this interrogatory," explain why you cannot answer it.

And, finally, bear in mind that wonderful mechanism that 33(c) gives you. Where the other side wants information that is contained in your client's records and your client does not object to letting the other side go through the records, your response to the interrogatory is essentially, "We will give you access to the records, you compile the information." And that is an adequate response to the interrogatory, the rule says so. You don't have to spend all kinds of time and effort compiling the information. Let the other side compile the information and it is extraordinary how often the other side loses its enthusiasm when it turns out that they have to put in the hundreds of hours necessary to compile this information instead of you.

Looking ahead a little bit to something we'll talk about, albeit very briefly, at the very end, interrogatories, as much as the oral deposition, lend themselves to abuse. The oral deposition lends itself to abuse when it's protracted as scandalously as that nine-and-a-half year deposition I mentioned a little bit earlier. The interrogatory is abused when it is multiplied to the point where nobody is going to sit and answer 10,000 interrogatories. Because no matter how dedicated you are to the practice of law, ultimately you're going to say to yourself that life is too short, I'm just not going to sit here and answer this kind of stuff, and you're going to walk away from it. Especially since the invention of what I call the memory typewriter—you know, the typewriter where you push a button and out it comes.

Interrogatories in enormous volume have come to be quite common. Volumes so enormous that I know of cases where they don't even bother to count the interrogatories, they simply weigh them. First set of interrogatories, 25 pounds. Second set, 40 pounds, and the like. I have seen interrogatories in antitrust cases where the first interrogatory was "What was the date of the marriage?" and the second interrogatory was "Where did the marriage take place?" And the memory typewriter is only a machine. It has in its memory every interrogatory that has ever been asked in every lawsuit that this office has ever handled. And somebody said to the memory typewriter, "Just regurgitate all of your interrogatories, whether they have to do with antitrust or not, because we're only weighing it out. We're not even going to read them, let alone answer them." And you hire a truck and you send it over to the other side and the other side looks at the 20 pounds of interrogatories and they call in some junior lawyer and say, "You're going to answer these things," and the junior lawyer just says, "No, I'm not and I'm going to go to dental school, and goodbye and good luck."

And ultimately this becomes a problem in the administration of justice. And I speak just as softly as I can. It leads to what? It leads to such phenomena—I'm sure many of you are familiar with them—local rules. Local rules of more than one United States district court. Saying what? Believe it or not, saying you may not serve interrogatories that have been typed on a memory typewriter. There is one, at least one federal court that has such a rule. Perhaps a little bit more focused—you may not serve more than 20 interrogatories at a time. And you know what happens the next day? The lawyer serves 20 interrogatories. Interrogatory 1A, B, C, D, blah, blah, blah, AA, AAA, AAAA, and so forth, so that the 20 interrogatories are really 20,000 interrogatories. And then you need an amendment to the local rule. No more than 20 interrogatories counting each subpart as an interrogatory. And you continue this duel between the court and the bar, with the bar trying to persist in using discovery in all kinds of abusive ways and the court trying to prevent it. Rule 11 ultimately will rear its formidable head, of course, but be aware that interrogatories are subject to this kind of abuse and let us move on to the next discovery device, which is discovery and inspection.

The mechanics are set forth in Rule 34 of the Federal Rules of Civil Procedure—discovery and inspection is a way of getting access to something tangible, be it documents in a file, be it the wreck of the car that was involved in an accident, or anything in between. Discovery and inspection is relatively inexpensive and where some tangible object is involved in a lawsuit, it is well to pursue discovery and inspection.

The tactical considerations, and I think they all militate in the direction of invoking discovery and inspection, are first, do it early, before people have had a chance to work on the object, to change it, to vet the files, or the like. Second, take a foundation witness with you. If you're inspecting real property, take a surveyor, take a photographer, take somebody like that, depending upon the circumstances. Next, take photographs in almost every instance. And, remember, a photograph would include Xeroxes or photostats or other kinds of photomechanical reproduction of documents. Take photomechanical copies of documents that seem to be important. Take photographs of the wreck of the car that was involved in the accident, whatever it may be. Frequently the photographs will be unnecessary, but it happens often enough that they become useful that it's well to follow the rule that you will take them in every case.

Which brings us, nearing the end, not of our consideration of discovery, but our consideration of the formal discovery devices, that brings us to the physical or mental examination, governed by Rule 35, and it permits one side to cause the other side to undergo a physical or a mental examination where physical or mental condition is relevant in the case. I think that the tactical considerations bearing upon physical or mental examination are best considered from the respective viewpoints. First, the lawyer who notices the examination and then the lawyer whose client has to go for the examination. If you are the lawyer noticing the examination, it seems to me that there are five important things that you want to have in mind. First, choose a doctor whom you would be content to call as an expert witness. Choose a doctor who's credible, who'll make a good impression, et cetera, et cetera. Bear in mind that in choosing the doctor to conduct a physical or mental examination, you are, in fact, pretty much choosing a witness. Second, do not permit that examination to go forward until you have received the medical records of the person to be examined and have supplied those records to the examining doctor. It is a waste of time to permit the doctor to examine the person without access to the records. And what opposing counsel will do is stall, try to bring it about that you've wasted the time. Don't let that happen. Just keep adjourning, putting off, postponing the physical or mental examination until, in fact, the records are in hand.

Next, here I incorporate by reference what I said earlier about experts in general and I guess I did not say, but might have said, about doctors in particular. They sometimes do very strange things. This third piece of advice from me to you has in mind that the doctor may do something strange. Make sure that your doctor understands that his job is to examine and formulate his opinion. He is not to treat. He is not to prescribe. I have heard of examining doctors who want to take out the hypodermic needles and start giving injections and the like. That's not his job. This person is not his patient. This person is simply someone he is to examine for the purpose of formulating an opinion, which opinion he may testify to in court.

Fourth, again, on the general principle that doctors tend to be peculiar and even if this is not a peculiarity, all doctors are always two hours behind, right? We've all gone to the doctor's or the dentist's office and you know that even though you've got a 3 o'clock appointment, you're going to sit there until 5 o'clock before he reaches you. Tell the doctor to be prompt. I will not mention this when I consider the tactics on the other side, but if it's my client sitting in the doctor's office to be examined under Rule 35 and the notice said be there at 3 o'clock, I don't want to be unreasonable, I'll wait 15 minutes. But at 3:15 I say to my client, "Get up and let's go." And my position is, you have waived your right to have a physical or mental examination. You waived it by not doing it at the time in your own notice you said you would do it, subject to 15 minutes leeway. You want to give him a half an hour leeway, whatever. But there comes a point when it's no longer reasonable to wait and I think it is a plausible argument that the other side has waived the right to take the physical or mental examination.

And finally, fifth and last under the heading of tactics for the attorney noticing the examination, make sure that your doctor takes a history from the person to be examined. Don't rely on the medical records. Have your doctor begin his examination with, "Mr. Smith, tell me the history of this thing. What happened?" And have your doctor take notes. Because the history you get from Mr. Smith may well be different in important ways from the history he has given his own doctor and you'd like to know that because you can do something with it at trial.

Now, switch over. You are the lawyer whose client is going to be examined. Let me give you five things that I would be concerned with. First, the notice identifies the doctor. To use the language of the teenagers, check him out. Look him up in the medical directories and make sure that he is the person he purports to be.

Second . . . now this one is a little bit, what shall I say, beneath the surface. The notice names Dr. Smith. We all know because we go to the doctor from time to time that most doctors these days practice in some kind of partnership, in an HMO, or whatever it may be. It may be just two or three doctors who get together and pool their practice so that every once in a while one of them can have a weekend off or take a vacation. So be it, perfectly reasonable. But this is a lawsuit and you give up nothing in a lawsuit. If the notice says that the examination is to be performed by Dr. Smith, Dr. Smith performs the examination. And if one of his partners in that medical practice undertakes to perform the examination, I get up and walk out. And my position is you have waived your right to a physical or a mental examination. You said it would be Dr. Smith and he wasn't there.

Next, implicit in what I've said, don't send the client unaccompanied to the doctor's office. You go or some other lawyer from your office goes, but I think it should be a lawyer. Someone reasonably conversant with what's going on and someone who will have the guts, if need be, to say to the client, "Let's get up and we're walking out of here."

Next, prepare your client on the history that the client is going to give the doctor. Rehearse it. Review the history that has previously been given by your client to be sure that the history given on this occasion is consistent with the earlier one.

And, finally, no injections, no treatment, no nothing. All the doctor does is poke and listen and ultimately formulate his opinion. And, by the way, my practice has been to insist that I be present during the examination. The doctor will resist it like mad because he regards it as an affront to his professional dignity. And I say something like, "Doctor, I understand that, but your professional dignity is not involved, this is not your patient, you're not treating the patient. This is a law matter. I'm the lawyer. If you're going to examine my client, I'm going to sit there while you do it. If you want me to look away at any particular moment, I'll look away, but I'm going to be in the room when you do it." Where you've got a cross-gender problem, bear that in mind. If you think that it makes sense to have a lawyer in the room at all times and the client, the person being examined is a woman, maybe a woman lawyer should go along to reduce the embarrassment and the tension of that kind of thing. But that's kind of common sense and I leave it to you.

This last of the formal discovery devices, ladies and gentlemen, is a very peculiar bird. It is traditionally viewed as a discovery device, but its nature is such that you cannot possibly learn anything as a result of using this device that you didn't already know. In short, it is absolutely without utility with respect to the classic purpose of discovery, finding out about the case. The sole purpose of Rule 36 is to give you a device that will be handy with respect to streamlining the proof and marshaling the evidence so that what you put before the jury or the judge in a bench trial is as interesting as you can make it and is forthright and moves quickly to a point. In short, so that you don't bore your audience. The request for admissions is the way you do it. The mechanics, as I've said, are set forth in Rule 36. But a brief reminder and, by the way, I remind you of it because in my experience, most lawyers make insufficient use of the request for admissions under Rule 36. I dare say most lawyers know about it, but they're just not accustomed to using it and I think extensive use should be made of Rule 36 because it permits you to try a better case. And remember, I, yours truly, your speaker today, is a trial lawyer as opposed to a litigator and I'm always concerned with what's going to make for a better trial.

You send to the other side a piece of paper that says something like, "For purposes of this trial and these purposes only, admit the truth of the following facts," and you list facts which in good faith you believe are not reasonably to be disputed. Alternatively, in this paper you say, "Concede the authenticity of the documents attached or the accuracy of the photographs attached." Now, remember, the other side is not conceding admissibility. They're free to argue irrelevance or the like, they're only conceding that the contract, a copy of which is attached to the request for admissions, is not a forgery, that it is authentic or that the photograph is, indeed, an accurate photograph of the IDS Building or the Empire State Building or whatever it may be. You see, then, that by adept use of the request for admissions, you remove areas of the case from controversy. There is no need to prove a fact which the other side has admitted. There is no need to indulge in the choreography otherwise required of you to prove the authenticity of a document or the accuracy of a photograph where those matters have been admitted by the other side. And how do they admit it? They admit it by failing to respond to your request for admissions. Silence is deemed to be an admission. Or if the other side is careful, they will respond, but they will say "I admit it." If they don't admit it, they're supposed to explain why. And remember that if the court later determines that the denial was unreasonable, even though the other side wins the case, they can be assessed the cost you were put to in proving those facts or in establishing the authenticity of those documents or the accuracy of those photographs.

It seems to me that lawyers should make ample use of Rule 36. I've already told you that I think most lawyers do not. Certainly, consider using Rule 36 to establish the authenticity of governmental and corporate records, the kinds of records that, in the real world, will not be forgeries. These are what they purport to be. We can argue relevance, but certainly there's no point in arguing authenticity. You'd be surprised how many cases involve family relationships. That A is the husband of the daughter of B and you can't prove it through birth records or you could prove it through birth records, but it would be very cumbersome and tedious. Who can reasonably dispute that kind of thing? Establish it by way of a request for admissions. We've already talked about the accuracy of photographs or maps. The authenticity of medical records, of age and employment records, really can't be disputed. They're tailor made for the request for admissions. Documents of title in a real property action work very well in connection with a request for admissions.

The only consideration on the other side of the ledger is a consideration most lawyers don't have to worry about because they're nowhere near this danger point. If you ask the other side to concede everything and the other side does concede everything. I mean everything but the one or two facts that really need to be tried, you risk losing drama. You risk taking all of the blood out of the case. And you don't want to do that, you want to strike a happy medium so that the tedium is removed from the trial, but the drama, the human aspect of it, is retained. And after a while, the experience, the feel for the courtroom will give you that happy medium. Ladies and gentlemen, that completes our discussion of the formal discovery devices, meaning the discovery devices that are set forth in the discovery article of the Federal Rules of Civil Procedure.

But let me go beyond that. And here I am putting before you information that I discovered kind of by accident as I engaged in my practice, such as it was, back east. I am not aware that you will find this in any of the treatises on discovery. I'm not aware that there's any case, that there's any law review article that talks about it. But it may prove to be as useful to some of you as it has proved to be useful to me.

There is one other discovery device. It is a formal discovery device in the sense that you use it in accordance with the terms set forth in the Federal Rules of Civil Procedure. But it's not a formal discovery device in that you don't find it in the discovery article. Nobody thinks of this as a discovery device. I just stumbled into the realization that this device is frequently the cheapest way to find out what the other side knows. It is the cheapest way to engage in discovery. And what is it but our old friend—because everybody knows it, but you know it from a different viewpoint—our old friend the motion for summary judgment, more precisely, the motion for partial summary judgment under Rule 56 of the Rules of Civil Procedure.

Now, remember when a motion for summary judgment or partial summary judgment is appropriate. When it appears that all of the evidence demonstrates that the facts are just one way. Since the facts are just one way, there's no reason to have a trial or at least a trial on this issue, because the purpose of a trial, after all, is to determine disputed fact issues. If the facts are all one way, you say to the court, "Let's not have a trial, let us proceed directly to the entry of judgment," and that's why you call it summary judgment.

I posit a situation in which you have evidence tending to show that the facts on whatever the issue is are A, B, and C. And if the facts are A, B, and C, you win, you are entitled to judgment. You don't know what the other side has. You might take a deposition, but that's going to cost you a couple of thousand dollars. You might try interrogatories, but they're going to obfuscate around and you'll never get the answer. Make a motion for partial summary judgment on the issue in connection with which you have the evidence that adds up to A, B, and C. And argue it just as powerfully as you can. There is no contrary possibility. The facts are A, B, and C. We are therefore entitled to partial summary judgment our way on this issue. And if that is the state of the record, it seems to me that you are perfectly compliant with Rule 11 requiring you to proceed in good faith and with the proper legal basis, and so forth. In your heart of hearts, it may be that you're prepared to admit to yourself, at 2 o'clock in the morning when you think about this, that you don't expect to win the motion. You're not making it to win, you're making it to get the other side's opposing papers. Because how does the other side oppose summary judgment? By demonstrating the existence of an issue of fact requiring a trial. And how do they demonstrate the existence of that kind of issue of fact? By showing the judge what evidence they have in the form of affidavits, copies of documents, or the like. And there it is. The papers opposing the summary judgment motion are discovery, pure and simple, in the handiest possible form. Here is the affidavit of the opposing litigant. Here are statements of witnesses on the other side. Here are the key documents attached to the affidavit, laid out. You're going to lose the motion for summary judgment, yes, because there is a fact issue to be tried. But you expected to lose it. You now know what the other side's proof is and you know it at the expense of preparing a motion for summary judgment—invariably much, much less than the expense of going through an oral deposition.

I commend it to you, and the *Celotex* case[2] in the United States Supreme Court, just 18 months ago, is an interesting example of what I'm talking about. It is a complicated case that, at first reading, has nothing to do with discovery. Read it again carefully and it's perfectly obvious, I know you will agree, that in the *Celotex* case, the side that ultimately prevailed in the Supreme Court made two motions for summary judgment. The first motion was designed to smoke the other side out, to find out what evidence they had. They found out what evidence the other side had and lost the motion for summary judgment. Now they made a second motion for summary judgment on a somewhat different footing, using the information that they had been given in opposition to the first motion for summary judgment. And on that they prevailed all the way to the Supreme Court. So the *Celotex* case is a laboratory demonstration of very skilled counsel using the motion for summary judgment as a discovery device. I urge you to consider using it as a discovery device. I think you will find it to be fruitful and I know that you will find it to be less expensive than an oral deposition.

Which brings us, ladies and gentlemen, to limits on discovery, a subject we adverted to, but essentially finessed, at the very beginning when we made the point that the scope of discovery under the Federal Rules and under their state analogues, is essentially infinite. It's anything that would be evidence or anything that might lead to evidence, and that means anything because you can always make an argument that A will ultimately

---

2. *Celotex Corp. v. Catrett*, 477 U.S. 317 (1986).

lead to Z. If you're a good enough lawyer and a good enough philosopher, you can make those arguments and lawyers are quite good enough to make such arguments. Anything is therefore discoverable. The argument that something is irrelevant is not likely to be a winning argument if by irrelevant you mean not within the scope of discovery. It may be irrelevant at the trial. It may not be admissible in evidence under the rules on relevance, et cetera, et cetera, at the trial. But insofar as the scope of discovery is concerned, anything goes. But there are exceptions.

The exceptions are three in number and I'm not going to pretend that anybody in my audience doesn't know these three exceptions, but simply so that it's been refreshed in your mind, let's review them. First, the Constitution of the United States and of the several states apply in discovery. You have all of the constitutional protections in the course of discovery that you otherwise would have. And the one that comes up virtually all of the time is the Fifth Amendment or its state equivalent, the privilege against self-incrimination. It comes up fairly rarely, so that many lawyers don't quite know what the law is on this, but the law is now well settled. You don't have cases in every single jurisdiction on it. For the most part, you've got no cases in any given jurisdiction. But a sampling of cases in a scattered few jurisdictions, a sampling that is large enough to make it clear that this is the state of the law.

Proposition number one, a party being deposed or being asked to answer interrogatories or the like, has the right to claim the privilege against self-incrimination. When I say a party, I mean anybody being deposed. If the person being deposed or otherwise responding to discovery is a third person, a bystander, that person may plead his privilege against self-incrimination. There is no way to prevent it. But by contrast with the situation in the criminal practice, comment may be made on the invocation of the privilege against self-incrimination. You may argue to the jury whatever inferences you think ought to be drawn and the jury draws whatever inferences they think are fair and proper, but the argument is a permissible one.

Suppose now that the person claiming the privilege against self-incrimination is a litigant—the plaintiff or the defendant. A litigant has a perfect right to plead his Fifth Amendment privilege, to plead his privilege against self-incrimination. But—and here's the point—you do not have a right both to plead your privilege and to continue to litigate this case. If you want to litigate the case, you've got to give discovery. And if you don't want to give discovery because of the Fifth Amendment, you don't have to, but then you don't litigate the case. Consequence. Assuming it to be an important matter—it's not some triviality—if a plaintiff pleads his privilege against self-incrimination, he may do so, but the complaint will be dismissed on the ground that he's refusing to make discovery, that's all. He has a right to refuse to make it. You're not going to punish him. But he may not have it both ways. If he wants to pursue this lawsuit, he gives up his Fifth Amendment right.

If the defendant pleads his privilege against self-incrimination, it's the same thing. He may not continue to litigate this case. He is deprived of a defense, which means what? Most lawyers and judges say that you strike his answer and you simply proceed to the question of a remedy. If what the plaintiff wants is money, you will have an inquest. You will have a trial, it's limited solely to the issue of damages. And that's exactly what you do whenever a defendant refuses to participate in discovery. Now, that's fairly rare, I'll grant you. That's why you have only a scattering of cases in a handful of jurisdictions. This does not come up every day.

What may well come up every day in the course of the busy litigation practice is the second exception to the wide-open scope of discovery that we have. And this second exception is the set of privileges that you find in the law of evidence, meaning to distinguish the law of evidence from the Constitution. There are privileges that are based upon the Constitution, most importantly the privilege against self-incrimination. There are privileges that are based upon the law of evidence. Call them evidentiary privileges. They are, in the instance of private litigants, the attorney-client privilege, the physician-patient privilege, the spousal privilege, and then, depending upon your jurisdiction, because not all jurisdictions recognize it, you may have a parent-child privilege, you may have an accountant-client privilege, you may have a social worker–client privilege and you may have a psychotherapist-patient privilege that's different from the physician-patient privilege. It covers the psychotherapist, who is not a physician. In short, you carry with you into the deposition session your knowledge of the jurisdiction's law of privilege.

Bear in mind that under the Federal Rules of Evidence there really is no federal law on privileges. In a case governed by state substantive law, the federal court applies the state law of privileges. In a case that is determined by federal law as a matter of substance, the law of privilege is common law. There's nothing in the Federal Rules, it's the judge doing whatever he thinks sensible and most judges will find the rule of privilege applied in that state to be very sensible indeed and that's what the judge will apply. So essentially there is no federal law of privileges, it's all state law of privileges. All right?

You must know what privileges are recognized by your state. Every state recognizes the attorney-client privilege. Every state in some fashion recognizes the spousal privilege and I think every state, at least in some measure, recognizes the physician-patient privilege. What happens if your client is asked a question, the answer to which is protected under one of the evidentiary privileges? Now this is . . . well, it's not really difficult, but it's a little bit slippery and it's slippery because the Federal Rules of Civil Procedure suggest an answer which is not the answer that all practitioners go by. What the Federal Rules of Civil Procedure say, you will remember, is that if an objection is made to a question, the witness or your client is supposed to answer the question. And then the judge at trial will rule upon the objection. Sustain it, in which case that's an end to it; or overrule it, in which case it's already been answered.

Anybody who has participated in depositions is familiar with the practitioner's objection that goes as follows: "Objection. I direct you not to answer it." You tell your witness or your client not to answer the question. That seems to fly in the face of what the rules say. The rules, remember, say you've got to answer the question to which objection is made subject to the judge's ruling later on, when you're before the judge at the time of trial. That is a bit of slipshod draftsmanship in the

Federal Rules of Civil Procedure. I have no doubt that every federal judge in the land will recognize the propriety in certain instances which I will describe in a moment, of saying to a client, "I object to the question, don't answer it." The instances where that's what you do are those instances in which to answer the question defeats the very purpose of the objection.

Now, if you object on the basis of privilege, what is the purpose of the objection? To keep this information confidential. Opposing counsel says to your client, "Did you meet with your lawyer, Mr. Younger, yesterday?" "Yes." "Tell me what Mr. Younger said to you and what you said to Mr. Younger." "Objection. Attorney-client privilege." But now if we were to permit him to answer the question, the whole thing is subverted because the information comes out and the judge, at the time of trial, will sustain our objection, there's no doubt about it, but you can't put the cat back in the bag. The information has been disclosed. So as a matter of common sense, if you will, the objection should be coupled with a direction to the client not to answer. And I personally have no doubt that that is proper.

Now, that's not the only kind of objection in which you will say to the client, "Don't answer." Where the objection is not based on an evidentiary privilege but is based on some formal problem or difficulty with the question. The question is bad as to form. Remember the nine possibilities we went through. You will make an objection and direct the witness not to answer in fairness to the witness. But the direction not to answer is only for a couple of moments. You direct him not to answer until the lawyer reformulates the question. If the lawyer says something like, "Do you know that I'm going to take the record of your testimony to the District Attorney and ask him to indict you for perjury?" you direct the witness not to answer that. That question is bad as to form. It is a bullying question. In fairness to the witness, the witness doesn't answer it. But if the lawyer will reformulate the question so that it's proper as to form, then you'll allow the witness to answer it. "All right, I'm sorry, I got carried away," says opposing counsel. "Mr. Witness, are you aware that you're under oath?" All right, that's proper.

Not terribly imaginative, but it is proper. The witness may answer it and on you go. Right?

So you've got the objection coupled with the direction not to answer where it's necessary to preserve the very point of the objection or where in fairness to the witness it's necessary. As to anything else, I think that our obligations as members of the bar and officers of the court are such that your objection is coupled, maybe sub silencio, with a statement to your client or witness as follows: "I've objected to the question. I'm sure the judge will sustain that objection, but answer it anyway." And that essentially is the objection on the grounds of relevance. Relevance. Not really relevant to the lawsuit. I object on that ground, but since the scope of discovery is wide open and since it doesn't really hurt anybody and it's not unfair to you, you may answer the question.

The third limitation on discovery is the so-called work product privilege. There's an enormous amount of litigation on this and properly so. I think it is a sensitive and important issue and it appeals to me as I dare say it appeals to everyone who is listening to me. The work product privilege, to begin with, is not an evidentiary privilege. It is a customary sloppiness of language that has us calling it a privilege. It is not a privilege in the way that the attorney-client privilege is or the spousal privilege is. It's not part of the law of evidence. It is entirely a part of the law of procedure. It is a necessary part of the law of procedure simply because of the adversarial system.

And you all remember that the work product privilege begins as a creation of the Supreme Court. It comes out of the mind of the Supreme Court in a case called *Hickman v. Taylor*[3] in which . . . I'm now sort of simplifying and typifying the facts of *Hickman v. Taylor,* but essentially this is what happened. In the course of discovery, counsel for the defendant says to counsel for the plaintiff,

"Have you prepared this case?"

"Yes, sir."

---

3. *Hickman v. Taylor*, 329 U.S. 495 (1947).

"Have you put a lot of time and effort into it?"

"Yes."

"And are you a good and imaginative lawyer?"

"Yes."

"And do you have a trial memorandum that sets forth for you and your partners' use how you're going to try this case?"

"Yes."

"Give it to me."

Well, under the scope of discovery, isn't it discoverable? It's evidence or it might lead to evidence. And yet it offends us all, just as it offended the Supreme Court in *Hickman v. Taylor*. And do you see why it's offensive? It permits lazy counsel to take a free ride on the energy and the diligence and the intelligence of counsel who is energetic and diligent and intelligent. And we don't want that kind of free ride to be taken. And so in *Hickman v. Taylor*, the Supreme Court said, "We carve out of the normal scope of discovery an exception for material which has been prepared by counsel and which in fairness ought not to be made available to the other side because the other side should do the same thing for itself. Be energetic, be creative. Go out and put in the time and effort that it takes adequately to prepare this case for trial."

Now, the work product doctrine of *Hickman v. Taylor* was codified by the Advisory Committee so that it's now part of the Federal Rules of Civil Procedure. You don't have to go to *Hickman v. Taylor*, you go to Rule 26(b)(3). And there you have the work product privilege and if you want to see how it works, apply to particular facts, you take a look at the more recent cases. I'm not going to parse hundreds of cases with you. I think the following is a fair and accurate summary of what the cases say and I think it's good enough for most trial lawyers to have in mind, recognizing that you'll go to the library, to the Lexis or the WestLaw keyboard if ever you have to investigate a particular problem involving the work product privilege.

If material has been prepared in order to try this case (to use lawyer jargon, if material has been prepared in contemplation of litigation) remember, that means it's not prepared in the ordinary course of the client's business, it's prepared to get ready to try this case. And it's prepared under the supervision of counsel. Sometimes it's by counsel himself, sometimes it's merely under his supervision. An investigator prepared it, an accountant prepared it, or the like. It is not discoverable. It is protected by the work product privilege, but the work product privilege is a weak privilege. It can be overborne. And if the other side can demonstrate that the information is not available to it upon the application of reasonable diligence and that a fair or just trial requires that this information be turned over, then the judge can overrule the assertion of privilege and say to the lawyers who have done a good job, "You've got to give your work product to the other side because they can no longer do it for themselves and it's necessary to a fair or just result."

For example, if a witness was interviewed at the very beginning and that witness is now dead, so that the other side cannot interview the witness, it may be that you're going to have to turn the stuff over. Now, there's always room for an argument, of course. The other side knew about this witness for two years, the witness only died last month. For one year and 11 months the other side has sat around doing absolutely nothing, just twiddling their thumbs. "Surely, Your Honor, that is not reasonable diligence. That's not a ground upon which to override my claim of privilege and turn me into a kind of paralegal working for the other side in this lawsuit." And on and on you go and if you ultimately touch the judge's nerve, the judge is going to say, "Damn, right. That's right. Objection sustained, you don't have to turn it over." So much for the exceptions to the normally wide open, virtually limitless scope of discovery.

Let me turn now to the use of discovery at trial, a subject in which, if anyone is interested in the impressions I get as a result of my experience, such as it is, lawyers do not have a very coherent picture in mind. This is a subject on which the rules are well settled. There ought to be no doubt or confusion at all, but lawyers are frequently in a great deal of doubt and confusion. How do you use discovery at trial? It's governed by Rule 32 and all Rule 32 really tells you is that discovery is usable at trial in accordance with the law of evidence. So you've got to know your law of evidence and apply it to the results of discovery at trial.

Now understand what we're not now considering. We're not considering discovery as a way of finding out about the case. You know, you read through all of the depositions and now you know all about the case. All right. That's done. We're not talking about it as a way of marshaling or streamlining the proof. That's done. We're not talking about it especially as a way of pinning down the other side so that they can't change their story between now and the time of trial. That's been done. We are on trial. What use may you make of discovery at the trial?

And I urge you to organize your understanding of how the law of evidence, as it were, intersects with discovery around three principal topics. First, impeachment. Impeachment is a more precise term, the looser form of which is cross-examination. Impeachment means that you examine the witness so as to show the judge or jury that the witness is not credible, is not worth believing. Now, one of the ways in which you may impeach a witness is with the witness's earlier inconsistent statement. The witness has said one thing in court on direct examination. Now on cross-examination we demonstrate that the witness at some time in the past said something different. So the argument is that the witness speaks with a forked tongue, talks out of both sides of his mouth, is not worth believing at either time.

Assuming that the witness gave you a statement in the course of informal discovery or you took the witness's deposition, formal discovery, the oral deposition, or even that the witness is the opposing litigant and he answered interrogatories for you, remember that the statement he gave you informally or the testimony he gave at the deposition or the answer to the interrogatory is . . . any one of those . . . is a prior inconsistent statement for purposes of impeachment. And all you have to do is impeach him with it. And how do you impeach him with it? Well, this is not the occasion to talk about the tactics of the courtroom or the kind of foundation that is required, but in a nutshell and making it very simple, it is usually a good idea to lay a foundation by directing the witness's attention to the time, place, and circumstances of the making of that prior inconsistent statement and then you confront him with it.

For example, the witness is T, a third person, a bystander, who on direct examination has said that your client went through the red light. At the deposition three years ago he said your client stopped for the red light. So, obviously, there is an inconsistency. How would you do it? "Do you remember, sir, that about three years ago you came to my office for a deposition? Do you remember that I was there, your lawyer was there, Mr. Smith was there, and Mr. Jones was there? Do you remember that? Do you remember that a court reporter was present?" And when you ask this question and you read it right from the transcript—"Question. Did the defendant's car stop for the red light? And did you give this answer—yes, the defendant stopped for the red light? Were you asked that question, sir? Did you give this answer? Did you give that answer?" If he says yes, you've done it, you've impeached him. If he says no, you're going to have to call the court reporter to testify that he did give those answers, but that is impeachment. It is perfectly permissible.

The only challenge is a challenge to courtroom craft to do it so that it has some impact upon the jury. And, most importantly, to this point in our analysis, there is no hearsay problem whatsoever. Why? Because, though the statement given at the deposition or the informal statement given to us when we interviewed this person at the very beginning of the case, even though those are out-of-court statements, they do not come in to prove the truth of what they assert, therefore, they're not hearsay by definition. They come in solely to discredit or impeach the witness. The opposing litigant gave us answers in the course of discovery. He answered a question at the deposition. "I stopped for the stop sign. I looked to the left, I looked to the right, I saw nothing, and then I proceeded." Well, in answer to an interrogatory, he said, "I was going 55 miles an hour," even though we know it's a 35-mile zone.

Can you put the answer to the question of the deposition or the answer to the interrogatory into evidence as part of your case? Yes, you can. Under what theory? On the theory that it's an admission by the opposing party. And if you want to be very careful about it, under the Federal Rules of Evidence it comes in on the theory that it's not hearsay because under the Federal Rules of Evidence admissions are not hearsay. That's how you explain their receipt in evidence. That's Rule 801(d)(2)—admissions, admissible on the ground that they're not hearsay. Remember, you put it in as part of your case and it serves as some evidence, if the jury is so inclined, that he looked to the left, he looked to the right, he saw nothing, and only then did he proceed. It serves as some evidence that he was going 55 miles an hour in a 35-mile zone. That is the nature of an admission.

Now put admissions together with impeachment. Suppose the opposing litigant takes the stand and testifies. What he testifies to on direct examination is that he came to the stop sign, he tried to look to the left, he tried to look to the right, but he couldn't see anything because the bushes were in the way. That's not what he told you at the deposition. Or he says, "I knew it was a 35-mile zone and I was going 35 miles an hour." That's not what he said in the interrogatory. May you impeach him with the testimony he gave at the deposition or the answer he gave to the interrogatory on the theory that it's a prior inconsistent statement? Yes, you may. And to that point, you have no hearsay problem whatsoever. But may the answer at the deposition or the answer to the interrogatory also come in to prove the truth of what it asserts? Yes. Why? Because it's an admission. It's an admission because this is not any old witness, it is the opposing party. And an opposing party on the witness stand who has made a prior inconsistent statement has always, by the same token, given you an admission. The prior inconsistent statement is an admission. It comes in to prove the truth of what it asserts as well as coming in to impeach the witness. All right?

And now the last situation. You took a deposition and the person you deposed is now dead or beyond the subpoena power or has disappeared off the face of the earth or whatever. In any event, in good faith, he cannot be produced at trial. Under what circumstances, if any, may the deposition transcript be received in evidence? Be received as if the testimony had been given in open court, right here in front of this jury? Be received as hearsay, as proving the truth of what is asserted in that deposition transcript? Suppose the person whose deposition was taken, but who is now dead, is the opposing party? Can the transcript of the deposition come in to prove the truth of what it asserts? Yes. How do you know? Because I just told you, it comes in as an admission. And, remember, under the Federal Rules the theoretical explanation is that it's not hearsay because admissions are not hearsay by definition under the Federal Rules.

But suppose the person who is now dead, whose deposition had been taken is T, a bystander, a mere witness, not the opposing litigant. You want to put that transcript into evidence to prove the truth of what it asserts. That means it's going to be hearsay. Is there any exception to the rule against hearsay that permits it to come in to prove the truth of what it asserts? And the answer is yes. And the exception is the former testimony exception, which you will find in Federal Evidence Rule 804(b), I think it's 2 or 3, subdivision 2 or 3. What is necessary for the former testimony exception is the following.

First, the person who gave the former testimony is now unavailable to testify and the best kind of unavailable, the best from the lawyer's point of view is death because there's no doubt about it. If you've got an unavailable declarant, the earlier statement is admissible, in a nutshell, if it was subject to cross-examination. Was the deposition subject to cross-examination? Well, of course it was. The other side was given notice of it, the other side was there. Maybe they even did cross-examine. It therefore comes in to prove the truth of what it asserts, it comes in as hearsay and the relevant exception is former testimony.

Test yourself now. Suppose the person deposed is T, a mere witness. He is not dead, nor is he beyond the subpoena power. He's just horsing around, he doesn't want to come to court. Can you put the transcript of his deposition into evidence? Nope. Why? Because it's hearsay and it doesn't fit the former testimony exception. Why doesn't it fit the former testimony exception? Because the declarant, the witness, T, is not unavailable. He's not dead, he's not beyond the subpoena power. He's simply misbehaving and misbehavior, refusal, for no reason or an arbitrary reason to come to court after being served with a subpoena, is not unavailability as 804 defines unavailability.

I want to add very briefly a section to the outline, ladies and gentlemen. The final section that we'll be talking about in just a couple of moments involves the abuse of discovery. We've already adverted to it and I'll talk about it some more. Let me add a section and the section might be headed, "Some Specific Suggestions for Conducting Depositions of a Recurring Nature." And before turning to that, let me address what you see at the very top of page 11. Where a deposition is admissible in evidence, because it's the deposition of a bystander who is now unavailable within the meaning of Federal Rule 804(a) or because it is the deposition of the opposing party and we wish to put it in as part of our case, this is a matter of courtroom etiquette more than of law.

If you are the side of the case offering the deposition, you offer those parts of it that you wish to offer. You are not obliged to offer the entirety of the deposition. And the way you normally do it is to read it to the jury. Now, that can be very boring. What I think any judge would permit you to do to bring it a little bit to life is to put a colleague on the witness stand, simply to sit on the witness stand, not to be sworn as a witness, and the colleague reads the answers and you read the questions. So you've got the two voices going back and forth and the answers seem to be coming from the witness stand, as they would if, in fact, this person were testifying in the flesh instead of through the deposition transcript. If you omit anything, the other side may read what you omit, if the judge thinks, in fairness, the jury ought to have it all. And if that's what the judge thinks, the other side can read it right then and there. If the judge says, "Well, the plaintiff has read everything that deals with issue A and the rest of the transcript deals with issue Z, so I see no reason to require that the jury have it all at once," remember that the other side, the defendant, can read the transcript dealing with issue Z to the jury as part of its case, so that ultimately the jury gets it all. So that the jury may get part of it on the offer of one side, the other side may get the judge to say, "You may read the rest of it to the jury right now." Alternatively, the other side may simply read the rest of it to the jury as part of its case. I repeat, this is etiquette more than law and you do it in whatever sensible way the judge says that you should do it.

But now let me turn to my added section—some specific suggestions for depositions or, conceivably, interrogatories in particular kinds of cases, recurring cases. And I do not pretend that any of this will come as news to those of you experienced in litigating this kind of case. But not everybody is experienced in every kind of case and it may be that, even though you're a very experienced lawyer, next month you're going to have your first class action or your first medical malpractice case or whatever it may be and let me give you a suggestion or two that might help.

First, suppose you are defending a class action. Remember that a class action is a very complex invention of the law. The elements which must be present before you can have a class action are clearly and unmistakably set forth in Rule 23 of the Federal Rules of Civil Procedure. Many lawyers overlook the possibility of taking the deposition of the plaintiff who purports to represent the class, not on the underlying issues, but on the elements which must be present if this is to be a class action. In short, you depose on the elements set forth in Rule 23. Numerousness of the class, typicality of this plaintiff's claims, the degree to which the plaintiff is in a position to represent the interests of the absent members of the class, and the like. The nature of the questioning I will not go into. You can get that by asking around. Common sense will give it to you. There are even form books that give it to you. But you may discover that you take a deposition limited to the elements of a class action under Rule 23 and, by God, this plaintiff is not a proper representative, which means you don't have a class action, which means all you have is the plaintiff's individual claim, which is trivial. What you were worried about was defending against a class action where you had a class of 100,000 claimants and you've managed to beat that.

Next, if you are litigating a medical malpractice case on behalf of the plaintiff, always take the defendant doctor's deposition. Well, remember my rule of practice. Always take the opposing litigant's deposition, so of course you will take the defendant doctor's deposition. If you don't have it clearly in mind, inform yourself, as a little bit earlier I suggested in a different context you do, inform yourself of the nature of impeachment out of a treatise. That's essentially Federal Rule 803, subdivision 18, and the commentaries on it. And depose the defendant doctor on authoritative treatises. That is, the question is simply at the deposition, "Doctor, you see this book? Is this book authoritative?" Get a yes answer and leave it at that. You're setting him up for impeachment at the trial. And the way in which you would impeach him at the trial will be perfectly obvious when you read at 803(18) or the commentaries upon it.

Next, if you are taking the deposition of an expert, remember, that's not matter of course. It's done by consent or on the judge's order. Where you are taking the deposition of an expert, let me repeat what I said before and in a different connection said just now. Make sure you understand how to use 803(18). How you use treatises when examining, whether on direct or cross, an expert and put the expert through the hoops on the deposition. I don't see any of you taking the deposition to begin with. I don't see any danger because the testimony can't change. "Doctor, is this book authoritative?" If he says no, find out why it's not authoritative and come up with the authoritative edition or whatever it may be. And then at trial you are in a position substantially to impeach him out of that treatise.

And, finally, a kind of deposition that I dare say most people in the audience have never taken. You know about it, but it's the kind of thing that very young lawyers do, sometimes even paralegals do it. Lawyers of standing rarely find themselves doing it and I once saw a master trial lawyer conduct this kind of deposition and it made such an impression upon me that I will never forget it and I want to pass it on to you. It is what in my home jurisdictions is called a supplementary proceeding. Now you may call it something else, but you have it. It is the deposition you take after the case has been tried and you have won. And the defendant is now not a defendant, he is a judgment debtor. You have a judgment against him for $100,000 and he's not paying. There is a panoply of discovery devices, essentially echoing what we have been discussing, available to you to help you find his assets. And, once you find them, to tie them up and apply them to the satisfaction of the judgment.

A supplementary proceeding is a deposition of the judgment debtor. And as most people take it, because most people taking supplementary proceedings are very unimaginative, it will proceed this way. Now, remember, we assume a judgment debtor who doesn't want to pay. He may have the assets, but he's hiding them. He doesn't want to disclose them to you and he's prepared to lie, if necessary, but he's not going to pay that judgment. Do you have a bank account? What answer do you expect? No. Do you own a car? No. Where do you live? A private house. Who owns the house? My wife. And on and on and on. You're just not going to get anything.

I once happened to be present when one of the great trial lawyers of his generation and his generation is the generation that's now dying out. This man is in his eighties, but still active at the New York Bar. I once saw him conduct a supplementary proceeding where you had someone you knew was dripping with assets, but was very clever at concealing them. And, of course, what it was was a matrimonial case, where this great lawyer represented the wife, she had a judgment for all kinds of money, support, alimony, et cetera, et cetera, against the husband and he just didn't want to pay her a penny. So he was, you know . . . monkey business is the only way to describe it.

You want to hear the first question on that deposition? And it was brilliant beyond imagining. The first question was, "Empty your pockets on the table." Out they came and, inevitably, you know what's going to come out? A key ring. That's what you watch for, the key ring. And you just pick it up and you say, "What's that key?" And at that point the judgment gets paid because you know what the key is? It's either the key to the safe deposit box containing the cash that the Internal Revenue Service does not know about, or it is the key to his girlfriend's apartment that he'd really rather not talk about. And you've got him sort of so bald faced that he can't lie his way out of it. So remember that little gambit and it may prove to be useful to you.

And let's use not all, but a part of the time remaining, ladies and gentlemen, to talk about discovery abuse, a problem of concern not so much from the viewpoint of the workaday lawyer who is trying cases, but it is a problem of concern to the profession generally, to the non-litigating branches as well as to the litigating branches. And simply as good citizens and as lawyers who wish to be upstanding members of the bar, we all have to be concerned with it.

It is the nature of discovery that it's susceptible of all kinds of misuse. Along the way we've mentioned some of the methods by which discovery can be used not to discover, not to marshal the case for trial, not to pin the other side down, not to find out what the other side knows—all perfectly legitimate purposes of discovery—but rather discovery can be used to frustrate, to oppress, to delay, to disappoint, so that the other side finally abandons the case or settles for what is essentially nuisance value.

The nature of the problem is known to the profession; its extent is far flung. And I could spend a great deal of time on citations demonstrating that point, but let me limit myself to one. When a justice of the United States Supreme Court, sitting in that ivory tower up on the hill in Washington acknowledges the existence of discovery abuse, you know that everybody is aware of it because once it reaches the Supreme Court, it has reached everybody.

In a case that is otherwise not relevant this afternoon called *Herbert v. Lando*,[4] known to all libel lawyers, but that's neither here nor there, decided in 1979, in a concurring opinion Justice [Lewis] Powell said and I quote, "[T]he widespread abuse of discovery . . . has become a prime cause of delay and expense in civil litigation."[5] Now that's a very polite way of putting it, but we understand that it's the Supreme Court or a Justice of the Supreme Court speaking and they habitually speak in polite terms. There is no doubt of the existence of the problem, there is no doubt of the scope of the problem. It exists and its scope represents a

4. *Herbert v. Lando*, 441 U.S. 153 (1979).

5. *Id.* at 179.

scandal in the administration of justice. Now what can be done about it?

In theory, if the other side misbehaves, you can make a motion for a protective order under Rule 26(c). And I don't believe in making motions for protective orders or the law with respect to protective orders more complicated than it has to be. Whatever kind of misbehavior the other side is indulging in the judge can discipline or rectify. Whatever remedial order is appropriate under 26(c), the judge can give you. The judge can cancel a notice of deposition, he can adjourn a deposition, he can say that certain questions will not be proper. The possibilities are virtually limitless. But the imagination and taste for ingenious misconduct on the part of many litigating lawyers is equally limitless and it's not much of a remedy to say to the innocent lawyer, "Go in and make a motion for a protective order," because you're put to the trouble and expense of making a motion, maybe you catch the judge on a bad day, the judge really doesn't want to read these papers about what's been going on in discovery, and you end up unprotected. And, in any event, a protective order only protects you with respect to what's happened. Now the other side figures out a new way of misbehaving and you're going to have to make another motion and you just end up more and more frustrated, more and more oppressed, and the client gets the feeling that money is just flowing out. He's hemorrhaging money and, after all, that is one of the purposes for which unethical practitioners use discovery or misuse it, I should say.

Now, what are some possibilities? One possibility is to handle the problem by local rule. You've got Local Rule 12(b) of the District Court for the Southern District of Indiana. No form interrogatories. In my lingo, no interrogatories that come out of a memory typewriter. At least let some human being read them. Local Rule 9(d) of Chicago, the Northern District of Illinois. Unless you get special leave of court, no more than 20 interrogatories and each subpart counts as an interrogatory. There's one judge in my original home court, the Southern District of New York, who when assigned a civil case tells the clerk to give the lawyers a Xeroxed sheet that the judge has prepared. And this sheet is entitled something like, "Special Instructions from Judge X"—I will not now name him—"With Respect to Civil Matters Before Him." One, the discovery article of the Rules of Civil Procedure is inapplicable. No discovery. Two, if you want to know something, ask the other side. Three, if they won't tell you, telephone me. And that's it. That's it. Those are the discovery rules. Every case before that judge is tried within 60 days of its being commenced. The lawyers groused and wept and, you know, complained limitlessly when the judge took the bench and those rules went into effect. These days lawyers celebrate when they get a case assigned to that judge because you know it's going to be tried in two months and what case can't be tried in two months? Which means what? It's not going to be tried in two months, it's going to be settled in two months. Most civil cases are not going to be tried, they're going to be settled, which means you're turning a case over very quickly. Turning it from an account receivable to cash in the bank. And, obviously, that's to a lawyer's advantage, so that judge is a hero among civil litigators in the district in which he sits. But not every judge is prepared to do that.

So obvious has the problem become that the American Bar Association itself, no example of fleet-footed justice, the American Bar Association. The American Bar Association has a special committee for the study of discovery abuse. That committee has been in existence, I think, for seven years now and they're still having meetings. And they've yet to come out with a report. I have no idea what they're thinking about. It's obvious that there's abuse. It's obvious that something has to be done to prevent it. If you want to read an article bringing you up-to-date as of 1979 on the work of that committee, there's an article by a former partner of mine who's a member of the committee, at 65 *American Bar Association Journal*, page 1050.[6] If you want to read a more formal piece of scholarship on the widespread incidence

---

6. Steve Umin, Discovery Reform: A New Era or Business as Usual?

of discovery abuse, there's a note, a rather good note, on it at 91 *Harvard Law Review*, 1033.

Everyone is aware of the enormous popularity these days of alternative dispute resolution. The origins of ADR, as it's called, lie with the business community—our clients, uniquely in a position to pay our bills, who suddenly realize that when they get into a dispute they don't regard it as a matter of truth, justice, and the American way. Disputes are an inevitable consequence of doing business and there's some price at which every dispute is reasonably to be settled. And they discover or they find that what lawyers are doing is engaging in a virtually limitless inquiry into the truth as it exists in the mind of God. And to this end, millions of dollars will be spent on depositions and interrogatories and all the rest of it, when all the litigant wants is a fast, inexpensive, and more or less rational method for resolving the dispute. And that's why alternative dispute resolution has come to be so popular. And you realize what it is—it's a rational method of resolving a dispute in hours with no discovery, no pleadings, no large bills rendered by lawyers to clients. How, then, are lawyers to educate their children, their grandchildren, and their great-grandchildren? We lawyers, we litigating lawyers had better look to it. It is a matter not just of good citizenship, it is a matter of bread and butter self-interest that we clean up our act. And the way to clean it up is to recognize that discovery has come to be abused and we better apply our collective ingenuity and imagination and good sense to coming up with workable devices that will bring about an end to this kind of discovery abuse.

Rule 11, applying a sanction when a lawyer engages in misbehavior, is a rough attempt in that direction. This is not the occasion for an extended analysis of Rule 11. In my judgment, it's probably a failure. It doesn't work very well, but at least it was well-intentioned. I think we've got to think beyond Rule 11. When we do think beyond it, we'll come up with a solution and we will then have preserved civil litigation as we have come to know and love it. And if we don't come up with that solution, civil litigation as we know and love it may well come to an end in our professional lifetime.

Ladies and gentlemen, I can't pretend that we've exhausted the subject and I'm not going to pretend that we have exhausted you, but I will frankly admit that we have exhausted me. So I thank you very much for being so gracious an audience.

Chapter 2

Expert Witnesses

DEAN STEVE EASTON: Welcome to "Expert Witnesses." Irving Younger recorded his classic series of CLE lectures in 1986 and 1987. His wisdom and eloquence are timeless and the suggestions he has for us as trial lawyers in dealing with expert witnesses are just as valid today as they were when he made these recordings.

There have been some significant changes in the law of expert witnesses, though, so I would like to briefly mention some of them. In 1993 the Supreme Court reached its decision in *Daubert v. Merrell Dow Pharmaceuticals, 509 U.S. 579 (1993).* That decision changed the landscape of expert witness testimony in federal courts and in those states where the state supreme court has adopted the *Daubert* approach. The *Daubert* case has essentially been codified into Rule 702 of the Federal Rules of Evidence with provisions that now state that an expert is allowed to testify if her testimony will assist the trier of fact and if the testimony is based upon sufficient facts or data, if the testimony is the product of reliable principles and methods, and, finally, if the expert has applied the principles and methods to the relevant data or evidence in a manner that fits the facts of a particular case and leads to a reliable result. That was the essential holding of *Daubert v. Merrell Dow Pharmaceuticals.*

The *Kumho Tire Company v. Carmichael, 526 U.S. 137 (1999),* case was important because in that case the Supreme Court made it clear that the *Daubert* approach to the district court's judgment about whether an expert witness should be allowed to testify applied not just to scientific experts, but to experts in other fields that arguably or certainly were outside of science. The *Kumho Tire* case involved engineering, but after *Kumho Tire* it is quite clear that the *Daubert* approach applies to an expert in a field such as accounting or economics or another field that we do not typically think of as science.

There have been other developments in the law of evidence with regard to the issues that Professor Younger is going to discuss, so let's briefly note a few of those changes. As Professor Younger notes in this seminar, at the time of the seminar, Disciplinary Rule 7-109(c) explicitly prohibited a contingent fee to an expert witness. Now the Disciplinary Rules have been replaced by the ABA's Model Rules of Professional Conduct and most states now have Professional Responsibility Rules that are based upon the Model Rules. Model Rule 3.4(b) now contains a prohibition against an attorney offering an inducement to a witness that is prohibited by law. Comment 3 to that Model Rule notes that under the common law of most states a contingent fee to an expert witness is prohibited. So the law really has not changed, but the prohibition is not as explicit as it was under the Disciplinary Rules.

Professor Younger will also discuss the admissibility of expert testimony regarding what is referred to as ultimate issues. The Federal Rules of Evidence, in Rule 704(a), now provide that in most instances an expert is allowed to testify with regard to an opinion on an ultimate issue. The major exception to that general grant of permission for such expert testimony is Rule 704(b), which prohibits expert testimony on one specific issue. That subsection excludes an expert opinion with regard to the mental state or condition of a defendant in a criminal case when that is an ultimate issue for the jury to decide.

Rule 703 of the Federal Rules of Evidence now explicitly allows an expert to base her opinion on otherwise inadmissible data, facts, or evidence as long as that data is of a type that experts in that field typically rely upon in reaching opinions or inferences. That raises another issue that Professor Younger discusses—if the expert is allowed to testify to an opinion that is based upon otherwise inadmissible data, is the expert then allowed to tell the jury about that inadmissible data? There is something of an answer to that question now in Rule 703, because that rule now provides that the expert may tell the jury about the inadmissible data behind her opinion only if the court determines that the probative value to the jury of hearing about that otherwise inadmissible data substantially outweighs the prejudice to the opposing party of admitting the otherwise inadmissible data.

Finally, as currently written, Rule 705 of the Federal Rules of Evidence does not contain an explicit provision allowing the use of a hypothetical question for an expert witness. However, most believe that a hypothetical question can still be used, if the direct examiner decides to present expert testimony in this way. The current language of Rule 705 states that an expert is allowed to testify to an opinion or an inference and give the reasons for that opinion, subject to what we just reviewed, without first testifying to the underlying facts or data. But then the rule provides that the cross-examiner is allowed to explore those issues on cross-examination, if she chooses to do so.

PROFESSOR IRVING YOUNGER: I will not belabor to this group of experienced lawyers the point that expert witnesses these days are crucial. With ever-increasing frequency, litigation in state and federal courts, civil and criminal, protracted and not so protracted, will turn upon the testimony of an expert. I think it's fair to say that these days no lawyer, no matter the nature of his or her practice, can function in a courtroom unless that lawyer has developed a fairly complete mastery of how to deal with expert witnesses—how to present them, how to attack them, how to argue their credibility. A very good part of the law of evidence deals with experts. A very good part of the craft of the courtroom deals with experts. And a very important part of the law of professional responsibility, as we will see, deals with experts.

Now, lest I leave you more than usually confused, let me tell you right at the outset how I propose to proceed. Rather than rehearsing the law of evidence or the craft of the courtroom, et cetera, et cetera, sort of in the abstract as a bunch of theoretical rules, let me raise with you the, whatever it is, five or so, principal questions that must engage the mind of a lawyer preparing and then trying a case featuring one or more experts. Let me raise those questions and answer them. In the course of answering them, I will weave together what the law of evidence has to say, what the craft of the courtroom has to say and, where appropriate, what the Code of Professional Responsibility has to say about these matters. Obviously, I cannot canvass every single jurisdiction. I will make no particular reference to cases in Georgia for the very good reason that my ignorance of the cases in Georgia is exceeded only by that of some of you in this room. But on the assumption that if you take a reasonably close look at the law in any one jurisdiction, it's not very hard to cross-reference it to another jurisdiction. I will refer as we move along to the Federal Rules of Evidence and to some leading federal cases, confident, though, I really don't have the basis for being so, that the law in Georgia cannot be different in any great respect from what it is in the federal court.

First question. Obviously a question you deal with at the threshold. Winning events of trying the case. How do you identify an issue in connection with which it will be proper to call an expert to the stand? On what kinds of issues may an expert testify to the opinion the expert has about the issue. I will grant you that in 999 cases out of 1,000, the answer is foregone. You don't even consider the issue because it's perfectly obvious that an expert may testify. But in one case out of 1,000 it will not be obvious and it's worth knowing how to answer the question.

Just to show you that it may not be obvious, here are the facts of the case. Couldn't be simpler. You've got a two-lane highway in a rural part of the state. Traffic moves in opposite directions. It's the middle of the night. Two cars moving in opposite directions are approaching each other. Each car is driven by a lone driver, no passengers. There are no bystanders. Suddenly, bam, a head-on collision and when the smoke clears you've got one car over there, another car over there, skid marks and debris scattered across the countryside and two dead drivers. One estate sues the other estate. On liability, the only question really is what was the point of impact because then you know which driver veered over to the wrong side of the road and you know who is at fault. On that question, the point of impact, an expert in accident reconstruction is called to the stand. Everybody agrees that this person is, indeed, an expert. The naked issue is the issue you deal with at the threshold. Is the question at the point of impact a question in connection with which an expert may testify? Those are not the facts of a hypothetical case, they are the facts of two real cases. Wholly obscure, there's no reason to go run it and look up the opinions. But it's just curious that the identical case comes up in two different jurisdictions.

One is the federal court in North Dakota and the other is a state court in New York. The federal judge, pre–Federal Rules of Evidence, relying though on a fair number of federal decisions, said the expert may testify. This is a question in connection with which it is proper to call an expert to the stand. On indistinguishable facts the state court judge says the expert may not testify and he's affirmed on appeal. So to a keen legal thinker it begins to be possible that you've got two different rules at work here. And you are right, there are two different rules at work. One rule, the rule that's hospitable to experts, that opens the door wide, that is generous in permitting them to testify, was applied by the federal judge. The competing rule, applied by the state court and principally in New York, by the way, is not hospitable to the receipt of expert testimony. It closes the door substantially.

The federal rule adds up to this. All the expert's opinion need do is help or assist the jury. And obviously that is not stringent. If it will help the jury, the expert may testify. The state rule is much more demanding. The opinion must be necessary to the jury's determination of this question. That it will merely help them is not enough. Those federal cases—and I think it's probably fair to say that it represents a majority of the states—but those federal cases have been codified in the Federal Rules of Evidence. It's Rule 702 and it says just what we've said. The expert may testify if his or her opinion will help or assist the jury.

And at this point, simply to relieve the increasing gloom and also just as a pleasant change of pace, stop taking notes and, indeed, you don't have to listen too terribly hard for the next two minutes. Whenever I talk about this issue, I like to put a case to the audience. And I'm going to put that case to you and ask each of you to be the judge and rule by a showing of hands. And then I'll tell you what the real case was and I'll explain why I do it. You are the judge and, indeed, you are a federal judge, so you're operating under the federal rule that we just talked about. The real case took place before the Federal Rules of Evidence, but the federal decisions were consistent with the codification that you find today in Rule 702. You are presiding over a criminal case. Every criminal case is important, but this one is especially important. It is probably the most celebrated federal criminal case of the century. You've been at it for many weeks. It's now sort of two-thirds or three-quarters through the case, right?

The indictment is a very simple one. It charges the defendant with doing a certain serious thing. The prosecution called a witness who testified that he, the witness, helped the defendant to do it. With his own eyes he saw the defendant do it. That prosecution witness was cross-examined for three days. He had used his testimony in every detail. The defendant has already testified and the defendant says unequivocally that he did not do it; that the prosecution witness is lying. The defendant was cross-examined also for three days and adheres to his testimony in every jot and tittle. There is corroborating evidence on both sides about equal in weight, it cancels out.

You are the judge. You're going to take the bench at 10 o'clock. It's now 10 minutes to 10 o'clock. You're sitting in the robing room doing whatever judges do 10 minutes before taking the bench. You're having your morning brandy perhaps, smoking a big cigar or whatever, when comes that knock on the door and, let me tell you, whether you're a judge or not, your heart always turns over. What's going to happen now? Who comes marching in but defense counsel, the prosecutor, and they've brought the court reporter to take it all down. And defense counsel now makes an application. He says, "Your Honor, we're now towards the end of the trial, the prosecution witness has testified, the defendant has testified. It is perfectly clear to all of us that when the jury retires to consider their verdict in this case, it turns upon their assessment of the credibility of that prosecution witness. If they believe him, the verdict is foregone—guilty. If they have doubts, the verdict is equally foregone—not guilty. That's all there is to it. Your Honor, we want to call an expert. He's a psychiatrist, but he's no ordinary psychiatrist. He is the immediate past president of the American Psychiatric Association. He is a professor of Medicine at the Cornell Medical School. He has just been appointed professor of Medicine at the Harvard Medical School, which position he will assume next September, and also become Chief of Psychiatry at the Massachusetts General Hospital. He is probably America's preeminent psychiatrist. He has never met or clinically examined that prosecution witness, but he has observed him on the witness stand. In addition, the prosecution witness is a professional writer. The psychiatrist has read everything the man ever published and the psychiatrist has been told the undisputed facts of the prosecution witness's life. On the basis of all of this, Your Honor, my expert, the doctor, is prepared to take the stand and tell this jury that in his, the doctor's, professional opinion that prosecution witness is suffering from a disorder of personality characterized by a tendency to make false accusations and tell lies. Your Honor, will you allow him to testify?" What's your ruling?

Rule: Don't call for your law clerk. There's nothing for your law clerk to tell you that you don't already know. The test is, will it help the jury? Apply the test. Can the psychiatrist testify? How many of you say yes? How many of you say no? It happened again.

All right, let me tell you, as I promised to tell you, that whenever discussing this issue I put that case to the audience. This is probably the fortieth time I've done it. Audiences of lawyers, of law students, of judges, and of laymen. The result is always what you just saw. The vast majority says I will not allow it; only a few say I will allow it. The majority is wrong. With all deference, Your Honors, I think that you are permitting your own skepticism about the testimony of that psychiatrist to interfere with the clarity of your judgment. It is not for you, the judge, to decide that the psychiatrist's testimony is a great big crock. Now, of course it is, but that is for the jury to decide. Your function is to just figure out whether it will help the jury. And, while it's unusual, I can't see how you can avoid concluding that it will help the jury.

The real judge moved correctly in the sense that it's a logical application of preexisting doctrine that the psychiatrist could testify, the judge recognized that it was as far as any federal judge had ever had to go in applying the rule that we're discussing. To this day, decades later, it remains the frontier case as far as any judge has had to go. Recognizing then that there ought to be a memorial of it, even though it was a trial ruling, which normally does not appear in the books, when the case was over the judge wrote a little memorandum about it, which is how one can look it up.

The judge's name was Henry Goddard. The psychiatrist's name was Carl Binger. The prosecution witness's name was Whitaker Chambers, and the defendant's name was Alger Hiss. It happened at the second trial, the one that produced the verdict of guilty. And, indeed, while you can't tell, still anybody who studied the trial would agree that in all probability the defendant shot himself in the foot by calling that psychiatrist to the stand. His testimony was in haec verba what you heard from me—that Whitaker Chambers is suffering from a disorder of personality characterized by a tendency to make false accusations and tell lies, whereupon Dr. Binger was cross-examined by one of the great, but unheralded, trial lawyers of our or any other time, Thomas Murphy, now a retired federal judge.

Most of you have heard me say that in my view cross-examinations should be short. Do you know how long Thomas Murphy's cross-examination of Dr. Binger was? It was three days long. Why did Thomas Murphy cross-examine Dr. Binger for three days? Because he was having too much fun to stop. It is the most devastating cross-examination of a psychiatrist, indeed, of an expert witness that I know of and if ever you get a chance to read the transcription, you should. We'll return to it when we talk about cross-examining or impeaching experts a little bit later on. But to this day I am told that when the dean of the Harvard Medical School speaks to incoming first-year students in the fall of their freshman year—you know the standard speech, get a white coat and get a good microscope and never go to court. He says, "Remember what happened to Dr. Binger. He was playing the lawyer's ball game by the lawyer's rules in the lawyer's ballpark. He didn't even know what the rules were, so of course he was made to look a fool." And that's a useful anecdote to have in mind, especially if you're fairly young, when you set out to cross-examine an expert. You may not be a doctor or an economist or an engineer, but you are a lawyer and it's a lawyer's game in a lawyer's ballpark by a lawyer's rules and you presumably know what the rules are. You can't devastate him every time out, but you can almost always lay a glove on him. And there are few things a lawyer does more pleasurable than pricking the balloon of some horse's ass of an expert. So that's to keep you interested until we come to cross-examination later on, but we must move along.

We will assume that you've got an issue in connection with which it will be proper to call an expert because it will help the jury. Next question which I raise not really to discuss into the ground, but simply so that our discussion is more or less complete. The next question, of course, will be how do you find the expert? And the answer, as anybody knows who's been around the merry-go-round a few times, is that you find an expert anywhere you can. You talk to other lawyers; you use the classified telephone book. Don't omit that, it's one of the great achievements of modern civilization. It's amazing what you will find in the classified telephone book. Do not neglect the catalog of your local university. There are ads in the *ABA Journal* and the like, people who are ready to testify as experts. There are agencies, booking agencies sort of, that you can call and you tell them what you want and they get it for you. And that's all to the good because there's a service that's available to private counsel comparable to the service that's available to federal prosecutors. When I was in the U.S. Attorney's Office, the FBI Laboratory was the booking agent. If you needed an expert, no matter how obscure the discipline, you called the FBI Laboratory and they had it for you. I'll never forget one day I called down and I said, "You're not going to believe this, but I need an expert in feathers, somebody who can look at a feather under the microscope and say, 'That comes from such and such a bird.'" And they said, "We got one. Here, he's on the payroll." A Ph.D in bird feathers, yet, from the University of Wisconsin. Up he came, testified to the bird feathers in a suitcase, which represented an important piece of circumstantial evidence to show that the defendant had carried birds in the suitcase, which led to other conclusions, et cetera, et cetera.

Next question. And here we're going to talk about some stuff that's very important pragmatically and also because, as I will try to get across to you, the law may well be changing in very important ways. You've got the issue on which you want an expert to testify and you've identified the person you would like to come be the expert, but now the question is how do you get him to show up? How do you secure the appearance of the expert in court? Let me give it some concreteness. I try to avoid war stories, but I must refer to my own experience. The first time I had to work at finding an expert, I'd left the U.S. Attorney's Office. I could no longer simply call the laboratory. I was in private practice on my own and it may have been the first personal injury case that ever came my way. It was certainly one of the first and it was a good case for a young lawyer to have, nothing especially difficult about it.

A little boy, the son of my client, who'd been going to school in an upper-middle-class residential suburb of New York City. And it was just down the street and across the roadway and there was the school on the other corner. And he was 10 or 11 years old, he'd done this for four or five years without anything happening. It was a nice clear day in the springtime, right around this season of the year. Nobody disputed the little boy's testimony. He went to the crossing, pressed the button, waited for the crossing light to be in his favor, and then started to cross the street. Suddenly, from his left, comes the defendant, total madman, driving a huge Buick about 100 miles an hour in this school zone. He's dead-drunk at 8 o'clock in the morning, hits the kid and the kid goes through the air like that and lands on the sidewalk 30 feet away. Picks himself up and says, "That was fun, let's do it again." No, no, no, kid, come on. You can't do it again, you've got to go to the hospital. They take him to the hospital and, you know, children survive these things because they do think it's fun. They don't tense up, they relax the way a good athlete should.

In the hospital, miraculously, there's nothing wrong with him. Bumps and bruises that are going to get better. But he has a ruptured spleen, that little organ back here that football players sometimes injure when they get tackled off balance. If the spleen is ruptured, it must be removed because it will not heal. And if you don't remove it, septicemia sets in and you're going to die. So they put him on the operating table. A very clever surgeon with golden fingers takes it out, taking about two minutes, and it's all done. It's the simplest kind of operation there is. They sew the kid up, six months later he's as good as new. The bumps and bruises are better. He's got a tiny little scar but that's of no surgical significance. Except he does not have a spleen because the spleen does not regenerate. He will never have a spleen.

The defendant concedes liability. The question is, what are the damages? Putting it as trial lawyers like to put it, what's a spleen worth? This is a spleen-out case, so what are the damages? And you can imagine that if you were the plaintiff, like me, you would ultimately argue to the jury what? Well, ladies and gentlemen of the jury, the spleen plays a vital, though as yet not fully understood, role in the body's immunological system. Without a spleen this little boy has a life expectancy that's a great big question mark. He may die of a common cold tomorrow. This case is worth what, $2 million at least.

And any one of us on the other side would argue, what's he talking about? Spleen is a vestigial organ left over from the days when we were fishes. It's nothing. He doesn't have it, but he's no worse off without it than with it. So what's it worth? $1.75, call it $2, huh? So I'm at millions and you're at $2 and how are we going to decide?

I will tell you what I discovered back then when I went to the books. Nobel Prizes in Medicine have been won on both sides of that question. The physiology of the spleen to this day is unknown. And great scientists have come to the conclusion that it does play a vital role in the body's immunological system and others have concluded that it's nothing, it's a vestigial organ like the appendix. Well, when the Nobel Prize winners disagree, who decides? There they are. See them? You see them? See those 6 or 12 post office workers, people who sell ribbons in the 5- and 10-cent store? They decide when the Nobel Prize winners are in disagreement. And it's the magic, the mystery, the miracle of our system that they do decide it remarkably well.

Well, to begin with, you've got to give them something to decide, so you need an expert, right? Obviously, the physiology of the spleen is an issue in connection with which an expert can testify. I went to the books and discovered—I was then in New York City—that the Nobel Prize in Medicine on the affirmative of that issue had been won by a professor at the NYU Medical School named Severo Ochoa, now dead. So he is the guy I want.

So now let's see what happens. You call him up, right? Dr. Ochoa, I've got this case, spleens, will you come and testify? Now, one possibility—he says, "Well, sure, I'll come and testify, but I've got to pay the grocer like everybody else and I have to be compensated." "Of course, Doctor, what do you think is fair compensation?" And he says, "$500." And you say, "Couldn't be more reasonable. You've got it, Doctor." Fine, there's nothing else to discuss. But that presupposes a client with $500 to put down. Suppose you don't have the $500. Suppose he gives you a figure that you just can't meet or you're representing someone who has nothing and couldn't pay $10, let alone $500. Now what do you do?

Well, you know, lawyers are nothing if not ingenious, especially young lawyers. That wasn't the situation in my case, but if it had been I can imagine Dr. Ochoa saying, "Well, if you can't pay me, I guess I just can't work for you." So . . . and then I would say, "Oh, Doctor, Doctor, don't hang up. Don't hang up. Doctor, I don't have the $500, but tell me, are you by any chance a gambling man?" And suppose Dr. Ochoa were to reply, "Well, now that you mention it, I kind of go to Las Vegas every weekend or so." All right. "Now, Doctor, it's a lot like rolling the dice at the crap table. I can't guarantee the outcome, but there is a possibility, Doctor, that, especially if you help me, we're going to win this case. And if we win it, Doctor, there is going to be a pot of gold, Doctor, and 10 percent of that pot, Doctor, will be yours." Do you have a deal? Sure, you have a deal. And what else do you have? Trouble with the bar association, as I am delighted to realize you know.

Disciplinary Rule 7-109(c) of the Code of Professional Responsibility that binds us all expressly forbids a lawyer to retain an expert on a contingency. This is no prefatory or hortatory language about be good to your mother. This is an unethical act and if you commit it, you have problems. Now, a keen thinker, especially one attuned to constitutional issues, is going to say why should it be that you can't hire an expert on the contingency? Can a lawyer? I mean, what's the reason for it?

The stated reason is that it will encourage litigation. But that's absurd. Lawyers can be hired on a contingency. Why? Because it encourages litigation. That's why we allow it. Because in the United States, most of the public's business gets done in the courtroom. We know that the legislatures are impotent and the executives don't know their left hand from their right hand, so we leave it to the judges to govern the country and that's what they've been doing, like it or not. Which means if you don't give people access to lawyers, you are denying them access to government. And the only way you can give a poor person access to a lawyer is to say you can hire the lawyer with the only thing you have—a piece of the action. So to say to a lawyer, you can be hired on a contingency, but you may not hire an expert on a contingency, is as much as to say, if your client doesn't have the funds to put down to retain an expert, we close the courthouse doors to them. And once you say that, aren't you saying that DR 7-109(c) is unconstitutional under the Equal Protection Clause as working an invidious discrimination against poor people? And that's more than a theoretical argument, it has persuaded at least one federal judge.

The late Judge [John] Dooling in the Eastern District of New York some years ago declared 7-109(c) unconstitutional under the Equal Protection Clause. Judge Dooling, alas, was reversed unanimously by the Second Circuit and the Supreme Court denied certiorari. I just don't know whether that case is in the materials, but I think its citation is there. It's *Person v. Association of the Bar of the City of New York (2nd Cir.)*.[1] And that is the state of the law. DR 7-109(c) is constitutional and unless you are prepared to fence with the bar association's Disciplinary Committee, you had better obey it and refrain from hiring experts on a contingency.

But that's not an end to this interesting issue, it is barely a beginning. Against the possibility that there are some of you who find yourself desperate for the wherewithal with which to retain an expert because

1. 414 F. Supp. 139 (E.D. N.Y. 1976).

your clients are indigent and you just can't help yourself, let me mention the possibility of using, even in Georgia or some other state other than New York, the *Matter of Shore* case,[2] which I trust is cited for you there. It's 415 N.Y.S.2d 878. It's the Appellate Division's Second Department, which is the intermediate appellate court in New York. In very brief terms, the Appellate Division, which is a court that commands wide respect among New York lawyers, held that even though DR 7-109(c) is part of the law of New York, as it is of virtually all states, if a lawyer retains an expert on a contingency, but with the following additional condition—Doctor, if we win, you get 10 percent or whatever it may be, but before I pay you the entire arrangement is going to be put before the judge and it's all subject to the judge's approval, so it's a kind of double gamble on both of our parts. If the judge thinks 10 percent is right, I'm going to pay it to you. If the judge thinks it's too little, it should be more, that's what I'm going to pay you. But you're at risk also. If the judge thinks it's too much and should be something else, you're going to get the lesser amount. In short, we have our deal, but it's subject to a kind of condition subsequent—namely, the judge's view of what's proper in these circumstances.

Now, the Appellate Division held that if you subject the contingency to that kind of condition, it is no longer violative of 7-109(c). It's now perfectly ethical to enter into that arrangement. And the importance of the case for a lawyer not in New York is this. If you rely upon it and enter into a contingent arrangement, but subject to judicial approval, à la *Matter of Shore*, your jurisdiction may decline to follow *Matter of Shore*. They may say, "No, no, no, it's really not proper, it's still subject to the proscription of 7-109(c)." But it's inconceivable to me that they would hold you at fault. After all, how can you be said to have acted unethically when you followed with scrupulous care an important appellate decision by an important court in a state as important as New York? Surely you acted in a lawyer-like manner. You're not dishonorable, you are wrong. But all of us are wrong at least half the time and, you know,

2. *Matter of Shore*, 415 N.Y.S.2d 878 (1979).

it sort of protects you, although it may be that your state will disagree with what the New York Court did. So there's *Matter of Shore*.

But let's turn now to the case of *Kaufman v. Edelstein*,[3] which I do want to discuss in some detail. I think you will agree with me when I tell you about it that *Kaufman v. Edelstein* potentially is the single, most important case in this field, probably of all time and certainly of many decades. And yet, to my astonishment, *Kaufman v. Edelstein* has gone widely unremarked by practicing lawyers, indeed by federal judges with whom I've discussed and to whom I've spoken about the case, and it's come as a great revelation. They just didn't know about it. The law reviews have not commented upon it and it really is something just potentially dynamite-like.

Kaufman v. Edelstein, ladies and gentlemen, was an offshoot of that celebrated, not to say scandalous antitrust trial that you read about in the *Wall Street Journal* some years ago. Remember, the government sued to break up IBM. A civil case tried non-jury before Judge Edelstein, then the chief judge of the Southern District of New York, for some seven or eight years. I have not misspoken. That's not seven or eight years of discovery, that's seven or eight years of trial following discovery, all of it non-jury. What in heaven's name were they trying for seven or eight years? It escapes me, but that's what they did. Both sides finally rested and when they were getting ready to put in the briefs, the new administration came in and threw in the towel, said, "Our complaint is wholly without merit, we withdraw it," and that was the end of it. Right?

Now, some of you have a lot of experience trying antitrust cases, but so that all of us have a certain sort of common foundation, let me tell you how a civil antitrust case is tried. With respect to what I like to call overt facts, you know, how many electric typewriters did IBM sell in 1979? There's no dispute, here it is. You know, that's the answer, there's nothing to fight about. Antitrust cases of that type invariably turn on expert testimony. The government, for example, in that case

---

3. 539 F.2d 811 (2d Cir. 1976).

called about 50 percent of the economics professors of the United States, each and every one of whom testified that IBM possesses monopoly power to such an extent that its continuation in its present form is a threat to the survival of the republic. We've got to break it up as a matter of self-preservation. And then the defense calls the other 50 percent of the economics professors, each and every one of whom testifies that IBM is a kind of mom-and-pop store that did well. And you just leave it alone and let it grow and we'll all be okay. And as between the two contending schools of experts, the poor judge has to decide.

Now, reading just a little bit between the lines of the opinion, but I'm sure this is substantially accurate, the following occurred. The government lawyers are sitting around talking about the case, several years into it, but it's still in its early stages, the trial is. And one of them says, "You know what I heard? I heard about two guys downtown on Wall Street. Now, one of them is a partner in one of the Big 8 accounting firms and the other is a partner in Arthur Little, the famous consulting outfit. Each of them has a graduate degree in economics or business administration, but each of them is a businessman, not an academic. In connection with his business, each of them has studied the computer industry and each of them is on record in the form of opinion letters and memoranda to clients of the firms that they are partners in that in their opinion, IBM does possess monopoly power and that it will work to the well-being of the American computer industry to break up IBM. In short, that the government is in the right in this case." And, you know, if you're a trial lawyer on the government's side of it, when you hear about this kind of thing, you start to salivate. You realize these guys are not pointy-headed academics, they're working businessmen. They are probably registered Republicans, for God's sakes and here they are, they have put it down in black-and-white attesting that the government should win.

So the government lawyers go to these guys and they say, "Will you come testify? All you have to do is come to court and tell the judge what you have already told the clients of your firm in black and white." And each of these guys says, "No, I don't want to come." And the lawyers say, "What's the matter? Is it a question of money? Name it. We print it, we'll print some more for you. Makes no difference." And they say, "No, it's not a question of money, it's a question really of the appearances of things, our position in society. Oh, we said that to our clients and we don't take back one syllable of it. We think IBM should be broken up, but we don't wish to appear in public to support the government's case."

So the lawyers now go back and they say, "What do we do? They won't come. They just won't come. It's not a question of money, it's a question of their just unwillingness to come." Now, if you were to go to the books, you would discover what those government lawyers discovered or already knew. At least to that point in our legal history, the experts had a perfect right to say, "No, I don't want to testify." An expert, traditionally, in the common law has been viewed as in a very different position from the ordinary witness. So the ordinary witness, John Q. Citizen, who happens to see two cars collide, has an obligation of citizenship to come to court and tell the judge and jury what he saw, an obligation triggered by the ministerial act of being subpoenaed and tendering the $2.50 witness fee or whatever it is in your jurisdiction. But an expert is different. An expert's opinion, the common law has said since essentially the days of Henry II, is his private property. He can give it away, he can sell it as he usually does, but it may not be compelled. Hence, at common law an expert may not be subpoenaed, which is why you get into these convolutions of trying to persuade them to come to court if you can't retain them on a contingency, et cetera. Can't compel them. Serve them with a subpoena? I mean, it's physically possible to do so, but the court will not enforce it. If you ask the judge to send the marshal or the sheriff out to arrest some doctor whom you've subpoenaed, the judge will laugh in your face and the doctor or the other kind of expert is free to tear up the subpoena and ignore you.

What are the government lawyers going to do? They decided to brazen it out. They sent the U.S. Marshal out with two ordinary witness subpoenas, one for each of those guys. They gave them the subpoenas, together with two subway tokens, which is the way you do it in

New York and say, "Here, ride the subway to the courthouse, take the stand and here's a token to get back to Wall Street." The guys aren't lawyers, they don't know what this means. So each of them picks up the phone and dials the senior partner of the Wall Street law firm representing the accounting outfit Arthur Little.

Now, I can tell by the white hair I see scattered around the room, some of which I possess myself, that a number of you are, in effect, partners in Wall Street law firms. I have been, too. And for the benefit of our juniors here in the room, let me sort of give voice to what I know now happened, though, again, it's reading between the lines. Each of these guys calls the senior partner. Okay? And says, "Guess what happened?" "What?" "The marshal came around and served me with a subpoena. Got to be in court three weeks from today. What do we do?" Senior partner, "Ohhhhh. Oh. We have a problem. But I tell you, we're going to solve that problem for you starting right now. I'm putting a task force together. I'm going to be at the head of it. Three junior-level partners, 5 associates, 10 clerks, 3 or 4 people to operate the Lexis machine, and three to go for coffee. And this task force is going to solve the problem." And, sure enough, $75,000 of client billable time later, the problem is solved. Each of those law firms has come up with a motion to quash the subpoena. And they march into Judge Edelstein's courtroom and they make their motion.

Now, I don't know whether the grapevine carried this far down, but at least around New York, it was quite clear during the trial of that case, up until the government raising the white flag, that Judge Edelstein was deciding against the defendants on everything. Anything the government wanted, the government got. And, indeed, there were a couple of mandamus applications of a fairly embarrassing nature along the way to air all this. So Judge Edelstein forthwith denied the motions to quash. He said, "These subpoenas stand."

The lawyers were prepared because they expected nothing less from Judge Edelstein. They instantly took the elevator to the 17th floor where the Second Circuit Clerk's Office is. Now, whether Judge Edelstein's order is appealable is subject to argument. So what they did was file a notice of appeal together with an application for mandamus, asking the Second Circuit to direct Judge Edelstein to quash those subpoenas. The mandamus application sort of came first in the papers, so that's why the case is not *United States v. IBM*, but rather *Kaufman v. Edelstein*. Kaufman is one of the witnesses and Edelstein is the judge. You know, in an application for mandamus, you sort of pretend that you're suing the judge and he becomes the respondent.

Now, all courts are entitled to our respect, but you know, courts are different and it seems to me that the U.S. Court of Appeals for the Second Circuit is a pretty damn impressive court, especially on an issue of this kind. And while all judges are also entitled to our respect, judges are different and when you're dealing with Judge Henry Friendly of the Second Circuit, you're dealing with an all-time great judge. The opinion in *Kaufman v. Edelstein* for a unanimous panel is by Henry Friendly. So considering the author of the opinion and the authority of the court, you've got to sit up and take notice. And it's an opinion that you must read for yourself. Please understand that I'm not quoting it, but I think that what I am about to tell you is a fair summary of Judge Friendly's opinion.

The application for mandamus is denied and, in effect, Judge Edelstein is affirmed. These subpoenas must be obeyed. Why? It may be that for hundreds of years the common law has treated the opinion of an expert as his property. He's free to give it away, free to sell it, but it may not be compelled, while an ordinary witness is in a very different situation indeed. But to continue that doctrine, in this day and age, when expert witnesses are so important, would be to say to experts—you may obstruct justice at will. Somebody who happens to see two cars collide must come to court. You don't have to come to court, even though your opinion may be at the heart of most lawsuits tried today. So, says Judge Friendly, "It's time to change the rule."

Now, recognize that there are limiting factors here. First, the experts don't testify for two subway tokens. They are to receive reasonable compensation. "But," says Judge Friendly, "we gather that that's not the problem. The lawyers can work that out. If they can't work it out, come back to us." They never had to come back. As I say, that wasn't the problem. Money was not at issue here.

Second, Judge Friendly points out what's easily overlooked, but is, indeed, a limiting factor. These experts are not being required to do any work beyond coming to court. They don't have to prepare, they don't have to go to the laboratory, they don't have to go to the library, they don't have to think about a thing. They have already studied the computer industry. They have already formulated their views. The only thing they're being compelled to do is come to court and tell the judge what those views are and presumably answer some questions about it. If you were to try to compel the expert to do preparatory work, no fooling, you'd have very serious questions under the 13th Amendment, you know, whether you can compel somebody to do that. But that's not involved here.

I said at the beginning that this may be the most important case, et cetera, et cetera. You can't be certain because, as I also said at the beginning, this case has gone widely unremarked. There's no progeny, there's no developing body of law following, illuminating *Kaufman v. Edelstein*. If we could reconvene 20 years from now, presumably we would know and we would see that either of these two possibilities have proved to be the fact. One is that the case 20 years from now will be seen as a kind of signpost, pointing out the direction in which doctrine will develop. What direction? That at least in some circumstances an expert may be compelled. You can subpoena an expert and require him to come to court. But the other possibility, of course, is that *Kaufman v. Edelstein* is a kind of sport in the law. We've all come across cases of this type. You usually say that they are limited to their facts so that you really can cite *Kaufman v. Edelstein*, if that turns out to be the situation, only the next time the government sues to break up IBM and a guy named Kaufman does not want to testify and the judge presiding is named Edelstein. Otherwise, don't rely upon it because you just can't count on it. We don't know. I leave that to the future and to you.

That brings us to the next question, which will occupy us for quite a while because it brings us into the courtroom. We have an issue on which an expert may testify. We have identified the expert we'd like to call. We have, in one fashion or another, secured the appearance of that expert in court. So now let's try the case. Obviously, if there's direct examination, there's cross-examination. Since direct examination comes first, let's talk first about direct.

Again, a brief roadmap. What I shall do is raise and discuss in turn the five principal questions of law, if you will, that are likely to arise in the course of the direct examination of an expert—any kind of expert in any kind of case. The answers to these problems are in part supplied by the law of evidence, in part by the law of procedure, and in part by the craft of advocacy, which of course, means that there are no right answers, but there are only thoughtful answers.

First question. What do you do first? And there's no one in the room who doesn't know that the first thing you do when undertaking the direct examination of an expert is qualify the expert. Indeed, you might think of it as follows. The direct examination of any expert on any subject in any case falls into two parts. The first part of the direct is qualifying the expert; the second part, eliciting the opinion, together with related matters.

Well, what about qualifying the expert? What's involved? Well, by way of background and to permit us to go forward, let me remind you of what's involved and it's really very simple and it's well-settled stuff in the law of evidence. An expert is permitted to give his opinion. That is the principal consequence of a witness being an expert. Normally, witnesses may not give their opinions. That is the famous opinion or non-opinion rule. Witnesses testify to what they perceive, not to what they opine. An expert, however, as an exception to the non-opinion rule, may give his opinion. You've got to have an issue on which expert opinion is permissible, to be sure, and the witness, indeed, must be an expert. Now, the term expert is a term of art. What I mean is not that he's a Nobel Prize winner, but do you know what it means? Very little. It means only that this witness knows more than the man or woman in the street, that's all. Knows more than the average person as a result of education, experience, whatever it may be. If the witness does know more, even only a very little bit more, the judge will say he may give his opinion under the expert witness exception to the non-opinion rule. That he doesn't know a hell of a lot more than the man in the street goes not to the admissibility of the opinion, but to its weight or credibility. And counsel may argue to the jury that, really, he doesn't know so much more, that he should be believed, et cetera, et cetera, et cetera.

Everybody knows that when you qualify an expert, you are in a manner of speaking saying to the judge, "Judge, I now show you that my witness knows more than the man or woman in the street, therefore you should allow him to give his opinion under the expert witness exception to the non-opinion rule." All too many lawyers think that that's all you're doing when you qualify an expert and that is a terrible mistake. The reason I say all too many lawyers is that an awful lot of lawyers, in my experience, sleepwalk their way through the process of qualifying the expert. They do it, of course, but they do it pro forma. There's no excitement, there's no psychic energy to it. And I suppose the reason they do it pro forma, sleepwalker style, is that you can't lose. All you've got to do is show the judge that he knows more than the man in the street—and of course he does. If it's the spleen-out case and the guy graduated from medical school last week, well, obviously he's not a Nobel Prize winner, but he does know more than the man in street. He took a course in spleens or whatever they do in medical school and that's more than Mr. and Mrs. Average Citizen. Since you can't lose, you don't work very hard at it.

Work hard at it. Prepare the qualifying of an expert with as much care as you would prepare a vital cross-examination or your summation. Because when you qualify an expert, always remember, you are talking to the judge in the manner that we have summarized, yes. But in addition, you are talking to the jury or the judge in his capacity as jury. And what you are saying to that jury as you qualify the expert is, "Listen to these credentials. Aren't they impressive? Don't they show you that this is a witness worth believing?" And we'll return to that when, at the very end, this afternoon, we talk about arguing the credibility of an expert. So, for God's sakes, don't do it pro forma. Do it the way it ought to be done.

Let me just take a minute—again, this is not realistic—but to give you the swing of it. As we've said, everything depends upon the circumstances and the personality of the expert and your personality. But, for example, if you had Dr. Ochoa—as I say, he's long since deceased and we settled my spleen-out case—but if we had to try it, there would have been Dr. Ochoa: a man about 65, Nordic, bright blue eyes, obviously strange last name—Ochoa—strange first name—Severo. He was a Finn. He was from Finland. He spoke with an accent, as he came to this country when he was 17 or 18 years old.

So you might begin, "Dr. Ochoa, I gather from your name and your accent that you were not native born. Where were you born, Doctor?"

"Finland."

"Oh, a lot of trees in Finland."

"Yeah."

"Yeah. And how old were you when you came to the United States?"

"Seventeen."

"And what did you then do?"

"I went to graduate school."

He was not a medical doctor, he was a Ph.D. in biochemistry or whatever.

"I went to graduate school and got a Ph.D."

"And then what did you do, Doctor?"

"Well, then I went right to the laboratory."

"And what did you do, Doctor?"

"Ha ha, spleens, spleens, spleens. That's day after night after day. Spleens. That's all I did for 35 years."

And you might want to bring out that, "Well, now, you're not a medical doctor."

"No."

"But you teach medical students."

"Yeah."

See, that gets a double benefit. He's sort of an honorary doctor and teaching doctors is even better than being a doctor. "And have you published and are you a member of the various societies?" and all the things that you don't need to be reminded of. But give it a pace and give it a shape and you might, in the instance of Dr. Ochoa, end up with, "Well, now, Doctor, after these endless hours, days, months, years of drudgery in the laboratory on spleens, spleens, spleens, Doctor, have you received any professional recognition from your colleagues in the field of physiology for your work?"

"Now what . . ."

"Come, doctor, this is no time to be modest. Tell us, have you received any professional recognition?"

"Well, I guess, yeah. Yeah, sort of, I guess you could say. So last year I . . . I kind of won the Nobel Prize." That's a good point to stop, right? Stop right there.

And then, depending upon who the judge is and your sense of the situation—this is not required, this is a matter of etiquette, really—you turn to the judge and you say something like, "Your Honor, I ask the court to declare Dr. Ochoa an expert on the physiology of the spleen." I'll tell you a secret. The reason you might want to do that—of course, you've got to know your judge—is this. Some judges not fully plugged in will hear that as doesn't he know more than the man in the street and so they will say, "Yes, I so rule." The jury hears it as, "Judge, isn't he terrific?" And the judge says, "Yes." See? Which means that you have associated the judge's authority with your witness's credibility, which is a way of enhancing the witness's credibility because, remember, the judge is the authority figure in that courtroom. But you've got to know your judge. Some judges don't like to be put in that position and, of course, they know how to deal with you if you make them uncomfortable. So know your judge and then you play the judge the way you play a fish on a line.

As in any aspect of a trial, you must recognize that for every move there's a countermove. For everything that a proponent ought to be doing, there's something for the opponent to be doing. So if the proponent has to concern himself or herself with qualifying the expert, the opponent has to be concerned with doing whatever can be done to prevent the jury from finding out, for example, that Dr. Ochoa, the plaintiff's expert, is a Nobel Prize winner in medicine. No guarantees that it will succeed, but you've got to know what's available, what are the tools that come to hand.

Well, anybody who's tried a case involving experts knows that if your opponent calls a Dr. Ochoa, obviously, he is going to be regarded by the judge, ruled by the judge to be an expert, hence entitled to give his opinion. You want to bring it about, if you can, that the jury never hears that this expert is a Nobel Prize winner. So most of you, maybe all of you, at this point would say what you do is offer to concede or stipulate. But if you're going to do it, for heaven's sakes, do it the right way. Leap to your feet the instant your opponent says, "My next witness, Your Honor, is Dr. Severo Ochoa," and what do you say? What you say is, "Your Honor, let's save time," like the invariably effective way of getting the attention of a trial judge. His mustache starts to wiggle when you say, "Let's save time." And then you would go on something, at least I would, something along these lines: "Your Honor, there is no need to spend endless hours going into the credentials of Dr. Ochoa. I am perfectly prepared to concede that he is an expert, hence entitled to give his opinion under the Expert Witness Exception to the Non-Opinion Rule." I would deliberately say it in such a manner as to make it likely that the jury has no idea what I'm conceding, assuming that we're doing it in front of the jury. And as the proponent, what should you do when I offer that concession? You should say, "Oh, no, he is offering to concede only one of the two things going on here. He's offering to concede that the expert may give his opinion. Of course he may. But he's not conceding the credibility of the expert and on that I have a right to put the credentials before the jury."

And finally we've got a case saying so—that's *Murphy v. the National Railroad Passenger Corporation case*[4] cited in the materials. A square

---

4. *Murphy v. National R.R. Passenger Corp.*, 547 F.2d 816 (4th Cir. 1977).

holding by the Fourth Circuit that the proponent of an expert has an absolute right to put the expert's credentials before the jury. Why? Well, because of the significance the credentials will have when the jury comes to deliberate upon the expert's credibility. Unless the opponent is prepared to stipulate the credibility of the expert, which, of course, he never will, you may put the credentials to the jury.

Not in the opinion, but I'm positive that it's implicitly there and I could not sleep tonight if I didn't mention it. There's no doubt in my mind that even under the *Murphy* case a trial judge has the power to impose a reasonable time limit on you, so that the judge may say, "Oh, I recognize, Counsel, that you have a right to put the expert's credentials to the jury but, for God's sakes, not two days. No, I'll give you 10 minutes or 20 minutes, or whatever," and so long as it's reasonable, that will satisfy the Appellate Court.

Let me mention now something that we'll talk about in somewhat greater detail later. Obviously, the opponent, quite apart from whatever he may do to prevent the jury from hearing about it, has a right to contest the expertise of the expert. Now, as a practical matter, it's almost never the case that there's a fair shot of persuading the jury that he is insufficiently expert to be entitled to give his opinion. I mean, you know, you don't call unqualified people of that kind. Obviously, the expert is going to know more than the man in the street and the judge inevitably will conclude that he may give his opinion. What you really do is question the expert on his credentials as a way of attacking his credibility. And, as we'll see, there are cases where that is a reasonable thing to do. It's not hopeless. It's not quixotic. It is the practice everywhere, so far as I know, that you may ask the judge for leave to cross-examine on the expertise, on the credentials, right at the end of that first phase of the direct. You don't have to wait for cross-examination proper, the theory being that if your cross-examination on credentials persuades the judge that he's not expert enough to give his opinion, he'll never give his opinion. Whereas if you wait for cross-examination at the close of the direct, the opinion will already have been given and the whole thing becomes a futile exercise. The phrase that's usually used to describe this advance cross-examination on the credentials is voir dire or voir dire—the same phrase that's used to describe the questioning of a prospective juror. And whether you want to wait for cross-examination later on or conduct a voir dire or voir dire now is entirely a matter of style and it will depend upon the circumstances before you. There's no general rule that I will suggest.

But consider the possibility of saying when the proponent of the expert, your opponent, says, "Your Honor, I ask you to declare Dr. Ochoa an expert on the field of physiology of the spleen," you might say, "Well, now, Your Honor, before you rule, may I voir dire the doctor on his credentials?" And the judge will say yes in all probability and what you now do is cross-examine, but solely on the credentials. Later on you will cross-examine on the opinion itself. What you might accomplish by way of cross-examining on the credentials we'll talk about under the heading of cross-examining the expert in 20 or 30 minutes, whenever we get to it. So much for qualifying the expert.

We turn now to the second phase or half of the direct examination of any expert on any issue in any kind of case—what I described earlier as eliciting the opinion and related problems. Now, those problems and eliciting the opinion add up to four principal issues, so let's talk about them. Together with qualifying the expert, you will have the five issues that kind of characterize the law with respect to direct examination of an expert.

First of the four—what about opinions on an ultimate issue? And you may remember this from law school. Indeed, if you went to law school about the time I did or as many years ago as I did, there came a day in the course in evidence when the instructor said something very much like this. He said, "Boys and girls, the cases are legion, holding that even though everything else may be appropriate for expert testimony, if the expert's opinion deals with an ultimate issue, he may not give his opinion. No opinions on ultimate issues." And at once a hand went up and when the student was recognized, the question was, "Professor, what's an ultimate issue?" And the answer would come, "Well, sonny or girly, as Justice Potter Stewart will one day say in a somewhat different connection, 'I can't define it, but I recognize it when I see it.'" The justice, of course, was talking about pornography, the evidence teacher is talking about the ultimate issue, but he's absolutely right in every way. The cases were legion, holding that an expert could not testify on an ultimate issue, and nobody had ever been able to define an ultimate issue, though usually you can recognize it when you see it.

I can't define it either, but in an effort to talk about it so as to convey some sense of what it is for those of you who don't know, an ultimate issue in my mind is nothing more than a ball game issue. Decide that issue and the ball game is over. There's nothing more to try.

Remember we began with the facts of the federal and the state case involving a head-on collision—where on the highway did the cars collide? That's an ultimate issue because once you decide where on the highway the two cars collided, at least on liability the case is over. You know which driver fell asleep at the wheel and that's an end, there's nothing else to talk about.

Take another example. Somebody buys a home stepladder, climbs up on the top and, while standing there, the thing collapses under him—dreadful quadriplegic injuries. Now, the claim is typical of product liability litigation. Not that the stepladder was manufactured in a defective way, but that it was designed improperly. It was not designed as safely as the state-of-the-art would allow. One side or the other calls an industrial engineer who testifies yes or no, it was or was not designed as safely as the state-of-the-art would allow. Well, that's an ultimate issue because, once you decide that issue on liability, the case is over.

Today it is the unanimous view of commentators and judges that those old cases forbidding an expert to testify on an ultimate issue are anachronisms. It's just not consistent with present-day thinking on what testimony should go before a jury. So the view today is that experts may testify on an ultimate issue, assuming no other impediments to their testimony. And that has been codified in Federal Evidence Rule 704, which says in so many words that an expert may testify on an ultimate issue. The Federal Rules do not define ultimate issue because they can't. They just leave it to all of us to recognize an ultimate issue when we see one.

The *Masson* case,[5] which is cited there by way of illustration, is not a particularly great case, but it's reasonably memorable on its facts and it sort of buttons it up and drives it home. So briefly let me tell you about the *Masson* case. It was a criminal case. The rule is no different in criminal cases, but because it is a criminal case, it has a certain cutting edge that civil cases don't have and it was a fairly unusual criminal case and one of the type that I find particularly amusing, I guess is the word.

For those of you who do not engage in federal criminal practice, it may come as a surprise to learn that there is a federal statute requiring bookies to pay an annual tax to the Treasury Department in receipt of which the bookie gets a great big stamp, a gummed stamp, which he's supposed to paste in the window of his bookie establishment. Now, it is not a federal crime to be a bookie, but it is a federal crime not to pay the tax and display the tax stamp. If you don't pay the tax and display the tax stamp and you are a bookie, you are guilty of a federal felony. If you pay the tax and display the stamp, you are not guilty of a federal felony, but of course, the locals then know to come around and arrest you because you're a bookie, you've got the stamp in the window. I am told, and simply pass it on for what it's worth, that since the days of Alexander Hamilton in the Treasury Department, precisely three such stamps have been sold, all three to stamp collectors.

In any event, Masson was on trial for running a premises for the purpose of taking bets on horses without having paid the necessary tax and displaying the necessary tax stamp. Now, Masson conceded that the premises were his. He conceded that he had not paid the tax. He conceded that the stamp was not on display. The only issue in the case was whether the government could prove beyond a reasonable doubt that the premises were used for the purpose of taking bets on horses.

---

5. *United States v. Masson*, 582 F.2d 961 (5th Cir. 1978).

Forgive me 30 seconds of a kind of personal soliloquy on the next phase of the case. The government had a wiretap. They had tapped Masson's phone. And that's not unusual, but as a sometime criminal lawyer, particularly in the federal courts, let me tell you that what was unusual here . . . two things. First, the tap was lawful. They had an order and the order was perfectly good. They had followed the statute in every detail. Second, and even more miraculous, the tap had worked. Boy and man, I have been involved in federal criminal litigation, much of it involving wiretaps and never, whether as prosecutor or defense counsel, have I been able to hear a damned thing on that tape. Invariably, when I'm the defendant, however, some FBI agent says, "Oh, I can hear it and here is a transcript of what I can hear," and sure enough, there it is, guilt writ large on the transcript. In this case, it was clear as a bell.

It was a lawful wiretap and it was like a high-fidelity symphonic recording. Every consonant and every vowel absolutely in place. The difficulty was one I know of only from reading the opinion. I tell you that gambling is the only vice to which I am immune, hence I know nothing about gambling. I gather from the opinion, however, that when people place bets on horses, they don't speak English. It's not even a dialect, it is wholly a foreign language and you just don't know what they're talking about unless you know the foreign language. So the government plays this tape for the jury. As I say, it's as clear as a present-day symphonic recording, but it might as well be a chorus of *Oedipus Rex* in the Attic Greek. They just don't know what it is.

The government calls an expert, an agent from the Treasury Department, who says, "I did not work this case. I don't know anything about this case. But over the years I have come to learn the language of placing bets on horses and that language is on that tape. That's the language of horse betting." Objection from defense counsel. "What's wrong?" says the judge. "Ultimate issue." It sure is an ultimate issue. That's the ball game, right? If this guy is permitted to testify to that opinion, defendant, pack up your toothbrush, you're going. Goodbye. Right? The judge says, "I will allow it." He's affirmed by the Court of Appeals. Why? Because, oh yes, it is an ultimate issue, but opinions on ultimate issues are permissible under the Federal Rules and any modern view of the Law of Evidence.

There is a foul line, however, over which the expert may not go. It's sometimes a little difficult to draw, but it's there. The expert may testify to an ultimate issue. He may say that's the language of horse betting, but he may not say what the verdict should be. He may not say Masson is guilty or that the jury should find him guilty. The industrial engineer may say that stepladder was or was not designed as safely as the state-of-the-art would allow, but he may not say the plaintiff should win or the defendant should win.

There's no citation for it, but let me briefly tell you about a case which drives that home and then we will move along. I know about it because a lawyer aware of my interest in the subject sent me the transcript. And so he sent me the transcript and a copy of the appellate opinion and, though it's not reported, there it is. It's a state case, but it is a state that has adopted the Federal Rules. So an expert opinion on ultimate issues, unquestionably admissible.

Criminal case, the prosecutor having read his state's equivalent of the Federal Ultimate Issue Rule, decides to do something clever. He calls to the stand an expert who testifies in summary fashion now as follows: "I am a professional investigator of criminal cases. I worked for the State Criminal Investigations Department for 35 years. I know all about how to investigate criminal cases. I have read the file of this investigation and, in my opinion, the defendant is guilty." That's what he said. Right. When they revived defense counsel, the defense counsel said, "I object, ultimate issue." And the judge, also the victim of too little learning, said, "Well, but we've got a rule now, it's like the Federal Rule, Rule 704, expert may testify to an ultimate issue. It sure is an ultimate issue, but that's what the rule says. I will allow it." "No, no, no," said the appellate court, "that's over the foul line. That's not an ultimate issue, that's telling the jury what the verdict should be and that no expert will be permitted to do."

Well, let's leave it at that and move to the next issue, which is one not frequently litigated, but particularly interesting at least to me. And perhaps it is because I have a longstanding interest in some of the modern problems of philosophy and science, epistemology, what is the nature of knowing, and things of that sort. I am not aware of any reported federal opinion dealing with the question. There are a number of state cases dealing with it, but it may come up and, in any event, it's worth knowing, so let's talk about it.

The best opinion I know of on this question is from the Appellate Division, that intermediate appellate court in New York. It is called *Ward v. Kovacs*.[6] And, for those of you who try product liability and medical malpractice cases, I urge you to read the opinion. I mentioned before and it's not the voice of parochialism, the Appellate Division in New York is an extraordinarily good court. Terrifically able judges on it, really better than the highest court of the state and especially good on commercial and tort cases. And the opinion in *Ward v. Kovacs* is a brilliant discussion of many of the problems, both of substance and of evidence and of procedure, that arise in those heavy tort cases. So any lawyer who practices in that field will learn a great deal from the opinion. But let me tell you what the issue is and then we'll see what *Ward v. Kovacs* does with it.

Putting it in the abstract, the issue is this: What is the degree of conviction the law requires of the expert? And to flesh that out a little bit—remember we said in a different connection a while ago that only the horse races go to trial. Where a case admits of only one resolution, it doesn't go to trial because lawyers are reasonable. The same thing is true of issues on which experts testify and it's why I am not too impressed by people who say that experts testify in accordance with their pocketbook. Whoever retains the expert gets the opinion. That's not what's going on at all.

In every field there are issues on which the professionals will not disagree. There is unanimity of view on this, that, or the other issue in medicine, economics, engineering, or whatever. Where a case presents

---

6. *Ward v. Kovacs*, 55 App. Div. 2d 391, 390 N.Y.S.2d 931 (2d Dept. 1977).

such an issue, the issue is not tried. Either the case is settled or it's tried without that issue. That issue is stipulated out of the case and that's why you never run into the phenomenon in the trial of lawsuits of experts on different sides of the case agreeing. In law as in medicine as in engineering as in economics, et cetera, there are issues on which people of impeccable professional credentials can, in good faith, disagree. Those are the issues that go to trial and that's why you have this phenomenon of swearing contests between the experts. They're not lying. They're not being insincere. In perfect good faith, the experts differ because there is professional disagreement in their field on these issues.

It follows, then, that no expert with any kind of professional self-respect will ever tell you from the witness stand that it's 100 percent certain. He can't because, by definition, the issue does not admit of that kind of certainty. Oh, he will tell you that he sincerely believes in his opinion, that in his subjective judgment it may be 100 percent, but as an economist or an engineer, he cannot tell you that all economists or all engineers agree. So the available degree of conviction is always less than 100 percent. Now, the man or woman is up there giving his opinion, so we understand that on a scale of 0 to 100, while it's less than 100, it's more than 0. Does the law require that degree of conviction to be at any particular point along the scale? And the answer is yes.

Now, doing it in numbers makes it a little easier to get at. One-hundred percent certainty will never be available. Obviously, it's more than 0. So where does it have to be at a legal minimum? Well, let's start with 50 percent, 50 on a scale of 100. And I suppose the verbal equivalent would be it's possible, maybe yes, maybe no. And every court that has considered the issue has said that if all the expert can say is that it's my opinion and it's possibly true, it's not enough. The opinion is not admissible. That testimony is incompetent. And while the courts are not very, what shall I say, learned in articulating it, the reason is pretty clear. Judges sense what any modern philosopher or physicist will tell you—anything is possible, literally anything.

That being so, to allow an expert to say that it's possible doesn't accomplish anything. It begs no laws. There's no forward motion in the case. So it's got to be more than possible. It's got to be more than 50 on a scale of 100. Which brings us, I suppose, numerically to 75 percent, the verbal equivalent of which would be probable. And that's what the law requires. The expert does not have to say, "I'm certain of it," but he's got to be able to say, "I think it's probably true."

Now, the consequence for a careful trial lawyer is that you must prepare your expert on the difference in a courtroom between the words possible and probable. To a layman, that is to say, to a non-lawyer, the words are more or less interchangeable—they mean about the same thing. But they are terms of art to a lawyer. They are technical terms and the expert must be clued in. In short this is part of, you know, the lawyers' rules that the lawyers play when they play this game.

Now, in the jurisdictions that I'm familiar with, where I try cases, there are certain formulae that have evolved over the years. And while the formulae will not bear logical analysis, they ought not to be analyzed logically, just use them because everybody knows what they mean. For example, when you put a doctor on the stand to testify to some medical issue, the phrase that's always used is, "Doctor, do you have an opinion which you can give us with a reasonable degree of medical certainty as to blah, blah, blah." Now, listen to me. Reasonable degree of medical certainty. If it's certain, then it's not to a reasonable degree, so it's inconsistent there. And what's a medical certainty as opposed to any other kind of certainty? But, as I say, don't analyze it, just use it, because it's a signal flag that you raise to the judge, saying, "It's okay, Judge, take it easy. You know, rest comfortable, I know what I'm doing." This expert is in effect saying to you, "Well, I may not be certain, but I think it's probably so."

Now, no form of words is required. If there are formulae that are commonplace in your courthouse, I advise using them. If there are no formulae, simply to prevent the issue from coming up and making trouble, on direct examination I would say to the expert, "Now, doctor or professor, whatever, do you have an opinion?" "Yes." "Before you give us the opinion, tell us, is it 100 percent certain?" "No, of course not, nothing in this field is." "Well, how certain are you?" "Well, I think it's highly probable." Enough. On we go.

Ward v. Kovacs, that opinion I urged upon you, a picturesque case. The plaintiff was a young woman of swinging lifestyle. Sort of the pendulum is coming back so that that lifestyle is not quite as popular as it was 10, 15, 20 years ago at the time of *Ward v. Kovacs*, but it becomes relevant as you will see. That's more than just a passing reference to the way the young woman lived. She took her vacation on Fire Island, a place some of you may know or have read of. It is a long, narrow beach to the south of Long Island and it's a place where swingers of all kinds go for vacation. And she is playing volleyball on the beach and she cuts herself somehow and it's rather a bad gash. So she goes to the local doctor who does whatever he does and sends her home. She wakes up that night and the hand has swollen to three times its normal size, it's terribly painful, it's throbbing. She is terrified. She manages to get across the bay to a general hospital where they take a look at her hand and they say, "Young woman, that's a fulminating streptococcal infection. The streptococci are reproducing without any defense from your body and that's a life-endangering condition; people can die of it."

So they put her in an oxygen tent and heroic medical measures are brought to bear and they save her life. But, in effect, she loses her hand. She comes out of this experience with her hand permanently clenched in that claw condition. Terribly unsightly—she is a young woman, after all—but it's nonfunctional. It's as if she has no right hand. Dreadful business. She sues the doctor claiming that whatever he did was malpractice. A number of issues in the case, of which one of them is the following.

Among the defenses raised by the defendant is that that young woman—remember my characterization of her lifestyle—was, at the time she cut her finger, aslosh with LSD. And one of the consequences of LSD in your system is that it reduces the body's ability to fight off bacterial infection. So that she was, at least in part, responsible for her own injury. All right. Can you prove it, Mr. Defendant?

They call to the stand a young doctor who does not practice; he's in the laboratory. And he says, in effect, "I'm a laboratory physician and I'm working on the biochemistry of psychic drugs." "And doctor, are you working on the effect of LSD on the system? "Yeah." "And do you have an opinion as to the effect of LSD on the human physiology?" "Yes." "And what is that opinion, Doctor?" "Well, I think that LSD reduces the body's ability to fight off streptococcal infections." You may inquire . . . now this is what happened.

The cross-examiner senses that the proponent has not prepared the doctor on the requisite degree of conviction and so he stands up and very mildly he says, "Now, Doctor, you gave us that opinion, but you're not positive of it." "Oh, no, no, no, we're working on it right now in the laboratory." "So what you're telling us all, Doctor, is that it's possible that LSD reduces the body's ability." "Yep, it's possible." Now, the proponent realizes that he's in trouble. Redirect. "Doctor, when you say possible, you mean, probable." "Right." Recross. "Doctor, when you say probable, you mean possible." "Right." Redirect. "No, Doctor, when you say possible, you mean probable." And back and forth, they whipsaw this guy, who is sitting there saying to himself, "What are these lawyers niggling about? I'm saying the same thing." But he's not. He's not. He just hasn't been told that possible and probable are very different things when an expert testifies.

The opinion by the court, as I say, is brilliant, persuasive, and it really hits the issue on the head and puts it out of its misery. First, no form of words is required. It would be nice for a lawyer to be careful and examine the expert in such a way as to eliminate the issue. But if he doesn't, it is not a fatal defect or deficiency. No form of words is required. When the issue is raised, the appellate court will examine the testimony in context in order to figure out what the witness really meant. On that record, the appellate court concludes that what the witness really meant was it's probable, therefore the testimony stands. If you concluded that what he really meant was it's possible, it must be stricken because, the Appellate Division says, as have the other cases to consider this issue, the law requires as that requisite degree of conviction that the expert tell us that his opinion is probably so or that it's probably certain.

Well, so much on the requisite degree of conviction. Let us move on to a matter which, if you are trying your case under the Federal Rules or some state equivalent, is particularly important for you, should you have learnt your evidence as I did, pre–Federal Rules. In this respect, ladies and gentlemen, I should tell you right at the start, I should confess a kind of interest or position here. We are dealing with what, in my judgment, is the single most radical thing in the Federal Rules of Evidence, the biggest change from the Common Law of Evidence. It is also, in my judgment, the wrongest thing in the Federal Rules, but that's a voice in the wind. The rules are the rules and if you practice under the Federal Rules, you'd better be aware of what the possibilities are. The rule is 703, specifically the second sentence. And the issue is what are the permissible bases of an expert's opinion? But I think that the way I ought to proceed here is first to remind you of the common law position and then to take a look at what the Federal Rules do.

Common law. An expert may give his opinion, assuming that everything is all right, and that opinion, of course, will rest upon certain items of data. Let's do it in algebra. Here is the opinion and it rests upon A, B, C, D, and E. We'll give you an actual example in a moment or two. The common law said that whatever the expert relied upon, A through E in my symbolic example, must be in evidence. That's a kind of shorthand. What the common law really says is that there must be enough evidence of A, B, C, D, and E so that a reasonable juror could reasonably find that A is the fact, B is the fact, and so on down the line. If the opinion goes beyond the evidence, if it rests upon data not in the record, the opinion is technically immaterial. How can the opinion help or be essential to the jury when the opinion rests upon material unknown to the jury? The opinion then is irrelevant to what the jury is doing and we call that immaterial.

All right, a real example. Now, I'll read an example and this is essentially *Sirico v. Cotto.*[7] Not a particularly great or class opinion, but it's a neat illustration of the common law rule at work and it has the special virtue, at least to me, of being an opinion I wrote myself. So, obviously, I think it's pretty snazzy. There were several issues I'm kind of simplifying, but not distorting.

---

7. *Sirico v. Cotto*, 67 Misc. 2d 636, 324 N.Y.S.2d 483 (Civ. Ct. N.Y. Co. 1971).

The expert is a doctor—a general practitioner, family doctor. And the issue is what ailed the plaintiff, an elderly woman. So dressing it up a little bit in lawyer talk, the opinion is going to be a diagnosis, right? What was wrong with your patient. And the testimony proceeded pretty much as follows:

"Doctor, did you examine Mrs. Plaintiff?"

"Yes."

"When you examined her, what did you find?" (And just by way of exercise or review, let's follow it along and see how you analyze it.)

"Well," says the doctor, "I looked down her throat and I saw red patches." Is that an expert's opinion? No. That's an ordinary witness's perception. Remember, experts sometimes testify as ordinary witnesses when they testify to their perceptions. I saw red patches. That is evidence of fact A. There were red patches. "I palpated the muscles at the back of the neck and they were in spasm." I felt that. That's ordinary witness testimony, it's evidence of fact B. She had spastic muscles in the back of the neck. "And the rest of my examination was clinically irrelevant. Nothing noteworthy was observed."

"On the basis, then, Doctor, of A and B, red patches, spastic muscles, were you able to arrive at a diagnosis?"

"No."

"So what did you do?"

"I sent her out to three specialists—an X-ray guy, a blood guy, and a nerve guy—for various work-ups. In due course, I received their reports."

"After reading their reports, Doctor, could you come to a diagnosis?"

"Yes."

"What was that diagnosis?"

"Objection."

"Sustained."

Why? This opinion rests upon five items of data. A, red patches in evidence. B, spastic muscles in evidence. C, the X-ray report. D, the nerve report. E, the blood report. Not in evidence—those specialists have not testified. The reports can't be in evidence—rule against hearsay, et cetera. By common law, how do you handle that?

"Doctor, step down."

My next witness is the nerve guy. He testifies to his findings. Or the X-ray guy or the blood guy.

"Now, Doctor, get back on the stand. Doctor, having in mind what you observed together with the findings of the neurologist now before the jury in evidence, could you come to an opinion?"

"Yes."

"What is it?"

On we go. Now, I'll grant you, that's expensive. I'll grant you that it's time consuming. But I'll also grant you that I don't see how else you can do it if you want the jury to decide the case in accordance with the evidence. The jury must know what underlies the opinion, otherwise they cannot assess the opinion. However, the critics of the common law rule, on the ground of expense and time, carried the day.

And so you have what you see in 703 second sentence. This is not a quotation, but it's pretty close to the exact language. An expert's opinion may go beyond the evidence. It may rest upon material not admissible in evidence so long as it's reasonable to do so. That's the dividing line. What's reasonable, what's unreasonable, with no attempt to define or characterize reasonable. All right? Let's be sure we understand what the law is and then we'll see how it works. Under the Federal Rules or a state version, the expert's opinion may rest upon A, B, C, D, and E, A and B being in evidence, B, C, D, and E or C, D, and E not being in evidence, so long as it's reasonable to do so. And the term reasonable, as judges have come to construe it, breaks down into two parts. First, is it customary for experts in this field to rely upon this kind of information and, second, does the judge think that the custom makes sense, that it's reasonable? So that if you were examining that general practitioner in my case today, you would say, "Doctor, what did you find?"

"Red patches, spastic muscles."

"Then what did you do?"

"I sent her to the three specialists."

"In due course, did you receive their reports?"

"Yes."

"Did you read them?"

"Yes."

"Were you then able to arrive at a diagnosis?"

"Yes."

"Is it customary for general practitioners to rely upon the reports they get from the specialists to whom they send their patients?"

"Well, of course, we do it all the time. That's how we practice family medicine."

"And Your Honor, I submit that it's a reasonable custom."

I should think the judge is going to say, "Yes, I think it's reasonable."

"All right, Doctor, what's the opinion? What was your diagnosis, even though three-fifths of what you base it on is not before the jury?"

How do you cross-examine? If the doctor bases his opinion on inadmissible material, does the inadmissible material thereby become admissible? Can the cross-examiner, if the cross-examiner wishes, put the inadmissible materials into evidence? The Federal Rules answer none of those questions. The cases really come to grips with none of those questions. Essentially, it seems to me, you are dealing with a rule written by people who have never tried a case. Oh, they think it's important to save time, et cetera, but they don't know what it is to cross-examine a witness, let alone an expert. You put an expert on the stand and he says, "Well, what I found on examination was not enough to support the diagnosis. But when I got the reports of the specialists back, then I could come up with a diagnosis and here it is." And now you have to cross-examine. You're going to ask him what was in those reports? Not on your life will you ask him what's in those reports because you're opening a Pandora's box, you don't know what's going to come out. It really is a very strange situation and it's why I call it the wrongest and the most radical thing in the rules.

Just to illustrate how strange this can be, here is a case—for some reason the opinion is unreported. It's a major opinion and it's four years old, of course it should have been reported, but I have never been able to find it. Many of you will have seen the name of Judge Sherman Finesilver. He is the chief judge of the U.S. District Court in Denver, Colorado—a very able and experienced federal judge. Many of you will recall, some of you, indeed, may have been involved in the wave of cases following the government program of inoculating people against a new strain of Asian flu some five or six years ago. Remember, I think Joe Califano was secretary of Health, Education, and Welfare. Joe said, "All right, you know, the flu is coming at us and we've got to inoculate all old people and babies against the disease." And it turned out that the inoculations caused more death and injury than the disease possibly could have done. What came upon people was something I can't pronounce but called approximately Guillain-Barré Syndrome. I will call it the GB Syndrome. Terrible illness and you can die of it. There was a lot of litigation involving this. Much of it was multi-districted before Judge Finesilver and one particular case I want to tell you about.

Judge Finesilver's case is called *Bean v. the United States*,[8] unreported, as I've said, but filed by Judge Finesilver on August 19, 1980. The government, as a matter of national policy, conceded in every one of these cases that if the disease, GB Syndrome, came on within a certain period of time of the injection of the stuff, call it *n* months, that causation would not be an issue. But if the disease came on in anything more than *n* months, then the plaintiff had to prove the causal connection between the disease and the inoculation. Bean was in that position.

The disease had come on in something more than *n* months, so Bean had to prove causation. Undertaking to prove that, Bean called to the stand a research scientist who testified to some experiments that he had done in connection with which he had come to certain conclusions. And the conclusions added up to a causal connection. Now, the experiments were a brand-new biochemical technique. And,

---

8. *In re* Swine Flu Immunization Products Liability Litigation.

just briefly, you know that the results of new processes of technology or science will be admissible when the court is persuaded that they have a scientific basis in the sense of general acceptance among scientists that this, indeed, has a basis in the laws of nature. When they got through trying out the issue, Judge Finesilver expressly ruled that the scientific basis of these tests was not generally accepted in the scientific community involved. Hence, the test results were not admissible. The doctor, the scientist was not allowed to testify as to his conclusions based upon his experiments.

Next witness is a doctor and the testimony goes just about this way. Now we're under the Federal Rules, remember. "Doctor, do you have an opinion to a fair degree of medical certainty as to whether there is a causal connection between the injection of the serum and the onset of the GB Syndrome?"

"Yes, I do."

"What is that opinion?"

"There is a causal connection."

"Now, Doctor, what do you base it on?"

"I base it on those test results." The test results the court has just held to be inadmissible because they don't have a proper scientific basis. Well, the doctor says, "It is customary among doctors to rely upon test results that are not fully validated because medicine is ongoing and, you know, you can't be a stick in the mud. You've got to be up-to-date and, even though it's not wholly free from doubt, it is customary for doctors to rely upon such results, even though they're necessarily incomplete, imperfect, and subject to a great big question mark."

And the judge says, "Okay, I believe it's customary and I think it's reasonable. How else will medicine progress? So I will not allow the results in because that is contrary to the Federal Rule on how you determine the admissibility of results, but I will allow the opinion in based upon the results because it's allowable under 703, second sentence. Even though the data upon which the opinion rests are not admissible in evidence, the opinion can come in," which strikes me as kind of topsy-turvy, but you know, there it is.

And I've got to leave it to you and to me, as the years go on, to struggle with this stuff. Perhaps I should mention that even though the second sentence says the opinion may rest upon data not admissible in evidence, there are limits, reasonableness in the sense of customary and does it make sense. Another lawyer familiar with my interest in this stuff sent me the page of a transcript from an antitrust trial which, so help me, went this way. The expert is an economist.

"Sir, do you have an opinion as to whether there is monopoly concentration in . . ." it was the business of selling golf equipment at retail. "So is there a monopoly concentration?"

"In my opinion there is."

"And what do you base that on?"

"Well, I base it on such and such a fact."

"And, Professor, where did you get that fact?"

And his answer, so help me, was, "A bartender at the country club told me." And the judge ruled, and here I must say the judge was very wise, that even though it is economics, this is too much. Just too much. Right? Right. You cannot rely on what the bartender at the country club told you. It may be customary, but it's not reasonable. And he ruled it out on that ground.

Fifth and last issue in connection with direct examination—how do you elicit the opinion? And, again, if we start with the common law, I think it'll be more efficient. The common law rule was—and in those states that still follow the common law of evidence, still is the rule—that putting aside marginal cases not really to the point, you elicited the expert's opinion by asking a hypothetical question. And the reason for requiring the hypothetical question was this. The expert's opinion had to rest entirely upon evidence in the case, so that the hypothetical became a way of making sure that the opinion did not go beyond the evidence in the case.

Let's go to my spleen-out case of years ago. "Dr. Ochoa, you have no personal knowledge of the facts here."

"No, of course, not. I'm not a medical doctor, I couldn't have had personal knowledge."

"Right. So, Doctor, assume a little boy was hit at a school crossing, taken to the hospital, diagnosed as having a ruptured spleen. The spleen is removed in a simple surgical procedure. He makes an uneventful recovery. Today he's normal except he doesn't have a spleen. On the basis of those facts, Doctor, do you have an opinion which you can give us with a reasonable or fair degree of medical certainty as to the consequences for that little boy of the fact that he doesn't have a spleen?"

"Yes."

"What is that opinion?" Blah, blah, blah, blah. As you ask the hypothetical, the opponent and the court can, in a manner of speaking, say, check, check, everything's in evidence, check, little boy hit by car, school crossing, taken to hospital. Everything is in evidence, therefore the opinion is permissible. If you put something in the hypothetical that's not in evidence, objection, sustained. Can't have it because it's not in evidence. The hypothetical question, which is really the only device I or anybody else has ever been able to think of for satisfying the common law requirement that everything the expert relies upon be in evidence, was used in an entirely different way by able trial lawyers. And you don't need me to tell you this. I mean, this stuff is particularly important in personal injury cases and no personal injury lawyer worth his or her salt would dream of asking the hypothetical of Dr. Ochoa as I just asked it. Oh, it does what the law requires, but that's the least important thing that's going on in a courtroom.

So long as, at common law, everything upon which the expert relies is in evidence, you can put anything you want into the hypothetical and so you know how it would be asked. You've all seen lawyers ask hypotheticals. And that hypothetical would take, in the hands of a master PI lawyer, at least 45 minutes, maybe a half a day.

"Now, Doctor, I'm going to ask you to assume certain things. Little Johnny got up about 7:30 that morning, Doctor. The sun was out, the birds were chirping. He came down to the kitchen and his mother was waiting. And his mother said to Johnny, Doctor, she said, 'Johnny, what do you want for breakfast?'" And on and on we go. So long as everything is in evidence, perfectly proper. Two hours later, right. We finally get to the question. The jury is crying. Why? Because in the hands of an artful lawyer, the hypothetical question was a free summation. You summed up in the guise of asking your hypothetical and you got to sum up next week when you really summed up. So you got to do it twice. And the scholar said, "Oh, this is a subversion of the real purpose of a hypothetical question. Its purpose is not to make the jury cry, it's to make sure everybody knows that everything is based upon evidence." But you can't abolish the hypothetical unless you're prepared to abolish that common law rule requiring that all the data be in evidence and it was well before the Federal Rules. Nobody was prepared to do that, so they struck a politician's compromise back in the Uniform Rules of 1940. The hypothetical question was no longer mandatory. Oh, it was permissible, but you didn't have to use it. And that Uniform Rule provision has been carried through in haec verba in the Federal Rules of Evidence, Rule 705. The hypothetical question is no longer mandatory, it is permissible.

In my experience, though, lawyers continue to use the hypothetical because of its utility as a free summation. But in theory, under the Federal Rules, now see what you can do. The expert takes the stand. Remember, his opinion may go beyond the record. It may rest upon data not in evidence. You don't have to use a hypothetical. So it may lack something in sex appeal, but just imagine. "Doctor," after you've qualified him, right? "Now, Doctor, the issue in this case is thus and so. What's your opinion? Thank you. Sit down." How do you cross-examine? It's like trying to get across a mine field without a map. You don't know what. "Doctor, for example, what do you base that on?" "Well, I base it on a piece of paper I found lying in the gutter." "Judge, come on." "Now, Counsel, you asked for it, you brought it out, so it's going to stay." You know, who knows what's going to happen. Really, I'm helpless to discuss it because I just can't conceive of how you can work under these rules. But it seems to be going fairly smoothly in the federal courts in major part, I think, because lawyers just haven't realized the damage you can do by making clever use of the possibilities implicit in these rules, which I think are rather poorly conceived and drafted. But judgments may differ on that and, in any event, we've spent enough time on direct examination. Let's turn to the cross-examination of an expert—a subject that I referred to earlier when talking about Murphy's cross-examination of Dr. Bingham.

I now speak for a few seconds especially to the younger lawyers in the room. I mean the less experienced lawyers. It is natural when you are at the early stages of your career to feel a certain trepidation at the prospect of cross-examining an expert. I mean, that guy's a doctor or an economist or an engineer or an accountant and I am not. And how, really, can I get to him? And you sort of shy off. Now, don't feel that way. For the third time, I remind you of what the dean of the medical school says. It's your ball game in your ballpark by your rules. And you can't always devastate the expert, but you can almost always lay a glove on him. You can make some points. So look forward to it rather with relish, not with trepidation, and enjoy it, because it is enjoyable.

Number one . . . again, it's a checklist. One, do not forget what many, many lawyers forget precisely because it is so obvious. An expert is, to begin with, a witness like any other. So that any impeachment that would be proper of an ordinary witness is proper of this witness, even though he is an expert. Now, that means you've got to look around to see whether you've got the ammunition for ordinary witness impeachment. And if you do, for heaven's sakes, use it.

Example: True story. Kind of a war story, but I was involved only as the judge. I was presiding. Many of you are familiar with how the personal injury practice works. In a place like New York, juries do not turn plaintiffs away without money. Invariably, there's a plaintiff's verdict. Defendants are not looking for defendants' verdicts . . . defense counsel are not. They are looking to keep the recovery down and if you keep it down below the amount that the claims manager has fixed in advance, that's a win. And so it becomes a contest between the experts. It's doctor against doctor because what's really in controversy is the amount of the damages.

And I discovered when I went on the bench and first learned about this field of practice that the doctors seemed to be full-time witnesses.

I can't imagine when they practiced medicine because the doctors are in court all the time. See, the juries don't know that. They see him only once, but the judge or the lawyers see him all the time. Here he is again. Every day he's in the courthouse. When is he in the operating room, for God's sakes? Moreover and even more appalling, the doctors come from the plaintiffs' stable or the defendants' stable and they never cross over. So that it's the same doctors for the plaintiffs time and time again, always testifying that the plaintiff is wholly disabled as a result of this accident. Totally out of it. He's a basket case. We'd bury him except we get a reading every time we stick the EKG in. Right? And the defense doctor in that very same case always testifies that there's nothing wrong with the plaintiff. He's a malingerer. He's better now than he was before he was run over. He ought to pay the defendant for having run him over. And as between the two, the jury somehow has to decide.

And there was one doctor in particular who kind of rubbed me the wrong way, I guess. I will call him Dr. Smith because that was his real name. Irving Smith was it. He was a defendant's doctor and, boy, was he good. Maybe that's why it rubbed me the wrong way. He looked like the . . . what shall I say, the early elderly Spencer Tracy. You know, kind of slightly enlarged in the middle, the lick of hair hanging down, guileless clear eyes and when he turned that witness chair halfway to the jury box, fixed them with those guileless clear eyes and told them that the plaintiff was a malingerer, it was like Spencer Tracy telling it to you and the jury just ate out of his hand. You didn't get defendants' verdicts, but you got verdicts down below where I thought they ought to be.

That doctor testified before me at least 20 times. Twenty times plaintiff's counsel got up to cross-examine and the cross-examination was feckless. It was wholly ineffective. Absolutely nothing was done until that 21st case when some plaintiff's lawyer stood up and, so help me, ladies and gentlemen, began the cross-examination as follows. "Doctor, have you ever been convicted of a crime?" I started going like that, you know . . . no, you can't ask that question without a good faith basis. I'm starting to . . . hey, I'd better take control here, something's going on. But before I can recover myself to talk, the doctor replies, "Yes." And the cross-examination, so help me, proceeded as follows:

"Was that in Federal Court across the street?"

"Yes, it was."

"About three years ago?"

"Yes."

"That was a felony, Doctor, wasn't it?"

"Yes."

"It was the felony of income tax evasion."

"That's right."

"You were found guilty after a trial, weren't you?"

"Yes."

"And you received a sentence of six months in prison."

"Yes."

"Which you served, didn't you?"

"Yes, I did."

The doctor was going to answer truthfully whenever the questions were asked. No lawyer had the wit or the energy to go across the street to the federal courthouse and look up in the defendants' name index to see whether the doctor was there. Shame on him. Because, in any event, about two-thirds of all doctors have been convicted of tax evasion, right? Chances are you're going to find him in the file and once you find him in the file, just think of what you can do. You won't be letting that guy get away with presenting himself to the jury as if he were Spencer Tracy. For God's sakes, he's a federal felon—make sure the jury knows about it. Now it's only the one case out of 20, to be sure, but still those are pretty good house odds. So remember, look around to see whether you've got the ammunition for ordinary witness impeachment.

Next on this sort of checklist. Apart from ordinary witness impeachment, there are under the Federal Rules and in the states and in the common law states generally as well—there's no big difference here—two methods of impeachment available only with respect to experts and you can't undertake a case involving experts unless you have mastered these methods of impeachment. They are commonly called impeachment out of a treatise. Now we see the word treatise. Remember here that treatise means simply a printed source. Treatise, textbook, article in a learned journal, whatever it may be.

Now, let's back up and review. Suppose the witness, the expert, has testified to ABC. This witness once published an article in which he said negative ABC, the contrary. May you impeach him with his own article saying a different thing? The answer is of course. And there's nothing unusual about it. That's ordinary witness impeachment, commonly called impeachment with a prior inconsistent statement.

Suppose you've got a witness who says ABC and somebody else once said negative ABC? When you're dealing with an ordinary witness, may you impeach with what somebody else said? No, it's just not allowed. You can impeach him with what he, the witness, once said, but not with what somebody else said. You can't tax him with somebody's else's comment. When the witness is an expert there are circumstances, however, in which you may impeach with what somebody else said, so long as what somebody else said is in a printed source and so long as you lay the proper foundation, to use the hideous expression that lawyers and judges always do use. Proper foundation simply means ask the necessary preliminary questions. And in the instance of impeachment with a treatise, it can be done in one question. Doesn't have to be one question and you don't have to ask it exactly this way; everything varies with the circumstances. But it must add up to what, simply for reasons of efficiency, I'm going to act out instead of discussing. I said there were two ways of doing it. Let's do them both. And to give it some concreteness, I select the following deliberately absurd situation, so that it's easy to remember and you don't waste mental energy coping with the facts.

The witness is a doctor. On direct examination he said that in his opinion the appendix is on the left side of the body. Of course, it's not—that's ridiculous. Here is *Gray's Anatomy.* He did not write it. But *Gray's Anatomy* on page 100 says, "The appendix is on the right side of the body." What can we do with it? Either or both of two things.

First way, the older way—the foundation question must add up to this. "Doctor, in the course of getting ready to testify in this case, did you consult this book, *Gray's Anatomy*?" You don't have to use the word consult—you can say referred to, read, look at, any such form of words, but it's got to add up to consult. That's the only question you need. If he says no, go to something else, it hasn't worked. If he says yes, and for reasons of etiquette and jury continuity, you might turn to the judge and say, "Your Honor, may I now read to the jury from page 100 of the book?" If the judge is plugged in, he will say yes. Observe. Under the Federal Rules, you are required to read it to the jury. You don't put the book physically into evidence, you don't tear the page out and mark it as an exhibit, you simply read it to the jury so that they do not physically have the book with them when they deliberate as an exhibit. If they want it read back, it's like ordinary witness testimony, the stenographer reads it back.

So let's do it again. "Doctor, in the course of getting ready to testify in this case, did you consult this book, *Gray's Anatomy*?"

"Yes."

"Your Honor, may I read to the jury from page 100?"

"Go right ahead."

Reading now, ladies and gentlemen, from page 100 of *Gray's Anatomy*. "The appendix is on the right side of the body." Slam the book shut, sneer at the doctor, and go to something else. That's all you do. Just that.

Now, the doctor is probably not going to say yes because he knows enough not to look at that book because that gives you the ammunition. That is why years ago the second way of doing it came into being and the second way is likelier to produce that necessary affirmative answer to the one foundation question. You don't have to do it as one question, but it can be done in one question. And it doesn't have to be in these words, but it must add up to this. "Doctor, is this book, *Gray's Anatomy,* authoritative?" Now, in front of a jury you wouldn't use the word authoritative and you don't have to. "Is this the standard reference, Doctor? Is this the Bible? Is this the book all doctors consult when they have to look up a question on anatomy?" or some such form of words. If you've selected the book properly, you know you're going to get a yes answer. And, again, turn to the judge, get the judge's permission, read it to the jury.

Let me take just a moment or two to illustrate what for some of you is still hard to believe, that this can be fun. I mean, to ask the doctor, "Is this book authoritative?" does the job, but it just sort of lies there in the bowl and sops up the milk. It's not doing anything. It doesn't add to the pleasure one takes in one's professional practice. So think of what you can do, especially with a doctor. Right? "Doctor, did you really go to medical school? Your Honor, I'm sorry, I'll withdraw that. I got carried away." "Doctor, when you went to this medical school you say you went to, did they have a course in anatomy? Did you take it? Did you pass it? Was there a book? Is that the book?" Right? You've got him. You've got him, right? He has to say yes. This is the textbook he used in medical school. Or, "Doctor, you have an office for the practice of medicine down on Main Street, don't you?"

"That's right."

"And that office consists of three rooms, it's a three-room suite, correct?"

"Correct."

"The outer office is where the patients wait."

"How did you know that?"

"Now, Doctor, I'm here to ask the questions, please. And the inner room is an examining room?"

"Yes."

"And the middle room is a kind of study where you sit and talk to patients."

"Yes. How did . . ."

"Doctor, please, just answer my questions. Now, Doctor, as you sit in that study, you are behind a desk, a large desk, isn't that right?"

"That's right."

"And as you look over your right shoulder there's a bookcase."

"That's right."

"And in the bookcase are books."

"That's right."

"And is this one of the books, Doctor?" You got him again. What's he going to do, tell the jury he practices out of quack books? Of course not. How did you know that this was a book he used in medical school? Go to the library. Every major library has at least on microfilm the catalog of every American medical school. You look the guy up in the directory, you know where and when he graduated. Medical school catalogues customarily print the title of the textbook together with the course description. You got him. How do you know what he has on the shelves? Well, this morning Paul Drake investigated prospective jurors. This time you called him in and you said, "Paul, you are about to have a stomach ache. And Paul, while you are taking off your pants, note what's on the shelves and if we're lucky, we're going to find a book on this field." Right? I have a friend whose judgment I trust who says that's unethical. I wouldn't do it myself, but I don't think it's unethical. If Paul Drake is willing to take off his pants, what the hell do I care? You may disagree. In any event, I raise the possibility that it's unethical.

How do you prepare your expert to deal with that kind of cross-examination? And remember, for every move there is a countermove. Let me make a suggestion or two. First and perhaps the most important of all, make sure that your expert understands that you understand that professional opinion in the expert's field may well differ on these issues and that you will not think any the less of your expert because it turns out that somebody wrote a book that says something different from what he thinks. Right? You've got to make sure that he understands that so that he does not hesitate to bring to your attention the contrary literature in his field and you've got to rely on him to bring it to your attention. So it's something like, "Now, Doctor, I understand that this issue is not free from doubt and while I credit and I'm sure the jury will credit your opinion, I understand that others in the field have taken a different view. Tell me what there is in print that takes a different view," and you take a look at it and now you get ready to deal with it.

One possibility . . . and it may or may not work. It's a possibility. I would always prepare the expert as follows. Make sure that your doctor responds to the other lawyer as follows. When the other lawyer pulls out the book, it's obvious what's about to happen. Tell your expert in a very low-key way, as a perfect gentleman, to stop and say something like, "Counselor, before you ask me the questions, may I see the book?" If it's in front of the jury and the other lawyer knows what he's doing, he will, of course, hand the book over. If he doesn't want to, you know, if he says, "I don't want to give you the book," the judge always will say, "Give the doctor the book." The doctor looks at the book and gives it back. That's all the jury sees, so there's no danger. What the doctor is doing is looking at the edition. And the book is genuine; you don't have counterfeit books floating around. But remember that in many fields of medicine especially, but not limited to medicine, knowledge is exploding. We just know that as newspaper readers. That in a field like immunology or genetics, if the printing presses could work quickly enough, you'd need a new edition every month. That's how fast developments are coming along. You don't get a new edition every month, but you do get a new edition every year in those fields. And if the issue falls within one of those fields, make sure that your expert is prepared as follows:

"Counselor, may I see the book?" And he gives it back. If it's the current edition, he answers the questions and you haven't lost anything. If its not the current edition, let your expert simply respond to the questions. "Now, Doctor," says your opposing counsel, "is that book authoritative?"

"No." Just that. "No." That's all your expert should say. And you will observe your opponent do a start and then say something like, "What do you mean it's not authoritative?" And then your expert, in that same, gentlemanly, low-key manner, should say, "Well, counselor, in medicine, as I assume in law, the book isn't authoritative unless it's the up-to-date edition. That book was authoritative two years ago, but it isn't anymore because there's been a more recent edition with all of the recent knowledge included in it." You see, if your expert does it in that low-keyed way, the only possible response from opposing counsel is, "Oh," and then he moves on. Which means your expert has educated opposing counsel in front of the jury and that's a wonderful way to enhance your expert's credibility.

If you can't do that, if there is something contrary in the literature, prepare your expert, and obviously this must be prepared, to explain it on redirect. And the explanation should go something along these lines. Obviously, the words will be the expert's words, but you work it out with him in advance. "The book is authoritative, I don't take back my testimony. Nor do I take back my opinion, which is contrary to the book." And then you might say on redirect, "Well, now, Doctor, how do you reconcile your opinion with the book?" And at that point the doctor is on his own. Sit down. Get out of the way. And if he's really in the swing of it, he will get it across the jury. And it should go something like this: "Well, you see, books necessarily have to be written about the average or typical situation and that book is a perfectly accurate description of the average or typical situation. But books can't anticipate the unusual, the atypical, the one-in-a-million and in this case we're dealing with a one-in-a-million situation. The book is correct, but this case is different from what the book is talking about. And that's why I don't take back my testimony about the book, but I don't take back my opinion either." I have found that juries regard that explanation as consistent with their instinctive sense of how the universe works and so they accept it.

And here's also a kind of subconscious flattery extended to the jurors. See, when the juror goes home tonight, he says to his wife, "Am I sitting on a big case. Boy, this is a one-in-a-million case. This is not your run-of-the-mill case." And the juror likes to feel that he's serving on an important case and this does something to give him that feeling. And, of course, he's grateful for that psychic pleasure and there's only one way in which he can make his gratitude known and that's the way we are talking about—namely, a favorable verdict.

Briefly, although it's a little bit off the subject of expert witnesses, but still related to it, suppose you are successful in using either or both of these methods of impeachment out of a treatise. And, by the way, in the materials you have *Ruth v. Fenchel*[9] cited in the Atlantic Second. Let me just draw that to your attention. *Ruth v. Fenchel* in the New Jersey Supreme Court back in, what was it, 1950 or so, is the single best discussion I know of these modes of impeachment. I mean, don't take it as an authority, you know, as a case that turns on its facts. It's just a wonderful discussion of every aspect and nuance of impeachment out of treatise. The case will have a special authority, you know, far beyond New Jersey, for this reason. The author of the opinion, then an associate judge of the New Jersey Supreme Court, is now William Brennan, associate justice of the United States Supreme Court, so you've got a, you know, especially powerful voice there. So it's worth having that case handy.

Back to where we were. Suppose at common law you impeach out of a treatise and you have now put before the jury that statement. "The appendix is on the right side of the body." Do you have a hearsay problem? And the answer in common law is no, because while the statement in the book is an out-of-court statement, it does not come in to prove the truth of what it asserts. Therefore, there's no hearsay problem. It only comes in to discredit the expert, which means what? If the expert testified that the appendix is on the left side of the body and you impeached him out of the book, the most the jury can do is simply ignore his testimony. Which means what? There is no evidence before the jury to support a finding that the appendix is on the right side of the body. If the statement in the book were taken as evidence that the appendix is on the right side of the body, it would be hearsay and we've got a rule against hearsay.

The Federal Rules change all that. The citation, as you see, is Federal Rule 803, subdivision 18, which permits no fewer than four ways of using a statement in a treatise as hearsay, as proving the truth of what it asserts. And, indeed, 803(18) of the Federal Rules is titled the "Learned Treatise Exception to the Rule Against Hearsay." Four ways.

9. *Ruth v. Fenchel*, 21 N.J. 171, 121 A.2d 373 (1956).

First, where you impeach the other side's expert out of the treatise, what you read to the jury comes in as it does at common law to discredit the expert, but it also comes in to provide the truth of what it asserts. To continue with my hypothetical, it serves as some evidence of the fact that the appendix is on the right side of the body. Second, if you call an expert and your expert along the way says that book is authoritative, you may read to the jury what you want and it comes in to prove the truth of what it asserts. So you've got a live expert, plus the book. Third, it's rare, but it's permissible under 803(18). If the judge will take judicial notice of the authoritative nature of the book, you may read to the jury what you will and it comes in to prove the truth of what it asserts.

And fourth—I have yet to see a case on it, but I'm sure that some lawyer soon is going to make use of it and, boy, it's going to be a lifesaver. Here, give it some concreteness. You've got the affirmative of a spleen-out case, that the spleen plays a vital, though as not yet understood, role in the body's immunological mechanisms. You'd like to have Dr. Ochoa, that Nobel Prize winner, on the stand, but you can't get him for the very good reason that he's now dead. You do not have the money to hire a physiologist to testify that in his opinion the spleen, et cetera, and that Dr. Ochoa's paper is the seminal classic paper on the physiology of the spleen. What do you have, the judge won't take judicial notice; he's never heard of Dr. Ochoa. Consider calling to the stand not a physiologist, but much less expensively, a medical librarian. A medical librarian whose testimony, in effect, would be, "I don't know a spleen from a lung, but I do know the literature of medicine and I know that when a young doctor asks for the classic paper arguing that the spleen plays a vital role in the body's immunological system, this is what you give him." In short, you call an expert whose expertise runs not to the underlying issue, but to the literature of the field. That establishes the authoritative nature of the work. You may now read it to the jury. It comes in to prove the truth of what it asserts and, in summation, you would hear me talking about Dr. Ochoa telling you the truth from the grave. Ten years dead, but he spoke to you through this article. You know, that kind of thing. And it's almost as good, maybe better, than having him there live. Why? Because, harsh truth though it is, you can't cross-examine the book, that's why. So maybe it's better than having him there alive.

I would not want to leave the subject of cross-examination without referring to a few particular modes of examination. I've already made advance reference to one of them. Let me talk about it and maybe one or two others. None of this stuff is proprietary. I've used all of these things, but learned them by watching other lawyers or reading it in transcripts and, you know, we all steal from each other. That's how we learn how to do it and if I were a young lawyer, I would not hesitate to copy something somebody told me about or that I saw a lawyer use. And if it works for him, it probably will work for me. And if it works for me, it becomes a permanent part of your repertoire.

Remember, I made some kind of mumbling reference earlier to cross-examining on the credentials, on the expertise. Maybe on voir dire, maybe on cross-examination. I freely concede that the possibility of getting the judge to hold that he's not an expert and is not entitled to give his opinion is nil. That's not going to happen. But you still may want to consider going into the credentials on cross-examination for a number of reasons. I'll mention one of them in a little while—but the other, let me talk about now.

Consider this possibility. It's not available every time, but it's available with some frequency. The expert is a doctor, no doubt about it. And he's a doctor of many years standing. But the issue, while it's a medical issue, does not fall within his particular expertise. Now, he's entitled to give his opinion because, as a doctor, he can give an opinion as to anything in the field of medicine. But you want to make sure that the jury knows that the thing he's testifying to is not within his field of expertise.

So, criminal case. Charge, bank robbery. Defense, temporary insanity. Psychomotor epilepsy. He went through the motions of a bank robbery but he was unconscious at the time. There is such a condition. It's mentioned in the books and if the defendant was suffering from it, there's no doubt that he's entitled to be acquitted. The defense calls a psychiatrist of 20 years experience to testify that in his, the psychiatrist's opinion, this defendant was suffering from psychomotor epilepsy. So one case out of 30 will permit this kind of cross-examination.

"Now, Doctor, you've been a psychiatrist here in town for 30 some odd years, isn't that right?"

"That's right."

"You've practiced downtown with great success."

"Well, I guess that's right."

"As a matter of fact, your reputation extends across the state and it's even national, isn't that so?"

"Well, I've heard it said."

"Isn't it true, Doctor, that within your field, within your specialization, if there's a problem anywhere in the country that the doctors really can't deal with, you are one of the two or three men they will consider calling in to consult?"

"Well, yeah, there's something to that."

"And, Doctor, your specialization within the specialization of psychiatry is the treatment of problems of sexual maladjustment, isn't that so?"

"Well, yes, that is so."

"And you are one of the two or three leaders in the world in studying that problem."

"Yes, that is so."

And that's it. Stop. Summation. Wonderful summation because jurors do not like the spectacle of professional men attacking each other. By and large, do not launch a direct attack on the other side's expert. To speak the rough language of the bar, not the bar association, you try to get in bed with the other side's expert. So it's confession and avoidance. Yes, he's terrific, but . . .

So, the summation. You know that wonderful doctor the defense called? Distinguished psychiatrist? I don't doubt that one bit. But what did he tell you? That for 30 years he's been working to achieve an international reputation as a specialist in the treatment of problems of sexual maladjustment. Oh, boy, he is terrific at it. If, God forbid, some member of my family, if I myself had such a problem, he'd be the first man I'd go to. But that wasn't the defendant's problem. His problem was not one of sexual maladjustment, his problem is that he likes to rob banks. Then you've gone right around it. You don't have to attack the psychiatrist. He's out of the case because what he's been working at for 30 years does not include precisely the issue involved here.

Let me get to just one other thing and then we'll turn to the last topic. This one, in my experience, is almost always effective, especially with doctors because of the sort of personality type that ends up being a doctor. They tend to be self-important and full of themselves and that's just a fact. I'm sure there are exceptions, but I haven't run into too many of them. What you're doing is getting across to the jury the idea—commonplace among lawyers, we spent a half an hour on it or so—that it's not certain. Oh, he believes it sincerely, but it's not certain. But there are ways of bringing it out so that it's dramatic and that it gives you the fun of puncturing the doctor, and so forth.

For example, I've seen a great trial lawyer do it this way. "Doctor, in your field you have a national, if not an international reputation, do you not?"

"Well, yes, I do."

"Doctor, if there's a problem in some part of the country and the doctors in attendance cannot agree upon the diagnosis, you are one of the two or three men who will be called in for a consultation."

"Yes, that is right. That is right."

"And, Doctor, that's happened many times in the course of your career."

"Yes."

"Where a couple of doctors treating a patient somewhere have had to call you in for a consultation because they couldn't figure out what was wrong."

"Yes, that's so."

"And on a number of instances, Doctor, has it happened that the two doctors had one diagnosis and you had a different diagnosis?"

"Yes, that has happened."

"And, Doctor, in some of those cases, in due course the patient died, an autopsy was conducted and the autopsy revealed, Doctor, that the other physicians were wrong and you were right."

"Oh, yes. Yes, that has happened." Do you see what's coming now?

"But, Doctor, has it also happened that when they conducted the autopsy it turned out that the others were right and you were wrong?" And it's worth doing just to look at him, just to look at him. And he turns all kinds of colors and, of course, he's got to say, "Yes. Yes, that has happened." And that's all.

And in summation you argue what? This is not arithmetic. It's not two plus two equals four. These are complicated issues on which professional people can differ. The doctor himself told you about occasions when he's been wrong. I don't say that he's lying, but I'm saying that there's a good possibility that he's wrong now. And if it ever happens, I mean, you laugh all the way to the bank. If the guy says, "No, it's never happened that I was wrong," stop. Right? If he says he's never been wrong, not another question. And in summation what do you say? You say, "Ladies and gentlemen, do you realize who that was on the witness stand? Oh, he said he was Dr. Smith, but really he wasn't. On cross-examination he told you who he was. That's the Lord God Almighty. He has never been wrong. And if you believe that's the Lord God Almighty, you can decide this case against me. All right?" And, of course, they're not going to.

Which brings us—and we'll get it done within seven or eight minutes—to the subject of arguing an expert's credibility on which, with a special emphasis, I remind you that everything I say is subject to the editorial with which we began. I think I'm right. It's proved effective for me. If it's effective for you, I'm delighted. But if you think it's wrong, feel free to reject it. How do you argue an expert's credibility given this very peculiar system of ours that has the jury of 6 or 12 lay people deciding the issue upon which the Nobel Prize winners are in disagreement?

I ask you to consider the following, which I do believe. The jury, no matter how carefully the case is tried and no matter how much time you spend on it, cannot be given the expertise of the expert's field. The jurors cannot become physicians or economists or engineers. From which I draw the following conclusion—that you never argue the underlying merits of the opinion. You don't argue medicine or economics or engineering, because it goes right over their head. They cannot cope with it. But you must argue an expert's credibility ,and the jury will ultimately resolve an issue of an expert's credibility. So what do you argue? What does the jury rely upon? It seems to me that while the mix will vary from case to case, there are four things upon which the jury will rely and it's from these four things—this is one final checklist—that you construct your argument.

First, already touched upon—the expert's credentials or qualifications. Do his credentials, do his qualifications, does his expertise include the issue in this case? Or a different aspect of qualifications—is there a disparity between your expert's credentials and the other side's? Jurors will be moved by that so long as the disparity is a gross one. Don't engage in lawyer quibbling about fine points. That your expert is seven years board certified and the other guy is five years board certified makes no difference. But if you've got a Nobel Prize winner and they've got a kid just out of medical school, that's a gross disparity and that's worth arguing. And don't attack the other side's expert. As I said, get into bed with him, build him up as much as possible and then, in a gentlemanly fashion, point out the difference, the disparity in credentials. And, assuming it's a permissible kind of argument, simply ask, if you had a problem, if your child had a medical problem, which one would you go to—the one just out of medical school or the one that after 30 years was awarded the Nobel Prize in Medicine? The answer is obvious and that's the answer in this case.

Second, do not neglect the possibility of delicately, of tactfully arguing common sense. Jurors do have a kind of laymen's sense of how the world works and if an expert has given an opinion that is contrary to that layman's sense of how the world works, you can use it to argue against the credibility of that expert. Now, I've never been able to put into words how you develop this sense of how laymen see the world, but I think a lawyer, trial lawyer especially, has a professional obligation to keep current with such things as the popular movies, the popular television shows. You read the *Wall Street Journal* and *The New York Times,* but you also read the popular newspapers and magazines. You want to develop a feel for how the man or woman in the street is thinking about things. And then in an occasional case you will make that part of your argument.

Third, must be done with great delicacy, but when it's done well, it can be very effective. Demeanor, as lawyers like to call it. The appearance of the expert. I'll take just a minute to tell you of something I did once. I'm not sure that you could get away with it today, but I got away with it then. When I was in the U.S. Attorney's office it was the first case I tried involving experts. The charge was interstate transportation of stolen property—a large and incredibly valuable late Degas painting. The defense, believe it or not, was temporary insanity growing out of a disappointed homosexual affair. All of the facts were conceded.

The question was what was the defendant's state of mind? And on that the psychiatrist testified and that was the whole case. My psychiatrist as well as the other side's psychiatrist said he was suffering from something called a fugue state. And you look in the diagnostic table and it exists. It's a recognized psychiatric disorder and if you're suffering from it, you can engage in activity so complex as stealing a painting, framing it, and shipping it to Texas, which is what this defendant did, from New York.

And the government psychiatrist said, we mean that it's homosexual makes no difference, it's a romantic disappointment. Everybody has it in the course of a lifetime, most of us more than once. You've got to learn to live with it. It's hardly a license to steal. Right? So it's between the two, the jury has to decide. And there I am, I'm trying virtually my first case, wondering what am I going to argue to the jury until finally I have a bright idea. I know what I'm going to argue to the jury. And I stood up in summation the next morning—this was 1960 and I remind you that 1960 was a presidential election year and the candidates were Kennedy and Nixon. I stood up and I said, "Ladies and gentlemen, these are psychiatrists of equal professional credentials. There's nothing to choose between there. And they gave their opinions and you're not psychiatrists, I'm not trained in psychiatry—who knows which one is more likely to be nearer the truth. But, ladies and gentlemen, you saw the psychiatrists on the witness stand. You heard how they talked." I should have told you before, my psychiatrist, purely by accident, looked like Van Johnson. You know, the boy next door, freckled face, sandy hair. You know, he just grew up and wanted to be a doctor, but he couldn't stand the sight of blood, so he became a psychiatrist. That kind of thing. And again, through no fault of his own, the defendant's psychiatrist had to shave four times a day, had long black hair combed straight back, and he had a perspiration problem. He was always sort of sweaty. So there I am, "You know, you saw them on the witness stand, you listened to them, you got a sense of the kind of people they were. So I ask you, which one would you buy a used car from?" That was the whole argument. These days, I would expect a bolt of lightning to come down from the judge, but nothing happened.

The jury retired and they came in many hours later with a guilty verdict. Defense counsel and I were friends. We ran out in to the corridor to say what took you so long, tough case figuring out which psychiatrist was telling the truth. And the jurors said, and this is a note on which almost to close, they said, "Oh, no, in five seconds we were agreed to disregard the psychiatric testimony. It was a great big nothing."

"So what took you so long?"

They said, "Well, we weren't going to convict that guy if it was just a romantic thing, you know, between him and his boyfriend. We were going to find him guilty only if he did it for money."

I said, "For money? That never entered the case. I never thought of it. You know, what do you mean he did it for money?"

"If the story about getting even with his friend was a made-up story, we weren't going to convict him, but if he did it for profit, then we were. And we finally concluded that he did it for profit."

"How did you conclude that he did it for profit? There's not a word in the case about that." Oh yes there was, and I told it to you. Remember where he sent the painting? Texas. They concluded that he sent it to Texas so he could get it across the border to Mexico and sell it on the international market for stolen artworks. Go figure. It began the development of my religious faith in juries.

Fourth and last and probably the most important—your credibility is your witness's credibility. If the jury concludes that you are an honest, honorable man or woman who will not mislead them, they will accept your witnesses as honest and honorable people who will not mislead them.

Chapter 3

Scientific Evidence

DEAN STEVE EASTON: "Scientific Evidence" is a rather remarkable seminar. In this lecture, Professor Younger discusses the *Frye*[1] test of general acceptance, which is the test that had been applied to scientific evidence for over half a century and which, at the time of this lecture, most evidence experts believed would continue to be applied to this type of testimony for many years in the future. *Frye* still applies in some states, so it is still important to have an understanding of *Frye*. In addition, even in the U.S. Supreme Court case that replaced the *Frye* test with another test, the *Daubert* case, which we will discuss in a moment, the Supreme Court said that the idea of general acceptance is still valid to the inquiry regarding whether or not expert testimony relying on a scientific principle should be admitted.

But what is amazing about this lecture is that, as you will see, after Professor Younger outlines the *Frye* test, at the end of the lecture, he predicts that the *Frye* test will soon be replaced. That was a rather unusual prediction at the time of this lecture in the middle of the 1980s and, yet, by the middle of the next decade that prediction had, indeed, come to pass when the Supreme Court reached its important decision in *Daubert v. Merrell Dow Pharmaceuticals, 509 U.S. 579 (1993)*. That was the case where the Supreme Court told the federal district court judges that they had an obligation under Rule 104 of the Federal Rules of Evidence to make a preliminary determination regarding whether testimony that claimed that it was based on science was, indeed, based upon sufficient data and upon scientifically valid principles and then,

1. *Frye v. United States*, 293 Fed. 1013 (D.C. Cir. 1923).

of course, whether those two things came together correctly in an expert's opinion. That is a development that, if you watch carefully, you will see that Professor Younger predicts at the end of this seminar.

There have been important cases that followed *Daubert*. In *General Electric Company v. Joiner, 522 U.S. 136 (1997),* four years after *Daubert*, the U.S. Supreme Court held that a federal appellate court reviewing a federal trial court judge's decision to exclude expert testimony under the *Daubert* test should review that decision under an abuse of discretion standard. As we know, if an appellate court applies an abuse of discretion standard, that is generally, though not quite always, going to lead to an affirmance of the decision of the trial court judge. So *Joiner* was important in telling U.S. district court judges that their decisions were often going to be affirmed in the area of scientific evidence.

The last case of what is sometimes referred to as the *Daubert* Trilogy is *Kumho Tire Company v. Carmichael, 526 U.S. 137 (1999).* It is important primarily because the Supreme Court said that this test of whether or not an expert's testimony was based upon reliable principles applied not just to "scientific" expert testimony, but to all other testimony that similarly relied upon application of a principle to a set of data. Thus, it applies to testimony from someone like an economist or an accountant or various other sorts of folks who show up as witnesses in federal civil trials.

State supreme courts have taken several different approaches to *Daubert*. Some have said that the *Daubert* test applies in their jurisdictions. Others have adhered to the *Frye* test that Professor Younger is going to discuss in this seminar. Still others try to combine the two tests. As a trial lawyer, you need to be aware of the state law applicable to your case.

In addition to those three important U.S. Supreme Court cases, there have been other developments in the 700 series of the Federal Rules of Evidence. Rule 702 has been amended to essentially codify the *Daubert* decision. Under language added to the rule based upon sufficient facts or data, expert testimony must be the product of reliable principles and methods, and must result from a proper application of these principles and methods.

Rule 703 of the Federal Rules of Evidence has also been amended. It now provides, with regard to an issue that Professor Younger will discuss, that an expert may base her opinion on inadmissible facts or data if those inadmissible facts or data are of a type reasonably relied upon by experts in that field to form opinions. Now, though, there has been an amendment to Rule 703 to deal with another issue that Professor Younger discussed: If the expert does indeed rely upon inadmissible data or information, is the expert allowed to tell the jury what that inadmissible data or information is in order to explain his opinion? After the 2000 amendment to Rule 703, the rule now says that that disclosure of the otherwise inadmissible basis behind the expert's opinion is allowed in direct examination of the expert witness only if the court determines that the probative value of the otherwise inadmissible information substantially outweighs the prejudicial effect of admitting otherwise inadmissible information. However, it is also important to remember that the Advisory Committee note to that rule tells us that if we cross-examine an expert witness in a manner that suggests that there is an inadequate basis behind the expert's opinion, those otherwise inadmissible bases of the opinion might become admissible in redirect examination.

PROFESSOR IRVING YOUNGER: Thank you, ladies and gentlemen. You will recall from your studies in classical rhetoric the device of the oxymoron. That is, the linking together of two words of opposed or antithetical meaning, such as the wealthy pauper or the youthful octogenarian, or science and law. Because, you see, by contrast with our colleagues in the natural and physical sciences, ours is an immature, not to say jejune, discipline. We lawyers and judges have not yet reached that level of sophistication obtained by the scientists some five or six centuries ago when they realized that the central principle of all intellectual work is, "Don't make it more complicated than it has to be." We lawyers have not yet reached that level. But there is one situation in which law has no choice—it must try to come to grips with science or technology. And that situation is the lawsuit in which one of the litigants offers scientific evidence.

I use the term scientific evidence to refer simply to that evidence which is obtained as a result of the application or use of some scientific or technological process or device. Scientific evidence has been a feature on the legal scene, I suppose, roughly since the beginning of the 18th century and the Industrial Revolution. But it comes to a head, it reaches the front burner, it becomes a major issue for the law approximately with the end of World War II. World War II sees an enormous expansion in science and technology and what science and technology produce will, more often than not, have utility in litigation. And so, in a rough and ready way, 1945 or 1946 marks the beginning of that trend of development which is at its height right now—a trend of development characterized by the need for a lawyer to persuade a judge that scientific evidence ought to be received.

Now, how do you do it? And lest I be accused of misleading anyone, let me drop a kind of scholarly footnote at this point and tell you that what I will be discussing for the next half hour or so, responding to the question I've just raised—how do you put scientific evidence in—will be found, ladies and gentlemen, in no treatise, in no textbook, in no law review article so far as I know, and in no judicial opinion. After all, if we measure from 1945 or thereabouts, scientific evidence has been with us for 40 years. And, as we all know, in the processes of the law 40 years is a split second; it is a flash of lightning. And so it is that the institutions of the law have only begun to recognize the problems presented when scientific evidence is offered.

Questions have begun to occur to the minds of lawyers and judges, but the profession has yet to work out commonly accepted answers to those questions. So what I am going to be setting before you is, I do believe, the way to do it. It is, I do believe, what the law requires of a lawyer who wishes to put scientific evidence in, but understand that I have no authority which with to support it. I believe that it's true, but as has been wisely said in another context, I will not go to the gallows for it. Okay? On that understanding, let's go to work.

How do you put scientific evidence in and, because all of us prefer to deal with a concrete case, I put a concrete case before you—one which I cannot identify by time and place, but which I am morally certain took place in more than one courtroom around this land sometime in the year 1946. A lawyer had to put before the court a new kind of scientific evidence—radar evidence. That is to say, the lawyer has to prove that the defendant is a speeder, that he was going 70 or 80 miles an hour in a 50-mile zone. And what does he discover available to him in the file as the means for proving that the defendant was a speeder but radar evidence.

And I must invoke the historical imagination. Remember, it's 1946. World War II is less than one year over and to a young lawyer sitting in a prosecutor's office in 1946, radar evidence is as much a mystery as it was to Hermann Goering, the commanding officer of the Luftwaffe, the German Air Force, in 1940 as the German Air Force tried to force England out of the war in the Battle of Britain. So come with me eastward in space and backward in time, not really to 1940, I suppose, but to the early 1930s.

The center of research in the physical sciences in England and in the world was a place called the Cavendish Laboratories in Cambridge University, England. A man named Robert Watson Watt, a physicist and engineer on the staff of the Cavendish Laboratories, invented a device that he called radar. It being 1934 or thereabouts, Robert Watson Watt realized that radar would have enormous utility in the event of another war and to anyone whose head was screwed on the right way in the early 1930s, it was perfectly obvious that there was going to be another war. More precisely, that World War I would break out again in a kind of second chapter that we called World War II.

Robert Watson Watt, accordingly, did not publish his new invention to the world. Instead, he took it to the British government, which, incredibly, had the sense to see that Robert Watson Watt was right. And so the British government saw to it that radar did not become available to the rest of the world. Instead, it was retained by the British government and used in connection with a series of radar installations facing the continent of Europe, installed all along the English Channel.

And now in 1940 comes the Battle of Britain. The forces of Hitler's Germany have occupied Western Europe to the Channel. The United States, of course, is not yet in the war. The only democratic nation left, the only nation between western civilization and barbarity is England. It stands alone. And you may recall from your readings in history—a handful of you are old enough to have a personal memory of it—Hitler's master plan was as follows. He did not wish to invade England if he could possibly avoid it. Instead, he thought that he would break the spirit of the English people, causing a general election at which

Churchill would be voted out of office. Then Germany would make its peace with England and the two countries, united, would turn to make war upon Soviet Russia.

That was the master plan. It required breaking the spirit of the English people and the way to do it, thought Hitler, was to bomb London into nothingness. And that was the mission of the Luftwaffe in the course of the Battle of Britain. By day and by night those bombers flew over London seeking to destroy St. Paul's. No German bomb ever touched St. Paul's, by the way—a miracle that nobody can explain to this day. Devastated all of downtown London, did massive destruction to the rest of London, hoping that ultimately the English people would say enough and get rid of Churchill. Of course, they never did.

They fought back and they fought back in one of the great chapters in the history of human heroism. The RAF, flying those wonderful airplanes, those Spitfires and those Hurricanes, remember with 18-year-old kids as the pilots, they were in the air constantly. From whatever point on the compass the German Air Force came, at whatever time of day or night, those Hurricanes and Spitfires were at the right point in the sky so as to come sweeping down and cleanse the heavens of that filth. And Hermann Goering, sitting back in Berlin, kept asking, "How do they know? Why are they always in the air at the right time? Why are they always where they ought to be in the skies? How do they know?" And the answer, of course, was radar. That's how they knew. And I suppose that at Nuremberg, before he took that final, fatal cyanide capsule, somebody told Hermann Goering that the answer was radar. So radar, for all practical purposes, saved western civilization in 1940.

By 1946 the war is over. Western civilization remains where we want it to be—front and center down the stage. And now the lawyers get hold of radar and turn it to civilian use. Having saved western civilization, radar becomes what in the hands of lawyers? You've got it—the means by which we convict speeders, that's what we do with it. And so there is some young lawyer, perhaps just out of law school or having served four or five years in the service of the colors, desperate to begin his or her career, working as a prosecutor in an office in New York or South Carolina or Missouri or California or anyplace in between—he opens the file and, for heaven's sakes, there it is—radar. And the young lawyer is going to say to himself, what is it? If Hermann Goering didn't know, why should I know? And if it's 1946, you're going to have to make inquiries and discover that radar is—and I will not bother with the technological details of which I am not the master in any event—but in a rough and ready way, today we all know essentially what radar is. All right? The young lawyer finds out what radar is, but now he's got the lawyer's problem. How do you get the evidence in?

And let me pause parenthetically to point out unnecessarily to an audience of this experience and sophistication that what the young lawyer had to do in 1946 in that very first radar case is what any one of you will have to do in 1985 or '86 or '95 or '96 involved in a case featuring scientific evidence. The general approach is identical, no matter the nature of the proof, be it radar, neutron activation analysis, the use of some chemical test to determine alcohol content of the bloodstream, blood tests in a paternity action—whatever it may be. The approach is the same. All right. Now, what's the question and, remember, we're doing it from the viewpoint of the prosecutor, the proponent of the evidence, the lawyer who wants to persuade the judge to let the evidence in, to permit the finder of fact, judge or jury, to take this evidence into account. What must you do? And if it's 1946 there's absolutely nothing in the law library to help you. If it's 1985 or so, there's very little in the law library to help you. What you've got to do, young lawyer, is think. All right?

To get that evidence in, the process of thinking ultimately will show you, you're going to have to prove three things. And these three things represent the approach to putting scientific evidence in in any kind of case, in any jurisdiction in the land, no matter the nature of the scientific proof involved. First, you're going to have to prove what I will call the reading. And I'm using that as rather a term of art. By the reading, I mean the scientific or technical process involved came to a certain conclusion. The nature of the conclusion and the form the conclusion takes will vary with the scientific device or technique involved. If it's radar, I suppose the reading is the equivalent of the needle pointing to the number 80, signifying that the car going through the radar field is moving at 80 miles an hour. In another sort of case, the reading might be that the chemical reagent turned from blue to orange. That's the reading you got. If the scientific device is a polygraph, a lie detector—we'll come to it in a little while—why, the reading is a certain set of squiggles on a line which can be construed by the polygraph operator as signifying that the subject is or is not telling the truth. All right? The possibilities are virtually infinite, but we understand that we must have gotten a reading, whatever it may be, on this occasion.

Is anything else necessary? Well, of course. A second element of proof in any case and no matter the nature of the scientific evidence involved, will be that the device was in good working order, which is, again, rather a term of art. And I mean by it nothing more than that in whatever way this device must be calibrated, must be oiled, in whatever way the equipment must be polished or handled in a certain way—that it's got to be plugged in, that the glassware is clean, that the chemicals were fresh, et cetera, et cetera. Again, the possibilities will vary from case to case with the nature of the scientific evidence involved, but you get the idea—that it was in good working order, that it was properly used on this occasion. I guess those are two different sides of the same coin.

So you've got to prove that you got a reading. You've got to prove that the device was in good working order. Pausing briefly to put that in the context of our radar case, the state trooper has to be able to tell you that we got a reading, the needle pointed to the number 80, signifying that the defendant's car that was down there in the radar field was moving at 80 miles an hour. Was the device in good working order? Well, the trooper will tell you, we calibrated it that morning, we had it plugged in. In the instance of radar, I guess you have to make sure that there's nothing in the environment that will throw the machine off. For example, it wasn't right next to an airport where all of the radar installations will throw the police device way, way off, and so forth.

But we'll assume you have all of that evidence. Do you need anything else? Unreflectingly, we might be inclined to say no, that sounds as if that's all you need. A moment's thought, though, will demonstrate that you need something else. You need one more element or prerequisite. And it's this third element or prerequisite that, as we shall see, is really the interesting one.

Just to recapitulate that for a moment, whenever scientific evidence is offered, the proponent, in order to get it in, is going to have to establish three prerequisites. There is, if you will, a three-step recipe to getting scientific evidence in. The first step, that you got a particular reading on this occasion. The second step, that the device was in good working order, that it was properly used and adapted to the circumstances of the nature of the proof, of course. And now the third step. What is that third step? And let me demonstrate to you, for those of you who don't quite see it, that a third step is absolutely necessary.

Recognizing that there is very little, if anything, in the books to help us on this subject, I ask you to become judges—each one of you is a judge—and respond instinctively, if not rationally. Respond, if you will, to the following offer in evidence of a piece of proof. You're the judge, I'm the prosecutor. I am laying out for you a case of speeding. It is my contention that the defendant, sitting over there, was going 80 miles an hour in a 55-mile-an-hour zone. And I say to you, Your Honor, to prove that he was going 80 miles an hour, I have some technical proof, some scientific evidence, if you will, and we're going to use it right here in the courtroom. Observe, Your Honor, that I hold in my right hand a sheet of plywood approximately 12 inches by 18 inches. On that sheet of plywood are painted the numbers from 0 to 100. In my left hand, Your Honor, I hold another bit of plywood, approximately three inches long, shaped much like an arrowhead. In the trade we call it a plectrum. Your Honor, I stand next to the defendant. I hold in my right hand the sheet of plywood with the numbers from 0 to 100 and I place it next to the defendant's head. I close my eyes, Your Honor. I put the plectrum on the sheet of plywood and observe that it moves, Your Honor, it moves without my controlling it and now it has stopped pointing to a certain number. The number is 80, Your Honor, I offer it in evidence. All right, Your Honor, how do you reason it through? Did you get a reading? I just gave you the reading right here in court. The plectrum pointed at the number 80. Was this device in good working order and properly used on this occasion? Let me tell you something I haven't to this point told you, Your Honor. I am the world president of the Ouija Board Association. And so I can tell you that this device was properly used. I know how to use it and it is, what we in this line of work, call a Ouija board. All right. Will you permit it to be received in evidence? And I need not ask for a show of hands because I know the answer. The answer is a unanimous no. And when asked to explain why the answer is no, Your Honor will reply, as many of us know judges are inclined to reply, "Counselor, I'm not here to answer questions, just move along." All right.

But if really forced to come up with an answer, let me suggest the answer every one of us would come up with and we're absolutely correct. The Ouija board result is not admissible in evidence, even though you've satisfied the first prerequisite, even though you've satisfied the second prerequisite, but it's not admissible because you haven't satisfied the third prerequisite, the really interesting one, as I said. And what is that third prerequisite? Well, we're talking about scientific evidence, aren't we? The third prerequisite to the receipt of scientific evidence is that this scientific process or device be scientifically valid, which again is a term of art that I've kind of coined, meaning that the device rests upon the laws of nature, that it's scientific in its operations such that if it was in good working order and you got this reading on this occasion, that the reading is reliable.

And do you see when you put those three elements together you've got a nice little paradigm, if you will, to account for the reliability of scientific evidence and, hence, for the phenomenon of its being received in evidence in the sense that the finder of fact will be permitted to know about it and to take it into account. It's not just the reading, it's not just that the device was in good working order and properly used, but that the device is scientifically valid, that gives it its reliability. So scientific validity is the third and, as you shall see, really, the most interesting of the three prerequisites.

Now, having established that scientific validity is the third prerequisite, we've got to face up to a problem, a problem which has come along in a lawsuit here or there scattered across the landscape, so that from time to time courts have been obliged to deal with this problem. And it's a little bit embarrassing to talk about, but we've got to talk about it because there's no other way to understand the development of the law with respect to scientific evidence. We say that the proponent must persuade the judge not just that you got a reading, not just that it was in good working order and properly used, but that the device was scientifically valid. How are you going to persuade the judge that the device is scientifically valid when the scientific basis of the device is, in fact, incomprehensible to His Honor?

Take radar. I will assume that nobody in this group is an electrical engineer or electronics expert qualified actually to understand the scientific basis of radar. We all understand it in a lay sense. It involves waves sent out and they bounce back and you kind of measure the bounce back ratio or something and you come up with the speed and the location of the device from which the waves are bouncing back. But that is hardly a demonstration of scientific validity. We all know enough about it to be aware that when you demonstrate the scientific validity of radar, when you actually put it before the court, it will involve what in 1946 was at the level of post-post-post-graduate work for a Ph.D in physics and today is at the level of, I suppose, a fairly bright undergraduate taking a freshman or sophomore course in physics. Even so, having posited a fairly bright undergraduate, we have passed most judges, have we not? And even if I have overstated the case with respect to most judges, once we get to the actual physics of it, we have left virtually all judges far behind.

Just imagine trying to make your favorite judge, whoever that man or woman might be, understand the scientific validity of radar. What are you going to do with those partial differential equations? Hmm? "Your

Honor, here's a partial differential equation." And his honor is going to throw you right out of the courtroom. His honor doesn't understand what you're talking about. He doesn't know what a partial differential equation is, let alone understand what it signifies. And as you try to sketch out for his honor the scientific validity of radar, why all you do is bore the court and leave the court not only not wiser, but not even better informed than the court was before you began this explanation. In short, how satisfy the third prerequisite? How demonstrate the scientific validity of a piece of scientific evidence when you are dealing with a judge who we can assume is scientifically illiterate? Because most judges are, because most lawyers are, because very few people outside the sciences these days are scientifically literate, that is to say, understand anything about how modern science works and understand anything of mathematics beyond the level of simple arithmetic. How are we going to do it? This is a problem that has plagued the courts for as long as scientific evidence has been around. It was way back, way back in the 1920s that a court called upon to pass on the question of the admissibility of a piece of scientific evidence first came to grips with this problem. How do you demonstrate the third prerequisite, which analytically is absolutely necessary? There's no doubt about that. But how do you demonstrate it to a judge who is incapable of understanding what it is that adds up to scientific validity?

The case in which the court came to grips with it is the *Frye* case. (The full text is appended.) And let me telegraph my punch by telling you that the *Frye* case is probably still, to this day, the single most important opinion in a case involving scientific evidence by any court in the history of the United States. As a matter of fact, we will be referring from time to time in the course of the morning to the *Frye* test or the *Frye* rule and it's this 1923 case that we will be talking about. I have not had the occasion to look up the cases in South Carolina, but if there is a case in South Carolina dealing with the admissibility of scientific evidence, I have no doubt that the court in South Carolina adopted the *Frye* test, cited and followed the *Frye* case that is here in the outline, and so South Carolina, I am quite certain, lines up with the vast majority, no longer the universe of, but the vast majority of American jurisdictions in following the *Frye* test right up until today, just 15 years or so from the turn of the century into the 21st century.

Now, what is the *Frye* test? First, a word about the case itself. It involved the offer in evidence of polygraph results, lie detector results. And we know that the prevailing American rule is that lie detector results are not admissible. But why are they not admissible? Analytically, how do you explain it? And the reason I use the word analytically is that, in my mind, for what it's worth, I distinguish between the judicial instinct and the judicial mind. The judicial instinct is to exclude polygraph results. I know that there are a handful of jurisdictions in cases going the other way, but the prevailing rule is lie detector results are not admissible. Why? Because the court's instinct tells it that it ought not to be admissible, and it's an instinct I share. I agree that it ought not to be admissible and it smacks too much of the black box, the magic, the crystal ball that somehow tells you the truth and makes all of these difficult problems easy and therefore readily solved and all the difficulties go away, et cetera. And in this veil of tears there is no such thing and we just don't want juries to be possibly misled by thinking that there is any such thing. But, of course, that's hardly a legal reason.

You need an analytical reason for the non-admissibility of polygraph results and the analytical reason goes this way. Did you get a reading on this occasion? Well, of course you got a reading. The little squiggles on the paper added up to that the subject is telling the truth or is not telling the truth. Was the device in good working order and properly used? Well, sure, we will call a qualified polygraph operator who will testify beyond per adventure of doubt that the machine was properly adjusted, that it was correctly used, that the techniques of questioning were in line with what is supposed to be done, and the like. Nevertheless, the polygraph results are inadmissible. Why? Because the court is not persuaded of the third prerequisite—that polygraph results, lie detector evidence has a scientific basis. The courts simply have not been persuaded that that is so.

In the *Frye* case, the District of Columbia, in those days functioning just as would a state, has to pass upon the question of the admissibility of the polygraph. And the Court of Appeals for the District of Columbia, then both a federal court of appeals and, as it were, a state Supreme Court, passing upon the question solely for the District of Columbia, says no, it's not admissible because of the failure to satisfy us of the third prerequisite, that the polygraph is scientifically valid, that it rests upon the laws of nature such that if it was in good working order and you got a reading, that the reading is reliable. We are just not persuaded of that third prerequisite. All right? That's interesting, but really relatively trivial.

The more substantial part of the opinion in the *Frye* case deals with the question, "How is a court to determine scientific validity given what we can take for granted—the scientific illiteracy of the judges who must make the determination?" In the instance of polygraph results, I guess the scientific sophistication necessary is in physiology, a little bit of biophysics, a little bit of electronics because of the way the machine works, and a great deal, I suppose, of laboratory psychology. I sort of had to invent that phrase to describe what I mean—testing human beings in the laboratory to see if you can quantify the way in which they react to such moral problems as telling a lie and the like. How is a judge to pass upon that?

The Court of Appeals for the District of Columbia, recognizing that the law was in a corner here, expecting judges to pass upon matters they were simply not intellectually equipped to pass upon, was very clever in painting its way out of that corner. And it came up with what has come to this day to be called the *Frye* test or the *Frye* rule.

In determining whether or not the third prerequisite is satisfied, in determining the scientific validity of the evidence which is being offered, the court does not pass upon scientific basis as such. Why? Because the court can't do it. The court doesn't know any science. The court doesn't know any mathematics. Hence, the court cannot decide whether this thing is scientifically valid. But what the court can determine—now listen carefully—is whether among the scientists concerned, whether among the scientists in this particular discipline there is general agreement that the device has a scientific basis. Judges can decide that and so, says the *Frye* court, that's how a court determines whether the third prerequisite is satisfied and that's the *Frye* test. Not that the device is scientifically valid, yea or nay, but rather do the scientists concerned seem to be in general agreement that the device is scientifically valid. In short, what the court does is count noses. That the court is well capable of doing. It's not up to the mathematics and the physics of radar or the physiology of a lie detector, but it's quite capable of saying, well, among physicists who specialize in this field is there general agreement that radar is scientifically valid? Count noses. *N* number of noses say yes, zero number say no, therefore it is scientifically valid. Is there general agreement among psychologists upon the scientific validity of polygraph tests? Count noses and among psychologists the answer is going to be substantially zero say yes, *n* say no. Therefore, it is not scientifically valid because there is no general agreement among the scientists that the device is valid. So do you see what's happened? We've gotten out of the conundrum of expecting judges to decide matters they're incapable of deciding by translating the issue into a different issue which judges are capable of deciding. Not scientific validity, but rather general agreement upon scientific validity among the scientists concerned. That's the *Frye* test. But there's yet more to be said about it.

Let's spend just a couple of minutes glancing at the way in which judicial notice will come into play in connection with scientific evidence. It's just the way of litigation, I suppose, that if scientific evidence is useful once it's going to be useful a second time, a third time, a thirtieth time, and a three-hundredth time. Once radar is invented and proves to be of utility in prosecuting speeders, there will not be one speeding case, there will ultimately be hundreds, thousands, and tens of thousands of speeding cases involving radar. If a certain test for determining the presence of alcohol in the bloodstream proves to be useful out there on the highway the first time, there will be a tenth time, a hundredth time and a thousandth time when it's used. And so for blood grouping tests and all of the other kinds of scientific evidence that we could enumerate.

Now, stick with radar as our example. Suppose the first radar speeding case is tried here in South Carolina in let's say 1946. The district attorney proves to the court that he got a reading, that the machine was in good working order and was properly used on this occasion, and that it's scientifically valid in accordance with the *Frye* test. That there is general agreement among electronics engineers and physicists that radar rests upon the laws of nature, hence it's scientifically valid. The judge says, "I agree," the evidence is received, there may be an appeal on whatever ground, conviction affirmed. And next week there will be the state's second radar speeding case and the week after that the state's third and fourth and fifth and so on. In each one of those cases, the prosecutor will go through the sequence of proof we have outlined here—that he got a reading, that the machine was in good working order and was properly used, and that it's scientifically valid as applied by way of the *Frye* test.

Now, there will come a point, ladies and gentlemen . . . I can't say that it's with the tenth case, I can't say that it's with the hundredth case, but at some point in the course of the development of this litigation pattern, an appellate court is going to say something like, hold on, we have now seen enough of these cases to be persuaded that it's inconceivable that any scientist in the field concerned is going to say that there is no general agreement about scientific validity. In short, it's inefficient. It wastes time and money to go through the steps of actually proving. The reading? No, that's going to have to be proved in every case. That it was in good working order and properly used on this occasion? No, that'll have to be proved in every case. But scientific validity in the sense of the *Frye* test. All right? That's what the appellate court will say at some point, be it the tenth case or the hundredth case, or something in between. That, the third prerequisite, scientific validity in the *Frye* sense, will from now on be taken for granted. We will not require the proponent to go through the steps, to spend the time, the money, and the effort on proving what is beyond question so that there is general agreement among the scientists concerned that the device has scientific validity. And so the court will say, "From now on we will take judicial notice of the third of the three prerequisites." Which means that from that point on, the proponent of the evidence need not prove scientific validity. For my money, what the proponent should do as a matter of both judicial etiquette and courtroom technique is say to the court, "Your Honor, I ask that you take judicial notice of the scientific validity of whatever the scientific evidence is." And assuming that an appellate court has said it's proper to do so, the court will say, "I take judicial notice of it." My impression is that that is rarely done, that the proponent of scientific evidence, given scientific evidence which is susceptible to judicial notice in this way, will simply shrug it off, will say nothing about it and that's a little bit of sloppiness, though it certainly doesn't affect the outcome or require the appellate court to get involved.

State v. Graham[2] case is an example of this phenomenon at work. It's the Supreme Court of Missouri in 1959, so you go from '45 or '46 to '59, roughly 15 years of radar speeding cases in Missouri. *Graham* is a radar speeding case. And in that opinion the Supreme Court of Missouri says, in effect, from now on in Missouri we will take judicial notice of the third prerequisite, of the fact that radar is scientifically valid in the *Frye* sense, that the radar people are in general agreement that this device does rest upon the laws of nature.

If you will permit me a personal note, I can't imagine anybody reading the opinion in the *Graham* case unless he had some special academic interest in it or perhaps unless you were a Missouri lawyer. But the Missouri court's opinion in *Graham* is worth skimming even if you have no particular academic interest in this subject and even though you are not a Missouri lawyer, and I'll tell you why. That opinion is an example of a very rare bird. And the rare bird is judicial humor. Conscious judicial humor. That is to say, comedy where the judge intends to be funny. That opinion, believe it or not, is an opinion in which the court is trying to be funny and, hoping that I will not destroy the humor of it, let me direct your attention in a general way to the part where the court starts to be funny.

---

2. *State v. Graham*, 322 S.W.2d 188 (Mo. Ct. App. 1959).

The court is leading up to the holding that judicial notice from now on may be taken of the scientific validity of the basis of radar. But to get there, the court decided that it's going to explain the scientific validity of radar for itself, not the *Frye* test. Simply count noses among the radar people. The court is really going to rise to the challenge and deal with the science. And so in the text of the opinion there's a paragraph on the scientific validity of radar that is absolutely incomprehensible and intended to be incomprehensible simply so that at the end of the paragraph the court can drop a footnote. And the footnote reads as . . . well, the paragraph begins with the words that signal to you that this is meant to be funny. It starts something like this. "This court yields to none in its ignorance of science in general and physics in particular. But assuming we understand what the physicists have been testifying to, here is the scientific basis of radar and then follows this incomprehensible jargon." And then at the end of it there's a footnote and the footnote reads as follows: "If this is unclear, we offer to the reader the following alternative explanation." And there then follows about three inches of mathematical equations, partial differential equations, which, of course, are even more incomprehensible than the text of the paragraph. And so if I'm any judge of these things, this is conscious judicial humor. The Missouri Supreme Court is trying to be funny. And I guess as judicial humor goes, that's pretty good. Grant you, by the standards of Bob Hope or Danny Kaye, I'm not so sure. But by judicial standards it's all right.

Now, before we move along, I want to say a final word not so much about radar, but about Robert Watson Watt. Remember, that man of the Cavendish Laboratories in England who invented radar back in '34 or '35. Robert Watson Watt survived well into the post-war era. If I recall correctly, he died somewhere towards the end of the 1960s. He became Sir Robert Watson Watt, an acknowledgment by the British Government of the extraordinary contribution his invention had made to the winning of World War II. After the war, of course, the world of physics and engineering was generally aware of radar and all of its even more refined contemporary developments. And Sir Robert Watson Watt, who was a very gracious, genial, articulate fellow, became much in demand as a guest speaker on university campuses all across the United States, let alone in England. And somewhere in the 1950s, Robert Watson Watt, Sir Robert as he was then to be called, made a tour of the United States. And I am told that because he wanted to get a sense of the country more than you would get sitting in an airplane flying at 25,000 feet in the air, he drove from campus to campus and he drove himself usually. And he was driving from one university campus to another in a state not very far away when, sure enough, he was pulled over by a state trooper for exceeding the speed limit in a radar trap. And when Robert Watson Watt tried to identify himself to the trooper, of course, it was in that plummy Cambridge, England, accent and the trooper thought that he was some kind of pervert. And, in any event, Robert Watson Watt did not have an AAA bail card with him, so the trooper took him in and held him overnight until the JP showed up the next morning.

Now, Sir Robert was not mistreated in any way, but he was held overnight in the jail and he was kind of calm about it; he thought it was sort of funny. And, as he sat there in the jail cell, a bit of poetry came to him. I really should call it verse, not poetry. And he jotted it down and it has come to my attention and I thought that I would do something to relieve the gloom that has descended upon you by sharing that bit of verse with you. This is Sir Robert Watson Watt speaking in that rural jail cell not more than 200 miles from where we are. He said, "Pity, Sir Robert Watson Watt, strange victim of this radar plot. And thus with others I can mention, the victim of his own invention. His magical all-seeing eye enables cloud bound planes to fly. And bites, no doubt, with legal wit the hand that once invented it." And so, having paid our respects to Sir Robert Watson Watt, wherever he may be, let's move along.

We understand that this three-step recipe represents how the proponent gets scientific evidence into court. We understand that under the *Frye* test, the third of the three steps, the scientific validity of the evidence, will be determined not by the courts looking to science, but by the courts looking to general agreement among the scientists that the device is scientifically valid—the *Frye* test. And as a by-the-by, we understand that judicial notice will come into play whenever the device has been used enough times so that the court sees that it's really inefficient, a waste of time and money, to insist upon compliance with that third prerequisite. And having reached this point, let me take just another minute or two just to give you some examples of the judicial notice pattern working with respect to other kinds of scientific evidence of the sort that we deal with every day today.

How about the tests of one sort or another for determining alcohol in the bloodstream, be it the breath test or the serum analysis test that the highway troopers use? Will judicial notice be taken of the third prerequisite of scientific validity? So far as I know, in every state in the land, the lawsuits involving that kind of scientific evidence have passed the point of judicial notice. Yes, the court will take judicial notice of the scientific validity of the breath test. Obviously, judicial notice will never be taken of the reading, will never be taken of the fact that it was in good working order, that the chemicals were fresh, the glassware clean, and the like. That will have to be proved. But scientific validity will be judicially noticed. With respect to polygraphs, we made the point that virtually all American courts have not been persuaded that there is general agreement among the scientists concerned as to scientific validity and so you've never even begun the development of this pattern which ultimately leads a court to take judicial notice of the scientific validity of the device.

With respect to yet other kinds of scientific evidence, well, let's take an example of something that's been used in litigation more than once, but not enough so as to reach the point of judicial notice. And that would be neutron activation analysis. I can't say that my count is absolutely correct, but it's been used in litigation perhaps seven or eight times around the country just in the last several years. Without getting into the science of it, it involves the resources of the nuclear physics laboratory of a major university and, in essence, it permits a determination as to whether this questioned material, for example, a bit of carbon left behind after a bomb explodes, whether this questioned material comes from a certain source, such as that woodpile or that closet in which the cardboard tubes are kept. And it sounds incredible, but it can be done. It's enormously expensive, enormously sophisticated scientifically. Because it's been used, so far as I know, only once in five or six jurisdictions, you haven't had the repeated experience with it of the radar case or the like, and so in no jurisdiction will judicial notice be taken of the scientific validity of neutron activation analysis. That will have to be demonstrated each time.

Take another kind of scientific evidence that's been used not five or six times, but 40 or 50 times in the last 20 or 30 years. This is the voice print analyzer, invented by a man named Kursta at the Bell Laboratories in New Jersey in the middle 1960s, I guess. What it does is this. It takes a questioned voice sample, such as the tape recording of the ransom telephone call in a kidnap case, compares that voice electronically with a known sample, such as the defendant reading the headlines on this morning's newspaper. And, according to its inventor, it will demonstrate infallibly that the questioned sample is the same as the known sample or that it's different, even if the voices are disguised, even if it's over the telephone, et cetera. If it works, it's obviously tremendously useful in kidnapping cases or any case in which you've got voice evidence. Does it work? Well, it's been offered in evidence 40 some odd, maybe 50 times around the country and the courts have split roughly half and half. About half the judges have said, "No, we are not persuaded that there is general agreement among the physicists and the voice physiologists that this device is scientifically valid, therefore it's not admissible." And in the other half of the cases, the courts have said, "We are persuaded that the device is scientifically valid in the sense of the *Frye* test or requirement, therefore it is admissible." So do you see, you're not yet anywhere near judicial notice. Judicial notice comes into play only when the courts are unanimous in seeing that there is general agreement among the scientists that it's scientifically valid. In the case of the Kursta voice analyzer, the courts go both ways and so obviously judicial notice, if it ever comes along, is miles and years ahead of us. Well, end of digression on judicial notice. Now let's go back to the *Frye* test.

The *Frye* test, which from the time of its invention up until relatively recent years, seemed so clever and satisfactory, a way to resolve the practical difficulty of a court which is scientifically illiterate in determining whether a device is scientifically valid. The *Frye* test, upon analysis, turns out to have three very important deficiencies. And we talk about those deficiencies, ladies and gentlemen, not because they are of theoretical or academic interest. I do not regard myself as a law professor sort of pontificating to working lawyers. I regard myself as a working lawyer trying to be helpful to other working lawyers and these deficiencies in the *Frye* test, as we will see, have enormous practical significance. This is not artsy craftsy stuff, this is getting right down to it as I will try to show you.

Now, what are these deficiencies? The first deficiency is that the *Frye* test, which has such immediate verbal appeal, is, in fact, indeterminate. It doesn't give you a reliable result. And by reliable I mean one that all of us can see is the correct result of the application of the *Frye* test. It's indeterminate in the sense that applying the *Frye* test will permit the court to come out any way it wants. And let me give a voice to my presuppositions here. Let me tell you my viewpoint when I talk about this deficiency of the *Frye* test, indeterminacy. I may be old fashioned and I may be unduly conservative, but I regard the law as essentially a regime of rules, and rules, to my mind, are rules—about which we can debate, of course. But once we have the rules of the game, I want the rules to be such that when you apply them, anybody sees that this is the correct answer, but that is the incorrect answer. I am made profoundly uncomfortable by a set of rules which can be made to support any particular outcome. You know, where you can make the game come out any way you wish. That's what I mean by indeterminate. And the *Frye* test is indeterminate in this sense. What does *Frye* tell the judge to do? "Your Honor," says *Frye*, "simply determine whether among the scientists concerned there is general agreement that the evidence is scientifically valid, that it rests upon the laws of nature," which means what? His Honor determines who are the scientists concerned and in making that determination you decide the outcome.

For example, do you want polygraph results to be admissible? Is that the outcome at which you wish to arrive? Easy. Simply define the community of scientists concerned as the community of polygraph operators and you've done it. Obviously, among polygraph operators there will be unanimity of view that the polygraph rests upon the laws of nature. But if you define the scientific community concerned as university professors of psychology, you get the opposite outcome because there there will be unanimity or nearly unanimity of view that the polygraph does not rest upon the laws of nature. Do you want the Ouija board to be admissible? Define the universe of scientists or technical people concerned as the members of the Ouija Board Society and the outcome is going to be that it's scientifically valid under the *Frye* test. Define the universe as anything other than the membership of the Ouija Board Society and the outcome will be different and so it's indeterminate. You've got to focus on who are the scientists concerned.

Second related deficiency and then we'll take an example of both in one. The *Frye* test, don't you see, ladies and gentlemen, it is an abdication of judicial responsibility. The *Frye* test says to the court, Your Honor, in order to determine whether it's scientifically valid, simply determine whether the scientists are in general agreement that it's scientifically valid. In short, you're saying to the judge, "You don't have to decide, leave it to the scientists to decide." But what we're deciding is ultimately an issue of the admissibility of evidence. And that's a judicial responsibility to decide, not a scientific responsibility. So that under the *Frye* test, the court has simply passed to the scientific community the responsibility of making a decision that most of us would agree, all of us would agree is a judicial responsibility, not a scientific responsibility. And that's struggling both philosophically and practically.

An example of these two deficiencies at work is the *Dowd* case.[3] And, as you see, we are no longer talking ancient or even medieval history. The *Dowd* case is approximately 12 months old. It was decided

3. *Dowd v. Calabrese*, 585 F. Supp. 430 (D.D.C. 1984).

just last year in 1984 by the United States District Court of the District of Columbia. I note in passing that the judge who wrote the opinion is Harold Greene, who will go down in history as the man who presided over the breaking up of the telephone company. That's this Judge Greene that we've read about in the newspapers, but he's long since done his dirty work on the telephone company and is now deciding other kinds of cases. In the *Dowd* case, a lawyer tried to persuade Judge Greene to receive in evidence certain polygraph results. Now, remember, this is the District of Columbia, the jurisdiction of the *Frye* case. And if any jurisdiction still follows *Frye*, it will be the District of Columbia. So how did the lawyer try to get it in? He offers the evidence. It's agreed that the reading was to the effect that somebody was or wasn't telling the truth. It's agreed that the device was in good working order, properly used. There's no point in contending on that score. But what about scientific validity?

Now, in my mind's ear, I hear Judge Greene saying to the lawyer who is the proponent of this evidence, "Aren't you familiar with the *Frye* case?" "Yes, I am, Your Honor." "Well, doesn't the *Frye* case hold that polygraph results are inadmissible?" "Your Honor, the *Frye* case concludes that polygraph results are inadmissible because the proponent in that case did not comply with what we have come to call the *Frye* test or requirement. I am prepared to comply with it. Your Honor . . ." and this is what he did, "I offer in evidence the result of a poll taken of polygraph operators on the question, do you agree or disagree with the proposition that the polygraph is scientifically valid." So do you see what we have? What is the relevant universe? Is it the universe of psychologists or is it the universe of polygraph operators? The proponent says it's polygraph operators. Moreover, he has taken a poll, and the poll, of course, shows overwhelmingly that the polygraph operators believe that the device is scientifically valid. Do you let the polygraph operators make a decision that all of us would agree really is a judicial decision—is the evidence admissible?

Well, whatever you might think about breaking up AT&T, Judge Greene is one smart cookie and Judge Greene says, "Oh, no. First of all, the defining of the community of scientists concerned is the key to this problem and you can't define it, I define it. And I'm not defining it as the universe of polygraph operators because . . ." well, for reasons that he sets forth in the opinion. Observe that Judge Greene accepts the *Frye* test. He's not going to fight the *Frye* test, he accepts it, but then works with it. And as to this business of taking a poll, I will not permit anyone to demonstrate compliance with the requirements of *Frye* by so mechanical a method as simply taking a poll. You're going to have to do more than that. You're going to have to call the scientists, at least a few of them, to the stand, subject them to cross-examination on their testimony as to general agreement in the scientific community about scientific validity, et cetera, et cetera. And so the polygraph results are inadmissible.

So what's wrong with *Frye*? First, it's indeterminate. Second, it bucks to the scientists a judicial responsibility for determining the admissibility of evidence. And third, since I promised you three deficiencies . . . third, most important, most dramatic and what shall I say . . . most troubling, but also most challenging in an occasional lawsuit—some of you may find yourself involved in such a lawsuit before too long, who knows? In any event, what's this third deficiency? The *Frye* test simply breaks down. It doesn't work when the scientific evidence is brand new. And do you see why? If the scientific evidence is brand new, it may be that there simply hasn't been time for the scientific community to become aware of it and if they're not aware of it, there cannot possibly be general agreement in the scientific community as to the scientific validity of whatever the science involved may be. And an unsurpassable example of the breakdown of the *Frye* test when applied to newly created scientific evidence is a case that I always look forward to telling about and I make sure that we have enough time to do in the kind of detail that gives it justice. And so for the next 10 or 15 minutes, ladies and gentlemen, let me tell you the facts of the *Coppolino* case.[4]

---

4. *Coppolino v. State*, 223 So. 2d 68 (Fla. App. 1968).

Now, some of you are old enough, perhaps, to remember that case as material for headlines in virtually every day's newspapers for as much as a year. And some of you may not remember the headlines, but you may have read about the case in the memoirs of a certain lawyer or a certain doctor whom I will be mentioning as we go along. But for most of you, I dare say that the name means little or nothing. I will therefore tell the story for the benefit of those of you who do not know it as you might have read it in the daily newspapers some 20 years ago. I guess it's a little bit more than 20 years ago and for those of you who already know the story, please be patient with me, forgive me for telling you what is already in your mind.

You begin in New Jersey, one of those upper-middle-class suburban communities right across the Hudson River, populated mainly by people who work in New York City. There was a fine home occupied by the Coppolino family. And the Coppolino family consisted of the father, Dr. Coppolino, who was a medical doctor and a qualified specialist in anesthesiology, who was in his middle or late thirties. Handsome man, physically attractive, seemingly in bursting good health, but with a curious fact in his background.

Some months before the time at which we begin this story, Dr. Coppolino had taken out a large insurance policy which guaranteed him very substantial monthly payments if he ever became disabled from practicing his profession, from working as an anesthesiologist. And lo and behold, not weeks before the time of which I speak, Dr. Coppolino had been diagnosed as having a serious heart murmur, a heart murmur, which the insurance company had been persuaded rendered him physically unfit to practice medicine, but which I tell you rendered him unfit for absolutely nothing else. He looked good, he felt good, and he was in full possession of all of his manly faculties. That was Dr. Coppolino, the father of the household.

The mother of the household, Mrs. Coppolino, was also Dr. Coppolino. She was a qualified physician. But because she had duties at home and there were young children, as you will hear, she did not practice medicine privately. She had a job with the laboratory of one of the big drug companies there in northern New Jersey and she went to work nine to five, Monday through Friday, so she had control over her hours of work.

There were youngsters at home, but there was plenty of income for the employment of governesses and the like to take care of the children. And so Dr. Coppolino stayed home because he couldn't go to work, because that would put at risk those very substantial checks received on a regular basis from the insurance company. He stayed home, but he had absolutely nothing to do. There were other people to take care of the house and to take care of the children. So he sat looking out the window.

And whom did he see? Well, before too long, his eye was caught by the lady that lived across the street. Her name was Marge Farber. Mrs. Farber was married to Mr. Farber, who was considerably older than she was. Now, Mr. Farber was a retired Army officer who had a job in the securities industry on Wall Street. He went to work every day. Mrs. Farber had no children and so she, too, essentially had absolutely nothing to fill up her day. She just sat looking out the window and before long her attention was caught by Dr. Coppolino looking out of his window directly across the street.

Now, I do not have with me a photograph of Mrs. Farber, but if you had been reading newspapers accounts at the time, depending upon the paper you read, Mrs. Farber would have been described as statuesque. Other newspapers would have said Junoesque. And newspapers designed for a more advanced readership would have called her perhaps Rubenesque, because Mrs. Farber had a great head of red hair and she was amply endowed with everything that a woman should be endowed with.

Well, Dr. Coppolino, as I said, was in the prime of life and, yes, he had that heart murmur, but that really didn't interfere with anything. And so you will understand that in due course nature took over, one thing led to another and Mrs. Farber began to nag Dr. Coppolino about getting a divorce. She said, "I can get a divorce from my husband, you get a divorce from your wife. We'll get together and have a life of our own." And Dr. Coppolino kept putting her off and putting her off and the affair got hotter and hotter. And Mrs. Farber became ever more insistent until one morning, incredibly, Mr. Farber simply failed to wake up. There he was, 7:30 in the morning, simply dead in his bed. Now, he was no longer a young man and he did have a history of medical problems and he sort of died of natural causes and he was buried.

But now Mrs. Farber was a widow. She was free to remarry and her urgings upon Dr. Coppolino became even more insistent. She said, "I am now free. All it will take is a divorce for you to become free. Do it and we can then get together." Dr. Coppolino's response to this high pressure from Mrs. Farber was not to get a divorce, not to break off the affair in a clean and straightforward way, but rather to pack up wife, kiddies, and household goods and move away from that town in northern New Jersey. They moved to Florida, to Miami as a matter of fact, and set up a new household there. And what do you suppose Mrs. Farber did? Mrs. Farber, not to be deterred, also moved to Miami and she rented a house around the corner from the Coppolinos. So she was no longer directly across the street, you had to go around the corner, but there she was. And she resumed her nagging of Dr. Coppolino. "Get rid of your wife so that we can get together."

Well, Dr. Coppolino in one way or another managed to stall her off. The days became weeks, became months and then, incredibly, Mrs. Coppolino failed to wake up one morning. There she was, dead in her bed. Now, no signs of violence, nothing, she just died in her sleep. Dr. Coppolino, who was a qualified physician, might have signed the death certificate, but I can't resist the temptation of telling you about this. He said he did not sign the death certification not out of considerations of tact—I mean, you know, it is kind of sleazy to sign the death certificate of one's own spouse, for heaven's sakes—but because if he had signed the death certificate, he was concerned that the insurance company would take the position that that was practicing medicine and cut off his disability payments. So what he did was call in a young physician, just a year or so in practice in the neighborhood, a young woman it was, and ask her to sign the death certificate. Well, Mrs. Coppolino did have a history of some heart trouble, but it was hardly, you know, fatal in nature. And this young doctor looks at the corpse lying there peacefully and fills out and signs my all-time favorite death certificate. And for those of you who may be aficionados of death certificates, it's worth having in mind. The death certificate says that Mrs. Coppolino died of heart failure. That's what it said. And I put it to you that in the history of the world, no one has ever not died of heart failure. To say that somebody died of heart failure is as much as to say that the person died of death. Well, of course. You know, that doesn't bake any loaves, let's move it along, huh? But the death certificate was accepted for filing by the county authorities and Mrs. Coppolino was buried down there in Florida.

And now Mrs. Farber comes to Dr. Coppolino and she says, "Now, no more fooling around. I'm free, you're free. Let's go see the JP and get married." Dr. Coppolino's response was not a simple no, it was not a simple we must terminate our relationship. His response was, to put it mildly, foolhardy, because what he said to Mrs. Farber was, "No, I'm not going to marry you because I have somebody else."

Mrs. Farber was now a woman not once, not twice, but thrice scorned. And she took all of her Junoesque beauty and her great head of red hair and she went directly to the district attorney's office down there in Florida and she said, "I tell you that Dr. Coppolino probably murdered his wife. And the reason I say probably murdered his wife is not that I know—I wasn't there to see it, I don't know. But I do know that he murdered somebody else the year before. And because he murdered that somebody else, he probably murdered his wife. And do you know who the somebody else is that he murdered? He murdered my husband, Mr. Farber. And I know that he did it because I helped him to do it. We decided to get rid of my husband. My husband was a very heavy sleeper. I let Dr. Coppolino into the house in the middle of the night. We went into my husband's bedroom, there he was asleep on the bed. Dr. Coppolino took a pillow, he held it over my husband's face. I helped him to hold my husband down. In due course, my husband died of asphyxiation and that's how we got rid of him. And I am prepared to testify to that effect."

Well, this was something, wasn't it? But you never know. All kinds of people come walking into DA's offices with all kinds of stories. You know, the full mooners that every prosecutor knows about. So the thing to do is exhume Mr. Farber's corpse and see whether you find any physical evidence to corroborate this wild story that Mrs. Farber is telling you.

So they exhumed the corpse up in New Jersey and because the medical examiner in New Jersey is not quite confident of his technical ability to conduct this autopsy, the corpse is sent over to New York City, to the office of the New York Medical Examiner, which these days is rather in trouble, but in those days was unquestionably the leading center for pathological work, for forensic pathology, in the world, not alone in the United States. And its head was Milton Helpern, now deceased, but then regarded as the dean, nay the founder of modern forensic pathology. And Milton Helpern, by the way, shortly before he died, published his own autobiography. It's easy to get hold of in the library and for anyone with an interest in this kind of work, well worth reading with a long chapter on the case that I am telling you about. Milton Helpern's autobiography is titled what else, "Autopsy," and it's about 400 pages long. The library will have it. It's not in paperback. If you find it in a used book store buy it at once. It will cost no more than 50 cents, so it's not a rare book, but it's kind of hard to get hold of.

In any event, Milton Helpern rolls up his sleeves—and I knew Helpern when I was in New York and I see him as I talk about him—a wonderful looking gray-haired man with a limitless fund of enthusiasm for cutting up corpses and seeing what you can figure out from that. And Helpern said that he, in his lifetime, had done autopsies probably on the order of 100,000. And he wasn't exaggerating. He was the world's master at this kind of work. So he rolls up his sleeves and he goes to work and, sure enough, what does he discover in Mr. Farber's corpse, but a fractured larynx—in effect, a broken Adam's apple. Now, as we all know, a male can die of a fractured larynx and it's the infallible sign of death by asphyxiation with a pillow being held over the face because, of course, the victim will struggle and the murderer has to hold the pillow down. And the way that your hands fall, the thumbs will be right over the larynx and that's what produces the fractured larynx. And Helpern said, "You find it every time you do an autopsy on an asphyxiation victim who has been asphyxiated in that manner. So I am now prepared to testify and I do testify before the grand jury in New Jersey that Farber died as a result of asphyxiation." In short, there's the corpus delicti. He's dead and he died otherwise than naturally. And as to who did it? Why, Dr. Coppolino did it and for that you just put in the testimony of Mrs. Farber.

So Dr. Coppolino is indicted for first-degree murder in New Jersey and he retains as his counsel Lee Bailey, who is, of course, still before the public, but sort of has fallen a little bit on hard times these days, I guess. But back in those days was at the very head of the criminal defense branch of our profession and whose brilliance was really beyond compare. He's an astoundingly gifted lawyer. Bailey says, "Okay, I will defend Dr. Coppolino at that trial in New Jersey."

And while it's not directly on point, I will take a minute or two to tell you of how Bailey handled the jury selection. Now, obviously, this was the most publicized murder case of the year and everybody in New Jersey was aware that the jury was going to be selected starting at 10 o'clock tomorrow morning and Bailey arrives at 5 o'clock the afternoon before at the Newark Airport. And, you know, Bailey is a pilot. Not just a pilot, but he's a jet pilot. So he flies in in his own jet plane and, of course, by prearrangement, all of the television stations are there. So the cameras are lined up and all the reporters are there with the microphones and Bailey is filmed getting out of the airplane with his helmet on. And he, you know, smiles at the camera and then he steps down and the Jane Fonda–type thrusts the microphone into his face and says, "Mr. Bailey, you're here to pick a jury in the *Coppolino* case tomorrow morning, isn't that right?" Yes. And, of course, Bailey is aware that every single person in New Jersey, every single prospective juror is going to be seeing this on the 6 o'clock and the 10 o'clock news that very evening. And they say to him, "Well, Mr. Bailey, what kind of jurors do you want?" And his answer was so clever. How many of you know what his answer was? He said, so that everybody in New Jersey saw it that night on television, "That's easy," he said, "I want the 12 most intelligent people in New Jersey." That's what he said. The next morning when he announced to the judge that the 12 people in the box were satisfactory to him, every one of the 12 said, "My God, Lee Bailey thinks that I'm one of the 12 most intelligent people in New Jersey." Terrific jury selection, but lest you unthinkingly use it next week, I digress to tell you that the bar association in New Jersey concluded that that was sharp practice, that it was undue use of television, et cetera, et cetera, and disbarred Bailey from trying any more cases in New Jersey. So, you know, got to be a little bit careful. And you may have more confidence in your bar authorities down here, but be aware that Bailey got into trouble.

In any event, Bailey's defense was absolutely brilliant. Let me just pick two of the highlights. Now what about the fractured larynx? I wasn't there, but I have read the transcript of that trial and Bailey established to my satisfaction in the sense that I've got a reasonable doubt about it that the fractured larynx which existed . . . I mean, he couldn't shake Helpern's finding that there was a fractured larynx . . . came about when one of the laborers assigned to exhume the corpse kind of misused the shovel. And the cutting edge of the shovel, it's like a blade . . . actually crashed through the rotting wood of the casket and caught the corpse right there so that the fractured larynx could well have come about after death as a result of that minor accident with the use of the shovel in the course of exhuming the body. As I say, it's enough to raise a reasonable doubt.

And then Mrs. Farber took the stand and she testified, "I stood there and helped Dr. Coppolino, the defendant, murder my husband." And Bailey conducted an absolutely coruscating cross-examination of Mrs. Farber as to how a woman could possibly do that and then testify about it, et cetera, et cetera. He cut her up into a million pieces and there was an acquittal. The jury acquitted Dr. Coppolino. Now, many of you are saying, but what does this have to do with scientific evidence? You are about to hear. Dr. Helpern, who had testified as to what he found in his autopsy of Mr. Farber, was absolutely beside himself for a reason that I tell you, and since it involves personalities, it's on the understanding that this is not to go beyond these four walls. Dr. Helpern was one of the sweetest and most interesting and charming guys I have ever met and he disliked very few people. But of the very few people he disliked, there was one he hated with a vengeance. And the person that Dr. Helpern for some reason hated with a vengeance was Lee Bailey. I don't know why, but he did. And when that New Jersey jury acquitted Dr. Coppolino, Dr. Helpern didn't care about Coppolino. You know, cards fall where they may on that. But he was flying around his office at the thought that Lee Bailey had gotten an acquittal in a case in which Milton Helpern had testified. And he said, not to himself, but out loud, "God damn it, he's not going to get away with this. I'm going to see to it that he doesn't get away with it." So Milton Helpern went to the district attorney in Florida and he said, "We can't do anything more about New Jersey because he's been acquitted. But we've got Mrs. Farber saying that he probably murdered his own wife down here in Florida." And the district attorney said, "Yeah, but, you know, we can't prove it. Mrs. Farber doesn't say that she was there to help him do it and, in any event, we have no reason to think that Mrs. Coppolino died otherwise than naturally." And Dr. Helpern said, "You leave it to me to find out what she died of. You exhume that corpse and you send it up to my laboratory in New York." And the authorities said, "Okay," and they exhumed Mrs. Coppolino's corpse.

Now, I don't want to discuss with anybody not too long before lunch, but you realize she had been in the ground not in New Jersey, but in Florida, where it's hot and it's wet and there are all kinds of creepy crawlies in the ground that you don't have in New Jersey. And when they exhumed that corpse, I'm told that it wasn't much more than green goo. It was just sort of Prell that they put into a cellophane bag and they sent it up to the laboratory in New York. But Helpern went to work and he conducted what he, himself, describes as the masterpiece of all autopsies in the history of forensic pathology. And this is what he discovered. He discovered that there was absolutely nothing in that corpse of clinical significance. Absolutely nothing to talk about.

It was a perfectly normal corpse with one exception and the exception was of a sort that only a Milton Helpern would have observed it. On the woman's left buttock, as I recall, there was a tiny puncture wound. Now, when I say tiny, I mean something less than what you would get if you sat on a thumbtack. It was sort of a bee sting, but it obviously was not a bee sting, it was a pin prick down on her left buttock. And obviously you don't die of that, whatever it may be. And surrounding that tiny puncture wound was a little bit of discolored tissue. That was all. That was all that he found that, by any stretch of the imagination, could be called out of the ordinary.

Now, if you read *Autopsy* you'll have Helpern's own account, not just of this particular operation, but of his philosophy of forensic pathology. Helpern thought that the pathologist ought to be the Sherlock Holmes in the case. It was the pathologist who really thought about the various possibilities for criminal activity here and putting that view to work, this is how Helpern reasoned it out. Let us assume for the sake of argument that this woman was murdered, that she did not die naturally. How was she murdered? It would have to be an injection of poison because there are absolutely no wounds, there are no signs of violence. If it was poison, this puncture wound is the wound left by the introduction of the poison into her body and it would be a pinprick. Not an injection of a hypodermic needle, a pinprick to her left buttock. Is there any poison that can be introduced under the skin by way of a pinprick in a quantity that minute—you know, whatever it would be, .00001 of a cubic centimeter—that would produce instant death? Because that's what you had here. There was no outcry, there was no struggle, there was no convulsion. And in addition would leave no symptoms in the body. There's absolutely nothing that you see. The kidneys are normal, the liver is normal, the lungs, the heart, all normal. Is there such a poison?

Now, Helpern didn't know. For that you go to the manuals of toxicology. He goes to the manuals of toxicology and discovers that there is a substance called succinylcholine chloride and, in essence, it is a liquid form of one of the nerve gasses that the government manufactures for use in the event of war.

Succinylcholine chloride, which I will represent by AB, is a very complex organic molecule which, introduced anywhere under the skin, produces instantaneous death in the sense that when you flip a light switch, the lights go out instantly. The central nervous system just conks out. The victim is unaware of anything happening, there is no outcry, there is no pain, there is no convulsion. There are no symptoms anywhere in the body. What is more, upon causing death, this succinylcholine chloride, AB, breaks down into the breakdown products A and B, each of which is harmless and is found naturally in the body. That's a perfect poison, isn't it? And who would know about it? An anesthesiologist, isn't that right? And do we have an anesthesiologist in the case? We sure do. Dr. Coppolino, remember, was a qualified anesthesiologist.

And so Helpern reasons as follows. This puncture wound is what's left from the pinprick by which Dr. Coppolino, using succinylcholine chloride, murdered Mrs. Coppolino. The way to prove it, since if that's all you have, he, Helpern, can't testify that it was an injection of succinylcholine chloride. The way to prove it, do you see, is to take that bit of discolored tissue and subject it to an analysis not for AB, not for succinylcholine chloride because it breaks down, remember, into the breakdown products A and B. You don't just test it for A and B because that's found naturally in the body. What you do is take that discolored tissue and test it for the amounts of A and B present in it, to see whether those amounts are far in excess of what you find normally. And if a biochemist can determine that the amount of the breakdown products A and B in that discolored tissue is 1,000 percent above what you would normally find, then Helpern would be prepared to take the stand in Florida and say that, in his opinion, Mrs. Coppolino died not naturally, but as the result of an injection of succinylcholine chloride and then circumstantial evidence makes the case against Dr. Helpern as the one who introduced the succinylcholine chloride into her body.

Now first, though, you've got to perform a quantitative analysis of that discolored tissue to determine the amount of the breakdown product. Helpern can't do that—he's a pathologist, he's not a biochemist.

But on the staff of the New York Medical Examiner's Office in those days was a biochemist of world standing who, for whatever reason, did not want and never did have a university position. He spent his entire career on the staff of the New York Medical Examiner's Office, but, as I say, he had a world reputation as a biochemist. His name was Joseph Umberger and he and Helpern were friends as well as professional colleagues. And Helpern called Umberger in one day and explained to him what I have explained to you about the scientific problem and the case that was before them. And Umberger in my mind's ear I hear, says to Dr. Helpern, "Well, Milton, what do you want me to do?" And Helpern says, "Joe, I want you to take some of that discolored tissue and conduct a quantitative analysis to determine how much of the breakdown product A and B is present." And Umberger said, "Milton, I understand what you want, but I can't do it." And Milton said, "Joe, what do you mean you can't do it?" And Umberger said, "Milton, I . . . I just can't do it." And Helpern said, "Joe, what do you mean?" And Umberger said, "Milton, I can't do it because biochemistry does not know how to do it." And Helpern said, "Joe, explain to me." And Umberger said, "Milton, biochemists do not have a technique for conducting a quantitative analysis for those products, A and B." And Helpern said, "Oh. In that case, Joe, invent it." And Umberger said, "Milton, I'll try." Dr. Umberger said to Dr. Helpern, "I'll try, Milton," and went to his laboratory where he stayed for some days or even a few weeks, in due course returning to tell Dr. Helpern that he had invented a technique, a technique of quantitative analysis for those breakdown products A and B. And, using the technique, he came to the conclusion that the amounts of A and B present in that bit of discolored tissue from poor Mrs. Coppolino's body were thousands of percents higher than what you would normally find. "Aha!" said Dr. Helpern, "That permits me to testify that the cause of death was not natural, it was an injection of succinylcholine chloride and that will make the case against Dr. Coppolino."

Helpern went to the authorities in Florida and, on the basis of the information that you now have, persuaded them to indict Dr. Coppolino for murder in the first degree committed in Florida. The victim, not Mr.

Farber. For that we had an acquittal in New Jersey. The victim, rather, was Mrs. Coppolino. And so for the second time, but in a separate case, Dr. Coppolino stood on trial for his life and, once again, at his side was Lee Bailey. And although, as we will hear, the outcome was somewhat different in Florida from what it had been in New Jersey, Bailey's defense was equally brilliant and not to say breathtaking.

Bailey said to that jury from the beginning that the defense in this case—and these are not Bailey's words, you understand. He wouldn't talk this way to a jury, but as lawyers we understand this is what he was saying. The defense is the defense of corpus delicti. I say to you that you will not be able to conclude beyond a reasonable doubt that that woman died as a result of some criminal intervention. And if you have a reasonable doubt of the corpus delicti, you must acquit. Now this is rare, we understand. Usually the defense in a criminal case will be of the final question—who did it? Can the prosecution prove beyond a reasonable doubt that this guy did it? Bailey's defense was that the prosecution is not going to be able to prove beyond a reasonable doubt that a crime had been committed in the first place. And he said, as I recall, right in the opening statement that if by any chance you do decide beyond a reasonable doubt that the crime has been committed, then you convict Dr. Coppolino because there will be no evidence to the effect that he didn't do it. He's not going to take the stand. There will be no other witness to testify that he didn't do it because there's nothing to deny doing. No crime has been committed. And, so you see, the battleground was what? Dr. Helpern and Dr. Umberger. That's what the trial was about.

Now Dr. Helpern was called to the stand and he testified about his autopsy findings. And if not in these words, to this effect, it went as follows:

"I found the puncture wound and I found the bit of discolored tissue."

"On the basis of those findings, Dr. Helpern, were you able to come to some conclusion as to the cause of death?"

"No."

So to that point, the prosecution has not proved the corpus delicti. The prosecutor says to the judge, "Your Honor, may Dr. Helpern step down and he will be recalled in a little while, but I wish to put on the stand Dr. Umberger." Dr. Umberger now takes the stand and Bailey is on his feet, saying, "Your Honor, before he testifies in front of this jury, I wish to conduct a voir dire, not in the presence of the jury, to determine whether his testimony, and we all know what it's going to be, is admissible in the first place." The judge said, "You may conduct that voir dire. The jury will be excused." And what we now had was the taking of testimony to help the judge decide whether Umberger's evidence would be admissible. And do you see, ladies and gentlemen, that we are dealing here with the phenomenon that is our subject this morning—scientific evidence and how a lawyer persuades a court to receive it in evidence.

And before moving along to tell you what happened in that voir dire, I just made reference to the judge saying to Bailey, "Yes, you may have your voir dire," and on a kind of point of personal privilege, let me tell you about something that happened to me a good many years ago. The judge presiding was Judge Silvertooth. That was his name, Judge Silvertooth. And by reputation he was about the ablest member of the trial level of the Florida state judiciary—a very knowledgeable guy in whom everybody had a great deal of confidence. Well, I've been kind of thinking about these problems for a long time and it was a good many years ago, ladies and gentlemen, that I stood before an audience at the National Judicial College in Reno, Nevada, addressing a group about the size of you, but a group of state court judges, on the problems that you get into when you deal with scientific evidence. And I was talking about the *Coppolino* case and I had reached just about this point in my account when I referred for the first time to the judge, Judge Silvertooth. And it entered my head to do what I then did. I sort of stopped and I looked out at the group and I said, "Does anybody here happen to know Judge Silvertooth?" And instantly a hand, I remember, right about there, went up. And I said, "Yes, sir." And the gentlemen stood and he said, "I'm Judge Silvertooth." Well, I want you to know that it concentrates the mind wonderfully to be talking about a case where the very judge who presided over it is sitting in the audience. But, unfazed, I continued my account, always keeping Judge Silvertooth in the corner of my eye and I'm delighted to report that for the rest of my narrative, Judge Silvertooth kept going, "Yep, that's how it was. Just like that. Yes, sir. Yes, sir." So I was kind of relieved to have the ultimate seal of approval from the judge who actually presided. In any event, back to that voir dire.

Bailey now stood up and, remember, his task was to question Umberger so as to show the judge that the results of the quantitative analysis were not admissible. Now, let's just pause and go through the thought process by which Bailey prepared for this voir dire. And I should tell you that now we're tracking what actually happened, first, because I've read the transcript; second, I've read all the briefs in the case; and, third, I've had the occasion to talk to the people involved—Bailey's then associate—about what they did here. It's no longer on the board, but we really don't need it.

Remember the three prerequisites that the proponent must prove if scientific evidence is going to be received. First, did you get a certain reading? Bailey would have said, if he were asked, "Of course, I acknowledge that Umberger got the reading. He's a biochemist of world standing and if he says that he got 1,000 percent of A and 2,000 percent of B, that's what he got and I'm not going to question it." Second prerequisite—was the device in good working order? Was it properly used in the context of this case? Was the glassware clean? Were the reagents fresh? Were the biochemical techniques what they ought to be? And, again, Bailey, if asked, would have said, "I'm not going to try to fight it on that ground. Umberger is a man whose professional credentials are beyond question. And of course his glassware was clean and his reagents were fresh and whatever a biochemist has to do, he did, so as to be able to say that this thing was properly used and the device was in good working order, et cetera. What Bailey would say if he were asked is that, "I was contesting the third prerequisite, the scientific validity of this technique." What's the technique?

A quantitative analysis of human tissue to determine the amounts of the breakdown products A and B. And Bailey would have said, "You've got a legal framework within which to work and then you prove your facts accordingly." What's the legal framework? The *Frye* test—the law in Florida, as it in the vast majority of American jurisdictions to this day. What is the *Frye* test? Among the scientists . . . in this case, I guess it would be the biochemists. Among the biochemists is there general agreement that the technique, the quantitative analysis for those breakdown products is scientifically valid? Right? That's it.

You know that Bailey established his factual basis in one question? The fact is, he asked two. The second question I think was a throwaway and there was no great risk because the jury wasn't there. I think he was showing off a little bit, but the first question did it for him. And do you know what that first question was? Breathtaking in its simplicity, but also in its brilliance. The question asked of Dr. Umberger—and by the way, for the trial lawyers in the room, Bailey had inquired around and discovered that Umberger had testified in other cases and the line on Umberger—you know, I'm speaking shop now, trial lawyers would talk this way about an expert witness. The line on Umberger was that he was not only a scientist of impeccable professional standing, but personally was a very conservative, quiet, sedate sort of man, who went right down the line. He was not pro-prosecution, he was not pro-defendant. He sort of called it the way he saw it and he didn't care much about anything else. And maybe that's why you could risk the second question. The first question, though, was simply this. "Dr. Umberger, have you published your results?" "No." Do you see how that's all you need?

Under the *Frye* test, if he hasn't so much as committed to print this newly invented quantitative analysis technique, how can you say that the biochemists of the world are in general agreement as to its scientific validity? They haven't heard of it and they haven't heard of it because this man has not published it yet. The second question, as I say, a little bit of showboating, really unnecessary, was, "Well, Doctor, are you ready to publish?" And the answer was no. He knew who he was dealing with. This conservative guy with impeccable professional credentials, who would not risk his scientific reputation. When he says he's not ready to publish, he means that he's not absolutely certain that he's got it right and so he's not willing to put his name on it and that's it. Bailey said, "Your Honor, that's my voir dire. I now argue that under the *Frye* test, Umberger's testimony is not admissible." And do you see the rest of what follows? If you don't have Umberger's testimony, Helpern is never going to resume the stand because Helpern will be unable to say, "In my opinion, she died as a result of an injection of succinylcholine chloride, which means there will be a total failure of proof on the issue of the corpus delicti, which means what? The indictment gets dismissed. It never gets to the jury. That's how Bailey was playing it. He said, "Your Honor, there is no proof of what the *Frye* test requires, general agreement among the scientists, therefore Umberger's results are not admissible."

And here was Judge Silvertooth's ruling. He said, not necessarily in these words, but it added up to this. He said, "Bailey, I understand your legal arguments and I see what you're doing. And what you're doing is very clever and, you know, it's to be applauded. But here's what I'm going to do. We're going to put the jury back in the box and you may cross-examine Umberger in front of the jury just the way you cross-examined him in front of me. But I'm going to let Umberger testify to his results, which means Helpern is going to get back on the stand and testify as to the corpus delicti and then you argue to the jury that they are unable to conclude beyond a reasonable doubt that she died as a result of an injection of succinylcholine chloride and we'll let the jury decide it." Bailey said, "If that's the ruling, that's the ruling."

The jury resumed its place. Umberger was cross-questioned in front of the jury as he had been in the voir dire and Bailey argued to the jury in summation and Helpern did testify that on the basis of Umberger's findings, together with what he, Helpern found in that autopsy, the woman died as a result of an injection of succinylcholine chloride. And there was circumstantial evidence as to who could have put the succinylcholine chloride underneath her skin by way of a pinprick, except Dr. Coppolino.

Now, Bailey's summation was as bold a summation as I've ever heard of. His summation was, "You cannot say that you're persuaded, ladies and gentlemen of the jury, beyond a reasonable doubt that that woman died as a result of an injection of this poison. But if you are so persuaded beyond a reasonable doubt, your verdict can be only one thing—murder in the first degree. Because if you are so persuaded that she died as the result of an injection of succinylcholine chloride, the only person who could have done it is Dr. Coppolino and the only possible legal characterization of what he did is murder in the first degree. In short, you either send him home or you send him to the gas chamber. There is nothing in between." That's what he said to them in summation. And it kind of takes your breath away until you realize that if it doesn't work and somebody goes to the gas chamber, it's Dr. Coppolino, not Lee Bailey. And I say that to the handful of you in the room who do criminal defense work. I used to do a great deal of that. Always make sure, when things are really dark and there's no light at the end of the tunnel and it appears that somebody's going to have to go to jail, make sure that it's the client who goes to jail, right? All the legal ethics, at least for criminal lawyers, can be summed up in that.

Well, back to the story. You have Bailey's summation. You've got to find him guilty of murder first or acquit him. The jury marched out and they came back with one of the most . . . I don't know that it's exactly the right word, but it kind of gets the idea across . . . one of the most lovable verdicts I've ever heard of. Do you know what their verdict was? Manslaughter. I believe that in Florida they call it murder in the third degree and in my home jurisdiction they call it manslaughter in the first degree. But what they were saying was he killed her sort of on the spur of the moment. Almost, as it were, by accident. He had this pin with succinylcholine chloride on it and he, you know, he lost control of his muscular movements, kind of got her in the left buttock with it, that kind of thing. And, as anyone who's tried criminal cases to juries will understand, what the jury was really saying was, you know, we have a reasonable doubt, but we also know he did it. Not only here, but in New Jersey as well. And God damn it, he's not going to walk away from it a second time. So you compromise with murder in the second degree.

Any criminal lawyer has run into verdicts of that kind, as has Bailey. And so when Bailey took it up, his real argument was in his second point. His first argument, I'm not so sure that I would have made it. The first argument was this is an irrational verdict. And the answer from the Florida Supreme Court is, of course it's an irrational verdict, but juries are entitled to bring in irrational verdicts. You're tempering justice with mercy, et cetera, et cetera., and you have nothing to complain of. And the Court's absolutely right.

The second point was the telling point. And Bailey argued forcefully and concisely and correctly that under the *Frye* test, which was and is the law in Florida, Umberger should not have been allowed to testify. Because under the *Frye* test, you have to say that his evidence is inadmissible. Why? There is no proof of general agreement among the biochemists that this device is scientifically valid. And the Florida Supreme Court, in an opinion that I whisper in your ear—I wouldn't want it published in the newspaper tomorrow—in an opinion that perhaps wants something in intellectual elegance, rejects Bailey's argument and says Umberger was properly allowed to testify because *Frye* was not the rule? Nope. *Frye* is the rule. Because we overrule *Frye*? Nope, we do not overrule *Frye*. To this day it's the law in Florida. But because in a case of this kind the admissibility of evidence is a matter within the sound discretion of the trial judge. That's all they say. They do not say what would have been understood in Florida at the time. Judge Silvertooth is a terrific fellow. Everybody has confidence in him and if he was willing to have the jury hear this evidence, we're not going to upset his ruling. Translated into plain English, maybe it shouldn't have come in and probably there's a reasonable doubt as to the corpus delicti, but we, too, know that he did it. And we're not going to stand by and let him walk away from it a second time. So there you have it.

Let me just anticipate a question that is always asked afterwards—whatever happened to Dr. Coppolino? Dr. Coppolino, under the Florida statute, got 20 years and he served whatever he served, 12 or 13, and he was then released. He is now out and when I last saw his name in the newspaper, it was, believe it or not, in connection with a lawsuit he had brought in New Jersey to regain his medical license, arguing that he had been acquitted in New Jersey and, as to the Florida conviction, well, you know, that really wasn't any concern of the New Jersey licensing authorities, that he should get his license to practice medicine back presumably so that he could resume collecting checks under that disability policy. But I really don't know about that.

The *Coppolino* case is a wonderful story and simply taking the Florida Supreme Court's opinion at face value, it represents a candid judicial acknowledgment of what all trial lawyers know—that you can spend all the time you want on these elaborate intellectual structures with respect to the admissibility of evidence, but ultimately it comes down to the trial judge's discretion. Appellate courts will rarely, if ever, disturb the determination of a trial judge in whom the appellate court has confidence with respect to the admissibility or non-admissibility of evidence. We all know that.

If you want to sort of step back and look at it from a different perspective and in a somewhat larger context, the significance of the *Coppolino* case to the student of the developing law of scientific evidence is that it is the first case that I know of in which a court departs from the *Frye* test. Now, we understand that the holding is limited and you can say all kinds of things to explain it, but the fact is the scientific evidence was held to be admissible despite the noncompliance with *Frye*. And so it represents the first occasion when a court steps back from *Frye*.

Why is that important? Because the *Frye* test, as we have said, while granted it has a certain surface appeal, in fact is deficient in three separate and substantial ways. Remember, it's indeterminate. It's jurisprudentially flawed in that it abdicates a judicial responsibility, passing the buck to the scientist. And, third, as we see in the *Coppolino* case, it simply doesn't work when you're dealing with brand new or newly created scientific evidence. Well, is there anything by which we can replace it?

One possibility is represented by the *Lopez* case.[5] *Lopez* is a district court opinion and perhaps we shouldn't lean too hard on a district court opinion, but the author of the opinion gives the opinion a special weight. The author of the opinion is Judge [Jack B.] Weinstein, now Chief Judge Weinstein of the U.S. District Court in the Eastern District of New York. What gives the opinion special weight is that Judge Weinstein, before he went on the bench, was Professor Weinstein of the Columbia Law School, evidence being his specialty. And Professor Judge Weinstein was a principal draftsman of the Federal Rules of Evidence and, as all federal practitioners know, the treatise to which you go to look up a question of federal evidence is Weinstein's Federal Rules of Evidence. That is the Weinstein we're talking about. So we're dealing here with a judge who is especially conscious of evidentiary matters and has a special competence to speak to them.

The issue is a simple one, because by now we're getting to be used to dealing with problems of the admissibility of scientific evidence. The scientific evidence concerned is, like radar, something with which every one of us is very familiar. But the scientific background of which is probably unknown to any of us and, until you read the opinion, you don't realize that that scientific background is as complicated as it is. You know what the scientific evidence is? It's the evidence you get when somebody walks through that frame at the airport. You know, the thing that goes buzz if you have too much metal in your pocket. Its trade name, apparently, is Friskem. I just get that out of the opinion, so I will call it the Friskem. In Weinstein's case there are many issues. I'm talking only about the issue of the admissibility of the scientific evidence. That three-element paradigm works yet again. Was there a reading? Yes. The Friskem went buzz; that's the reading. Second, was the machine in good working order and was it properly used? And the answer is yes. There is a way of calibrating and setting up those machines and whatever that

---

5. *United States v. Lopez*, 328 F. Supp. 1077 (E.D.N.Y. 1971).

way is had been done. Third, is the scientific validity of the Friskem such that you can admit the buzz and rely upon it as some evidence that the person walking through the frame actually has a quantity of metal in his pockets? Now, if you were to apply *Frye*, you would say is there general agreement among the electrical engineers that this Friskem rests upon the laws of nature? Judge Weinstein does not want to apply *Frye* because Judge Weinstein, as a student of the law of evidence, is aware of these three basic deficiencies in the *Frye* test. And I'm now psychoanalyzing. You're not going to see this in the opinion, but my hunch is that Judge Weinstein wanted to write an opinion that would be there in the books for any lawyer to point to if the lawyer wished to argue for a departure from *Frye*. Obviously, it was not there at the time of the *Coppolino* case, so it couldn't have been cited to the *Coppolino* court.

What Weinstein does is the act of a very sophisticated lawyer, now judge, writing an opinion. And I'm paraphrasing and simplifying, but I think this is what it adds up to. He says, "I hold that the Friskem results are admissible. As to the third prerequisite, scientific validity, I find that the *Frye* test is satisfied. There is general agreement, et cetera, et cetera. But independently, as a kind of alternative holding, I find as a fact myself that the device is scientifically valid." So you see what he's done? If you want to replace *Frye* with a test that says the court, however difficult it may be, must decide for itself that the device is scientifically valid, here's a precedent for you, albeit by way of alternative holding. Now Judge Weinstein says, "I find as a fact that the device is valid and in finding that fact," remember he was sitting as jury, "in finding that fact I have relied upon," and he cites various articles and electronics books and the like and he says, "I have deposited with the clerk of the court copies of those articles and any counsel in the case may read them and if anybody wishes to contest my finding, that lawyer is free to do so."

Editorial by yours truly. Even though few, if any, of us are equipped to understand the scientific basis of the Friskem, every one of us would agree that it is scientifically valid. You know, it's like radar. Obviously, this is not a Ouija board; it operates in accordance with the laws of nature. Second, Weinstein says that he has read these various technical materials and deposited them with the clerk. If he says he read them, I believe that he read them. Did he understand them? My view is no, he did not understand any two consecutive words of that technical material. Why then does he say, "And any lawyer who wishes to challenge me may do so"? Because no lawyer is going to challenge him for two reasons. First, it's absurd. Even if you are an electrical engineer, what are you going to do—establish the Friskem as a Ouija board? Of course not. It is scientifically valid. And, second, the odds are overwhelming that no lawyer is going to be able to pick up the challenge because no lawyer is in a better position than Judge Weinstein to understand the technical data that appears in these materials. So it's a fairly easy out, but there it is, waiting to be cited by any lawyer who wishes to argue to a court that the *Frye* test should be departed from.

Now, are there grounds for argument? Is the *Frye* test doomed to be replaced in the course of legal development by another test? Yes, I think there are grounds for argument and if I had to, I think that I could make the argument. Let me show you in the time that remains to us this morning what that argument is.

Now, once again, ladies and gentlemen, I've got to repeat what I said at the outset. I can give you cases by way of example, but everything that we have talked about this morning is sort of among us. There's no book, there's no article, there's no judicial opinion in which all of this is laid out. I believe what I'm saying to you, but I have no way of documenting it. I believe that the *Frye* test is in its last days. The *Frye* test was universally followed as recently as the *Coppolino* case. The *Coppolino* case was the first departure from the *Frye* test and, as of today, you heard me say *Frye* is no longer universally followed. It is followed in the vast majority of jurisdictions, but my sense is that in every jurisdiction in which a lawyer makes a serious argument for departing from *Frye*, for replacing *Frye* with something else, that argument is going to prevail. That is the trend. That is the direction in which doctrine will develop.

And the reason we've got this trend, the reason doctrine is moving away from the *Frye* test is that the *Frye* test, we now acknowledge, is simply not very good. We're not persuaded still of its merits, either because of the first deficiency, that it's indeterminate, or the second, that it abdicates a judicial responsibility, or the third, that it doesn't work when you're dealing with newly created scientific evidence. Courts are prepared to say we've got to depart from it and replace it with something else.

Now what is to take its place? What is the direction in which the law on scientific evidence is going to develop? Acknowledging that my crystal ball is as cloudy as the next fellow's, this is what I see in my crystal ball. An increasing, albeit inarticulate, awareness on the part of courts that the way we have, we the law, has responded to the phenomenon of scientific evidence was flawed from the outset. It was an unconsidered and, therefore, unintelligent response. And do you see what that response was? Think back, if you will, a couple of hours or so to our beginning this morning with the hypothetical, but historically accurate, case of the first offer of radar evidence. Or, as a matter of fact, just consider the facts of the *Coppolino* case or any other of the cases that we've looked at. Even the *Lopez* case in which Judge Weinstein dealt with the Friskem. The habit of mind used by the lawyers and judges involved in those cases might be put into words as follows. Scientific evidence is evidence different in nature from any other kind of evidence. And so we need special rules to determine the admissibility of scientific evidence. Special rules that can be summarized as the three prerequisites and then *Frye* as a gloss on the third prerequisite and all of the complications that come with that.

If you will permit me a legal tag, this is scientific evidence vel non. Scientific evidence considered as an entity unto itself, characterized by law applicable only to scientific evidence. That is the way the law has looked at scientific evidence and I think it's wrong. Scientific evidence should not be treated as evidence different in nature from any other kind of evidence. Scientific evidence should not be treated as something different from the evidence John Q. Bystander gives you when he says, "I was standing at the street corner and I saw that the traffic light was green." What we should do, I put before you, and as we will see, just in the last year or so courts are waking up to this alternative method of dealing with scientific evidence. What we should do is consider scientific evidence not as a species of evidence unto itself, but rather as a kind of evidence you get in certain ways. And the law should focus on the ways in which we get the evidence. In short, look at the means, not the end. If the means are acceptable, if the means are in accordance with the rules that we have, the evidence is admissible. Call it scientific, call it non-scientific, call it what you will. And you don't have to concern yourself with the three prerequisites for *Frye* or any such thing. All right?

Getting away from the scientific evidence vel non approach, I say, you focus on the means by which the evidence is adduced. And those means can be either of two. And those two means for introducing scientific evidence will be discussed one after the other and will keep us busy until it's time to quit for the morning.

The first, obviously, is scientific evidence that is offered by way of a document, a report typically, and I'll develop that in just a moment. And the other way is scientific evidence that is offered not through a document, but through a living witness, a scientist, whom we lawyers would call an expert witness. And to recapitulate it, and then we'll talk about each of those means for adducing scientific evidence, I say that what the law should do and what the law is now beginning to do is focus on the document or focus on the expert witness. And if you've determined that the document is admissible, do not worry about the nature of the evidence that comes in through the document, which will be scientific evidence. If you determine that the expert is entitled to testify, that's it—the court need not concern itself any further with the substance of the testimony and that substance will be scientific evidence.

Now, let's look within the limits of the time that is available first at scientific evidence as it comes in through documents and then at scientific evidence as it comes in through the expert. First, with respect to documents, I paint with a broad brush acknowledgedly, but still I think it is essentially true and for those who have not had any experience in the field, it's needful to have a bit of background. Typically we're talking about tort litigation here. Not necessarily, but typically. And it's tort litigation of the kind that is getting to be a commonplace here in 1985 going on to 1986. Before you know it, it's going to be the 21st century. Tort litigation that I ran into in the early days of my years in practice almost always was what you might think of as one-on-one. The blue Buick collided with the yellow Plymouth. Driver sues driver. Who went through the red light? That's the question. So you see my one-on-one idea. Generalizing a little bit, in your typical tort case, invariably the kind of case that would have been tried 30 years ago and still fairly common today, the public has no particular involvement beyond the generalized involvement that the public has in the trial of any lawsuit. The trial of any lawsuit is a matter of public concern and so the public is interested. But there is no direct, there is no immediate involvement on the part of the public in this case between one driver and another driver. The only people directly involved are the drivers themselves.

But life, technology, society, the modern world have become so complicated that an increasingly large fraction of tort litigation these days involves litigation where the public is directly involved. A couple of examples. When the skywalk collapses in the Hyatt Hotel in Kansas City and kills 114 people and desperately injures perhaps 500 more, and not so desperately injures another 1,500, all of those injured people or their heirs are directly involved. But the public feels itself to be directly involved as well. Do you see why? What caused that skywalk to collapse? Is there something wrong with the engineering and architectural techniques by which such large public buildings are built? "Do I have to worry," the member of the public says to himself or herself, "the next time I walk into a hotel that the thing is going to collapse around me?" Or when the engine falls off the left wing of the DC-10 taking off from the O'Hare Airport in Chicago, well, directly involved will be the heirs of the 300 some odd passengers who are killed. But every other air traveler, which is essentially every other American, is also going to start asking what caused the engine to fall off the wing. "Are these planes safely designed, safely built, and safely maintained? I am directly involved as an air traveler." Or take just one last example. Every one of us knows, either through experience as a lawyer, conceivably through experience as a victim and certainly through experience just reading the newspapers, that toxic shock syndrome is a major public health problem in the country. And toxic shock syndrome is a bacterial infection that particularly afflicts women, but is not limited to women. And it can cause death and is always very serious and the legal issue is what causes it. And, as it comes up in litigation, the contention of the victim will be that what caused it is the use of a tampon, a sanitary napkin of a certain design and that produced the bacterial infection. And these cases are all over the country. There are hundreds, if not thousands, of them. And do you see how it's not just this plaintiff and this defendant who are involved? Every woman who uses tampons of this kind or conceivably anybody, because males occasionally come up with the disease, feels directly involved because you want to know what causes it so that we can do something to control it.

AIDS has not yet hit the courtroom, but it will before long. It's going to be the next plague upon us and, obviously, everybody is going to have to worry about AIDS because every one of us, apart from sexual habits or whatever, is potentially at risk. So when the public is involved, there will be a public response to what the public perceives to be the problem—a problem which presents itself in this lawsuit, but which goes beyond the four corners of the lawsuit. And when the public cries out for something to be done, when the public does respond, what can the public ask for? Well, within the realm of reason, all the public can ask for is an investigation. We want an investigation. We all know it from newspaper editorials. What caused the skywalk to collapse? Why did the DC-10 crash? What is the cause of toxic shock syndrome? Or do something about AIDS. Government, do something. We read about it every day today. Put money into research. Find out what causes it so that ultimately we can come up with a preventive or a cure.

The consequence of that public outcry will be that government does do something. Whatever the level of competence, we're not talking about that now. But ultimately government does something.

It conducts an investigation and produces a report. The investigation bears fruit in the form of paper and on the paper will appear the report of the investigation. And that investigation or that report of the investigation will always be in two parts. I mean, you may dress it up all you want, you can make it as complicated as you want, but when you boil it down, it's in two parts. The first and longer part adds up to this is what we did. Here's the investigation that we conducted. And the second part, sometimes one page long, is here are our conclusions. The skywalk collapsed because . . . the engine fell off the wing of the airplane because . . . the likeliest explanation for toxic shock syndrome is . . . and so on down the line.

All right. Now back to the courtroom. You are a lawyer trying a skywalk collapse case, a DC-10 case, or a TSS case. Whether you're the proponent or the opponent, the issue is really the same. It just depends upon how you shape the issues. But for convenience, let's look at it from the viewpoint of the proponent. You are helped in this case by the investigative report and specifically by the conclusions. For example, you're trying a toxic shock syndrome case. You represent a woman who came down with this disease. You are suing the manufacturer of the tampon that she used. Your legal theories are the standard theories you find in a product liability case. The ground of contention, the battlefield, if you will, is causation.

It's agreed she came down with the illness. It's agreed she used the tampon, but did the use of the tampon cause the illness? And here you've got a governmental report and it says that the explanation for TSS or the likeliest explanation is the use of these tampons. If you are the plaintiff, boy, do you want that report in evidence. And I can think of at least three reasons why you want the report in evidence. First, it's inexpensive. Instead of the hundreds or thousands of dollars it will cost to produce an expert, you've got a couple of dollars in xeroxing and there it is. Second, there is an actual report of the kind I am talking about and it's a report of the Center for Disease Control in Atlanta, Georgia, an official agency of the United States Government and the world's leading center for research in epidemiology. What a wonderful thing to have a document bearing the imprimatur of the United States Government before the jury—a document that comes out on your side of the case. And third, once again, I've got to note that I say it quietly, confident it will not go beyond these four walls because someone who's not a lawyer might misunderstand me. You want that document in evidence precisely because it cannot be cross-examined. You get it in and the opponent can't possibly ask it any questions. If the opponent wishes to ask questions of someone, it's the opponent who must go to the time, trouble, and expense of causing the expert from the Center for Disease Control to come to court. That's a wonderful burden to shift to your opponent. It is a wonderful advantage to have that your evidence cannot be cross-examined. And so, obviously, if you are the plaintiff in that TSS case, you want that report in evidence.

Now, let us think together. The report is hearsay. It's an out-of-court statement and you will be offering it for no purpose other than proving the truth of what it asserts. The first part of the report—these are the investigations that we at the Center for Disease Control conducted—are essentially inconsequential. Nobody's going to fight about that, but that doesn't do much for you in the case. It's the conclusion, the second part, that you want and the conclusion of the actual report says, "The likeliest cause for the epidemic of TSS is the use of this kind of tampon." That's what you want in evidence and you want it in as hearsay. Now I will be referring to the Federal Rules of Evidence. I know that South Carolina has not adopted the state version of the Federal Rules of Evidence, but I should think that your cases in South Carolina pretty much approximate what you'd find under the Federal Rules of Evidence, but please understand that I make no representations about the state of the law of South Carolina. Indeed, I make no reference whatsoever to the law of South Carolina for the excellent reason, ladies and gentlemen, that my ignorance of the law of South Carolina is exceeded only by that of some of you in this room. But I do know a little something about the Federal Rules of Evidence and so I shall refer to them, leaving it to you to translate to what you need when you're in a state courthouse.

Is there a rule against hearsay in the federal courts? Well, of course—Federal Rule 802—hearsay is not admissible with exceptions. Is there an exception that may help us get this governmental report in? There sure is. Look at Federal Rule 803, subdivision 8, the exception for governmental reports. And that's a fairly long provision and much of it is not relevant to our purposes here. But there is one part of it that obviously bears upon our case, our toxic shock syndrome case. It's 803, subdivision 8, sub-subdivision c. And what that says, using the key words of the rule, is that yes, a governmental report such as the Center for Disease Control Investigative Report, is admissible as an exception to the rule against hearsay insofar as it sets forth factual findings. That's the word or the phrase, factual findings. Well, is the conclusion, which is what we're interested in, a factual finding? Remember, the likeliest explanation for the epidemic is the use of this kind of tampon. Is that a factual finding? Well, if you look at it at this instant, it sort of looks like a fact, but if you look at it in the next instant, it looks like an opinion. It's kind of somewhere between the two. So not finding an answer to our particular question in the text of the Federal Rules, we've got to go to the cases.

You go to the cases and you will find that the original and still most important case construing the term factual finding as used in 808(8)(c) is the *American Export* case[6] decided by a U.S. District Judge in the Southern District of New York back in 1977, two years after the Federal Rules went into effect. He was dealing with the investigative report of the Coast Guard looking into an accident that occurred in New York Harbor. The report was very complicated in its nature, but when you boil it down, it fits the form or the format I have suggested to you. First part—this is what we at the Coast Guard did. Second part, our conclusion—the cause of the accident was blah, blah, blah.

Judge Tenney, the judge writing the opinion, says that the conclusion, which in his case, as in our toxic shock syndrome case, is what really is the ground of contention. That conclusion is not a factual finding as used by the draftsmen of the Federal Rules of Evidence. Judge

---

6. *Complaint of American Export Lines*, 73 F.R.D. 454 (S.D.N.Y. 1977).

Tenney said, Call it an evaluative finding. See, in grammatical form it's a fact, but it's really an opinion. It's an evaluation based upon what the Coast Guard as the investigating agency did. And said Judge Tenney, Simply construing the Federal Rules in accordance with Congress's intent, as I understand it, it was not Congress's intent to permit evaluative findings to come in as factual findings under 803(8)(c). So under *American Export*, we the plaintiff are out of luck and if you're the defendant you're in luck. Your objection to the receipt of the conclusion of that Center for Disease Control investigative report will be sustained.

Now, if that's all there were to say, I wouldn't have spent this much time on it. But there's a good deal else to say. The *American Export* case, though it's a district court opinion, had come to be understood as stating federal law and, as a matter of fact, it was followed in a good many state courts as well. Evaluative findings are not admissible as part of the official investigative report. It had been cited and followed by U.S. courts of appeals, which normally do not like to cite and follow district court opinions. If you look at Shepherd's or Lexis, you will find hundreds of references to it.

But then last year the Fourth Circuit decided the *Ellis* case.[7] And if I were practicing in this field *Ellis* is an opinion that I would carry in my briefcase at all times. The *Ellis* case is, in fact, the toxic shock syndrome case that I've been using as an example or hypothetical. The plaintiff is a woman who came down with TSS. She did not die, but had serious injuries. She sues the defendant, claiming that they manufactured the tampon which caused the injury. Did she use the tampon? Well, of course—that's not what we're fighting about. Did she come down with the disease? Of course—we're not fighting about that. What we're fighting about is causation. The plaintiff has a report of the Center for Disease Control, an official agency of the United States Government and, as I said a couple of minutes ago, the world's leading center for epidemiological research. The Center for Disease Control, responding to public outcry about this TSS epidemic, conducted an

---

7. *Ellis v. International Playtex Co.*, 745 F.2d 292 (4th Cir. 1984).

investigation and concluded in its official report that the likeliest explanation for TSS was the use of this kind of tampon.

"I offer it in evidence," says the plaintiff. "Objection," says the defendant, "803(8)(c) is the relevant Federal Rule, but it's as construed in *American Export* and evaluative findings are not admissible." "Objection sustained," says the district judge, "we must follow *American Export*." The plaintiff is non-suited. The plaintiff has no other evidence on causation, complaint dismissed. Up we go to the Fourth Circuit and the Fourth Circuit reverses. This is a holding in unmistakable terms. The Fourth Circuit reverses because the Center for Disease Control report insofar as it sets forth that evaluative finding about the likeliest explanation for TSS is admissible and a judge will be reversed for excluding it. This is a departure from *American Export*. This is a new venture under the Federal Rules of Evidence and under the Common Law of Evidence and a very important one.

Among its reasons, the court says, first, the Center for Disease Control is the world's leading epidemiological research center. If the CDC, the Center, was willing to publish this report as an official CDC report, was willing to put its imprimatur on it, it's about as reliable as anything you're going to get in this world. And in any event, it's the best there is. There is no better evidence than this. That being so, it is not unfair to shift the balance to the defendant or the burden to the defendant of causing the scientist to come to court and respond to questions if the defendant wishes to ask questions. We will give the plaintiff the benefit of the exception to the rule against hearsay. I've already referred to my cloudy crystal ball. Looking into my cloudy crystal ball, I would say that the *Ellis* case is going to be followed elsewhere. That's why I would carry it in my opinion and in my briefcase and as long as it helps me, of course, I would urge upon a court that *Ellis* ought to be followed, that evaluative findings ought to be admissible as exceptions to the rule against hearsay.

Now, by way of a parenthesis, let me point out some problems that lawyers are going to have to deal with—not involved in the *Ellis* case, but that are obviously on the horizon. In *Ellis* the investigating agency was the Center for Disease Control, which is unquestionably the world's leading epidemiological research outfit. Their professional credentials are beyond cavil and their impartiality may be taken for granted. What do you do when the investigating agency is—and I mean to tread on no toes and I don't want to have an argument with anybody—but what do you do when the investigating agency is the county sheriff? And the conclusion, the evaluative finding is that your client is a speeder? What do you do when the investigating agency is—this is a real case presently in litigation in the federal court in New York—is the Federal Trade Commission? And you know what the conclusion is? That a certain line of commerce has been monopolized and your client is charged with being the monopolist. It's a civil case, so you know, you don't have to be concerned with the problems peculiar to criminal matters. Is that evaluative finding, that there is monopolization in such and such a line of commerce, admissible as part of the Federal Trade Commission investigative report? Which means that you can't cross-examine it. Is that what *Ellis* means? And, although it's unseemly in a way, you know what the argument that's going to be made is? The Center for Disease Control is an outfit staffed by people who, for the most part, graduated in the upper 20 percent of their medical school classes. The Federal Trade Commission is an outfit populated for the most part by lawyers who graduated in the lower 20 percent of their law school classes. And that makes the difference. The Center for Disease Control is reliable, the Federal Trade Commission is not. You see what I mean by an unseemly argument. You don't feel comfortable making such an argument, but obviously such arguments are going to be made because the *Ellis* court itself relies so heavily on the credentials of the Center for Disease Control. Well, obviously, we're dealing here with a brand new development. Its implications and its future direction really cannot be marked out with any precision.

Let us turn now to the second of the two means for putting evidence before the jury. Remember, my point is that the courts will focus on those means rather than on the evidence itself, hence getting away from the approach I have called scientific evidence vel non. The second means is the witness, the expert witness, and the approach, I guess, would be this. We have well-settled rules for determining whether an expert may testify. Assuming that under those rules this expert may testify, the law should not concern itself one bit with what the expert tells the jury. If what he tells the jury about involves scientific evidence, so be it. But the law does not have to analyze that scientific evidence or deal with it except insofar as it deals with the propriety of this expert testifying. In short, we get away from scientific evidence vel non, we avoid the problems of the *Frye* test, and we put in its place the well-settled rules with regard to the propriety of an expert testifying. And we can hit the highlights of those rules in the time remaining.

Highlight number one: Right at the threshold I ask, when may an expert testify? On what sort of issue is it permissible for an expert to give his opinion to the jury? Once again, referring to the Federal Rules of Evidence, the answer is as you find it in Federal Rule 702, which I would expect to be followed in any state court in the land. If the expert's opinion will assist the jury, the expert may testify. Just that. Obviously, a hospitable rule. A rule that opens the door wide to those occasions when an expert may testify.

So I guess we should imagine ourselves in the shoes of a judge here. You say to yourself not is this scientific evidence admissible under five blah, blah, blah. You say to yourself, the evidence, whatever it may be, is going to come in through the testimony of this witness. Now this witness is the kind the law calls an expert. First, is the witness giving an opinion that may assist the jury? If the answer is no, he doesn't testify. If the answer is yes, we go on to the next issue as we will in just a moment. Though Federal Rule 702, ladies and gentlemen, was written as a kind of grant of admissibility, a charter expanding the occasions when an expert may testify, there is, I believe, a developing trend among federal judges that I want to talk about.

Now, once again, I've got to tell you I can't cite you to anything. But for my sins I spend a fair amount of time sort of in groups of federal judges, various educational groups and things of that kind. I'm not a federal judge myself, but there I am with federal judges and, once again, since it's all in the family and it's not going to go beyond just the group of us, federal judges, like judges generally, like to adjourn to the bar at the end of the day. I don't mean the bar association, I mean the bar. And after the third or fourth martini, everybody's kind of relaxed and, you know, what do you talk about except the one thing you have in common, which is law business as conducted in the federal courts.

On the basis of such conversations, which I'll grant you are two or three or four martini conversations and, therefore, must be taken perhaps cum grano salis, I put it before you as worth considering that some federal judges are taking a new look at Rule 702. Rule 702 appears to be a grant of admissibility. The expert may testify if it will assist the jury. That doesn't demand very much. That's a very low threshold requirement. But you know what some federal judges are doing? They're saying, wait a minute, this can be read and applied as a kind of way of keeping experts off the stand. It can be regarded as a blank check by which a judge is given authority to reduce the number of occasions when an expert testifies. So that if the judge is prepared to rule something as follows: "I think that this expert's testimony is going to be such gobbledygook presented in such impenetrable jargon to the jury that it can't possibly assist the jury, that it can only obscure what the jury does, I will keep the expert off the stand. I will simply not allow the expert to testify." So you see what we do? We don't waste time listening to the gobbledygook. We don't leave it to the good sense of the jury to ignore this garbage. Instead the judge takes control right at the outset and says the expert may not testify because his testimony is such a mishmash that it can't possibly help the jury. I know of a number of federal judges who have so ruled, but I'm not aware that any of those rulings has been mentioned on appeal or has yet gone up on appeal, so you just don't know whether an appellate court is going to agree that the federal judge, district judge has the authority under 702 to do this. My own bet is yes, he does have that authority.

For what it's worth to you, each and every instance in which a federal judge has so ruled has involved a certain kind of expert. You know who? The statistician or the economist whose testimony is particularly obnoxious in the sense that it's absolutely opaque. And yet, if you study it long enough, you get the sense that all the expert is doing is talking about matters of common sense, but dressing it up in this absolutely convoluted jargon so as to impede the jury's ability to see what common sense suggests. And so federal judges are saying, look, juries have lots of common sense. Let the lawyers argue common sense to the jury and we don't need the jargon from the expert to obscure things, so I will not permit the expert to testify. Be aware that this may be a developing trend among federal judges and we must move along.

The next issue that is likely to arise is the issue touched upon but not fully developed in the *Bean* case.[8] And it's kind of a striking one and in its way teaches volumes about the utility of this approach to scientific evidence focusing on the expert, rather than the original approach focusing upon scientific evidence vel non. Start with the general question: Upon what may the expert rely? Assume that the expert's opinion does deal with something that will help the jury. So we get over the threshold requirement. Now the expert has an opinion and he bases it upon A, B, and C.

What does the law say about A, B, and C? And we must distinguish here between the common law rule, the rule that I dare say is followed in the state courts of South Carolina and the ruling you'll find under the Federal Evidence Rules. The common law rule was and is as follows: The expert can rely upon whatever he or she wishes, so long as everything upon which the expert relies is in evidence. The expert may rely upon A, B, and C, but each of A, B, and C must be in evidence. To put it the way trial lawyers usually put it when they talk shop, the expert's opinion may not go beyond the record. It must rest exclusively upon the record because, after all, the opinion is admissible because it will assist the jury. Assist the jury in doing what? In understanding the evidence. If the opinion rests upon material not before the jury, not in evidence, how in heaven's name can that opinion assist the jury?

---

8. *Bean v. United States*, 533 F. Supp. 567 (D. Colo. 1980)

So, at common law, go back to the *Coppolino* case. "Dr. Helpern, what did you find?" "I found the puncture wound on Mrs. Coppolino's left buttock." That's now in evidence. He found it, he saw it, he's testifying to it as an ordinary witness. It didn't go this way, but it could have. "Doctor, on the basis of what you've just told us about, your finding of the puncture wound, do you have an opinion as to the cause of death?" "No, I do not." At common law in Florida at the time of the *Coppolino* case, could Dr. Helpern go on to say, "But I give you the cause of death as an injection of succinylcholine chloride, basing my opinion in part upon what Dr. Umberger found"? No. Why? Dr. Umberger's findings are not in the record. They're not in evidence. That's why Helpern is excused, Umberger is put on the stand, and why we now interrogate Umberger in the manner that we described.

Take one other example. Family doctor on the stand. "Doctor, did you examine your patient?"

"Yes."

"What did you find upon examination?"

"I found red patches down her throat and spastic muscles at the back of the neck."

"On the basis of those findings, Doctor, could you come up with a diagnosis?"

"No."

"So what did you do?"

"I sent the patient to a neurologist for certain nerve tests."

"In due course did you receive the neurologist's report?"

"Yes."

"Did you read that report?"

"Yes."

"Then were you able to arrive at a diagnosis?"

"Yes."

"What was that diagnosis?"

"Objection."

"Sustained."

Why? The diagnosis rests upon red patches, in evidence; spastic muscles, in evidence; and the neurologist's findings, not in evidence. The report is hearsay, it cannot come in, the neurologist has not yet testified.

So what do we do? What was done in Florida in the *Coppolino* case. General practitioner, step down. Neurologist, step up. What did you find? Blah, blah, blah. Step down. Put the general practitioner back on the stand and say, "Now, Doctor, taking into account your findings of red patches and spastic muscles and the neurologist's findings now before this jury of thus and so, were you able to arrive at a diagnosis?" "Yes." "What was it?" And then it counts. That is the common law way of doing it. Is it cumbersome? It can be. Is it time consuming? Usually. Is it expensive? Very. Because it takes two experts instead of one.

The draftsmen of the Federal Rules of Evidence criticized the common law rule on the grounds of cumbersome-ness, consumption of time, and expense. Their view was that the expert ought to be able to testify in a manner consistent with the way in which the expert practices his own profession. He ought not to be obliged to play by the lawyer's rules. That view carried the day and you will find it expressed in Federal Evidence Rule 703, second sentence. And what does that say? It says that the expert may go beyond the record. The expert may rely upon material not in evidence with an outer limit. Of course, there's a foul line over which the expert may not go and the outer limit is that it must be reasonable for the expert to rely upon this non-record information. Reasonable. And the way federal courts have come to construe that word reasonable is a two-step process. First, is it customary in the experts field to rely upon such information and, assuming that it is, is the judge prepared to say that it's reasonable?

So back to our general practitioner. "Doctor, you found red patches and spastic muscles."

"Yes."

"Was that enough for a diagnosis?"

"No."

"What did you do?"

"I sent the patient to a neurologist for certain nerve tests."

"In due course did you receive the neurological report?"

"Yes."

"Did you read it?"

"Yes."

Just yes or no. "Were you then able to arrive at a diagnosis?"

"Yes."

"Now, doctor, in the practice of family medicine, is it customary for the general practitioner to rely upon reports received from the specialist?"

And I suppose the answer is going to be, "Yes, we do it all the time." And then you turn to the judge and say, "And Your Honor, I submit that that custom is a reasonable one." And I would expect the judge to say, "Yes, it is a reasonable custom." "Doctor, what was your diagnosis?" And in it comes, even though one of the three items upon which the diagnosis rests, namely the neurologist's findings, is not in evidence.

Let me take a moment to tick off some unanswered questions. Is Rule 703, second sentence, a grant of admissibility? Can you continue with the general practitioner as follows?

"Doctor, now what was your diagnosis?"

"Blah, blah, blah."

"And you've told us that you based that diagnosis on the neurologist's report?"

"Yes."

"Is this the report?"

"Yes."

"I offer it in evidence."

In short, 703, second sentence, represents a new exception to the rule against hearsay. Another unanswered question: Can the opponent put the report into evidence? The proponent elicits the general practitioner's diagnosis and sits down. Opponent: "Doctor, your diagnosis rests in part upon the neurologist's report. Isn't that correct?"

"Yes."

"Is this the report?"

"Yes."

I offer it in evidence and now the proponent who elicited the opinion based in part upon that report, says, "I object." Will the objection lie in his mouth? Must it be sustained? We don't know. The Federal Rules don't say and the litigation in the ten years since the going into effect of the Federal Rules does not give us the answer. Rule 703, second sentence, is very problematical, very troublesome, especially difficult for trial lawyers, but we've just got to leave it at that. We don't know the answer.

And now let's apply what you see in Rule 703 against the background of the common law to the problem in the *Bean* case. That's the case with which we began. And the *Bean* case is yet another lawsuit that turned upon scientific evidence. Remember some years ago there was a tremendous public fight about swine flu. A new strain of influenza virus had apparently shown up in the Far East and the newspapers had us believe that it was going to sweep eastward and there would be all kinds of influenza outbreaks in the United States and most of us, if not all of us, would die, and it was going to be the end of the world as we know it. So the government said, "We come to the rescue. We know what to do. We will inject everybody with swine flu vaccine and then nobody will die." And there was a certain protest about the government getting involved in this kind of thing and what finally was done is that the influenza vaccine was available to those who wanted it and there were special urgings to the very old and the very young to get it, old people and babies being especially at risk. And do you all remember the upshot? There was no new strain of virus. There was no swine flu influenza epidemic of any kind. But the vaccine that was injected into so many people produced an awful lot of illness and some death. And so there were lawsuits brought all around the country against the government under the Federal Tort Claims Act, raising various products liability theories, seeking damages for the illnesses or the death.

These cases were so numerous that they represented a considerable logjam in the administration of the law in the federal courts, so what was done was that these cases were collected together and assigned to a handful of federal judges in various parts of the country. Judge Sherman Finesilver, who is now the chief judge of the U.S. District Court in Denver, Colorado, was one of those judges and the *Bean* case is one of the cases over which he presided. Now, they're under the Federal Tort Claims Act, so they're non-jury.

The government took the following statesman-like position. Since in virtually every one of these cases, there's no doubt that the plaintiff got sick or in some instances died, and there's no doubt but that the plaintiff received the swine flu injection, insofar as liability is concerned, the issue, the ground of combat, is going to be causation. Did the injection cause the illness or the death? And the government said, "This is what we're going to do. If the illness came on within *n* days, whatever the number may be, of the receipt of the injection, we, the government, concede causation. But if the illness came on *n* plus days after the injection, we do not concede causation, the plaintiff must prove it." All right?

In the *Bean* case, the plaintiff got sick. The plaintiff had received the injection, but the injection had been given the plaintiff more than *n* days before the illness came on. So the ground of combat, the skirmish, was on the issue of causation. The plaintiff calls to the stand a scientist whose testimony in condensed form is scientific evidence testimony. I have conducted certain laboratory experiments and the results add up to causation. The details need not detain us. And Judge Finesilver writes an opinion—remember this is non-jury so everything is on the table and articulated. He writes an opinion saying this is a problem in the admissibility of scientific evidence.

Now, these are my words, not Judge Finesilver's words, but this is the decision tree of the decision. This is the computer program that the judge's mind applies. He says first, did we get a reading? Yes, we got a reading. The scientist says that the conclusion of his experiments is that there is causation. Nobody quarrels with that, that is the reading. All right? Was the test properly used, in good working order, et cetera? Sure. The glassware was clean, there was no contamination, et cetera, et cetera. I, the judge, can conclude that the test was in good working order. The real issue is the third prerequisite and observe what the judge is doing is treating it as scientific evidence vel non. He's treating scientific evidence as a problem unto itself.

The real issue is the third prerequisite, the scientific validity of these tests. And Judge Finesilver is not prepared to go with Judge Weinstein in the *Lopez* case or with the Florida Supreme Court and Judge Silvertooth in the *Coppolino* case. He says, as to scientific validity, it's *Frye*. Is there general agreement among the scientists concerned that these tests are scientifically valid? On the evidence before me, I conclude that there is no such agreement, therefore the third prerequisite is not met, therefore the scientific evidence is inadmissible. With me? Okay. The scientific evidence, not admissible, next witness. And the plaintiff says, "Your Honor, my next witness, still struggling with this issue of causation, will be the treating physician."

And listen to the testimony. "Doctor, did you treat the woman?"

"Yes."

And observe that without anybody being aware of it, we have switched from scientific evidence vel non to emphasis upon the vehicle by which the evidence comes in, namely the expert witness.

"Did you treat this woman?"

"Yes."

"In the course of treating her and thinking about the case since then, have you come to an opinion as to the cause of her illness?"

"Yes."

"What is that opinion?"

"Her illness was caused by the injection."

"What do you base that upon, Doctor?"

"I base it upon the laboratory tests that have just been ruled inadmissible."

But now we continue. "Doctor, is it customary in the practice of medicine to rely upon laboratory results whose scientific validity has not yet come to be generally accepted?" And the answer and all of us know enough about medicine to know that this is a straight answer, is yes. By and large, doctors know nothing. It is why they like to say that the practice of medicine is an art, not a science. And rather than fly absolutely blind, the doctor will grasp out for anything available, any information, no matter how flawed, simply because anything is better than nothing. And so in the really difficult and interesting reaches of medicine—you're not setting a broken bone or delivering a baby here—this is very sophisticated stuff. You rely upon these laboratory results that are published in the journals, even though their scientific validity may turn out to be worthless. It's because we have nothing better; we do it all the time. And the judge says, "I guess that's right and that seems perfectly reasonable to me. I therefore permit the second witness to give his opinion that the illness was caused by the injection, even though the opinion is based upon scientific evidence which I have just ruled to be inadmissible." Isn't that amazing, really? Seemingly inconsistent and yet perfectly consistent with the logical structures that we've been sketching out, the ruling on scientific evidence is consistent with *Frye* and scientific evidence vel non. The ruling allowing the second doctor to testify to his opinion is authorized under Federal Rule 703, second sentence, and highlights the difference you get when you focus on the vehicle, the expert witness, as opposed to what the vehicle gives you, the scientific evidence vel non.

Well, so much for the basis of the evidence. Let's talk for the time remaining about a fairly subtle issue which is raised from time to time, though not frequently, and which is characteristic, I suppose, of the kind of evidence you get from an expert working on a frontier issue such as toxic shock syndrome, such as the syndrome involved in the swine flu case, in the *Bean* case before Judge Finesilver. The issue is the requisite degree of conviction. Putting it in colloquial, if somewhat slipshod, English, how certain does the expert have to be?

The reason this will come up is that, as we all know, very few experts will profess absolute certainty. It is a commonplace among non-lawyers to say that all experts are kind of whores, prostitutes simply selling their opinion to the highest bidder. And while I kneel to none in the degree of my cynicism about the processes of the law, I must say that here we're looking at a bum rap. I don't think that experts are whores or prostitutes selling their opinion to the highest bidder. I know of many a dispute in which the experts on both sides were in perfect agreement and their professional self-respect would prevent them from taking the stand to testify to anything else. And I suspect that those kinds of disputes are not so rare. But they don't go to trial. They don't go to trial because the experts on both sides are in agreement. You may have a lawsuit commenced. There may be some poker playing to enhance the amount of the settlement or diminish it or whatnot, but there's not going to be a trial. Counsel on both sides, if at all experienced, know that there will never be a trial.

Those cases that do go to trial are those cases in which experts of equal professional standing with perfect self-respect can give you diametrically opposed opinions on the same issue. Why? Because the experts cannot be certain. If the question is where in the human body do you find the appendix, you're not going to have a lawsuit because there's no doctor in the world that will tell you anything but it's on the lower right side of the abdomen. But if the issue is what role does the spleen play in the body's defense mechanism, you're going to have a lawsuit because the doctors are not in agreement. As a matter of fact, Nobel Prizes in Medicine have been won on both sides of that question. Is the spleen a vital organ in the body's physiological defenses against bacterial infection or is it simply a vestigial organ left over from the days when we were fishes, worth absolutely nothing? That's the kind of case that goes to trial. And it's why the degree of the expert's conviction will never be 100 percent. I'm sure you've run into that. No matter how honestly the expert believes in his opinion, he's not going to present it as 100 percent.

A brief vignette illustrating it that some of you may know or know by reputation, Judge [William J.] Bauer for the U.S. Court of Appeals Seventh Circuit, sitting in Chicago. He was a state prosecutor before he became a federal judge. As a state prosecutor he prosecuted a fraud case. The nature of the fraud is that the defendant was selling shares in a business that purported to be able to turn water into gasoline. So Bauer, as the prosecutor, calls an expert to the stand, a petroleum chemist. And he says, "Doctor, in your opinion, can water be changed into gasoline?" And the expert replies, "Absolutely not, so far as I know." All right? That gets the idea across. He's pretty certain, but it's not quite 100 percent.

Now, since he's giving an opinion, it's got to be more than zero and the question the law asks is where on the scale does it have to fall? Well, how about 50 percent? 50/50. Is it possible? And every one of the handful of courts that has considered this question has said it's got to be more than 50/50. It's got to be more than a possibility. So I guess it's got to be 75 percent, the verbal equivalent of which would be it's probable. Remember, those numbers are just for illustration, don't lean on them too heavily. It's got to be probable and that is the requisite degree of conviction, that is what the law requires of the expert. He doesn't have to be absolutely sure, but he's got to be able to say that it's more than a mere possibility, that it's a probability. We don't have time to go over it, but *Ward v. Kovacs*[9] is an illustration of a court applying that rule.

Perhaps the most important lesson of what I've said in *Ward v. Kovacs* is that we lawyers have the obligation to prepare our witnesses, the experts, as to the significance of the requisite degree of conviction. You see, to a non-lawyer the words possibility and probability tend to be interchangeable. In the courtroom they are not. The expert must be prepared to say I think that my opinion is probably true, and he must understand why it's important to say probably rather than possibly. And how you bring it out, well, those are matters of courtroom technique that we don't have the time to go into.

Now, in the last year, ladies and gentlemen, I find three high courts of their respective jurisdictions that have avowedly turned their back on *Frye*. They don't overrule *Frye* as such, they say in just about these words that *Frye* is an anachronism. It is no longer necessary because in this jurisdiction from now on our approach will not be scientific evidence vel non. Instead our approach will be to focus upon the vehicle

9. *Ward v. Kovacs*, 55 A.D.2d 391, 390 N.Y.S.2d 931 (2d Dept. 1977).

by which the scientific evidence is elicited. And in these three cases that vehicle is the expert witness. And we will simply expect the trial courts to determine whether the expert may testify. Is this an issue on which an expert may testify in the first place? Is the expert relying upon things that he may rely upon? Is the degree of his conviction what the law expects of him? If so, the expert may testify and if what he testifies to is what people want to call scientific evidence, so be it, but the law imposes no particular rules with respect to that scientific evidence, so long as the determination is properly made that the expert may testify.

The Supreme Court of Oregon[10] and the Supreme Court of Wisconsin[11] and the U.S. Court of Appeals for the Third Circuit[12] have all so held within the last 15 months or so. The particular facts are not important, the point of each case is what's important and the point is what we've said—that it's not scientific evidence vel non any longer, it's not the *Frye* test any longer. Rather it's "May the expert properly testify?" and, if the answer is yes, the opinion comes in and the law need not concern itself with scientific evidence as such.

And let me spend the last minute and a half, ladies and gentlemen, pointing out a problem which has not yet come to the fore in any appellate opinion so far as I know. It's there in the trial courts. I'm sure that more than one of you in the room has dealt with this problem. And I think it will be the next stage in the story of the grappling of the law with science in the courtroom. Anyone who knows anything at all about modern science knows that for the most part the results are expressed statistically.

When the Center for Disease Control studies toxic shock syndrome, the conclusion is not that the cause of toxic shock syndrome is the use of this kind of tampon, but rather that the likeliest explanation for the cause of toxic shock syndrome is the use of this tampon and, as

10. *State v. Brown*, 687 P.2d 751 (Ore. 1984).

11. *State v. Walsted*, 351 N.W.2d 469 (Wisc. 1984).

12. *United States v. Downing*, 753 F.2d 1224 (3d Cir. 1985).

I recall, the CDC actually can quantify it that the chances are, whatever, you know, 99.8 percent that the use of the tampon causes the illness. Anyone who's familiar with the very sophisticated blood tests that are now used in fraternity rape actions and the like, that they are expressed in statistical terms. If the question is who is the father of this child, given the blood chemistry of this child, the father would have to have a certain blood chemistry. It's more than the old blood types that we studied in high school. And out of a universe of 100,000 males, only eight would have that blood chemistry. And the respondent on trial has that blood chemistry, but that's all the expert can tell you. That's the most that science can do for you. That out of a universe of 100,000 only eight will have this blood chemistry. Of those eight, only one can be the father, of course. And whether this man on trial is one of the other seven or that one, science can't tell you. In short, the law over the centuries has been accustomed to proceed in a polar fashion. Yes or no. The light was green or it wasn't green. And there are no possibilities in between.

Modern science, modern epistemology, modern philosophy tends to proceed in statistical terms. The chances are such and such that this, that, or the other thing is or is not true. The mesh between the two, how the law will adapt to this kind of statistical proof is, I would predict, the next issue the courts will need to deal with. I repeat what I said before. My crystal ball is as cloudy as the next fellow's, but I have a feeling that that is what some of you will be dealing with over the next several years and what some of our judges are going to have to cope with. How the judges will cope with it, the kinds of arguments that will be made, I really don't know. And in any event, time does not permit us to go into that.

Chapter 4

Hearsay

DEAN STEVE EASTON: This program covers a part of the law of evidence that is vital to every trial lawyer—hearsay. The program is a fabulous review of hearsay law. In it you will see many aspects of Irving Younger's background as a trial attorney and a professor. You will see from his experience as a trial attorney and a trial court judge that he focuses his attention and therefore our attention on those aspects of the law of hearsay that actually do come up in the cases that you and I try before juries and judges. You will also see Professor Younger's background as a law professor, because he does a great job of explaining the logic and the public policy or, in some cases, the lack of logic and public policy, behind aspects of hearsay law. Finally, and in some ways most importantly because it makes this program so enjoyable, you will see his background as a lover of legal history and a story teller. The stories you are about to see do a great job of explaining hearsay, but, quite frankly, they are also a lot of fun to read.

As Professor Younger explains, the law of hearsay is ancient and quite well established. There have been very few changes in the law of hearsay since Professor Younger's untimely death in March 1988. There are a couple of relatively minor changes. Professor Younger discusses the business records exception to the hearsay rule, which is codified in Rule 803(6) of the Federal Rules of Evidence. Now, in Rules 803(6), 902(11) and 902(12), there is a process by which documents can be self-certified, contain a certification from the custodian or another qualified person so that you do not have to bring a witness to authenticate the documents in some instances. Another relatively minor change involves the catch-all, sometimes referred to as the residual, exception to the hearsay rule. There used to be two catch-all exceptions—one in Rule 803 and the other in Rule 804(b). As Professor Younger notes, they were identical in language, but found themselves in those two portions of the Federal Rules of Evidence. Now they have been removed from 803 and 804(b) and put into a new rule, Rule 807, titled "Residual Exception." There was no change in the law, but if you are looking for the residual exception, now you need to look in Rule 807. In many states with Rules of Evidence. the catch-all exceptions are still in Rules 803 and 804(b).

Also, if you are involved in the trial of criminal cases, you'll want to take a look at the important Supreme Court case of *Crawford v. Washington, 541 U.S. 36 (2004).* It dealt with the confrontation clause issues involved in the presentation of hearsay evidence by a prosecutor in a criminal case. The Supreme Court cases after *Crawford* seem to change the law of confrontation frequently, so I will not attempt to summarize them here.

IRVING YOUNGER: What is it that is characteristic of a common law trial? What makes it different from a trial under some other system of law, for example, the civil law followed on the continent? And they came up with an answer and that answer, we will see, generates our topic this morning. The signal feature of a common law trial those English judges and lawyers realized is cross-examination, meaning the right of the advocate to ask questions of the witnesses called by the other side. In the civil law there is something that looks a little bit like cross-examination, but it's essentially interrogation by the magistrate inquiring after the truth. Our kind of cross-examination, common law cross-examination, is the advocate's cross-examination designed to persuade the finder of fact that the opposing witness is not worth believing.

That kind of cross-examination, to the mind of a lawyer trained in our system, the common law system, is the ultimate guarantee of reliability, the assurance of fairness. And once you've come to that perception, it's a very short step to articulating a rule of law, of evidence law. And that rule, taking it in slow steps and painting in broad strokes, would be this. If cross-examination is the signal feature of a common law trial, if to a common law lawyer cross-examination is the ultimate assurance of reliability, why it follows, doesn't it, that if you can't cross-examine it, it ought not to be received in evidence against you. In short, evidence which one side does not have the opportunity to cross-examine should not be received on the offer of the other side.

Now, of course, to say that if you can't cross-examine it, it ought not to be received, covers much too much territory. Simply as a matter of what you observe happening in the courtroom, all kinds of evidence is received, though you can't cross-examine it and no one would dream of suggesting that the inability to cross-examine is a proper objection to the evidence. Every time a tangible piece of evidence is received, for example, you can't cross-examine it because it's inanimate. But nobody would regard an objection on the ground of inability to cross-examine as the appropriate one.

So those professional cousins of ours across the water came up with a technical term to describe that evidence which will not be received precisely because of the inability to cross-examine. And the term they came up with is hearsay. We'll define it in a moment, but let's just see how it works. If hearsay is evidence which will not be received because the party against whom it's being received cannot cross-examine it, we are in a position to state the keystone rule in the law of evidence, the most litigated rule, probably, in any area of the law. The rule that will be our subject matter this morning. The rule against hearsay is simply that hearsay, to be defined in a moment, is not admissible. Hearsay, that evidence which will not be received precisely because the opponent cannot cross-examine it, is not admissible. And those four words state the rule as you will find it, for example, in the Federal Rules of Evidence, Rule 802. Hearsay is not admissible.

I understand that South Carolina is essentially a common law state when it comes to evidence. You have not adopted the Federal Rules of Evidence and the common law cases will frequently use that four word formulation—hearsay is not admissible—though some judges, inspired by a desire to be succinct, get it down to three words. Hearsay is inadmissible. And I don't hear any difference between the two formulations. A couple of years ago, standing before a class at the Georgetown Law School in Washington, I said, "Four words or three words, makes no difference to me, but I don't think you can get it down to less than three words." Instantly a young woman in the front row raised her hand and said, "I can get it down to less than three words," and I said, "Let's hear it." And she replied, "No hearsay." Perfect. It wants something in grammatical polish, I suppose, but it gets the idea across. So be it two words, three words, or four words, there you have the rule against hearsay. Hearsay is not admissible, with exceptions, to be sure, which we will come to very soon. But still, you've got to start with the rule.

Well, having started with the rule, we turn now to the task of defining hearsay. Defining it so that we can recognize it when we see it, so that we know when an objection will lie on the ground of hearsay. And just to revert a moment or two to the point I was making about not everything being inadmissible because you can't cross-examine it. Inanimate evidence, real evidence is frequently offered in evidence and yet you can't cross-examine it. Let's just be sure we understand that. Suppose the prosecutor is examining the medical examiner, the coroner in a homicide case. Many of you have been involved in such cases and you know the questioning; it's almost formulaic.

"Doctor, did you perform an autopsy on the body of the victim?"

"I did."

"In that autopsy, Doctor, did you determine the cause of death?"

"I did."

"What was the cause of death?"

"A bullet in his brain."

"Doctor, I hand you a bullet previously marked as Prosecution Exhibit 1 for identification. What is that?"

"That's the bullet I found in the victim's brain."

"Your Honor, I offer it in evidence."

Defense counsel: "I object. Hearsay."

No, no. No. No. No. The slightest instinct for how you try these cases will tell you that whatever objection defense counsel may want to make, hearsay is really not one of them. And if you were to ask him, "How can you object on the ground of hearsay?" and he were to reply, "Well, I can't cross-examine the bullet," you'd just laugh at him. Of course you can't cross-examine the bullet. But the inability to cross-examine the bullet is irrelevant. That's not what we're talking about when we refer to hearsay; hearsay is something else. Well, what is it?

The problem of defining hearsay has engaged the attention of lawyers and judges for a very long time. We can afford only two or three minutes on it, but I assure you that it's a very difficult intellectual problem. And by way of briefly sort of embodying the difficulty, let's talk about two cases. Both of them are cited in the materials. They are not famous cases, but they're memorable by way of illustration. The first of them is the *Mima Queen* case.[1] In the United States Supreme Court Reports, way back in the early 1800s, there it is at the bottom of page two. And you will forgive the very brief autobiographic note. I kind of rediscovered that case. I had never seen it cited—indeed, I did not know of its existence. And several years ago while putting together a case book on evidence, I said to myself, as law professors are wont to do in editing case books, "Let me find the earliest case in the Supreme Court in which the concept of hearsay was discussed." And, being as old as I am, I can't go to Lexis and ask the machine to do it. Indeed, given my mechanical aptitude, I know better than to even put my hand on that keyboard because I'm positive that were I to touch a Lexis keyboard, I would instantly short out the Strategic Air Command and leave us naked to our enemies. So I go to the digest. You know, the old-fashioned digest, and you turn pages and you work your way backward in time. And in that old-fashioned manner, I finally came across *Mima Queen* and the hair on the back of my neck stood up. And perhaps you will respond in the same way.

Mima Queen was a slave. She was an elderly woman whose name was Mima Queen and she brought an action in the courts of Maryland for what we would call a declaratory judgment declaring her not to be a slave, but to be free. And I was not really amazed, but surprised, to discover that there was a recognized form of action in every state of

---

1. *Mima Queen and Child v. Hepburn*, 11 U.S. 290 (1813).

the union in the days of slavery whereby a slave could bring a lawsuit for a declaration of freedom. Now, as you know, the records of the early cases in the Supreme Court were lost in a fire a long time ago, so that when you're looking at a case in 11 U.S., all you have is what appears in the volume. There are no documents to go look at in the Supreme Court Clerk's Office. Reading a little bit between the lines, it seems to me that this was probably an action brought on behalf of Mima Queen by a local abolitionist society seeking some kind of favorable ruling of law that would help other black people in a similar situation. All right. So much for the procedure.

Mima Queen brings an action asking for a declaration that she is free. What is the substantive rule applicable to such a lawsuit? It's a very easy one. The slave who brings the lawsuit must prove that some direct ancestor of his or hers was himself set free. In short, once a slave is freed, that freedom flows down to one's children, grandchildren, great-grandchildren and the like. Mima Queen's position in that trial was that her, if I remember correctly, great-great-grandfather, going four generations up the ladder, had been set free by his then owner. Now, there was no statute of frauds. A slave could be manumitted, set free orally. There was no need to have a writing. But, still, it was necessary for Mima Queen to prove by admissible evidence that her great-great-grandfather had, indeed, been set free. In attempting to carry that burden, Mima Queen called three or four witnesses, each of whom testified essentially to the same thing. And I don't have a blackboard to sketch it out, but I think I can make it clear enough.

Each of those witnesses testified in essential terms as follows: "I was told by my father that his father had told him that his father's next-door neighbor, the person who owned Mima Queen's great-great-grandfather had set the great-great-grandfather free." In short, you had people a couple of generations ago telling people a generation ago, telling people today, who told the person on the witness stand that Mima Queen's great-great-grandfather had been set free. Mima Queen lost and the abolitionist society took an appeal which ultimately went to the United States Supreme Court. And the author of that opinion was John Marshall himself. And, really, it repays study, not really because it teaches you about the law of hearsay—that's relatively trivial—but because of the insight it gives you into American history in those years.

Marshall says that we recognize that the issues in a case of this kind are troublesome and especially . . . he doesn't say appealing, but require careful consideration. He says, however, that the rule against hearsay is an established part of our law of evidence and you must stick with established rules because great property interests depend upon them. What an extraordinary expression in a case involving a human being. "Great property interests depend upon them." John Marshall says the evidence offered by Mima Queen was hearsay. Because it was hearsay, it runs afoul of the rule against hearsay. Hearsay is not admissible. Since that evidence was not admissible, there is no proof on behalf of Mima Queen to establish that key proposition that her ancestor had been set free by the ancestor's then owner. Hence, Mima Queen loses her lawsuit and remains a slave.

I cannot resist the temptation to tell you that if you go to the books and look up that opinion, after you read John Marshall's opinion, turn the page to a dissent by an otherwise totally obscure justice named [Gabriel] Duvall, who sat on the Supreme Court for 20 some odd years under the administration of John Marshall. We all know that John Marshall was a titanic personality and one did not lightly disagree with John Marshall on anything. And it took more than heroism to dissent publically from a John Marshall opinion. You're aware that there are almost no dissents in cases written by John Marshall. But Duvall writes a dissent—the only one in 20 some odd years on the Supreme Court. His only dissent and his only claim to a place in the history of American law. And the dissent is remarkable because it says in virtually these words, "I am outraged by this decision. Remember what's involved. A human being's liberty is involved and when a human being's liberty is involved, you don't worry about such concepts as hearsay and the rule against hearsay," et cetera, et cetera. So a kind of silent round of applause for Justice Duvall, but we will return to John Marshall's opinion.

He says that the evidence offered by Mima Queen was hearsay and why was it hearsay? Well, in very close to these words, John Marshall says it's hearsay because hearsay is defined as follows. And if you take the terms of the definition and match against those terms the evidence offered by Mima Queen, why you see that it's hearsay. And I'm formulating it a little bit more cleanly than Marshall does in the opinion, but I'm not distorting it. This, he says, is the definition of hearsay: hearsay is evidence which depends for its probative value upon the testimony of someone who cannot be cross-examined at this time. And that's the way you bring it about that your term hearsay covers evidence which will not be received precisely because of the inability to cross-examine. If it depends for its probative value upon the credibility of someone who cannot be cross-examined, why then it's hearsay.

Now, what was the evidence? The evidence, of course, was the evidence of what the owner of Mima Queen's great-great-grandfather said 40 or 50 years ago. And upon whose credibility does the probative value of that evidence depend? Well, it depends upon the owner's credibility 40 or 50 years ago, plus the neighbor who heard him say it, plus the person to whom the neighbor told it, plus that person who was told it by the . . . and so on, working through the chain. So we see that the probative value of the evidence depends upon the credibility of three, four or five other people. Those people are long since dead. In any event, they have not been called to the stand at this trial. Hence, there has been no opportunity on the part of the adversary to cross-examine. Hence, it's hearsay.

And there, teased out of John Marshall's opinion in the *Mima Queen* case, you have what I like to call the complicated definition of hearsay, because it is complicated. It's hearsay if it depends for its probative value upon the credibility of someone who cannot be cross-examined. And the reason a complicated definition is not entirely useful for us is a reason that's worth spending just a moment giving voice to.

I am kind of fascinated by the law of evidence as opposed to the law of something else because the law of evidence is peculiarly applicable to the courtroom, and I love the courtroom. Rules of evidence are not really there for manipulation by appellate lawyers and law review commentators. The rules of evidence are the working rules of the game that we trial lawyers play in the courtroom and, as one trial lawyer talking to other trial lawyers, I know that I tell you nothing that comes as a surprise. The tensions, the pressures of the courtroom, the complexity of what's going on when you try a case are so great that you just don't have the psychic wherewithal for complicated concepts and complex definitions. Now you all know that.

You're sitting there on the verge of collapse. Your chief witness is being examined or the chief witness on the other side is being examined by your opponent. And suppose your opponent is one of those lawyers, who, like me sometimes, prefers to go at a machine gun clip and the questions are coming out like that. Question, question, question. And you're sitting there with the drops of perspiration running down your face and you're saying to yourself, "Should I object? Should I object? Wait a minute, that question maybe calls for a hearsay answer. Let's see, John Marshall come to my rescue. Does the evidence depend for its probative value upon the credibility of someone who cannot be cross-examined? Yep, it does. I object." What do you mean object? The witness has answered the question, the examination has been completed and the next witness is on the stand by the time you get finished applying that complicated definition. And as an alumnus of the Judges Union, permit me to break one of the union rules—secrecy—and tell you that even for the judge who has to pass upon the objection, complicated definitions are really not very helpful.

You see, the judge can take all the time he wants. You know, the judge can say, "Hold it, hold it," and think about it. Well, let's see what happens. The judge is sitting there, it's 3:30 in the afternoon, he's had a wonderful several glasses of lunch. He's kind of resting easily. I don't suggest that he's asleep. Of course not—no trial judge is ever asleep. But occasionally the trial judge is not functioning on the one cylinder God gave him. You know, he's sort of taking it easy when you disrupt the even tenor of the afternoon with an "I object!" "What's the matter?" says the judge. "Object, it's hearsay." The judge says, "All right, hold off. Does it depend . . ." So if it's going to take you five seconds to apply that definition, it's going to take His Honor the same five seconds and while His Honor is thinking about it, the jury is sitting there. And what's the jury saying to themselves? What's wrong with the judge? Why doesn't he talk? Right? And once a jury starts asking themselves questions like that about the judge, why the judge is never going to become governor, is he?

So, you see, for somewhat other reasons that complicated definition will not work for the judge, just as it will not work for us, the working lawyer, down there in the trenches. And, curiously, that perception came to the barristers of England not very long after the hearsay rule was first articulated and that complicated definition, which shows up in John Marshall's opinion, began to be worked out by the English judges. The barristers of England, the trial lawyers of our live bar across the water, recognized, as we all recognize, that while there may be much to be said for a rule against hearsay, there's a great deal to be said against the complicated definition. And so those barristers said to themselves something very much like this. Is it possible to come up with a definition of hearsay that will cover the field, that will describe the evidence you mean to exclude because of the inability of the adversary to cross-examine it, but which will have a kind of mechanical ease and certainty of application? Rather than the complex definition which, as we see, is simply too slippery to be effective in the courtroom. And in a little while those barristers in England managed to come up with what they thought was a definition just as accurate, just as theoretically precise as the complicated definition, but which had the ease and certainty of application of sort of 2 + 2 = 4, because that's what you need when you're trying a case. When I'm trying a case, I guess I can manage 2 + 2 = 4, but go beyond that and I'm pretty much helpless. I just don't have what it takes up here to deal with complicated issues while a trial is going on.

Now, the mechanical definition that those English lawyers came up with is the definition that has occupied the terrain. This is the definition that you will find in every modern hearsay case. It is the definition that you will find in every modern codification—the Federal Rules of Evidence, the Uniform Rules of Evidence, the Model Code of Evidence. And in just about these words, it goes as follows: Hearsay is the evidence we mean to exclude precisely because of the inability of the opponent to cross-examine. Hearsay is an out-of-court statement offered to prove the truth of what is asserted in the statement. Observe, then, that the definition is in two parts.

First, it must be an out-of-court statement. And that's very easy. And don't make it more complicated than it need be. An out-of-court statement, the cases aren't uniform in holding, is simply anything other than what this witness says from this witness stand in front of this jury right now. Anything else is an out-of-court statement. That it's in writing doesn't matter. That it was under oath doesn't matter. That it was in a different courtroom before a different judge and jury last week across the corridor doesn't matter. If it's not from this witness stand right now, it's an out-of-court statement.

But not every out-of-court statement is hearsay. That is the curve ball to watch for. And at least in the jurisdictions in which I practice, many judges, especially older judges, don't seem to understand this and you've got to get it into them. An out-of-court statement standing alone is not hearsay. It becomes hearsay depending upon its relevance. See the subtle interplay between relevance and hearsay? Relevance simply means that evidence is offered to prove something. Here's an out-of-court statement. What is it being offered to prove? Until you answer that question, you cannot answer the question, "Is it hearsay?" If the out-of-court statement is being offered to prove one thing in the universe of possible relevances, then it's hearsay. And what is that one thing that it's being offered to prove the truth of what it asserts? If the out-of-court statement is being offered for any other purpose in the world, it may or may not be admissible in evidence depending upon all the rest of the law of evidence, but hearsay will not be the applicable issue.

The other case[2] is a very obscure New York state case and there are probably hundreds, if not thousands, of cases like it in the books. But it illustrates the difference. In that New York case what you had was a criminal prosecution. There is a policeman on the stand and in simple, but not distorted, terms the policeman says, "I was present at the line-up and at the line-up, the victim of the robbery or the mugging looked at the four or five people standing there," and there's no distracting factor here. Assume it's a fair line-up and et cetera. We just focus on the hearsay issue. "The victim," says the policeman on the stand, "pointed at the number two man, who is the defendant in this case, and said, 'That's the man who robbed me.'" Out-of-court statement? Well, sure, it's an out-of-court statement. It's the policeman telling you what the victim said in the station house when the line-up was conducted last year. And what is the relevance of that out-of-court statement? It's being offered to prove the truth of what it asserts. The prosecutor says, "I'm offering it to prove that the defendant committed the robbery," therefore it's hearsay. But the victim, the out-of-court declarant, was sitting in the front row, had testified in the course of the trial, and was available to be recalled to the stand on the request of anybody and, certainly, upon the request of defense counsel if defense counsel had said, "I wish further cross-examination of the victim." Do you see that under John Marshall's definition that's not hearsay? Because the evidence, the statement in the station house, "That's the man," depends for its probative value upon the credibility of whom? The credibility of the victim. And the victim can be cross-examined just by asking, "Please take the stand again." But under the mechanical definition, it's hearsay and it's the mechanical definition, I repeat, that has occupied the field. It's the definition that you will find in the codifications and in all of the modern cases.

---

2. *People v. Michael J.*, 387 N.Y.S.2d 875 (App. Div. 1976).

Let's just run through three or four examples to make it clear and then we will move on. And the reason I spend these additional few minutes on it is that it has seemed to me, as a law student, law teacher, practitioner and judge that whatever difficulties the law of hearsay may present, most of those difficulties will be resolved when the lawyer becomes adept at recognizing hearsay. If you're good at recognizing hearsay, everything else kind of falls into place. The difficulties arise when the lawyer or the judge just can't see that it's hearsay. All right. Example. Assume it's some kind of admiralty case. It is relevant, there are no booby traps in these hypotheticals. Just look at the question, "Is it hearsay or not?"

Witness on the stand: "I was there when the captain of the ship went on board and as the captain went on board, the captain said, 'This ship is safe.'"

Out-of-court statement? Yes. Is it hearsay? You all see that you can't tell whether it's hearsay or not because I haven't told you what it's being offered to prove. And if a hearsay objection were made at that stage and the judge were unclear in his or her mind as to what it's being offered to prove, the judge, assuming good judicial craftsmanship, should say to the proponent, the lawyer offering that evidence, "Counselor, what are you trying to prove?" Then you listen to the answer, that gives you the relevance of the out-of-court statement and permits you to decide one way or the other whether or not it's hearsay.

For example, "Your Honor, I am trying to prove," says the proponent, "that this witness on the stand who heard the captain say, 'This ship is safe,' therefore believed that the ship was safe." Is that hearsay? No. Why? The out-of-court statement is not coming in to prove the truth of what it asserts, that the ship is safe, it's coming in to prove something else. What? Something about the state of mind of the one who heard the statement. Remember, we have assumed that that state of mind is relevant. The statement may not be true, but the inability to cross-examine the captain is beside the point. The captain made the statement. Whether or not he knew what he was talking about, it induced the captain's hearer, the one who is there to listen to the statement he made, to believe that the ship was safe. Therefore, not hearsay.

Witness on the stand: "I'm the captain. The ship was unsafe."

"Captain, when you went on board, didn't you say the ship was safe?"

"Well, yes, I did, but I was fooling or didn't know what I was talking about," et cetera. Right? So he acknowledges the prior inconsistent statement. At common law do you have a hearsay problem? No. Why? You've got an out-of-court statement. Yes, the captain's own out-of-court statement, but it's not coming in to prove the truth of what it asserts. What is it coming in to prove? Something about the credibility of the captain. Namely, that he's not worth believing because he says one thing today and another thing tomorrow. The relevance of the statement, then, is to discredit the one who made the statement, not to prove the truth of what is asserted in the statement.

Now, a somewhat subtler one. Same witness, same testimony. "I, the witness, heard the captain say, 'This ship is safe.'"

"Objection. Hearsay."

"Counselor, what are you trying to prove?"

Response: "Judge, I'm trying to prove that the captain, the one who made the statement, therefore believed that the ship was safe." Assume that the captain's state of mind is relevant. Is it hearsay? And there are two different analyses and one is not better than the other, each is acceptable. It's a matter, really, of taste, of aesthetic style. The two analyses lead you to different conclusions and yet both are correct. And that should not trouble any lawyer who has long since learned that the law is nothing more than an infinitely flexible set of methods for devising arguments. The law doesn't give you the right answer to anything. There are other things to give you the right answer.

All right. How would you argue that it's not hearsay? The out-of-court declaration is this ship is safe. The out-of-court declaration is not being offered to prove that the ship is safe, but it's being offered as circumstantial evidence of the state of mind of the speaker, the one who made the statement, that he believed the ship to be safe, otherwise he would not have said, "This ship is safe."

And if you don't see it, here's another hypothetical illustrating that very same principle and I think it'll be very clear indeed. A lawyer wants to prove that A dislikes B. Witness on the stand: "I heard A say to B, 'B, you're a son of a bitch.'" Out-of-court statement? Plainly. Hearsay? Obviously not. Why? Not offered to prove the truth of what it asserts. Not offered to prove something about B's pedigree or the state of his parents' marriage or anything of that kind, but rather to prove circumstantially the state of mind of the speaker, the one who made that statement—namely, that he dislikes the person he's calling a son of a bitch. So it's not hearsay.

Alternative analysis, rather more elegant. Also more complicated and for that reason, perhaps, to be disfavored. As a matter of English usage, when the captain says, "This ship is safe," that being something not subject to direct perception, what he really is saying is, "I believe that this ship is safe." But it's a commonplace of the language that we understand "I believe that." You don't have to include that; it's understood. Reframing the statement then so that it says exactly what it means, the out-of-court declaration is, "I believe this ship to be safe." What is it being offered to prove? Exactly that. Now it's hearsay because the statement proves or is offered to prove exactly the truth of the matter asserted in the statement. And it may well be admissible under an exception to the rule against hearsay, but the analysis is very different, we see, in the second example when you contrast it with the first example.

That's all that time will allow on recognizing hearsay, let's turn now to the issue generated by my third example, I guess it was. The captain on the witness stand says, "The ship is safe."

"Captain, did you not say on such and such an occasion that the ship is unsafe?"

"Yes, I said it, but I was fooling around or drunk. I've changed my mind or whatever."

Out-of-court statement by the witness. At common law we said no hearsay problem because the out-of-court statement is offered to prove something about the credibility of the captain, the one who made the statement. It's not being offered to prove the truth of what it asserts. That simple hypothetical has given judges and law professors and people concerned with evidence generally more trouble than any other issue in the law of hearsay and arguably in the entire law of evidence. If ever you have occasion to look into it, the label you will commonly find on this problem is the evidentiary status of the extrajudicial, meaning out-of-court, statements of witnesses. You see what you have? You've got a witness on the stand and what is offered is an out-of-court statement by this witness. And this witness is answering questions. He's not taking the fifth or pleading some other kind of privilege or claiming loss of memory. He is answering questions. Which version is the truth? The jury will decide, but [the witness is] being responsive.

Now, if you apply the complicated definition, you come to the conclusion that it's not hearsay, because the out-of-court statement depends for its probative value upon the credibility of the one who made the statement and that, sticking with my example, is the sea captain on the witness stand answering questions. So the opponent is not being deprived of the opportunity to cross-examine. Shouldn't it then be received either as non-hearsay or, if you want to stick with the simple definition, call it hearsay, but receive it under an exception—an exception you might say for hearsay statements by those who are now witnesses who are available for cross-examination? This problem has engendered more difficultly than any other single problem in the law of hearsay. Judges and lawyers have cracked their brain over it. Many judges and lawyers get it wrong. But it's inexcusable to get it wrong, because the right answer is clear in the cases.

And I think the easiest, most efficient way for me to make it clear is to talk about three federal cases that lead to the provision you will find in the Federal Rules of Evidence on this issue, but contrast those cases with the common law generally, which I take it for granted is the law that would be followed in a state court here in South Carolina. The *Biener* case[3] is a federal case, but it precedes the Federal Rules of Evidence and represents a judge applying the common law rule as of 40 some odd years ago, the time of the *Biener* case, or today in a jurisdiction which has not adopted the Federal Rules of Evidence. I like the *Biener* case because it's a picturesque illustration of a principle that's sometimes hard to picture in one's mind, but is not otherwise a celebrated case, so it has a certain freshness to it. As you will gather from its style, it was a federal criminal prosecution. And, as one who learned the trial business, or began to learn it, as an assistant United States attorney many years ago, prosecuting criminal cases in New York, it has additional charm.

Biener was indicted in one count for violating the Mann Act. For those of you who do not know criminal work, or who do not know federal criminal work or have otherwise led a sheltered existence, I will tell you about the Mann Act briefly because it's necessary to understand the hearsay point. The Mann Act is a statute in which Congress in its well-nigh limitless wisdom said that it's a serious felony for anyone "to transport in interstate commerce a female for immoral purposes." That's the statute.

And if ever a statute were unconstitutional on its face, there it is, for no fewer than two independent reasons. First, at least to my mind, it's void for vagueness. It says "for immoral purposes." What's an immoral purpose? You know, you can go from all the way on the left to all the way on the right—a spectrum of immorality. What is intended to be proscribed by the statute? An actor cannot know. He's entitled to reasonably precise notice of what will be criminal and I say the statute is void for that reason. Other reason for its unconstitutionality: Only a female can be transported in interstate commerce for immoral purposes. Is not that statute then bad for wont of equal protection? Why can't a male—me, for example—be transported in interstate commerce for immoral purposes? Now, it seems to me that the statute should have been laughed off the books by the Supreme Court, but the Supreme

---

3. *Unites States v. Biener*, 52 F. Supp. 54 (E.D. Pa. 1943).

Court, in its limitless wisdom equal to that of Congress, many years ago rather wittily said that the statute is valid as an exercise of Congress's power to regulate interstate commerce.

So there we have it. And it is the FBI that is charged with investigating violations of the Mann Act and, at least in my day in the federal prosecution business, those FBI agents who had proved their incompetence at absolutely everything else, were assigned to the Mann Act squad. If they proved unable to investigate bank robberies, hijackings, and were sent out to Montana to guard the sheep and the wolves came and ate the sheep, then they brought them back to work on Mann Act cases.

Biener was charged with transporting a young woman for purposes of prostitution from Chicago to Philadelphia, if I recall correctly. And the young woman was a kind of helpless, uneducated, really, you know, 19- or 20-year-old girl, all alone in the world. The FBI gets her in, and I don't want to cast aspersion on the FBI, but we've all seen enough of this on movies or television, if not in the daily practice, to know what happens. The FBI says, "You're in trouble, kid. You want to go to jail?"

"No, I don't want to go to jail."

"Well, you know what you have to do?"

"What do I have to do?"

"Do you ever wash your hands?"

"Yeah."

"Can you wash one hand without washing the other?"

"No, you can't."

"Now, do you know what you have to do?"

"I guess so."

"Was Biener the guy who was transporting you in interstate commerce for . . ."

"Yes, yes, he was."

"Write that out for me." And she writes out a statement in her own handwriting that Biener did it. The salacious details need not concern us. Just Biener is guilty, that's what it adds up to. And she signs her name to it. And they say, "Okay, now you're free to go and we'll call you when we need you for the trial." And in my mind's eye—obviously, you don't have this in the opinion—I see her walking out of the courthouse and she says, "I'm free to go, but where do I go? I have no place to go. In my whole life, only one man has ever been good to me—Biener." So she goes to the telephone booth and calls Biener. Fade out.

Fade back in. Time to try the case. There's Biener sitting there in the chair reserved for the defendant and the prosecutor calls his only witness—the little girl. And, as one who has been there, you know what you do. She's 19 years old—you have her in a long skirt and a nice white blouse, just a touch of subdued color at the neck. And she takes the witness stand and she looks like a kid right from a high school graduation. He said, "Do you know that man, Biener, over there?"

"Yes, I do."

"Did he ever transport you in interstate commerce for immoral purposes?"

"No," says she. The prosecutor now goes like what? See, these are in the old days before the Federal Rules, when to impeach your own witness, you had to show surprise and prejudice. Well, the prejudice is obvious—she says he's not guilty. And the way you showed surprise was just that way. The judge said, "Younger, I guess you're surprised." Boy am I surprised. All right. Go ahead and impeach your own witness.

Now, we pull her statement out of the file and we say, "Young woman, is that your handwriting?"

"Yes."

"Is that your signature?"

"Yes."

"Did you write that statement at the request of the FBI agents?"

"Yes."

"Did they beat you?"

"No."

"Did they threaten you?"

"No."

"Did you write that statement of your own free will?"

"Yes."

"Well, doesn't that statement say that he's guilty?"

"Yes, it says that he's guilty, but I was joking with the FBI agents."

I offer the statement. It's received in evidence and the prosecutor sits down. You can't do anything more than that. Defense counsel in the *Biener* case—bless him, retrospectively—knew his business. What do you do if you're a defense counsel? And that's the testimony on direct examination of the only witness against your client. What do you do? You know what you do. Many of you have heard me tell you what to do in those circumstances. What? Nothing. It's not that you stop—don't get started. The guy hasn't laid a glove on you, don't ask him a single question. And that's what defense counsel does. He says, "I have no cross-examination, Your Honor," and he sits down. That's it. Government rests.

"Defendant, do you have a case?"

"Nope."

"What's your motion, Mr. Defense Counsel?"

"I move for a directed verdict of acquittal. There is no evidence to give to the jury."

And this is actually what happened in the *Biener* case. The judge said, as I whisper in your ear, many judges today in federal courts and state courts would say, "What do you mean there's no evidence of guilt? Are you out of your mind? The woman at first said, 'Yes, he's not guilty.' But then that statement she gave to the FBI agent was received in evidence. The statement says that he's guilty and the jury can decide whether she's telling the truth here or whether she told the truth when she gave the statement to the FBI."

"Oh, but it's hearsay, it's hearsay."

"What do you mean it's hearsay? It's the young woman who signed the statement. She's here to be cross-examined. You didn't want to cross-examine her. If you want cross-examine her now, I'll let you do so. But that statement goes to the jury and the jury can take it for what it's worth. The jury will know what to do with this case."

Defense counsel says, "I don't want to ask her any questions and I just stand on my motion."

The judge gives the case to the jury, charges them, goes up to chambers. Again I'm reading between the lines here, but I'm sure something like this happened. And the judge walks into chambers and the steam is coming out of his ears. And there's the law clerk sitting there. Now, the law clerk was not appointed by the President, nor confirmed by the Senate. But the law clerk maybe read a couple of cases a year or two ago and he had the evidence course in law school. And so the judge with the steam coming out of his ears says to the law clerk, "The nerve of that lawyer, asking me to direct an acquittal on the ground that there's no evidence of guilt when the woman gave that statement to the FBI," et cetera. And the law clerk says, "Hey, boss, hang on. Maybe we'll pull Wigmore off the shelf." And there you see it—that simple mechanical definition of hearsay has occupied the terrain. If it's an out-of-court statement offered to prove the truth of what is asserted in the statement, it is hearsay. You don't revert to the John Marshall complicated definition. And not only is it hearsay, but perhaps this is the telling part. In no jurisdiction is there an exception that permits the hearsay to come in simply because the out-of-court declarant is now on the stand answering questions subject to cross-examination. Now do you see what the judge did? The judge gave that young woman's out-of-court statement to the jury, telling the jury in substance, "If you believe the out-of-court statement, you can take it as proving the truth of what it asserts—that Biener did these things, that he is guilty." That means it's hearsay—an out-of-court statement offered to prove the truth of what it asserts. The maker of the out-of-court statement is the young woman on the stand answering questions, but that is irrelevant. The proper characterization of her prior statement is that it's hearsay and there is no exception that will permit the hearsay to come in just because the young woman is now answering questions.

And, again, reading between the lines, the judge sees all that in Wigmore and you know what judges do in those circumstances? Judges pray. And the prayer is, "Jury, bail me out. Bail me out, jury." Comes the knock on the door; it's the bailiff. "They have a verdict, Your Honor." I'll also tell you a secret. The bailiff always knows the verdict. I don't know how, but he knows the verdict, so that the judge can be thinking on the way to the courtroom, what am I going to do? And, of course, the verdict was guilty. And the judge now did something sensational. The judge takes the stand and proceeds to dictate to the reporter the opinion, which polished up a little bit is what you will find in the Federal Supplement. It's the oral opinion delivered moments after the jury's verdict has come in.

And what that opinion says is, "I made a mistake." And I wonder if that's as rare in your jurisdiction as in mine. In my jurisdiction, judges commonly tell lawyers that the lawyers made a mistake. It's not uncommon for appellate judges to tell trial judges that the judge made a mistake. But for a judge at any level to say, "I made a mistake" is virtually unprecedented—so unprecedented that you might almost say that it's grotesque, relatively speaking, of course. In any event, this judge says, "I made a mistake because the out-of-court statement given by the woman to the FBI was admissible, yes, but not as hearsay." It was admissible solely to discredit her, so that if the jury took that statement for the maximum utility the law of evidence allows, do you see how it would work? The woman on direct examination said, "He's not guilty." This discrediting statement, at most, can persuade the jury that she's not worth believing. In your mind, then, cross out the not guilty. What's left? Nothing. Absolutely nothing. Which is why defense counsel was right when he said you can't give this case to the jury, there is no evidence to support the conclusion that he is guilty. The judge says, "I reverse myself. I should have given a limiting instruction to the jury and on the record before me there is no evidence that the jury could have used in coming to its conclusion of guilt. I therefore set the verdict aside and dismiss the indictment for failure of proof."

Now, there is what you might call a hard illustration of these common law rules that some judges and lawyers find it impossible to accept. It's hearsay, even though the out-of-court declarant is present in court, available for cross-examination, and there is no exception to the rule against hearsay at common law that permits it to come in simply because the out-of-court declarant is available for cross-examination. Now, many of you will practice from time to time in the federal courts and, in any event, it may well be that in due course South Carolina, as roughly half the states so far, will adopt the Federal Rules of Evidence. So let's take a look at the next federal case, which then becomes codified in the Federal Rules and represents as far as any jurisdiction has gone on this issue.

The next case is one of the great federal cases on evidence. It's *United States v. DeSisto*[4] and it's one that I always come to with a special enthusiasm because, I had better tell you, I am acquainted with everybody in that case. The judge is an old friend of my wife's family. The prosecutor and defense counsel are both buddies of mine at the New York bar. I had been introduced to the principal witness, whom you will be hearing about, and I even know the defendant, at least to nod to, because I used to see him in the Federal Detention Headquarters every once in a while.

The *DeSisto* case is a case of the kind that you typically get in the Eastern District of New York. I can't expect you to know New York City the way I, as one born there, would know it. But Southern District is Manhattan, Eastern District is Brooklyn and Queens. All hijacking cases are in the Eastern District because that's where the airports are, and it's where the freighters unload. To the extent that we still have passenger ships, they unload in Manhattan, but nobody hijacks human beings. They hijack loads of cameras and silk and high-tech stuff coming in from Japan and you get away with a truckload of that stuff and you've made yourself a great deal of money tax free. In New York, hijacking tends to attract the interest of the ablest members of the criminal classes. And, by the same token, the FBI assigns the best agents to the hijacking squad. That's a plum assignment in the FBI office in New York and the guys there are rather swashbuckling and they all look like movie actors and, you know, play the part accordingly.

In the *DeSisto* case a ship was being unloaded—silks or cameras, as I recall. In any event, highly valuable, readily salable merchandise.

---

4. *United States v. DeSisto*, 329 F.2d 929 (2d Cir. 1964).

And the way the industry is organized is this. You can unload the ships only at two times every 24 hours because of the tides. So they always pick the time that's sort of offbeat, when the streets are going to be empty. You don't pick rush hour. Hence, it may be, depending upon the season of the year, that you unload the ship at 2 o'clock in the morning. You load up the truck and you have a short haul driver who gets behind the wheel—he's all alone—and he will drive the truck through the streets of Brooklyn, over the bridges or through the tunnels, into New Jersey, just to get out of the stream of traffic. There he will turn the truck over to the interstate driving team, typically two men or women, who will drive the truck off to Cleveland or Chicago, wherever it goes. And then the short haul driver just comes back to pick up his next load. Well, that's what happens here. The short haul driver is a fellow universally known as Wimpy and throughout the opinion, which is by Henry Friendly, you know, formidable federal judge indeed. Even Judge Friendly calls this guy Wimpy throughout the opinion. And for those of you are too young, Wimpy was Popeye's friend in the comic strip who ate too many hamburgers, he was fat, et cetera, and Wimpy was kind of fat and liked hamburgers. Everybody called him Wimpy.

Wimpy gets behind the wheel of the truck and starts to thread his way through the curving streets of Red Hook, the neighborhood near the ports in Brooklyn, when suddenly, out of nowhere—and it's 3 or 4 o'clock in the morning—there comes the famous Oldsmobile that just suddenly appears in front of him as he's on the entry ramp to the Brooklyn/Queens Expressway. The Oldsmobile jams on its brakes, so Wimpy has to stop the truck. Wimpy is stopped and, before he knows what happens, a guy gets out of the car. He is wearing khaki pants and a T-shirt, he is undisguised, he is carrying a revolver. He jumps up on the running board, he puts the revolver to Wimpy's head and he says, "Wimpy, do as you're told or I'll kill you." Wimpy does as he's told.

The fellow says, "Give me the keys." Wimpy gives him the keys. The fellow says, "Get out." Wimpy gets out. The fellow reaches into his pocket and takes out a pair of 5- and 10-cent store sunglasses with plumber's black masking tape over the lenses and he puts that on

Wimpy. You see, these guys know their business. What he wants to do is blindfold Wimpy. You use a handkerchief and it's obvious to any passing policeman that you've got somebody blindfolded there and the hue and cry will be raised. But you put these sunglasses on him, it's August, it's summertime. To a passing policeman or motorist, it's just a guy wearing sunglasses, but it's an effective blindfold.

All Wimpy knows now is that he's put in the back of the Oldsmobile, the Oldsmobile drives off and the truck disappears. And, as a matter of fact, I'm told that it has never been found, that the merchandise was somehow gotten into the stream of commerce and the truck was probably dropped into the bay somewhere. In any event, Wimpy is unharmed. They drive him for 15 or 20 minutes to the Belt Parkway, a major commuter highway coming into New York from the prosperous suburban communities along the south shore of Long Island. The Belt Parkway was built by Robert Moses, who planted trees alongside the highway and those trees by now are very large. So the hijackers take Wimpy and they put him around a tree, handcuff him there and leave him. So there's Wimpy wearing the eyeglasses, handcuffed around a tree, and it's now 5 o'clock in the morning.

Six o'clock in the morning or so; it's broad daylight. The commuters start to drive by. One, two, five, nine. Does anybody stop? No. Why? This is New York. You never stop for anything in New York and if you notice that there's a guy around a tree, you say to yourself, "It's a tree freak, that's all," and keep going. Okay?

Finally, and this . . . my friends involved in the case have told me all of these details. Much of this is in the opinion, but some of it, obviously, will not be. Finally, a tourist driving along says that's not a tree freak, that guy is handcuffed around the tree. Let's stop to see what's up. So they stop and instantly Wimpy cries out, "Get the cops, I've been hijacked." Well, they wait a few minutes and a squad car pulls over. The squad car contains two of New York City's finest, each a veteran of 20 years on the New York City Police Department, every day of those 20 years spent cruising the highway, giving out traffic tickets. This is beyond their experience—a guy handcuffed around a tree.

So you know what they did? They went to the regular issue kit that's in the trunk of every squad car and they took out the saw and they set to work sawing through the tree. That is just what they did, with Wimpy handcuffed around it. They get about halfway through when it dawns on them that another few strokes of the saw, the tree goes over, Wimpy is still handcuffed around it and goodbye witness. So this is a job for the emergency squad.

So they put out a call for the emergency squad, which shows up in ten minutes, and they've got a hacksaw. So they cut though the handcuffs. Meanwhile, of course, the word has gone out to the FBI office, then on East 67th Street, that a hijacking has occurred. And those elite members of the hijacking squad have gotten ready. They tell the policemen, "You get Wimpy to our office, we need to talk to him at once." So they cut through the handcuffs, they put Wimpy in the back of the squad car, get the siren going and they go like a bat out of hell directly to East 67th Street where the FBI is waiting.

Now, what the FBI has done in anticipation of Wimpy's arrival is this. Since obviously this hijacking was done at a very professional level, whoever did it has a last name that ends with a vowel. So you go into the file . . . this is what they did . . . and you pull out the photograph of everybody you have whose last name ends with a vowel. You then look in the other file to see who is presently in jail. You put those photographs back in the file and the rest you lay out on the table. They bring Wimpy in and the FBI says, "Wimpy, look at these photographs and see if you recognize the guy who jumped up on the running board." Wimpy looks and he says, "That's him," and he picks out DeSisto.

They go and they arrest DeSisto who, to this day, denies any involvement. They have a line-up, a line-up whose fairness has never been questioned, and Wimpy picks out DeSisto unhesitatingly. They put Wimpy before the grand jury and in the grand jury they kind of have a photographic line-up and Wimpy identifies DeSisto. DeSisto is indicted. He is tried. Wimpy identifies DeSisto at the trial. DeSisto is convicted. It is reversed for irrelevant reasons and sent back for a retrial and it's the events of the retrial that concern us here.

At the retrial DeSisto is represented by a lawyer different from the lawyer who represented him at the first trial. And just let me impose upon your patience for 30 seconds because it is a matter of kind of, oh, I don't know, personal something or other that impels me always to say this whenever I talk about the *DeSisto* case, about the defense lawyer. In New York and I dare say in Columbia and every other town or city, there are lawyers who spend a lifetime practicing law at the highest levels of professional honor and competence. And, except for those who knew them while they practiced, nobody remembers them. They're not Clarence Darrows and they're not people whose names become part of the history books, but they represent really the best of our profession. And the man who represented Wimpy at the second trial was one of those men. He's in retirement now, but still alive, so I'll speak in the present tense. His name is Jerome B. Lewis. He's now well into his eighties. He was an assistant U.S. attorney way back when and left the U.S. Attorney's Office to make a career defending serious federal criminal cases. That's all he did. He did it with enormous professional skill. There was never a breath of scandal or disgrace attached to him and if you're defending criminal cases for a lifetime, that itself is extraordinary. And he was generally loved by everyone. One of the reasons we all loved him is that Jerome B. Lewis worked as a criminal defense lawyer against the grain. You see, if you're going to spend a lifetime defending federal criminal cases, you ought to look like Gregory Peck. Jerome B. Lewis, to begin with, insisted that he be called by his nickname, which was Jerry. So you're calling a guy Jerry Lewis there in the courtroom. Moreover, he's about 5'4" tall and he has round apple cheeks and black button eyes and a kind of Adolph Menjou mustache. So he looked like the little man on the wedding cake, which is not what you should look like if you're defending federal criminal cases. Moreover, Jerry is bald. Well, that's just nature, there's nothing to talk about there. But Jerry insisted upon wearing a toupee and that toupee could not have cost Jerry more than $1.75. And it sat there on top of his head, saying to the jury, "I am a toupee, I am a toupee, I am a toupee." And yet he tried cases and got marvelous results and was loved by everyone.

And this is what he did in this trial. Now, remember, he was not there at the first trial, so all of this came, to say, as a shocker, a bolt out of the blue, is to understate the situation. It happened within syllables, exactly as I will describe it to you. Wimpy takes the stand and on direct examination testifies to the story as I have described it to you—that the fellow jumped up on the running board and did what he did and it was DeSisto and he points him out.

Lewis on cross-examination: "When this man jumped up on the running board, was he disguised in any way?"

"No."

"What was he wearing?"

"What I've told you—khaki pants and a T-shirt."

"By a T-shirt, do you mean man's underwear, cut pretty short at the arms?"

"Yes."

"Did you get a good look at those arms?"

"I sure did. One of those arms was holding a gun to my head."

"Was there anything unusual about that man's arms?"

"No."

And at that point, Lewis turned to DeSisto and said "DeSisto, stand up. Take off your jacket." He took it off. "Roll up your sleeves." He rolled up his sleeves and there was an audible gasp in the courtroom because from wrist to shoulder, both arms were tattooed like the tattooed man in the circus. The government stipulated that DeSisto had been tattooed in that fashion at the age of 20 some odd; he was now well into his forties. And Lewis sat down. That's it. What more can you do on cross-examination? You have raised a serious question not as to whether there was a hijacking, not as to whether somebody didn't jump up on the running board, but as to whether Wimpy has identified the man who did it correctly.

Redirect examination. What's the purpose of redirect? Repair the damage, of course. And what the prosecutor does on redirect is bring out the prior identifications. Did you pick him out of the photographs at the FBI? The line-up? The grand jury? The first trial? Brings them all out. Now, just stop and in your mind see a blackboard and imagine our charting it out on the blackboard because I don't have a real blackboard here. On direct examination Wimpy testifies to circumstances, which add up to guilty. DeSisto is guilty. The cross-examination raises a real doubt as to the accuracy of the identification. Call it NG for not guilty. Now, redirect examination brings out those . . . what are they? They are out-of-court statements. Out-of-ccurt statements by Wimpy. Statements which add up to what? G for guilty, right?

Lewis, who is a good lawyer as well as a good jury lawyer, at that point, stands up and says to the judge . . . now listen to this. He says, "Your Honor, I do not dispute the admissibility of those out-of-court statements by Wimpy so long as they come in only insofar as they bear on Wimpy's credibility, either as impeaching the cross or buttressing the direct. It doesn't matter which way you take it. But they cannot come in to prove the truth of what they assert." Do you see why? Because then they're hearsay and the fact that the hearsay declarant is Wimpy, on the stand, answering questions makes no difference and if you needed a citation, it would be the *Biener* case. So all I want is a limiting instruction to the jury. I will yield to the temptation for 10 seconds to speak as a student of trial tactics. Do you really want a limiting instruction to the jury? Anybody who's tried to defend in criminal cases knows of course you don't want a limiting instruction to the jury. You think you're entitled to one, but you don't want it. Why? Because if the jury gets it, there's no error. And if the jury gets the limiting instruction, it doesn't do anything for the jury. They don't know what the judge is talking about. We barely know what the judge is talking about. So how do you expect the jury to follow that stuff? So I'm sure Lewis is saying, "Judge, I want a limiting instruction. Pray God don't give me a limiting instruction." And the judge, who is a very able judge, in due course chief judge of the Eastern District, now Senior—Judge Jacob Mishler, a friend of my wife's family—said, as did the judge in the *Biener* case, as would many a judge today, "No limiting instruction."

He writes, really, a terrific opinion. It's obvious that he finds the facts as amusing as we all do, because he spends a lot of time on them. And then he says, "The limiting instruction, if required in the first place, came too late." Because you can't really expect the jury to remember back the four or five days and apply the limiting instruction, so we decide the case as if no limiting instruction had ever been given. Hence, we've got to deal with the issue—should it have been given in the first place? We've got to assume that the jury took those out-of-court identifications by Wimpy as proving the truth of what they assert. Are they entitled to do so? Actually, to use Judge Friendly's exact words in stating the issue, "And so we reach the issue, which in a certain other case we left for another day as to the evidentiary status of prior statements by witnesses," and they affirmed the conviction. Not that there was harmless error, but that there was no error. And for a while that was taken by law teachers, myself included, as standing for the proposition that, at least in the Second Circuit, perhaps in the federal courts generally, there was an exception to the rule against hearsay for hearsay statements where the declarant was on the stand, available for cross-examination. We called it the *DeSisto* exception to the rule against hearsay.

Subsequent cases in the Second Circuit suggested that the Second Circuit did not intend so broad a holding. And, in any event, when the draftsmen of the Federal Rules set out to write a rule dealing with the evidentiary status of statements by witnesses, this is what they did. It is not coherent, it represents a political compromise, which is perfectly understandable and honorable if you remember that the Federal Rules of Evidence became a subject of political controversy in Congress. Remember, it wasn't just one of these things where Congress let it become effective in 60 days. They stopped the clock, they rewrote it and they held hearings because it became involved with Watergate, you may recall. But that's a story for another occasion. What they did was strike a compromise, and in some measure this is a codification of the holding in *DeSisto* illuminated by subsequent cases in the Second Circuit. They said that in certain circumstances out-of-court statements by a witness will be received to prove the truth of what they assert on the theory that they're not hearsay. In short, you go back to the John

Marshall complicated definition. Comes in to prove the truth of what they assert because it's not hearsay.

But what are those circumstances? They are the *DeSisto* circumstances. That's what they've come to be called. And here they are. The out-of-court statement must have been made by someone who is now available for cross-examination. Answering questions, not dead, not disappeared, not taking the Fifth, not pleading some other privilege. And, in addition, you must have at least one of the following three factors and these have been called in years since the *DeSisto* factors. Observe. It's in the disjunctive. You've got three factors, but you need any one of them.

First factor: The out-of-court statement by the witness is admissible anyway as a prior inconsistent statement to impeach or discredit. And, as part of this factor, it was under oath. Admissible anyway to impeach and under oath. Second factor: Admissible anyway as a prior consistent statement rebutting a charge of recent fabrication. In short, admissible to accredit and observe it need not be under oath. Third factor: The statement is the kind involved in the *DeSisto* case—a simple statement of identification, a that's the man kind of statement. Nothing much more than that—that's the man. If you've got one of those three . . . or here . . . get the logic of it under the Federal Rules. If you've got an out-of-court statement by a witness and you have one or more of the *DeSisto* factors—it comes in to prove the truth of what it asserts, but the proper label is not hearsay. If you've got an out-of-court statement by a witness in the federal courts today and you do not have one or more of the *DeSisto* factors, you revert to the common law position. It's hearsay if it's offered to prove the truth of what it asserts and there is no exception to the hearsay rule that permits it to come in simply because the out-of-court declarant is now on the witness stand. All of that will be found, should you need it in a federal action, in Federal Evidence Rule 801(d)(1). Rule 801(d) is captioned statements that are not hearsay and the first paragraph deals with this *DeSisto* case and what we've been discussing.

And just to wrap it up, to drive it home, a federal case, post-Federal Rules of Evidence, the *Palacios* case.[5] I suggest you follow it along and just see if, you know, you come to the answer and if you do come to the right answer, you can be confident that you now have this stuff pretty much at your fingertips.

Palacios was a very bad guy, apparently a big time narcotics importer. And the agents have been after him for a long while, but he's pretty smart and, to speak the language of the cops and robbers business, he makes sure that he never touches the money, he never touches the drugs. And if you're ever going to get him, what you need on the prosecutor's side is for someone to come over the wall—that's the expression. And if you have a different way of looking at it, what you need is a canary, someone who will take the stand and sing.

Well, they finally do get someone and you know who it is? Palacios's longtime live-in girlfriend. So far as the authorities claim, she did not, herself, participate in the conspiracy, but she was there to observe many things that happened in the course of the conspiracy, including participation in the conspiracy by her boyfriend, Palacios. I don't know what motivated her, but she sits down with the Feds and she writes out a long, long statement, a 20-page narrative in circumstantial detail of all kinds of horrific malefactions by Palacios. She signs it. They send her home. She is not found in an alley with her throat cut. Instead, at trial, she takes the stand and the U.S. attorney says, "Did you live for 15 years with Palacios?"

"Yes."

"And did you see him do all kinds of bad things?"

"Never. Never. He never so much as crossed the street against the red light."

Well, it's under the Federal Rules, you can impeach your own witness at will. We pull out the statement.

---

5. *United States v. Palacios*, 556 F.2d 1359 (5th Cir. 1977).

"Is that your statement? Twenty pages in hair-raising detail about all of his wicked deeds?"

"Yes, that is my statement. Nobody beat me, nobody threatened me. I gave it of my own free will, but it's a joke. I now take it back."

The judge gives the case to the jury. That's the only evidence of guilt, by the way, if it is evidence of guilt. The judge gives it to the jury. Observe the uncanny resemblance to *Biener*. The judge gives it to the jury, the jury finds the guy guilty, and the judge gives him 20 years, as I recall, every day of which he richly deserves, so long as we have convicted him fair and square.

Up we go to the Fifth Circuit. The Fifth Circuit says this prior statement by the woman will support the verdict if you can receive it to prove the truth of what it asserts. What it asserts essentially is that Palacios is guilty. Can you receive it to prove the truth of what it asserts? Under the Federal Rules of Evidence, only if it's admissible as non-hearsay under 801(d)(1). Is it a statement by a witness? Yes. Is the witness now answering questions? Yes, she is. She's not pleading the Fifth or anything of that sort. But you must have at least one of the *DeSisto* factors. Is this a statement admissible to impeach and under oath? It's a statement admissible to impeach, but it's not under oath. Is it a statement admissible to accredit, rebutting a charge of recent fabrication? No. Is it a simple statement of identification—that's the man? No. Therefore, you lack any one of the *DeSisto* factors. Therefore, you're back to the common law position. You can't receive the statement to prove the truth of what it asserts because that would run afoul of the rule against hearsay. That being so, there is no evidence of guilt. Verdict vacated or judgment vacated, indictment dismissed. Total failure of proof. Right. There's the special situation you would have in a Federal Rules jurisdiction.

In a non–Federal Rules jurisdiction, such as South Carolina, the common law, I assume, would be applicable and an out-of-court statement even by a witness presently answering questions is hearsay if received to prove the truth of what it asserts and there is no exception to the rule against hearsay that would justify its receipt in evidence simply because that declarant is now answering questions.

Let me turn to a wrinkle in connection with which I'm hard put to decide whether to spend 30 seconds or 30 minutes on it. It is a wrinkle that traditionally has fascinated teachers of evidence and I'm no different—it fascinates me. It's rather easily handled if you're in a Federal Rules jurisdiction. And in a non–Federal Rules jurisdiction, truth to tell, it's usually handled by being ignored. The fact that the Federal Rules deal with this issue may well have sensitized lawyers and judges to the existence of this issue. It is the issue, you may recall from your law school course in evidence, commonly described as "conduct as hearsay." The implied assertion.

Go back to those hypotheticals with which we began an hour ago. Witness on the stand. "The captain said to me, 'The ship is safe.'" Right. Same case, same issue, but change the testimony of the witness. The witness says, "The captain didn't say anything. He just went on board and sailed off into the blue." That's conduct by the captain. He went on board. Is there even arguably a hearsay objection? And at common law, the answer is it's beyond document. There is a hearsay objection. And do you remember the case that first pointed out that hearsay can be contained implicitly in conduct, in acts by people rather than statements?

Well, the case which was at least mentioned, no matter where you studied evidence and whichever book you used, was *Wright v. Tatham*. I dare say that the name strikes reverberations in your mind. It's an English case decided by the House of Lords, which, remember, sits as the Supreme Court of England, in 1838. So we're dealing with moderately ancient history here. And if you ever need *Wright v. Tatham* or want to cite it, its citation is rather special. It's 5 Clark and Finnelly 607, House of Lords 1838. 5 Clark and Finnelly 607. The English call those the nominative reporters. They go by the name of the people who actually compile the opinions. So Clark and Finnelly compiled the opinions. And the reason I say it's a special citation is that if ever you're before a judge and this issue comes up and the judge says, in the manner of all judges, "Do you have a case?" You say, "Of course I have a case, Your Honor." "What's your case?" "*Wright v. Tatham*." "Well, where do I find that?" "5 Clark and Finnelly, Your Honor." The judge always says, "Of course, of course. Right, right, right," and it kind of adds to your legend, you see, that you're citing 5 Clark and Finnelly.

For those of you who do not have a vivid recollection of it, remember that Warren Marsden had died, leaving a will, and the will transferred a great deal of very valuable property to people over here. Call them A. Now, if that will is invalid, the property passes under the intestacy laws and B over here will get the property. So it's a contest between A and B. There's no doubt that the will was signed by Marsden. So the contestants, B, say, "Yeah, he signed the will, but he lacked testamentary capacity. He was off his rocker. He didn't know what he was doing. " Hence, the will is invalid and the property passes under the intestacy laws.

The proponents of the will, the people occupying position A, offer in evidence the following celebrated items of proof. First, that Marsden's solicitor wrote Marsden a letter suggesting the terms under which a certain dispute might be settled. Second, that a curate, an ecclesiastical official, wrote Marsden a letter thanking Marsden for some favor that Marsden had done him. And, third, a cousin of Marsden wrote him a long letter recounting the details of a sea voyage from which the cousin had just returned. Remembering the years, for all I know it was the Bounty and, you know, he was there with Captain Bligh, but that's by the by.

The proponents offer that proof in evidence and the opponents object on the ground that it's hearsay. And it works its way to the House of Lords. Now, in the House of Lords, there are professional judges who are nominated by the government, or at the suggestion of the government by the Crown, to sit for life as Law Lords. That's the colloquial expression. The actual expression is Lords of Appeal in Ordinary. Isn't that wonderful? And there are whatever the number is . . . it's an odd number. It's more than 9—13 sticks in my mind, but I may be wrong.

And they are the Supreme Court of England. In theory, they sit as a committee of the House of Lords and any member of the House of Lords is entitled to sit with them. And as a committee of professional judges, they then decide the case. And in passing I say that in theory any member of the House of Lords is entitled to vote on the decision of the case. But, as you know, most members of the House of Lords have hereditary syphilis and are hardly in a position to vote on anything. And I mention that because just this year, for the first time in anybody's memory, one of these decadent, you know, son of a son of a son of a son of a son, sitting in the House of Lords, you know, with barely a 75 IQ, insists upon voting in some complicated commercial appeal that the judges have decided and nobody knew what to do. Not that his vote would have changed the result of the case, but if you allow him to vote, the next thing you know, the whole House of Lords is voting and the whole system of English justice crumbles.

Well, in England they have wonderful ways of handling this. The clerk simply didn't hear him. He just didn't hear him and so didn't write down that he was voting and only the Law Lords voted. The way they handle it is that the barristers appear in the well of the House of Lords. They argue orally, unlimited in time. There are no written briefs and the judges normally, right after the arguments, though not always so, individually announced their opinions. And instead of opinions, they call them speeches because they are delivered orally, though being barristers, they've usually got a very high degree of verbal polish.

Many of you will recall, perhaps, reading one or more of the speeches in *Wright v. Tatham*. For professional reasons, I have read those speeches perhaps 15 or 20 times. I can read them another 15 or 20 times. Indeed, I could read them every day until the day I die and I will not understand them, nor will you. They are total gibberish. All you know, though, is that the case was decided. And it is the commentators in the years since who have articulated the reason for the decision. The decision is that that evidence is inadmissible because it's hearsay. It runs afoul of the rule against hearsay. But what's the analysis?

In simple, but not distorted terms, it goes this way. Keep your eye on the evidence. The evidence that is being offered is not really those letters. They are out-of-court statements, of course. The evidence, rather, is the act of writing the letter by the solicitor and the curate and the cousin who just came back from a sea voyage. That is evidence of conduct. But the conduct implies a statement and the implied statement is being received to prove the truth of what it asserts, therefore hearsay, therefore the issue conduct is hearsay. Now, the conduct sitting down to write the letter. What's the implied assertion? Something like this.

Marsden, the person I'm writing the letter to, my addressee, is sane, otherwise I wouldn't be writing him a letter. That implied statement, "Marsden is sane," is being received precisely to prove the truth of what it asserts. Therefore, hearsay. And, as a matter of fact, in one of the speeches, one of the judges who votes with the majority to say this cannot come in because it's hearsay offers a hypothetical illustrating the principle. And you know what the hypothetical is? A ship has been lost at sea. Lawsuit on the question—was it safe. Evidence offered by the opponent of safety. The witness says, "I saw the captain go on board, taking with him his wife and children." In those days the voyage might be for three years, so the captain might well take his family. Just that—the very example I've been using with you. And the judge, the Lord of Appeal in Ordinary said, "That's hearsay." The conduct of the captain in going on board with his family implies a statement, "This ship is safe." That implied statement is being received to prove the truth of what it asserts, therefore hearsay.

There's one difficultly with *Wright v. Tatham*. Not a difficulty, but a talking point. And the talking point is this. The assertion "Marsden is sane" is one that that was not intended by the actors. There was no will contest, there was no threat of a will contest. It never entered the mind of the letter writer to be understood as saying Marsden is sane. It is the law that reads the assertion into the conduct, but it's not the actor who puts the assertion into the conduct. The line was drawn by the commentators as follows. There are two kinds of conduct—assertive and nonassertive. Assertive conduct is conduct intended by the actor to be understood as implying a statement. Examples. If you lend me your eyes, I'll give you two examples right here. Here's one. That's conduct. Well, obviously it implies a statement. Yes. Here's another. "Sir, do you see standing in this lineup the man who mugged you?" There's conduct, but it implies an assertion plainly—that's the man.

To be contrasted with assertive conduct is nonassertive conduct, such as the act of the letter writers in writing the letter to Marsden in *Wright v. Tatham.* Nonassertive conduct, the commentator said, for reasons too complex to spend time on here, ought to be treated as non-hearsay, just by definition. Just don't get involved in the implied assertion, don't get involved in the hearsay issue. Which means *Wright v. Tatham* would be differently decided by those commentators. That view that there's a distinction between assertive and nonassertive conduct carried the day with the draftsmen of the Federal Rules of Evidence. And so in Rule 801, the definitions rule at the beginning of Article 8 dealing with hearsay, you see definitions as follows. Hearsay is an out-of-court statement offered to prove the truth of what it asserts.

Assertive conduct will raise a hearsay problem because assertive conduct is intended to stand for a statement and if that statement is being offered to prove the truth of what it asserts, you've got hearsay. But if it's non-assertive conduct, by definition it's not hearsay. We just define the problem out of existence and in it comes.

Well, let me give you a fast example and this is the *Grimes* case.[6] A district judge in Alaska writes a splendid opinion dealing with any number of difficult evidentiary issues and the opinion is marvelously helpful on all of them. But we will deal only with the conduct as hearsay issue and it comes up in a context that has been before many of you in your daily practice. If you're here, I assume it's because you're interested in trying cases or you do try cases. If you do try cases,

---

6. *Grimes v. Employers Mutual Liability Insurance Company*, 73 F.R.D. 607 (1977).

some of you from time to time will try personal injury cases, whether for plaintiff or defendant. And, as you all know, if you've got a catastrophic injury case, at least in my neck of the woods in places like New York, Washington and Los Angeles, with a catastrophic injury you don't really expect a defendant's verdict. The jury is going to give this dreadfully injured person something, there's no doubt about it. If you're defending the case, you're trying to keep it down, you know. And if you keep it down below a certain level, that's really a win. And if you're the plaintiff, to use the argot of New York City, you're trying to ring the bell, which these days means $2 or $3 million because juries in New York City give away money in a way that's hard to conceive of.

Well, how do you get a jury to give $2 or $3 million? And the answer is make them feel in their own bodies the dreadful thing that has happened to the plaintiff. And you know how you do that. It's the day in the life movie or video. You don't put the plaintiff on the stand to tell about the horror. You know, that's pretty bad, but you can make it even worse. And that's what was done in the *Grimes* case. The plaintiff was a paraplegic. Instead of carrying him in in a wheelchair, they sent a video maker to his house and there he was in bed. And the video maker said, in effect, "Show us how you get out of bed in the morning." And the camera turns and the guy crawls out of bed. You know, you can imagine how affecting it is. And then how do you go to the bathroom; and how do you brush your teeth; and how do you, etc. He lived alone. How do you make a cup of coffee for yourself. And you see the guy dragging himself on the floor and the awful agony it is to do the things that the rest of us take for granted. This movie is offered in evidence.

Well, there are such objections as undue prejudice, Federal Evidence Rule 403. There are objections with respect to the accuracy of the film. All of those are surmounted by the proponent and now we come to the most troublesome objection, and I wonder how many lawyers would be sharp enough to make it—hearsay. Now, it's a silent movie, there are no out-of-court statements. What the jury sees is out-of-court conduct by the plaintiff, dragging himself out of bed. But do you have the argument? This is assertive conduct. When the jury sees the video of the man dragging himself out of bed, it's conduct intended by the actor to stand for the assertion, "This is how I get out of bed in the morning." And that implied assertion is being received precisely to prove the truth of what it asserts. Therefore, hearsay under the Federal Rules and common law unquestionably because in common law you don't distinguish between assertive and non-assertive conduct. So it is hearsay.

Just so that you know what you have in the case, the judge concludes to admit it under an exception to the rule against hearsay. But an exception you would have only in the federal court, not at common law, the so-called catch-all 803(24) [now 807]. You know, any other hearsay can come in, blah, blah, blah.

There is one aspect of conduct as hearsay that I should touch upon if only to inform you of its possibilities and maybe to sort of alert you to deal with it. There is a certain kind of trial lawyer, and I must confess I am one of them, who frequently finds himself defending or prosecuting cases that want something in merit. They can be tried anyway and one of the ways you handle yourself, of course, is you try to drive the judge crazy or your adversary crazy. If you succeed in driving your adversary crazy, maybe you'll settle at something, more or less depending on the side, than you otherwise would. If you drive the judge crazy, who knows? You know, who knows what's going to happen. And one of the ways to drive judges crazy, you all know, is to make precise and technically imaginative use of the Rules of Evidence. Because I trust I commit no act of lèse-majesté, many judges really don't know much about the Rules of Evidence. They operate on instinct and common sense. Instinct and common sense will almost always give you the right answer, but they don't help you sometimes when a lawyer is insisting that you face up to some formal problem.

Well, conduct as hearsay—in a federal court, it's got to be assertive conduct. So be it. In a common law jurisdiction, assertive or non-assertive. What about this?

Witness on the stand. "Well, I saw the two cars collide."

"What time was it, sir?"

"Ten o'clock in the morning."

"How do you know it was 10 o'clock in the morning?"

"Well, I looked at my watch and my watch . . ."

"Objection. Hearsay."

"What do you mean hearsay?"

It's conduct by the watch, isn't it? Put the little hand on the 10, big hand on the 12. And it's assertive conduct. The very way we say it in English points it out. The watch said it's 10 o'clock in the morning. I object on the ground that that's hearsay.

Now, common sense and just a general instinct for what to do will show a judge that the right answer is, "Shut up and sit down, your objection is overruled." But suppose you say, "I insist upon an articulated reason for your ruling"? And the judge will say, "I'm not here to give reasons, you just move along," right? But some judges don't like to do that, they like to explain and how do you explain it? And the answer, of course, would be it's not conduct because it's not animate. It's a machine and machines can't make statements, whether verbally or otherwise and on that ground your objection is overruled. And, by the way, if you would go to the library, you would find a scattering of appellate opinions to the effect that machines do not make statements. By machines we mean inanimate objects. So when somebody says, "It was Broadway and Main and I knew it because the street sign said so," that street sign is not hearsay. It was 100 West 100 Street because the door had a number on it—that's not hearsay, it's inanimate. So it's got to be animate.

But then what do you do with the following? If you ever want this case, you will find it . . . it's an obscure state court decision. Give me just two minutes to tell you about it. It's called *People v. Centolella*. It was decided by a county court judge, a former colleague of mine—the same level court, but a different county—in 1969 and it's reported at 61 Misc. 2d 723. That's the official reporter for trial court judges' opinions in New York State. Normally, trial court judges don't and state courts don't write a lot of opinions, but this judge wrote the opinion that you will find there in the books. And he wrote it and caused it to be published because he was so proud of it. And it's rather a special opinion because it is an example of something very rare. It's an example of judicial humor—unconscious judicial humor, to be sure, but still judicial humor. It is very funny, though the judge didn't know that he was being funny.

Oneida County is a very rural county in upstate New York. There was a little sort of grocery store that occupied a structure that contained only the grocery store. And it was at the side of the road in the middle of the woods. There was no habitation, there was no town for miles around. And one night when nobody was there, the bad guys came around and they used a stick of dynamite to blow out the back of the building and they got into the store and took whatever was worth taking and disappeared. The next morning, the store owners arrive, they go to open up the store and they realize, my God, we've been burglarized. Call the sheriff. They call the sheriff and, sure enough, in a few minutes the sheriff arrives and whom do you suppose the sheriff has brought with him? The county bloodhound. And the county bloodhound sniffs around the back of the store and then takes off like a shot through the woods, and the sheriff goes huffing and puffing afterwards. And five minutes later, there you are in the middle of the woods, there's a great big tree, at the top of the tree, the defendant, at the bottom of the tree, the dog, going, "Woof, woof, woof."

We're now at trial. The sheriff is on the stand. "This is what I did, the dog went through the woods, there I found the dog at the base of the tree. At the top of the tree, the defendant, at the bottom of the tree, the dog. And the dog goes . . . "

"Objection."

"What's your objection?"

"Hearsay."

"It's not even conduct as hearsay."

"The dog is speaking. It's dog language to be sure—woof, woof—but we all know what the dog means. He means, 'That's the man.' And that out-of-court statement is being offered precisely to prove the truth of what it asserts, therefore hearsay. And don't tell me, Your Honor, that the dog is a machine. The dog is obviously not a machine. We all know dogs. Dogs may not have the capacity, the moral capacity to lie, but they fool around, don't they?"

Defense counsel, I can imagine, said, "You bring that son of a bitch in and let me cross-examine him."

The judge, as instinct would tell any judge, would say, "Shut up, sit down, your objection is overruled." But the judge did not have the sense to rest content with that instinctive ruling. Instead he wrote an opinion. When the case was over, he wrote an opinion and that's the opinion in the books. And the opinion is wonderful because what the opinion says, after recounting the facts, is that defense counsel objected on the ground that it's hearsay. Hmm. Well, defense counsel has an objection, but it's not hearsay. He misconceives what he should be saying. You see, when the dog says, "Woof, woof," what the dog really means is, "In my opinion, that's the man." So the real question is whether the dog is an expert entitled to give his opinion. And then the judge, with a straight face, starts talking about the dog's education and experience and concludes that he is an expert entitled to give his opinion.

Now, that, of course, is a humorous case and it's once in a lifetime. If you try criminal cases, you're going to run into dogs. You know that the authorities are using dogs to spot narcotics. And when the German Shepherd goes, "Woof, woof," or whatever they do, saying, "I smell whatever in there," there's an out-of-court statement and does it raise a hearsay problem? Under the Federal Rules, no, because the Federal Rules by definition got rid of the problem. Hearsay, 801 says, is an out-of-court statement, et cetera. And an out-of-court statement is a statement made or an act done by a person. So if it's not by a person, by a watch, by a street sign, or by a dog, by definition, there's no hearsay problem.

At common law, however, I think you do have a hearsay problem. Not when it's a machine—I'll go with the judge on that. But when it's an animal, almost always a dog, I think there is a problem. Now, should you ever be faced with a trial under the common law rules and you've got an out-of-court declaration by a dog, I urge you to insist upon your right to cross-examine the dog. And don't smile. Say, "I want the dog brought in and I will cross-examine him." And I'm not going to take the time now to tell you how it might be done, but if you ever have the occasion to do it, I invite you to telephone me, wherever I am, collect, and I will tell you how to cross-examine the dog.

Let's pick up with the exceptions to the rule against hearsay. Whether you are working at common law in a state court, for example, or under the Federal Rules of Evidence in the United States District Court, there are a large number of exceptions to the rule against hearsay. We will talk about the three, conceivably four, most important in my judgment. I think it fair to say that if you're going to try cases effectively on a day in, day out basis, there are probably seven or eight exceptions that you ought to be familiar with. But if you have unlimited time in the library and wish to paint with a very fine brush, you could probably come up with close to 100 separate exceptions to the rule against hearsay, a good many of those 100 coming along once in a career, if then.

As you know, under the Federal Rules, the draftsmen worked with a moderately broad brush and they came up with 27 enumerated exceptions and a catch-all at the end. To a trial lawyer then, who's got to carry much of this stuff in his or her head, the first question will be, "Is there any coherence to the exceptions? Is there some golden thread that binds them all together so that you don't have to remember discrete miscellaneous rules for each exception, one after the next?" And I'll just tell you that there really is no coherence, there is no pattern, there is no golden thread, at least none that anybody has ever been able to determine.

This is a rule of thumb. Do not take it as an expression that will work with mathematical precision. But as a rule of thumb it's easy to remember and it kind of gets you going in thinking about exceptions to the rule against hearsay. In a rough and ready way, for every exception to the rule against hearsay, there will be two factors that you can identify and those factors are inversely related. That is to say, the more important one, the less important the other, and vice versa.

The two factors are, first, the need to receive the hearsay. That need can be either relative or absolute. Relative need means you can prove this fact without the hearsay, but it's awfully expensive to do so, taking a few seconds with an example. It is hardly a matter of once in 100 years occurrence that a lawyer has to prove the closing price of a stock on the New York Stock Exchange. Can you do that without hearsay? Yes, you can. You would start from the *Wall Street Journal,* let's say, for that day, go to the Dow Jones broad ticker tape, which comes before it, then the Dow Jones narrow tape, which is before that. Ultimately, you would track down the slip representing the last transaction on the floor of the Exchange, which gives you the closing price. There would be the symbol for the buyer and the seller. You'd have to go find them, put them on the witness stand to testify to that last transaction. It can be done, but it's going to cost you $50,000 in discovery time and so what, for heaven's sakes. Common sense tells you that the *Wall Street Journal* is as good as anything else that you can get.

Absolute need would be represented by an issue which could not be proved without hearsay. The only way to prove it is with hearsay. Example. Some historical fact, let's say 100 years ago . . . last night at dinner, talking to a native South Carolinian and being something of a Civil War buff, we got to talking about General Sherman and how his march to the sea came through Columbia and to this day you can see the place where the match was struck to the bale and downtown Columbia was burned. I have no idea on what day that occurred, but suppose, for some inconceivable reason, you had to prove the precise date on which Sherman and his troops burned Columbia. Well, obviously (putting aside judicial notice), there's no way to prove it, except by hearsay. There is absolute need. And the law generally favors the resolution of controversies on the merits, not because of technical failures of proof. So that the need really means the desire of the law institutionally to get the case decided on the merits. So receive the evidence, even though it is hearsay. There is the need factor.

Bear in mind that when hearsay comes in because there's a need to receive it, it does not change its character. It's still hearsay. Meaning what? It's uncross-examined. The vice of hearsay is that you can't cross-examine it. And what were the first words we said this morning?

To a common law lawyer, cross-examination is your ultimate assurance of reliability. So for every exception to the rule against hearsay, there will be a factor that you might describe as follows. A substitute for cross-examination, some alternative assurance of reliability, some alternative to cross-examination. So you've got need and reliability and they're inversely related in a rough and ready way. The greater the need, the less the guarantee of reliability. The greater the guarantee of reliability, the less the need.

With that brief preface, let's take a look at the major exceptions from a pragmatic viewpoint, the ones that come up most often in the trial of lawsuits and see what the common law situation is and then briefly, for each one, what the situation is under the Federal Rules.

First exception. In my experience, the one that comes up most often, it is a very rare case, civil or criminal, state or federal, in which this exception will not be invoked. It is an exception to the rule against hearsay at common law. Under the Federal Rules, for reasons I will not go into, this "exception" is treated not as an exception, but as an example of non-hearsay. Beyond that difference in approach it works pretty much the same way. The exception is the exception for admissions. So if you're looking it up in a common law jurisdiction, the category is probably the principal exception to the rule against hearsay—admissions. If it's the Federal Rules you look at 801(d), Statements Which Are Not Hearsay; (d)(1), Out of Court Statements by Witnesses, the *DeSisto* case, already discussed; (d)(2), Admissions.

Now, I urge you to fall into the habit, if you have not already acquired the habit, of calling this the exception for admissions or the non-hearsay exception as we call admissions under the Federal Rules. By the way, I prefer the common law, so from now on I'm going to talk about admissions as an exception and you can understand the way in which you'd reformulate it if you were before a federal judge. Okay. It's the admissions exception, not admissions against interest. First of all, admissions against interest is not the name. Second, you risk confusing admissions with declarations against interest, a very different exception. And, third, if you call it admissions against interest, you may be misled because an admission is not recognized or characterized by the fact that it's against the interest of the declarant. I'll give you an example of that in a moment.

I think that the most efficient way to proceed would be as follows. If you would look at the Federal Rules, 801(d)(2), you see just about everything you need to know about admissions except for one thing. Nowhere do the Federal Rules define an admission. And it's very rare to encounter a definition in a common law opinion. And the reason, I think, is that the direction of the Federal Rules and common law judges generally figure that anybody who's trying a case recognizes an admission when you see it, so there's no need to define it. But I think it's helpful to have a definition and let me give you one of my own coinage. This is a kind of formal definition which has packed into it almost everything you need to know about admissions. An admission is a statement made or, I would insert, an act done by a party to a lawsuit which is or which amounts to a prior acknowledgment that some fact is not as the party now claims it to be. Let me gloss each word or phrase and you'll see how much of the law of admissions is packed up in there.

An admission is a statement made, obviously, because we're talking about an exception to the rule against hearsay, hearsay or statements, so it's got to be a statement or an act, because acts can generate hearsay problems if the act implies a statement. So it's a statement made or an act done by a party to a lawsuit. And there is the key to grasping the admissions exception. Admissions are pegged to parties, meaning in a civil case, the plaintiff or the defendant—in a criminal case, the defendant. And if some of you have sharp ears, you'll realize I left out the prosecution in a criminal case. There is one appellate opinion in the history of the common law holding that the admissions exception is not available against the sovereign when the sovereign prosecutes. That was a federal case, so I guess you've got to limit it to the federal sovereign. And there's nothing to the contrary, so you've got to take that as the law. Admissions not against the prosecution, certainly against the defendant and against either side in a civil case. All right. Statement made or an act done by a party to a lawsuit which is, meaning on its face it is, or which amounts to, meaning that a jury could reasonably take it to be. Why? A prior acknowledgment. Prior to when? Prior to right now. So it could be 30 seconds ago, 30 minutes, 30 days or 30 years ago. That some fact, any fact, is not as he now, at trial, claims that fact to be. And how do you know how he claims the facts to be? Any way that makes sense. Look at the pleadings, listen to the opening statement, listen to the testimony, ask the lawyer what he contends the facts are. The feel of the courtroom will give you what he contends the facts are. And if at any time he acknowledged a fact to be different from what he now says it is, that's an admission, whether or not it was against his interest at the time.

And here's my illustration of that. Policeman has a suspect in the back room of the station house. It's Boston 20 years ago. Says the policeman, full compliance with the Constitution, "You're the Boston Strangler."

"I am not," says the suspect.

"Well, on such and such a day a woman was strangled here in Boston. Where were you on that day?"

"I was in New York on that day,"

"I believe you," says the policeman, "You're free to go."

He's now on trial in New York for holding up a gas station on that day. Is his statement to the policeman in Boston admissible against him as an admission in the New York trial? Yes. Perfectly consistent with his self interest at the time he made it, but it's contrary to a position he takes at trial in New York. His not guilty plea negates, puts in issue every fact essential to the prosecution's case. Obviously, the presence of the defendant in New York on the day the crime was committed is a fact essential to the prosecution. His not guilty plea negates or negatives that. Here is a prior acknowledgment that some fact is not as he now, at trial, claims it to be. So in it comes as an admission.

Now, that formal definition might be okay as a kind of note taking device, but going back to the definition of hearsay, if you're sitting there trying a case you really don't want to fiddle around with something 20 words long, whatever that may be. And so let me give you my trial lawyer's rule of thumb. This is my invention, but it works, it's infallible, and it permits you to operate very quickly, indeed.

Put aside any constitutional problem. You know, the cops didn't beat him up or anything of that sort. Either side to a lawsuit may put into evidence anything the other side ever said or did, so long as it's relevant. Or at common law we would say so long as it's material. So long as it's logically connected to an issue in this case. One side may put into evidence anything the other side ever said or did, so long as it's relevant. Conduct or silence. None of this is very difficult so long as you keep your eye on either the formal definition or the trial lawyer's rule of thumb that I've suggested to you.

This is by way of example. It's a real case, though nothing that I can cite because there is no citation. One of my colleagues, in the days when I was in the judging end of the business, was presiding over a criminal trial in The Bronx. And The Bronx is kind of a hairy borough in New York City—it's sort of down at the heels and sort of strange things are happening there. The courthouse is a couple of blocks down from Yankee Stadium. If you've ever visited Yankee Stadium, your eye probably passed the courthouse. And it's sort of a zoo. You know, it's overcrowded and many of you have probably seen courthouses like it, but it being New York City, this is 50 times worse.

A defendant is on trial before my colleague for some species of narcotics offense and it's the first day of trial and the prosecutor puts into evidence the several bags of heroin seized from the defendant at the time he was arrested. Received in evidence. There are no problems of unlawful search and seizure or the like. It's now 5 o'clock, the day is over. The defendant is out on bail. The judge says to the clerk, "You take possession of the evidence," and the clerk locks the bags of heroin in a steel locker that is in the courtroom. Everybody goes home. Except the defendant, he does not go home. He goes to a bar across the street and he waits until it's midnight. Now, he knows a lot of law—street law. And I'm sure you've got street law in Columbia; we have an awful lot of it in New York. For example, a contract signed with a ballpoint pen is not valid. Did you know that? Everybody walking the streets of New

York knows it. You can say anything you want to the cops as long as it's not in writing and they can't use it against you. Yeah, an awful lot of people are in jail who think that's the law. And third, and relevant to this case, if they don't have the narcotics, they can't convict you of selling it. Absolutely nothing to that. I mean, we all know that. They don't need it. They use it to impress the jury and so forth, but they really don't need it. In any event, the defendant thinks if he can get rid of the several bags of heroin that are in that steel locker, he walks.

So it's now midnight. He goes creeping up the front steps of the courthouse. Being a very adept pick man as well as a pusher, he picks the lock on the front door and goes in, up the stairs, to the courtroom, picks the lock, goes in, picks the lock on the locker, takes the heroin, goes directly to the men's room, flushes it down the toilet, and now goes home, figuring that tomorrow, he walks. Unbeknownst to the defendant, he was observed throughout this by the clean-up guy who saw him do it and just stayed in the shadows and watched him go about this set of activities.

The next morning you can imagine the consternation in the courtroom. The clerk of the court is crying, you know, "Who took my narcotics? Who took my junk?" Right? The judge, "Who took that stuff?" The defendant, "Uh uh uh uh," you know, ready to walk. The prosecutor says, "Don't get excited, gang, I have a witness—the clean-up guy. Take the stand." And he now offers in evidence the clean-up guy's narrative of what he saw the night before. Right. Let's get at it this way. This is not a trial for burglary, for obstruction of justice, or anything of that kind. It is a trial for selling heroin to school children last year. Is this evidence relevant? And the answer is, of course it's relevant. And you reason it out, if you have to, something like this. It is conduct by the defendant, conduct which implies an assertion. And what's the implied assertion? I am guilty of the charge on trial here, selling heroin to school children a year ago. It's because I'm guilty that I've got to destroy evidence. That implied assertion comes in to prove the truth of what it asserts. That makes it hearsay, but it's admissible as an admission and that's how you see that it's relevant in this case and also admissible with respect to the potential hearsay objection.

Conduct as hearsay. So common is that kind of conduct that it's got a special label. It's shorthand for the analysis I've just put before you, albeit in a nutshell. Spoliation. Spoliation of evidence. Destruction of evidence is an implied assertion of guilt or liability of the underlying charge. Same kind of analysis applies to fabrication of evidence, creating false evidence, threats to witnesses. Flight—he ran away, implied assertion. I'm running away because I'm guilty. That makes it an admission and in it comes. And finally, silence. Silence can be an admission. But no one should be misled, no one will be misled. Remember that in a criminal case, the defendant's silence when in the hands of the police may never be used against him. Oh, there may be some aberrational cases at the margin, but that's still accurate enough. If you are in the hands of the police, recognizing can sometimes be a difficult concept; that when are you in the hands of the police you have an absolute right to remain silent and your silence may never be received against you. But in other circumstances your silence can be received against you in a criminal case and in a civil case. In a criminal case when it's not silence, when in police custody in response to police questioning, in a civil case any time. When?

Perhaps it will be easiest if we state the rule and then, by way of illustration, take the New Jersey case, *Ollert v. Ziebell.*[7] The rule is this. When something is said to someone who is now a party, which a reasonable person in these circumstances would reasonably be expected to deny and the person did not deny it, his silence is deemed to be an acknowledgment of its truth. That is sometimes called an adoptive admission. You didn't deny it, so even though you didn't say it, you heard it and you have adopted it as your own by failing to deny it.

Now, in a given case we can quarrel about whether a reasonable person would have denied it in these circumstances and that's necessary to remember when you look at the facts of *Ollert v. Ziebell*, an absolutely unforgettable case because . . . well, you'll hear about it in

7. *Ollert v. Ziebell,* 114 A. 356 (N.J. Err. & App. 1921).

a moment. It's not the only case on silence as hearsay. The *Kilbourne* case[8] is a contemporary illustration of silence as an admission in a criminal case. But in *Ollert* it's a civil case and it's unforgettable because it's a wrongful death action brought against a dentist. And all of us have sat in the dentist's chair while the dentist did the awful things that the dentist does. And, you know, when it's all over you realize that it's an unalloyed blessing. Just think of the misery that we're saved because we live in the times of modern dentistry. But still, when it's going on you can't help but wonder, you know, what if his hand slips? What if he drives that thing into the roof of my mouth? It'll go into my brain. I'll be turned into a vegetable. All of that thinking when you're lying there and the dentist is drilling or doing whatever.

In the *Ollert* case, in simplified but not distorted terms, a woman goes to a dentist, the dentist does something wrong, and she dies as a result. She dies. And a malpractice action is brought against the dentist. It's a wrongful death case, arising out of dental malpractice. The plaintiff is the woman's survivor, her husband, and he's got the burden of proof. And he's going to introduce evidence that, if believed by the jury, would support the conclusion that the dentist did something wrong. And, as you see, the case is 60 years old or so, at a time when it was very difficult to get medical experts to testify for the plaintiff in a malpractice case. We may touch upon that this afternoon.

I'm not suggesting cynically that there was a certain amount of self-help here, but this is the evidence that is offered by the plaintiff. The husband takes the stand and he says, "My wife was dying." She came home from the dentist, took right to her bed, and three days later she died. While she was dying the dentist, the defendant, came to pay a courtesy call. Can you imagine? That's heroism for you. The dentist, having killed the woman, comes to say goodbye. According to the husband, the dentist is standing at the woman's bedside when the woman said, not in these words, but this is what it amounts to, the woman

8. *United States v. Kilbourne*, 559 F.2d 1263 (4th Cir. 1977).

said, "You committed malpractice upon me," and the dentist failed to reply. The argument is that's an admission by the dentist.

Now, if it is his statement, if he adopted it, obviously, it's an admission. It adds up to "I committed malpractice." And his position at trial is that he did not. The claim is that he heard it and that a reasonable person, similarly situated, would have denied it were it untrue. Since he did not deny it, he is deemed to have acknowledged its truth and it comes in as an admission. Now, on the facts, I find that kind of hard to accept. I mean, if the dentist did kill her, never mind whether he's liable or not, and she's dying and she says, "You committed malpractice upon me," what is the dentist supposed to do, slap her in the face and say, "I did not"? Of course not. You know, you hold your tongue in extraordinary circumstances of that kind. I suspect it was result oriented. They wanted to make sure that the plaintiff won. Do you know, they jiggled the rules a little bit. But people can differ on that and there you have an unforgettable example, I should think, of silence as hearsay.

Let's turn now to what I said a moment ago was the most controversial issue in connection with the admissions exception and here, while I cannot profess to a knowledge of the South Carolina cases, chances are we will be looking at a major point of difference between practice in the state court and practice in the federal court. Assuming that on this point a South Carolina judge would follow the common law, as would a judge in my home state of New York, you've got to switch gears rather substantially when you walk into federal court from what you do when you walk into state court. It is the problem of the vicarious admission. That's the general tag attached to this issue in the literature and to make it more precise, it is the problem of when, under what circumstances, will A's statement be received against B, the party, as if B had said it. So it's B, the party, concededly said nothing. A said something. When will we allow that statement to be treated as if B said it? And the issue first surfaces in the cases in every jurisdiction early in the history of the automobile. It's automobile accident litigation that particularly requires courts to work this out. And sort of the archetypical case is as follows.

You've got an accident with a plaintiff catastrophically injured. The plaintiff was involved in a collision with a huge interstate truck owned by the ABC Trucking Corporation and driven by the trucking corporation's employee, Charlie Truck Driver. The plaintiff sues the trucking corporation. Well, all of us recognize that under substantive principles of tort law, specifically Respondeat at Superior, the corporation is liable for the negligence of its employee. And the corporation has lots of insurance, lots of money, that's the deep pocket. You go against the corporation. That's not the problem. That issue the law settled a long time ago.

The problem arises in the, what shall I say? It's not the usual case, but it's not the rare case, in which the only evidence of the truck driver's negligence consists of the following. Not a bystander who says, "I saw the truck veer over to the wrong side of the road." Not physical evidence from which an expert in accident reconstruction can say, "Now, the truck was on the wrong side of the road." Instead, all you have is something like this. The policeman, "I responded to the accident call. I did not see the accident. I have no firsthand knowledge of what happened. When I got there, the plaintiff was in a coma, which he is still in. Charlie Truck Driver was sitting by the side of the road, shaking violently, covered with blood, throwing up, perhaps. It was only five minutes or so after the accident. I said to him, 'Charlie Truck Driver, what happened?' And he replied to me, 'My God, I fell asleep at the wheel.'" All right? If it comes in to prove the truth of what it asserts, it plainly gets you to the jury and supports the jury's verdict.

But does it come in to prove the truth of what it asserts? Assume Charlie Truck Driver is dead. It's unimportant, just . . . can it come in, whether or not he's around? It's an out-of-court statement offered to prove the truth of what it asserts. Charlie Truck Driver is not the defendant, the trucking company is the defendant. Under what circumstances will the truck driver, the employee's statement, be admissible against the trucking company, the employer, as if the employer had said it? The vicarious admission of the employer.

Now, if you go back to the early cases, on the pages of the reports, you can see judges scratching their heads and saying, "What the hell do we do with this?" Because, after all, the admissions exception came into being at a time when life and, hence, litigation was very simple. It was one-on-one litigation. Mr. Plaintiff sued Mr. Defendant and everything went according to plan. But now you've got corporations and other aggregates of power. Corporations, lawyers pretend, are individuals who can sue and be sued. Well, it's only a pretense. It's a legal fiction, we understand. But how do you determine the admissibility of the employee statement when judges are confronted by a new problem? And 70 years ago this was a new problem.

Judges traditionally resort to legal reasoning and legal reasoning, I need hardly remind you, is reasoning by analogy. What kind of analogy? Almost always false analogy. Right? You know, that's typical legal reasoning. You say that something is like something else, you then treat it as if it were the something else even though it's totally unlike. Judges looked at this fact pattern and said, "We've got to find something it's like. Ah, aha. The relationship between the trucking company and Charlie Truck Driver, that we're familiar with. It is the relationship of principal and agent." So you will treat this issue of the admissibility of evidence as if it were an issue of agency law because agency law is a mature subject. As of 1910 it was a mature subject and judges knew how to treat it. If you went to law school as long ago as I did, you took an entire three-credit, one-semester course in agency. These days, it is covered in five minutes. Five minutes is too long. You can imagine what a one-semester, three-credit course was. The entire law of principal and agency can be stated while standing on one leg. I shall do so. If the principal authorized it, he is stuck with it. Everything else is commentary.

So if the principal authorized it, he is stuck with it. Is the truck driver's statement to the policemen admissible against the principal? Yes. When? When the principal authorized the statement to be made. Otherwise . . . oh, it may be admissible against the truck driver, but he doesn't have the insurance, so it doesn't help us. Only if it's authorized by the principal will it come in. Consequence in this case is that it doesn't come in because the trucking company's lawyer stands up and says, "I object. It can't come in against my client because it's settled and it can come in only if my client authorized it. Was Charlie Truck Driver an agent for my client? Yes, he was, but what was the scope of his authority? To drive trucks, not to make speeches. Therefore, it's not an authorized statement, therefore it can't come in." And that is the common law rule to this day.

I've got at my fingertips the New York cases. As recently as three years ago, an appellate court in New York . . . New York, you know, one of the two most important commercial states with California these days. Very sophisticated judiciary. It's 1982. They look at this issue and decide it the way they would have decided it in 1882. If the principal didn't authorize it, it's not admissible against him. Just to give you the facts of that New York case, it's a construction accident. The construction company is being sued. The cause of the accident was an overloaded temporary elevator that the workmen were using. The foreman on the job, the construction company's foreman, says to the investigator from the Building Department, "I overloaded the elevator." Can't come in against the construction company because their agent's authority was to supervise construction, not to make statements to investigators. Therefore, inadmissible as the vicarious admission of the trucking company. A very troubling result, but it flows from this false analogy between evidence and agency.

It was the sainted John Henry Wigmore who first pointed out that it was a false analogy and suggested an alternative test. That alternative test has been picked up in the Federal Rules of Evidence so that if you're trying your case before a federal judge, there is a much greater scope for receiving the statements of the agent against the principal. You'll find it in 801(d), remember, statements which are not hearsay. Not (1)—that's witnesses' statements—(2), admissions. And you'll look at sub-sub-subdivision (c) and (d) together. And what it adds up to is this. The common law test is continued, of course. If the agent was authorized to make a statement, it comes in against the principal. But in addition, sub-subdivision (d)—this is the Wigmore test taken right out of Wigmore's treatise. If the agent made the statement at a time when he was the agent of the principal, in short he was then employed by the principal, and while not authorized to make a statement, what he made a statement about was within the scope of his authority. Then it comes in as the vicarious admission of the principal. Back to the truck driver. Was he employed as the truck driver at the time he made this statement? Well, of course. Was he authorized to make this statement? No. But what is the statement about? It is about how he drove the truck. That was his authority and, therefore, the statement comes in.

Just to recapitulate it, I suppose the most commonly encountered example of an agent authorized to speak, and I always like to mention this because, surprisingly, some of us forget it. You know what the most commonly encountered example of the speaking agent is? The answer is us—lawyers. We are agents for our clients who are principals and we are authorized to speak for them. Many of us don't realize it. When you speak to the opponent in a lawsuit, for example, there can be no possible claim of attorney-client privilege, you're speaking outside the relationship to someone who is a stranger to the relationship—in fact, your opponent. And anything you say about the matter which is the subject of the professional representation can come in against your client as a vicarious admission, subject to privileges, such as in the course of settling a case. Obviously, we know that there are privileges which will prevent it from coming in. Subject to the kinds of signals lawyers use because we frequently have to talk to opponents and we don't have to want to worry about it coming in. You know those signals—off the record; without prejudice; if you quote me, I'll deny it—things of that kind.

If ever you get involved in this, go to the books and you will find criminal cases in which a defense lawyer in the course of talking to a prosecutor in unprivileged circumstances—actually, there probably is no privilege for negotiating a guilty plea—for example, said to the prosecutor, "You know, he was there, but he didn't participate in the robbery, so let us plead to a misdemeanor." The plea negotiations fail. That concession that the defendant was there comes in as an admission against the defendant, so you'd better watch it when you talk to the other side in a civil or a criminal matter.

On the Federal Rules view, this is not a reported case, but it's a real case that came to my attention, to give you some example of really what teeth this kind of thing has. Antitrust investigation. The U.S. attorney has been trying to pin a price-fixing indictment on the defendant corporations for a long time and he just can't do it. And it happened literally this way. The U.S. attorney is sitting at home when there's a knock on the door. He opens the door and in walks a vice president of one of those corporations. And the vice president says to him, "I want to get something off my chest." (Footnote: it turned out that the vice president had just come from his doctor who said, "You have cancer and three months to live," and that's why the guy wanted to clear his conscience.) He said, "I want to get something off my chest. My corporation has been fixing prices for years and I'm the guy who does it. I meet with the officers of the competing corporations and we fix prices, we allocate markets, et cetera, et cetera. And I'm ready to go before the grand jury and say so. And there are no deals. Obviously not—I'm not going to be around to have to face the music." They put him before the grand jury the next day, he testifies in a fashion clearly showing guilt on the part of the corporation, and in three months he dies.

It's a year later, the corporations are now on trial for price fixing and the prosecutor offers the grand jury testimony of that employee as an admission against the corporate employer. The corporate employer not only had not authorized the employee to testify, they didn't know that he was testifying and if they'd known that he was going to testify, they probably would have hired a hit man to rub him out. Hmm? It comes in as their admission. Why? He was the vice president at the time he testified and he was testifying about something he was supposed to do, namely fix prices and allocate markets. That is big medicine, let me tell you. But we're not finished with it.

Back to our common law judge, be it 1910 or be it today. And I'll speak for myself and I think in doing so I speak for virtually every judge. You're in a common law jurisdiction, you've got the plaintiff who's in a coma, he's never going to come out of it, it's going to take $2 million to provide medical care and reasonably decent circumstances for the rest of his life expectancy. The defendant is a multi-billion dollar corporation with that many billions more in insurance. There's no doubt that Charlie Truck Driver fell asleep at the wheel. Somebody's got to pay for that poor injured plaintiff and you certainly don't want it to be the taxpayers. But all the plaintiff has is the policeman to say, "The truck driver said to me, 'My God, I fell asleep at the wheel.'"

"Objection," from the trucking company lawyer.

"What's your objection, counselor?"

"The driver was not authorized to make statements and under the settled rule in this jurisdiction, reaffirmed by the High Court as recently as yesterday, it may not come in because the agent was not authorized to speak."

And what is any right thinking judge going to do? It comes as no surprise to you, any judge who's screwed on the right way is going to say, "Your objection is overruled."

"How can you overrule my objection?" says the trucking company lawyer. "The High Court yesterday reaffirmed the common law principle."

What does the trial judge do when called upon to explain something which cannot be explained? You all know what a trial judge does is talk Latin. And so the trial judge will say to that trucking company lawyer, "Oh, counselor, I understand, but that statement cannot come in as a vicarious admission of your client. It doesn't come in on that basis. Rather, it comes in as part of the res gestae." What's the res gestae? Well, for those of you who haven't had the benefit of a Jesuit education, I tell you to begin with that it's res gestae, that literally translated it means the things done. Yes, yes, yes, but what does it mean? And the answer is, nothing, absolutely nothing. An appellate court once said that the use of the term res gestae by a trial judge is an open confession of a refusal or an inability to think. You can't get any sharper than that.

If I were talking to a group of judges I would say, but I say anyway talking to a group of working lawyers, the term res gestae should be eliminated from your vocabulary if it's there now. It plays no part in the law of evidence anymore. We now understand, because we've got the benefit of decades of experience, that the term res gestae was a Latin tag cloaking the following phenomenon: The judge is receiving hearsay and he doesn't know why. Or, in my example, he can't explain why, because it violates what the High Court just said.

There are four or five lines of cases which begin with judges receiving hearsay on the grounds that it's part of the res gestae. Each of those lines of cases we now see represents a separate, well-recognized exception to the rule against hearsay, and a careful, precise, technically, highly tuned lawyer or judge, should use the correct label. What the truck driver said to the policemen in my hypothetical is admissible, not as the vicarious admission of the principal because we understand you need authority to speak and you don't have it. But if you can get it in under some other exception, more power to you. And you can get it in under another exception. Which one? Not res gestae—that doesn't exist, if it ever did. But one of those four or five streams of cases has now matured into what should be called the exception for excited utterances.

It's a very useful exception, coming up over and over again in both civil and criminal litigation. It's in the Federal Rules of Evidence as 803, subdivision (2), but it's well recognized in the common law case. I have no doubt that it's part of the law of South Carolina and it works the same way everywhere. It doesn't matter whether Charlie Truck Driver is dead or alive, available or unavailable. Doesn't matter at all. If there was an exciting or unusual event, such as the collision, and some person in a position to know, participant or bystander, under the exciting influence of the event, cries out and what he cries out tells you something about the exciting event, that outcry comes in to prove the truth of what it asserts and you call it an excited utterance.

Need to receive it? Well, I guess the need is that it's really the best available evidence. It's what was said right at the time. Guarantee of reliability? The excitement, which of course, is the key fact. The statement must have been made at a time when the declarant was excited. And, as a matter of green thumb psychology, we all know that when you are excited, it's impossible to lie. You can't prevaricate when under the influence of some extraordinary event. You may be so excited that you don't know what you're talking about, that your perceptions are upside down, but you can't lie. That has been enough for the law. Since you can't lie, that's enough of an assurance of reliability and in it comes.

Give you a rule of thumb. I once had occasion to look, I can't say at every American case, but an awful lot of them. And this is a fair description of what you'll find in the cases. If an out-of-court declaration begins with the words, "My God," it's probably admissible. And it's admissible as an excited utterance. Okay. So much for the excited utterance and, by the same token, so much for admissions.

Let's move now to what is, in my view, the second most important exception and some people might say it's really the first most important, with admissions coming second. This is an exception which is treated as an exception under the Federal Rules and at common law and at every jurisdiction in the land. You can't try a civil case, and you can try very few criminal cases, without using this exception. It is the exception for business records, sometimes called business entries. This exception, to spend just two seconds on its history, for various reasons was not recognized by common law judges, meaning judges in the early days, particularly in England.

Just yielding to the temptation to drop an interesting personal footnote, this is one of several examples that I've collected over the years of a legal development, primarily in England, that can be traced to an underlying class hostility between the judges and the litigants. And the class hostility was the businessman as litigant and the judge as aristocrat. And, remember, that's what it was roughly through World War II. A well-to-do or titled family produces several sons. The first son inherits the title and the wealth and so you don't have to do anything. Go to the House of Lords. Right? Second son goes into the Army or the Navy. The third son is called to the bar, meaning barrister, never solicitor. Solicitor is a bourgeois occupation and aristocrats didn't do that. But the bar, yes. If you're a barrister, you might easily become a judge. All judges of the High Court are drawn from the ranks of practicing barristers and there you are, a member of the hereditary nobility, and the litigant is a member of the rising middle class, the businessman. And there's really a very great hostility, a feeling of antagonism and class interest between the two.

Fletcher v. Rylands,[9] the famous case on land use, is best explained as an example of that. And the refusal of judges to recognize an exception for business records is similarly motivated—a feeling that businessmen will do anything, including create false records, in their self-interest and they're just not going to let the record come in. That carried over to the United States, probably unthinkingly, and it was only in the 1920s that legislation was enacted in every single state legislature. In a period of two years, every single state legislature enacted a statute recognizing the business records exception. Congress did also. It was the one hearsay exception that in the federal courts rested upon a statute before the Federal Rules of Evidence. That statute in the federal court has been supplanted by 803, subdivision (6). New York has a statute, I dare say South Carolina has a statute. The statutes may vary in detail, but in essence, the exception works the same way everywhere. Any memorandum, or in whatever form, kept of any transaction, which memorandum was made in the regular course of business, the transaction occurring in the regular course of business is admissible to prove the transaction, to prove the truth of the out-of-court statement, to prove what the record says—the truth of what the record says.

Business means business, professional occupation, or calling of any kind and lack of knowledge on the part of the entrant or maker affects weight, but not admissibility. All right. Now, adding all that up, what does it mean? It means that any enterprise which generates records on a regular basis is a business for purposes of this exception. Sears Roebuck to be sure, but the state government, this university, the local draft board, the public library, a criminal enterprise, the Mafia—if it creates records on a regular basis, yes, all of those are businesses for purposes of the business records exception. That the clerk who actually

9. 159 Eng. Rep. 737 (Ex. 1865).

makes the entries did not participate in the transaction reflected by the entry affects weight, but not admissibility.

Assuming that the record was regularly made, it comes in to prove whatever the record says. The assurance of reliability is the routineness, the regularity with which the record is made. Error is always possible, but routineness tends to minimize the occurrence of error. We all know that in 95 cases out of 100 this is the easiest exception to invoke. Indeed, in my original neck of the woods in New York, it is usually the case that when a lawyer offers business records, the opponent will instantly stipulate their admissibility. You never even have to lay the necessary foundation.

The kind of case in which a lawyer will stipulate admissibility, the 95 cases out of 100 where this is the easiest exception to use, will involve the traditional accounting record, be it the bookkeeper's ledger page right through to a computer printout. It really makes no difference, but you've got debit and credit entries—numbers. And if the record consists of those numbers, it will be received in evidence so long as you go through the footwork to lay the foundation should that be required of you. How to do it is for a course in trial techniques, not for a course in evidence. In any event, I'm sure all of you know how to do it.

For a course or sort of mini-course, mini-lecture on hearsay, what remains to be considered is the issue that can come up when certain kinds of business records are offered in evidence. And for a while this proved an excruciatingly difficult issue for courts to deal with. The issue comes up every single day. It no longer should be difficult, excruciating or otherwise, because we now know how to resolve this issue. We know how to answer the question. So let me tell you what the issue is and show you how it should be answered. And, by the way, here Federal Rules, common law, it makes no difference. The Federal Rules simply codify the common law view. So be it South Carolina state court or federal court, you work the same way.

The issue should be present in your mind, that is to say, be alert for it. Whenever a business record is offered which contains not numbers, but words. Now, that doesn't mean that it's inadmissible, it just means that it's a special kind of business record. Instead of debit and credit entries it has such things as the doctor's diagnosis. Patient received in emergency room, fractured left femur. Or the prognosis—guarded, as is always the case these days. Or to take the actual record from the case in which the issue first came up.

This is a New York case, which has lent a name to the issue *Johnson v. Lutz*,[10] the Federal Rules of Evidence cited it. This is the problem of *Johnson v. Lutz. Johnson v. Lutz* was a wrongful death case. To make it easy, I'm not going to talk about decedent, et cetera. I'll talk about plaintiff and defendant.

The plaintiff was driving a motorcycle, collides with the defendant driving a car and ends up dead. Everybody agrees he's dead; everybody agrees that there was an accident. The question is, who went through the red light? On that question, the defendant puts a policeman on the stand. This is within months of the enactment of the Business Record Statute in New York. And the policeman's testimony goes essentially as follows: "I did not see the accident. I don't know what happened. All I know about it is that this is the accident report written by the investigating officer." Is the police department a business within the meaning of the statute? Yes. Was this accident report regularly made within the meaning of the statute? Yes. "I offer it in evidence," says the defendant. Instantly you should be alert to the issue because the accident report does not contain accountant's entries, not numbers, not debit and credit. Instead, insofar as the case is concerned, the report contains a section headed "bystander statements" and the reporting officer, the policeman who signs the report, puts down in that section that three bystanders said to the policeman, in effect, the plaintiff went through the red light.

"Objection. Hearsay," says the plaintiff.

"Well, of course it's hearsay," says the defendant. "But there is now an exception to the rule against hearsay for business records. The police department is a business within the meaning of that exception and the record was regularly made within the meaning of that exception and those are true statements. Nobody contends otherwise."

---

10. *Johnson v. Lutz*, 253 N.Y. 124 (1930).

"Ah," says the plaintiff. "The policeman had no personal knowledge of who went through the red light. He's only reporting what he was told by bystanders."

"That's right, but what does the statute say? Lack of personal knowledge on the part of the injured only can affect weight, not admissibility. And so I press my offer," says the defendant.

And the judge says, "I will not receive it. Don't ask me why. I don't know why. But my instinct tells me that it's not admissible despite the legislature's having enacted the Business Record Statute a couple of months ago." It goes to the New York Court of Appeals. That's the court of Cardozo, the greatest common law court that ever sat. And they wrote a wholly unsatisfactory opinion affirming the trial judge, but not telling you really why. They say the police report, insofar as it gives you the statement of the bystanders, is inadmissible. Why? And this is all the opinion says by way of explanation. There was no business duty on the part of the bystander to speak to the policeman, by which, with all deference to Cardozo and his colleagues, I would say, well, what's a business duty as opposed to another kind of duty? Second, doesn't a bystander have a duty to talk to the policeman investigating an accident? This is not a criminal case with privileges against self-incrimination at work. And, third, where in the statute does it say you've got to have a business duty? It doesn't. You're construing a statute, after all, so where does it come from. And, fourth, how do I recognize it the next time around? No answers to those questions in *Johnson v. Lutz.*

The same court, differently constituted many years later, decided a case called *Kelly v. Wasserman,*[11] also cited by the Federal Rules of Evidence. And if you have *Kelly v. Wasserman* in mind with *Johnson v. Lutz,* you will forever after be able to solve this problem, the problem of *Johnson v. Lutz,* business records that contain statement. *Kelly v. Wasserman* was a little old lady case. And that's not a sexist remark, it's a perfectly accurate description of the case, as you will hear.

---

11. *Kelly v. Wasserman*, 5 N.Y.2d 425 (1959).

There was a little old lady whose husband dies and leaves her with one asset in the world, a small apartment building in Queens, as I recall, in New York City. A couple of apartments upstairs, the little old lady lives in one of them. Downstairs, some stores. She acts as the janitor, the custodian. She shovels snow in the winter, she hauls in coal, she takes out the garbage, and she lives on the rental income from the apartments and the stores. But she's getting on in years and she's no longer strong enough to do the physical work. So she goes to the pharmacist, who rents one of the stores downstairs, and she says, "I tell you what. I will give you the building. Give it to you in fee simple, absolute outright. It's yours. And you shovel the snow and bring in the coal. No price, it's yours free. The only condition is that I live in my apartment the rest of my life. I've got certain payments coming to me from the Social Welfare Department, that will be enough for groceries, et cetera." And, according to the little old lady, the pharmacist said, "It's a deal." And she transfers the building to him.

What does the pharmacist say? He says, "She came to me and said she was no longer strong enough to do the work. She said she would give me the building in fee simple, absolute. She said I didn't have to pay a thing. There was a condition, but the condition was not, as she says, that she can live in the apartment the rest of her life. No. The condition was she can live in the apartment for two years. The two years are up. I want her out."

Now we know who's going to win that case, don't we. And that's why you call it a little old lady case. The little old lady has to win that case. But we've got to manipulate the doctrine to make sure it comes out right. Since the deed is absolute on its face, the law cannot help the little old lady. We speak now as legal historians. She must go to the chancellor and invoke the chancellor's foot, which means we go to equity and we bring an action to impress a trust upon that deed, that the deed transfers title to the pharmacist, but he holds that title in trust. What's the nature of the trust? If the little old lady wins, that she can live in her apartment the rest of her life. But she's got to prove that was the condition.

In aid of that burden, the little old lady calls to the stand a supervisor from the Social Welfare Department, who says, in essence, "I do not know anything about this dispute. I have no personal knowledge. But this is the little old lady's file from the Social Welfare Department and the only part of the file that we're concerned with is the docket sheet that appears on top." Is the Welfare Department a business within the meaning of the statute? Yes. Is the docket sheet regularly made within the meaning of the statute? Yes. What does the docket sheet say? It says, in abbreviations, but everybody agrees that when you spell it out, this is what it says. The pharmacist had said to the old lady, "I want you out." She doesn't know what to do. She's desperate. She has no friends. She goes to the Welfare Department and she walks into the office and she's crying. And the Welfare worker says, "Sit down, have a cup of tea, tell me what's wrong, and maybe I can help."

And the lady says, "He wants to throw me out. I don't know what to do."

The worker says, "Let me call him up and see what he says." She calls him up and notes this right on the docket sheet. Telephoned the pharmacist, asked what about the old lady, and he replied, "Don't worry, she can live there the rest of her life." It's right on the docket sheet. Why they don't call the caseworker, I don't know, the case doesn't explain. It's offered through the docket sheet.

"Objection," says the pharmacist's lawyer.

"On what ground?"

"Under *Johnson v. Lutz*." He had no duty to speak to the caseworker. He was not receiving benefits. He's a mere volunteer when he made this statement. He's an idiot for having said it, but still it can't come in against him because *Johnson v. Lutz* says that that's the outer limit of the business records exception. Observe that what we're dealing with is a business record that has words on it, not numbers, which instantly should trigger this problem.

The trial judge said, "I agree with you. Objection sustained under *Johnson v. Lutz*," and the little old lady lost. So we go to the highest court of New York—no longer Cardozo's court, it was Conway's court.

He was the chief judge and he wrote the opinion. And of course, he reversed. The little old lady wasn't going to lose that case. But how do you explain it? The opinion is as unsatisfactory as the opinion in *Johnson v. Lutz* because what the opinion says is, "The trial judge sustained the objection. He was wrong. We reverse *Johnson v. Lutz*. End of opinion." That's what it says. That's why at the beginning I said the courts have had a lot of trouble with this. But there's no need to, because when the issue comes up the next time in a case you are trying, you have the benefit of *Johnson v. Lutz* and *Kelly v. Wasserman*, which those judges did not, after all.

Though the opinions are opaque, I put the following propositions to you. Each case is correctly decided. They are perfectly consistent with each other. And if you see why they are consistent, you will be able to deal with this problem the next time it comes up. Remember, you're construing a statute. If the record is regularly made within the meaning of the statute, the record comes in to prove what? To prove the occurrence of what is written on the record. That's the key perception. In *Johnson v. Lutz*, the record was regularly made, so it does come in to prove what? The occurrence of what is written on the record. What's written on the record? That the bystander said to the policeman, "The plaintiff went through the red light." That doesn't end your analysis, it just brings you to the last step.

And what's the last step? Having proved that the bystander said it, is the bystander's statement itself admissible? Yes or no? And I'm sure you won't say the answer is yes in *Johnson v. Lutz*. In *Kelly v. Wasserman* the docket is admissible to prove that what the docket contains occurred. What is that? That the caseworker telephoned the pharmacist and he said, "Don't worry, she can live there the rest of her life." We've proved that. Now the next step is, is the pharmacist's statement to the caseworker itself admissible? And the answer is yes. And do you see why it's admissible? It's an admission contained within the business record. In *Johnson v. Lutz*, the bystander's statement is naked hearsay contained within the business record and so it can't come in.

You want a generalizing principle? Any business record that contains words is an example of statements within statements. The business record is the outside statement and whatever it says is the inside statement. There must be, assuming you're offering it to prove the truth of what it asserts, some exception to the rule against hearsay for each level of statement. In *Johnson v. Lutz*, the outside level, the policeman's accident report, you've got an exception, the business records exception. The inside level, the bystander's statement, there is no exception so it can't come in. *Kelly v. Wasserman*, the outside exception, business record. The inside exception, admissions.

Change it. Suppose you have a police accident report and the policeman says, "I got there within minutes of the accident and there was Charlie Truck Driver, who's now dead, trembling by the side of the road and he said, 'My God, I fell asleep at the wheel.'" Is it admissible? Yes. Outside level business records exception. Inside level, excited utterance. See? That is codified in Federal Evidence Rule 805. And all it says is what we've said—you need an exception to the rule against hearsay at each level. And that is understood to be the teaching of *Johnson v. Lutz*, *Kelly v. Wasserman*, and, actually, you may be interested to know that there are tens and probably hundreds of cases on the *Johnson v. Lutz* issue before and after the federal rules. Almost always, the courts get it right. But nowhere do they explain it. It takes Federal Rule 805 finally to give you the key.

Once again, I make bold to put before you a trial lawyer's rule of thumb, a gimmick if you will. This is my absolute favorite because it works in a split second. Again, it's infallible and it will always give you the right answer to a *Johnson v. Lutz* problem. Whenever a record is offered, which record contains words, imagine that the record comes to life. The record is the recording person. He is now on the witness stand and what he says is what he wrote down in the record. Will the judge allow a witness to say that? And there's your answer. When the police record in *Johnson v. Lutz* comes to life, what does it say? It says, "I'm the policeman and a bystander told me he went through the red light." Can't come in. In *Kelly v. Wasserman*, the record comes to life. It says, "I'm the caseworker. I called him and he said, 'She can live there the rest of her life.'" Clearly an admission.

Now, let's go beyond it to the kind of *Johnson v. Lutz* problem many of you deal with every day, and that is the *Johnson v. Lutz* problems presented when medical records are offered in evidence. Now, a medical record can be a list of numbers, you know, the accounting part of a hospital admission. That we're not concerned with. That's always uncontroversial. But what about date of entry, date of discharge, diagnosis, course of treatment, prognosis? Apply my rule of thumb. When the record comes to life, it's the doctor. If the doctor on the witness stand would be allowed to say these things, it can come in through the record. So date of entry, date of discharge, okay.

How about diagnosis? Fractured left femur, whatever it may be. Can that come in through the record? Yes. Why? It's the doctor making an entry, which is identical with what he would be allowed to say if he were here. It comes in through the entry as hearsay, but you've got a business records exception to let it in and the 805 *Johnson v. Lutz*–type analysis tells you that it's admissible, yielding to the temptation to drop a footnote to one line of cases, which I rather cherish in the District of Columbia, holding that a physical diagnosis is admissible, but not a psychiatric diagnosis. That can't come in through the record. The reason being that it's such bullshit anyway that it's just not fair to deprive the opponent of the right to cross-examine. That's one panel in the District of Columbia that decided a series of cases to that effect. Absolutely persuasive, but it's just one panel.

How about prognosis? Well, it's an opinion, but the doctor would be allowed to say it. You know, his forecast of the future. And the part that's most troublesome—the medical history. You've all run into that. They bring the patient in and the the doctor says, "You've got a broken leg, what the hell happened?" Patient says, "I crossed against the light. I'm such a fool. And I got run over." And the doctor jots that down. And you know what happens. The patient is now the plaintiff, suing the motorist who ran him over and he says, "The motorist jumped the red light. Of course, I didn't cross against the light." And there it is, right in the history. Is it admissible?

On the assumption that at least some of you deal with that all the time, let me take two minutes to give you the key to unlocking that problem. I am omitting an analysis of the cases. The cases support this key, but there's no one opinion that says this is the way to do it. But I tell you that this is the way to do it. When there is offered in evidence the history as part of the medical record, the emergency room record, the doctor's office statement, or whatever, you need a two- or possibly three-step analysis.

First step. Is this statement by the patient about what happened part of the record? Now, we understand it's physically written there, but you know, a marginal notation or a doodle can be physically written there, but it's not part of the record. So first you've got to determine whether it's part of the record and the test for doing that is this. Was it relevant to the doctor doing the doctor's job to know this? If yes, it's part of the record. If no, it's not part of the record. If the answer is no, end of analysis, it's not part of the record, even though physically written there, and it cannot come in. If yes, it is medically relevant, and just, by the way, on that question when the patient says, "I crossed against the light and got run over," is that something the doctor needs to know? I mean, when a patient is brought in semicomatose, having collapsed while walking down the street and the patient said, "God, doctor, I suddenly felt a surging pain in my left chest running up the back of my neck and everything began to go around and I couldn't catch my breath and I felt clammy all over and then I passed out," the doctor damn well has to know that because that's a heart attack. But when the patient says, "I crossed against the light," to the doctor, who the hell cares?

I know of two cases—one in the High Court of New York, one in the High Court of Missouri, going in opposite directions. And one case says, yes, the doctor needs to know that; the other says no, the doctor doesn't need to know it. But, you know, fighting on the facts are what lawyers are accustomed to do and that's unimportant for us.

Assuming it is medically relevant, it's part of the record. If it is part of the record, then use your *Johnson v. Lutz* analysis. Imagine that the record comes to life and it speaks. Would a witness be allowed to say that? Let me show you. Assume we're in a jurisdiction that says that when the patient tells the doctor how the accident happened, it is medically relevant. That happens to be the Missouri case. Suppose what's written there is, "Doctor, I crossed against the light and got run over," now offered by the defendant motorist at the trial. Is it medically relevant? We've stipulated yes, so it's a part of the record. Applying our gimmick, the record comes to life. It's the doctor saying, "The patient, now the plaintiff, said to me, 'I crossed against the light.'" Admissible? Yes. Why? It's an admission.

Change it. Stay with me now. The patient says to the doctor, "I crossed with the light and the son of a bitch motorist knocked me down," offered by the plaintiff at the trial. Is it medically relevant? Yes, we've posited that it is medically relevant, so it's part of the record. But is it admissible? No. Why? Use the gimmick. It comes to life. It's the doctor saying, "The patient, now the plaintiff, who has called me to the stand said, 'I crossed with the light.'" Is it an admission? No, because it's not something the other side said, it's something he said. Is it an excited utterance? Probably not, to which time went by and he didn't begin with "My God." Is it anything else? No. So it's naked hearsay and it can't come in. And that will put the cases into a pattern. There are cases all over the lot, but that will kind of line them up so that you can deal with them. So much for admissions, excited utterance, the business record.

Let me spend just five minutes on the state of mind exception and then we'll turn to our conclusion. Things like the dying declaration and so forth come up so rarely that I will not talk about them. Just looking ahead a bit, the learned treatise exception is very important these days, but I had planned to deal with it this afternoon because it works better if we talk of it in the context of examining an expert witness. So really we will have covered a good deal of the material. The state of mind exception, frequently overlooked or misunderstood by lawyers or judges, and it's a very useful thing to know. It exists in the federal courts, it exists at common law with really no differences of detail worth talking about. If you're equipped to deal with it in one jurisdiction, you're equipped to deal with it in the other jurisdiction. It is a matter of some frequency that a lawyer has to prove the state of somebody's mind. Now that covers a lot of territory. Emotion, knowledge, whatever. Belief, anything of that sort.

The rule is that if X's state of mind is in issue in the sense that it's a fact directly in contention between the parties, X's declaration of that state of mind is admissible to prove the truth of what it asserts. Without more, it's admissible. What's the need? The need is that if you've got to find out what's going on in somebody's mind, the best and sometimes the only evidence is what he, himself, says, because nobody can get inside somebody else's head, and frequently you have no circumstantial evidence of conduct illustrating state of mind. So, for example, if somebody has to prove that A disliked B and the witness says, "I heard A say, 'B, I dislike you,'" that's hearsay, but it comes in under the state of mind exception.

Some of you may have been involved in cases in which people offer an opinion poll. Here's the way the analysis goes. It's a case called *Zippo Manufacturing v. Rogers Manufacturing*[12] in the Southern District of New York in the mid-1960s. The opinion is by Judge Feinberg when he was a district judge. He's now chief judge of the Second Circuit. It's an unfair competition case. Zippo is the plaintiff. They claim that the defendant manufactured a cigarette lighter that looks exactly like the Zippo lighter and, hence, the defendant is taking a free ride on the good will attached to a Zippo cigarette lighter. In support of their case, the Zippo people offer a poll. The poll shows that consumers, presented with the defendant's lighter, responded, "That's a Zippo," even though it wasn't. But we assume that the poll was taken in accordance with good polling principles. That's something the judge decides at the threshold. How do you get over the hearsay analysis?

12. 216 F. Supp. 670 (S.D.N.Y. 1963).

The poll results consist of 1,000 or 5,000 people saying what? When shown a Zippo they say, "I believe that that is a Zippo." That comes in to prove the truth of what it asserts, but it comes in under the state of mind exception. The state of mind of those members of the public being an issue, because that kind of confusion is an element of an unfair competition case.

The *Adoption of Harvey* case[13] is a common law case that's just another illustration of how it works. A young woman has a baby out of wedlock. She gives the baby up for adoption, and then, shortly afterwards, changes her mind. She wants the baby back. The litigation is between the adoptive parents and the natural parents. Under the Pennsylvania substantive rule of law applicable to these disputes, the adoption is final if there was physical abandonment of the child together with a particular state of mind on the part of the natural mother, an intention to abandon. Physical abandonment is conceded. She gave the baby up for adoption. But she says, "I did not intend to abandon."

Suppose the defendant, the adoptive parent, calls a witness who says, "I heard the adoptive mother at the relevant time say, 'I intend to give the baby up for adoption.'" Admissible? Yes. Why? It's an admission.

What the case is about, however, is a witness called by the natural mother who says, "I visited her in the hospital room shortly after she gave birth and she said, 'You know, I've signed the adoption papers, but I really don't intend to abandon.'" Is that admissible? We all know judges who would say it can't come in because it's self-serving. Like res gestae, self-serving is a concept unknown to the law of evidence today. There is no such objection to the receipt of evidence. Sure, it's self-serving in the sense that it helps the natural mother's case, but whether it's admissible or not turns upon your analysis of the hearsay issue. Is it an out-of-court statement? Yes. Is it being offered to prove the truth of what it asserts? Yes. We all see that. "I do not intend to abandon the child"—and that's precisely what it's being offered to prove. Therefore, hearsay.

---

13. *Adoption of Harvey,* 99 A.2d 276 (Pa. 1953).

Is it admissible? Only if it fits an exception. What exception? Not an admission. It's not being offered by the other side, it's being offered by her. Is it an excited utterance? No. Is it a business record? No. But is it state of mind hearsay? Yes. Therefore, admissible, which is precisely what the court holds.

Separate from those cases on state of mind in issue are the cases involving what I like to call state of mind nearly relevant. Here the leading case is *MLI v. Hillmon.*[14] It has a special authority because it's a United States Supreme Court decision. It also is one of the few cases cherished by all teachers of evidence and many of you will recall it. It actually plays a fairly important part in the history of the populist movement in the midwest. The legislature of Kansas actually enacted a statute forbidding the defendant insurance companies from doing business in Kansas unless and until they settled this case. And it went to the Supreme Court three times.

Hillmon had a life insurance policy, actually several life insurance policies, involving a lot of money. He has disappeared. Certain human remains were discovered up in the hills in Colorado. Hillmon's heirs bring a lawsuit in which they say, "You're the insurance company, admitted. You wrote a policy on Hillmon's life, admitted. We are the named beneficiaries, admitted. We have made claim, admitted. You have not paid us, admitted." So what's left in the case? Is Hillmon dead? That's the issue. The plaintiffs say those remains are Hillmon and it was the 19th century, forensic pathology had not really been well developed and nobody can say yea or nay whether that's Hillmon. It's pretty much a grease spot on the ground after the Indians got finished with him and it can be just anybody. The defendants come in—the names have come back to my mind—and they say, "No, no, those are human remains, but it's not Hillmon. We'll tell you who it is. It's Walters." And in support of that contention, the defendants argue that Walters rode out from Wichita, Kansas, went up into the hills in Colorado, he got into trouble, and he's the guy who's there on the ground. And the evidence in

---

14. *Mutual Life Insurance Co. v. Hillmon*, 145 U.S. 285 (1892).

support of that claim consists of letters Walters wrote to his girlfriend. And the letters say, "I intend to ride out into the Colorado Hills." Forget about hearsay. You see the argument to the jury? He said he intended to ride out, therefore he did intend to ride out, therefore he did ride out, therefore he got into trouble, and therefore the remains are those of Walters. But you see that means it's hearsay.

Out-of-court statement in the letter. "I intend to ride out." Offered to prove precisely the truth of what it asserts, therefore hearsay. Is it state of mind in issue? No. Walters's state of mind is relevant because it helps the insurance company make the argument that I've just summarized. But his state of mind is not an issue in the sense that it's a fact directly in contention between the parties. The Supreme Court said it's admissible.

In *Shepard v. United States,*[15] the Supreme Court dealt with an attempt to push that phase of the state of mind exception one step farther. Dr. Shepard was tried for poisoning his wife. Of course, she was dead. His claim was that she hadn't been poisoned. The prosecution offers the following evidence. The nurse who attended the lady in her last day or two testifies that on the night she died, she was very sick, but she was in full possession of her faculties. The victim said to the nurse, pointing to a decanter of whiskey on the bedside table, and these were her exact words, "This is what I drank last night. It tasted funny. Dr. Shepard is trying to poison me." The last part is plainly inadmissible as an opinion, speculative, et cetera. Stick with the first part. "This is what I drank last night. It tasted funny." The prosecutor wants to get that in to show that she was poisoned, that there was something in the whiskey.

Now, it's being offered to prove the truth of what it asserts, so it is hearsay. The prosecutor's contention in the Supreme Court was that it comes in under the *Hillmon* case—state of mind relevant. What state of mind? Memory. She remembers drinking it last night. She remembers that it tasted funny. If she remembers it, it probably happened.

---

15. *Shepard v. United States*, 290 U.S. 96 (1933).

And if it happened, there was some foreign substance in the whiskey. What foreign substance but the poison that nobody but Dr. Shepard could have put there. And no less than Benjamin Nathan Cardozo says, "No. We don't take back the *Hillmon* case, we affirm it. We affirm it." But observe the difference. The *Hillmon* case pointed that way, into the future, I intend to go. The *Shepard* case involves a statement pointing backwards into the past. "This is what I drank last night. It tasted funny." And when it's state of mind not in issue, but nearly relevant, that's the limit. A statement of intention casting light on the future is admissible to prove the intention to prove it likely that the person did what he intended to do. But a statement of memory looking backwards into the past offered as tending to prove that something did indeed happen is not admissible. Why, says Cardozo? Because if you put in the memory statement or if you allow the memory statement to come in, that is an end or nearly so to the rule against hearsay.

Those are his words, to which an intelligent response might be, "So what? So what? You know, we're only talking about hearsay. This is not nuclear weapons." Still, you know, it's been around a long time and we don't seem to be ready to give it up. And if you look at 803(3) of the Federal Rules, while it's put a little bit cumbersomely, that is exactly what the draftsmen have said. If it looks to the future, if it's intended, something that's going to be done, it comes in. If it looks to the past, memory, can't come in. So much for state of mind in just a couple of minutes.

Let me speculate a little bit on the future of the rule against hearsay. And in doing so, let me tell you about something that I did many years ago and, as a matter of fact, wrote it up as part of an article which appears in the *South Carolina Law Review*, so it's with a special sort of enthusiasm that I mention it. It's in the *South Carolina Law Review* some seven or eight years ago. It's called "Reflections on the Rule Against Hearsay."[16] I wanted to put to the test something that seemed to me true, but it was based upon my experiences as a trial lawyer—experiences that I dare

---

16. 32 S. Car. L. Rev. 281 (1980).

say are shared by all of you who are trial lawyers, but one's own experiences are a kind of infirm basis for generalization.

It seemed to me that hearsay was almost always admitted. Now, it was admitted because there was some exception to the rule against hearsay or it was admitted without an exception to the rule against hearsay, but common sense suggests that it ought to be admissible. Or, finally, it's admitted, it's error, but it's harmless error. So that whatever the justification, hearsay usually comes in. And having told you about my fear of touching the Lexis keyboard, I put an engineer who had gone to law school to work on this and he figured out a way to do it with Lexis. And what he did, essentially, was say to Lexis with respect to a sampling of jurisdictions, "Lexis, Lexis on the wall, tell me, from the beginning of time to today, in how many cases has hearsay been offered in evidence?" And you get a number. And then the next question is, "Never mind the reason. In how many of those cases was the hearsay received in evidence?" And you get a number and that gives you a percentage.

Now there are flaws to this. Obviously, it's statistically unsound and so forth. But we did it for a rural jurisdiction, for an urban jurisdiction, for a middle type jurisdiction. We did it for federal courts. We did it for state courts. And the numbers came out the same or almost the same every time. Upwards of 80 percent of the time, the hearsay is admitted. Four times out of five, the hearsay is admitted. So assume that I'm off for statistical reasons by 20 percent, which is an enormous margin of error, so three times out of five the hearsay is admitted. And I put it to you that any logician, any mathematician, any scientist would tell you that if three or four times out of five the hearsay is admitted, you don't have a rule against hearsay, you have a rule in favor of hearsay. A rule that says hearsay is admissible. Perhaps with an exception, but that's the rule.

Do you know that in the very first draft of the proposed Federal Rules of Evidence, that was the rule? Hearsay is admissible with an exception, just one exception. And the bar went berserk. You can imagine the reaction every one of us would have. We would say to the draftsmen who dared to propose such a rule, "I sweat bullets. I sat in that dank, large classroom in the University of South Carolina listening to that maniac rant for three hours to try to get a handle on this stuff and now you want to give it away? You want to let the kids coming up the pike now get along without it? No, no, no." Well, with that kind of outcry, the draftsmen of the Federal Rules, being good politicians, immediately pulled in their horns and changed it to hearsay is not admissible, the orthodox, the classic form, with a lot of exceptions. But if 80 percent of the time the hearsay is admissible, the lesson is first, to a judge, I guess, when in doubt, admit the hearsay. To a lawyer, though the evidence is hearsay, don't be afraid to push it. Judge Littlejohn, who is an acquaintance of mine—we were chatting just during the break and he said how often, when he was a trial judge, a lawyer would question the witness and say, "Well, what happened then?" And the answer would be, "Well, A then said to me . . ." "Objection, hearsay." And the proponent would immediately withdraw the question. And Judge Littlejohn said, "I was perfectly prepared to overrule the objection." The out-of-court declaration usually is not hearsay and even if it is hearsay, it's probably admissible.

And even if it's not admissible, they admit it anyway. The appellate court doesn't care. You know, the most they're going to say is it's harmless error. And if you look at the most recent attempt to codify the law of hearsay, it's Article 8 of the Federal Rules of Evidence. There is the famous catch-all at the end of 803 and 804. Rule 802, hearsay is not admissible. Rule 803, 23 exceptions which may be invoked even though the hearsay declarant is available. 804(b), four exceptions, which may be invoked only when the hearsay declarant is unavailable. In addition to the foregoing, any other hearsay will be admissible if it tends to prove an important fact, if it's better than any other evidence that's available, if it has indicia of reliability, and you give the other side due notice. A kind of blank check inviting federal judges to receive hearsay.

And while we don't have the time and this isn't the occasion, I've been keeping up with the federal cases and I tell you that there is virtually not a single case in the last nine years, since the enactment of the Federal Rules, when hearsay has been excluded simply because it's hearsay. Those cases in which hearsay is excluded involve constitutional issues, such as confrontation and the like. Extraordinary hearsay comes in under the Federal Rules and my crystal ball as to the state of the future of hearsay 20, 30, 40 years from now is that because of the inherent conservatism of the profession, we will continue to have a rule against hearsay. Hearsay will not be admissible, but the exceptions will be so numerous and so broad, with the catch-all, the blank check provision coming to be so commonplace, that for all intents and purposes we will have a rule that admits hearsay with one exception—when the trial judge in his or her sound discretion thinks it unfair to receive the hearsay.

Chapter 5

Jury Selection

DEAN STEVE EASTON: Jury selection is an interesting topic, because it is that part of the aspect of trying cases where seasoned, skilled trial attorneys differ the most from one another. On direct examination, cross-examination, opening statement, and closing argument, if you watch 10 different strong trial attorneys conducting those tasks, you will see them doing essentially the same thing. But in jury selection, we disagree about the best approach. It will help all of us to go back to the master of trial advocacy, Irving Younger, and remember what he had to say about this important topic.

In the time since Professor Younger's death in March 1988, there have been developments in the law of jury selection. In fact, toward the end of the presentation, you will see that Professor Younger quite astutely predicts some of those developments and some of those questions that the Supreme Court has addressed—essentially overturning the *Swain v. Alabama, 380 U.S. 202 (1965),* case that Professor Younger discusses. In a case that we trial attorneys are quite familiar with, *Batson v. Kentucky, 476 U.S. 79 (1986),* the United States Supreme Court overturned the conviction of an African-American defendant because the prosecutor in that case had exercised peremptory challenges to strike all four potential African-American members of the jury. In *Powers v. Ohio, 499 U.S. 400 (1991),* the Supreme Court indicated that a white defendant could object to the prosecutor's striking of all available African-American jurors. In *Edmonson v. Leesville Concrete Company, 500 U.S. 614 (1991),* the Supreme Court applied this prohibition of the discriminatory use of peremptory challenges to a civil case.

In *Georgia v. McCollum, 505 U.S. 42 (1991),* a white defendant was accused of assaulting two African-American males, so it was the defense attorney who exercised the peremptory challenges to strike potential African-American members of the jury. The Supreme Court held that the prosecutor had standing to object to the defense attorney's discriminatory use of peremptory challenges. And in *J.E.B. v. Alabama ex. rel. T.B., 511 U.S. 127 (1994),* the Supreme Court held that "gender, like race, is an unconstitutional proxy for juror competence and impartiality."

IRVING YOUNGER: I believe certain things about the trial of a lawsuit, ladies and gentlemen, and because those items of belief of mine will inform everything else that I have to say, let me begin by telling you what they are.

First, I believe that the trial of a lawsuit is an art and, like every other art, it involves a combination of talent and of craft. The talent, the spark that God gave you, I have nothing to say about beyond naming it. It is the craft of a part of trial advocacy that is our subject matter today. By craft, I mean the technical skill, which in the instance of a painter, involves how to hold the brush and in what manner to apply the paint to the canvas. There is a technical skill that underlies trial advocacy. I believe that it may profitably be studied, that it can be taught, and virtually anybody with a modest amount of intelligence and a liberal application of energy can learn that craft. Now, I believe that this craft of advocacy is independent of the jurisdiction in which you are trying your case. It makes no difference whether the case be federal or state; within the state system in whichever court the case may be pending, the craft of advocacy remains constant. There will be differences of detail to be sure and we will mention some of those differences as we move along. But they are only differences of detail and really need not detain us unduly.

I think that the craft of advocacy is independent of the nature of the case. Be it civil, be it criminal, be it protracted, be it short, the craft of advocacy is unchanging. And, finally, the craft of advocacy in my view is independent of the side of the table at which you sit. If it's a civil case, whether you're plaintiff's counsel, defendant's counsel, on the criminal side of the calendar, whether you're the prosecutor, whether you're the defense lawyer, it really makes no difference—the craft of advocacy is the same. In my mind's eye I see this craft of advocacy as existing, as it were, in between the law of procedure on the one hand and the law of evidence on the other, with a certain amount of overlap at the margins, to be sure, but still the craft of advocacy is a body of doctrine, if you will, a way of looking at things different from the body of doctrine we know of as the law of procedure and the law of evidence.

And finally, I believe that the craft of advocacy, though, of course, related to the law of evidence and the law of procedure, is very different from those subjects in one principal way. When you come to consider the craft of advocacy, you are confronted, of course, by a host of interesting and challenging and difficult and sometimes vexing and always interesting and amusing questions. But unlike the phenomenon that you see when you look at a body of learning such as the law of evidence or the law of procedure, almost always in the craft of advocacy it is true that there is no right answer. If by right answer you mean an answer that is the right answer for virtually all of us, there is no such thing in the craft of advocacy. So much depends upon your particular style, so much depends upon the nuances of the lawsuit being tried, so much depends upon the feel of the courtroom on that day, at that hour, at that very moment, that it's impossible to speak in generalities which are true for all of us all the time.

The most that you can do when you come to consider the craft of advocacy is to think about these questions. You have a kind of obligation to yourself and to your client and to the profession to think about the questions and arrive at thoughtful answers, answers which represent the application of intelligence to these questions. And if you have come up with thoughtful answers to these questions, I think you can go to bed with a clear conscience that night—you have done everything that you can expect of yourself.

Now, let me say it once so that I need not waste time saying it each time as we move along. I will make bold to put before you answers to a good many of these questions that will confront a lawyer picking a jury or trying a case which turns upon expert testimony. Please understand me to have stated each time I put one of these answers before you that this is an answer which seems to be the right one for me. Do not understand me to be saying that it's necessarily the right one for you. Of course not. Nor is it a better answer to these questions than other lawyers may come up with. It is simply the answer to the question that has proved over the years of my practice to be effective and useful and efficient for me. If it proves to be those things for you, I am delighted. Take it—I give it to you. And if it turns out not to be so right for you, don't waste a moment worrying about it. Reject what I suggest, substitute for it something that seems more in keeping with your style, your taste, the courtroom in which you are working. But think about it and I will be at some pains to suggest those factors which ought to play a part in your thinking about these questions. So much for credo at the beginning. Now it's time to go to work on jury selection.

I always turn to the first aspect of it with some hesitation, concerned that some of you will think it almost too elementary to talk about. And it may be elementary, but it sure is desperately important. And for a lawyer at the early stages of his or her career, it is especially necessary to keep it in mind. For a lawyer who's been around the merry-go-round several times and bears the scars of it, it's still useful to be reminded.

Jury selection, more so than any other aspect of the trial of a lawsuit, involves the lawyer knowing things that cannot be looked up in a book. If you're about to undertake the selection of a jury in a civil case in federal court, you, of course, will want to know how many peremptory challenges you have. That can be looked up in a book. Or, if you go to the library, take a look at Title 28 of the Federal Rules of Civil Procedure and you have your answer. But that's about all you can look up in a book with respect to jury selection in that federal courthouse. And I take it for granted that the same thing applies to jury selection in your state courts. It is certainly true in the courts in which I have practiced. Virtually everything a lawyer needs to know about jury selection rests in local custom, the traditions of the courthouse and, not to be scoffed at, the, what shall I say, the proclivities of the individual judge who will preside over your jury selection.

And so first and foremost when getting ready to select a jury, inform yourself of, what I will call for shorthand, local custom. And how do you do that? Well, it's common sense. There are any number of ways. To begin with, talk to other lawyers. If you practice in an office in which you have colleagues, talk to your colleagues who have picked juries in that courthouse and, ideally, before the very judge you will be before next week when you pick your jury. If you don't have colleagues to talk to, talk to other lawyers at the bar or the bar association. After all, what is there to talk about at the bar or bar association meetings but professional matters. And this is a very important one to keep high on the list of things to discuss.

And the best way of all to inform yourself of local custom is to take a couple of hours off several days before you have to pick your jury and go to the courthouse, the courtroom, and be before the very judge who will preside over your jury selection. Sit there and watch. See how that judge likes to do it. Because on the principle of you don't fight with City Hall, the way the judge likes to do it is the way to do it. Why begin with friction? Why begin with some nonsensical misstep, which perhaps gets the judge a little bit angry at you and, if it occurs in the presence of the jury, begins to suggest to the jury that you don't know what you're doing? And remember, the process of persuading the jury begins with the very instant you are in the presence of those prospective jurors. And so you've got to be concerned from that first instant with communicating to the jury your professionalism, your mastery of the situation; hence, know what the judge wants.

Now, I am a not-so-infrequent visitor to Atlanta, as many of you know, but I've never had the pleasure of trying a case in either federal or state court here in Atlanta. So I have no way of knowing what your judges are like. But as a former member of the union, I take it for granted that your judges are no different from the judges I know in New York and Washington. Each and every one of them is rather eccentric. Splendid pillars of the law, to be sure, but each of them has sort of peculiarities of personality and since that's the judge, you know, he sort of makes known what his peculiarities are. There's no reason for him to be tactful about it, and it can be very unsettling to walk into a courtroom to pick a jury unaware of the eccentricities of that particular judge. I have in mind a judge of the general jurisdiction trial court in New York City, now deceased, so I make free to tell stories about him. A very able lawyer with a very distinguished professional background, and you would think that going into his courtroom to pick a case is pretty much appearing before any competent judge anywhere in the free world. How would you know that that judge has his own rule with respect to the appropriate neckwear a male lawyer should wear? And if you are wearing a bow tie, you have violated that rule. And you walk into his courtroom and you happen to be wearing a bow tie and the judge will look down from the bench and say, "Take it off." "Take it off? What do you mean take it off, Judge, the jurors are about to come in." He will say, "I don't care, take it off." You've got to take it off and, believe it or not, the judge will then hand you a long tie. He keeps one on the bench, but it's only one. Whatever it is, that's what you get and you put it on hastily, before the jurors come in. And so you've got to stand up before those jurors and your tie doesn't match your suit. Talk about humiliation. Hmm. And you're not on the way to winning that case because the jurors get to thinking, why doesn't his tie match his suit? He's careless. He doesn't pay attention to the details and, if the jurors begin to think that about you, you're on the way to losing. I'll return to that many times in the course of the morning.

Lest you think that the judge is sexist and has it in only for male lawyers, he also had a rule with respect to female lawyers. And there are a good number of women trial lawyers in New York, and among the best of them—she's still around, but now sort of semi-retired—is a friend of mine and a very effective trial lawyer—she's tried many criminal cases—is a woman named Enid Gerling. And Enid, from the beginning of her career at the bar, adopted as a kind of trademark the wearing of large hats. And, as you know, it is acceptable etiquette in our society for a woman to wear a hat indoors. And what she would do is try her cases wearing the hat. And, you know, that's kind of formidable because it sort of hypnotizes the jury and if you were a man on the other side, there wasn't much you can do about it. You can't very well ask her to remove it, et cetera, except the judge I have in mind had a rule for women—no hats, no hats. And, so help me, this happened the first time Enid Gerling walked into that judge's courtroom to try a case. He looked at her hat and said, "Take it off." And she said, "No." And he said, "Perhaps you didn't hear me. I said take it off." And she said, "No." And he said, "I'm the judge and I'm telling you to take it off." And she said, "I don't care, I'm Enid Gerling and I'm going to keep it on." And he said, "I'm going to send you to jail for civil contempt. You're going to go to jail and you're going to stay there until you take it off." She said, "Send me to jail." He sent her to jail. She went to jail, to the Women's House of Detention, and she sat there a first day, a second day, and then a third day when the warden called the judge and said, "Judge, she's never going to take it off. So you'd better let her out, otherwise it's a life sentence." And then he let her out. Right. And the newspaper coverage of that episode was worth hundreds of thousands of dollars to Enid.

As I said, the judge has passed on, so you don't have to worry, if you're ever called to New York to try a case, about being before him. But lest you think I invent these things, it occurs to me that I ought to tell you his name. His name was Irving Saypol. And if you know anybody in New York, you might sort of ask about, you know, sort of the gossip at the bar about Judge Saypol and you will be told he was a terrific judge and, especially if you had a tough commercial case, you couldn't get anybody better than Judge Saypol. But don't wear a hat if you're a woman and don't wear a bow tie if you're a man. So enough said on that. You will inform yourself of local custom.

No, perhaps not enough said. Let me tell you, I try to stay away from war stories, but to give you an example perhaps a little less idiosyncratic than Judge Saypol of the importance of knowing local custom and, in addition, driving home the idea that this phrase "local custom" applies to an awful lot of things you just wouldn't think of if you sat in your office trying to think through the process of picking a jury. I began to try cases in the federal courthouse. Not my first job in the law, but my first job in which I actually stood up in front of a jury, was as an assistant United States attorney, trying criminal cases in the Southern District of New York a good many years ago. And I thought I knew about everything you could learn in the law library and I was right, I did know about everything you could learn in the law library, which is about "that much" of what you need to know to be a lawyer.

Well, I knew you have so many peremptory challenges. I knew that the judge pretty much conducted the process of questioning the jurors. I knew that my job was to kind of look at those jurors and somehow psych out which ones I ought to challenge.

And finally we reached that point in the jury selection in my first case when my conscious mind told me that it was now time to exercise peremptory challenges. And, to my horror, the clerk who worked in that courtroom suddenly picked up from his desk a large wooden frame containing 12 small metal springs. He used each spring to affix to the frame the jury slip, the little piece of paper bearing the name of each one of the 12 jurors sitting in the box. He affixed each slip to one of the springs. He then took the frame, now bearing the 12 slips of paper, and handed it to me. What do I do now? I realized in a general way I was now supposed to exercise my peremptories, but I didn't know how to do it. I had never seen it done and I had never thought to ask somebody, "How do you exercise your peremptories? What is the footwork? What is the choreography that you go through?" And here's the clerk handing me the wooden frame.

Now, one possibility is to stand up and say, "Judge, I really don't know how to do this. Will you tell me how?" And the judge, milk of human kindness running in his veins, would undoubtedly tell me how to do it. But the jurors are sitting there and what are they thinking? Here's a lawyer who doesn't know the first thing about trying a case. See, they would say to themselves, I, the juror, don't know how to do it, but I'm not supposed to know how to do it. The lawyer is supposed to know how to do it. And you're on your way to losing that case. You might, you know, cry or do something of that kind and it gets you a little time, but, again, it doesn't communicate to the jury that kind of infinite self-assurance that is the hallmark of successful work in front of the jury. And I just had to flub my way through it, but of course, the next time around, I knew.

Had I taken the trouble to go watch a jury being picked in federal court before I did it myself the first time, I would have discovered that in the Southern District of New York—I have no idea whether this is so anywhere else—the custom, the choreography, the minuet with respect to exercising peremptory challenges is as follows. The clerk hands you that frame. You look at the jurors. You decide which ones you're going to challenge peremptorily. You take the slip of paper bearing those jurors' names and turn the slips upside down and put them back in the spring and return the frame to the clerk. Rather elegant, reminiscent of English clubs, isn't it? It's a kind of genteel blackballing. You just turn the card over. Who, in heaven's name, would know that unless somebody had told you or you had gone to court and seen it for yourself? So now I can say it, I'll stick to it—enough on local practice. Desperately important, but I suppose that we've said everything that we should say about it.

Let's turn now to the mechanics of picking a jury. In order to give some life, some substance, some point to this discussion of mechanics, let me take just a moment to put before you my view of the purpose of jury selection. This is sort of pious and general and it's not particularly helpful, I suppose, but it's necessary to begin with a statement of what you think you're up to when you pick a jury. And, as a footnote here, let me remind you that what I'm about to say is independent of the jurisdiction, the nature of the case, or the side that you are on.

When you took procedure in law school, it may be that you spent perhaps a half an hour talking about jury selection. Few teachers of procedure in law school spend anything on it and those who do spend time on it will devote perhaps half a class to it. So enormously important an aspect of trial practice, but in the minds of the theoreticians of the law of procedure, there just isn't very much to say. And what there is to say probably went something like this. The purpose of jury selection is to find those 6 or 12 impartial, unbiased, and open-minded citizens who can try the case solely in accordance with the evidence, apply the law in a dispassionate manner and arrive at a just verdict. And if that's what you think is the purpose of jury selection, you ought to turn in your ticket. The teachers of procedure say it because they believe it and they believe it because, for the most part, they have never tried a case. Indeed, for the most part they have never practiced law. As a matter of fact, the higher you go in the pecking order, the more nearly you come to the very first drawer, the elite of law schools, the more likely it is to be true that the teacher has never practiced—an extraordinary and, in my view, scandalous situation, but you're a captive audience and I ought not to burden you with that.

If you are not looking for an impartial, unbiased, and open-minded jury, what kind of jury are you looking for? And the answer, of course, as every one of us who's ever tried a case knows, is that you are looking for a biased, prejudiced, closed-minded jury absolutely incapable of deciding this case fairly. You're looking for the jury that is capable of deciding the case in only one way and that way is your way. So what you want is a jury of 6 or 12 bigots. Yes. People who cannot conceive of any result other than a result favorable to you. And while it's mildly amusing, I suppose, it is not cynical to say that that is the purpose of jury selection because, remember, when you pick a jury, when you try a case, you are not playing solitaire. There is another lawyer on the other side of the table who is trying to do exactly what you're trying to do, but in the opposite direction. And the magic of the system—and it really is a magical system—is that it's in the clash of the opposites, in the contest between the advocates, that things seem to work well. But let one of the advocates suddenly undertake to be a statesman and to act in accordance with the principles of pure justice and mercy, and the system falls apart. It just doesn't work anymore.

So when you set out to pick a jury, you are looking for 6 or 12 clones of your client. I guess that's what it comes down to. Your client will know how to decide his own case. Of course he will. And those are the kinds of people you want in the jury box.

Which leads to what I think is a more useful, a more accurate formulation of the phrase that describes the process you are participating in when you pick a jury. And I just used the customary phrase—pick a jury. That's the way you see it everywhere—picking or selecting a jury—and it's the way it appears in these materials. But, really, you don't pick or select a jury, because "pick" or "select" connotes that the lawyer plays some part in determining the identity of the people who will ultimately constitute the jury. And, of course, the lawyer plays no part whatsoever in that. Chance determines the identity of the people who will ultimately decide this case. The most the lawyer can do—by using the devices that we will be talking about in a little while—is to bring it about that certain of those potential jurors do not sit; that they are removed from the group, sent to be on a jury in another courtroom, in another case, on another day. In short, you don't pick the jury. Rather, within limits, you unpick the jury. You don't deal the cards, fate deals the cards. But within limits the law says that you may remove certain cards from the deck, so that you're always unpicking rather than picking. And I think that this is more than a niggling of words. I think that it has a real cutting edge for a lawyer. What my experience has demonstrated to me is that the question you ask yourself as you sit there picking the jury, whatever the nature of the case, whatever the jurisdiction, however the judge wants you to do it, you never say to yourself, "Who's best? Who's the right juror in this case?" Because that's the question that would make sense if you were picking the jury and you're not picking the jury, you're unpicking. Hence, the question you ask yourself always is, of these 6 or 12 or whatever the number is in your courtroom, who's worst for me?

You might think of it this way. You have determined, well before you went to court to pick that jury, the profile of the ideal juror, the person who, if this were a perfect world and you could have your way, you would want to sit in that jury box. You use that profile as a kind of measuring stick and you measure the prospective jurors by it. And you ask yourself not who comes closest to the ideal, but who departs farthest from the ideal, who is the worst for me. And you bring it about, if you possibly can, that those people do not serve, that those cards are removed from the deck, so that you're constantly unpicking, not picking.

Now, how do you remove a card from the deck? What are the mechanical devices available to you for accomplishing this rather obvious purpose of jury selection? No matter the jurisdiction, there will be five ways of removing jurors from the panel. You may call them different things from one courtroom or one jurisdiction to another, but they're there in every common law jurisdiction. Let's talk about them. And, because this is the first time we have come to what ultimately will be some 15 or 20 checklists you will get from me in the course of the day, let me point out that it is a checklist—a very useful device—but you should not deceive yourself as to how you make it work for you. A checklist avoids undue work. You don't have to reinvent the wheel. The checklist, in a manner of speaking, gives you the universe of possibilities, but by no means should you automatically use every item on the checklist. Of course not. You use those items which make sense in your case, given the circumstances before you. But you run through the checklist as a kind of menu of possibilities and, from that menu, you draw the one or more which make sense in the problem before you. Right?

Checklist: the five possible ways of bringing it about that some prospective juror does not serve in this case. First, frequently overlooked because it's so obvious, at least in one of the jurisdictions in which I've practiced, it is far and away the most important. That jurisdiction is New York. Agreement. Where the lawyers agree that a particular person should not serve on the jury, that person doesn't serve. And because it's by agreement, it's not chalked up against the score of either side. In New York civil practice, 98 to 99 percent of the time that is the way it's done. As a matter of fact, let me tell you because it's of passing interest, I suppose, that in civil cases in New York state, the jury selection is conducted by the lawyers without the judge being present. The judge is not there. It's just the lawyers and the prospective jurors. At the beginning of things in New York—and it has become part of the tradition, indeed, it's part of the codified law—the lawyers went off in a room by themselves and selected the jury. No judge was present. In theory, it saves time and it does, in fact, save time because the judge's attention is almost never required.

What causes the lawyers to behave themselves? How come things work the way that they're supposed to? And the answer is, the sanction is the sanction of the jurors' response to lawyer monkey business. Jurors are very sensitive to unprofessional conduct. They may not be able to give it a name, but they recognize it when they see it, and if a lawyer is guilty of unprofessional conduct, that lawyer will be punished by the jurors. So the lawyers behave themselves; they conduct themselves with dignity towards each other, to the court, and to the jurors, and the thing works very smoothly indeed. Because there is no judge present it has become a habit that the lawyers not worry about formal exercise of peremptory challenges. If the plaintiff's lawyer says to the defendant's lawyer, "Charlie, I'm inclined to challenge number six." Charlie will say, "You know, I thought you were going to do that. It's agreed, he's excused." Because Charlie knows that, when his turn comes, he will get the same kind of treatment from plaintiff's counsel, so that the thing works by consent rather than by operation of law. Do not neglect it as a possibility for removing jurors.

Second possibility, rarely encountered for I suppose most of us; never in the course of a career, for many of us, perhaps once for others. When you do encounter it, it's always anticipated well in advance, carefully researched. There's time to go to the library to lay out the law on this. It's usually fairly dramatic. It's done on papers. You never do it just right out of your hip pocket. But it has its place on our checklist. This is what is everywhere called the challenge to the array. The challenge to the array says not, "I wish to remove certain cards from the deck." Rather, the challenge to the array says, "I want a whole new deck. All of these people should be sent home and a new panel given to me." Now, the basis for a challenge to the array is invariably some claimed flaw or deficiency in the process by which prospective jurors are selected, so that the deck is not a fair deck. Now, it will vary from case to case, but the deficiency will always be in the nature of a constitutional violation, such as a process for selecting prospective jurors that is not race-neutral, that favors whites over blacks or blacks over whites, that favors males over females or vice versa, that favors old over young or vice versa—whatever it may be. Something that is not designed, a system that as a system, is likely to produce a stacked deck, a deck that is not fair, that is not a cross-section of the community. All right. So, obviously, it's anticipated, you plan it, you will prepare papers on it, and I will have nothing more to say about it. But there it is on the checklist.

Next, a challenge which comes up as a matter of fact fairly infrequently, although the name of this challenge falls trippingly from the tongue of trial lawyers all the time. As I'll mention in a moment, the name is, in fact, misused. This is the challenge for cause, which, at least in my neck of the woods, will be heard probably about on the average once in the course of every jury selection. And in my neck of the woods, almost always the term is being improperly used by the lawyer. It's, in fact, not a challenge for cause, it's something else.

Just because terminological precision is the hallmark of a careful lawyer, let's get the terms down right. A challenge for cause is a challenge to some prospective juror resting upon circumstances in that juror's background. But here's what makes it a challenge for cause. Given those circumstances, the juror must be excused. It is mandatory. If you like to put it this way, the law requires that the juror be excused. The judge has no discretion in the matter whatsoever. And the grounds that will support a challenge for cause will be set forth in the statutes or the cases in your jurisdiction. And, at a minimum, relationship within a certain degree of consanguinity between the prospective jurors and the litigant will support a challenge for cause.

Now, just so that the melody of it becomes clear, not trying to act it out in a way that's absolutely realistic, if you're in a courtroom in which you are permitted to question the prospective jurors and you turn to juror number two and you say, "Juror number two, do you happen to know the defendant, Mr. Smith, who's sitting over there?" "Well, yes, I do." "Well, how do you come to know Mr. Smith?" "He's my brother." Judge . . . judge. Do you feel it? If the judge were to say, "Well, the juror looks like an honest man to me, I think we'll leave him on this jury," that's wrong. That is error as a matter of law, because a juror who is so closely related to a litigant cannot sit, and the judge must grant your challenge. That is a challenge for cause. And if you pick juries in a large city, just the odds on it are such that a true challenge for cause, a challenge for cause correctly understood, will come up very rarely indeed.

It is the next kind of challenge, number four on our checklist, which is, in fact, what most lawyers are referring to when they use the phrase challenge for cause. Among American lawyers, we don't have a separate name for it because we sloppily use the phrase challenge for cause and so I have helped myself to the term that our professional cousins across the water, the barristers of England, use. They refer to this as a challenge to the favor. And it's an old-fashioned and archaic way of referring to a challenge which, of course, rests upon circumstances in the juror's background, but where those circumstances invite the judge to use his or her discretion. It is a discretionary ruling whether or not to excuse the juror and if anybody . . . of course, some of you . . . many of you, I know, have been through it. You will know that the ruling is virtually unreviewable. In the first analysis and in the last analysis, it's left to the common sense of the judge presiding and the appellate court will not concern itself with the ruling on a challenge to the favor.

Again, to sort of get the melody of it, "Juror number two, do you know the defendant, Mr. Smith, who's sitting over there?" "Yes, I do know him." "Well, how do you know him?" "Well, we were in junior high school together." "And how long ago was that?" "Twenty-seven, twenty-eight years" "Were you particularly good friends?" "No, I wouldn't say particularly good." "Did you ever visit his home?" "I think once." "Did he ever visit your home?" "No, I really don't think so." Judge, how about it? And your ear tells you that the answer is yes or no and either one is the correct answer. The judge may say we'll excuse him or we'll not excuse him. The ruling is entirely discretionary and that is the challenge to the favor.

Fifth and last, and I suppose statistically most important in that you use it more than any of these other challenges, is the peremptory challenge, in some jurisdictions simply called the strike. Whatever you call it, we all know what it is. It is, as lawyers say when they speak loosely, the challenge which may be exercised for no reason. And always that loose. I'll accept it, but only if we understand that that's very sloppy talk. Shame on you if you ever exercise a peremptory for no reason. Of course you will have a reason.

Until very recent years—and what's been happening in recent years we will be concerned with a little bit later on in the course of the morning—until very recent years, it was possible to say that the peremptory challenge was a challenge exercised for a reason, to be sure, but a reason that was private to the lawyer. Under no circumstances could a judge ask you what your reason was and doubly under no circumstances could a judge second guess you and tell you that the reason is wrong or unworthy or unlawful. As many of you know and as all of you will be told in due course this morning, that's changing with respect to one kind of reason for exercising a peremptory challenge. We'll review the nature of the change and take a look at some of the cases later on. So cross-referenced to a later discussion, let's leave it that the traditional view, subject to a question mark in very recent years, is that the peremptory challenge is a challenge that is exercised for a reason kept within the mind of the lawyer, shared, if with anyone, only with his client.

The single most important thing to remember about a peremptory challenge, assuming that you've got a reason for it, is that while you have peremptory challenges in every case, in every jurisdiction, you have them to a limited number, and that number is always low. What the number is will vary from state to state and from jurisdiction to jurisdiction. Of course, you look it up in advance. And, as you exercise peremptory challenges, in the forefront of your consciousness should always be what? Not how many do you have. That partakes of picking a jury. Remember, you're unpicking a jury, so that the question in your consciousness as you exercise peremptories is always how many do I have left?

Thus, if you're in a jurisdiction in which you've got three peremptories, it's now time to exercise them. You look at those 6 or 12 people sitting in the jury box. Juror number four, he makes your flesh creep.

Why does he make your flesh creep? I'll tell you why, because you make his flesh creep. It is always reciprocal. Should you get rid of him? Of course you should get rid of him. I say now and will say at the very end, play your hunches. That's the single best thing you have going for you. What your instinct, your bones, the seat of your pants tells you, that's what do to. Because in the last analysis this is a process of trying to guess something about human nature, and all of us are pretty good at guessing it, but it's impossible to articulate it. Something in you tells you to do it, but you can't put into words why. That guy makes your flesh creep? Okay, get rid of him. Use a peremptory, which means what? You've got two left.

That's what you say to yourself as you examine the rest of those jurors. Look at number eight. He makes your blood run cold, because you make his blood run cold. So what should you do? Get rid of him, right? Now how many do you have left? One. Now it gets interesting. See juror number one? Something about him. I'm just not sure. Now, it doesn't rise to the level of he makes my flesh crawl or my blood run cold, but I'm uneasy. The novice will say, "Get rid of him, you've got the one challenge." That's picking a jury. The older hand, battle scarred as we are, will say, "Wait a minute, you've got the one challenge, but if you use it to get rid of juror number one, how many do you have left? " Zero. And what will you be looking at? An empty chair. And will some other person be called to sit in that chair? Yes. And can you do anything to determine the identity of that person? No. And once that person is called to sit in that chair, will you be able to excuse him peremptorily? No. You will have none left. So what do you do? Do you get rid of number one or do you not get rid of number one? What do you do? I don't know.

I said there are no answers here—that's part of the fun of the game. You think and you think and you think and you get it down to the finest point that you possibly can and you know what ultimately all of us do? You close your eyes, and hold your nose and jump, praying that there's water in the pool. That's all you can do. Nobody can guarantee anything and nobody can give you a list of right answers or recipes that are going to bake the cake every time.

You've got the five methods of excusing a jury. Now, let's pause very briefly before turning to the heart of the matter for some advice, or at least commentary, on my part on how to kind of have the table arranged in front of you. This may seem like stuff so picayune it's unworthy of discussion at a program presented by the Atlanta Bar Association. What do you mean the table in front of you? How many pencils to have? What kind of notebook? Yeah, that's exactly what I mean. Yes, it is picayune, it is a matter of detail. But it's by paying attention to those picayune matters of detail that lawyers win cases. Nothing should go unconsidered. I leave it to you to assess your professional colleagues.

Let me give you my assessment—not really an assessment, a description—of what I have seen over the years trying cases and presiding over cases from the middle in New York and then, more recently, in Washington, D.C., with a handful of cases from other jurisdictions scattered in. An awful lot of lawyers do a credible job of jury selection, but somehow trip over their own feet when it comes to the notes and what to have on the table in front of them. It's especially vexing to see because it's so unnecessary.

And on the chance that what I have to say about it may help some of you, let me give you my view of what to do about the notes. The one thing I'm certain of is that you should not do what so many lawyers are guilty of in the places where I practice, and if I tell you about it, I'm sure you will recognize that at least some of your colleagues are guilty of the same mistake. Indeed, I whisper softly, perhaps some of you. You're in a courtroom in which you are allowed to question the jurors and the lawyer will stand up with a yellow pad and a pencil and he will say to juror number one, "Where do you live, sir? And what do you do for a living? And are you married, sir?" Writes down every answer and by the third or fourth question, those other jurors are about to explode with boredom, right? Because it so impedes the flow of things that it just loses all interest. And, as I will be saying in due course, one of your obligations as a trial lawyer, an obligation that is no small part of jury selection, is to interest those jurors.

Number one, don't take notes. Now, there is a way of getting the basic information that you need that I will suggest to you. It's something that I was taught by my elders at the very beginning. I have made it an habitual part of my trial practice and I've run into lawyers from other parts of the country who do the same thing.

Take a look at the jury box in your courtroom before you start the jury selection. In large courthouses, I have found that the courtrooms are designed according to either of two blueprints. There are left-handed courtrooms and right-handed courtrooms, depending upon which side has the jury box. And I assume that in your jurisdiction, as in every one I know, the places are numbered. Well, make sure you know how they number them. It takes us back to the beginning. Local practice—do they begin over there or do they begin over there? That's the difference between a right-handed and left-handed courtroom. So is that one, two, three, four, five, six or one, two, three, four, five, six? If you have six plus jurors, more than six, know whether seven is up there or up there. Whether you sort of double back or make a U-turn or what do you do? How is it counted? Then diagram the jury box, ideally using a loose-leaf notebook, not a yellow pad, and that diagram should be about the size of the page. Give yourself plenty of room.

And, because I believe in writing down everything that I can think of in advance, because I'm going to write virtually nothing during the trial and the more I write in advance, the more likely it is that my eye will do the work my brain is too feeble to do, I actually number the boxes so that if this is a left-handed jury box, that becomes one, so on down the line to six. And that will be either seven or that will be seven, depending upon how they do it in your courtroom. There's no standard practice, you just have to know the way it's done. Then, as names are called, assuming what is likely to be so, that the clerk calls out names and those people come up and sit in seats 1 through 6 and then 7 through 12, as the clerk calls the name, write it down. And as you see that's the only writing that I'm going to do. So you have the names here, which means you have before you a diagram of the jury box. The diagram visually matches what you see as you stand in front of the jury box. You don't have to go through any mental arithmetic in figuring out that whether this name goes with that person or with that person. Your eye does it instantly for you and that's all you will have as you talk to the jurors.

Don't take notes because, first, it impedes the flow and it makes your presentation less effective. And second, it detracts from the eye contact, which is probably the single most important thing you have going for you when it comes to persuading the jury. And third, perhaps most important—it's not necessary. It's not necessary, because, though many of you think you do need it, you can remember everything that you need to remember if you will let yourself do so. Each one of us has a power of concentration, an ability to absorb information for a short time, but in enormous quantities, beyond what we realize. We use the notes as a crutch to assist our nervousness. Perfectly understandable, but you've got to get over the nervousness. Or you really don't get over it, but you learn to master it. And give it some practice and you will discover that you don't need the notes. You can remember who's married and who's not and in any event, those little details are much less important than a general feel for the personality of the prospective juror and giving that juror a feel for you. And you do that by looking at the juror and talking to him in a direct way rather than taking notes as if you're a court stenographer, sitting there listening to a deposition and writing everything down.

If, for whatever reason, you find it absolutely essential to have in written form something about the jurors, have a colleague take notes. Don't you take the notes. Somebody else sits in the audience or at the counsel table and takes the notes. You just talk to those jurors while looking at them.

Whether you find it useful, I don't know, but let me tell you that there was one other kind of box score that I learned to keep at the beginning and still keep. Because it is so important not to lose track of it, I put over on the side or on another page something that looks like an inning-by-inning baseball box score and that's the way I keep track of the peremptory challenges. And that'll be for the plaintiff, that will be for the defendant. Enough boxes to add up to as many peremptories as there are. And it is almost like formal box score keeping in baseball. It would work this way.

Suppose the plaintiff exercises a peremptory with respect to juror number one? I put number one in that first box, representing the plaintiff's first peremptory, draw a line through that first prospective juror, and write in the next person's name who is called to sit. You can now, if necessary, reconstruct what happened. The plaintiff exercised his first peremptory on juror number one. Mrs. Smith was excused, Mrs. Jones was called to take her place. And your eye now tells you that you have that many peremptories left on the plaintiff's side and so many on the defendant's side—whatever the numbers may be. Sometimes it comes in handy and I guess, engaging in a little bit of self-psychoanalysis, putting the numbers down and drawing the lines does something to vent that nervous tension. It gets you doing something that keeps things to a manageable level. But that's all—the chart of the jury box, the box score with respect to peremptory challenges and no notes beyond that.

Just pausing to generalize, many of you have heard me say it, because I do say it when we talk about trial practice generally, I believe that most lawyers take far too many notes in the course of a trial. I think that the least productive thing you can do when your opponent is conducting the direct examination of an important witness whom you will cross-examine, is to take notes on the direct examination. Shame on you if you don't know what the man's going to say. Of course you know what he's going to say. Listen and watch. Get a sense of the witness. His facial expressions will give you a clue as to the weak spots and how to get at them in cross-examination. Much more important to use your eyes and all of your perceptions than to sit writing things down and then try to read through it while you conduct your cross-examination. But that's for another occasion. End of generalization.

With respect to jury selection, I apply what I believe in general. Minimum note taking. It's simply not necessary and it interferes with the effectiveness of your presentation. Now, we talk about the effectiveness of the presentation. What is it that you are trying to do on jury selection? Well, we said that you're unpicking the jury, you're trying to get rid of those people who depart farthest from the ideal. But that is so vague and all-embracing a way of saying it that it doesn't particularly help, so let's begin to refine it. Again, it's a checklist. Not everything on this checklist will be achieved every time, but it represents what, to my mind, is the universe of possibilities.

When you pick a jury, no matter the nature of the case, no matter the jurisdiction, there are, at most, three things that you can accomplish. You will not necessarily strive to accomplish each of these things simultaneously, but at any moment in the course of jury selection, you should be able to say, right now what I'm trying to do is one or two or three, or possibly a combination of them, possibly. You owe it to yourself to know what you're up to at each moment in the courtroom. Indeed, I would say that the beginning of developing an effective courtroom style is to be self-conscious about it. Not self-conscious in the sense of hesitant and abashed, but self-conscious in the sense of always thinking about what you are doing. Never do anything without a reason. So three purposes of which the first is, I suppose, the most obvious. You're trying to acquire information about the prospective jurors. To what end? The more you know about the prospective jurors, the more accurate you can be in measuring the juror by the measuring stick represented by the profile of the ideal juror you want in this case, and then determining who among these prospective jurors departs farthest. Whom am I going to try to get rid of?

You want information about prospective jurors and it seems to me—again, it's a checklist—that there are five possible ways of acquiring information about a prospective juror, not all of them available in every jurisdiction. As a practical matter, not all of them may be available simply because of limitations of money, resources in the case. But, as we'll see, what in my mind are the most effective ways of acquiring information about jurors are available in every courtroom in the land, the jurisdiction makes no difference and the only thing you need is energy. No money is required. Now, what are the five ways?

First, available in every jurisdiction, in virtually every case, but, as we'll see in a moment, it is expensive—advance investigation. And somebody who's never been through the mill will say, what do you mean advance investigation? I mean, investigation of the prospective jurors before they are called to sit in the jury box. And then the question will be, so whom do you investigate? You told us and everybody knows, a lawyer plays no part in determining the identity of the prospective jurors. How, then, can you investigate them in advance? As follows. An occasional melodramatic criminal case aside, it is true generally that the list of prospective jurors, of panelists, whatever you call them in your jurisdiction, summoned for jury duty that week or month or term of court, is a public document. The name and address of every person who gets a jury summons for that month is available upon application to the clerk and the payment of whatever the Xeroxing fee is. Now, in an urban jurisdiction, that will be a long list, because a lot of people are summoned. It may be 500 names long. But your 6 or 12 will come from those 500. And so the advance investigation that you do is to get the list as soon as it's available and then you call in Paul Drake or whoever does that work for you, and you say, "Paul, go out and investigate all 500." You've got to investigate the 500 to have something useful for the 6 or 12 who ultimately sit in that jury box. And there's the expensiveness of it.

Now, if you're going to do it, obviously only once in a great while, for heaven's sake, make sure that Paul does it tactfully. You are investigating the jurors who are going to sit in your case. And it may strike some of you as unduly cynical, but I ought to say it and certainly it will not go beyond these four walls. The jurors ought not to know that they're being investigated, because the instant they know that they're being investigated, they take offense and you have lost that case. So the investigation cannot be calling upon the neighbors and asking whether the fellow over there has wild parties or something of that kind. It cannot involve the public examination of the garbage of the prospective jurors. But other kinds of discreet inquiries will be made and it will occasionally produce extraordinary results.

Let me give you some suggestions for what may be done. I don't know, but there may be a couple of people here who are government lawyers, be it local government or the federal government. Well, the possibilities there are astounding. I mentioned that I was an assistant U.S. attorney all those years ago. The resource available was the FBI. It's so expensive, however, that even if you are working for the federal government, you've got to get clearance from a higher level to do this. It was called a name check. You took the list of 500 or so people summoned for jury duty and three FBI agents sat and ran those names through the central index. It was before the days of computers, so it had to be done manually. And it took the three agents something like three days. That's nine man-days—that's a lot of money. And it produced a whole bunch of useless information, plus, with respect to one juror in an internal security case, information that you could not possibly have acquired in any other way. And on the basis of that information I did exercise a peremptory challenge of the juror. I don't want to make it more dramatic than it was, but it approached the discovery that juror number six was a Soviet spy. That's pretty useful to know in an internal security case, right? So the guy was bounced. I'm positive he was a spy because he waited until the next recess and got me out in the corridor and very politely said, "Why did you excuse me?" You know, he just sort of seemed to be a citizen who was curious as to why a lawyer got rid of him. I'm sure you've been asked that question by jurors. Some jurors really are curious. I think this guy wanted to know whether his cover had been blown. So, of course, what I said was, "I don't like people with mustaches," wholly invented, but the guy had a mustache, so he went away wondering whether he'd been had or not. A very expensive peremptory challenge.

You may not have the resources of the FBI or the local police department, but let me point out that a reasonable amount of energy and ingenuity can give you access to sources of information. Your client may have files. Remember that there are credit privacy statutes, which you may have to worry about, but we'll assume that you've made sure that you're not violating any of those statutes. Banks have files on people. Insurance companies have files on people. It's expensive, but not overwhelmingly expensive, to pull credit reports on people. Other ways of getting information will occur to you, but there's one way that may not. And let me give it to you and I have found it to be very useful, pretty much in inverse relationship to the size of the community.

In a place like New York City, Los Angeles or, I suppose, Atlanta, this may not prove very useful. But in a town with 10,000 residents, this is going to be terrific. If I were practicing in such a town or were about to try a case in such a town, I would make it my business to be introduced to the managing editor of the local newspaper simply so that I could then ask, as a favor, to be allowed to use the morgue. And I'm sure you know, the morgue is the clipping file that every newspaper maintains. It's not a public facility. That's why you've got to make friends and ask for permission to use it. But there's nothing dishonorable about it—the reporters use it all the time. Whenever an item appears in the newspaper about John Smith, it'll be clipped and placed in a file on John Smith. Where it's *The New York Times* or the *Atlanta Constitution,* the universe is too great for it to be particularly useful, but in a smaller town the newspaper is printing items of exactly the sort you would want to know about when picking the jury. Who was involved in a small accident? Who got into some kind of juvenile trouble? A school record, domestic difficulties, things of that kind, are in the newspaper and there they are in the morgue. That's free. All you have to do is put yourself out to get access to it. Right? So remember the possibilities of advance investigation.

The five-item checklist of ways of acquiring information about the jurors is a phenomenon of fairly recent development. Not all of us will believe in it and not many of us will have the opportunity to use it. To do an adequate job of discussing it will take more time than we can afford to give it. So I freely confess that all I'm doing is naming this resource and just talking for a minute or two about it.

This is the assistance that, in recent years, has come to be available for social scientists—the psychologists, the sociologists, the social psychologists who, typically for a fee, stand ready to advise a trial lawyer on any aspect of trial practice, but most importantly on jury selection. Now, I dare say the vast majority of us have never had the opportunity to use these people. So let me tell you in very broad terms, really in a nutshell, what the sociologist or the psychologist can do for you. Obviously, this must be done well in advance. Remember we talked about the profile of the ideal juror, which you will use as a measuring stick to determine who on that panel departs farthest from the ideal and, thus, ought to be excused if you can manage it. The psychologist or sociologist, using what he is pleased to call exquisitely sensitive sampling and polling techniques, will go out and study the community where your case is going to be tried. And, on the basis of those polling techniques, he or she will come up with a statistically demonstrable profile of the ideal juror in this case, considering who the client is, the nature of the cause of action, the community, what's going on in the world, what people are worrying about, the kinds of people who live in this town and therefore will be on the jury, et cetera, et cetera. You, the lawyer, then take this profile and you use it as the measuring stick to determine who departs farthest and therefore ought to be excused.

Now, I've been involved in cases in which we've used the social scientist and many of my acquaintances have been involved in those cases and let me tell you that my own experience and the experience of all of my acquaintances is identical. The social scientist will produce a very persuasive result in the sense that the profile of the ideal juror that the sociologist comes up with after doing a sampling, et cetera, et cetera, is invariably identical with the profile you would have come up with simply on the basis of intuition and common sense. And many of you are smiling because you say to yourself, well, if the sociologist comes up with something identical to what your own intuition tells you, why do you have to spend $75,000 of the client's money to conduct one of these polls? And the answer, again in the family, not to go beyond these four walls, is that it's very reassuring to the client to have the "scientist" tell him that the lawyer knows what he's doing and, especially secretly, I whisper in your ear, it's very reassuring to the lawyer to have the scientist tell you that the seat of your pants is telling you the truth.

Just one anecdote to wind it up. It's not a case I was involved in, but it's a case all of us recall. The lawyer who tried it is a friend of mine and he has told this story publicly, so I make free to tell it to you. Remember many years ago, John Mitchell, Nixon's attorney general was tried. Not in the Watergate case in Washington, in which he was convicted, but in New York on an indictment charging Mitchell and Stands, the secretary of Commerce, and a few other people, with attempting to fix an SEC investigation on behalf of Robert Vesco, the fugitive financier. In that case, everybody was acquitted. It was much in the newspapers, both because of the identity of the defendants, and because it was the first time John Dean testified and was cross-examined.

A New York lawyer, extremely able, named Peter Fleming, a good friend of mine, represented John Mitchell and got him acquitted. So more power to him. Peter used one of the social scientists. Now, this goes back 10 or so years, so it was very early in the history of this phenomenon of social science assistance to trial lawyers. He sent the social scientist out to conduct a poll and come back with a profile of the ideal juror in that case. Now, remember, it's Watergate, New York City, the defendant is John Mitchell, charge is attempting to fix an SEC investigation. The pollster comes back some weeks and many thousands of dollars later and says, "Peter, the profile of the ideal juror in this case is a white male at least 55 years old, earning $100,000 a year, a registered Republican." You realize what he's done is describe John Mitchell, right? Of course. We all knew that. We knew that an hour and a half ago. You want jurors who are clones of your client because your client will know how to decide his case.

In passing, and because we're friends and, you know, I know it will not be misunderstood by anybody, it's the Southern District of New York. That's Manhattan and the Bronx. Not people who work in Manhattan, but people who live in Manhattan. Well, who lives in Manhattan? You know, a couple of millionaires who get off the jury list and for the rest it's Harlem and the South Bronx. The pollster has described the smallest minority there is in the Southern District of New York. There are no more than 12 people in the Southern District of New York who can show up for jury duty who satisfy that profile. And, do you know, the odds were billions to one, all 12 were in the jury box. Peter has said that from the instant the jurors were called, he knew he was going to win that case because he had 12 clones of his client sitting there. And, of course, his client would know how to decide his own case. It was kind of miraculous and once in a lifetime and it's not going to happen to Peter ever again or probably to any of us, but be aware that the social scientist is there to help. The nature of the help ties in with what trial lawyers have been doing, if not since the days of Clarence Darrow, probably even longer than that.

Next, we begin to discuss means of acquiring information available ad lib in every case. It doesn't involve money, it simply involves lawyer dedication and determination and the application of energy and perhaps a certain amount of practice. I guess it's a skill, but it's a skill that anybody can learn.

The third method of acquiring information is what I call using the information on the jury slip. Now, that terminology may be foreign to you, but what I'm talking about is not foreign to you. You may not call it the jury slip. You may have a different way of doing it, but let me show you that we're talking about something that's part of your practice as well as mine. In every jurisdiction in the land when the jurors are called to sit in the jury box, when the prospective jurors are selected, some paper is given to the lawyer. Now, in the courts of the northeast, the ones with which I am familiar, both state and federal, the paper is literally a slip. It is about the size of a business card. It's the thing the clerk pulls out of the wheel when he selects the 6 or 12 people to come and sit in the box. It is called a jury slip and it contains minimal information. In New York and in the District of Columbia, name, address, and sometimes occupation. That's all that's on the slip. In other courts, especially in the midwest, I know, from talking to friends of mine, the lawyer gets a rather lengthy document about the jurors. When the jurors report in for jury duty, they are given a poll, much like a census poll, with all kinds of information about their personal background. They fill it out and that questionnaire is automatically given to the lawyer when the juror is called to sit in the box. So whether it's the short form of New York or Washington or the long form of a place like Kansas, I am positive you get some document, some piece of paper containing information, be it minimal or maximal, about the prospective juror. Right? My point is that you must learn to use that information and learning to use it means recognizing that the information, the data on the jury slip, will suggest much more information that is probably true. You can't be positive that it's true, but it's probably true. And, after all, probabilities and hunches, in the ultimate analysis, are all you have to go on in this process of jury selection.

A few examples, not necessarily applicable in every case, but let's see how it would work. And in turning to these examples, I have to call things by their right name. We understand that when you pick a jury, invariably you've got to take into account racial, ethnic and religious stereotypes. You don't live your personal life that way. You recognize a stereotype for what it is. You don't judge people and you judge them for themselves, not for accidental circumstances of their background, but you have so little to work with in a courtroom that you have an obligation to make use of these stereotypes, if only because they're stereotypes precisely because there's a certain amount of truth in them. And you just take it into account as part of the mix.

So with that editorial, so that there are no misunderstandings, I put it to you that religion or ethnic background is something you want to know about jurors. Of course you want to know about jurors. I mean, you don't have to be a master psychologist, you don't have to be Shakespeare or Chekhov to know that Jews are different from Germans or that somebody whose grandparents came from Scandinavia is different from somebody whose grandparents came from Italy. Yeah, the grandchildren, the people who are being called to sit on this jury, were born in the United States, but still from where your grandparents came affects who you are. It's in the genes, and if it's not in the genes, you remember grandfather, grandmother. This is the way they were and it plays a part in determining who you were.

And it's absurd, it's stupid not to recognize that, while all people are equally valuable, Scandinavians are different from Italians. You're from

Scandinavia. It's cold all the time. It rains all the time, and life is hard. And it produces a certain kind of personality. Tends to be judgmental, vindictive, so that if you represent the plaintiff in a civil case or the defendant in a criminal case, no. But an Italian, it's the shores of the Mediterranean. May not have much money, but the sun shines. Life is sweet and the flesh is weak. That plays a part in determining the personality of the grandchild and if you're representing the plaintiff in a civil case or the defendant in a criminal case, you begin to like that person and various other importances of ethnic and religious background we'll talk about later on when we go through that checklist of things that you want to watch out for.

But how do you find out whether someone's grandparents came from Italy or whether someone is Jewish? Assuming a jurisdiction in which you can ask questions of the jurors, let me say it now—there's no law on this. Insofar as the law is concerned, you can ask absolutely anything you want. I mean, the questions the law forbids are absurd. No lawyer would dream of asking questions of that kind. Insofar as the law is concerned, you are perfectly free in a courtroom in which lawyers conduct the voir dire, to ask a juror what his religion is. But you don't dare. Of course not.

Why? More important than the rule of law is the rule of thumb. When you question jurors, ask any question you want so long as you would ask it of a new acquaintance, someone you had just met at a cocktail party. Because to the perspective juror you are a stranger talking to them. They're not familiar with the procedure of the voir dire, of jury selection. They don't have a professional attitude towards it. And they will accept a question or comment from you if they would accept it of someone they had just met at a backyard cookout, cocktail party, or the like. And that's how to test a question that you're inclined to ask. And if you have any doubt about it, if you think I'm not telling it to you right, when you go to the cocktail party the next time, or a backyard cookout this weekend and you meet somebody, try it. Okay? "How do you do, I'm Irving Younger. Are you Jewish?" You know, you just don't do things like that.

Well, within limits you don't have to. It's obvious enough, but how many lawyers fail to take advantage of the information on the jury slip? Look at the name. Not always, but much of the time the name gives you the religion or the ethnic background. Now, I'll grant you, as the generations go by in the United States, the ethnic identification is increasingly ironed out. Before too many generations, everyone is going to be named Smith. But still, we're not yet at that point and occasionally there will be a Mr. O'Brien. He's probably not Jewish, huh? Right? And you can go on from there.

All right. Less obvious and very important. In addition to religion, ethnic background, and the like, you want to know economic class. You want to know his income because economic class plays a vital role in determining how people look at the world. And, really, what you are doing as you engage in this process of jury selection, of acquiring information about the jurors, is trying to get a fix on how this juror is going to respond to the world you present to him or her in the course of trying this lawsuit. Can you ask how much money did you make last year? Of course you can ask it, the law doesn't care. But you can't ask it by application of the cocktail party rule. You know, income is the great forbidden of American life. It is more acceptable these days to say to a total stranger, "How's your sex life?" than "How much money did you make last year?" But you don't have to ask it; look at the address and 999 times out of 1,000, the address gives you the economic class.

If you're going to pick juries in Atlanta, you've got to know the neighborhoods of Atlanta the way the postman knows them. You've got to know where apartment buildings are, where private homes are. If it's a private home neighborhood, you've got to know whether they are $50,000 or $500,000 homes. A glance at the address gives you the class.

To drive this home, many of you will know, or know of, a sensationally able and successful personal injury lawyer in Chicago named Phil Corboy. He's a friend of mine and I'm authorized to tell you this. It's just something that he's used over the years. In a heavy case he regards it as so important to get the economic class of the jurors and, aware that he can't ask the question, that he's got to get it from the address, and since he tries most of his cases in Chicago, he cannot know the neighborhoods as well as he does, he has an acquaintance of his who has spent a lifetime as a taxi driver in Chicago whom he pays to sit in the courtroom when he picks the jury. And he just finds an opportunity to have this taxi driver look at the addresses on the jury slip and clue Phil in as to what the neighborhood is. Usually the taxi driver can even tell him about the nature of the very street on which the building or apartment building or whatever it is is, and then Phil goes from there. Right. Whether you carry it to that length or just rely upon your own knowledge of the neighborhoods, make sure you have some knowledge of the neighborhoods and, for heaven's sake, make use of it.

Let's wind this up with an example. And simply because I don't know Atlanta well enough and I don't want to offend anybody, I draw it from my former hometown, the place in which I was born, New York. Look how much you can do with a jury slip, recognizing that these are only probabilities, but probability is what you have in a courtroom. Here's the slip on juror number three. Remember, it's minimal information—name, address, and occupation. You look at it. Right. You now know, he's a white male, maybe 40 years old. Name, John Smith. All right, doesn't tell you much about the ethnic background. Address, 10 E. 78th Street in Manhattan. And, for those of you who don't know it offhand, that's right across the street, across Fifth Avenue from the Metropolitan Museum of Art. It is the highest rent high-rent district in the world. A one-room efficiency apartment in any building in that neighborhood goes for about $200,000 a year. You want a separate bedroom, $400,000 a year. Mmm hmm. So now you know that guy makes a lot of money. Look at the occupation. I tell you from my own experience that invariably, the person I have described living in that kind of neighborhood puts down as his occupation self-employed. Now you know what he does—pushes heroin, obviously. And I'll grant you, he may not push heroin—so he pushes something else. What does it matter? It really doesn't matter, but he's a pusher. And when you come to pick a jury, standing alone that doesn't mean anything. It's not to condemn him, it's not to praise him, it is simply a factor that you want to take into account along with everything else in determining whether this is the person you want serving on this jury. I guess that's about all we can say about the jury slip.

And to recapitulate, we're talking about the methods of acquiring information about the prospective jurors. We've considered the possibility of advance investigation. We've considered the assistance available from the social scientists. We've talked a little bit, but as much as time will allow, about making lawyer-like use of the information on the jury slip.

We turn now to the fourth method of acquiring information, a method available in all jurisdictions without expense. It is simply a matter of developing the habit of using this method. And if you detect an unusual level of enthusiasm in me as we discuss this method, it is because, I inform you, I have found that, for me, this fourth method of acquiring information is by far the most productive. I would use it above any of the other four. It may be a peculiarity of my personality and it may be, of course, that I am deceiving myself, but I don't think so.

Remember that, whatever the choreography expected of you with respect to jury selection, the one thing you can take for granted, be it federal court, state court and no matter how tyrannical the judge presiding, is that you will be in the physical presence of the prospective jurors, which means that you can look at them. Do so and see what is there to be seen. This fourth method of acquiring information about the prospective jurors is simply observation. One of the reasons, I suppose, that I find this method so productive and so engaging to my mind is that you can practice it all the time. Obviously, you cannot practice social science all the time. You can't practice advance investigation all the time. But observation, seeing what is there to be seen, you can practice literally every waking moment. As you walk down the street you can say to yourself, let me imagine that the pedestrians moving in the opposite direction are prospective jurors. In the few seconds that I have to look at them, what can I learn? And it's amazing what you can learn. Every human being, I put it to you, is a walking advertisement for the inner man or woman. You just must become adept at reading the signs, at seeing the advertisement that is being worn.

What I'm talking about here is, I suppose, the faculty that all of us associate with Sherlock Holmes. Every one of us read some Holmes stories in our adolescence and I urge you to make that part of your repertory as a lawyer. Remember, Holmes said again and again to Watson that he, Holmes, did not have vision more acute than anybody else, but rather that Holmes saw what was there to be seen and that's what most people did not do.

And if it's been a long time since you read Holmes or you think it might be helpful to get some additional inspiration here, let me suggest that you read or reread one particular story. You will find it in any collection of Sherlock Holmes. It's about 12 pages long and its title is *The Adventure of the Greek Interpreter*. And if you don't have time for even 12 pages, read the first four or so. And let me tell you what happens. The client comes to Holmes and he gives him the problem. And Holmes is stuck, he can't get the handle. So he decides to consult with his smarter older brother. And for those of you who are not Holmes fans, it may come as a surprise, Sherlock did have a smarter older brother named Mycroft, who, believe it or not, was employed by the Navy office as a sort of human computer. They just gave Mycroft all of the documents and he put everything together and told them what was going on in European politics. In any event, Sherlock goes to consult Mycroft in the Diogenes Club, a fictional club in the heart of London. And before getting down to the problem of the Greek interpreter, the two brothers, Sherlock and Mycroft, stand at the window of the reading room and they look through the plate glass at the pedestrians walking on that street in London. Now, they cannot hear what the pedestrians are saying because there's a plate glass window, but they can see them. And the two brothers vie with each other at figuring things out about those pedestrians. It's very amusing, it's very clever, and it's just inspirational to see how much you can figure out just from looking at people. And you can't become a Sherlock Holmes, I assume, but a little bit of that you can make part of what you bring with you to the courtroom.

A couple of examples. I assume that, at least in Atlanta and perhaps even in the other communities here, the way in which the prospective jurors are handled is pretty much the way it is in New York or Washington or Chicago or Los Angeles, the places where I've seen it done. The jurors come in in the morning and they assemble in a large waiting room, typically called the Central Jury Part. And if it's New York City or Washington or Los Angeles, that room is larger than this room. It looks like the railroad station downtown in a huge metropolis. And it's about as dingy and depressing as the waiting room in a railroad station. The lights are terrible, the smoke of countless cigarettes and cigars hangs in the air. There are no windows. The paint has long since peeled off. It's just awful. And they understand and, indeed, they are told in the little mimeographed instruction that comes with the jury summons that they will spend most of their time waiting. And if you don't want to go out of your mind with boredom, they are told, bring something to read, because there's nothing there. They don't have television sets. They don't have a lending library. So you bring whatever it is you're going to read to pass the time. And when the juror's name is called out as now being a member of the panel to go down to the courtroom where you are waiting to select the jury, the clerk up in the Central Jury Part says, "If you brought reading matter with you, take it along to the courtroom because, if you leave it behind, it will be stolen." So everybody picks up the newspaper or the book or the magazine and, as they walk into the courtroom, they are carrying it.

Now, you sit there and look. Don't stare. Remember the rule of thumb, you can do anything you would do at a cocktail party. You don't stare at people. So when they come walking into the courtroom, don't turn around like that and look at them. It makes the jurors uncomfortable. I said you have to be a little bit of a postman and know the neighborhoods. To a little extent, you've also got to be a fighter pilot. You've got to have peripheral vision. You know, you've got to see them coming in from your right there. So you're looking straight ahead, apparently, but really you're looking at the jurors and you're just watching them out of the corner of your eye. And, among the other things you are noting, is what are they carrying? Because the reading matter, as the clerk calls it, is right there in the juror's hand. So is it the *Wall Street Journal* or is it the *National Enquirer*? There's a difference. And you begin now to know something about those people. Many of them carry books. You're going to have to be a librarian as well as postman and a fighter pilot. You don't have to have read every book in the world, but you have to know enough about the genres, the categories of book that people are reading to recognize what it is and then use it. And there's a very good probability that what you can glean about the human being from the nature of the book that person is carrying is an accurate insight into the personality.

For example, there's somebody carrying an Agatha Christie mystery story. You don't have to have read that mystery story and you don't have to be a mystery story fan, but you've got to have some sense of what these mystery stories are. After all, he reads the thing because he gets a kick out of it, he enjoys it. And what is it that he's reading? It's done to a formula. There are 250 pages. 249 pages make it seem all that way and then when you turn over to the 250th and last page, my God, it wasn't that way at all, it was this way. And if I'm picking a jury for the defendant in a criminal case, I begin to like that fellow. Because when I defend a criminal case, invariably that's what I'm arguing to the jury. Oh, I know it all seems that way, but really . . . Right? And here's someone whose mind may respond to that kind of argument.

All right. Here's somebody else reading a great, big, fat paperback of Barbara Tuchman's *A Distant Mirror*. Do you remember, it was a best seller years ago? She's probably our best non-academic historian. She wrote an 800-page book describing life in a section of 14th-century France. Now, why is that juror reading that book? He does not have any professional interest in life in that far-off place so long ago. He reads it for the same reason people read Agatha Christie. He gets a kick out of it. He enjoys it. Well, what is it that he's enjoying? I suppose it's the experience of reading a book in which the author takes thousands, tens of thousands of little bits of information and puts them together into a mosaic, a coherent picture of life in that mysterious place so long ago.

Well, if you're the prosecutor or the plaintiff in a civil case, you begin to like that juror. Because, after all, what do you do as the plaintiff or the prosecutor but take hundreds or thousands of bits of evidence and try to show the jury that they do fit together to form a mosaic, a coherent picture of something that happened in the past. And here's a juror whose mind may respond to that.

Pay attention to clothing. In all seriousness, if you're going to pick juries, if you're going to be a jury lawyer, you must spend a moderate amount of time informing yourself of fashions, of what people wear. It means glancing every so often, even though otherwise you wouldn't do it, at the windows of the fashionable stores in town. In New York I'd say it means that you do go through the annual sections *The New York Times* publishes on Sunday on men's fashions and women's fashions just to get a sense of what's up to date. And to look at a woman and to realize that she is dressed in the height of fashion, or a man, makes no difference—or the other way, that what the person is wearing is perfectly respectable, but it's five years out of fashion—tells you something about the person.

It's a commonplace among people who talk about what you can learn by looking at people that, always look at a man's shoes. The shoes tell you something. Most men pay no attention to things like a shirt. A very little bit of attention to the suit. But you've got to pay attention to your shoes, if only to make sure that they fit properly. And there's a wide range of styles, so the style tells you something. And, more than the style, look at the state of the heels because that's something you've got to take care of. If you don't want to walk around with worn-out heels, you've got to take the shoes to the fellow who puts new heels on them. So that a man wearing shoes with absolutely square-cut heels you know is an anal neurotic. You know, you're not a psychiatrist, you don't care one way or the other. It's not a value judgment, it's simply a factor to take into account along with everything else.

Jewelry. You realize everybody wears jewelry. Everybody does. Meaning by jewelry what's on your hands or your wrists. You've been looking at me now for two hours. What jewelry do I wear? If I you're a trial lawyer, it should be second nature that you scan everybody who comes into your field of vision to pick up such things as wedding rings. Am I wearing a wedding ring? No? Now for a man it doesn't tell you much. For a woman it tells you something right off the bat. There's a datum that you now have. Am I wearing a Mafia diamond pinky ring? No, because I'm not the type and, in any event, I'm not. Am I wearing any jewelry at all, and the answer is yes, I am. No rings, but the watch. The watch is jewelry. And in my experience, especially for men, the watch offers a vivid insight into the personality of the wearer.

Now it may not be true here in Atlanta, but it's certainly true in New York and in Washington that invariably the male juror, who is 30 years old and works in a bank or in the back room of a brokerage house, is wearing a certain kind of watch. Now, I always ask myself when I look at that prospective juror, how can a young man spend his life working in a bank office or the back room of a brokerage house? You realize whether he does it with a computer or by hand, he is sitting there day after day after day, adding up numbers. That's all he's doing. Why doesn't he go berserk? If I had to do it, I'd last five minutes and I'd be bonkers. How can he do it day after day? Look at his watch, his watch will tell you. Invariably, that guy, the man I have described, is wearing the kind of watch they made for astronauts to wear when they walk on Mars. You press one button and a radar screen lights up. You press another button, the poison gas comes out and so forth. So you see, he can sit in that back room adding up numbers because in his mind, which is where it counts, he's not adding up numbers, he's an astronaut walking on the surface of Mars. Which means what? That guy, who at first glance is a humdrum clerk, in fact leads a rich inner life. He's got an active imagination and that's an important thing to take into account in determining whether you want him on your jury. For example, if I'm picking a jury for the defendant in a criminal case, I grapple him to my soul with hoops of steel because, defending criminal cases, I need jurors with a rich imagination.

On the other hand, suppose the guy is wearing not the sort of watch they made for astronauts to wear, but you can't see it, so I'll tell you, it's the kind of watch I'm wearing. It's a $40 Timex with no added features whatsoever. Which tells you what about its wearer? He has no imagination at all. None whatsoever. And if it's that juror who sits in the back room of the brokerage adding up numbers, you now know that he does it because he likes it. But look at what that tells you about him as a juror. There is a man who likes it because, at the end of the day, it balances. The debit entries equal the credit entries, which means he is probably psychically incapable of grappling with a situation in which they don't balance. That's a situation of infinite stress for him, which means what? That if you are the defendant in a criminal case, you can't let him be on the jury, because a defendant's verdict in a criminal case is a concession that life is full of loose edges, that things sometimes just don't add up, that in good conscience, you can't always say it's clear beyond a reasonable doubt. He is incapable of saying that. Right? So you don't want him on that jury. And other kinds of implications will be clear for all of us.

In any event, I think I had better move along to the fifth and last mechanism for obtaining information about the jurors, the one that most of us would put first and some of us would think of as the only method of acquiring information. As you see, it's one of about five and, in my judgment, I think it's the least important. At least for most lawyers, it is the least productive, in my humble opinion. And that is why I don't get unduly excited about the issue, do you want lawyer-conducted voir dire or judge-conducted voir dire? This fifth method of acquiring information is voir dire. In any event, questioning the prospective jurors. And we all know that, generally speaking, there is a division between federal judges and state judges. With just a few exceptions, federal judges all around the country do not let the lawyers question the jurors. The judge questions the jurors. The most the lawyers can do is suggest to the judge what questions or some of the questions to be asked. In the state courts though there are exceptions, the lawyers question the jurors. I've told you in New York it's even done not in the presence of the judge. In other places, the lawyers do it, though the judge is sitting there on the bench.

I said that, for my money, this is the least important method of acquiring information and I think I also said at least with respect to how productive it is for most lawyers. Let me tell you why. I've seen an awful lot of lawyers question prospective jurors and, while it is not true across the board, it is true of most of them, that they accomplish virtually nothing. They have, for all practical purposes, unlimited time to ask questions, they can ask any question they want, and I don't think they end up six hours later knowing much more then they knew at the beginning. And it's because they don't ask the right kinds of questions.

It appalls me that lawyers who have the opportunity of talking directly to the prospective jurors, because that is the practice in that courtroom, waste it so inexcusably; and they waste it by asking questions along these lines. These are not the exact questions, but it's something like this. "Sir, are you married? How long have you been married? How many children do you have? How old are the children? What do you do for a living? What does your wife do?" and so on down the line. They are asking questions designed to elicit what, in these days, the age of the computer, I guess you would call a byte of information, the kind of thing you could feed into a computer, a datum about the juror. And, I'll grant you that it's better to know it than not to know it, but in the long run, knowing that kind of stuff does not help you decide whether you want this juror to be on the jury or not.

Please remember that qualification. This is me talking and if it seems useful, use it, but if it seems wrong to you, reject it. Much more important than having that kind of demographic profile of the prospective juror to me is getting a sense of the personality, the contour of the human being who inhabits that skin. That's what I want to know, because that gives me a sense of how the person will respond to the world that will unfold before him in the course of trying this case. I want to know something about the real person. And to know that he's married or has three kids or whatever, I suppose, helps. I can't say that it hurts, but that doesn't give it to me. It's very difficult to put into words, so let me use an analogy. When you meet somebody—never mind courtrooms—when you meet somebody in a social or professional setting and you want to get a sense of who this person is, what do we do? All of us do it because we've developed the skill simply by reason of having survived to the age of 25, 35, 45, 55, or whatever you are. You know, the next time you meet someone in whom you have some faint spark of interest, step back a little bit and watch yourself; you will see that you're doing it almost unthinkingly. And, as you watch yourself, you will be teaching something to yourself about how to question jurors. When human beings meet and they want to find out who they are, you will notice that what we do is find a way to talk to each other at some length. And by some length I mean on the order of two minutes. That's a long time to talk.

If it's more than casual conversation just designed to smooth a social situation, when you run into someone who, you know, that's somebody I may be interested in, I may want to become his friend or her friend—I want to know something about them—observe what we do. We find something that we can talk about and then we talk about it. It's not cross-questioning each other. You know, are you married and how old are you and how many kids do you have and so forth—that's too smooth a social situation. But when we want to know about each other, it's not necessarily this, but along the lines of so what do you do for a living? You know, what it's like? Do you like it? You know, are you happy? You know, I mean, what's your life like? Something like that. Talk to me and then I will talk to you about something. And two minutes a piece, three times around, three stretches of two minutes a piece and I may not know how many kids you have, but I know what kind of person you are. And I certainly know enough about you so that I would know whether I want you on my jury the next time out.

So the lesson for the lawyer picking a jury in a case where lawyers question the jurors is get the jurors to talk to you. Don't ask those questions inviting a monosyllabic answer that can be fed into the computer. Find a way to get the juror to talk. It doesn't matter what it's about, get the juror to talk to you. And after 90 seconds or two minutes, if only you can get the juror to talk, you will know more about that juror than you ever knew about a prospective juror in your life. You will know the contour of the personality that inhabits the skin and then you can begin to make an intelligent decision as to whether you want that person to sit on this jury.

Now, getting a juror to talk is a very hard problem. It's hard because the jurors are embarrassed, they're not accustomed to speaking in public. There's a certain intimidation that comes from the mere juxtaposition of lawyer and not lawyer. The juror may not be able to put it into words, but the juror knows that essentially our profession is the use of words. We're men and women of letters, that's what we are. It's the spoken word and the written word. We are professionals at speaking. And here is someone who knows that he's not a professional at speaking being invited by such a professional to make a speech. That's terrifying. He's never made a speech in his life. So you've got to find a way to get them to talk. Obviously, there's no guaranteed way to do it and there's no right way to do it. There are different ways for different people. Everything will vary with the circumstances, but find something.

Again, to give you the melody of it, "Sir, I see from the jury slip that you're a garbage man." "That's right, kid." And you heard it? See, he assumes that you're now going to make fun of him because people have been making fun of him for 30 years because he's a garbage man. And you're a lawyer, the beneficiary of seven years of higher education, and you're going to lord it all over him. So you've got to turn that around right away. And at the same time, we're trying to get him talking. So he called me kid, so I think of myself as still 25 years old and he's 45, so immediately say, "That's interesting, sir. Seems to me I read a couple of months ago in a newspaper that garbage collecting is the most dangerous kind of municipal work there is, that more garbage men are injured on the job than policemen and firemen put together. Is that right, sir?" "That's right, kid." See, you're beginning to turn him because you complimented him instead of made fun of him. "Well, why is that, sir? How come so many get injured?" And maybe you can get him talking about that. Rule of thumb. People who are unaccustomed to speaking can be drawn out on the details of their occupation. They know it. They can talk about it.

Tell you another secret. It's enormously interesting to everybody else. The more detailed it is, the more fascinated the other jurors will become. And to the extent that you can keep them interested in what's going on, you're doing your job as a lawyer. We'll be talking about that in a little while overtly. Draw him out on something. And you may discover after the guy talks for a minute or so about garbage collecting and the dangers that go with the work that, though he's got only a sixth-grade education and he is only a garbage collector, that guy probably is the most intelligent person on the panel with the strongest personality and he is going to lead that jury deliberation. And that doesn't necessarily mean you want him—it may mean you don't want him, but it's certainly the kind of thing you have to know. Much more important than how many kids he has or is he married or something of that kind. So get them to talk.

Let me drive this home and conclude this particular point with really an extraordinarily significant, in the true sense of the word, anecdote. We all know that federal judges, by and large, do not let lawyers question the jurors. Consider the following the next time you are before a federal judge and, even if you don't try cases in the federal court, if you do question the jurors yourself, take this as further illustrating my point that getting jurors to talk is the most useful thing you can do for your cause on voir dire.

About three years ago, a great civil antitrust case was tried in the federal court in Chicago. The plaintiff was MCI, the defendant was AT&T and, remember, the verdict after trebling was the largest verdict in the history of the United States. It was well over a billion dollars. On damages it was reversed by the Seventh Circuit and it's going to be retried any day now. The lawyers on both sides are acquaintances of mine and I've talked to them about that case. The judge presiding is a federal judge in Chicago, one of the very able people there. His name is John O'Grady. And he handled the jury selection as follows. This was a practice of his that I had never heard of before. I have since used it. I have asked federal judges to do it in place of the sort of random and useless questioning that they normally engage in. They've done it each time and it has proved to me as useful as it was to those lawyers in

MCI v. AT&T. The judge had each juror in turn stand up and what the judge said was, "Sir or madam, talk to us about anything, whatever you want to talk about. Talk about your job, talk about your children, talk about your war experience, talk about politics, anything you want to talk about. Talk to us for a couple of minutes." That was what the judge did. Each juror stood up and it took a little coaxing and tooth pulling, of course, but ultimately each of them did ramble on and the lawyers on both sides said that after that process, which took an hour, they felt that they knew more about the prospective jurors than they had ever known in any other case.

And I think the pudding that is being proved there is that if you get the jurors to talk about anything at all for a couple of minutes, you will know about those jurors more than you can possibly know by eliciting bytes of information. Well, that doesn't exhaust the subject, but with an eye on the minute hand, it's about all that we can do with it, so let us leave the first purpose of jury selection, acquiring information about the jurors, and turn to the second, which is the obverse, I suppose. Very important, but there isn't that much to be said about it.

This is communicating information to the jurors and the key word here is information. It's information that is now flowing from the lawyer to the juror. By way of background, I would say that in my view and a view, I dare say, shared by all of you or most of you, certainly, a trial among all of the other things that it is, is an exercise in education. The lawyers know about the case, the jurors do not, by definition at the start. And one of the things that a lawyer must do—not the only thing by far—but one of the things the lawyer must do is educate the jury. If you can't teach the jury about the case, there is no chance of winning their verdict. Now, educating them is not all that there is to it. You've got to persuade, et cetera, et cetera, et cetera, but everything rests on information the jurors must have about the case. It can only come from you or through you from the witnesses and you begin that process the instant you start to talk to them.

If you are selecting a jury in a courtroom in which you are not permitted to talk to the jurors, there is very little you can do on this. It doesn't mean that the next ten minutes or so are wasted, it just means that what I have to say about the next ten minutes essentially gets transferred to the opening statement. Assuming, however, that you are in a jurisdiction in which you are permitted to question the jurors, start the process of educating them the instant you say your first word to them. Don't wait for the opening in two days. You continue the process then, but you begin it now. And what you begin is the process of educating, of communicating information to the jurors. Assuming a courtroom in which you may talk to the jurors, there are just two ways of doing it, which is why we will not spend that much time in discussing it; there are only two methods available. And the burden of what I have to say is remember to do it. If you remember to do it, you'll do it and you'll do it well. There's no great magic to it. First way, so obvious it amazes me that so many lawyers do not do it. Assuming that jurisdiction in which you may question the jurors, when you first stand up at the very beginning, whether you're a plaintiff or defendant, you may make a brief preliminary statement. As a matter of course the judge will allow it. Now, I'm not talking about an opening. This is not a half an hour speech. But it's a couple of minutes of talk from lawyer to prospective jurors. For heaven's sake, remember that you can do it, prepare it, and do it.

In my experience, at least half the lawyers don't do it and they don't do it, I think, because they haven't prepared it. And they haven't prepared it because they didn't remember to do it. They realize as they stand up, my God, I really could say something to the jurors now, but since I don't know what to say, I will forego the opportunity. Shame on you—a chance to talk to the jurors and you give it up. If you remember to prepare, you'll have something useful. Obviously, this is not the time to make the jurors cry, but this is the time, perhaps, to tell them who you are. They don't know anything. Who the opponent is, something about the case—whatever it is you think they should know right off the bat. And beyond that, there's really nothing that I can say that's going to be helpful. If you remember to do it, you will do something effective.

Second way of communicating information to the jurors: The nature of the English language is such, recall, that any declarative sentence can be turned into an interrogative sentence. Any statement can be made a question. That is to say, you may question jurors not to get an answer. Here you don't care about the answer. This is not seeking to accomplish purpose number one, acquiring information about the jurors, this is accomplishing purpose number two, communicating information to the jurors. The answer is unimportant, it's the question that's important because the question contains a piece of information that you want the jury to have.

"My name is Irving Younger," is a declarative sentence. "Did you know that my name is Irving Younger?" is an interrogative sentence. I have asked a question. I don't care about the answer, but you now know my name. "This case is about an accident that happened at the corner of Main and Market," is a declarative sentence. "Did you know that this case is about an accident that happened at the corner of Main and Market?" is a question. The answer is relatively unimportant. But the jurors, having heard the question, now know something about the case. So, consider using the voir dire not only to acquire information about the jurors, but to communicate information to them. And I will very soon return to this and develop it, but as a rule of thumb, the things I want the juror to know about the case as early as possible, before the opening statement, are the weaknesses in my case. Whatever is bad I want the jurors to know about as soon as I can tell them. Why? Because that's the way to make it something that's not bad. That's the way to handle problems in the case. Lay your cards on the table; tell the jurors about it. How do you tell them about it? By asking a question.

Civil case. My client has a criminal record. That's bad because he's going to have to take the stand. When he takes the stand under the applicable rules of evidence in this jurisdiction the criminal record is going to come out. For God's sakes, I'm going to bring it out as quickly as I can. I want the jurors to feel that they can trust me because I will not fool them and whatever they ought to know, I'm going to tell them about myself, even if it doesn't help me. "Did you know that Mr. Smith, the man I speak for in this case, has a criminal record?" "No, we didn't know that." But they know it now, don't they? And then if you want to, "Is that going to affect your consideration of the case?" "No, no," of course it will. That's why we're dealing with it right now. But they always say no. I don't care about the answer. I just want them to get the idea that in fairness they ought to recognize that the criminal record has no relevance to the circumstances of this accident. Okay, we're going to be returning to that and bringing up other examples, so let's leave it at that.

Asking questions to communicate some piece of information to the jury. That, together with a brief preliminary statement, are the only ways I know of to seek to accomplish this second purpose, which brings us to the third purpose, which in my judgment, is far and away the most important aspect of jury selection. Its nature is such that by and large you can work at it only in a jurisdiction in which you can talk to the jurors. I'm still going to spend 20 minutes or maybe even a half an hour talking about this aspect of jury selection because of its importance, and if you customarily try your cases in the federal court where you don't get to talk to jurors, the next half hour will not be wasted. Take everything I say and apply it to the opening statement, your first opportunity to talk to jurors. I will assume, however, that at least to supply a context to this discussion, that your first opportunity to talk to jurors comes in the jury selection.

Again, a bit of background. Let me back up even beyond that. One of the reasons, perhaps the principal reason, ladies and gentlemen, why I presume to stand up and speak to lawyers, some of it having been at it longer than I have or having, as lawyers, tried more cases than I have. I've tried a lot of cases, but lots of people have tried more. I suppose of all of us in the room, I am the only one to have had the—I'll call it the advantage—at least the marvelously interesting experience of having served as a trial judge. A trial judge in New York City, the busiest metropolitan trial court in the world. And while the New York court system is very complicated, judges get moved around to different courts so that the gist of the six years' experience was anything that happens in a trial courtroom, I have presided over. Civil, jury, criminal, adoptions, the works.

So it being New York, with the congested calendars and the like, that experience has given me a vantage point that probably none of you have. I have seen thousands of lawyers at work. And if your experience is that exclusively of a practicing lawyer, you cannot have seen more than hundreds. You've tried 200 cases—that's an enormous number. So you've seen essentially 201 lawyers at work—yourself and your 200 opponents. But as a judge, especially in that court system in New York City, you see at least two lawyers every day. Sometimes more because of the way we try cases in New York. Actually, there was one day that I tried, in whole or in part, four cases. At minimum, eight lawyers. Over six years, which isn't that long, but it was how long I served, you add it up. You see thousands of lawyers and you get a sense of what it is to be a trial lawyer. More precisely, what it is to be a good trial lawyer and what it is to be a bad trial lawyer. And that, I suppose, is why I have the temerity to talk about these things.

So let me tell you what that experience has brought home to me, tempered, of course, by my own experience as a trial lawyer. People get into all kinds of disputes and they bring those disputes to lawyers. And lawyers are rational people. We can make fun about the profession sort of in the family, but by and large, we've all got our heads screwed on the right way. Most disputes admit only one possible resolution. There's no two ways about it. You're either in the right, Mr. Client, or you're in the wrong. And those disputes do not go to trial because we are intelligent people. You don't go to trial simply to get your head handed to you. Now, granted, there may be a criminal case every once in a while that you'll take to trial on the principle of who the hell knows, you know, the world may come to an end. But you know he's going to be convicted, but let's give it a shot. On the civil side, an experienced lawyer can always tell when it's a dispute that admits only one resolution and that invariably will be the resolution. Those cases don't go to trial, they're settled. On the criminal side, most of them will be settled by way of the guilty plea or occasionally the prosecutor will see the error of his ways and withdraw the indictment.

That means that a fascinating process of selection precedes the commencement of the trial of every lawsuit. And you know what that process of selection is? The obvious ones are weeded out. The ones with the predetermined correct answer are weeded out and those that go to trial are horse races. There is no predetermined correct answer. It can be decided either way, depending upon how the case is presented to the jurors, how the case strikes the jurors. What makes the difference then? And the difference, in my experience, is that lawyers determine whether the case is going to be won or lost. Now there are some cases that no lawyer, not even the best, could win.

Those cases don't go to trial. There are other cases that no lawyer, not even the worst, could lose. Those cases don't go to trial. Those cases that do go to trial can be won or lost and the quality of the lawyer is the single most decisive factor. Now, when I say the quality of the lawyer, I assume a certain amount of technical competence, et cetera, preparation, time spent, et cetera, et cetera. But I want to go beyond that. What is it that marks the successful trial lawyer? And I have some answers. While necessarily they're tentative and I may be wrong, I'm going to put them before you. Please understand that it's only my own inability to phrase it properly that will make it seem as if this is written on the wall in letters of gold. I can't get across with the vividness I want that everything depends upon your style; that there's no one right way to do it; there are as many right ways to do it as there are intelligent lawyers. But having seen that enormous number of lawyers at work in courtrooms in New York and, to a lesser extent elsewhere, these do seem to be the characteristics of the able lawyer. And the able lawyer wins more cases than he loses.

The quality of the lawyering counts. It makes a difference in the result. It's not all there is to say, but let me talk about three particular qualities of the effective trial lawyer, qualities that you should begin to communicate the first instant you talk to the jurors. So where it's lawyer-conducted voir dire, you do it the instant you begin the process of selecting those jurors. First, the ably effective trial lawyer trying a case to a jury is always clear. And by clear I mean nothing more complicated than using plain English. That's very simple, but for most of us, very hard to do, at least at the beginning. There are no exceptions to the following statement: Every experienced trial lawyer I have ever seen or the transcript of whose work

I have read has reacquired the habit of speaking plain English. And I say reacquired because we all had that habit before we went to law school. Law school consists essentially of three years of practice—intensive practice—at distorting the English language. We learn a jargon, a dialect of English spoken only by lawyers and, by and large, understood only by lawyers. And it's the invariable mark of the beginner that the man or woman stands up in court and sounds like a lawyer. It's the kiss of death. It's the guaranteed way to lose a case.

Now, granted, in law school we've all heard law professors say you've got to sound like a lawyer, you've got to learn to talk like a lawyer, you've got to learn to think like a lawyer. I guess that is the hallmark of success in law school, but it's not the hallmark of an able trial lawyer, for many reasons of which two are principal.

First, perhaps less important of the two, if you talk like a lawyer to a jury, you will not be understood. Jurors are amazingly intelligent and insightful, but most of them lack polish. They are not the beneficiaries of all of those years of higher education that we are. So things that we take for granted in the language may not be taken for granted with jurors. Do you realize only lawyers say "prior to" when they mean "before?" Only lawyers say "subsequent" when they mean "after." Of course we know what "prior to" means. Of course we know what "subsequent" means. But you can't assume that that sixth-grade garbage collector knows what it means. And if he's sitting there worrying about what it is you're driving at, he's not paying attention to you. And if he's not paying attention, you can't possibly persuade him.

There's yet another reason, perhaps more important, one that cuts more deeply. You want to win cases and, as I will develop in somewhat greater detail in the last analysis, at the heart of it, the secret of winning cases with a jury is to make the jury trust you. That's why the first thing you do on voir dire is tell the jury about the problems in your case. Make them trust you.

Here's an aspect of striking the jury as a trustworthy person that I will not talk about later on. You realize you're a lawyer, so to begin with they don't trust you. That's not a joke; it's a phenomenon. That is true of western civilization and has been true for as long as there have been lawyers. And it's hackneyed to refer to Shakespeare, *Henry VI*, Part II—a character called Dick the Butcher taking part in Jack Tyler's rebellion, says, "First thing we do—let's kill all the lawyers." That's the voice of the people speaking as of approximately 1580. Little too old for you? Bring it up to date. Some of you will know the work of Carl Sandburg, a poet of the last generation. Not a very good poet, but he worked hard, trying to give voice to the American Spirit. The book in which he tried hardest to do it is called *The People, Yes*. There are just two lines of verse in *The People, Yes* about lawyers—"Why is there a secret singing every time a lawyer cashes in? Why does the hearse horse snicker hauling a lawyer away?" Hmm? That's America talking about us.

So if you stand in front of a jury and in words or substance, to sound like a lawyer, say, "Hey, folks, I'm a lawyer," you're on your way to losing that case because they won't trust you. You can't say it overtly, but what you want to get across to that jury is something more like this: "Ladies and gentlemen, it is true that I'm a lawyer, but it's a misfortune that happened to me. I didn't want to be a lawyer. My mother made me. So, I mean, this is what I do for a living, but please don't hold it against me. And, for God's sakes, I'm not going to act like a lawyer here. I'm not going to be a pettifogger, I'm not going to pull the wool over your eyes, I'm not going to fool you about anything." And you realize, when you say "prior to," when you say "subsequent," when you question a witness with a question like "What did you then do with respect to the operation and control of your motor vehicle?" instead of "How did you drive your car?" what you are saying to the jury sub silentio, subliminally, but they're hearing it, is, "I now remind you, ladies and gentlemen of the jury, that I'm a lawyer." And every time you remind them of that, you enhance the likelihood of an unfavorable verdict. So, for God's sakes, be clear. Speak plain English, both to be understood and to convey to the jury that impression that you're not really a lawyer or, you know, you're not the stereotype of a lawyer.

Second, again, I wish I had the skill to say it so that there's no possibility of misunderstanding. You must interest the jury. I don't mean that your job before a jury is to stand up there and be Milton Berle, a Fourth Circuit comedian. That's also a guaranteed way to lose a case because it's wholly out of keeping with the nature of the exercise that's going on in a courtroom. It's not comedy; it's not entertainment as such. Your task as a trial lawyer is to persuade. You cannot persuade if they're not listening. And they can't listen—it's just not possible for human nature to pay attention—if they don't find it interesting. So you have a professional obligation to be interesting to that jury.

Now, how do you do it when you're conducting voir dire? It's difficult, but I think there are things that anybody can do or learn to do with a modest amount of practice. It may strike some of you that for me to say you've got an obligation to be interesting is an exercise in futility. Some people are inherently interesting. I mean, one would guess that at birth they were fascinating people and, typically, they are movie stars. Cary Grant is, you know, just interesting. We all watched the Academy Awards ceremony. The guy is 80 years old. He walks out and says, "I'm Cary Grant," and you're in love with him. Katherine Hepburn on the female side is, at least for me, somebody like that. She's also almost 80. She's got five different fatal illnesses and I tell you right now, if anybody knows her, pass it along—I am ready to run away to sea with her instantly. I'll leave, I'm ready to go, all right, if she'll have me. But, of course, she won't, alas. Not many of us are Cary Grant or Katherine Hepburn and if you are Cary Grant or Katherine Hepburn, you're not in this room, you have a different way of earning a living.

Most of us bore ourselves and if we bore ourselves, how can we be expected to interest other people? I assume that there is nothing inherently glamorous about you. There are technical procedures that anybody can master with just a little bit of practice that will raise your interest quotient enormously. How many lawyers have you observed conduct a voir dire something like this—I'll start with juror number one.

"Juror number one, what is your name? What is your address? How old are you? Are you married? Do you have children?" By about that point, everybody else is asleep. It is so dull, and it's dull because you are dull, and all you're doing is asking questions and the juror has no reason to be interested. And it's just so monotonous and everybody's asleep. And if they're asleep, they're not listening. And if they're not listening, they can't be persuaded. You've just defaulted on your obligations as a lawyer.

How to make it interesting. We'll assume that you've got to ask the questions. You must get the information. The secret of being interesting is variety. No matter how well you do anything, you know if that's all you do, it gets to be dull after a while. So you've got to change it constantly. Don't ask questions of one person interminably—finish the process and then go to the next and go to the next. That's just 6 or 12 of these exercises in boredom. If there are 100 questions that you have to ask of each juror, bounce around—ask two of number one and then three of number four and so on down the line. And you will say that you won't be able to keep the answers straight. And I tell you that even without notes, you will remember enough so that it will prove useful, but more importantly, the contact with the jurors, the looking at them, the eye contact, as it's called, will do much more for you than a careful notation of the information. So that recognizing that it just gives you the drift of it, the swing of it, it should sound something like this.

"Juror number one, what is your name? What is your address? Juror number four, have you ever been involved in an automobile accident? Juror number seven, did you serve in the Army? Juror number one, are you married?" And you keep bouncing around that way. Ultimately, you'll get all the information that you need and it will be interesting to the jurors because of the change in voice, the change in personality, the change in rhythm.

I have observed a second consequence of bouncing around, and I think it's real. And I think it's worth noting and putting to use for you, though some of you will say people just aren't like this, it doesn't happen this way. I differ—people are like this. By the second or third bounce, all 6 or 12 people in the box recognize that you're going to bounce around, that you're not going in any particular order, that the next question may come at them. And there's, if not a physical, a kind of psychic leaning forward. It's getting ready. Sort of, you know, I'm playing volleyball and the ball is going to come at me, so I want to be ready to get it. They don't want to be embarrassed by having to say, "Oh, I wasn't listening. Would you repeat that?" That's embarrassing with the other jurors. They want to be ready. So they're participating with you. Do you realize they're playing the game with you? They're part of your volleyball team. And while it's way deep down, it's working. When you participate in a team sport, when you're on the beach playing volleyball, you've got to trust your teammates. If you don't trust them, the game doesn't work at all and that's what's going on. They begin to play the game with you, they're on the team with you, they know that they've got to trust you. And that's where we're going to end, as it's where we began. Get the jury to trust you and you're on your way to winning.

So don't ask questions at length of any one juror and there's yet another way, very easily mastered with sort of one case of practice to bury it. Every once in a while throw in a question to the entire panel, so that putting the two together it goes something like this.

"Juror number one, what is your name? Where do you live? Juror number three, have you ever been involved in an accident before? Who on this panel has had military service of any kind? Juror number five, are you married?" And so on. So you've got two different kinds of variation going on and it's amazing how interesting it becomes. All right. You've got to be clear; you've got to be interesting.

And now, let me talk overtly about something I have addressed more or less in passing now three or four times. You've got to make the jurors trust you. If you make the jurors trust you, you're going to win that case and you're going to win most of your cases. As a matter of fact, let me back up and refer to that experience observing so many lawyers on the bench as well as a fair number, as have many of you, in the course of an active trial practice. Because of the lifelong interest in this aspect of lawyering, what goes on in a courtroom, really, I've wasted the flower of my youth studying it, doing it, observing it, trying to figure things out about it. I have been trying to come up with an answer to the question "What is it that marks a good lawyer?" I've told you, I don't have any doubt, based upon my experience, that good lawyers are more effective than bad lawyers. There's a bread and butter reason to try to be a good trial lawyer. You will win more cases than your less good colleague or opponent.

But what is it that makes a good trial lawyer? I've said before and I say again, there's no recipe, there's no way of writing it out so that any one of us can become a good trial lawyer. But having observed so many good trial lawyers and believing, by the way, that at this instance, somewhere not too far away in Atlanta, the lawyers are trying cases. If all 400 of us could be turned invisible and transported to a courtroom where lawyers at this instant are trying a case, the 400 of us standing in a corner invisibly would watch the two lawyers and if, by any chance, one or both of them is a good lawyer, every one of us would recognize it. We would not be able to articulate it. We wouldn't be able to write out the recipe, the list of ingredients that go to the making of that good lawyer, but we'd instantly recognize the good lawyer. Moreover, we'd all agree that there's no one way. If there are a thousand good lawyers in Atlanta, there are a thousand different ways of being a good lawyer, but what is it that we recognize when we see a good lawyer at work? And the only way I can put it before you is a kind of metaphor.

I'm going to take the couple of minutes to put the metaphor before you and, in order for it to mean anything, I have to tell you just a little bit about my personal background. It's of no particular importance, but it puts the story in its context. I was born and brought up in New York City, and my parents were very poor people. Wonderful parents and they loved me and I loved them, but they never had any money and were working all their lives, seven days a week, just to make ends meet. I grew up in a neighborhood that might moderately be described as a noisome slum. I was the first child and the problem was how to get me more or less to adulthood without some moral or physical catastrophe occurring to me.

Well, from September to roughly July 4th there was no great difficulty. Once I was old enough to be out of the house, I was old enough to go to school. So my mother took me to school every day, Public School 132. She sort of turned me over to the teacher, who locked the front door. At 3 o'clock the teacher unlocked the front door, let me out, but there was my mother waiting for me to take me home, lock me into the apartment and I was good 'til the next morning. And so the time passed.

But come July 4th school was over and it didn't start again until Labor Day. So what do you do during the summer—send little Irving to camp? Don't be silly, there's no money. Put him in some kind of municipal program? There may have been municipal programs in those days in New York, but if there were, my parents didn't know about them. So what are we going to do with Irving? Very clever answer.

Like all New York City kids, I knew my way around the city. There was a trolley car. They had street railways in New York in those days. There was a trolley car, the old trolley car, that stopped right in front of our house. The fare was a nickel. At about 9 o'clock every morning in the summertime, my mother put me on that trolley car with a nickel for the fare box. It was exactly eight minutes on the trolley car and you got off in front of the Yankee Stadium. At 9 o'clock in the morning, they opened the gates to the bleachers. Price of admission? A quarter. You go in and, in those days, once you were inside you were perfectly safe because there were attendants, there was no rowdiness and there was no rough stuff. You just sat there and waited for the game to start. A long time to wait, but if you're a kid, it's okay because you're waiting to see the ballgame.

Come 1 o'clock or so, you had to have something to eat—hot dog was lunch. Cost a dime. Game was over 4:30, 5 o'clock, take the trolley car right there. Seven minutes, you're home. So for two fares of a nickel; plus price of admission, a quarter; plus a hot dog for 10 cents. Forty-five cents a day. Perfect babysitter.

The consequence was, ladies and gentlemen, that I spent the long summer days of my childhood and early adolescence watching the Yankees play ball. Now, I am not as old as I look. I never saw Babe Ruth. I was watching the Yankees all of you have heard about and everybody has read about. These were the Yankees of those great, great teams. Remember? Charlie Keller, Joe DiMaggio, Tommy Henry, Bill Dickey, Buddy Hassett, George Stirnweiss, Phil Rizzuto, Red Ruffing out on the mound—great, great men, every one of them. And, as you see, I made it through adolescence. Finally, I went off to college and I was pretty much on my own. My parents had done a terrific job.

I finished college and the one thing I thought I knew about me and my future was that I never again was going to see the inside of a classroom. I had had it with school. If anyone had given me a crystal ball and in that crystal ball I had seen myself ultimately returning to school, becoming a lawyer and a sometime law teacher, I would have vomited in my shoes. The only thing I knew was that I was finished with school, I was going to come to New York and be a newspaper man, which is what I was. I got a job with the *Mirror*—Hearst's tabloid, his attempt to compete with the news; wonderful newspaper. And in which to learn the business, terrible newspaper. Sort of in the abstract, but it was a great place to work. I started as a copy boy, the way everybody does, and in due course, I got to be a sports reporter. I covered the New York Giants in the days when they were the New York Giants and, indeed, those were Willie Mays's early years. And I couldn't believe it—I was 21 years old and I was a sports reporter for a New York City newspaper. They paid me to go to the Polo Grounds and sit in the press box above the home team dugout.

And it being the *Mirror*, you understand, sports coverage was a little bit odd. It was assumed that all *Mirror* readers were lip readers and so you really, really couldn't print anything for them to read. What you did was you put in the box score and a lot of pictures. And my job as the reporter was to sit there and make notes of what the photographer was taking pictures of so that when the photo editor selected the photographs, I could write the caption. See that thin line of text under the photograph, that was the way we covered the games. So, since I was a kid and the photographer was very senior, I would sit there and take notes.

And when the game was over, the photographer would give me the plates and I would take them down to the City Room. The photographer would go home. I would turn them over to whoever to get developed and wait for the photo editor to pick the pictures and then I would write the text. Well, while I was waiting, I would sort of overflow with enthusiasm to my older colleagues, these guys who had seen Babe Ruth and some of them had seen Cy Young pitch his first game—that's how long they'd been around. And being 21 years old and excited out of my mind at the idea that here I was covering the New York Giants, I would say to them, "You know what I saw today, fellows?" And they'd say, "No, kid, tell us what you saw." I'd say, "I saw Willie Mays make the greatest catch I have ever seen. The batter hit the ball out to center field. With a crack of the bat, Willie turned his back to home plate and ran 60 miles an hour right out into center field. He gets about 10 feet in front of the fence, he looks over his shoulder, the ball was coming down. He's going too fast to stop, he doesn't have room to stop, so he turns himself into a human donut and he rolls to the fence. And, as he rolls, he gets his glove up between his legs and he catches the ball—the greatest catch I have ever seen. That guy has to be the greatest center fielder who ever lived." And my older colleagues would say, "No, kid, no. Willie's very good, there's no doubt about that, but he's not the greatest center fielder who ever lived." I said, "What do you mean? You're out of your mind. Well, if he isn't, who is the greatest center fielder who ever lived?" And they'd reply, "Well, all things considered, the greatest center fielder who ever lived was probably Joe DiMaggio." And I'd say, "What are you talking about? I spent every single summer day of my childhood and early adolescence sitting in Yankee Stadium watching those Yankees play ball. I must have seen the Yankees play hundreds of games, DiMaggio in center field in every one of them and not once, not bloody once did I ever see Joe DiMaggio make the kind of catch you see Willie Mays make every day." And they said, "That's right, kid. Joe DiMaggio never made a spectacular catch. You see, when Joe DiMaggio played center field and the batter hit the ball into the outfield, as the ball reached the peak of its trajectory, no matter where it was, and turned to begin its descent to the ground, there, standing under the ball, calmly tapping his glove, was Joe DiMaggio. He put his glove out, the ball infallibly landed in the glove and, with an almost insolent grace, he returned the ball to the infield as if to say, 'I hereby permit the game to continue.'" That was Joe DiMaggio.

As I reflect on it, I think my older colleagues in the City Room were right. At his peak, he was the greatest center fielder who ever lived and, more than being a wonderful spectacle of the art of athletics, it is by way of image, a wonderful metaphor for the art of being an effective trial lawyer. Although there are as many ways of doing it as there are trial lawyers, every trial lawyer I have ever seen, every trial lawyer whose transcript I have ever read, in his or her own way, manages to communicate to that jury what Joe DiMaggio, playing center field, symbolizes.

I can imagine that if you were pitching for the Yankees in 1938 or 1939 or 1940 and the batter hit the ball on the fly to the outfield, you didn't even turn around. There was no need to. DiMaggio was out there—of course he was going to catch the ball. That kind of absolute professionalism, total competence, the kind of competence that leaves the pitcher not needing to turn around to see whether the ball is going to be caught, is what a good jury lawyer conveys to the jury. It is what I mean to convey when I have said several times already, make the jury trust you. If they trust you, you will win the case.

Now, juries can't put it into words because they lack the professional background that we have, but juries know that every case that goes to trial is a horse race. There's no such thing as a perfect case. Every case has problems; every case has weaknesses. And what they want from you is straight shooting. Put your cards on the table. Do not try to fool them. So you're going to be clear, you're going to be interesting, and you're going to be trustworthy. And if you manage to be all of those three things you will have the results that a good trial lawyer has. That is to say, you're going to win more cases than your not so good opponent across the way.

Now, let me apply this to the real world of practice and take some recurring problems in cases and suggest to you ways of handling them. Let me take five problems, one of which we've already touched upon.

Begin with the one we've already talked about and that is the problem of a client or a witness who has a criminal record. And perhaps it'll be helpful to you if I just give you the rule that we're illustrating here. It's the rule that puts to application this general comment that what you want to do is convey to the jury your trustworthiness; that they can rely upon you. And the rule I extract from this is that the problems and weaknesses that produce lost cases for many lawyers will become irrelevant to the outcome if you handle the problem or weakness. And, by and large, the way to handle it is to tell the jury about it. The nature of a problem or a weakness is such that there's nothing you can do to fix it. I mean, you've got a gap in the case. There's some unexplained inconsistency in the evidence. There's something in a witness or client's background that is troublesome. You can't change it, but you can alleviate its consequences by telling the jury about it, by laying your cards on the table, by speaking to them something like, "There's a problem, but that's life. Life is full of problems. And the one thing you can be sure of is that I will never mislead you. I'm telling you about it myself."

So let's take that first example: you represent the plaintiff or the defendant in a civil case. He's got a criminal record. The criminal record is logically irrelevant. We, as trained lawyers, as thinkers, know that it's irrelevant. But to the jury it's not irrelevant. Somebody with a criminal record is very hard to find in favor of. They don't like them. They want to stay away from them. And we can't change the fact that he has a criminal record. It will be necessary to put him on the stand. Under the rules of evidence, the jury is entitled to know about that criminal record, impeachment, et cetera.

So how many lawyers would say it's a problem and the way to handle a problem is the way the ostrich handles problems—you put your head in the sand and pretend it's not there. Well, to pretend it's not there does not mean it goes away. You put the client on the stand, he says, "I was standing there and I got run over." Now, cross-examination. "Isn't it a fact that you were convicted of burglary three years ago?" and the jurors start to shake. My God, there's a burglar, a felon here on the stand. You, the lawyer, you caused a felon to appear in our midst.

Right? So what are you going to do? Handle it. How? Tell the jurors about it as soon as you can.

Lawyer-conducted voir dire. "Ladies and gentlemen, did you know that my client has a criminal record? " No, of course they didn't, but now they do. "He was convicted of a burglary two years ago. Did you know that? Is it going to affect your consideration of the case? "Well, of course it will, but now we're doing something to alleviate it. Now you can bring it out yourself on the stand or, if the other side goes after him like a tiger with the saliva dripping down its jaw, "Isn't it a fact that you were convicted of burglary?" You know what the jury is saying to themselves? What's he getting so excited about? We've known about it for four days. The more they know about it, the easier it becomes to deal with. It's really irrelevant to whether or not he was run over at the street crossing and suddenly the problem isn't there. And if it is there, the impact of the problem is much less than it otherwise would have been.

Next, remember things, that as lawyers we have a professional obligation to do, and which most of us actually enjoy doing, to a jury are at best boring, and at worst, irritating. For example, objecting. The need to object is part of our professional task. It can be rather fun if you're doing it. But if you're in the audience, that is to say in the jury box, trying to get a sense of the narrative that underlies this case, of the flow of events, every time a lawyer objects, you know what your reaction is. "Goddamn lawyer. Why doesn't he stop being a lawyer? Why doesn't he let the witness talk?" But sometimes you're going to have to object.

You know, by and large, the rule is don't object. Don't. It's much more important to let the jurors get a sense of the flow of the trial. But sometimes you have to. So it's a problem in the case. How to handle it? Tell the jurors right in the voir dire. "Ladies and gentlemen, do you understand that, as a lawyer, I've got a professional obligation from time to time to make objections?" Now they know, now they know. And I'd also say, "And do you understand that Mr. Smith, the other lawyer, has the same professional obligation, so that from time to time, both of us are going to have to make objections? And when we do that, we're not trying to interrupt the trial, it's just that it's work that lawyers have to do and that's the way you do it. Do you understand that?" Yeah. Now when you make the objection, what's the reaction? Goddamn lawyer? No. Now the reaction is, well, he's a goddamn lawyer, but he's only doing his job. Right?

Next, cross-examination is a challenge and rather a pleasure for most of us. Let me take another analogy from the world of sport, though a different sport. Cross-examination when well done is also enjoyable to the audience, the jury, so long as the cross-examination seems fair to them. And a fair cross-examination is one that would be fair as a prize fight. That's my analogy. Remember, in the world of prize fighting, heavyweights fight heavyweights, lightweights fight lightweights and you don't mix the two. So that the heavyweight champion of the world, weighing 225 pounds, is not going to fight some guy who weighs 120 pounds.

Be alert to the cross-examination that you conduct that will strike the jury as unfair because it is a mismatch. Now, we're not talking about physical weight, of course not—but mental weight. If you, an experienced lawyer with all of the technical skills at your command, must cross-examine a 10-year-old child or an elderly person, that's a mismatch and it will strike the jurors as unfair. So deal with it as a problem, which means tell them about it upon voir dire. "Now, ladies and gentlemen, it's no secret that in the course of this trial, Mr. Smith, the other lawyer, is going to call as a witness little Annie Jones, who's 10 years old, lovely little girl. Now, you know, don't you, that my job as a lawyer is to see to it that you have all the information you need to decide this case fairly and justly and that to see to it that you have all that information, I'm going to have to ask little Annie some questions. And you know that when I ask her those questions, it's only to be sure that everything comes out. I have no desire to be mean to her or to make her cry or any such thing." Something along those lines. And now you've done it. And when you stand up to cross-examine that child, the jury is saying to itself, not that you're a bully, but that you're only doing your job and, of course, you cross-examine with kid gloves anyway.

Next, this is going to be particularly useful to some of you because it's something I more or less stumbled onto by accident myself. I didn't learn this from anybody else, but it has proved to be enormously useful. Many of you try commercial cases. The problem that I discuss is characteristic of commercial cases, but is not limited to commercial cases. But in commercial cases especially, you will, with some frequency, need to read at length from depositions or documents. And any of you who has done it, knows that it's incredibly boring to the jury. There is no way to avoid it. There are certain things that can be done to liven it up just a little bit. If you're going to read one hundred pages of deposition, typically you put a colleague on the witness stand, he reads the answers, you read the question, you try to bring it to light that way. But, even so, it's very boring. In your courts perhaps, certainly in the courts that I know, if you want the jury to know the terms of some 20-page corporate indenture, by and large the judge will insist that you read it to them. Can you imagine? A 20-page document, printed in type so small that only an insect can read it? And you've got to stand up there with a magnifying glass and read that thing to the jury or read a lengthy deposition? And anybody who's done it knows that within 30 seconds the juror reaction is not really one of boredom, it's one of fury. They're saying, "Why does this lawyer do that to us? Why did he do it? This is so bor . . . goddamn it, I'm going to go to sleep." They go to sleep. They're not listening, but worse, they're angry with you. So, deal with it.

How to deal with it? In the way that I suggest—tell them about it. And I am not kidding. Tell them about it. "Ladies and gentlemen, I want you to know that Tuesday or Wednesday, once we get going, you're going to see me stand up and I'm going to read to you from a document lawyers call a corporate trust indenture. Never mind what that is, you'll recognize it when we get to it. Did you know that the court rules require that I read that to you?" They didn't know—now they know. "And did you know that it's going to be the single, most boring thing you have ever heard in your entire life? Did you know that?" No. But now they know it, right? "I want you to know I can't help it, I've just got to read it to you."

Now, you see, when you stand up and you read that document, what is their reaction? Their reaction is something like this, "Why, those goddamn lawyers . . . hey, wait a minute. He told us it was going to be boring. Let's go to sleep, we're in good hands. He'll wake us up when it's over." See? Of course they go to sleep—human nature can't be changed. But it's the attitude in which they go to sleep that makes the difference. They know that they are in good hands and that means you're on your way to winning that case.

Next, fifth and last of recurring problems, and I guess in a way I have misled you by calling this a recurring problem. It's not recurring, it comes up every once in a while. When it comes up, it is just awesome in its difficulty. But, luckily, most of the time you can just pay no attention to it.

This is the problem of the other lawyer; and I have a sort of personal belief here. I should tell you that I am a lawyer because I like it. And if I didn't like it, I wouldn't do it. I try cases because I enjoy it, and the instant I stop enjoying it, I'm going to stop doing it. Life is just too short to spend any part of it on something you don't like. And part of what I like about it is the professional kinship that binds us all. And I really believe it. Too often, to my taste, the opposing lawyer disappoints me. But I'm not going to get sucked into it. I really want to conduct myself the way our professional cousins across the water in England conduct themselves. The barristers just regard it as their first obligation to be gentlemen and gentlewomen to each other. It's an obligation that takes precedence over the obligation to the client or even to the court. You never embarrass your colleague, you don't mislead him, you don't do anything that would cause people to be reluctant to have a drink with you at the bar later on in the day. And that's the way I try to conduct myself, which means that if the other lawyer misbehaves, most of the time I pay no attention to it. I just don't want to be sucked into that. I just don't like it and so I will not do it. Let him misbehave all he wants; ultimately the jury will realize that he's misbehaving and they will handle him more effectively than I could possibly handle him.

The problem I'm thinking of is not the misbehaving lawyer, but the lawyer who is so much better than you are that you've got to treat it as a problem in the case. And since experience is a necessary requisite to effective trial work, I will make it easy to think of by telling you that the other lawyer is so much better simply because he's very good, but he's also much more experienced than you are. To be inexperienced is not a moral failing, it is simply a description that, at one point or another, is true of all of us.

So you are there trying your first case. Actually, let me give you something that is a real world happening. It actually happened—not to me, but to a friend of mine who is now a federal judge in another jurisdiction. But he had gone to work right out of law school for an older lawyer. It was just a one-man practice. He had been on the job for about a year. He'd been to court to argue some motions. He'd taken some depositions. He had seconded his boss in preparing a certain case for trial. It was now ready for trial. He really knew the case much better than his boss and his boss hadn't told him until the night before jury selection was to start that this was going to happen because the boss didn't want him to just dissolve in nervousness.

But the night before jury selection was to start the boss said, "Herb, you've been at this business for a little more than a year. You've been to court, though you haven't tried a case. You've prepared this thing with me. You know it as well or better than I do. There's no way to start but by starting. It's time for you to fly solo. Tomorrow morning you go down, pick that jury, you try the case. And I'm not going with you because that's just going to increase the nervousness. I want you to go do it, come back when it's over, tell me you won it, tell me you lost it, that doesn't matter. But tell me you did it—you tried the case."

So you can imagine, Herb starts to hyperventilate. You know, danger of cerebral accident overnight, but somehow he gets through it. He goes down the next morning and, honest to God, he walks in to pick the jury. It is his first trial and the other side has called in trial counsel. He didn't know about it because there's been no application for an adjournment, they're ready to go. But they've got a lawyer who's come in overnight, who's picked up the file and he's going to proceed. And it was Edward Bennett Williams. Now, let me tell you as a partner of Edward Bennett Williams, that he is the greatest lawyer in the world.

There's just no doubt about it. And you are not. More than that, you are trying your first case and the disparity has to be treated as a problem. So what do you do? There's a way to handle it. You say to yourself, all right, the main thing is to tell the jury about it. And that may not make the problem go away, but it will certainly alleviate it.

And so what Herb did was something like this, and I don't know that anybody here has yet to try his first case or will do so against somebody like Ed Williams, but here we go.

"Good morning, ladies and gentlemen. My name is Irving Younger and I'm here to represent the plaintiff. Have you seen who's here to represent the defendant? Ladies and gentlemen, that's Edward Bennett Williams. He's the most famous lawyer in America because he's the best lawyer in America. That's who's here to represent the defendant. And I'm representing the plaintiff. Now, ladies and gentlemen, if you're going to decide this case as if it were a contest between me and Mr. Williams, I'm going home right now because I can't win. But you understand, don't you, that it's not a contest between me and Mr. Williams? Of course not. No lawsuit is a contest between the lawyers. It's not a contest. It's a dispute. But you have to decide on the basis of the evidence and the law that His Honor is going to explain to you and justice controls, not which lawyer is better. So you understand that, don't you? Right. I can see that, from your faces, that you do. So I tell you, I'm not going to go home. I'm going to stay and I'm not very good, but I'm all my client has. And I'm going to rely on you to decide the case fairly, not to be swayed by Mr. Williams's skill and brilliance." And you see, you've told them.

And then, as the trial proceeds, every time you screw up, what does the jury say? The jury says, "He's doing it again. But he told us he would. I mean, the kid's no good. He admitted it. But he's only a kid. Everybody has to learn. The main thing is he's not trying to fool us." And if that's their attitude, it's a fair contest, even if it is against Edward Bennett Williams.

Now, looking around at some of the gray beards in the room, I think I ought to say, well, what if you're Edward Bennett Williams on the receiving end of that? What do you do? And my answer is that if you're Edward Bennett Williams on the receiving end of that, you will know what to do.

I propose, ladies and gentlemen, to wind up our discussion of jury selection by talking through a fairly lengthy checklist of matters in connection with which one would like to secure information together with some comment from me, necessarily idiosyncratic to my experience and outlook, on the significance of this information. Let me briefly repeat what I said this morning, that in order to be of use to you, I must call things by their right name. And so we talk here about ethnic stereotypes, the significance of race and the like, in a way which, of course, is inconsistent with our personal outlook on life, and the way in which you lead your own life but constitutes part of what a lawyer must use when picking a jury, if only because the stereotypes have, on occasion, some merit to them.

Every lawyer knows that you want to find out whether a juror is acquainted with the litigants, with the witnesses, with the parties, with the other people involved in the case. But an aspect of juror familiarity with the lawsuit frequently overlooked is the juror's familiarity with a physical location that is important in the case. Physical location will be important in automobile accident cases, of course, but remember that it's not limited to that. For example, in a criminal case where the charge is bank robbery or something of that kind, you will probably want to find out whether a juror is familiar with the particular bank that was robbed or the particular corner at which the episode occurred.

The reason for wanting to know whether a juror is familiar with the location is this. Being familiar with the location, it seems to me, is not probably going to bias or prejudice a juror one way or the other. But when they retire to deliberate, if one of the jurors says to the others, "You know, I know that store," or "I know that location," human nature is such that that juror becomes an expert in the jury room. The other jurors will accept as gospel what their colleague tells them about sight lines, for example, the physical circumstances of the location, what can or cannot be seen or done. And that may or may not be accurate and in any event, it is certainly going to play an unduly weighty role in affecting the way in which the jury deliberates and the outcome. That may help you, it may hurt you—there's no way of determining that in the abstract, but it's certainly something that you want to know about and take into account.

A juror's occupation, of course. At least in my cities, you had to be fairly sensitive in asking about a spouse's occupation, particularly a wife's occupation. A way of doing it—not necessarily the best way, but a way that keeps you out of trouble—is always to say to a man, "Are you married?" And if the answer is yes, the invariable next question, simply so that you don't forget and then come back to it in a way that is awkward or harmful to you—"Are you married, sir?" "Yes." "Does your wife work outside the home?" That way you've gotten over the awkwardness. If he says yes, what is her job? If he says no, you can say something like, "Well, I guess she's got her hands full at home." But, you know, you've sort of taken it for granted that every woman works, whether it's at a job outside or taking care of the house.

As to form of address, also sensitive these days among women, I have found that the best thing to do is simply to ask each woman how she prefers to be addressed. Sometimes you do it before asking whether they're married. You know, "Ma'am, before we proceed, would you tell me how you prefer to be addressed? Is it Miss or Mrs. or Ms.?" And just do it the way the woman says and you've gotten over that problem.

With respect to gender, obviously, you don't ask questions, you observe and there it is. You know who's a man and who's a woman. Let me pass on to you, perhaps unnecessarily, what you might call sort of folk wisdom among trial lawyers. But this is folk wisdom among the trial lawyers that I know. That tends to be big city and coast, either east coast or west coast. Whether it's in accord with your experience, who knows? But think about it. Generally speaking, lawyers of my acquaintance—and I must say, I share this view—are concerned about the reaction of female jurors to female litigants. There seems to be an undercurrent of hostility, especially if the juror is a bit older than a younger litigant and particularly a young, attractive woman litigant. And you've just got to be sensitive to it. The male response to a female litigant is obvious and there's no reason to pretend that it's not there. And I suppose the other way around, if you've got an attractive male litigant with a susceptible female juror. You know, sex appeal is basic to human nature and if it's there, you might as well take it into account and if you can make it work for you, so be it.

It's not the kind of thing on which you will ask because it's so awkward, but you can usually pick it up by observation. And that is what I call health, but I also include age. The signs of the person who is not in good health either because of illness or because he's 80 years old and, you know, it's just natural not to feel too good when you're 80 years old. Now, you will pick up those signs by careful observation. Obviously, someone who is disastrously sick is not going to be there in court. But you watch for the restlessness, the shifting in the seat, the sallow complexion, the other signs that we spot at once as long as you're alert to it, but are sometimes difficult to put into words. And I would venture to articulate the significance of less than good health something as follows.

If it's a long trial, the juror might find it physically difficult or impossible to sit through it. And so a day or two into a trial, the juror turns off the sort of a mental hearing aid, is not listening anymore and, in any event, is resentful at being put through this experience, which is turning out to be painful for him or her. Even in a short trial, a juror who is in less than good health will respond to that physical condition this way. In my experience, generally, low vitality, low energy goes with less than perfect health. So that the trial may be only a two-hour trial, the juror does not find it physically difficult or impossible to sit through it, but when they retire to the jury room, that low vitality, that diminished dynamism has this kind of effect. The juror will sit there passively through the deliberation, will vote his or her mind, but will not have much, if anything to say. So that what you've got is a vote, but not a voice. And that may be good for you, it may be bad for you. There's no way of telling. But it's part of what you take into account in trying to predict the dynamic of that jury deliberation.

Let me turn now to the question of race, on which there's a fair amount to be said, because it's in connection with the question of race that the law, with respect to peremptory challenges, may be changing. Remember, I adverted to that at the very beginning and I said cross-reference to it, we'll come to it later. Again, some aspects of the folk wisdom of lawyers with respect to race. A case on its merits may be race-neutral in that there's no reason to think that race is going to play any part. It's not a question of police brutality or something of that kind. And there's no reason to think about race when looking at the litigants or the witnesses. Still, race may play a part in any part of the country where you've got blacks and whites living together so that you've got blacks and whites on the jury. The case may be race-neutral, but you want to consider the effect of two black people, or more than two, on the jury.

The folk wisdom tends to run this way. In a race-neutral case, the fact that a juror is black is of absolutely no significance. He or she will participate and vote in accordance with how he or she sees the case and there's nothing more to say. But you've got two black people on the jury and it becomes much more complicated and impossible to predict in the abstract. Some lawyers think that when you've got two black people on the jury they will almost always vote together just for sort of subliminal or unconscious reasons of race loyalty. On the other hand, some lawyers think or can talk about cases in which it turned out that precisely for those reasons of racial sensitivity, two blacks will not vote together on a race-neutral case. They just don't want to seem to the other jurors to be together. and so you're going to have a difference of view and, of course, that affects the way in which the jury considers the case.

Other aspects of the jurors' race in a race-neutral case will occur to you as you think about it. In order to have time to discuss it, though, let me turn now to situations in which race is relevant. Now, relevance will come up most obviously if you've got a black litigant, be it a civil or criminal case, doesn't matter. Here the folk wisdom—and I must say this is in accord with my own experience and, of course, that's essentially the northeast and big cities, et cetera—is not quite consistent with what one's immediate reaction would suggest to be the case. I have found, for example, that in personal injury cases where what you're looking for is a large award of damages and the plaintiff is black, black jurors are not going to vote against the plaintiff. They're not going to vote for a defendant's verdict, but they seem very reluctant to vote for a large recovery.

Normally you would say that juries in New York City are very liberal in giving away defendants' money. It's in New York City that you ring the bell time and time again. You know, the verdicts are now, as a matter of course, breaking a million dollars. You know, they're heading to 5 and 10 million dollars in New York City and, yet, black people seem to be much more conservative in assessing a black plaintiff's damages than will a white. Again, saying it straight out and not getting into any quarrels over it, it has been suggested with some appeal to me that what's happening there is that a white jury in a place like New York is essentially expressing an attempt to make reparations to a black plaintiff in the way that a white middle class conscience would find appealing. And that brings the verdict way up.

In a criminal case where the defendant is black, and I have a great deal of experience on this, I almost never permit a black person to stay on the jury. That's assuming there's no issue of police brutality or something of that kind. It's race-neutral apart from the fact that the defendant is black. And I'll give you my surmise as to the reason why. The nature of jury selection is such that anyone sitting in that jury box—black, white, yellow, or anything else—is middle class, has a job, works for a living. Which means what? That person has money or property that is at risk. And a black person living in a black neighborhood in New York sees himself as the victim of crime, not as the victim of police misconduct.

The most law-and-order groups in New York City are groups of black parents in places like Harlem and the South Bronx. Their view of what ought to be done to drug pushers is that they ought to be shot between the eyes on sight by the police. Never mind fair trial—it's their children who are primarily at risk. You put one of those people on the jury with a black defendant and, apart from the race of the defendant, there's nothing racial about the case, and you guarantee a vote to convict. It's that juror especially who wants to clean the streets of that kind of person, meaning the defendant. But now, assuming a lawyer-conducted voir dire, how do you get at racial attitudes among the perspective jurors? It is very difficult to do, simply because it's just about impossible for most people to speak forthrightly about racial attitudes and, even if they are speaking forthrightly in the sense of telling you what they believe to be the truth about themselves, frequently they don't know the truth. They're unaware of their own biases or prejudices.

So with respect to race, I think it is especially important for a lawyer to watch—we all know the phrase body language. I've deliberately avoided it until now. It's a very heavy meal made of some very simple but very useful stuff. Body language is a true language. People are telling you things quite apart from the words they use. Telling you things by tone of voice, by facial expression, by body movement, by the way in which they sit, by posture, et cetera. And just a little bit of practice watching will show it to you. It is amazing how people communicate what's really going on in their minds and how frequently what's really going on in their minds is at odds or at variance with what they are saying. And so where you conduct the voir dire and you're concerned with race, I suppose what I would suggest doing is to stand up and talk about race. Get the juror to talk about race in any way and in any aspect, and then watch the juror. And it's the body language that's going to communicate something to you. Not necessarily that . . . of course, not the best and not necessarily the only way to do it.

Suppose you're standing there picking a jury in a civil case, your client happens to be black, but apart from that the case is race-neutral. So you go, "Now, ladies and gentlemen of the jury, obviously John Smith, whom I speak for in this case, is black. He's a member of the black race. Now, this is not the occasion to have a debate on bias or prejudice, but I simply want to ask each of you whether you can give Mr. Smith the kind of fair trial that you would want for yourself if you were a litigant, exactly the same as if he were not black, but were white or Asian or a member of any other of the human races. Can you give Mr. Smith equal justice? Do you have any difficultly? Do you have any discomfort with that idea?" And on and on and on. Of course, the answers to all of those questions are going to be the commendable answers. No, I have no difficulty, perfectly fair. But watch them when they say it and it's what you *see* rather than what they *say* that is important. I have seen a very able lawyer end that kind of questioning with something like this. He said, "Now, if you have any hesitance about your ability to put race out of your mind in this case, in fairness, this is what I ask you to do. Excuse yourself right now. Nobody will quarrel with you. Nobody will ask you to explain. Just say to me you'd rather not serve in this case and you'll be excused." Every once in a while somebody does and you've done the job.

Now, what about the situation of black jurors, and let's start with the most melodramatic situation—black prospective jurors sitting in a criminal case in which the defendant is black. Now, I've just told you in my experience as defense counsel, I don't want black jurors as a general rule. But in other parts of the country that may not be so. In any event, the litigation that has surfaced in the last several years involves situations in which the lawyers apparently operate on the following assumption—that black jurors will not vote to convict black defendants. So that prosecutors do not want blacks on the jury and defense counsel will at least argue for blacks on the jury, whether or not they really want them—it's impossible to tell. But there you have it.

What will a prosecutor do? Let's assume that you've got blacks and whites in the box. The prosecutor has peremptory challenges sufficient in number to excuse most or all of those prospective black jurors and he does so. And if you were to ask him why after the trial, he might say, "It's none of your business," or "I don't have to tell you," or, "If I do tell you because it doesn't make any difference now, I excused those jurors because they were black because I thought they would vote to acquit and it's my job to get a conviction and I have a right to exercise my peremptories for any and every reason. Nobody is entitled to know those reasons and no judge is entitled to tell me that the reasons are unlawful or unworthy."

And if you ask the prosecutor for authority to support that rather bald proposition that he can exercise the peremptories on any grounds, including race, he'd have very good authority. It's *Swain v. Alabama.*[1] A not terribly ancient Supreme Court case in which, in an opinion by Justice White, the Supreme Court held that peremptories could be exercised for any reason at all putting extreme situations to one side. Where there's a history of blacks never serving on the jury, sure, that will be regarded as a due process violation.

But apart from that, when it's a matter simply of what the prosecutor is doing in the individual case, to use Justice White's language, peremptories may be exercised for any reason. You may excuse all white people, all black people, all blue-eyed people, all accountants, all dentists, whatever you want, within the limit of the number of your peremptories. And there is no due process violation when that is done. Now, of course, the due process referred to is 14th Amendment due process. That is to say, federal law applicable, of course, to the states. As of *Swain v. Alabama*, you would have said then that you may exercise peremptories to the limit of the number of peremptories that you have for any and every reason and you're never going to have to explain.

Then along came *People v. Wheeler,*[2] now eight years ago. Black defendant. Prosecutor excuses all prospective black jurors because he has enough peremptories to do so. There is a conviction. The conviction is reversed by the California Supreme Court on California constitutional grounds. Not resting on the due process clause of the 14th Amendment, resting on California's constitutional guarantee of a jury drawn from a fair cross-section, holding it is violative of the California Constitution for the prosecutor to exercise peremptories solely on racial grounds. Well, that's California—our most popular state, very influential.

On the other hand, being realistic about it, you can always shrug off California Supreme Court decisions on the ground that they're a bunch of crackpots anyway. And as of the date of *People v. Wheeler*,

---

1. *Swain v. Alabama*, 380 U.S. 202 (1965).
2. *People v. Wheeler*, 22 Cal. 3d 258, 583 P.2d 748 (1978).

remember, they were sort of having televised hearings on which of them was a liar and which of them had done things judges aren't supposed to do; it was generally a circus. So that the authority of *People v. Wheeler* was much enhanced when just a year later, so conservative a court as the high court of Massachusetts, called the Supreme Judicial Court, the SJC, held identically that a black defendant on trial for his life—it was a capital case—at whose trial the prosecutor uses peremptories to excuse almost all black jurors, has been deprived of a right guaranteed by the state constitution.[3] A footnote to that case is that the prosecutor did not excuse all blacks. One black remained on the jury, selected by the other jurors as the foreman of the jury. And they nevertheless convicted the defendant of killing a Harvard football player, by the way, in a bar celebrating Harvard's win in that year's Yale/Harvard game. SJC reversed on the ground that the use of peremptories to excuse black jurors violates the state constitutional guarantee.

Now, there are a number of lower court decisions and if you find yourself dealing with this issue, please remember to use Lexis or Shepherd's because it's come up a number of times in other states. Now, you've got the law in California, you've got the law in Massachusetts set forth for you definitively in those cases. In other jurisdictions you're not in the high court of the state, so it's not definitive and, while I haven't counted, it's working out about 50/50. A number of states have rejected this argument, have stuck with what underlay *Swain v. Alabama* and have reaffirmed the traditional view that even race may be used to support a peremptory challenge. Or, in any event, you can't second-guess a lawyer. You can't be a Monday morning quarterback as to whether his or her reasons are worthy or honorable.

Now, all of the cases are criminal cases; whether the use of race as a basis for exercising peremptories is even arguable in a civil case, we just don't know. But some lawyer some day is going to raise it. Moreover, each of the reported cases involves peremptories exercised

---

3. *Commonwealth v. Soares,* 377 Mass. 461, 387 N.E.2d 499 (1979).

by prosecutors. No case that I am familiar with involves a claim that it's unfair for a defendant to exercise peremptories for racial reasons. And that's a terribly tough one. You know, if I'm representing the defense lawyer, no judge is going to tell me that I can't excuse a juror simply because I'm afraid that that juror is going to be inclined to vote to convict. No, sir. I just can't see that, though it may happen.

And also remember that, with the one exception I'm about to mention, all of these cases involve race. It's not hard to make an argument that there are other aspects of a prospective juror's position in the world which perhaps, not quite as sensitive as race in the United States, or almost as sensitive. How about religion? We talked abut that back at the beginning. There is one lower court case in New York in which the defendants were named Moskowitz and Weinberg, well, obvious enough. So the prosecutor is using his peremptories to excuse every juror with a Jewish surname. So it's the prosecutor using peremptories not for racial, but for religious reasons and he was called on it. What happened was the judge said, "Will you tell me why you are excusing these jurors?" And the prosecutor said, "No, I don't want to tell you because I don't have to tell you. It's private. Private business. You know, it's up here and you have no right to second guess me." And the judge said, "All right, I'll just take it at face value. It looks to me as if you're excusing jurors solely because they're apparently Jewish and I think that violates the Constitution." That judge was subsequently reversed on that case, to the extent that you've got any learning on it. It seems to be that religion is not subject to judicial inquiry in the way that race is.

And, most importantly perhaps, just months ago a federal judge, a U.S. district judge in the Eastern District of New York, named Judge Eugene H. Nickerson, a very able and widely respected judge, in a case called *McCrea v. Adams*, Eastern District of New York—I have not seen it yet in the reports, but in any event, it'll be in the Second Circuit before long. If you've got to track it down, it's habeas corpus, so it's technically civil, 83 Civil 4406 in the Eastern District of New York, decided December 19, 1983. A state prisoner applies for federal habeas corpus, arguing that the state prosecutor used his peremptories to excuse all the black prospective jurors so as to produce a lily-white jury. The state's response is what's he talking about? *Swain v. Alabama*. It does not violate federal due process to excuse black jurors for any reason, including the reason that they are black. And Judge Nickerson said, "That's what *Swain v. Alabama* holds, but I don't think the Supreme Court would hold it today. It's only 20 or so years ago, but I think they would take a different view of it and I, therefore, take a different view of it." And he granted habeas corpus, holding that due process was violated by the use of race as a basis for peremptories. Now, obviously, that's been appealed and in due course we'll have something from the Second Circuit and, presumably, something, if not in this case, in another case from the Supreme Court reconsidering the issue of *Swain v. Alabama*.

To wind up, if I were defending a criminal case in which the defendant, well, no matter the race of the defendant, I would watch the prosecutor's use of peremptories. And if it seemed to me that the prosecutor was using peremptories on any basis arguably unconstitutional—race, religion, age, anything at all, I would raise it. And if I get knocked down, I get knocked down. But at least there's an arguable point on appeal that the prosecutor should not be doing it.

And just, finally, my own view of the real explanation of these cases—the *Wheeler* case in California, the *Soares* case in Massachusetts, et cetera, is that these are not due process or fair cross-section of the community cases. No opinion says this. I said it in an article, but nobody stood up and saluted, but who knows. I think that what the courts are really talking about is the special obligation of the prosecutor to see that justice is done. A prosecutor has obligations beyond that of the ordinary advocate and those obligations include, these cases teach, an obligation to see to it that the defendant gets a jury that's more or less a cross-section of the community with people on the jury who, at least with respect to race, are like the defendant. So that this is an obligation that rests on the prosecutor in criminal cases only. It has nothing to do with civil cases, has nothing to do with defense counsel, et cetera, et cetera.

Let's leave it at that and briefly look at a few more items on this checklist. Related to race is nationality or ethnic background. We touched upon it earlier. We said you've got to be a little bit of a postman, you've got to be a fighter pilot, you've got to be Sherlock Holmes, you've got to be all kinds of things. And if you're going to pick juries in any city in which the population is mixed, ethnically mixed—people come from all parts of the old world—you've got to be something of an historian. You've got to know what groups don't like other groups. This has nothing to do with the individual's personality, it has to do with memories that people have.

Turks and Greeks hate each other. They've hated each other for generations and they're going to hate each other for the rest of time in all probability. If your client is obviously Turkish by reason of surname or appearance, you can't let Greeks stay on the jury. Indeed, I would consider a challenge to the favor, asking the judge to rule as a matter of discretion that those national groups are not to serve.

Recently, in the papers back home, the Turk-Armenian hatred has come to life again. You know that there are Armenian hit squads going around the country assassinating Turkish diplomats and vice versa, because of the slaughtering of the Armenians, when was it, 1915. So you've got to be careful. Irishmen and Englishmen tend to dislike each other because of the civil war over Irish independence. And underlying that, of course, is that it's a war of religion, which makes it all the more bitter, so you've got to be very careful there.

You don't have to be much of a modern historian to understand that Germans and Jews don't get along, even 40 some odd years after the event. If your client is obviously German, is sitting there with a roll of fat at the back of the neck, his head shaven, he obviously spent the early 1940s torturing people in death camps. You can't let Mr. Weinberg stay on the jury. Weinberg is incapable of giving that guy a fair shake, and you don't want a fair shake, you want the shake that's in his favor and you're certainly not going to get it from the Jewish juror.

Okay, enough on that. Next, be alert to circumstances that may indicate that a prospective juror will, albeit unconsciously, respond as would one who has a stake in the outcome. And sometimes this requires that you look a little bit beneath the surface. Homeowners pay real estate taxes so that if you are suing the county, a verdict against the county will be sensed by this juror as a verdict that will raise his own taxes and that's going to play a part in his view of the case. People who are customers of utilities pay gas and electric bills and that will play a part in their consideration of a case against a utility. People who carry insurance pay insurance premiums. Life insurance is not really to the point here, but property insurance, casualty insurance. Hence, verdicts that require the payment of large sums of money by insurance companies result in raising the premiums. Almost everybody owns an automobile, everybody has automobile insurance—that's going to play a part. Remember that the insurance industry engages in advertising to the effect that verdicts are astronomical, et cetera. I'm not taking an editorial position on it. I just remind you that it's there and you've got to consider its effect upon jurors.

Next, always remember to acquire whatever information can be acquired about a juror's previous litigation experience and, by juror's experience, I include the experience of people close to him—friends, members of the family, and the like. Remember that a previous experience with litigation may have soured the juror. In any event, when he talks to his colleagues in the jury room, if he's able to say, "I once was a juror on a case," or "I was a witness or a litigant," he becomes an expert in the jury room and his voice carries a special weight with his colleagues on the jury.

And sometimes you've got to look beneath the surface. For example, you're representing a plaintiff in an injury case and one of the jurors once experienced a similar injury himself. Right. To that point, you'd figure, boy, the plaintiff wants him and the defendant doesn't want him. But now add something to it. His, the juror's injury, came on the job, so that the only compensation he got was workman's compensation. He's probably going to be inclined to find in favor of the plaintiff, but I'm not so sure he's going to be inclined to award a lot of money. He only got the modest amount workmen's compensation gives him, so why should he give a sort of windfall bag of gold to this fellow who suffered an injury pretty much the same as his own?

Previous experience on juries in a large city is something you usually don't have to worry about. People don't sit that frequently and it's sometimes hard to find out. But in a smaller community, people may sit on juries with some frequency and, by and large, somebody who's been on two juries or more than two—two is the limit—more than two, I would move heaven and earth to get rid of them on either side of the case. They've just been around too often; they've seen it before. It's no longer, you know, a trial, but rather the kind of partial charade or theatrical performance that we, as lawyers, know that it is, but for perfectly good and honorable professional reasons. That juror may not understand that.

Be sure to find out and, if so, take advantage of it, whether the law of your jurisdiction permits the question, "Do you have an interest in an insurance company? " Many jurisdictions permit that question, though it comes as a great shock to a lot of lawyers. In my own former home state of New York, there is a statute widely unknown by lawyers that specifically permits the question "Do you have an interest in an insurance company?" And, not to be unduly cynical about it, the question is put not really to find out whether the juror does have an interest, but to remind the jurors that lurking behind the defendant here is an insurance company. Hence, you're giving away insurance company money, not defendant's money, which brings us to the next question.

Suppose there is no insurance? Do you still ask the question? The statute doesn't say no, so why not? On the other hand, it is kind of misleading to the jury and if the plaintiff does ask that question, should the defendant now be permitted to tell the jury that there is no insurance? I don't know the answer, but it just shows the complications that you get into here.

Next, consider the extent to which particular occupational groups are at a public relations advantage or disadvantage with the jury. It may not be so in your community but, for example, by and large, employees of utility companies—not just sort of favorable to utility companies, but generally speaking, they are not pro-plaintiff. No matter the nature of the case, they will incline to vote against the plaintiff. People in the health professions as well as policemen—that is to say policemen, nurses, of course doctors, people who work in hospitals, doctors' wives—may be sympathetic to a plaintiff in an accident case in that there's no reason to expect them to vote against the plaintiff, but you don't get enormous verdicts from them. And my theory as to why you don't is that they've seen worse. No matter how bad your injury is, they've seen worse. And, hence, they don't get that excited about it. We mentioned antipathy to lawyers. There is also not quite as intensive antipathy to doctors, so watch out for the possibility of juror antagonism to a litigant who is a lawyer or a doctor.

Remember to deal with the issue of damages, whichever side of a civil case you are on. Many jurors do not find the idea of awarding money to be comfortable. They may understand as a matter of words that it's all the law can do, but still, it's kind of crass and they're not used to doing it, to say that a right arm is worth so much or a child's life is worth so much. So you've got to get them ready for it in the way it's communicating something to the jury, a way of looking at this problem. From the plaintiff's point of view, it may be something along the lines of, "Now, we're going to be asking you, ladies and gentlemen, for a very substantial sum of money at the end of this case. Now, do any of you have any problem with the idea that if Mr. Smith's injuries are shown to you to have been enormous, then he's entitled to enormous damages? Just as in a case where the injuries are very slight, the plaintiff would be entitled to very slight damages. Do you have any difficulty with that? Can you imagine a case in which the injuries were so tremendous, so catastrophic, that the only fair compensation is a sum in excess of $5 million? Can you imagine such a case?" And you begin to see people shifting in their seats. You realize that whatever they may tell you, they find it hard to imagine such a case.

On the defense side, you've got to be aware of an attitude that laymen frequently have that just because somebody started a lawsuit they're entitled to something. Something. You don't send anybody away with no remedy whatsoever. So deal with it now by laying it on the table. "Does anybody here think that just because a plaintiff starts a lawsuit, he's entitled to recover? Did you know that the law says that people are entitled to recover only if they prove that they're entitled to recover? Are you aware that the plaintiff is here, asking to shift his own loss to somebody else and the law says that that can be done only if it's proved to be right? " Something along those lines to get them ready for it.

Watch out for jurors with some training in law. Not just did you ever go to law school, but at college did you take a law course? In high school did you take a course in law? Increasingly, high schools offer courses in law. And, remember, a juror who has any kind of familiarity with the law invariably has it wrong and will speak with a special authority in the jury room. Every experience I've had with jurors with any kind of contact with the law has proved to be a sour experience, so just stay away from jurors with law. The system presupposes jurors who know nothing about the technical part of it. We're supposed to know the technical stuff. What they bring to it is that layman's response to the case. And all of that is complimentary and if a juror is a lawyer or a lawyer is a layman, it just doesn't work.

Next to last. No jokes, no humor in the courtroom. It is totally out of place and, especially, I look around the room, I see that a good many of you are fairly young. There are jurors who are older than you. Just take it as an absolute rule—you cannot make jokes in a courtroom where there are jurors older than you. Only if you are older than every one of the jurors can you use humor and then very delicately. The situation is a serious one in court, no matter the nature of the case. The jurors know it and if a lawyer starts to horse around, it seems to the jurors that the lawyer is not taking the proceeding seriously. And if he's not taking the proceeding seriously, why should they? And you're on your way to losing that case.

You can turn it to advantage if your opponent indulges in humor by pointing out to the jury essentially what I've just pointed out to you. Your opponent uses humor and, you know, there are lawyers who make it a style and are very good at it. And, you know, he has them laughing. He's a good comedian. You know, it's not that it's corny or falling flat, it's working, which means you better respond to it. And whether it's in jury selection or later on, you say to the jury something like, "Now, ladies and gentlemen, this is a serious affair. Mr. Smith lost his right arm, that's nothing to joke about. And Mr. Jones over there is a splendid comedian and some other time we'd love to hear his jokes, but not in this trial. It's totally out of place here." Something like that.

If it is a lawyer-conducted voir dire, have prepared in advance some kind of obvious last question or final comment to get you off your feet in a way that's crisp. I mean, don't peter out. Don't sort of, you know, you've all seen it—some guy goes through his notes one last time and he says, "Well, I guess I've asked everything, so . . ." That's not Joe DiMaggio. Remember, part of the elegance of DiMaggio's performance was not just catching it, but the way in which he returned the ball to the infield. Remember? In such a way as to say, "I permit the game to continue." It doesn't take much, but it should be something crisp that says to the jury, not vocally, but it does say it—I have done what I set out to do. Having done it, I now sit down. That communicates to the jury that mastery, that ease with the situation that's part and parcel of conveying the trustworthiness which I think is at the heart of being a good trial lawyer.

And simply so that we do end with it, having promised to end with it, for God's sakes, for all the checklists, for all the folklore, for all the analysis that you can bring to it, play your hunches. The only experience I've had with that is sort of the reverse. I think most of the time, without really being aware of it, I am playing hunches. On the few occasions I am aware of, when I deliberately did not play a hunch, I regretted it. Somehow we all have very sensitive radar to each other. The radar tells us that somebody's going to be good, somebody's going to be bad. You don't know why it's telling you that. You can't really read the waves on the pattern, but your stomach is telling you get rid of that guy or keep that guy. Play your hunches—they are better than anything you can reason out in words.

Chapter 6

Credibility and Cross-Examination

DEAN STEVE EASTON: You are in for a real treat. This is an outstanding program that brings to bear Professor Younger's vast array of experience, as not only a trial attorney who both prosecuted and defended criminal cases and tried civil cases both for plaintiffs and defendants, but also his experience as a trial court judge who heard and saw lots of other lawyers try cases. He was also a law professor of great renown, and he was the first person to actively teach us, the trial attorneys, how to better try cases. He is remembered for all of those things, but he is perhaps best remembered for his 10 Commandments of Cross-Examination, a portion of the program that you're about to see.

Since Professor Younger's death in March 1988 there have been a few relatively minor updates in the law that he discusses, the law of credibility. In 1990, Federal Rule of Evidence 609(a) was amended. Prior to 1990, Rule 609(a), which discusses the admissibility of the prior convictions of a witness, explicitly stated that such prior convictions could be admitted during cross-examination. In 1990 that reference to cross-examination was eliminated from the rule, so now quite clearly the rule allows the proponent of the witness's testimony, the attorney conducting the direct examination, to make the jury aware of a prior conviction. Frankly, people were doing that long before 1990, but it is now recognized officially in the rule. Rule 609(a) was more recently amended to provide that an attack based on a non-felony is allowed only if the elements of the crime of conviction required proof or admission of a false statement as an act of dishonesty.

Also, there was a 2003 amendment to Federal Rule of Evidence 608(b), which Professor Younger refers to as the Prior Bad Acts Rule. Now that rule only allows the use of a prior bad act to attack (or less often, support,) the witness's character for truthfulness. Prior to that time, the rule said that you could use such instances for the purposes of attacking or supporting credibility, a somewhat broader term. So we have now narrowed the admissibility of prior bad acts so that they have to be precisely about character for untruthfulness. So, in fact, Professor Younger's example that you will soon see about the prior bad act of selling heroin to school children would probably not be allowed under the current version of Rule 608(b) of the Federal Rules. Similarly, be aware that Rule 610 of the Federal Rules of Evidence excludes evidence of religious beliefs when used to attack a witness's credibility. Other oath-related inquiries are presumably still allowed in cross, however.

IRVING YOUNGER: You're trying a lawsuit, ladies and gentlemen, any kind of lawsuit in any court in the land. You call a witness. You are desperate to have the jury believe that witness. When your opponent calls a witness, you are equally desperate to have the jury disbelieve your opponent's witness. The lawyer's word that we use to describe what is at work here is credibility, and it has been said with some justice that credibility is the overriding issue whenever a witness testifies as to any subject matter in any kind of case in any courtroom anywhere in the common law world. Credibility is the overriding issue connoting a rather complicated and subtle concept. By definition, the jurors know nothing about the transaction that constitutes the subject matter of the lawsuit. Had it turned out that any prospective juror saw the accident or was present at the bank when the bank was robbed, that person would not be on the jury box.

We take it for granted, then. It's a kind of presupposition of our litigation system that the jurors can never, of their own knowledge, know the truth. The most the jurors can do is respond to the credibility of the witnesses who testified before them, meaning what? The jurors assess the appearance of reliability, the likelihood that a witness is telling the truth, and all of that is connoted in the single word credibility. I think it's therefore fair to say that, from the viewpoint of the working trial lawyer, not the theoretician, not the author of articles in the law reviews, but the working litigator out there in the trenches—that part of the law of evidence and that part of the craft of the courtroom dealing with credibility is the single most important part of the law of evidence and the craft of the courtroom. And, as we will be seeing this afternoon, the law of evidence has a great deal to say about credibility.

Now, technical terms which we all know, but let me say them briefly at the start so that there's a sort of common denominator. Credibility applies to the issue that's presented whenever a witness takes the stand and it suffices, I suppose, to articulate that issue something as follows. To what extent will the jury conclude that the witness seems to be telling the truth? Because it is so important an issue, the law has evolved a number of rules, which are available for you, the working trial lawyer, to use, the purpose of which is to build up the appearance of believability. And we call those the rules of accrediting a witness, bolstering believability, enhancing the likelihood that the jurors will conclude that the witness is telling the truth.

There are a rather larger number of rules that are available for you to use, the purpose of which is to make it appear to the jury that the witness is not worth believing. If you will, then the purpose of these rules is to help you attack or negate credibility. And we call these the rules of discrediting. So you've got accrediting and discrediting. Simply because I may slip back and forth, the word discrediting has a synonym and that synonym, of course, is impeachment. So to impeach a witness is the same as to discredit a witness and what you are doing, whichever way you call it, is trying to show the jury that the witness is not worth believing.

Well, let's begin our canvass of this so important portion of the law of evidence by looking at the rules that apply to direct examination. They are simple, they're uncontroversial and they are essentially the same, no matter the court in which you are trying the case. It's direct examination, meaning you call the witness to the stand. Almost always, your purpose will be to persuade the jury that the witness is worth believing. The temptation that you will experience then is a temptation to accredit your witness, to do whatever the law of evidence permits you to do to bolster, or build up, the believability of the witness you have called to the stand. And here we will be met by what is the established common law rule. It continues under the Federal Rules of Evidence and any other state's modern codification of the law of evidence. You may not accredit your witness.

Let me sort of spell that out in somewhat longer form, but plainer English. When you call a witness to the stand, when you are the proponent, when it's direct examination, you may not do anything the law makes specially available to a lawyer for the purpose of building up believability. In lawyer shorthand, you may not accredit your witness. Oh, you'll want to, of course. And in due course it may be permissible to accredit the witness, but not now. Reason? Save time. You see, to accredit is to build up believability. And in its well-nigh limitless wisdom, the law says why spend time accrediting when it may turn out to have been unnecessary? When will it be unnecessary? When the witness's credibility has never been attacked. When there is no discrediting, why then it follows that there's no need for accrediting. So you call the witness to the stand. Obviously, there's been no discrediting. The opponent has not had a chance at that, so you may not accredit. When may you accredit? Only when, and not until, your witness has been discredited. So accrediting follows discrediting. And putting it in the context of the sequence in which a witness testifies, it almost always works out, as you well know, that you accredit on redirect examination. You call the witness on direct examination, you do not accredit because it's improper, because it's premature. Typically, the opponent discredits on cross so that you come back on redirect and accredit. To use the lawyer slang for it then, the purpose of redirect is to repair the damage. And how do you repair the damage? By accrediting.

What are the rules of accrediting? We will talk about them, but not now, because if we talked about them now it kind of would not be symmetrical, as it is at trial. You use the rules of accrediting on redirect examination, after the witness has been discredited, typically on cross-examination. So let us save our discussion of accrediting to follow our discussion of discrediting on cross-examination. So we'll talk about accrediting, I promise you, but at the very end.

Now, simply so that we've mentioned it, there are three exceptions to the rule that forbids accrediting your witness unless and until the witness has been discredited. I have not gone through and counted up jurisdictions, but these three exceptions are pretty generally recognized. They exist in common law and I dare say that, if you're interested in the cases in any particular state, a fast trip to the library, use of Lexis or the Digest will turn up cases recognizing that these exceptions will be followed in whatever state you're interested in. Let me just expand upon it a little bit so that everybody sees what they are.

Claims of coerced confession, where it's typically a hearing, not a trial, and the witness is the defendant in a criminal case who is raising the contention that a confession should not be received in evidence against him because it was coerced. All right? That's the substantive issue of criminal law or criminal procedure. In every jurisdiction, so far as I know, when you put the defendant on the stand, you, the defendant's lawyer, the proponent of that witness, on direct examination, will be allowed to elicit the fact, if it's so, that this suspect made prompt complaint of the coerced confession as soon as he could. For example, he was arrested on the street, they took him to the back room of the station house, they beat him up, and he confessed. They then took him to the courthouse and they arraigned him. The instant he appeared before the magistrate, he said, "They beat me up. They made me confess." You have him on the stand now at the hearing in connection with the motion to suppress the confession. You may elicit that prompt claim of coercion.

Now, if you analyze it, you see that it's an out-of-court statement. It's not coming in to prove the truth of what it asserts, it's not coming in to prove that, in fact, he was coerced. That would be hearsay, and we've got a rule against hearsay. It's coming in solely as it bears upon the credibility of the defendant. How does it bear on the credibility of the defendant? It accredits him. He's testifying that he was beaten up and here, on the first occasion when he appeared before a magistrate, he made complaint of a coerced confession. So it's accrediting. Before he's been discredited, yes, but it's allowed.

Second, and it's essentially the same principle at work, the testimony of the prosecutrix in a rape case. She testifies that the rape occurred. The proponent, the prosecutor, of course, on direct examination may bring out the fact that as soon as she could do so, she made complaint of the rape. She escaped from the place where she was being held, immediately called the police and said, "I've been raped." Or went, rang a neighbor's doorbell and made complaint of the rape, whatever it may be. Same analytics. Out-of-court statement. Not coming in to prove she was raped—that would turn it into hearsay and raise problems under the rule against hearsay. Rather, it comes in as bearing upon her credibility. How? Accrediting. At the first reasonable opportunity she complained of the rape. It's accrediting before discrediting, but it is permissible.

And, finally, in many, if not most, jurisdictions, when the witness on the stand is the victim in a criminal case, the victim identifies the defendant. That's no problem. The victim simply says, "That's the man who mugged me," or the like. The victim will be allowed on direct examination to testify to his, the victim's, earlier identification of the defendant as the assailant. So it's something like this.

"Now, Mr. Victim, you've identified the defendant, but let me take you back to the afternoon of the morning you were mugged."

"Yes."

"Where were you?"

"I was in the police station."

"Was there a line-up?"

"Yes."

"And at the line-up did you pick somebody out as the person who mugged you?"

"Yes."

"Who did you pick out?"

"The defendant."

Prior identification of the defendant, admissible not to prove the identification—again, that would be hearsay—but admissible as bearing on the victim's credibility. How? Well, he picked him out before, so chances are he's picking him out accurately this time. It accredits, but it's accrediting before he's been discredited. But it is permissible simply because that's one of the three exceptions generally recognized to the rule forbidding accrediting before there's been discrediting.

We know what discrediting means. To use one of the rules, the purpose of which is to permit the lawyer to attack credibility. Since we're discussing direct examination, let's stay with it, but turn from accrediting to discrediting. You wish to discredit your own witness. It's not as rare an occurrence as a novice lawyer might think, although I'll grant you it doesn't happen necessarily every day of the week. Here you must distinguish between the practice at common law and the practice under the Federal Rules of Evidence or in any state which has enacted the Federal Rules of Evidence.

At common law you were forbidden to discredit your own witness, the reason having to do mainly with legal history—some traditions and customs rather than any careful thought. And reducing it to a very small nutshell, at common law, when a lawyer called a witness to the stand, the lawyer was deemed to represent to the jury that that witness would tell the truth. That was called vouching for the credibility of your witness. So it was an easy logical corollary to say that since you vouched for his credibility, since you represented to the jury that he would tell the truth, you cannot now attack his credibility, you cannot suggest to the jury that he's not worth believing. Hence, you may not discredit your own witness. That represents an unrealistic view of the world of litigation as it exists in the latter part of the 20th century, of course. It was accurate as of the 12th century. But, after all, from the 12th century to the 20th century is only 800 years, and in 800 years you cannot expect the law to change its view of these matters. The law does not work that quickly. It is a conservative profession, as you know.

I began to learn the business in the state courts of my original home state of New York, which to this day is essentially a common law state. You call a witness to the stand because he's John Q. Bystander. He happened to be standing there when my client's car collided with the defendant's car. I didn't pick him out. If I had a choice, my witness would be Cardinal Cook. But I can't call Cardinal Cook for the very good reason that he didn't see the accident. So who is it I have to call? He's really not John Q. Bystander, he's Frank Costello. Can't help it. Still, in its limitless wisdom the common law says, "Younger, you call that guy to the stand and you vouch for his credibility and you will not be permitted to discredit him," with an exception.

To every rule there's an exception. I can't imagine that there's anyone here who does not, however vaguely, recall the exception from your studies in the common law at law school, if not afterwards. At common law, if one was surprised by the testimony of one's own witness, and was prejudiced by it, then you were allowed to discredit your own witness. You had to be surprised and prejudiced. And, as I had to learn the business, that's how you showed it. That demonstrated to the judge that you were surprised. That you were prejudiced.

Briefly, to recapitulate, the common law rule forbids one to discredit one's own witness and one's own witness is any witness you call to the stand, any witness of whom you are the proponent. The exception is for surprise and prejudice. Given the existence of those elements you may now discredit or impeach your witness as if it were cross-examination. Now, it may be a misplaced concern for the niceties, but there are a series of commonly recurring trial situations that do not run afoul of the common law rule and raise no particular problems under the contemporary Federal Rules of Evidence. Let us, as briefly as we can, run through those situations just to get a feel for it.

First, a distinction not commonly made by judges and lawyers. If you call a witness who testifies to A and then you seek to show the jury, by attack upon that witness, that he's not worth believing, you are discrediting or impeaching that witness. Now contrast that situation with the following situation. You call a witness who testifies to fact A. You now call a separate witness who testifies that the fact is not A, but B. Both witnesses cannot be correct. The fact is either A or B. One says A; the other says B. It may be tactically imprudent to call that second witness, but there are no doctrinal prohibitions against doing so. As a practical matter, when you call the second witness to testify that the fact is B, the jury may well be inclined to disbelieve your first witness, who said that the fact was A, or vice versa. But the law characterizes that not as discrediting or impeaching either witness. Rather, that is called contradiction, when the second witness contradicts the first witness. And while it may be tactically unwise to do, you are free to do it if you choose to. You may contradict a witness ad lib, at will. Contradiction is different from impeachment.

Second, I suppose, again, this is just a concern for precision of language. I can't imagine that anybody here is confused about it, but briefly, to review it, you call a witness, it's a direct examination. At common law, you're not permitted to discredit them. In any event, you don't want to discredit this witness. But the witness suffers a failure of recollection and anybody who has tried cases has had that happen. And it happens not because anybody has been reached or threatened or bribed, but because putting aside the professional witness—the doctor, the FBI agent, or the like—most people have never testified; most people have never seen the inside of a courtroom. You put Mr. or Mrs. Bystander on the witness stand to testify to what they saw because they happened to be there at the intersection when the two cars collided, and they are absolutely terrified. It is a degree of cold, unreasoning fear known to every one of us because it's what we all experience when we stand up to try a case. We, however, are accustomed to controlling it. The witness is not accustomed to controlling it, and that is why all kinds of things happen.

I don't know what your experience has been, but it can't be so different from mine. I mentioned this morning that I served a time as a trial judge in New York. I did not have this happen to me, but three of my colleagues did. Witnesses died on the witness stand. Can you imagine? That is not a failure of recollection, it's the angel of death came for them before they could answer the question. Out, out, out, just dead and right in the arms of the judge.

I have had it happen to me that you ask a question and it's of so inconsequential in nature as what happened next or even, actually, I'll never forget—what is your name? It began with what is your name? Absolutely nothing comes out. The witness has frozen at the stick. At the other extreme, even with an experienced witness, what happened next? So much has happened, I just don't remember what happened next. What do you do now? Well, the answer is that you've got to help the witness to remember because if the witness does not remember, the witness is incompetent, may not testify, goes home. That witness is over; maybe the case is over.

So how do you help a witness to remember? This problem of the forgetful witness in good faith, the witness who, through pressure or whatever reasons, cannot remember, has been around for so long that it's essentially the barristers, our professional cousins across the water, who evolved the courtroom techniques for handling the situation and those courtroom techniques have become rules of evidence law. Actually, two of them have become rules of evidence law. The first two don't lend themselves to being codified as rules, but still, what are they? There are four ways to handle the problem of the witness who forgets.

First, so obvious, don't overlook it. Ask for a recess. It may look a little bit awkward to the jury, but sometimes you can't help yourself. Ask for a recess, talk to the witness, presumably things get back on track, and off you go.

Second, ask a leading question. Normally, you can't ask leading questions on direct examination, but there are many exceptions. One of the exceptions is that you may ask one or two leading questions to refresh recollection. This is not impeaching or discrediting your witness, it is asking a leading question. They are not the same thing. "So what is your name?" "Ah, ah, ah . . ." "Your name is John Smith, isn't it?" "If you say so, I really don't remember."

It hasn't worked, so now we proceed to the third of the four possibilities. And this is just by way of naming it. I don't want to get into it, it's really a little bit off of the direct line for us. Present recollection refreshed.

Anything may be made available to the witness. It is for the witness's use only, it doesn't go into evidence, it's not for the jury. The witness reads it, tastes it, smells it, whatever. And then we see whether the witness now remembers. If he does, fine. He testifies on the basis of a present recollection that has now been refreshed. If he can't remember, we've got problems, but there's a fallback, as we'll see.

"What is your name?"

"Ah."

"Come on, your name is John Smith, isn't it?"

"I really can't say."

"I hand you what has earlier been marked plaintiff's exhibit A for identification. Read it to yourself." It's his birth certificate, okay? "Have you read it?"

"Yeah."

"Now do you remember what your name is?"

If he says yes, on we go. If he says no, we're in trouble.

Fourth possibility, fallback. Can't remember. At a time when he did remember, he wrote it down. And if he didn't write it down, somebody else wrote it down, but he reviewed it at a time when he remembered. And while he can't remember today, he does know enough to be able to tell us in whatever fashion that that writing is accurate. Okay.

"Have you read your birth certificate?"

"Yeah."

"Now do you remember your name?"

"No."

"Have you ever read that before?"

"Yes."

"When?"

"When I got married."

"Do you remember what you thought to yourself when you read it on the day you got married?"

"Yeah."

"What did you say to yourself?"

"I said, 'Boy, this is accurate, that is my name.'" Right?

"I offer it in evidence." And in it goes as an exception to the rule against hearsay. The birth certificate stands in place of the witness's forever unavailable recollection.

But again, that's not discrediting or impeaching. That really has nothing analytically to do with credibility, it's just helping the witness remember so that he is competent. The *Riccardi* case[1] is the best opinion I know discussing present recollection refreshed and the fallback when you put the birth certificate into evidence called, as of course, everybody knows, past recollection recorded. The *Riccardi* case tells you everything you need to know about it and there are no differences today from what was the state of affairs in 1949 when the *Riccardi* case was decided.

Next, a term that everybody knows and, if one is concerned with nicety of terminology, I think you'd have to say that most people misuse it—the hostile witness. Hostile witnesses are, in fact, very rare. The term hostile witness should be applied only to that witness who demonstrates by his demeanor on the witness stand a personal, belligerent hostility to the lawyer asking questions. That the witness on the stand is the opposing party doesn't make him hostile. For example, I represent the plaintiff. I call the defendant himself to the stand. That's not a hostile witness, at least assuming no misbehavior on his part. I'm suing the ABC Trucking Company and I call to the stand their employee, the truck driver who drove the truck that collided with my client's car. That truck driver is probably sympathetic to his employer. He's not sympathetic to my client, but that does not make him a hostile witness. A hostile witness is one who demonstrates by his demeanor that kind of belligerent hostility. Because most people are too frightened to misbehave on the witness stand, you don't run into hostile witnesses too often. When you do, it is highly dramatic, even melodramatic.

A true example drawn from a lawsuit some of you may know something about. Some of you may get involved in defamation work. One of the great libel cases of all time was brought by Quentin Reynolds

---

1. *United States v. Riccardi,* 174 F.2d 883 (3d Cir. 1949).

against Westbrook Pegler, *Reynolds v. Pegler*.[2] And if you don't remember reading the opinion, it was turned into a successful Broadway play and a movie and a television show called "A Case of Libel." It was one of Louie Nizer's famous trials. He represented Quentin Reynolds and he won that case.

Westbrook Pegler, for those of you who don't remember—he's been dead for a while—was a very successful, extremely conservative, very pugnacious columnist for the Hearst newspapers. And that's what he was in personality as well as in literary persona. He took the witness stand and he was being examined by Louie Nizer. And as Nizer walked towards him to ask a question, Pegler interrupted to say, and I quote it from the record, "One step closer, you son of a bitch, and I'll punch you in the nose." That is a hostile witness, right? Right.

What the law says about a hostile witness is simply that you may, even though it is direct examination, if it is a witness you call to the stand, you may now interrogate by leading questions. That doesn't mean you may impeach or discredit. No, no, no. It just means that you may ask leading questions because there's no real danger of putting words in the witness's mouth or suggesting the answer and we've got to get the thing moving along.

The unwilling witness is a witness whose demeanor is reasonably polite and acceptable, but who simply seems reluctant to testify. You know the expression, "It's like pulling teeth." That's the kind of witness we're talking about. If it's your witness, for that reason you can't discredit, that he's unwilling. But you may ask leading questions. Again, do not confuse leading questions with discrediting or impeaching.

And, finally—and this applies at common law as well as under the Federal Rules—when you call the opposing party himself or herself, you represent the plaintiff, you call Mr. Defendant to the stand or vice versa, that direct examination is equated to cross-examination. So you may ask leading questions and you may impeach or discredit to your

---

2. *Reynolds v. Pegler*, 223 F.2d 429 (2nd Cir. 1955).

heart's content. It is simply not regarded as direct examination. That witness is not your witness in the traditional or usual sense.

So much for these niceties and, in any event, unless you are concerned with practice of common law, it's probably unnecessary to think about. Because under the Federal Rules enacted substantially in your jurisdiction, this old idea that you vouch for the credibility of your witness goes out the window. And its anachronistic view of litigation is replaced by a contemporary view, which recognizes that, for the most part, you don't pick your witnesses; chance picks your witnesses. You have no way of determining who sees the accident or who's involved in the dispute that gives rise to the lawsuit. Since chance picks your witnesses, you ought not to be regarded as vouching for their credibility. And, hence, the provision that is Federal Rule 601. (A piece of legal trivia—that is the shortest rule in the federal codification just by number of words.) "The credibility of any witness may be attacked by any party, including the party calling him." So you don't have to worry about surprise or prejudice or anything else. Any witness may be discredited by anybody ad lib. If you happen to be the proponent, it makes no difference.

Given the realities of the trial of lawsuits and that you generally don't call people simply to attack them, as a practical matter, even under the contemporary rules, it's going to look a lot like a common law trial. You're going to call witnesses whom you want the jury to believe. The other side will call witnesses they want the jury to believe. The other side will cross-examine your witnesses, you will cross-examine their witnesses. And it's on cross-examination that discrediting will take place. Which brings us to cross-examination. I remind you that, at the very end when we come to redirect, we will talk about the rules of accrediting.

Cross-examination will keep us busy for the greater part of the afternoon. And I suppose it's only fair to acknowledge, ladies and gentlemen, that nothing that a trial lawyer does is simple or easy. But of all the things that a trial lawyer must do, the hardest, the slipperiest, the likeliest to go wrong is cross-examination. Now, cross-examination is a term that has a very simple and mechanical meaning. It's a term understood by lawyers, but misunderstood by all laymen. On the off chance that any layman is listening, let me remind you that cross-examination is a label we attach to the stage of the testimony of a witness. It tells you nothing about the emotional temperature of that examination.

One lawyer or the other lawyer calls a witness to the stand. The lawyer who calls the witness to the stand, the proponent, by custom, asks questions first. That's direct examination. That's all it means—questioning by the proponent. When the proponent gets done, the other lawyer—each of them, if more than one in the case—now has a right to ask questions. Those questions, put to the witness by a lawyer other than the proponent, are cross-examination. That's all it means—questioning by a lawyer other than the proponent. It tells you nothing about the thrust, the direction or the purpose of the cross-examination.

Now, much of the time, maybe most of the time, the purpose of the cross-examination is to persuade the jury that the witness is not worth believing. Hence, what goes on at cross-examination is discrediting or impeaching the witness. So it is that among laymen the term cross-examination is used interchangeably with discrediting or impeaching. People will talk about cross-examining a witness when a lawyer speaking precisely would say discrediting or impeaching a witness.

I need hardly remind this professional group that it will happen sometimes that you are cross-examining your own client. You represent the defendant. Plaintiff's counsel calls your client to the stand. In a civil action that's not unheard of. That's direct examination when the plaintiff's lawyer questions your client. It will be equated to cross, yes, for purposes of leading questions and the like, but it is direct examination. And when it's over, you stand up and you question your client. You did not call him to the stand, so that the accurate label to attach to your questions is cross-examination. And, obviously, the emotional temperature will be warm. You are not there to attack the credibility of your own client. And for the next hour or so, that's not the cross-examination I will be talking about. It will happen more frequently than novices and people outside the profession realize—that while it's cross-examination, you're not really concerned to attack the credibility of the witness. For example, the other side called the policeman who happened to investigate the accident. That policeman knows four things—A, B, C and D—about the accident. The other side brought out A and B. You do not challenge A and B, you simply wish to bring out the rest of what the witness knows—C and D. So you use your cross-examination to bring out C and D. You haven't attacked him, you haven't built him up. You might say that the emotional temperature of that cross-examination is neutral. And that's not the kind of cross-examination I will be discussing for the next hour or so.

The kind of cross-examination I will be discussing is the most common. It is what all laymen, and most lawyers, mean when they use the term cross-examination. It's the kind of cross-examination that is the most difficult to do and raises the most intractable problems. Cross-examination where the purpose of the cross-examining lawyer is to impeach or discredit—to persuade the jury that the witness is not worth believing.

Now, I take it that each of you in some manner has some interest or experience in litigation—you try cases. Then you're bound to have had the experience that I and my friends have over and over. If you go to a cocktail party and you're introduced to someone who is not a lawyer, you know, what do you talk about? Yeah, so what do you do for a living? I'm a dentist. Oh, that's very interesting. And what do you do? I'm a lawyer. Oh, what kind of a lawyer? I'm a trial lawyer. Immediately do you know what the dentist is thinking? You cross-examine people. Because to the non-legal mind, trial lawyer equals cross-examiner. It's the Perry Mason phenomenon. You know, as the result of the ubiquity of those television shows a half a generation ago, anybody who is a trial lawyer stands up in court day after day and makes people cry on the witness stand. That's what you do. Now, we, as professionals, know that that's not what you do. Oh, yes, you stand up and you cross-examine, you attempt to discredit or impeach, but you don't make people cry.

Every trial lawyer has an occasional sleepless night. It's what the Russian novelists call white nights. You have counted sheep. You have rehearsed the rule against perpetuities. You have had four or five stiff bourbons. Nothing helps. It's 3 o'clock in the morning and you are still awake. And some of you must be like me—you give up. You're just not going to get to sleep that night. So what you do is daydream. Now, it's the middle of the night, but it's daydreaming. You live out in your mind the kinds of things you would like to do in the real world. And if you're a trial lawyer, in your mind you are standing up in court and you are cross-examining that son of a bitch, huh? To make him cry? No. To strike him dead on the witness stand, that's what you're doing in your mind's eye. And it's worth it once in a while yielding to the temptation to indulge in that daydream, because it has a certain pedagogic value.

Compare, ladies and gentlemen, only to yourself—no one is going to be asked to recite out loud—those brilliant cross-examinations that you conduct in your mind at 3 o'clock in the morning that strike the witness dead on the witness stand with the cross-examination that you conducted let's say your first time out. And truth to tell, your second time out, your third time out, and for most of us, whenever it was that you last cross-examined a witness. Okay? Why this enormous gap between the cross-examinations that you conduct in your mind at 3 o'clock in the morning and the cross-examinations that you actually conduct in the courtroom? With respect to the ones that you actually conduct, did you strike the witness dead? No. Did you make him cry? No. I speak for myself and you decide for yourself whether your experience is like this. The first time I cross-examined a witness, as a direct and immediate consequence of my cross-examination of that witness, my client went to jail. Right? It took me a long while to realize that there is something with which to reassure yourself. No matter what you do, it's the client who goes to jail, right? As a matter of fact, it's irrelevant, but still it's worth knowing. My former law partner, Ed Williams, likes to say that the only rule of legal ethics you need to remember is just this: when things are darkest and you see no light at the end of the tunnel, and you don't know where to turn, remember, make sure it's the client who goes to jail.

Yes, your cross-examination lost the case for the client, but without being excessively comic about it—so what? The "so what" is that you have done worse than lose the case. Or, speaking for myself, I had done worse than lose the case. In consequence of my cross-examination of that witness my first time out, I wanted the ground to open up beneath me. I would sink in, the ground would close up over me and I would never be heard from again. It's not that I had lost the case, it's that I had humiliated myself. And if you're the kind of person I think you are, that's the worst of all consequences.

Well, why this gap, as I said a moment ago, between the brilliant cross-examinations you conduct in your mind's eye and the actual cross-examinations conducted in the real world of the courtroom? I don't know whether it's of use to anybody, but it strikes me, having wasted the flower of my youth thinking about this stuff and practicing it and observing it and trying to learn what there is to learn, that to be a brilliant cross-examiner, to be that kind of cross-examiner that every one of us wants to be, requires three talents or qualities. They must come together in the given lawyer. And what are they?

First, most obviously, is technical ability, or technical knowledge, if you will. And by technical knowledge, I mean a detailed knowledge—a knowledge the hand has of the glove it wears—of three bodies of legal learning: the law of evidence, the law of procedure, and what I think is a separate body of legal learning, the craft of the courtroom or trial technique. You've got to know that up, down and sideways, plus enough residual scholarship to be able to work up whatever area of the law is applicable to your case or this witness—antitrust law, family law, whatever it may be. And virtually every one of us has or can acquire that requisite technical ability. Look, we're all very smart, otherwise we wouldn't have gone to law school. We're all accustomed to working hard and what you don't know, you can learn just by going to the library and reading.

And if you've been around the merry-go-round enough times, as a large number of you have been, you know the evidence and the procedure and the trial technique that you need and you know how to work up whatever the substantive law is that's applicable to the case. So you've got the first of those three requisites. Then why the hell is brilliant cross-examination so rare? And the answer is that there is a second prerequisite and the second prerequisite—and this I address principally to the youngsters in the room—is experience. There are no child prodigies at litigation. There are no Mozarts in the courtroom. You cannot begin to function effectively at anything in the courtroom, and certainly not at cross-examination, without a fair amount of experience. And while I can't prove it and each of us may have a different idea, my sort of guesstimate as to the requisite experience is 25 jury trials. Doesn't matter the nature of the case, doesn't matter which side of the table you sit on, doesn't matter what the courtroom, but 25 jury trials before you have your sea legs—that ability to sense what's going on behind you as well as what's going on in front of you. That knack of reacting faster than you know how to think, so that you can't believe what you hear yourself saying, but somehow it's almost the right thing. That's what I mean by the consequences of experience. But to say that you're inexperienced, I hasten to point out, is not a moral criticism. It is a description, and everybody was inexperienced at some time. So if you lack the 25 jury trials or whatever you think it is that you need, well, a little bit of luck and you make sure that you're in a position to try cases and you try them. And after two years or three years or four years, you've got the experience. Technical ability, of course. Experience, ah, you'll have it.

Then why is brilliant cross-examination so rare? And the answer, I do believe, ladies and gentlemen, is because of the third quality. Now, I say this with diffidence. I am aware that it's unfashionable to speak in this manner these days. It is elitist, anti-equalitarian, and perhaps even antidemocratic, but it is, alas, true, that to be a brilliant cross-examiner takes talent. You either have it or you don't have it. And if you don't have it, there's nothing on earth that you can do to acquire it. Having observed thousands of lawyers try cases and having read transcripts galore from before the days of Abraham Lincoln through today, I tell you that so far as I can tell in the history of the common law, no more than seven or eight people have had that talent. Chances are, then, that no one in this room has it. I can speak of a certainty about only one person in this room—myself. And I tell you right now that I don't have that talent.

Well, assuming I'm right, what do you do? If you don't have the talent, you're never going to be a brilliant cross-examiner. You're never going to be Clarence Darrow. Toss in the towel. Go to dental school. A little late in the day for that and, really, do you want to spend the rest of your life looking into people's mouths? I certainly don't, but I have a reassuring piece of news for you, a note of good cheer. Granted, I don't have the talent and let's assume hypothetically that you don't either. Given that technical mastery and given that requisite experience, every one of us can become not a brilliant cross-examiner, but a reasonably competent cross-examiner, and that's an achievement worth working for.

I cannot speak to the situation in your state or in your city, but I can speak to the situation in the city in which I practiced longest and was a trial judge for six years—New York City. Do you know that in the courthouse in which I presided—a very large, well-designed courthouse, as I said before, the busiest metropolitan trial court in the world—when a lawyer conducted a cross-examination that was reasonably competent, they rang a bell on the roof of the courthouse and lawyers would come from the four corners of New York City to sit in that courtroom and watch a lawyer who could conduct cross-examination of a witness without humiliating himself. And that is my standard. If you can cross-examine day in and day out without humiliating yourself, you can cross-examine with reasonable competence and anybody can learn how to do it. Oh, it takes some practice. Yes, the experience is necessary. But technical mastery means what? An intimate knowledge of that part of the law of evidence we have begun to discuss and will continue discussing that part of the craft of the courtroom that we will be talking about. Put it into practice, make it second nature so that you can do it unthinkingly, and you will be a reasonably competent cross-examiner and that, itself, marks you out as one lawyer out of thousands.

If I'm wrong and one or more of you has that third quality, the requisite talent, I stand in awe of you, and I have nothing to teach you. I cannot teach anybody how to be a brilliant cross-examiner. You make your own technique as you go along. But on the off chance that you do lack the talent, perhaps I can be of help and, if I can be of help, I have spent the day profitably, and I will be delighted.

The two big questions that the law can answer for you, assuming that you don't have that third requisite, that you don't have the talent, that you're not the kind of person who can create his own technique as he or she goes along, the two questions that the law can answer for you are, first, what do I ask on cross-examination? Remembering that we've agreed that cross-examination means to discredit or impeach. What questions do I ask to persuade this jury that the witness is not worth believing? And, let me say it again, because it was an astounding revelation to me when I realized that this was so, and it may come as a surprise to some of you. The answer to that question is furnished to you by the law of evidence. The law of evidence that I studied in law school was a host of negative rules that tell you what not to do and what's wrong or incorrect can be turned around and used affirmatively as a set of rules to tell you what to do. And specifically as a set of rules that give you a kind of checklist of things to consider asking about in order to discredit a witness.

And the parenthesis, personal parenthesis—forgive me—the reason the law of evidence can be stated that way is, in major part, and certainly with respect to credibility, the law of evidence is nothing more than a codification of generations of experience of trial lawyers—English and American. This is what works in the courtroom, this is what's fair. This is reasonably economical of time and effort. You turned it into a rule of evidence law, but you can turn it right back into a rule of effective courtroom practice.

The second question, looking ahead, is how do you ask it? Not what do I ask, but how do you ask it? And there I think the craft of efficacy has some guidelines that will help. But let us begin with "What can I ask about?" Now, remember this is a checklist in the sense that we are reviewing all of the possibilities. Please, do not be so foolish as to use any of them unthinkingly. You've got to consider the circumstances before you, the nuances of your case, the feel of the courtroom—as lawyers like to say—and decide what makes sense. But if you have this checklist in mind, you know what the possibilities are, because this checklist exhausts the universe. This is what there is to ask about. Some of it may not be apposite in your case. So be it. But you run through the checklist and you're ready to proceed. There's nothing magical about the way in which I present this stuff or talk about it or review it, but over the years it has seemed to me that this is the most useful way to organize it because it comes out most quickly when you need it in the hurly-burly of the courtroom. When you're under fire, you don't have time to think complicated thoughts. This somehow acts as a kind of mnemonic device, helping you to remember.

Under the Federal Rules of Evidence and at common law, there are nine ways to discredit a witness. Not 10, not 11—9, that's the maximum. A handful of states recognize only eight of the nine. But all of them are recognized under the Federal Rules of Evidence, assuming that's the jurisdiction in which you're trying your case. If you know these nine, you will know how to discredit a witness, what to ask about. And the nine are not miscellaneous, they're not incoherent. They have a kind of internal organization and it works this way. There is a first group of four and a second group of four and then there is one mode of impeachment that kind of stands by itself. And that's what you have. And if you think of them in this way it kind of falls into place, because the first group of four are related among themselves, but essentially unrelated to the second group of four. The second group of four are related among themselves, but unrelated to the others, and that ninth one stands out there all by itself.

First group of four. Think back to basic evidence, roughly the third week of the course when you took it in law school. What are the elements of competence today? Meaning, assume that we've got no incompetence by status. I mean, no matter your religion, no matter your race, no matter whatever, you're competent to be a witness so long, remember, as four simple prerequisites are met. Remember what they are? You have to take the oath or some substitute for the oath, the affirmation; you must have perceived something of the transaction which constitutes the subject matter of the lawsuit; you must remember what you perceived; and you must be able to communicate what you remember perceiving. Oath, perception, memory, communication.

Competence simply means that the witness is eligible to take the stand and testify. If there is a question—for example, the proposed witness is 11 years old. Does this child understand the nature and significance of the oath? That's for the judge to decide. Competence is a question of law. The judge decides it. But, obviously, with respect to fully grasping the significance of the oath, degree of perception, completeness of memory, eloquence of communication—nobody's at 100 percent, we all have deficiencies. In order to be competent, essentially you've got to be more than zero. You must have perceived something, remembered something, be able to communicate something, even if it's not very much. And the judge will say, "That's enough, take the stand and testify." As to these shortcomings, as to these deficiencies in perception, memory, communication, that's for the jury to weigh when assessing credibility. We're all familiar with that tag phrase. That goes not to competence, but to weight. If you wish to pursue it, counselor, do so on cross-examination and argue it to the jury as affecting credibility. Well, there you have it. Take the elements of competence, turn them around, use them destructively to show the jury that the witness is not worth believing. Now, how you do it will be up to you, your style, the circumstances of the case, but see what the possibilities are.

First, the oath. Now, you don't have to be Clarence Darrow to understand that to come at the witness like a raging tiger with the ferocious question, "When did you last go to church or synagogue? When's the last time you saw the inside of a house of God? " Right? You start asking questions like that and the jury's going to be laughing at you. Juries are very mature. The only thing they lack on us is technical lingo. They're quite as smart as we are and usually smarter. And you start horsing around with a witness like that and a jury's going to say to itself, that lawyer is the ass. If that's the kind of question he's asking, he doesn't have a case. Jurors have no patience with that kind of thing. And that sort of kid stuff is articulated in Federal Rule 610. You see, evidence of religious belief or practice or the lack thereof is not admissible by way of impeachment. But that doesn't mean that you don't have this first possibility of attack. Read Rule 610. It's evidence of religious belief or practice that you may not go into.

But assuming that you wanted to and assuming that the circumstances are right, you can still attack on the grounds of the oath and I'll give you a celebrated example drawn from the trial of Alger Hiss. Now, not talking about the cross-examination of Carl Binger, but the cross-examination of Whittaker Chambers at the first trial, which was defended on Hiss's behalf by the then-ablest criminal lawyer in practice, Lloyd Paul Stryker.

Whittaker Chambers had testified before the House on Un-American Activities Committee in extenso and had never mentioned espionage. He had testified before the grand jury a couple of times without ever mentioning espionage. He testified at a deposition in the libel action that Hiss brought against Chambers and never mentioned espionage. And now here he is on the stand, testifying about Hiss bringing documents from the State Department for transmittal to the Soviet Union. Right? So you've got maybe 10 versions of Whittaker Chambers's story, all given under oath, and not one of them mentions the crucial set of transactions involving espionage. Does anyone, I wonder, happen to know the first question Stryker asked on cross-examination? The first question of Whittaker Chambers asked by Lloyd Paul Stryker was, "Mr. Chambers, do you know the meaning of an oath?" Huh? Is it proper? Never mind is it wise, is it prudent? Never mind do you like the style. Is it technically proper? Answer: Yes. If the prosecutor had objected, the objection should be overruled. Why is it proper? It goes to the oath. Not religious belief or practice, but simply the extent to which this man acknowledges the obligation of telling the truth after he takes an oath.

Now, that's going to be rare, I'll grant you. It's going to be an Alger Hiss, Lloyd Paul Stryker, Whittaker Chambers. Perception is much more common. You just attack the witness's ability to perceive what the witness claims to have seen. And, again, everything depends upon the circumstances, but run through the checklist. He says he saw it. How far away was he? What were the lighting conditions? Night or day?

Were there trees in the way? Was he wearing his glasses? Identification. Identifying the kind of person he is accustomed to seeing so that he recognizes subtle differences of facial structure, or is it a member of a minority group and they kind of all look the same to him—that kind of thing. It's a commonplace of the courtroom and you see where it fits into the analytical framework. It is attacking perception.

Take just one example and, I repeat, I deliberately make these examples absurd so that they do demonstrate, so that they do illustrate and they're easy to remember. The witness on direct examination says that he saw your client's car collide with the other fellow's car right in front of the general post office in Minneapolis. Cross-examination, right? Okay. The oath . . . now who cares when he goes to church. We're not going to do that. But how about perception?

"You say that you saw the two cars collide in front of the post office?"

"Yes."

"Now the post office is at Marquette and 1st Street, isn't it?"

"Yes."

"Where were you?"

"I was at Marquette and 10th Street."

Right? What do you do now? You know what to do, but will you do it? No, you will not do it. You will not stop, right? You will ask the next question, right, and you know that the next question is:

"Well, then, Mr. Bigshot, you say that you saw the two cars collide in front of the post office when you were nine blocks away at Marquette and 10th Street?"

And every time you ask that question, you know that you get the answer:

"Well, Counselor, I was on the observation deck of the IDS building, looking through high-powered binoculars when I saw the whole thing."

Now asking the extra question is a phenomenon we'll talk about later when we discuss how to ask the questions. I raise it now simply to get your interest and I remind you that my only concern at this point is that you see that you attack perception as a way of suggesting to the jury that the witness is not worth believing.

The third element of competence—memory, recollection, remembrance. Call it any of those words that you like. The witness must be able to remember what he tells you he perceived. And the passage of time, of course, attenuates memory. Other things that may have happened will attenuate memory. Handle it very delicately, but if there's nothing about the episode to make it memorable, then you argue to the jury that it's kind of hard to take that he does remember, but be very, very careful.

Let me take an example from a field in which I was once in very good practice indeed—prosecuting and then defending complex federal conspiracy cases. At least in my neck of the woods in those years, a complex federal conspiracy case was, if you were in the business, defined as 13 defendants whose last names end with a vowel, plus a stool pigeon. Right. That was a conspiracy case. And there was a certain charade that the prosecutors went through, because typically there was an overt act in the indictment and it was something as inconsequential on its own as that on a certain date your client, my client I'll make it, my client registered at the Waldorf-Astoria Hotel. You know, so here we are on trial today. Nineteen-eighty, four years ago, on such-and-such a date, you registered at the Waldorf-Astoria Hotel. And there are all the defendants seated on the chairs that have labels on them and the labels say these are where the defendants sit. They're not allowed to sit anywhere else. And the government will call to the stand the desk clerk at the Waldorf-Astoria. Right?

"Sir, are you employed?"

"Yes."

"What's your job?"

"I'm the desk clerk at the Waldorf-Astoria."

"Were you employed in that capacity on such-and-such a date in 1980?"

"Yes."

"Were you on duty on that day?"

"Yes."

"Did you register people?"

"Yes."

"Now I want you to look all around this courtroom and tell me, yes or no, whether you see present in court anyone you registered that day."

And let me take a moment or two to tell you the way it would be done in the Southern District of New York in those days. "Take a moment, look around the courtroom and tell us." First the fellow takes his eyeglasses off. Then he turns to the judge. And then to juror number one and so on down the line. And realize this takes minutes and minutes in the courtroom, an eternity. And the tension begins to build as he works through the jurors, then the lawyers, and then he comes to the chairs where the defendants sit. It's a charade. Everybody knows those are the defendants.

"There, I see him! I see him!"

"All right. Point out the one you registered."

And he points out your client. You may inquire. All right, now let's see . . . you're going to ask him when he last went to church? Ah, come on. You going to ask him whether he had his glasses on when he registered them? Come on. But memory—there's something about this that doesn't ring true. So let's give it a shot, right?

"The Waldorf-Astoria is one of the world's largest hotels, isn't it?"

"Yes."

"How many days a week do you work?"

"Five."

"How many weeks a year?"

"48."

"On an average, how many people a day do you register?"

"Oh, about 412."

"How many years had you worked there before the day in question?"

"About 20 years."

"And you've been working there since then, another four years, is that right?

"Yes."

"Then by my count, as of the time you claim to have registered Charlie sitting over there, you had registered 182,412 people, isn't that correct? And in the four years since, another 27,812. Correct?"

"Correct."

What do you do now? Hmm. Will you? No, no. No, you know what you're going to do.

"Right. Now how come out of these 150,000 people you can tell this jury that it's my client whom you registered on that day?"

And every time you ask that question the answer will come:

"Well, you see, counselor, your client walked up to me and took out a gun yea big and held it to my head and said, 'Register me, Buster, or I'll kill you.' That's how I know it was your client."

Now, again, we'll talk about that later, but that's why.

Four, communication. It doesn't come up too often, but often enough so that it's worth being on the alert for it. Typically it's going to be a matter of your ear. You hear the opposing witness use a word or a phrase that's just not his word or phrase. It clinks, it doesn't ring true. They call the witness to the stand. Your radar is, of course, always on in the courtroom. You recognize at once that that witness is a moral leper. More than that, he has an IQ of no more than 40. Right? So he's put on the stand, slobbering, moaning, drunk . . . I mean, obviously, a halfwit of some kind. And suddenly there he is using the word "antidisestablishmentarianism." Something's wrong, right? So you might consider such a question as, "You remember that word that you used?" "Yes." "What does it mean?" Just that, right? Never mind whether you think it's astute, wise or effective. Is it technically proper? If the other side objects, what will the ruling be? If the other side objects, you know, when you say, "What does that word mean that you used on direct?" "Objection, objection, blah, blah, blah." Objection overruled. You are discrediting by inquiring into his communication. Is he, in fact, communicating what he remembers perceiving or is he simply repeating back what the opposing counsel or the prosecutor told him to say? Perfectly proper. You are free to do it.

Now, I've said each time, putting aside considerations of tactics, strategy, whether it's going to be effective or not, let me drive that home. When you are impeaching using any one of these first four, there are no preconditions by way of doctrine. There are no rules that must be satisfied. You may impeach by going into the oath, perception, memory or communication, so long as you think it's going to help you to do so. You can go fishing. That's what I'm saying. We all know the expression, "It's a fishing expedition." You have a right to go fishing. And you don't need me to tell you, don't get bullied around on it. If you decide to go after perception by saying, "Now, Mr. Witness, you say that you saw thus and so."

"Yes."

"You're wearing glasses, aren't you?"

"Well of course I'm wearing glasses."

"Were you wearing your glasses at the time?"

"Objection. He's going fishing."

"Damn right I am and I have the right to go fishing."

Now, I run the risk of an adverse answer, but I am entitled to ask that question. As we will see, that's not so when you come down here, which is why it is so important to have some sense of the pattern, the coherence of these rules, because then you understand what the limitations are or, as in this first group of four, the freedoms are. You're free to go into it, so long as you think it makes litigation sense to go into it and you run the risk of an adverse answer. All right. So much for the first four.

This second four are more complicated. There are rules. There are conditions that must be met, as we shall see. I call these the special modes of discrediting. I say special in that it's not the reverse of the elements of competence or something as elementary as that. These are the rules specially given by the law of evidence to help you discredit a witness. I've tried as hard as I can to find the simplest way of stating these rules. Let me state them as simply as I can and then illustrate them out of real cases, in the instance of some of them, or just little hypotheticals that I'll make up as to others. Now, these four, as I say, are related to each other, but not related to the first four. The order in which I do them is just the order that I'm accustomed to; there's no magic to that.

First, any witness may be impeached or discredited by asking questions designed to show bias, prejudice, interest or corruption. Those are four qualities, but they add up to the first mode of impeachment: bias, prejudice, interest, corruption. On many occasions in the literature, that's shorthanded to bias. But there are four different qualities at work there and, if it helps anybody, let me take a moment to define them. Bias is an irrational predisposition in favor. Prejudice is an irrational predisposition against. Interest is a stake in the outcome—an economic stake, an emotional stake, what have you. And corruption is simply bribery. Dishonesty, affecting the testimony.

Now, there are some conditions. There are some prerequisites, but they apply to all four of that middle group and so we will discuss them at the end, after we've discussed the four. Assuming compliance with those prerequisites, assuming that you have done what the law requires to be done by way of condition, the precedent before using this line of attack, this line of attack is an absolute right in any court in the land. No one can prevent you from going into bias, prejudice, interest or corruption and, if you are prevented, it's probably reversible error.

And one of the more dramatic examples of that that I know is this *Tla-Koo-Yel-Lee* case in the United States Supreme Court in 1897—a long time ago, to be sure. But this doctrine is today exactly what it was in the 19th century, in the 18th century, and even beforehand. So deeply rooted is this idea of bias, prejudice, interest, corruption, impeachment in our law of evidence, that there's not a word about it in the Federal Rules of Evidence. Not because they mean it not to be available in the federal court, but because there was no need to write a rule. Everybody knows that this is powerful stuff. When you've got the goods on a witness, you can really do damage with bias, prejudice, interest, corruption and you must be given the right to do that damage.

Some silly examples, then I'll briefly tell you about that case in the Supreme Court. By silly examples I don't mean they're silly, but fast examples to drive it home.

Bias:

"Sir, you say that the other driver had the green light?"

"Yes, I do."

"Well, you're the other driver's brother, aren't you?"

"Objection."

"Overruled, bias."

Irrational predisposition in favor of his brother:

"Sir, you say that my client went through the red light?"

"Yes, sir."

"Well, you observe that my client is black, a member of the black race, and I see that you're a life member of the Ku Klux Klan, aren't you?"

There are a lot of judges who would say that's not proper, that's irrelevant. They'd probably say it's peripheral to the case. It's off the bullseye, it's off the target. No. No, it's not. It shows prejudice, an irrational predisposition against black people, and you have an absolute right to ask that question.

Interest. Stake in the outcome. It's easy:

"Sir, you say that my client went through the red light?"

"Yeah."

"And that you had the green light?"

"Yeah."

"You're the defendant, aren't you?"

"Yeah."

"That's interesting."

Right. Always done by an adept prosecutor in a criminal case when the defendant takes the stand. It is usually the first or the last question on cross-examination. You're the defendant, aren't you? And it's devastating from the vantage point of the jury box. It brings it all out. He has the most obvious and substantial kind of self-interest in lying.

And then corruption:

"You've been bribed to give your testimony, haven't you?" That's an end of that witness, which is why we've got to have some conditions and limitations on this, but there you get it.

That case in the Supreme Court[3] is not much more complicated an example, but it shows you the teeth this doctrine has, that nobody can deprive you of the right to use it. It's a federal case because it arises in the territory of Alaska. The defendant is charged with murder. The theory of the prosecution is that the defendant murdered the victim and that the bystanders, the two witnesses, were another man and his wife, that is the defendant's wife. The defendant's wife testifies against him and her testimony is to the effect that he did it. Technically, former husband, but she was married to him at the time. "My former husband did it." Impeachment by the defense lawyer:

"Ma'am, are you married to him now?"

"No."

"Are you married to anybody now?"

"No."

"But are you living with someone?"

"Objection. What does that have to do with anything? That's collateral." You've all heard that expression. Trial judge sustained it. Give yourself a little exercise here. Is that the correct ruling? Absolutely not. Why? The person she was living with was the other man who purportedly was with her when they witnessed the murder. The argument would be she is living with this other guy, this other guy and she may well have committed the murder, and she is motivated to testify against her former husband to get him out of the picture. I don't care whether you're persuaded by that argument, but it's a plausible argument, a colorable argument and it supports the contention that this is impeachment of the witness to show prejudice, really, against the defendant, about whom she is testifying. The trial judge sustains the objection. When you get to the United States Supreme Court, the Solicitor General confesses error. He says, "There is no way to support that ruling. Defense counsel had an absolute right to question on matters showing bias, prejudice, interest, corruption. That they were

---

3. *Tla-Koo-Yel-Lee v. United States,* 167 U.S. 274 (1897).

peripheral, collateral, in the sense that they had nothing directly to do with the homicide is irrelevant. The trial judge's ruling was insupportable, the conviction must therefore be reversed." And all the Supreme Court says is, "We agree, reversed." So it shows what teeth, what sharpness this doctrine has. Okay.

Next, second of this middle group of four, a mode of impeachment commonly encountered in criminal cases but available, as a matter of theory, in civil cases as well. There's a long history to it, which I shall refrain from recounting, but a moment or two of reference to the history is necessary to make clear what's been happening in these last few years. And if you're not up to date on it, let me tell you that a lot has been happening in these last few years.

It is impeachment by bringing out that the witness has been convicted of a crime. And I put it that way to emphasize that the two key words are "convicted of a crime" and we mean exactly what they say. A conviction is a conviction. You were found guilty after trial or you pleaded guilty. An arrest is not a conviction. An indictment is not a conviction. It's a conviction for what? For a crime—typically felony or misdemeanor. Not a traffic violation, not a hunting law violation, not a juvenile delinquency adjudication, not a youthful offender adjudication—those are adjudications of status. This is a conviction of a crime.

Now, just briefly, what is the history of it? At common law, meaning 300 to 400 years ago, anyone convicted of a crime was, forever after, incompetent to be a witness, ineligible to testify. The rule didn't cause much controversy because at the time the rule came into being, the penalty for virtually any kind of crime was death. As a result, you had very few people walking the streets who were in a position to witness an accident and then take the stand and say, "Oh, but by the way, I was convicted of a crime," because they were hanged or, if they were lucky, transported to Australia.

In due course, the rigors of universal capital punishment were mitigated, so you began to have people walking the streets who had been convicted of crimes, but still they were incompetent to testify and it led to unsatisfactory results. Cases were not being decided on the merits.

And so the common law just turned 180 degrees and said, oh, anyone who's been convicted of a crime is competent. That person may testify. But the fact of conviction may be brought out to affect credibility. And that was the common law rule and I guess still is in some jurisdictions. Any witness in any kind of case may be impeached by showing that the witness has been convicted of a crime. The instance that gives rise to troublesome consequences is the instance of the witness who occupies the very special status of the defendant in a criminal case. Now, the defendant is entitled to have his guilt determined solely on the basis of the evidence tending to show that he did the thing charged in this indictment. In theory, nothing else counts. That is our vision of how criminal justice ought to work. That is the common law view of it. That is what is included, along with other things, of course, in the concept of due process.

In Europe, as you know, they do things differently. It's equally civilized, but a different way of doing it. Some of you may know Camus' wonderful novel, *L'Étranger (The Stranger).* A magistrate's inquiry into a murder. Why did Meursault kill that Arab on the beach? And the first question the magistrate asks is, "Why didn't you cry at your mother's funeral?" But to a common lawyer that's irrelevant. Doesn't matter why he didn't cry at his mother's funeral; what matters is just—is the evidence showing that he did what this indictment says he did.

Now, you put the defendant on the witness stand and he tells the jury whatever his defense is. Alibi. "I was in the movies, I didn't do it." Or I saw it done, but I wasn't participating in it. Or it was an accident, I didn't have the necessary mental element or whatever it may be. And now the prosecutor stands up to impeach with convictions. And all of you have been around enough to know what happens. The prosecutor stands up and, you know, "You've been in trouble before, haven't you?"

"Yes, sir."

"Five years ago you were convicted, weren't you, of selling heroin to school children?"

"Yes, sir."

"And two years after that, statutory rape?"

"Yes, sir."

"And last year, kidnapping?"

And you see what's happening. The jury starts to say the world would be well rid of this guy's shadow. So let's get rid of him. Let's lock him up and throw the key away because he is a bad guy and that may be a perfectly understandable reaction from the jury, but it is contrary to what is supposed to be our system. His guilt is determined, not because he's got a criminal record, but because the evidence shows he did this thing.

Just briefly, there were various palliative devices that developed. Defense counsel, for example, would be permitted to bring out the criminal record. Have you ever seen that? Analytically, you can't defend it. I mean, if you think of it as accrediting, you're accrediting before he's been discredited. If you think of it as discrediting, there's no surprise in prejudice, but defense counsel brings it out in a softer way and that makes it different. I have, myself, seen it brought out as follows. This literally happened. Put the defendant on the stand, begin the direct examination this way.

"Charlie, you've had a lot of trouble in your life, haven't you?"

"Yeah."

"Been convicted?"

"Yeah."

"Tell the jury how many times."

"Five and this'll make six."

That's the kind of thing that would happen in the old days. Well, there were a lot of attempts to restrict the right of the prosecutor to use convictions. There was a lot of controversy back and forth. The short of the story is that in virtually every jurisdiction today, you have a rule, a statute, or a case that limits the right of the prosecutor to impeach a defendant with convictions. In the federal courts, that limitation is contained in Federal Rule 609, a very complicated rule set forth verbatim in the appendix, and I don't think it would serve any purpose for me to stand up here and go through it parsing it out. It's too complicated and badly drafted, but there it is. It limits the kinds of crimes, it limits convictions that are more than a certain number of years old and it provides, in certain instances, for the judge to exercise his discretion in telling the prosecutor not to use a particular conviction.

The *Santiago* case[4] in Hawaii is interesting in that it's out there all by itself, but it's as far as any court has gone with that. In the *Santiago* case, the Hawaii Supreme Court held as a matter of due process under Hawaiian law that whenever the defendant in a criminal case takes the stand, he may not be impeached with convictions. The prejudicial impact upon the jury is so great as to outweigh any real relationship the convictions have to credibility. So no impeachment with a conviction under any circumstances. Seems to me that that's about all that we properly should do with impeachment by conviction. I repeat, if you're working with a situation governed by Rule 609, you've got to spend a lot of time threading the needle, seeing exactly what its mechanics are.

It's unnecessary, I know, but let me remind you in 10 seconds of where we are. We are discussing this middle group of four modes of impeachment. The first was impeachment by showing that the witness is biased, prejudiced, interested or corrupt. The second, showing that the witness has been convicted of a crime subject to the qualifications, limitations, and exclusions set forth, for example, in Federal Evidence Rule 609. We come now to the third of this middle group of four.

Here we impeach by asking a question designed to show that the witness has committed some immoral, criminal, or vicious act, sometimes called simply a bad act. Now, not meaning a conviction, but rather meaning an act which perhaps did not result in prosecution or the act that underlay a conviction. So it's not "Were you convicted of selling heroin to school children?" Rather, when you're using the third mode of impeachment, it is "Didn't you sell heroin to school children? Did you not assault such-and-such a person? Did you not do whatever the immoral, criminal or vicious act may be?" This is the one mode of

---

4. *State v. Santiago*, 492 P.2d 657 (Hawaii 1971).

impeachment of these nine which you may well find not to be permissible under a given state's law of evidence.

For example, if recollection serves, in California this mode of impeachment is not permissible. There was a time when it was thought that this mode of impeachment was not permissible in the federal court. This was before the Federal Rules of Evidence. But the Federal Evidence Rules contained Rule 608(b), and Rule 608(b) says, in my paraphrase, one may impeach by asking a question designed to show that the witness has committed some bad act, so long as the bad act has some relationship to credibility and is subject, in any event, to the judge's discretion to exclude the bad act if its prejudicial effect upon the jury will outweigh any light it may shed on the witness's credibility. There's really little more to be said than that, so let's pass to number four.

This fourth and last mode of impeachment involves showing that the witness, on some occasion in the past, has said something different from, inconsistent with, what he has said on direct examination here. So we call this impeachment by prior inconsistent statement. The theory of it is obvious. The witness speaks with a forked tongue. He says one thing today and another thing tomorrow or yesterday, hence he's not worth believing. Having said that, you've said about everything there is to say, save for the common law requirement of a foundation. Worth mentioning because, at least to some extent, it is continued under the Federal Rules of Evidence. Now, briefly, once again, I remind you what a foundation is. It's a very simple idea. There's no reason to make an unduly heavy meal of it. Over and over again our law of evidence says to you, the trial lawyer, something as follows: Counselor, is that what you want to do? You want to do that over there? You may do that, so long as you do something else first over here. And the generic name that we give to the things that you have to do first over here is the foundation. You lay the foundation here for what you want to do over there.

There's no one way to lay a foundation. There are as many ways to lay a foundation as there are rules of evidence that say you've got to do something first before you do something else. So with respect to the impeachment with a prior inconsistent statement, there are certain foundations to be laid. I speak in the plural because at common law there are two different foundations, depending upon whether the prior inconsistent statement was oral or in writing. If the prior inconsistent statement was oral, the foundation consists simply of two, three, four questions, as many as you need, to direct the witness's attention to the time, place, and circumstances of the making of that prior oral statement. We've all done it. We've all seen it done.

Assume that the witness on direct examination said that the traffic light was green. Our investigation reveals that a couple of weeks ago at the bar down the street he told the bartender that the light was red. How do you lay the foundation?

"Mr. Witness, do you remember a couple of weeks ago you went to the bar down the street? Do you remember you spoke to the bartender? Do you remember the conversation turned to this accident?" We've laid the foundation. Now you may impeach him. "Didn't you tell the bartender that the light was red?"

Suppose the prior statement is in writing? The foundation is laid differently, but even more simply. The foundation is laid merely by showing the witness the writing and giving him a few moments to look it over. Just that. After he's looked it over, you are free to question him in any way you care to about the prior inconsistent statement contained in that writing.

Now, the Federal Rules of Evidence, as you see when you look over Rule 613, in some circumstances, abolish the requirement of a foundation. In some circumstances, you will be permitted to proceed directly to confront the witness with the prior statement, be it oral or in writing. But how it works is best reserved for a little bit later on. If I were to talk about it now, it would be at best inefficient and at worst probably incomprehensible. That completes our canvass of this middle group of four modes of impeachment—bias, prejudice, interest, corruption, convictions, bad acts, prior inconsistent statements.

Now, remember, I said that there were some conditions, there are some special rules applicable to the use of this middle group of four.

Let's talk about those special rules now. First, the so-called collateral or not collateral issue. An awful lot of judges and an awful lot of lawyers seem to have trouble grasping this and it ought not to be troublesome because it is really very simple, so long as you see clearly what the issue is. With respect to this middle group of four, one asks the impeaching question and you get an answer. And the answer can be yes or no. Are you not a life member of the Ku Klux Klan? Yes or no says the witness. Were you not convicted last year of perjury? Did you not sell heroin last year to a school child? Did you not tell the bartender last week that the light was red? Right? If the witness says yes, if the witness acknowledges the impeaching information, as a matter of courtroom technique, if nothing else, move on. Go to something else. Don't dwell upon it. You've already accomplished everything you reasonably can hope to accomplish.

But if the witness says no, do you see what we're concerned with? The witness denies the impeaching information. Then we've got to deal with the collateral/not collateral issue. The term collateral or not collateral is best understood as not referring to the impeaching question. Are you a life member of the Ku Klux Klan? Were you convicted of such and such a crime? Did you do such and such a bad act? Did you tell the bartender something different? The propriety of the impeaching question is determined simply by seeing whether it fits one of these modes of impeachment, whether it is permissible under the law of evidence. If it is permissible, it's a proper question. But if the witness denies the impeaching information, then you've got to ask yourself, "Will I be allowed as part of my case to prove the contrary of the denial?" Do you see it? To introduce evidence to show that the witness really is a member of the Ku Klux Klan, really was convicted, really did commit that bad act, really did tell the bartender something else. And the term collateral or not collateral refers to introducing evidence to show the contrary of the witness's denial.

Now, once you understand that, it's not hard to remember the rules because the rules are very clearly established at common law, in the federal court in any jurisdiction that follows the Federal Rules of

Evidence. And the rule varies with the mode of impeachment, which is why it is so important to have some kind of device to keep this stuff organized in your mind. And I will simply tell you what the rules are. When it's bias, prejudice, interest or corruption and the witness denies it, it is not collateral to prove the contrary of the denial. You have a right to introduce independent evidence to show the bias, prejudice, interest or corruption. Please understand that. It may be unnecessary, but give me 30 seconds and be patient with me while I drive that home.

The question is who went through the traffic light in this ordinary automobile accident negligence case. Witness. "Sir, you say that my client went through the red light?"

"Yes, I do."

"You see that my client is black?"

"Yes."

"Aren't you a life member of the Ku Klux Klan?"

Many judges would sustain that objection. That's wrong. The question is absolutely proper as showing prejudice. "No, it's not true that I'm a member of the Ku Klux Klan." Now, as part of my case, perhaps on rebuttal, I wish to introduce records to show that he is a life member of the Ku Klux Klan. Many a judge would say, "What are you doing? This is not a case of a Ku Klux Klan membership, it's a case about the red light." That's right, but the law is well settled, the cases are legion, that a showing of bias or prejudice goes so centrally to the question of credibility, which is the overriding issue whenever a witness takes the stand, that we will spend time going into these matters, even though that's not what the case is about. But the case is about credibility. So if a witness denies it and it's bias, prejudice, interest, or corruption, you may prove the contrary of the denial.

If it's a conviction, the witness is not likely to deny it because it's a matter of record. But should the witness deny it, here is the rule. It's not collateral. You may prove the contrary of the denial, but you will be required to do so in the most economical way that there is. And the most economical way is by the record of conviction. You will not be allowed to call the judge who presided at the trial at which he was convicted or the foreman of the jury or a bystander to say, "I heard the jury found him guilty." You do it by the record of conviction, appropriately certified or exemplified.

Bad act, that's the curve ball. Under the Federal Rules and in those jurisdictions which do not follow the Federal Rules, but which allow this mode of impeachment, here is the rule. You may ask the impeaching question, "Didn't you sell heroin to school children?" whatever the bad act may be. If he says yes, you've done it. If he says no, that's an end to the matter. It is collateral to prove the contrary of the denial. There's a lawyer's expression to say that. You can ask the question with respect to bad act impeachment, but you must take the witness's answer. If he says no, you know, you can badger him a little bit and, depending upon your style, you know, pretend to be upset and yell and scream. But if the witness insists upon no, that's it. You've got to accept it. You will not be permitted to prove the contrary of the denial. That will be collateral.

As to impeachment with a prior inconsistent statement, there is no rule that can be stated to cover all cases. Essentially, it comes down to this. If the inconsistent statement deals with the important matter in this lawsuit and the witness denies making the inconsistent statement, it's not collateral to prove the contrary of the denial. We will take the time to hear the bartender's testimony about what the witness said concerning the color of the light, whatever it may be.

If the inconsistent statement deals with an unimportant matter in this trial, it is within the judge's sound discretion to say, "You can ask the impeaching question, but you've got to take the answer. I will not let you call other witnesses to testify to the contrary of the denial." Now, the Federal Evidence Rule on laying the foundation for impeachment with an inconsistent statement—in the first instance you don't have to lay a foundation. You can proceed directly to tax the witness with the inconsistent statement. And if he admits making it, there are no further difficulties. But if he denies making it—and this is going to sound very awkward, but it's the way the rule is drafted. If he denies making it and you are going to try to prove the contrary of his denial because it is an important matter, before you can prove the contrary of his denial, before you can call independent witnesses to say, yes, he did make that inconsistent testimony, you must lay the foundation. You must somehow direct his attention to the time, place and circumstances, or show him the writing. Only after you've done that—giving him a chance presumably to change his answer—will you be permitted to prove the contrary of his denial. Awkward, cumbersome, but that is what the draftsmen intended in Rule 613.

That's it because that's really all there is to say about the collateral or not collateral issue. One other limitation—it should be self-evident, but let's make it explicit. We said, and I do not now change, but I just refer to it to remind you, that when you impeach up here, the reverse use of the elements of competence, you may go on a fishing expedition if that's what you want to do. The law of evidence says go right ahead. It's your risk, but you may ask even though you don't know the answer.

When you get down here it's a little bit different because, as any trial lawyer will recognize, when you ask questions about bias, prejudice, interest, corruption, convictions, bad acts or inconsistent statements, the mere asking of the question affects the way the jury looks at this witness. And, you know, any kind of trial lawyer's instinct will tell you that. "Are you a life member of the Ku Klux Klan?" "No." Already the jury is saying of course he's going to deny it. It's a disgraceful thing and it's true. The mere asking of the question begins to poison the well with respect to this witness. The law of evidence has recognized that for a long time and so, with respect to the middle group of four, you cannot conduct fishing expeditions. Meaning what? You may ask the question so long as it fits one of those four modes, but you may ask it only if you have a good faith basis for doing so. That guards against the pure fishing expedition. And this requirement of a good faith basis is the way it's put in all the cases in all the jurisdictions. What constitutes a good faith basis is essentially a judgment call by the judge. You know, it's hard to say in the abstract that so much constitutes a good faith basis, but another quantum of proof does not.

Lest anybody have any question about it, you can have a good faith basis even though what it rests upon is not admissible in evidence. It might be hearsay upon hearsay, but if it adds up to what the judge thinks is a good faith basis for asking the question, you may go right ahead. You may have a good faith basis, but for tactical reasons decide that if the witness says no, you will not seek to prove the contrary of the denial even though you have a right to do so. "Aren't you a life member of the Ku Klux Klan?" "No, I'm not." I'm going to leave it at that. I will not go back to it as when I come to putting in evidence or on rebuttal. You're free to make that tactical choice, but when you ask the question are you a life member of the Ku Klux Klan, were you convicted of whatever it may be, did you do that certain bad act, did you tell the bartender something to the contrary, there must be a good faith basis.

It is rarely done, but you might consider the following. This is a question of courtroom tactics or strategy. The other side asks such a question of your witness. Now, you know the opposing lawyer. There are opposing lawyers who, by and large, play the game by the rules. You wouldn't dream of doing this to such an opposing lawyer, but suppose it's an opposing lawyer who doesn't play by the rules or may not know what the rules are. Consider an objection. Not on the ground that the question on its face is improper—on its face it is proper because it matches one of those four modes of attack. But on the ground that there's no good faith basis—and I say to you that you have a right to know that good faith basis. The jury doesn't know about it, of course not. That's not admissible in evidence, but I've seen it done, and I've done it myself.

The question is asked—now remember, this magnifies the question because the jury sees all kinds of commotion going on, so that there are some risks as well as advantages. But I would say, "Objection, Your Honor, may I approach the sidebar?" At the sidebar, "Your Honor, I challenge my opponent to state the good faith basis for asking that question. And I ask that we go into the robing room to have him do so." And I would insist that he represent as a member of the bar what his good faith basis is. And I know of a couple of cases where there was no good faith basis, where the lawyer said, "Why did I ask him is he a life member of the Ku Klux Klan? I'm testing credibility." That's usually what they say—"I'm testing credibility." You can't ask that question without a good faith basis. What is your good faith basis? Well, I guess there is none.

Take it one step farther. Consider this possibility—he doesn't have a good faith basis. Go back in front of the jury and, you know what? Put him on the stand as part of your case. Put him on the stand and say, "You remember asking that question?" Everybody's hair stood on end. The jurors began to shake and quake. "Did you have any basis for thinking that my client was a member of the Ku Klux Klan?" "No." "Thank you." End of case.

There is at least one reported appellate decision approving that mode of procedure. It's risky; it's hairy. It probably won't do much for your reputation as a congenial fellow in town. But, you know, sometimes you have to play it that way, so consider it. Enough on this middle group of four.

Now, as to this last one, unfortunately, to talk about it at all adequately takes five minutes and probably five minutes is more than it's worth. You just don't run into it with any kind of frequency and when you do run into it, it's not a hand grenade going off in the jury box. It just doesn't do that much. But it's there, it's available under the Federal Rules of Evidence, it is available at common law.

Let us briefly recapitulate. A witness is called to the stand. He testifies on behalf of your opponent that the traffic light was green. It's your position in the case that the traffic light was red. Let us assume that we are operating in a jurisdiction that permits all nine modes of impeachment. Let us assume that, where necessary, you have a good faith basis for asking the question. And, finally, let us assume that you have made a tactical decision to launch an all-out attack on the credibility of this witness. So the impeachment would go something like this:

"Mr. Witness, do you know the meaning of an oath?"

"No, I do not."

"You say that the traffic light was green."

"Yes."

"But you were in Vietnam that day, weren't you?"

"Well, yes I was, now that you mention it."

"You say that you remember that the traffic light was green?"

"Yes."

"But your brain was surgically removed last year, wasn't it, so that you remember nothing?"

"Oh, now that you remind me, I guess that's right."

"You say the light was green?"

"Yes."

"What does the word green mean?"

"I really don't know."

"Aha! Now, sir, you've been bribed to give your testimony, haven't you?"

"Yes, as a matter of fact, I was."

"And you were convicted last year of perjury in circumstances uncannily similar to these, were you not?"

"Yes, I was."

"And last year you sold heroin to junior high school children, didn't you?"

"Yes."

And now laying the foundation, "Do you remember last week you went to the bar down the street?"

"Yep."

"Talked to the bartender?"

"Yep."

"Conversation turned to this case, didn't it?"

"Yep."

"Didn't you tell the bartender that the light was red?"

"Now that you mention it, I did."

And if that's not enough, we now proceed to the ninth and last mode of impeachment which involves, note, not one more question on cross-examination. Get that. We impeach our witness 1 (W1), but not on cross-examination. Instead, as part of our case, we call another witness—witness 2 (W2), this being W1, the prime witness. Now, let's go back to the common law. The common law said we will allow W2 to take the stand and testify in essence now—never mind technicalities—in essence that W1 is a liar, because we're concerned with credibility. So W2 will testify in essence that W1 is a liar. The technical question is how W2 says that. And there are only three possibilities. First possibility—W2 testifies to specific instances when W1 told a lie. Second possibility—W2 testifies to his own opinion, "In my opinion, W1 is a liar." Third possibility—W2 testifies to gossip in the community as to whether or not W1 is a liar.

Those are logically the only three possibilities, and to the minds of those English judges who for the most part created our law of evidence for us—now we're speaking about the 18th century here—of those three possibilities, only one had real probative force and that one was gossip. And so the common law rule was that W2 could take the stand and testify that the gossip in the community was to the effect that W1 was a liar. Observe, this is not character in a criminal case. This is not a character witness testifying for a defendant. This is an attack upon credibility available as to any kind of witness in any kind of case. Whoever W1 is, whatever he has testified to, you are the opponent, you are discrediting by calling W2, who at common law says the gossip is that W1 is a liar.

Now, gossip is what it is, but our professional cousins in England and our judges and law professors today share a common professional trait. They do not like to speak—indeed, some would say they are incapable of speaking or writing plain English. So they would never say gossip, but rather reputation. Never reputation for being a liar, rather reputation for lack of veracity. So there it is. W2 testifies to W1's reputation for lack of veracity. And it goes approximately this way. It sounds a lot like a character witness in a criminal case, but it's not.

"W2, do you know W1?"

"Maybe yes, maybe no." That doesn't matter.

"But have you ever heard of W1?"

"Yes."

He must have heard of W1. "In what connection?"

"We're members of the same Boy Scout troop. We live in the same town." Whatever it may be.

"Have you heard people talk about W1 over the years? "

"Yes, I have."

"As a result of what you've heard, have you come to be familiar with W1's reputation for lack of veracity?"

"Yes."

"What is that reputation?"

"Lousy."

You may inquire. That's it. And obviously it's awkward, doesn't do much and you run the risk of the jurors saying if this Mickey Mouse is what the guy has to do, he doesn't have much of a case. But there it is. Reputation or lack of veracity.

Now, that's the common law as of 1750. We're now working in 1984, but most of us will be practicing in the 21st century, at least in the early years of it. And it occurred to the draftsmen of the Federal Rules of Evidence that when a witness today says that W1 has a reputation, he really doesn't mean a reputation, because virtually no one today has a reputation for anything, good or bad. Most of you live in a moderately large city, and I used to live in an extremely large city. I'm sure your experience is the same as mine. You don't know the name of your next-door neighbor. You expect your neighbor to know something about you or you to know something about your next-door neighbor? Most of us know nothing about our spouses or the people we lived with. Who knows anything about our children—they're total strangers to us. I put it to you that in the United States of America, in the last 20 years, there is only one man who has the reputation of being a liar. And look what it took to get him that reputation. See?

So when a witness takes the stand today and says, "Oh, W1's reputation is lousy for telling the truth," what he really means is, "In my opinion he's a liar," and he's been coached, prepared to say it in the right way. I think there's a lot to that point. And so the Federal Evidence Rules said, this is still permissible. We continue the common law rules, but we add to it the possibility of the witness saying what he really means. So we will allow W2 to testify to W1's reputation if he wishes, but also to say, "In my opinion, W1 is a liar," because that, after all, is what he really means.

Still, not specific instances, but only W2's opinion or W2's sense of the reputation of W1 for lack of veracity. Right. I remind you that W2 is now a witness like any other. The proponent of W1 may attack W2. "Do you know the meaning of an oath?" And so and on and so on and so on—all nine modes of attack, including calling W3, who testifies that W2's reputation is one of lack of veracity or that W3 has the opinion that W2 is a liar and so on and so on.

Federal Evidence Rule 608(a) gives it to you and we turn now not to accrediting—that will come at the very end—but rather to the second big question to which I promised you at least a kind of tentative first draft of an answer. The first question, remember, is what do I ask about? And I put it to you an hour and a half ago that the law of evidence tells you what to ask about when you are attacking credibility. I shall not again return to it, but there you have my answer to the question "What do you ask about?"

The second question is, "How do I ask it?" And there it's not the law of evidence, but rather the craft of the courtroom, the technique of advocacy as it's beginning to be understood by lawyers and academics who think about this stuff. That supplies the answer. I repeat, for those of you who have that God-given gift, for those of you who are the Darrows and the Sir Edward Carsons of your generation, all of this is meaningless. You will make up your own technique. But if, like me, you need all the help you can get, there is help available. You can conduct a cross-examination to impeach or discredit every single time without humiliating yourself if you will follow this approach. And I guess there are a lot of ways of enunciating it, but let me use this one simply to try to bring it to life.

Imagine that I had up here on the platform with me some intelligent man or woman who is a lay person with respect to the law. Reads the newspapers, goes to the movies, et cetera, but has no technical knowledge of the law. And suppose we were to say to this lay person, "Sir, madam, would you tell these lawyers how you think a lawyer goes about preparing a case and then trying it?" I dare say the layman's response would be something like this: "Well, you study the file, you talk to the witnesses on your side, you learn everything you can about your part of the case and your opponent does the same with respect to his case. And then you go to court and you present your witnesses as effectively as you can and the other side presents their witnesses as effectively as they can. And, of course, you cross-examine the other side's witnesses and they cross-examine your witnesses, trying to show the jury that the other side's witnesses are not worth believing. And then comes the day when both lawyers announce, 'We rest,' and the judge says, 'At 10 o'clock tomorrow morning you sum up to the jury.' And now you go home and you pace the living room. Round and around you go, saying to yourself, 'What can I argue to that jury about the credibility of these witnesses tomorrow morning? What can I argue?' And then you look at your watch and, my God, it's 7 o'clock in the morning, you haven't even gone to bed, but it's time to go back to the courthouse. So you take a shower and you go down to the courthouse and you're still trying to think of what to tell the jury about the credibility of your witnesses and the lack of credibility of the other side's witnesses and finally you've got to stand up and say whatever you thought. So you stand up and you say whatever you can say about the credibility of the witnesses on both sides and the other lawyer does the same thing at his turn. Now the judge charges the jury and the jury goes out to deliberate and the pacing really starts now. Up and down you go, smoking three cigarettes at a time. Up and down, waiting for that verdict. And finally the verdict comes in. You win, you lose. If you won, you run to the bar across the street and have a drink. And if you lost, you have two drinks. And so on to the next case." Hmm? That is what our layman would probably say in response to our question and we know, as professionals in the enterprise, that while it's the layman's conception of how a lawyer should prepare and try a case, it is dead wrong. It is absolutely upside down. And if that's how you're going to prepare and try cases, you really ought to turn in your ticket.

The ideal—and I put it that way because all of us cut corners—nobody can practice perfectly, the pressures are too great. But you strive for the ideal always. The ideal is something like this. Whatever the nature of the case, whatever the circumstances of your practice, you will have some time before the trial starts to prepare—be it an hour, a week, a month, or a year. Whatever the time you have, that case will occupy your consciousness to the exclusion of everything else. You eat it, you sleep it, you breathe it—that's all you think about. Why? There is no enterprise a human being can engage in more complicated than trying a case. I do believe that. There are so many variables at work in that courtroom that there's no equation that will hold them in place. It is impossible to respond extempore in the courtroom and get it right, but it's sometimes possible to respond if you have prepared in advance to respond and then you get it right. So you concentrate with the zeal of a fanatic to the end that you anticipate everything that's going to happen in that courtroom. And, of course, you never succeed perfectly. Things will come as a surprise, but if more than, say, 20 percent of that trial unfolds by way of surprise, you have not prepared properly.

What follows from this? What follows from this is that before the first juror is impaneled, you can sum up. You can deliver your summation into a tape recorder one week before the trial starts. Try a two-month security fraud case. Tape record the summation you actually deliver at the end of the trial and then compare the two. And if they're not within 80 percent of each other, you have not prepared properly.

What follows from that? You know before the first witness is called by the other side what you are going to say to the jury in summation about the credibility of that witness. You know in advance what argument to make to seek to persuade the jury that the other side's witness is not worth believing. And if you're with me to that point, you have my approach to effective, reasonably effective, competent, non-self-humiliating cross-examination. You will cross-examine only to the extent necessary to secure the information that you need to support the argument that you have planned well in advance to make in summation about that other side's witness. And when you have secured the necessary information, what do you do?

Well, you all know what to do, but nobody ever does it. What you do is stop, sit down, no more questions. That four-letter word, S-T-O-P, is the single most important word in a trial lawyer's vocabulary.

When things are going great, what do you do? Stop. When they're not going great, what do you do? Stop. When you haven't the vaguest idea what's happening, what do you do? Stop, stop, stop! I put it to you as baldly as this: No trial lawyer has ever made a mistake by stopping. But almost invariably, when you don't stop, you live to regret it.

Let me talk about a not uncommon application of that simple rule. I guess it's mainly for the benefit of younger lawyers. You have an argument that you've prepared in advance to make in summation about the other side's witness. You need certain information to support that argument. Lo and behold, the direct examination conducted by your opponent brings out the information that you need. Right? Let me hear your cross-examination. That's it, I just heard it. Don't stop—rather never start. Why? You don't need it. Young lawyers especially seem to think that there's a kind of professional obligation to cross-examine every witness called by the other side. No, there's a professional obligation not to screw up the case. That's your professional obligation. And much of the time by cross-examining, that's all you accomplish—you screw up your case.

I mean, if you want to begin to develop some kind of style, though, especially if you're a beginner, don't just say no cross-examination, take advantage of the situation. You're not going to cross-examine, but make some points with it. So stand up and there should come across your face a smile, reflecting what Mark Twain once described in somewhat different circumstances as the calm confidence of a Christian with four aces. "Is there any cross-examination?" "Your Honor, I have no cross-examination." And sit down. And I'm telling you that especially if you're a lawyer under 35, that has enormous impact in the courtroom. In the back of the courtroom the lawyers who come to watch will suddenly say, "Who is that lawyer? A young lawyer with the guts not to cross-examine—what is his name, what is his address?" And, you see, your legend begins to build right there. And, after all, that's one of the things you want to accomplish when you try cases. So don't stop—never start.

Sometimes it's necessary to start. You must elicit the information that's necessary to support the argument that you're going to make.

You've got to cross-examine. Well, how do you do it? We understand what to ask about, reference to the law of evidence. How to ask the questions?

Over the years, I have come up with a set of suggestions, guidelines, if you will, which if made part of your intellectual repertoire and made to become second nature, will guarantee—and I am choosing my word carefully—will guarantee that every cross-examination you conduct is reasonably competent. It will not be a flash of lightning. No, it's not going to be Clarence Darrow. No. But you will never humiliate yourself. You will never throw the case away on cross-examination. So desperate am I that everybody achieve that really minimum level of professional competence that I withdraw here and now my designation of these things as guidelines or suggestions. They are not guidelines or suggestions, they are commandments in the sense that you must follow them. If you do not, if you violate them, you will pay the price. There are 10 of them. But because we've been together all day and start to be friends, I wish to make a confession. There really aren't 10, there are only 6 or 7. But I say some of them in different words to make it add up to 10. Because 10 commandments has a literary ring that I find appealing. Okay? And so, especially towards the end, if I seem to be repeating myself, do not rise in your places and denounce me. I know that I'm repeating myself in order to get it up to 10.

I have struggled to reduce each commandment to the fewest possible words. It's a matter of a half an hour to memorize the 10 commandments, probably less. Probably many of you know them already. I tell you from harsh experience that to know them in the sense of being able to write them down, 1 through 10, is not to have made them part of one's intellectual repertoire. You must school yourself to cross-examine in accordance with these commandments. At the beginning, irresistible temptation is to violate the commandments. You've got to make yourself do it in accordance with these commandments. If you're about to hear them for the first time, I guarantee that the next time you cross-examine a witness, you're not going to do it any better than the last time you did it, but this time as you violate the commandments you will know that you're violating the commandments. You will know which commandment you are violating. You will realize that with some questions you violate all 10 commandments in one question, but you somehow can't help yourself, it comes out that way. But the next time around and the next time around it gets to be a little bit easier. And by the 25th jury trial you don't have to think about it anymore. Well, you've reached that level. One lawyer out of 1,000 able to conduct a cross-examination with any kind of witness in any kind of case without humiliating himself.

In no particular order, just the order in which I have written them down, the first commandment: Be brief. Remember that unless you are Clarence Darrow or unless you are Thomas Murphy cross-examining Carl Binger, cross-examination should be a commando raid. In and out. It's not the invasion of Normandy. And there are a number of reasons why that should be so. Let me take just one of those reasons. The purpose of cross-examination is to persuade the jury that the witness you are cross-examining is not worth believing. You can't always persuade them, but sometimes you can. You can't begin to persuade them unless they remember what you did on cross-examination. They are listening to it; they're not reading it. Every human being has a very limited capacity for absorbing information through the ears. Jurors, like everybody else, are accustomed to absorbing large amounts of information, but through the eyes, by reading or watching television. This is listening. Here in the head, between the ears there's a little cup representing the jurors' capacity to absorb information through the ears. It is a very small cup. It is soon filled, and if you try to add more to that cup once it has been filled, many of you know, it's not that the excess overflows, but somehow the cup tips over, everything runs out, and they remember nothing. And if they remember nothing, you're never going to be able to persuade them.

Applying this commandment, I am accustomed to using the word point to refer to an argument I will make in summation about this witness's credibility. Never try to support more than three points on cross-examination. Two points are better than three and one is best of all because you're guaranteed to have the jurors remember it. So be brief.

Second, acquire the habit—perhaps I should say the art—of asking short questions using plain words. After all, we went to law school and law school, among other things, is three years of intensive practice at distorting the English language. That is why every lawyer who wants to be a trial lawyer, that is to say who wants to try cases to juries of ordinary people, must reacquire the habit of speaking plain English. If you're a corporate lawyer, I suppose you don't ever have to reacquire that habit because you're going to spend all your time drafting corporate trust indentures. Well, shame on you if you question a witness so that it sounds as if you're dictating a corporate trust indenture. I told you that I sat on that metropolitan trial court, presiding essentially over automobile accident cases—hundreds, maybe thousands of them. Not once did I ever hear a lawyer say to a witness, "How did you drive your car?" Not once. It was always, "What did you then do with respect to the operation and control of your motor vehicle?" Hmm? Just like a corporate trust indenture. And the jurors are sitting there saying, "What the hell does a vehicle mean? You know, what is it?" You know, remember, we know now because we're the beneficiaries of all of those years of higher education. The jurors don't know. They spend their time wondering what it means. Perhaps they decide to go on what it sounds like. If you don't know what the word vehicle means, it kind of sounds like the sidecar on a motorcycle. So suddenly the juror is saying, "What motorcycle? There was no motorcycle. Where did the motorcycle come from?" And they're not listening to your cross-examination.

Moreover, to the extent that you talk like a lawyer, you are reminding the jurors that you are a lawyer, and that is the fastest way to lose them. To the extent that you remind the jurors that you're a lawyer, precisely to that extent, they will not trust you. The essence of the art of getting the jury to trust you is to say to them essentially, "I mean, I know I'm a lawyer because my mother made me go to law school. But I really didn't want to be and it's an unhappiness in my life that I am. And don't hold it against me. I've got to earn a living somehow. I'm just a plain fellow like you and I'm not going to fool you and this is what the case is all about." And if you can get that across to the jury, you're going to win. But to the extent that you stand there and say, "I'm a lawyer." Right, we know about lawyers. String them up from the nearest lamppost, get rid of them all. That's the way to make life better. But to the extent that you're saying that to the jury, of course, your case is going down the drain. So short questions, plain words.

Third, never, never, never on cross-examination ask anything but a leading question. A brief and unnecessary review of the law of evidence, which is childishly simple on this point. On direct examination, no leading questions with many exceptions. On cross-examination, the law of evidence says it's a matter of indifference whether you ask leading questions or not, anything you wish. The craft of advocacy tells you that when you cross-examine to discredit a witness, only leading questions. What is a leading question? A question that suggests the desired answer, that puts words in the witness's mouth. Well, that's why you can't ask it on direct examination—you're not supposed to put words in the witness's mouth. But on cross-examination, that's the whole idea. You control that witness. You make that witness say what you want him to say. So that an effectively-conducted cross-examination to discredit the witness is an aria sung by the lawyer, interrupted only by an occasional monosyllable from the witness. Shame on you if you ever let that witness say anything more than yes, yes, yes, yes, yes. That's all, that's all. You testify for him.

"You got up that morning at 9 o'clock, didn't you?"

"Yes."

"By 10 o'clock you were fully clothed?"

"Yes."

"You went down on the street."

"Yes, I did."

"And the first place you went was the supermarket."

"Yes."

"And there you proceeded directly to the fresh fruit counter?"

"Yes, I did."

"And you measured out six ripe oranges and put them into a cellophane bag, didn't you?"

"Yes."

"You then went to stand on the checkout line."

"Yes."

"And as you stood on the checkout line, you looked out the plate glass window at the street, didn't you?"

"Yes."

"And there you saw an octopus coming out of the manhole, didn't you?"

"Yes."

"Thank you," and sit down. You've done it. You have told the story for him, he has merely confirmed its accuracy. That is why when a lawyer on cross-examination says to a witness "Why did you do that?" the judge has cardiac arrest. Right? Why? I mean, that's a leading question? Or, "What did you do next?" Or, "What happened then?" No, no, no! You control the witness on cross.

Some of you may like to go horseback riding. You ever ride a horse up into the mountains? And then you get off and you say, "Hi, horsie, here's the rein. Wait for me." And you walk away, huh? What does the horse do? He takes off for home. Right. You've got to control the horse and if you have to control the horse, let me tell you, you've got to control that human being on the witness stand who has every reason to give it to you. And the way to guard against it is to testify for him by leading questions.

This always comes as a shock to novices, to law students, to people who don't know much about the trial process, but it's perfectly obvious that this must be one of the commandments. Ask only questions to which you already know the answer. Do not ask a question to which you don't know the answer, because if there is any answer in this universe that will harm you, that's the answer you're going to get.

Cross-examination is not a deposition. It is not the occasion for finding out about the case. That occasion was discovery. We're long past that stage. What you're doing now is getting the information you need to support the argument, an argument that you have planned in advance. You know the case. You know some arguments are supportable and some are not. And so it follows, of course, that you know the information that you can elicit, and you ask only those questions to which you are certain to get the answers that you expect.

If you don't know the answer, don't ask it. Two exceptions—one sort of obvious. You may ask a question to which you don't know the answer if you don't care what the answer is. But I repeat myself, I know, but it's that important. Be sure you don't care what any answer might be because if there's some answer that's going to hurt you, that's the answer you're going to hear. Essentially, this is the rhetorical question, you know: "You've been bribed to give your testimony, haven't you?" "Yes." "For $300,000, you agreed to come and tell lies about my client." "Yes." "And everything you've said about my client is a lie." "Yes." "Aren't you ashamed of yourself?" I don't know the answer to that last question, but I really don't care, so I will ask it. And I mean it just that way. You've got to know what the answer is or else don't ask it.

Next, it's a little hard to get across, so I'm going to give you a suggestion for further reading that you might enjoy at your leisure to illustrate this phenomenon. The older hands, the battle-scarred veterans in the room, and there are some of you, have long since observed this and learned how to do it for yourself. Anybody can learn it, but it takes a certain amount of practice. It is what in my neck of the woods is called escalating. It is sometimes also called closing doors. You close doors to possible answers and then the door that you leave open is the one answer that you're going to get. Escalating means at the bottom of the escalator, you don't know what the answer is that you're going to get to the question you put at the top of the escalator, but you somehow rise up on the escalator and by the time you get there, you know what the answer is going to be. There is a question that you'd love to ask. It's important. It's more than important. It's at the heart of the case. One possible answer helps you; another possible answer devastates you. But you don't know which answer you're going to get. There is a way of asking questions seemingly inconsequential. The spectators, the other lawyer, the judge, the jury will, at worst, think that you're wasting time, but you're not wasting time. What you are doing is finding out what the answer to the payoff question will be. And if you sense that the answer will not be favorable, you drop it, go to something else in a clatter of dust, and nobody is the wiser. And you certainly haven't hurt yourself. But if you begin to get the sense that the answer to the payoff question will help, you pursue it and, you know, a certain amount of gamble and luck, of course, but by and large it'll work out all right.

The best example I know of that kind of escalating cross-examination occurred in a famous trial and, because it is much written upon, all it takes is a trip to the public library. Not even the law library, the public library, and you'll be able to read it for yourself. It is a cross-examination that occurred in the trial of Lizzie Borden. You know, the New England woman who took an ax and gave her mother 40 whacks and when she saw what she had done, she gave her father 41. Lizzie was indicted for the really hideous ax murder of her stepmother and father. Unless you're an aficionado of the case, you wouldn't know that Lizzie was very wealthy. She was a millionairess and could afford the best counsel of the time. Her lawyer was a man named Robinson who had been governor of Massachusetts. He was called Gov. Robinson and was probably the leading trial lawyer in New England. Now, I personally have absolutely no doubt that Lizzie was guilty, but she was acquitted and she was acquitted in major part because Robinson conducted a brilliant, brilliant defense.

One of the things that he was working on was this. Lizzie was tried in Fall River. She was in her early 30s. She had lived all of her life in Fall River. She was an extremely prim and proper American Victorian heiress. Indeed, I think what underlies the case, what explains it is an explosion of sexuality of a kind that was inconceivable to Victorians. What was inconceivable to those jurors was that this little girl, whom they had seen grow from her birthday until today, 33, 34 years old, could not have carried out these hideous murders. These people were hacked to pieces. The physicians who arrived to look at the bodies threw up. That's how bad it was. They'd never seen anything like it.

Well, Robinson was gambling on that—that sort of sense of psychological impossibility for Lizzie to have done it—helping him with the jury.

In order to support that, he wanted to establish that there had been no quarrel in the home that morning. The homicides took place at about 10 o'clock. Breakfast had been served at 8 o'clock and the person who served breakfast was Bridget, an 18-year-old Irish immigrant girl, actually illiterate. She couldn't read or write, but she was quite intelligent and spoke well and so forth. And she was called by the prosecution to testify to something about the doors having been locked, so no intruder could have gotten in. So who could it have been but Lizzie?

Cross-examination of Bridget. Robinson wanted to ask the following payoff question and it was almost in these words. "When you served breakfast that morning, Bridget, was everything calm and peaceful and happy?" And do you see the importance of it? The answer had to be yes. If the answer was no, there went this subtle defense of sort of psychological impossibility. He didn't know what answer he would get. He asked about 15 questions, each one of them seemingly inconsequential, and he uncannily found out through those 15 questions what the answer to the payoff question would be.

There was an English lawyer who left the practice to make a career of writing about true crimes and real criminal trials, named Edgar Lustgarten. Lustgarten wrote a book about the Lizzie Borden case. He was, himself, a lawyer, remember. As an appendix to Lustgarten's book about the Lizzie Borden case, he prints Robinson's cross-examination of Bridget, the maid, and annotates each question, giving you his, Lustgarten's, idea of what Robinson was up to, what door he was closing, how he was gradually finding out what the answer to the payoff question would be. And it's a marvelous thing to read and, as I say, the best example I know of this kind of escalating cross-examination, so I commend it to you.

Fifth commandment. Whatever you do on cross-examination, for heaven's sake, do not let it be simply the occasion for the witness repeating his direct testimony. Now, I have no quarrel with you if you set up the target on cross. For example, you've got a prior inconsistent statement. He told the bartender last week that the light was red. He's just testified on direct examination that it was green. So you might set that up—this is what I mean by setting up the target—with, "Now, are you certain the light was green?" "Yes." "Okay. But now didn't you go to the bar last week? Didn't you talk to the bartender? Didn't the conversation turn to this accident and didn't you tell the bartender that the light was red?" making it quite clear to the jury what it is you're hitting at. That's not what I'm talking about.

I'm talking about the kind of just dunderheaded cross-examination that I heard over and over virtually every single day sitting on that bench in New York City, that would go something like this. The witness on direct examination said the light was green. The cross-examining lawyer's job is to show the jury that he's not worth believing. It is his position in the case that the light was red. The cross-examination always begins this way. "Mr. Witness, there are a couple of things about your testimony that are unclear. Let's clear them up." No, no. If there is anything unclear, it's not the cross-examiner's job to clear it up. Leave it unclear, you idiot. And, in any event, there's probably nothing unclear, it's just a way of covering his nervousness. He doesn't know what to say, so he's babbling. That's what it is.

"A couple of things about your testimony that are unclear. Let's clear them up. What color was the light?"

"Green."

"Are you sure?"

"Yes, I'm sure."

"Then tell us again, what color was the light?"

"It was green, you imbecile."

"I observe that you're wearing your glasses."

"Yes."

"Were you wearing your glasses that time?"

"Yes, I was."

"And what did you see as you looked through your glasses?"

"I saw the green light."

"I remind you that you're under oath. Now tell us what color the light was."

"It was green!"

And the fellow sits down. That's the end of the cross-examination. Okay? You ever heard of that kind of cross? I'm sure you have. On direct examination he said that the light was green once. The cross-examination brings it about that the jury hears it 10 more times. All right. And you know the rule of thumb, if the jury hears it once they may or may not believe it. If they hear it twice, they will probably believe it. If they hear it three times, they will certainly believe it. And if it's in writing, nothing on this earth will persuade them that it's untrue. So the lawyer has not just damaged his case, he's really lost his case by conducting that kind of clumsy cross-examination.

Six, it's implicit in what we've already said; it's one of the repetitive commandments. Don't let the witness explain. It's implicit because, of course, if you ask leading questions only and only questions to which you know the answer, there will never be an occasion to explain. But if a witness for some reason tries to get away from your control and says, "I want to explain that," don't you allow it. Now, I'll grant you there are judges, a lot of them, who don't like a lawyer who tries to control the witness on cross-examination. There are judges who will say, "No, if the witness wants to explain, let him explain." That's a can't help. There's nothing to do about that. But don't you yield the point. You insist upon yes or no answers to your leading questions and you all know how to do it. You say, "No, I didn't ask you for an explanation." Or, "Your lawyer will ask you questions in a little while, that's the time to explain." Or, "Just answer my question yes or no or I can't answer it yes or no, we don't need anything else." The various ways you bully a witness to keep him under control. But if a judge intrudes and says, "Oh, no, no, no, let him explain," well, that's the way it's going to be.

Why insist that the witness refrain from explanations and just respond to your questions? Well, a couple of reasons, one of which is why you play tennis with the net up. The game is more elegant that way and I don't want to be charged with undue cynicism, but one of the reasons you engage in this really life-wearing kind of work is that it is a game and it can be enjoyable and you want to play it for all it's worth. But turning to a reason that's perhaps a little bit more substantive, if the explanation comes out later on redirect examination, it's the same explanation you would have given now, but if it comes out then, it smacks of the afterthought. It has less persuasiveness with the jury than it would have if it comes out now. And then, finally, you play for the house odds, right? Sure, on redirect examination the explanation may come out and 19 times out of 20 it will come out, but the one time out of 20 the opposing lawyer is asleep at the switch, he's afraid to bring it out, he doesn't know what's going to happen, maybe a bad situation will become worse. You play for that 5 percent, right? The one time out of 20 when it doesn't come out. And I repeat, even when it does come out, it lacks a certain something when it comes out on redirect.

Seventh commandment. This one came to me a little bit later than the others and it came to me as a result of pondering the question of why did a certain phenomenon take place over and over again. I'm sitting there as the judge, so I don't have to worry about, you know, playing the game. I'm just the umpire. I'm relaxed and I'm in a position to observe and ask myself questions and try to analyze the proceeding that is unfolding before me. Here's a lawyer. He's not very good, but even a not-very-good lawyer doesn't strike out all the time, right? So he's cross-examining a witness and he asks exactly the right question and he gets exactly the right answer from his point of view. It devastates the other side's case. It makes the cross-examiner's case and time after time after time the lawyer did nothing with it. He did not pursue it on cross-examination and, more tellingly, did not talk about it on summation. And I kept saying to myself, why doesn't the lawyer do something with this wonderfully helpful piece of evidence that he elicited on cross-examination? It's as if he never heard it. And then it came to me. The reason the lawyer doesn't do anything with that piece of helpful testimony elicited on cross-examination is that, in fact, he didn't hear it. He didn't hear it because he was heedless of the seventh commandment, which is: listen to the witness's answers. Seems self-evident, but, you know, you've got to make yourself do it. I speak on behalf of everyone in the room who's ever cross-examined a witness, to those of you who have yet to do it for the first time, you can't believe how frightened you are—the lawyer. And to give a voice to what is happening internally, it goes something like this: "Mr. Younger, you may now cross-examine." "Oh my God, what am I gonna do? What am I gonna do? Why did I ever get into this kind of work? I should have gone to medical school the way my mother . . . why am I here? I don't want to be doing this. 'What is your name?' Oh, I got it out, I got it out. All right. I'm still going strong. What should the next one be? 'Where do you live?'" All right. And, you see, you're so wrapped up in your own psychic turmoil that there is no energy left over to listen to the answers.

Now, I tell you that you will never get over that turmoil. Indeed, one of the benefits of experience is that you learn to turn it to advantage. Do not believe for one minute that you are ever cured of it. The thousandth time you try a case, you will be as terrified as you were the first time you tried a case, but you turn it to advantage through a physiological process, which I cannot explain, but which every trial lawyer experiences and, after a while, comes to master. That terror produces a flow of adrenaline that is beyond belief. I am positive when I try a case that if a madman came running up with a .38 revolver and from six inches away pulled the trigger twice, the bullets would bounce off. If a locomotive came through the back wall of the courtroom, with one hand I could stop it.

That is why every trial lawyer does things in the courtroom, on his feet when on trial that he's not smart enough to do in the office. You hear yourself saying things and, my God, that's clever. Am I really saying that? It's as if somebody else has taken over. And it is somebody else—it's you with adrenaline running through your bloodstream. Now, you pay a price for it, of course, because adrenaline is essentially Drano and there it is, going through your veins and your arteries, working away from inside. And that is why when doctors get together, they talk about the litigators' cardiac syndrome and when psychiatrists get together they talk about the trial lawyers' anxiety syndrome. That stuff is working from within, sapping away and you pay a price, of course. But what you're paying a price for is this superhuman quality that we have in the courtroom. And what you are able to do after a while is put a cap on it. You make the adrenaline work for you. You still feel it in the pit of your stomach. It still takes you hours to come back to the ground.

I don't want to be personal, but when I try a case, my wife is a lawyer, so she's kind of sympathetic and she knows. You know, you come home at the end of a day in court and the aftermath in the office and you ring the doorbell and she opens it. She's got the pitcher of martinis and she pours it over my head because there's no time to get it down. And it's only after the pitcher of martinis has been absorbed that I'm civil enough, you know, not to bark to the kid, kick the dog and, you know . . . there's that much going on inside you. So you want to put a cap on it so that the adrenaline is there working for you, but at the same time there's a little bit left over for listening to the witness so that you can respond if you get that occasional extraordinary answer.

I have an anecdote that I like to tell to illustrate this, but I don't want to be misunderstood. This is not literally true. You all remember it's an increasingly long time ago, like 10, 11, 12 years ago, the Ervin Committee was conducting the Watergate impeachment inquiry. And remember it was on television every day and the entire nation was watching television. The more you think about it as the years go by, the more amazing those years become. It was as close as any of us will ever get to having been a citizen of fifth century Athens. Through the miracle of the technology, we were sitting not in a stadium watching a Greek tragedy unfold, but watching a kind of political tragedy unfold and there was pity and there was terror and all 250 million of us were an audience of one.

Well, do you remember the senators sat in a semi-circle and the ground rule was, I think, that each senator had two minutes or so to ask questions. And then it went to the next senator and then to the next. Now, I don't want to get into political quarrels with any of you, so I just tell you where I stand. I think that those senators deserve the thanks of the Republic because I think that they probably saved the Republic. But, having said that, I would be the first to admit that none of those senators was an intellectual giant. All right? And of all of those senators, there was one that instantly became and has since remained my favorite, but I think out of tact I will not name him. But in case you have a vivid picture of those senators, he was the one who was Central Casting's idea of a United States senator. He had gray hair, every thread of it in place. Sharply chiseled features, the perfect tanned complexion. And once you caught on you realized that what you had to do was watch that senator at all times because when he wasn't asking questions, he was giving himself facials, making sure that every muscle was just right, combing his hair. Now the senator in front of him was asking questions and now, bang, the red light went on the camera and Senator Blank was before the nation. Now, he had the questions written out on a card in front of him. And I'm not quarreling with the questions—the staff wrote those questions. But this is the way Senator Blank would interrogate the witness.

"Now, sir, did you enter the Oval Office?"

"I did."

"And when you entered the Oval Office, what did you see?"

"Well, Senator, I walked into the Oval Office and there was President Nixon, naked as a baboon, prancing around on all fours with the Gemstone file in his mouth."

"Ah," says the senator. "And when did you next see the President?" That's not listening to the answer, and every once in a while you get an answer as extraordinary as that. For God's sakes, hear it so that you can do something with it and you will hear it if you remember that commandment. Listen to the answer.

Eighth commandment. Many lawyers think that this is a rule of the law of evidence, that you must not ask argumentative or quarrelsome questions. I'm not so sure that it's a rule of the law of evidence, but I am sure that it's a rule of the craft of the courtroom. Never argue with the witness. Now, it's hard to resist, because if you are a trial lawyer, you have a belligerent personality. That's the kind of person who becomes a trial lawyer. You enjoy combat.

Now, that's not a joke. It doesn't mean we're alley fighters. We don't get out there with knives and stab people in the back. It's the combat of the chess board. It's highly regulated with a lot of rules, but that's the kind of combat we like. That's why we do it. But deep down there is that belligerence that has a tendency to come out when we are cross-examining an opposing witness, especially one who we feel is lying, not just making a mistake or something of that kind, but lying. And you want to start slapping him around. Don't do it for a number of reasons. First, it looks terrible and it detracts from the artistry of your presentation, the elegance of the way you try the case. Second, if you ask a question and you get an answer that is inconsistent with all the other evidence of the case, it is contrary to the laws of the universe. It can't be so. Go to something else. Or better, stop right there. But if you start quarreling with the witness—"How dare you say that, sir? Don't you realize, blah, blah, blah, blah," you have signaled to the witness that he has given you an answer harmful to him and helpful to you and he will immediately wiggle off the hook by saying, "Oh, I didn't mean to say that," or "You misunderstand me," or "I misunderstood the question," or whatever it may be. Don't signal anything. Go to your next point or sit down and argue it in summation.

To illustrate this, I have a favorite anecdote and this one, to balance the one I just told you, is true. Most of us have at least some kind of memory of World War II, and I am a particular sort of buff of World War II. Hence, it's with a special enthusiasm that I tell you about this. As a history buff and a World War II buff, and then a lawyer as well, it will be understandable to you that I have had a fascination for many years with the Nuremberg trials, especially the first one, where the leading German leaders were put on trial. All of us have seen pictures of it. Remember, they used the meeting room in the old Nuremberg City Hall, and they built a huge defendant's box and there was Hermann Goering, the highest-ranking survivor in seat number one and all of the others were sitting there. And, remember, you had the four Marine sergeants in the four corners and the judges, one from each of the major powers, and it really was an extraordinary thing. One can argue its wisdom, but it was something really unheard of in the world's history.

I had read a lot about it and even had access from time to time to the transcripts. I haven't read them all, they're much too long. But along the way I came across a wonderful fact not widely known. The

British government was aware that posterity would want to know what it was really like. Not what does the transcript show, but what was the feel of the courtroom? What were people doing when something was going on on the record? What was the expression on Goering's face? What happened when the verdict was announced? Things of that kind. The British are very sort of sensitive to these considerations.

The British government—Clement Attlee was the Prime Minister—sent to Nuremberg as a regular member of the prosecuting team a professional historian named John Wheeler Bennett. He was not a lawyer, but he was a specialist in the history of Europe in the 20th century. He knew the major languages, and his job was to sit there and observe and take notes and leave the notes in the file for posterity to read and use, by way of reconstructing the actual atmosphere of the courtroom.

Well, that was very interesting, and then imagine my glee when some years later—I was then teaching at a university somewhere else—there came across my desk an announcement from the History Department that Sir John Wheeler Bennett, as he then was, was going to be in residence at the university for a semester teaching courses in European history. So I cashed in some social IOUs and got myself invited to dinner with John Wheeler Bennett. And with the finesse and the aplomb that I know that by now you associate with me, I walked in and said, "Sir John, tell me about Nuremberg." And he said, "Yeah, sit down, I'll tell you about Nuremberg." And the things he told me. . . .

I know some of you know, but I wonder whether everybody knows that three of the defendants were acquitted. They were acquitted. And because the judges had something of a sense of humor, when they came in on the day the verdicts were to be announced, they did not read the verdicts in the order of the defendants or in alphabetical order, they purposely took the three acquittals and read them first so that the prosecutors sat there saying to themselves, "We blew it." Can you imagine? "We blew it, we have lost the Nuremberg case." No, it was the first three. And Sir John told me what happened when the first acquittal was announced. Terrific story, but it's not to the point here, so I'm not going to tell it. And so on and so on.

What I will tell, however, is Sir John's description of what he, as a non-lawyer, said he recognized as probably the dramatic highlight of the trial. And I'm going to give it to you exactly as Sir John gave it to me. He said:

"Hermann Goering took the witness stand. Hermann Goering had been head of the Luftwaffe, number three in the German command, a very smart and well-educated man who, towards the end of the war, gave way to narcotics and sexual perversion, etc. But he pulled himself together for the trial and he was at his best, fighting not for his life—of course not. He knew he was going to be convicted, sentenced to hang, and do you remember what they found when they came to get him that morning to hang him? He was dead in his cell, having taken a cyanide pill and, to this day, no one knows how he got the cyanide pill. That's what was ahead of him. He was on the stand fighting for his place in history, a much more important matter to a man like Hermann Goering. And because it was Hermann Goering, the head of each of the four allied prosecuting teams personally cross-examined. I'm not in a position to assess the professional competence of the cross-examination. I am not a lawyer. But I am in a position to tell you that, uncannily, each prosecutor perfectly reflected the national stereotype."

"First, Robert Jackson, associate justice of the United States Supreme Court. Went to Nuremberg to prosecute."

Can you imagine an American Supreme Court Justice cross-examining Hermann Goering within six months of the end of the greatest war in the history of the world?

And Sir John said:

"Jackson was frequently brilliant, but sometimes Goering got the better of him and that was when Jackson was not prepared. And he was not well prepared on a number of occasions in that cross-examination. The Englishman did very little. What he did, he did to perfection and all he did was to bail Jackson out of his difficulties. The Frenchman was wholly charming and wholly ineffectual. It was just a laugh from beginning to end.

"But best of all was the Russian. The Russian prosecutor was the highest-ranking officer in the Russian Army's version of the Judge Advocate General Corps. So he was a lawyer, but a two-star Russian general. And he was stamped out of the mold that they used to create all Russian generals. He was five feet tall and five feet wide. And throughout the trial he wore his overcoat with those huge epaulets coming out with the two red stars on them. And he had an enormously loud, gruff voice and, of course, it was in Russian."

(John knows Russian and Goering used the little ear thing to have it translated into German.) And Sir John said:

"This is how the Russian cross-examined Hermann Goering. He took his position sideways to the witness stand so that Goering was sitting over there, looking over here. The Russian is this way, looking this way. And in front of him he had a table. And on the table a modest pile of documents. And he began as follows. He picked up the first document and he said, 'Hermann Goering, I hand you a document. Read it. Have you read it? Does it bear your signature? Do you now confess yourself to be a fascist beast?' 'No.' And he picked up the next document and did it again. And again and again."

Now, that question, "Do you now confess yourself to be a fascist beast?" is quarreling with the witness. And I give it to you as a kind of tuning fork. You carry it in the back of your mind here and whenever you are tempted to ask a question that makes the tuning fork vibrate, that has the air of, "Do you now confess yourself to be a fascist beast?" don't ask it for all of the reasons that we've touched upon, summarized as it will violate the eighth commandment.

Ninth commandment. I include this essentially out of a perhaps misplaced sense of obligation to the next generation. This is not really a commandment of cross-examination, it's part of the lore of trial work. But each generation must pass it on to the next ninth commandment: don't ask one question too many. And you will always recognize the one question too many immediately after you ask it. All right? If you apply all of the other commandments, you will never ask the one question too many. But if you ignore them, you'll invariably ask it. My illustration is a true story, and it involves my law partner until January 1 of this year, Edward Bennett Williams, who is, for my money, the best trial lawyer of his generation. He is amazing. He has confirmed to me the truth of the story and authorized me to tell it in public.

Williams got out of law school. All he wanted to be was a trial lawyer. In due course, he got a job that would permit him to try cases every day. That's what he wanted and that's how he learned the business. He was trying cases for the old District of Columbia Street Railway Company, the trolley car, and he began as you begin, trying soft tissue cases. And from soft tissue cases he went to suture and broken bones cases. And then he was pretty good so he went to leg off and arm off cases. And after leg off and arm off cases he was trying—this is the height of it, of course, the pinnacle—death cases, cases in which the trolley car had killed someone. This was a death case. The victim was a notorious old drunken bum, who used to live on the street in Washington where the drunkards and the winos hung out.

Now, this guy was an old man. He hadn't been sober for 40 years, and he was hit by the trolley car and killed. The defense was that he was drunk, he staggered in front of the trolley car. The difficulty for Williams was that, for some reason, there had been no autopsy, so he had no scientific evidence as to alcohol in the bloodstream and, incredibly, when the cops picked up the body, there was no whiskey bottle in his pocket or in his hand. For the first time in 30 years he didn't have a whiskey bottle on his person. How do you explain it?

The investigator finds a bystander, perfectly solid citizen, whose testimony is as follows. "I was at the other end of the block, so I saw generally what happened, but I can't tell you in detail. I saw the trolley car hit the old man. The old man dropped to the floor, the trolley car stopped. Sitting on the curb, 10 feet from where the old man was lying was another drunken bum. Believe it or not, the old man's son. The son got up and ran to his father's body, bent down and did something, then stood up and went away."

"Aha," said Williams, "that's it." What the son did was take the whiskey bottle out of his father's hand and somehow lose it so that the claim would be that his father wasn't drunk, et cetera, et cetera. Sure enough, the plaintiff proving damages, et cetera, puts on the victim's survivor, the middle-aged drunken bum who was the son of the decedent. And now Williams stands up to cross-examine him and, as he tells it, he did it as follows.

"Now, mister, you were sitting on the curb when the trolley car hit your father, weren't you?"

"Yes, sir."

"And you saw the trolley car hit your father."

"Yes, sir."

"And the first thing you did when you saw the trolley car hit your father was get up and go over to where your father was lying. Isn't that right? "

"That's right."

"Now, you just listen to me, mister, and answer my questions yes or no. When you got to where your father was lying, you bent down, didn't you?"

"Yes. "

"And you did something, didn't you?"

"Yes."

"And then you stood up."

"Yes."

"And you walked away."

"Yes."

What should you do now? What should you do now? Stop. You have everything you need to make the argument to the jury about what happened. As Williams tells it, "Irving, I did not have enough sense to stop. Right? I asked the next question." Observe that the next question is a leading question, but it's probably arguing with the witness and, more to the point, Williams does not know the answer. What he said was, "Now, listen, mister, when you bent over your father's body, what you did was take the whiskey bottle out of his hand, isn't that right?"

And the guy said, "No, Mr. Williams, that's not what I did at all."

And Williams says to me, "Irving, even then I didn't have enough sense to stop," because now he asks plainly the one question too many. Observe that it's not leading, he doesn't know the answer, et cetera, et cetera, et cetera. It's also giving the witness a chance to explain. Williams is a great big man. He stands up to his full height and he says, "All right, mister, you tell these ladies and gentlemen of the jury what you did when you leaned over your father's body."

And the answer came. "Well, Mr. Williams, he may have been a drunken bum, but he was my father and what I did when I leaned over his body was kiss him goodbye." Well, huh? That's the kind of answer you will get even from a drunken bum when you ask that one question too many.

Well, and now the tenth and last commandment, which in a way is my favorite. It's my favorite, I suppose, because you don't need it every time out. For many people, you don't need it in the course of a career. But for those however many of you who will have the occasion to make use of this commandment, it may be the most vital of all. And let me just back up a little bit and kind of re-gather your attention to this. I know some of you slightly; I know most of you not at all. However, we're all human beings and, in that sense, we all know something about each other. Though I know nothing particular about any of you, I have to assume because you are all human beings that each one of you has an object of heart's desire. I don't know what it is, but I know that you have it—some one primary goal in life. And whatever that goal may be, if you're ever going to get it, it's through being a lawyer. You see, we all are what we're going to be when we grow up. It's too late to become a basketball player, a movie star or anything else that may appeal to you. This is it, fellows and ladies, this is what we are. So whatever it is you want—you want to be famous, you want to have a lot of money, you want to have a lot of power? Whatever it is, you're going to get it, if at all, only through being a lawyer.

Now, imagine that it's next week, you're in the office waiting for the next client to come along when the next client does come along and it's a client with a lawsuit to try. And you don't have to have been around for very long to recognize that this lawsuit, if won by you, is going to bring you the object of your heart's desire, whatever it may be. Right? All you have to do is try it and win it. So for six months you concentrate with the zeal of a fanatic upon this case. You eat it. You sleep it. You breathe it. You do nothing but let this case occupy your mind. You realize, finally, that the case will turn upon the jury's assessment of one witness. You try to come up with the argument in advance to be made in summation about the credibility of that witness and, sure enough, you come up with that argument.

Now you need the cross-examination that will elicit the information to support that argument that you've planned in advance to make about the credibility of the witness and, by God, you have it. And it's a cross-examination that can be conducted in absolute compliance with the nine commandments we've already discussed. And that's when you need the tenth commandment. That cross-examination, precisely because it will comply with the nine commandments already discussed, will not be fully understood by the jury. And the temptation that you, the cross-examiner, must resist is the temptation to spin out the cross-examination to the end that the jury understands then and there how clever you have been. The jury does not have to understand it then and there, they have to understand it when? In summation, that's when. Let me give you an example. I've already told you what I think about Watergate.

If there was one case that I suppose for personal reasons I would loved to have tried, it would have been the prosecution in Washington, D.C., of the Watergate defendants. You know, John Mitchell, Erlichman, Haldeman, and those other guys. And, obviously, I would have wanted to be the prosecutor, putting those guys away. And I must tell you that as to Haldeman and Erlichman—ah, you know, they're sons of bitches, they frankly concede that they're sons of bitches, there's not much to say. But I am willing to tell you in public and on video that the defendant I really would have wanted was John Mitchell. Yeah, you remember him? Attorney General of the United States with the wattle swinging back and forth.

And, remember, he took the witness stand on direct examination and he testified for several hours that he did nothing wrong, that he knew nothing wrong, that if he had known about it, he would have stopped, that he was as innocent as a newborn babe. And, oh, I want that guy. And if I had been the prosecutor, I would have stood up and my cross-examination would have been one question. "John Mitchell, you were born on March 10, 1912, weren't you?" "Yes, sir." And I'd sit down. Do you feel it? Do you feel it? Those jurors are saying to themselves, "What the fuck is that all about?" That's what you want them to be saying. The trial can continue for another six months and that's all they're saying to themselves, "What was that all about?" You see, unsatisfied curiosity is a wonderful way to hold people's attention and that's the beginning of persuasion.

And now it's six, seven months later, it's a year later and look what you can do in summation. "Now, ladies and gentlemen, I know that it was a long time ago, but do you remember my cross-examination of John Mitchell?" "Mmm hmm. Mmm hmm." "Did you understand what I was getting at?" "Mmm mmm." "Well, let me tell you what I was getting at." You tell them. They're six inches off the chair. They don't even want to retire into the jury room. They've got their verdict already.

And what is it you want, huh? Money? Well, beyond the dreams of avarice. Fame? There's *People* magazine, you're on the cover already. Power? You know what they play when you walk down the front steps of the courthouse? "Hail to the Chief." All because you remembered the 10 commandments.

Ha, but we're not finished. I promised you that before we're done we'd talk a little bit about accrediting. Remember, accrediting comes almost always as a redirect examination, which follows cross-examination. We've talked about cross-examination, so let's talk about accrediting.

Under the Federal Rules or at common law, there really are no great differences here. There are three ways to accredit. First way, you can say it in a single word: explain. Have the witness explain. Now, you better know what the explanation is and that means very careful preparatory work. I cross-reference to the redirect examination of your expert who has been impeached out of a treatise. Remember? Do you want to take back your direct testimony? No. Do you quarrel with what's in the treatise? No. Do you stand on both? Yes. Well, you'd better explain that to the jury, just that way. Explain it to the jury, but be certain that the witness has an explanation that may move the jurors.

The *Johnson* case[5] is an interesting illustration of a phenomenon every experienced lawyer is aware of. Perhaps I should better say beware of. If the cross-examination brings up A and a full explanation of A requires otherwise inadmissible material to come out, it comes out. The cross-examiner is said to have opened the door to the receipt of that otherwise inadmissible material. I have known instances in which a lawyer sets up his opponent. You call a witness, praying that the witness is impeached in a certain way so that on redirect examination the door is open to putting something into evidence. And if that's a little bit too clever, shame on the cross-examiner who barges in so clumsily as to make it possible for the opponent to explain in a way more helpful than the damage done on cross-examination.

Example. And this is essentially *Johnson v. Minihan*. Witness on direct examination says the light was green, red, whatever—says green. Cross-examination. "I hand you a piece of paper. Does it bear your signature?" "Yes." We're laying the foundation for impeachment of the prior inconsistent witness statement. Okay? "Look it over. Have you looked it over?" "Yes." "Did you sign that?" "Yes." I offer it in evidence and it's a statement that says the light was red. Inconsistent statement. Redirect examination. "Mr. Witness, how did you come to sign that statement?" And the answer is, "An insurance adjuster representing the defendant came around and said, 'We will settle your claim as the passenger if you will sign a statement as follows.'" So you've

5. *Johnson v. Minihan*, 200 S.W.2d 334 (Mo. 1947).

brought out the fact of insurance, settling with the passenger, et cetera, in order to put the prior statement in context. All of that context information is inadmissible standing alone, but it is admissible by way of accrediting the witness under the rubric of explaining. It opens the door to what otherwise would be excluded.

Second, the prior consistent statement rule is not very hard, although it is widely misunderstood. Many judges, let alone lawyers, think that the rule is, or that there is a rule to this effect: One may accredit a witness by showing that on some occasion in the past he made a statement consistent with, the same as, what he has said in court. There is no such rule. Other judges and lawyers think that the rule is you may never accredit a witness by showing that he has said the same thing in the past. There is no such rule.

The actual rule under the Federal Rules and common law both, no difference, is in the middle. A witness may be accredited with a prior consistent statement when his testimony in court has been attacked in such a manner as to suggest that he is lying and he made the prior consistent statement at a time before there was a motive to fabricate. That's why it's sometimes called the recent fabrication rule. The claim is that his testimony is a recent fabrication. Here's a prior statement consistent with his testimony made before there was a motive to fabricate.

The New York case *People v. Singer*[6] is a textbook illustration of that rule at work. Remember, though, that it's a rule not peculiar to New York. All jurisdictions follow it; Federal Rules the same.

And you never run into it, but the third way, just so that it's complete, is reputation for veracity. Not lack *of* veracity, but veracity. You accredit W1 by calling W2 to testify under the Federal Rules that W1's reputation is that of a truth teller or, that in W2's opinion, W1 is a truth teller. The Federal Rule sets it forth and so let's leave it at that.

If I may impose upon your good nature for just at most five minutes more I will have done everything I wanted to do and we will then quit.

---

6. *People v. Singer,* 300 N.Y. 120 (1949).

I promise to end with some speculation akin to the speculation with which we ended the segment on expert witnesses. Some thoughts, useful I hope—if not useful, feel free to reject them—on the kinds of arguments you want to make to a jury. Earlier we talked about the kinds of arguments you make about expert witness credibility. Now I want to talk about the kind of argument you make about ordinary witness credibility.

It strikes me that the effective jury argument on witness credibility will always satisfy three requirements. Saying it a little bit differently, there are three touchstones that the effective jury argument on witness credibility will reflect. First, the effective jury argument on witness credibility must always be tactful. Here is why I think that is so. In my experience, jurors invariably want to do the decent thing. They take their work as jurors with the utmost seriousness. They may not like it. They don't want to be here, they want to be somewhere else, but when they get right down to it, they want to come out in the way that wisdom and decency and justice require them to come out.

There's a special something that takes over when people are sitting there in the jury box and when they retire to the jury room to deliberate. I am in the habit of reading whatever is published by jurors about their deliberations, so there's a fairly large shelf of stuff to read and the place to begin, if you are interested, is an essay by a well-known English writer of the late 19th and early 20th century—some of you may know of him—called G.K. Chesterton. Chesterton once was summoned to serve on a jury in the Old Bailey. It was a jury of 12 men and they passed on a burglary case. Chesterton, as you know, is a devout Roman Catholic and so he has a certain way of looking at the world and a certain set of images. Chesterton writes a wonderful essay called "The Twelve Men" about his experiences on that jury. And he said that when the bailiff closed the door to the jury room after the judge had charged the jury and turned the key, locking them in, and they became aware that those 12 had to pass upon the liberty, the fate of their fellow citizens sitting out there, said Chesterton, "The Holy Ghost actually descended and was physically present in the room."

Now, that may not be your bag, I'll grant you, but it gets the idea across. And something like that happens when jurors retire to deliberate and that is why you must handle arguments on credibility with great tact. You are not discussing an abstraction, you are talking about a human being who took the witness stand in their presence yesterday or the day before and swore to them that he was going to tell the truth and now you want to argue that he wasn't telling the truth or at best is not worth believing. That's difficult to get down with the bark on. So you've got to take the bark off. You've got to make it as smooth as you possibly can.

Let me wind it up with just a brief illustration. There is a case that's well known to teachers of the law of evidence. It's name doesn't matter. And what it adds up to is this—that a lay witness may testify to an opinion on somebody's sanity or insanity. And the case is as follows. The defendant was a young man charged with murder and the prosecution had five eyewitnesses, three admissible confessions, 12 valid wire taps and a videotape of the murder being committed, so it was awfully hard to come up with a defense on the merits. But there always is a defense—insanity. That was the defense. Did they have a psychiatrist? No. A psychologist? No. A doctor? No. Who is always available when you really have trouble? The answer is your mother. And so the sole witness called by the defense in support of that insanity claim was the mother, and she testified that the boy lived with her at the time and that he was out of his mind, et cetera.

When I was a kid just learning how to try cases, not knowing enough to be tactful, I suppose that I would have argued mother's credibility to the jury something like this.

"Now, ladies and gentlemen of the jury, what is the defense in this case? Insanity, we all know that. And who has been called by the defendant to support that defense? Some psychiatrist who has devoted his professional life to the study of mental and emotional illness? No. Some next-door neighbor who observed the defendant? No. Who has been called in support of that defense? The one witness called by the defendant to support this claim of insanity is his mother. Goddamn liar!" That's probably what I would have done when I was 25 years old and I can tell by your response that that's not going to work. That's not going to work. Everybody understands that mother will lie for her son. But you've got to do it tactfully.

"Now, ladies and gentlemen, what is the defense in this case? Well, we all know what it is, it's insanity. And who has been called in support of that defense? A psychiatrist, who's devoted his professional life to the study of mental and emotional problems? No. Some neighbor, some disinterested person to tell you how the defendant was at the time in question? No. Who was the only witness called by the defendant in support of this claim of insanity? His mother." And go on. The shrug of the shoulders does it for you. And when the jurors retire to deliberate and the bailiff turns the key in the lock and the Holy Ghost actually descends and is physically present in the room, those jurors look at each other around the table and they say, "Well, what is the defense? Clear insanity. And who did he call in support of that defense? His mother. Goddamn liar!" See, they will take the step for themselves that they will not permit you to take for them, so you must be tactful.

Second, you must be simple. The kind of lawyer-like argument that got you a pat on the back and an A+ from the tax teacher in law school will not do. And you can almost let your ear be your guide. It's a kind of musician's ear. Stand up at home, deliver the argument to the mirror or the wall or whoever it is at home, and just listen to yourself. And if it's a wonderful lawyer's argument with convoluted subordinate clauses and the like, it's no good. Your ear will tell you. It's got to be a straightforward argument or else it won't work with a jury.

And, finally, I've said it before, but I do believe it with all the strength I can command—those jurors cannot be fooled. Collectively they remember every word of the trial and are smarter than you and me and the judge all put together. Don't ever try to fool them. Respect their intelligence and perhaps you have a chance. If you can come up with an argument about witness credibility that makes the three light bulbs go on—it's tactful, it's simple, and it respects the jury's intelligence—you're probably going to persuade them. If you can't come up with that kind of argument, well, life is hard and this is a very difficult business. Then you go with the best you have, you cross your fingers, and you just hope that at the end of a career you have batted 500. Thank you very much.

Part II

Chapter 7

Ulysses in Court

PROFESSOR IRVING YOUNGER: On the morning of February 2, 1922, two parcels wrapped in plain brown paper were delivered to the conductor of the Dijon–Paris Express that ran between those two cities in France. The conductor's instructions were to deliver these parcels to a messenger who would be waiting at the Paris depot. The messenger was indeed waiting; he took the two parcels and brought them to Sylvia Beach, the proprietor of a bookshop in Paris that did business under the name Shakespeare & Company. Ms. Beach undid one of the parcels; it contained a book and she placed that book in the window of her shop. She took the other with her that evening to Ferrari's Restaurant, where in a private room was held the fortieth birthday party of James Joyce. Joyce sat at the head of the table and at the end of the dinner, Ms. Beach presented to him the parcel. He unwrapped it and there he found a printed copy of his novel *Ulysses*; a novel that has been called the very bombshell of the century. Some view it as the greatest novel ever written in the English language.

Those literary judgments are not our concern here.

Our concern is with litigation. The fact is, that paper-backed volume of some 700 pages was not the first appearance of *Ulysses* in print. Its earlier manifestation had generated a lawsuit in the state courts of New York; a lawsuit which has been pretty much lost to professional memory both among lawyers and among scholars of the novel. In addition, the definitive publication of the novel was to result in one of the great federal cases on the law of obscenity.

My purpose in this presentation is to tell you the story of those two lawsuits—the one in the New York state court and then the federal case, which is still one of the sources of what we know of our law on obscenity.

I will not occupy you with an excess of footnotes. I tell you that what you are about to read is based upon research in the standard resources of the law library. In addition, three of the lawyers who, at various points of my work were still alive, were infinitely patient with their time, their personal recollections, and their files. In addition, two of the great law firms of New York City that were involved in those pieces of litigation gave me full access to their files. And finally, the manuscript and rare books collections of Cornell, Harvard and Columbia Universities, as well as that of the New York Public Library, were thrown open to me. Suffice it to say, for every sentence there could be at least one footnote. For some, two. And for a few, three. In short, I have invented nothing. It happened exactly as I am going to relate it to you.

First, for those of you who read *Ulysses* a long time ago and no longer remember it, I will remind you that the novel is a picture of one day in the life of a group of citizens in Dublin, Ireland. The physical background of the novel is the geography of the city presented in microscopic detail. There is a host of characters, starting with Malachi "Buck" Mulligan, the medical student who is discovered on the novel's first page, standing stately and plump at the top of the stairs getting ready to shave, and, just to mention the other principal characters: Blazes Boylan, Gerty MacDowell, Stephen Dedalus, Leopold Bloom (the protagonist), and ending with that celebrated last episode of the thoughts of Molly Bloom, Leopold's wife, as she drifts off to sleep at the end of the day.

Each of the novel's chapters and characters has an analog in Homer's *Odyssey.* Leopold Bloom represents Odysseus, or, in its Latin form, "Ulysses," hence the novel's title. Molly, his wife, represents Penelope. Stephen Dedalus represents Telemachus, and so on.

James Joyce was one of the absolute lords of language. He was a master of English prose in all of its periods and styles, as well as the possessor of some dozen languages other than English. And what Joyce does is to adapt his style to the action: sometimes where he finds English innocent of the word he needs, he invents the word, and he freely uses multi-lingual puns. The consequence of all of this is that the novel is a masterpiece. Everyone would have to agree with that. An astonishingly beautiful masterpiece, but a most difficult one. And since the principal inter-concern of the novel is the mental life of each of the characters—human beings what they are—a fair portion of the novel deals with their sexual lives.

Our story begins with a lawyer. A lawyer named John Quinn, who was a distinguished practitioner in New York City in the early years of this century. He was the founding and senior partner of a firm that specialized in foreign international transactions and banking work. In addition, he was a power behind the scenes of Democratic politics. The recipient of an enormous income with no family upon which to spend it, he devoted himself by way of avocation to the arts. He was extremely sophisticated in the Modernist movement in literature, the visual arts and music, and consequently made use of his money to finance struggling writers, struggling painters and struggling publishers.

Among the struggling publishers with whom Quinn became acquainted were two women named Margaret Anderson and Jane Heap. Margaret Anderson was a native of Chicago, where, in 1914, she founded a magazine she called the *Little Review.* She described the *Little Review* as "A magazine of the Arts, making no compromise with public taste." In short, this magazine was concerned with the avant-garde in all of its manifestations.

Shortly after founding the magazine, Margaret Anderson met Jane Heap, who soon became her partner in the publishing venture as well as her erotic partner. In 1916 or so, finding Chicago rather confining, they moved their magazine and their personal existence to New York City.

They were committed to finding and publishing a work from the edge of the Modernist movement in Europe. To that end, having met

Quinn, they asked him for a sum of money with which they might retain an agent who would bring to their attention important work being done by writers in Europe. Quinn gave them that sum of money—$750 per year. With that sum Anderson and Heap retained Ezra Pound as their European agent.

Ezra Pound was personally acquainted with James Joyce, who, as of the spring of 1917, had published a collection of short stories called *Dubliners,* a play titled *Exiles,* and a novel called *Portrait of the Artist as a Young Man,* as well as scattered poetry. Pound wrote to Joyce asking whether he had anything that would be suitable for publication in the *Little Review,* and referring to the magazine as, "A place where the current prose writings of James Joyce, Wyndham Lewis, T.S. Eliot and myself might appear regularly, promptly, and together."

In November or December 1917, Joyce sent Pound the manuscript of the first three episodes of *Ulysses;* known as "The Telemachiad," because it concerns Stephen Dedalus primarily, whose counterpart in the *Odyssey* is Telemachus. Pound was the first person outside of Joyce's family circle to read the opening pages of *Ulysses,* and he commented to Joyce in a letter written in the voice of Artemus Ward:[1]

> Well, Mr. Joyce, I reckon yure a damn fine writer, that's what I reckon, and I reckon this 'ere work of yourn is some consurned litrature. You can take it from me, and I'm a jedge.

Pound sent the novel on to Anderson and Heap. They read it, and Margaret Anderson responded to Pound:

> This is the most beautiful thing we'll ever have. We'll print it if it's the last effort of our lives.

Pound warned them of trouble with censors, of whom there were many in those days—remember, this is not 1988; it is now the early months of 1918. The March 1918 issue of the *Little Review* published the first appearance in print anywhere in the world of any part of

---

1. Artemus Ward was the pseudonum of Charles Farrar Browne, American frontier humorist of the 19th century.

Ulysses, the first three episodes, *The Telemachiad.* The entire issue was immediately seized by the United States Post Office and publicly burned. The January 1919 issue contained the next episode of *Ulysses,* titled *Lestragonians.* The first few copies were mailed to subscribers, the Post Office saw what was in that issue, and immediately entered an order forbidding the mailing of any additional copies to subscribers.

In April 1919, the *Little Review* published the next episode, based upon the Scylla and Charybdis segments of the *Odyssey.* This third segment was bowdlerized—was edited—by Anderson and Heap with an eye to keeping the censors at bay. What they did was print in that issue of the magazine an editor's note, referring to the seizures and orders forbidding mailing:

> . . . . To avoid similar interference this month, I have ruined Mr. Joyce's story by cutting certain passages in which he mentions natural facts known to everyone.

Through this period of time the lawyer Quinn was getting angrier and angrier—that tended to be his personality. In addition, so far as I can make out, Quinn simply found these women distasteful for personal reasons. He just didn't like them. He was concerned with the ultimate fate of *Ulysses* and James Joyce, whom he recognized to be a great writer. And, you see, his judgment was a lawyer's refined judgment: Publish what you wish in a book and you will get away with it, but if you publish in a magazine (circulated primarily through the mails), you will get into trouble with the Post Office, and if that trouble comes first, it may prevent the ultimate publication of the book.

If Quinn had had his way, he would have had nothing appear in the *Little Review.* He would have waited for Joyce to finish *Ulysses,* then publish it as a book. As Quinn put it in a letter to Pound:

"There are things in *Ulysses,* published in number after number of the *Little Review* that never should have appeared in a magazine asking the privileges of the mails. In a book, yes. In a magazine, emphatically no!"

This brings us to the July/August 1920 issue of the *Little Review* and the famous Gerty MacDowell episode. I can't give you the text here, it runs some 80 or 90 pages. But I will tell you its gist so that you can understand the lawsuit that followed its publication.

In the Gerty MacDowell episode, we see Leopold Bloom wandering more or less at random around Dublin and finally settling at the beach, where he simply leans against a stone wall and watches some young women at play. The analogy in the *Odyssey* is the episode in which Ulysses, having been shipwrecked, is washed up on the beach of a land unknown to him. He is utterly exhausted and he is naked. He goes to sleep under a bush and is awakened by the sound of voices of young women. He peers out from under the bush and there he sees Nausicaa, the daughter of the king of the Phaeacians, playing with her handmaidens. Ulysses stands up, taking care to keep the bush between himself and the young women, because he is quite literally naked. He addresses Nausicaa and her companions, introduces himself, and Nausicaa instantly falls in love with this masterful figure who appears out of nowhere. They dress him in their own clothes and lead him to the palace, where he is entertained as befits one king receiving another, and in due course leaves to continue his adventures.

That episode is what is in Joyce's mind as he writes about Leopold Bloom there on the beach. He watches some young women playing—total strangers to him. One of them is Gerty MacDowell, a young Dublin girl who happens to have a limp. She is there with some friends taking care of some younger children. The friends move down the beach. Gerty realizes that she has attracted the attention of Leopold Bloom, a distinguished looking old man. Rather toying with Bloom, she sits down on a swing there on the beach, and proceeds to swing herself while a display of fireworks is being shot off in the sky. She swings herself higher and higher. With each rising arc, more and more of her leg becomes visible to Bloom. Remember, this all takes place in 1904, when the sight of a woman's ankle (let alone any portion of her leg above that) was extraordinarily exciting.

Well, Bloom becomes extraordinarily excited! Until, at the climactic point of the fireworks going off in the sky, and Gerty having reached the high point of the arc of her swing, Bloom experiences an orgasm.

This episode appears in the July/August 1920 issue of the *Little Review.* Immediately, one John Sumner, then the secretary to the New York Society for the Suppression of Vice, swore out a warrant against the owners of the Washington Square Bookshop, a bookstore down in the Greenwich Village area of New York, charging them with disseminating an obscene object. The police came around and seized the bookstore's copies of that issue of the *Little Review.*

Pound wrote to Joyce:

> Nausicaa has been pinched by the police!

The Monday after the seizure, recognizing that the situation had reached crisis proportion, lawyer Quinn convened a conference in his office. Those attending were Margaret Anderson, Jane Heap, the owners of the bookstore, and the bookstore owners' lawyer. Quinn opened the meeting by saying, "I don't give a damn for the *Little Review.* I wouldn't waste two minutes on it. It would serve you," turning to Anderson and Heap, "damnably right if it were excluded from the mails."

At that point, Margaret Anderson began to speak of broadening the public. Quinn said, "You'll be broadening the matron at Blackwell's Island one of these days, and serve you damn well right." (Blackwell's Island being the women's prison in New York City.)

Anderson replied, "We're following the wishes of Pound and Joyce, who want the thing printed without changes."

Quinn responded (rather intelligently), "Pound and Joyce are in Europe. You are in New York. Europe is old. New York is young. Europe is civilized. New York is not. It's all right for artists such as Joyce to ask for no changes, but the editor of a magazine ought to have knowledge of the conditions of the place where the magazine is published and exercise independent judgment—not be a mere adding machine to register the punches of those who play it.

"Well," Quinn said. "Let's stop stalking. Let me call Sumner and see what I can do." As he placed the telephone call, he said, "Nothing is gained by spitting in the eye of a public official, even though it's a small eye." He got Sumner on the phone and sweet-talked him into agreeing to a luncheon appointment for a few days later. Quinn met with Sumner tete-a-tete and asked Sumner to drop the complaint, in exchange for which, Quinn suggested, "No more excerpts of *Ulysses* will appear in the *Little Review.*" In short, no further magazine publications as Joyce wrote them.

At that point, Sumner revealed something extraordinary. He said, "The Society for Suppression of Vice did not originate this case. What happened was that the daughter of a Wall Street lawyer received a copy of the *Little Review* in the mail. She read it and was outraged. She showed it to her father, who was also outraged, and her father went to the district attorney. The district attorney said, "I would rather not institute the case myself. Let's call Sumner at the Society for Suppression of Vice." And so Sumner signed the complaint. "As a matter of fact," said Sumner to Quinn, "I have never before this heard of James Joyce and haven't read a single word he ever wrote." Sumner said, "I will agree to do what I can. At most, that will be to attempt to persuade the district attorney to drop the case. What we can agree upon, though, is that if the case isn't dropped, the owners of the bookstore will be excused, and substituted as defendants will be Margaret Anderson and Jane Heap, who, after all, published the thing and properly ought to be the defendants."

Quinn now made a tactical mistake. He sent Anderson and Heap down to the courthouse to accept service of the summons in place of the bookstore owners and didn't go with them. What Anderson and Heap did when they got to the courthouse was convene a press conference on the sidewalk in front of the courthouse. They made speeches defying the district attorney and daring him to do his worst. So, of course, the district attorney declined to drop the case and moved on to a preliminary hearing before a judge to decide whether there was cause to proceed with the trial on the merits.

The hearing was held on October 21, 1920, at the old Jefferson Market Police Court at 6th Avenue and 9th or 10th Street in New York.

(For those of you familiar with the neighborhood or those of you who may wish to visit it, the building still stands. Several years ago it was restored by a very able architect and is now used as a branch of the New York Public Library called the Jefferson Market Library.)

The judge for the hearing was Magistrate Corrigan, a personal friend of Quinn's. At this preliminary hearing the defense had the right to take the stand and testify. Quinn waived that right. He said Anderson and Heap would not testify. The prosecutor simply offered Sumner's affidavit as his case. He said, in effect, "This is the affidavit upon which this whole thing began, and on that I rest."

The lilt of the language may interest you. The affidavit read:

> The defendants are accused of publishing, manufacturing, and preparing a certain obscene, lewd, lascivious, filthy, indecent, and disgusting magazine, which said magazine represents in its description of scenes of lewdness and of obscenity, and which magazine is so obscene, lewd, lascivious, filthy, indecent, and disgusting that a minute description of the same would be offensive to the court and improper to be placed upon the record.

The Magistrate was having none of that, and said, "I'm not going to act simply on the basis of an affidavit. I want to read the episode." So they gave him a copy of that issue of the *Little Review.* Corrigan said, "Everybody wait here, it'll take a half hour of so. I'm going into the robing room to read it and then I'll come back and announce my decision."

Quinn said to him, "Before you go, your Honor, you ought to know that James Joyce is a serious artist and that any reader who understands this stuff could not be hurt by it. And, if, as will be with most readers, the reader doesn't understand it, then obviously they can't be hurt by it."

The Magistrate said, "We'll see," and went into the robing room. He came back in a half hour and said, "No, I've got to hold the defendants for trial in Special Sessions (the court in which misdemeanor cases were then tried), because," said the Magistrate, "there was one incident which anyone would understand. That was the incident when the man went off in his pants. That, I think, is smutty and filthy within the meaning of the statute." The Magistrate fixed bail at $25 for each woman, and so the case then passed to the Special Sessions Court.

John Quinn that night wrote a long account of what had occurred before Magistrate Corrigan and sent it to Pound, expecting—as indeed it does turn up—that Pound would pass it on to Joyce. Pound did pass it on to Joyce and Joyce then replied, in a letter directly to Quinn:

> I was very much amused by your letter. I hope the Magistrate enjoyed himself in his chambers as much as he appears to have done in court. Ulysses causes a great deal of trouble to everybody, not excluding myself. He is one of those world-troubling seamen.

Special Sessions Court no longer exists. It was the court which functioned on in New York City for the trial of misdemeanor cases and was way before *Duncan v. Louisiana* involving jury trials in such matters. What you got at Special Sessions was, at the defendant's option, either one judge or three judges. Quinn opted for three judges.

The trial began on February 14, 1921, before Special Sessions Judges MacAnerny, Kernahan and Moss. MacAnerny and Kernahan were rather elderly, white-haired, Irish politicians who moved onto the bench. Moss was somewhat younger, very much brighter, and far and away a better lawyer than either of the other two. Not a civilized or cultured gentleman, but certainly someone with an I.Q. beyond that of MacAnerny and Kernahan.

Anderson and Heap, once again acting beyond the instructions of Quinn, came to the trial with a crowd of sympathizers and supporters. Once again, they held a press conference on the sidewalk outside the courthouse, at which Margaret Anderson made the following statement: "Twenty-five years hence the world will stand aghast in amazement at the people of 1921, who in the slightest questioned Joyce's story from a moral standpoint. John Sumner is not qualified to judge *Ulysses*. Judgment on what is obscene literature should be left to experts."

"Well," the prosecutor said, "my *prima facie* case consists of the magazine. I will have no witnesses, except possibly in rebuttal." He put the magazine into evidence and that was that.

We now turn to the defense.

Quinn stood up and described James Joyce. He identified the books Joyce had published and began to say something about Joyce's standing in the world of letters. At this point he was interrupted by one of the judges, who said, "What does all that have to do with the issue? I don't care who James Joyce is or whether he's written the finest books in the world. Our only function is to determine whether certain passages violate the statute." Quinn, being a very able lawyer, knew that when a judge says something like that, you go with the judge.

Quinn said, "Very well, your Honor, I will call my first witness."

His first witness was novelist and essayist John Cowper Powys, who testified in substance that *Ulysses* was too obscure and philosophical a work to be in any sense corruptive. Quinn then call as his second witness Philip Moeller, the president of the Theatre Guild, a theatrical producing organization in New York, who testified that the objectional chapter is "an unveiling of the subconscious mind in the Freudian manner, and I see no possibility of these revelations being aphrodisiac in their influence." Whereupon, one of the judges said, "Here, here, you might as well talk Russian. Speak plain English if you want us to understand what you're saying."

Another judge picked up the colloquy and said, "What would be the effect of this chapter on the mind of the average reader?" Moller responded, "Well, your Honor, I think it would mystify him." And the judge said, "Yes, yes, but what would be its effect?"

For the life of me I can't figure out what was on the judge's mind.

At this point, the testimony having been rather tedious, Quinn was prepared to agree with the prosecutor that all the other witnesses would testify to the same effect. So it was on the record that there was no need to call the other witnesses. Quinn now stood up to make his final argument. He said, "*Ulysses* might be called futuristic, but it was neither written for, nor read by schoolgirls. It may be disgusting in part, perhaps, but no more so than Swift, than Rabelais, than Shakespeare, than the Bible. It may incite to repulsion, but it does not lead to lascivious acts." He ended up saying, "I myself do not understand *Ulysses,* but I think Joyce has carried his method too far in this experiment." And one of the judges interrupted to say, "Yes, it seems to me like ravings of a disordered mind. I can't see why anyone would want to publish it."

At that point, you realize, Anderson and Heap, sitting in the first row, had not been introduced to the Court. They hadn't testified and there had been no need for any witness to refer to them. So the judge, having said, "I don't see why anyone would want to publish it, it's so obscure," looks up and sees two women sitting there. He says, "Oh my goodness, the district attorney is probably going to read passages to us in his argument. I think those young ladies ought to be excused." Quinn said, "Your Honor, they are the publishers." Whereupon the judge said, "Oh, I'm sure they didn't know the meaning of what they were publishing."

The judge was absolutely right in anticipating that the prosecutor and assistant district attorney, a man by the name of Forester, was going to read. His final argument consisted simply of reading the material that had appeared in the *Little Review.* He began by saying, "This Nausicaa episode violates the law. And no matter how great a writer James Joyce may be, he's not entitled to break the law."

And he began to read. As he began to read—in the manner of a good many Irishmen—he got very excited and red in the face, and it was obvious that his blood pressure was approaching the boiling point. As this point approached, Quinn jumped to his feet, and though you are never supposed to interrupt your opponent, could not resist the temptation.

He shouted out, "That's my best exhibit!" pointing to Forester. "There's proof *Ulysses* does not corrupt or fill people full of lascivious thoughts. Look at him! He's mad all over. He wants to hit somebody; he doesn't want to make love to anybody! Which is exactly what *Ulysses* does. It makes people angry. But it doesn't grind them into the arms of some siren!"

The judges were fairly amused by this incident. They declared the argument at an end, but they also said "We're not going to decide without reading it. So we're going to adjourn the case for a week. Everybody come back then, at which point we will have read this episode and you'll have our decision."

They came back a week later, now February 21, 1921, and the decision was announced unanimously by the three judges. The defendants were guilty and the penalty was a $50 fine.

Quinn, as I previously suggested, was in the habit of writing long accounts to either Pound or to Joyce of each stage in this historical litigation. He wrote a long account directly to Joyce of what happened in the trial, which gives you the flavor of the courtroom far beyond anything you can reconstruct from the newspaper accounts—there is no stenographic transcript. But for a lawyer, much of the fun of the following letter is that it shows Quinn, the high-powered counselor, letting off steam after having lost the case. Every lawyer who tries cases loses them. What you do when you lose is go to the bar and have a few drinks and curse out the judge. This letter is a wonderfully articulate cursing-out of the judge. This is what Quinn wrote to Joyce a couple of days after the verdict was returned:

> I took the only [at]tack that could be taken with the three stupid judges and that was that no one could understand what the thing was about. I nearly got away with it. I got two of them to admit that they could not understand it. After the witness was examined, they said they wanted to read the magazine, so there was an adjournment of a week until February 21st. I knew that two of the judges were more interested in eating and smoking, and perhaps drinking and poker playing, probably, than they were in reading the *Little Review* and there was no chance that they'd read it in the meantime. But the third judge was one of those nervous asses. He reminded me for all the world of one of those restless hyenas that move up and down and backwards and forwards for days. He is an ass without the slightest quiver of culture, but he knows the meaning of words. I made what many people called a brilliant argument, and my assistant, Mr. Watson, felt when we got through that the case was won. Two of the judges had agreed with me that they could not understand it. I made an analogy to cubist painting and so on. The case for the prosecution was argued by an Irishman named Forester, a typical Irish patriot of the vintage of 1882 and prior to that time. A blatant, flatulent windbag patriot, an Every-Saturday-in-confession-Every-Saturday-night-a-bath-Every-Sunday-to-communion Patriot.

He then describes Forester's reading of the extract and becoming more and more excited and what he [Quinn] had done to interrupt. He continues:

> The judges were rocking with laughter, and again I thought I had them. But that 1% judge and 99% baboon carried the other two who

> had not read the book. Heap and Anderson were each convicted and found guilty and sentenced to pay a $50 fine. In fact, I had to certify to the judges that that chapter was the worst in the book or they might have been sent to prison.
>
> Sincerely yours,
> John Quinn

In addition to paying the fine, the law required the defendants to be fingerprinted. Up to this point they had not been arrested and therefore no fingerprints had been taken, so they had to be printed. I believe you will enjoy as much as I did Margaret Anderson's accounting of the handling of the fingerprinting episode:

> We were led through many corridors by an Irish policeman, passing John Sumner, who was standing at some distance. He raised his hat high in the air as if in tribute and then, adieu.
>
> We entered a room; several men were in attendance. I examined the finger fluid (that's the fingerprint ink) into which I was supposed to dip my well-kept fingers, and then insisted on elaborate advance preparations to guarantee its removal. They hadn't enough towels to reassure me; they rushed out to find more. I didn't like their soap; they provided another kind. I insisted upon a nail brush; this gave them difficulty, but they found one. Then I managed to make them suffer for my indignity until they were in a state bordering on personal guilt. I finally offered my fingers with the distaste of a cat, and it became their personal responsibility to convince me that there would be no permanent disfigurement.

No appeal was taken, because Quinn was concerned that an affirmance would represent an appellate court's view of the obscenity of the novel and might act as a substantial impediment to the appearance of a formal edition in the United States of the completed novel. Now remember, the novel came off the presses in France in February 1922; indeed, on the day of Joyce's 40th birthday. Some 10 years later, as of 1932, that edition was widespread in Europe, and indeed, throughout the world. There had been an English edition with no legal incidence to speak of, but there was no American edition. Every publisher who had considered producing an American edition had finally decided that the legal risk was too great.

As of the early months of 1932, the publishing firm of Random House was in its infancy. It had been founded by Bennett Cerf, a young man who had been educated at Columbia and from college had immediately gone to work for Alfred Knopf, the great publisher. After three of four years of a kind of apprenticeship, Cerf, anxious to have his own publishing company, established Random House with a partner. Those of you my age will recall Bennett Cerf as a leading figure in the American publishing industry; those of you somewhat younger will remember him as a panelist on *What's My Line?* This is the Bennett Cerf to which I refer.

Bennett Cerf realized that it would be rather a coup for him and for the infant Random House to publish the first American edition of *Ulysses.* Through an intermediary—a relative of a relative—he managed to get a message to Joyce asking for a meeting and the return message came that Joyce would be glad to meet with Cerf on a given day at Shakespeare & Company, the Paris bookstore run by Sylvia Beach, under whose aegis the first edition had appeared in France. On the appointed day, at the appointed hour, Cerf walked in and found Joyce sitting in the bookshop with a bandage around his head, his arm in a sling and his foot bound up and extended on a chair.

Said Sylvia Beach, "Oh, Mr. Cerf, don't think he always looks this way. He was so excited about meeting you that on his way here he was run over by a taxicab. But he insisted on seeing you because he needs money and he thinks maybe you're going to get some for him." Cerf said, "Well, I'm certainly ready to give him some." Cerf then turned to Joyce and said, "I don't know whether we can win a court case or not, but I do think the climate is changing in America, and I'm willing to gamble on it. I will give you $1,500 with the understanding that if we legalize the book it is an advance against regular royalties of 15 percent. If we lose the case, you keep the $1,500." Joyce said, "I don't think you'll manage it and you're not going to get the $1,500 back." Cerf said, "Of course not, it will serve to make the deal binding."

Joyce agreed, accepted the $1,500 and Cerf had the American publishing rights.

Cerf returned to New York and on March 28, 1932, met with the lawyers he thought ought to handle the matter. Those lawyers were Morris

Ernst and his young partner, Alexander Lindey. The Ernst firm went out of existence some few years ago. It was called Greenbaum, Wolff & Ernst, and on the off chance that some of you are not immersed in the lore of the New York Bar, let me pause to tell you a little about Ernst and his law firm.

Ernst was a kind of refugee to New York City. He was born in one of the Southern states, but came to New York as a young man, where he established a very prosperous practice. The law firm did commercial work of all kinds, but was particularly active in First Amendment and literary property matters. Before the term was commonplace, they would have been described as civil liberties lawyers. They represented a good many of the publishers in New York. They were active in virtually every major lawsuit challenging censorship on the grounds of obscenity—or any other grounds. Ernst was an extremely able lawyer and rather a figure of note around New York. He was extremely articulate, extremely hardworking, enormously productive, wrote some 10 books related to his life as a lawyer, but not of a technical nature—books addressed to general readers.[2] In addition to which, he smoked five packs of cigarettes a day and was a generally memorable person.

Cerf met with Morris Ernst and Alexander Lindey and said, "I want to retain you to do whatever you think ought to be done to make it possible to publish *Ulysses* in the United States. Now, I don't know what ought to be done. That's for you to decide, but will you take it on? I can't pay you very much; essentially it has to be on a contingency basis."

Ernst agreed to take on the case, and you may find the terms of the retainer fascinating. There was a cash down payment of $500. Random House was to lay out all expenses for the litigation ultimately brought. If the lawsuit went to trial, Ernst and his partners and associates were to receive an additional $50 a day. Assuming the lawsuit was successful and there was an American edition, Ernst's firm's contingency was a percentage of the revenues generated by the edition. Five percent on

---

2. Books by Ernst on related subject matter are *The First Freedom* and, with W. Seagle, *To The Pure: A Study of Obscenity and the Censor.*

the trade edition, two percent on reprint editions and five percent of any book club payments. I am told, but I don't know whether it is true or not, that it turned out to be the single largest fee the law firm ever received.

Ernst now engaged in an absolutely brilliant piece of thinking that is "lawyering" at its best. A less skillful lawyer, a lawyer less exquisite in his analytic powers would have said, "Go ahead and print the edition and if they come around and arrest you, we'll fight like hell and maybe we'll win." And that's not prudent advice for two reasons. First, you risk the entire edition—hundreds of thousands of dollars down the drain if the book is seized—and, ultimately, Ernst loses the battle. But from Bennett Cerf's personal point of view, and perhaps closer to the bone, you risk criminal prosecution. If Ernst loses the battle, he doesn't go to jail. Bennett Cerf goes to jail, and that's not too cheerful a prospect.

Ernst came up with an incredibly clever alternative. He had the wherewithal to think of this because some years before he had assisted a United States Senator in a study of and partial revision of the revenue statutes under which the Customs people operate. Ernst had the bright idea of using the Customs procedure.

In outline, this is how it works: An article is sought to be imported into the United States. If the Customs Service deems it to be non-importable (non-importable items include anything from heroin on the one hand to obscene books on the other), they seize the particular items sought to be brought into the United States. No one is arrested; it is a seizure directed at that specific item. Anybody with an interest in the item is entitled to be heard in court. The question is: Is is importable? Is it seizable under the statutes? If the answer is that it is importable, the Customs Service gives it back to you. If the answer is that it is not importable, because, for example, it is obscene, the Customs Service destroys the item and that's the end. What is at risk? The one item you import. Putting aside the legal cost, what is involved is $3.50 and nobody goes to jail. It is an entirely civil proceeding which can be handled quickly, expeditiously, and with minimum exposure to unpleasant consequences.

Ernst came up with this bright idea: "We will cause one copy of *Ulysses* to be imported into the United States. We'll import openly and when the Customs people seize it, we will have a proceeding to determine whether or not it is obscene and we hope we'll win. At least that's the format for this approach. The first question now is the tactics—there's the strategy, but now let's decide the tactics. The first question is: To whom should the book be addressed? We're going to import one copy of *Ulysses*—who should be the addressee?"

Bennett Cerf was a man not only of great imagination and courage, but of incredible nerve. In March 1932 he wrote the following letter:

> Dear Sir:
>
> Some two years ago you were kind enough to send us an unsolicited note complimenting the Modem Library which Random House publishes, on the publication of its one-volume edition of the philosophy of Spinoza. We wrote to you at that time telling you how much we appreciated your interest. We are about to embark now on a really exciting publishing venture, and I am writing to you now because you can be of inestimable help to us, if you so desire, without the slightest effort on your part.
>
> We want to publish James Joyce's *Ulysses,* complete and unabridged, in America. With this end in view we have signed a contract with James Joyce, paying him a substantial advance royalty and agreeing to foot all the expenses of the legal battle that looms in the offing. We have engaged Mr. Morris Ernst as our counsel in the fight to legalize this great book.
>
> All of us feel that now, if ever, is the time to remove the idiotic ban from the great works of literature of modern times. We plan to open our legal battle by having a copy of *Ulysses* mailed to this country from Paris. We will notify the Customs Service that the book is coming, since it is imperative for our purpose that it be seized. We will then be able to fight for the book without having to go through the very expensive procedure of having it printed in America. If the book is once cleared by the U.S. Court, we feel that we will be justified in going ahead with our plan to publish.
>
> If you will permit us to do so, I would like to have this Paris copy of *Ulysses* addressed to you. There is no man in the entire country whose name, given in connection with this case, would be more helpful in swaying any member of the judiciary. By the same token, i feel that there is no man in this country more apt than you to be willing to lend his name to this fight to win James Joyce the due that has so long been coming to him for *Ulysses* in the United States. If you are at all interested in hearing further about our plans for *Ulysses,* I will be delighted

> to write you in greater detail, or even come down to see you personally. I look forward anxiously to your reply.
>
> Sincerely yours,
> Bennett Cerf

The addressee of that letter was Justice Oliver Wendell Holmes, Washington, D.C. Holmes was not then an active member of the court. The letter was written in March 1932 and Holmes had resigned earlier that year, and of course died in 1935.

I have reviewed the Holmes papers, which are in the possession of the Harvard Law School, to see if there was a response. There was none; even in draft. I went through the Cerf papers, which are deposited at Columbia University, to see if perhaps some handwritten postcard had come in, and there was none. I determined who was Holmes' law clerk at that time, because he had law clerks even after he left service on the Court. His law clerk is the senior partner of a great law firm in Cleveland, Ohio. I called him and he was kind enough to speak with me. I asked whether he remembered the letter or anything Holmes might have said about it. He said he really didn't remember it, but he had a vivid recollection. He couldn't place it as it related to the receipt of the letter, but he did have a vivid recollection of Holmes sitting down to read *Ulysses*—what he was reading was the Paris edition, of course. He got to about page three or page four and then just said, "I can't understand this," and read no more. It looks as though Holmes simply ignored the letter, but who knows, someday maybe a response will turn up.

Not having received a response, Cerf recognized that he would not be able to play tricks with the identity of the recipient, so the recipient would simply be Random House of New York.

Ernst discerned another problem to which once more he had an extraordinarily imaginative solution. The proceeding that would take place in Federal Court once the Customs Service seized the book would be very simple, that was its utility from Cerf's point of view. It was fast, it was inexpensive, and it was danger-free. In essence, the book would be given to the judge. The judge would read the book, look at the statute, and decide whether the book offended the statute. The procedure did not permit a trial to take place; it did not permit the calling of witnesses. In effect, this was summary judgment and nothing more.

Ernst's concern was that the judge might not know who James Joyce was. He might not realize that Joyce was regarded by many as the greatest living writer in the English language. Not knowing who Joyce was, it was quite conceivable that any well-intentioned judge might read *Ulysses* and decide simply that it was a dirty book and that would be the end to the proceeding to determine whether one could publish or import it lawfully. How, within the confined nature of the seizure proceeding, do you make sure that the judge knows who James Joyce is? "Ah," said Ernst. "The copy of the book that we import, the thing that will be before the judge when the seizure proceeding starts to unwind, will be a specially prepared copy." And he gave instructions to Joyce as to what to do. Joyce and his secretary, a French lawyer named Paul Leon, did it. They took one copy of the book and, using a razor blade, opened the binding. They then secured copies of some 32 critical reviews about Joyce and *Ulysses,* all hailing Joyce as the new great novelist of the English language and acknowledging *Ulysses* as one of the masterpieces of the form. They took this collection of critical writings and pasted it into the book. They just stuck it in there right at the beginning, and glued the binding back into place so that what they had was, literally, a unique copy of *Ulysses.* A copy of *Ulysses* with an anthology of critical writing about Joyce.

[Just by the bye, the copy itself was from the 11th printing of Sylvia Beach's 1922 edition. The number is not given, but thousands are listed. It was in the 28 thousandth echelon of that printing.]

The way things worked—remember, in his letter to Holmes, Cerf said, "We're going to have it mailed to the United States,"—was that the book was delivered to the postal authorities abroad. The postal authorities would tell you on which ship it would cross the ocean, and then if there was going to be a problem about getting it through Customs, the recipient was notified of the name of the ship so that they could meet it and deal with the Customs people there at the pier.

Paul Leon, Joyce's secretary, cabled to Cerf, in late April 1932, that the parcel had been given to the Post Office—the parcel containing the specially prepared copy of the book—it would be shipped on the *S.S. Brennan* and someone should be there to meet it.

The Brennan steamed across the Atlantic Ocean and arrived in New York on May 8, 1932. That day was the hottest May 8 in the history of New York City. The ship tied up at one of those piers on the Hudson River and, as you know, people and merchandise come off ships—huge, enclosed ships. Not only is there no air conditioning on this ship, but there isn't a breath of fresh air. It's like being in a warehouse with no access to the outside world. The temperature inside that ship exceeded 120 degrees Fahrenheit. The consequence being that the Customs agents on duty wanted only one thing—to get rid of the passengers, get rid of the merchandise, and get the hell out of there. They were clearing everything without opening it.

There was some young executive there from Random House, whose job it was to see to it that the book was seized. Well, this is what happened:

He went to the counter where you go to pick up packages, and takes his to the Customs agents. The Customs agents are, indeed, stamping everything without looking at it. The Random House executive at this point began to get nervous, and when the Customs agent took the parcel and raised his right hand to bring down the stamp, the messenger from Random House said, "I insist that you open that package and search it." The Customs official looked at him as if he were a lunatic and replied, "Look, buddy, it's too hot."

The Random House man said, "I think there's something in there that's contraband and I insist that it be searched!"

At that point, thinking it would be faster and easier to get rid of this lunatic by doing what he wanted rather than quarreling with him, the Customs officer opened the package and there was James Joyce's *Ulysses,* doctored in the manner that I have described.

As the novel fell out onto the counter, the Random House representative said, "Aha! Look at that, look at that!" And the Customs agent said, "Oh, for God's sake. Everybody brings that in. We don't pay any attention to it!"

(T.S. Eliot was a visiting professor of English at Harvard that year. He taught a course called "The Modern Novel," in which *Ulysses* was required reading! What was it the students read? They read a copy of Sylvia Beach's edition that their parents had brought home from Europe. In those days, virtually every American who visited Europe came back with a copy of the book. So common was the book around the country that it had been made required reading at a course at Harvard.)

The Random House representative, becoming frantic and sensing that his job was on the line, said, "I demand that you seize that book!" At that point, figuring that he indeed had a lunatic on his hands, the Customs officer called over the inspector in charge and said, "This fellow wants me to seize that book." The inspector started to argue, "That's ridiculous. We never seize that book."

But the Random House executive begged and pleaded, and finally, to get rid of him, the inspector said, "All right, all right, you can have your way." And to his agent, "Seize the book."

Notification was sent to the United States attorney for the Southern District of New York, which includes Manhattan. The matter was turned over to the chief of the Civil Division, a very able lawyer, a wonderful man named Samuel Coleman, who was a colleague of mine in the years that I served on the court in New York. Coleman was a rather learned fellow; someone with more than the usual just-nodding-acquaintanceship with the world's literature.

Coleman brought in Assistant U.S. Attorney Nicholas Atlas to work on the matter with him, an equally able, equally wonderful man, and also a person of more than the usual background and culture. Coleman knew who Joyce was. He had read *Portrait of the Artist as a Young Man,* but had read no part of *Ulysses* to this point and wasn't familiar with what had appeared in the *Little Review.* He and Atlas read the novel. They decided to recommend that the U.S. attorney—the Justice Department—back up the Customs Service and take the position that the book was not importable. They notified Random House to that effect and began what is called a libel. This proceeding is deemed to be an admiralty proceeding, so the legal language is the language of admiralty law, not the language of ordinary civil procedure with which you are familiar. The caption—the style—of this libel was "United States of America against One Book titled *Ulysses* by James Joyce." So they are going after the book and that is all that is at risk.

Ernst, on behalf of Random House, filed the necessary papers to signify that Random House was intervening, was claiming the book, and was prepared to argue that it was properly importable, the seizure was unlawful, that the book did not violate Section 305 of the Tariff Act (which, in essence, says that obscene matter may not be imported). There were various papers of no great significance, and ultimately it all added up to Cross Motions For Summary Judgment.

The Government says: "Judge, read the book, look at the statute, and hold that the book is obscene." Random House says: "Read the book, look at the statute, and hold that the book is not obscene."

But the problem at the outset was finding a judge. The matter was first assigned to Judge Cox, and for reasons that I cannot determine, and on which I can only speculate, Judge Cox didn't want it. It went back to the calendar, to a second judge who didn't want it. It went to a third judge who didn't want it, until finally, on July 25, 1933, the matter was assigned to the judge who ultimately decided. That was Judge John Monroe Woolsey who had gone to the court some years before out of a very successful practice, principally in the admiralty field.

A word about Judge Woolsey. He was then 56 years old. He was a South Carolinian who had come to New York for law school. He'd gone to Phillips-Andover, Yale, and Columbia Law School; obviously a person of some family means. A very able judge, a life-long bachelor, by the way, who indulged himself in some fairly eccentric hobbies. He collected pipes, and smoked them as well, using some strangely blended tobaccos; he also knew a lot about old clocks and about antique furniture. The one sport he played was golf and he was a great reader of the novels of Anthony Trollope. He had a round face and a totally bald head with large eyes set very far apart. He wore old-fashioned rimless glasses and very strong lines ran from the side of his nose down to the corners of his mouth. And as of 1933, men were beginning to dress in the manner that we associate with today's fashions, but Judge Woolsey affected something of the older fashion. He wore a starched white shirt with a high collar and he always had a gold collar pin holding his tie in place.

Judge Woolsey, I would guess, was kind of pleased to get this matter. He liked it because he knew something of English literature and he was aware that the quality of the lawyering was going to be rather high. What Judge Woolsey did was suggest that briefs be submitted and he then scheduled it for oral argument at whatever time seemed to be convenient to him. The government submitted no brief. They just relied on the book. Random House submitted, through Ernst of course, a fairly short memorandum doing nothing much more than asserting their position that the test of obscenity is a living standard and by that standard *Ulysses* is not obscene; that it is a literary classic, it has been generally accepted by the community (in that so many libraries are anxious to have copies), that it is taught in university courses on the modern novel, and hence it cannot be obscene. Finally, they asserted that it must be judged as a whole; that you can't take particular words or phrases or episodes out of context. You've got to read the novel and come to a judgment based on the novel in its entirety.

Judge Woolsey—my hunch is that he was anticipating a great deal of publicity, which there was[3]—set the matter down for oral arguments. Not in the courthouse, but rather in a wonderful, dignified, beautiful meeting room in the house of The Association of the Bar of the City of New York. It is on 44th Street between 5th and 6th Avenues; upstairs is this magnificent room full of antique furniture. In this room on November 25, 1933, the argument took place. There was the judge, Ernst for

3. See *New York Times,* June 24, 1933, 14:4; July 12, 1933, 15:1; Aug. 30, 1933, 16:5; Nov. 26, 1933, 16:3; Dec. 7, 1933, 21:2; March 13, 1934, 19:3; March 18, 1934, 6:6; May 13, 1934, 17:4; May 17, 1934, 21:6; Aug. 8, 1934, 15:3.

Random House, Sam Coleman for the government, and an awful lot of spectators—newspaper reporters, Ernst's wife, Bennett Cerf, Donald Klopfer (Cerf's partner), two of Cerf's principal editors, and a good many other people whom I have not been able to identify.

There is no transcript of the argument, but this argument is kind of the keystone of the history of the federal lawsuit. I have reconstructed as carefully as possible, from the notes and recollections of the participants, as well as from contemporary news accounts, something very close to a verbatim transcript. It is not as long as the real argument was, obviously, but it gives you the high points. And I think it's interesting to a student of the law of obscenity, to a student of litigation, and certainly, to a student of human nature.

Judge Woolsey, because it was not the courtroom, sat smoking a pipe—wearing his robe, but smoking his pipe—and he told Ernst to feel free to smoke his cigarettes. The judge began by saying, "This is not an easy case. My own feeling is entirely against censorship; I am opposed to it; I think things should take their chance in the marketplace. Otherwise you have bootlegging; everybody sees about the same amount of activity as though the traffic were openly permitted, but the profits all go to persons illegally engaged." Then he looked perplexed and he took a puff on his pipe and he said, "Still, there is that soliloquy in the last chapter. I don't know about that, but let's go ahead. Let's hear your arguments."

Coleman, for the government, went first; they had seized it. So he said, "There are good old Anglo-Saxon words in many books that have been passed on by courts, but obscenity is in the very texture of *Ulysses* and could not be eradicated without destroying the essential values of the book. No one would dare attack the novel's literary merit; I myself like *Ulysses,* but there is obscenity in it."

Judge Woolsey, "Yes, there's some pretty rough stuff in *Ulysses,* but I haven't yet reached a decision. You know, I took it with me on vacation this summer. Some of it was so obscure and unintelligible that it was difficult to understand at all. It was like walking around without your feet on the ground. I spent nights reading and rereading the book and became almost frantic trying to get the author's idea. That one scene in Nighttown where all the characters are tight, and having visions and dreams was a perfect phantasmagoria. Before I got to the soliloquy of Bloom's wife, I was going to say the book was not obscene, but that last chapter is pretty rough stuff. But still, I may have to decide on the book as a whole. The last scene may represent the reflections of a woman of rather promiscuous habit: I dare say it does. The thing that bothers me is that now, after practically finishing the book, I seem to understand it."

Ernst, at that point, sensed danger, so he jumped up and said, "I didn't understand the book either, your Honor, when I first read it." Coleman, not wishing to be one upped, said, "Well, I did, and you're right, your Honor. The most obscene thing in it is Molly Bloom's soliloquy."

Judge Woolsey: "Mr. Ernst, suppose a girl of 18 or 20 read the soliloquy of Molly Bloom, wouldn't it be apt to corrupt her?"

Ernst: "I don't think that's the standard we should go by. The use of four-letter Anglo-Saxon words is cleaner and less revolting than paraphrases of those words. There is nothing in the book taken as a whole that would corrupt anybody."

Judge: "Mr. Coleman, do you agree that a book is not obscene if it does not excite sexual feeling?"

Coleman: "No, I don't agree. I don't think that obscenity should necessarily be limited to exciting sexual feelings. I can understand people reading something that does not excite them in such a manner, but which they might still conclude was obscene. I can say a thing is obscene by the ordinary language used and by what it does to the average reader; indeed, not necessarily by what the author intended. On these grounds, I think there are ample reasons to consider *Ulysses* to be an obscene book."

Ernst, I think now trying to be the scholar: "I have made a study of what language in books does to the ordinary reader. And I have yet to find one single instance where it could be proved that the reading of any book had led to the commission of a crime of passion. Life is full of corruptions. A movie or a tabloid can provide sexual excitement in some persons."

Coleman: "If a producer tried to present *Ulysses* as a play, it would be too obscene for the public."

Judge Woolsey: "To observe the mores of the country at large would be to observe all the restrictions that Will Hayes enforces. (Hayes was then the movie censor.) To challenge Rabelais now would be absurd. Now, Mr. Coleman; how does *Ulysses* differ except that it isn't an old book?"

Coleman: "Under a strict interpretation of the law, Rabelais' works would be banned, though I personally would not ban them."

Woolsey: "Then what is the exact location of the line between tender and shame?"

Coleman: "I beseech the Court not to think me a puritanical censor."

Ernst at this point jumps in: "Libraries and private persons all over the country have already accepted *Ulysses* as a classic through bootleg sources and the law should follow the will of the public."

The judge—my hunch is Judge Woolsey was not finding this especially useful to him—interrupted, saying, "Mr. Ernst, were you really able to read the book?"

And Mr. Ernst replied, "When the book first came out, I had one of those bootleg, blue-bound copies. I started to read it but I couldn't finish it. Last summer, however, I had to read every word in preparation for this argument. While I was lecturing about the bank holiday (Remember, these are the early years of F.D.R.—Roosevelt had closed the banks.) in the Unitarian Church in Nantucket."

At that point, the judge, a little bit impatient, says, "What has that to do with my question? Have you read *Ulysses*?"

Ernst, claiming lawyers should never back down, says politely but still firmly, "Well, your Honor, let me explain."

And when you put it that way, the judge will almost always say what Woolsey said: "Go ahead."

Ernst continues: "While talking about banks, I realized that I was thinking not only about banks and banking laws, but also about the clock at the back of the hall, the gray-haired woman sitting in the front row, the tall shutters at the sides and innumerable other physical objects that were in front of my eyes. Just as, now, while I have been arguing about *Ulysses,* I must admit that at the same time I was thinking of my arguments, I was also thinking about the gold ring around your Honor's tie, I was thinking about the picture of George Washington behind you and the fact that your robe is slipping off your shoulders." At that point there was laughter.

Woolsey said, "Now for the first time I understand the significance of this book. I have listened to you as intently as I know how and still I must confess that by listening to you I have been thinking at the same time of the Hepplewhite furniture behind you." At this point the judge entertained the room with a discourse on Early Colonial furniture, coming back to the point as follows: "Mr. Ernst, I know your client is anxious one way or the other about this book, still I must take a little more time to make up my mind. I have only 10 more pages to read."

Coleman, trying to get the last word in for the government, says, "Those are the best 10 in the book! Or the worst, depending on how you look at it."

And the judge ends with saying, "Well, I'm very puzzled what to do about it. Decision reserved. "

On December 6, 1933, the opinion was final. You will find it at 5 Fed. Supp. 182 and of this judgment I have no doubt whatsoever. From the point of view of literary merit, it is unquestionably the best opinion ever to appear in the Federal Supplement. For those of you who say that's not much praise, I would be inclined to agree. I will not give you the entire opinion, but just a representative paragraph or so, and really, it is just so beautifully done.

Referring to the use of foul language, Judge Woolsey writes:

> The words which are criticized as dirty are old Saxon words known to almost all men, and I venture to many women, and are such words as would naturally and habitually be used, I believe, by the types of folk whose life, mental and physical, Joyce is seeking to describe. In

> respect of the recurrent emergence of the theme of sex in the minds of his characters, it must always be remembered that his locale was Celtic and his season Spring.

And the concluding paragraph, the decretal paragraph, as it were, reads:

> I am quite aware that owing to some of its scenes, *Ulysses* is a rather strong draft to ask some sensitive though normal persons to take. But my considered opinion after long reflection is that whence in many places the effect of *Ulysses* on the reader is undoubtedly somewhat emetic, nowhere does it tend to be an aphrodisiac.

That was December 6, 1933.

The next day, December 7, Bennett Cerf issued a press release announcing that the presses were rolling and that the Random House edition would be on the streets January 20, 1934, just some five weeks away at the price of $3.50. On that day, the day after the decision, Cerf wrote to judge Woolsey as follows:

> Dear Judge Woolsey:
>
> When one's private interests are as deeply involved in a matter as mine are in James Joyce's *Ulysses* at the present moment, it is hard to distinguish in one's general reaction to the decision which emotions are purely selfish and which are generally disinterested. Nevertheless, I'd like to tell you again that regardless of how it affects my own personal fortunes, I consider your decision on *Ulysses* one of the most far-reaching and important in the history of literature in America. I intend to print your decision in full in our edition of *Ulysses* and I look forward to the pleasure of sending with my compliments the first copy that comes from the bindery.
>
> Cordially,
> Bennett Cerf

And to this day, the Random House or Modern Library edition of *Ulysses* has a preface—Judge Woolsey's opinion.

Coleman issued a personal press release welcoming the decision and informing the press that he, Coleman, had recommended to both the United States attorney and to the attorney general that no appeal be taken. He said, "The decision is fair and I have no desire to be a prosecuting censor."

Ernst's statement to the press was as follows: "The first week of December 1933, will go down for two repeals. That of Prohibition and that of squeamishness in literature. We may now imbibe freely of the contents of bottles and of forthright books. It may well be that in the future, the repeal of the sex taboo in letters, inherent in Judge Woolsey's decision, will prove to be of greater importance. The victory of *Ulysses* is a fitting climax to the forward march of our course."

Joyce authorized his secretary, Paul Leon, to announce that "Mr. Joyce finds the judge not too devoid of a sense of humor."

Now, this was early 1933. Of course, Franklin Roosevelt had been elected in November 1932 and had taken office in January 1933. Coleman had been serving under the Hoover administration. Some time after Judge Woolsey's decision, the new administration came in and a man named Martin Conboy became the United States attorney. Of course, the United States attorney is entitled to his choice of chief of division, so Sam Coleman resigned and went into private practice. Conboy and the Justice Department decided not to follow Coleman's recommendation, but rather to take an appeal.

The appeal was taken to the United States Court of Appeals for the Second Circuit. The government's brief was rather skimpy; it simply states that under the test that goes back to the English case of *Regina v. Hicklin* (L.R. 3Q.B. 360 [1868]), *Ulysses* is obscene. The test is whether the work will deprave and corrupt and by that test *Ulysses* is obscene. And Morris Ernst's brief expanded upon the themes that were sounded in the oral argument before Judge Woolsey.

The case was argued in the Second Circuit on May 16, 1934. The three judges were Learned Hand, Augustus Hand and Martin Manton.

[I need hardly say anything about the Hands. Some of you may not know that Martin Manton, chief judge of the Second Circuit, was, not too many years later, indicted for accepting bribes in connection with his judicial work. He was convicted of that crime and sentenced to serve a two-year term in federal prison.]

A contemporary newspaper account describes the judges as sitting there rather self-consciously, each looking at the copy—the Random

House edition—of *Ulysses* that had been placed before him. The government was the appellant because they had lost below. Speaking for the government was Martin Conboy, the United States attorney himself, a very distinguished looking, no longer quite young gentleman who had been extremely successful as a litigating lawyer in private practice.

Conboy began the argument by saying, "This book is filthy, it is offensive to modesty, it is subversive of decency, therefore it complies with all the definitions of obscenity I have been able to find. The government's case is that this is an obscene book. The only exhibit is the book itself." Learned Hand then asked, "Do you believe the court should read it?" And Conboy said, "No, I will read aloud a generous sampling from this product of the gutter. I do not believe it will be necessary for your Honors to read the entire work. All vices," continued Conboy, "and all sensuous thoughts are set forth without restraint and without attempt to palliate or minimize their offensiveness. Sexual practices, normal and abnormal, are dealt with, as are the use of contraceptives. A large part of the book is taken up with minute descriptions of performances and conversations in a brothel where the supposed hero spends a lot of time."

Conboy began to read excerpts. He read excerpts for 40 minutes, at which point they were at the end of the session. Court adjourned, with the argument to continue the next day. When they left the courtroom, Ernst sent his young associate, just a couple years out of law school, to the library to see whether there was any authority to support the proposition that it was improper to read excerpts; that the entire allegedly obscene work had to be read to the court. The associate worked literally all night without sleep, reporting back the next morning that he could really find nothing to support that proposition. Of course, the argument had been made and would be made.

[The associate, I mention in passing, was Benjamin Kaplan, later a very distinguished law professor and a former Justice of the Supreme Judicial Court of Massachusetts.]

Ernst, trying to do something to strike back at Conboy's tactic, spoke to reporters at the end of the session. And what he said to the press was, "I will ask the judges to read the book in its entirety before coming to their decision, as it is manifestly unfair to take selected passages out of context and come to a conclusion about the book as a whole."

The next day the court reconvened, Conboy stood up and began to read more and more excerpts. Learned Hand finally lost his patience and said to Conboy, "Are you going to read the whole book to us?" Conboy said, "Well, I'll give you a generous sampling." He read another fifteen minutes and then pointed at the book, which was on the lectern in front of him, and said with a quavering, loud voice, "It is obscene, it is obscene!" and sat down.

The copy that Conboy was reading from was the specially manufactured copy that had been sent here on the freighter, and he had marked with a penciled "X" in the margin each excerpt that he read. I have seen that manufactured copy and I know what he read in court. To give you some of the flavor of Conboy's performance, I will give the first and last excerpts. The first appears on page seven of Sylvia Beach's edition:

> "God," he said quietly, "Isn't the sea what Algy calls it: a grey sweet mother? The snot green sea. The scrotumtightening sea."

And the last was the very end of the novel, the conclusion of Molly Bloom's soliloquy and these are the words:

> . . . . and Gibraltar as a girl where I was a Flower of the mountain yes when I put the rose in my hair like the Andalusian girls used or shall I wear a red yes and how he kissed me under the Moorish wall and I thought well as well him as another and then I asked him with my eyes to ask again yes and then he asked me would I yes to say yes my mountain flower and first I put my arms around him yes and drew him down to me so he could feel my breasts all perfume yes and his heart was going like mad and yes I said yes I will Yes.

Ernst stood up and said, "Every university library in the country has a copy of this book. Those few that have not, want one. It is a great work of fiction and James Joyce is a majestic genius. More than 50 critics have written about the book and only 1 purported to be shocked. The real arena of action in *Ulysses* is not a Dublin brothel, but a human skull. English 26 at Harvard would not be a real English course without *Ulysses.* You cannot take excerpts from this book and know it.

You must take the entire book. No great work of fiction that has survived is without sexual stimulation. We cannot bind the masses to the rule of the saints. Not only in sophisticated New York, but in the small towns of the South and Middle West, *Ulysses* is sought in every library.

"There are two questions pertinent to the issues in this case. The first is: Has the book been accepted and dealt with openly or has it been dealt with under the counter? The answer is that it has been dealt with openly. The other question is that of the intention of the author. As to that, I do not think there can be any serious derogatory comment. This book was written to present a study of the human mind and emotions in certain phases and it has not been hawked about in a coarse, grasping sense. Those shouting loudest for censorship are the big business fellows who tell dirty stories in Pullman cars. If you blush, it minimizes the corruption and acts as a repellent."

One question was asked by Learned Hand. He said, "You can imagine writings that are rude without being lustful; they would be merely disgusting. Is that your point?" Ernst: "That's right, your Honor. If reasonable men differ on *Ulysses,* then according to the precedents in our law, the decision of Judge Woolsey must stand."

The vote of the panel was 2-1. Augustus and Learned Hand voted to affirm Judge Woolsey; Judge Manton dissented. Judge Augustus Hand undertook to write the opinion. Rumor around the courthouse is that Learned Hand, proud of his reputation as a stylist, did not wish to write the opinion because it would mean head-to-head competition with Woolsey's opinion and he was unwilling to engage in that competition, so Augustus Hand took on the job. His law clerk is now a lawyer retired from practice in Washington, who has told me that Judge Hand did not think it fair to write the opinion without reading the entire book and he decided to read it while riding back and forth on the commuter railway, from his home to the courthouse. As he was a little reluctant to be seen reading this book, he had his law clerk take plain brown paper and make one of those covers that school kids use, so that he could read the book on the train without being seen to do so. The Second Circuit's opinion affirming Judge Woolsey's is reported in 72 Fed. 2d 705;

there also you will find Judge Manton's dissent. Some of you may be interested to read the opinion. I think it's fair to say the restatement of the idea contained in Judge Woolsey's opinion was presented in a manner less distinguished by Judge Hand.

Two weeks or so after the Second Circuit's opinion was filed, the government notified Morris Ernst that no appeal would be taken; that the Second Circuit's word was the last word.

Joyce, when informed about the Second Circuit's affirmance a couple of days later, was reported as saying, "Three cheers for me, says I to myself, says I."

There you have the story of *Ulysses* in court. It is a story of lawyers able and not so able; of judges brilliant and not so brilliant. The story sounds themes which are important in the law of obscenity to this very day: That one must consider the artist's purposes. That one must consider the likely audience of the work. That one must treat the work as a whole, rather than by excerpts, and that the standard by which it is determined whether a work is obscene is a changing standard, a living standard, essentially set by the community.

But lest we become too solemn about it all, I shall close by telling you that a few days after the Second Circuit's decision, James Joyce and his wife Nora went to dinner at the apartment of a friend in Paris. Four or five other couples were present, including Saxe and Dorothy Commins; Saxe Commins being a senior editor at Random House, one who played no direct part in the *Ulysses* litigation or in Cerf's decision to publish the novel. After dinner, the men went to one side of the living room and the women sat on the other. Dorothy Commins was there with the women. And of course, since the Second Circuit's decision was only a few days old, the talk was principally of Joyce and *Ulysses* and of the decision which made it possible to continue to publish the novel in the United States. One of the guests said to Nora Joyce, "Nora, there is so much talk going on about *Ulysses*. The ban is lifted once and for all now and your husband's book will reach out everywhere. You must be very proud of him." And Nora Joyce, who was a poor girl from the west country of Ireland replied, "Indeed, I'm proud of Jim, he's a good man, a very good man; but he's got such a dirty mind."

Chapter 8

The Trial of Alger Hiss

IRVING YOUNGER: When I was a lad, ladies and gentlemen, I was lucky enough to serve a term as assistant United States attorney for the Southern District of New York. Now, not least among the attractions of that marvelous job was that one had full access to the private library of the United States Attorney. There in the files were memoranda of law by Felix Frankfurter, briefs by Thomas Dewey, and, of course, transcripts of all of the great trials which have taken place in the Southern District of New York. The *Rosenberg* trial, *Provo, Lanton, Dennis*. But the one that instantly became and has since remained my favorite is the trial of Alger Hiss. It seems to me that the fascination of that trial, ladies and gentlemen, rests upon four things.

First, the confrontation of the two protagonists has a kind of Shakespearean intensity. Second, simply as a mystery story, it's as good or better than anything Alfred Hitchcock ever put on film. Third, the case is an important chapter in American history. It is a symbol of the disappointment of the years following World War II, of what some have called the treason of the intellectuals, of the corruption of liberalism, of the God that failed. And, fourth, to a trial lawyer the case has endless professional interest. Now, one or more of those reasons will appeal to everyone and so it is, I suppose, that everyone has an opinion on the guilt or innocence of Alger Hiss. Yet, very few of us know much about the trial itself. And while the trial is not all there is to consider on the question of Hiss's guilt or innocence, surely it is the place to start and that starting point is my subject this afternoon. And a voluminous subject it is.

There are 3,307 printed pages of testimony. There are another 1,000 pages of exhibits. There are 595 pages of lawyers' briefs and affidavits, and three judicial opinions. Now, out of this welter of materials, let me try to winnow for you the answers to two questions. First, what was the evidence and second, does the evidence justify or support the jury's verdict of guilty?

Now, in telling the story, ladies and gentlemen, I shall be relying almost entirely upon the transcripts, the exhibits, and the briefs and, to a very great extent, I shall tell the story largely in the words of the witnesses and the lawyers who participated. Please understand that I have no new information to offer, I have no revelations to make. I should say at the beginning that I am personally acquainted with none of the participants except the prosecutor, Thomas F. Murphy, who in 1951 became a federal judge before whom I tried several criminal cases in the early 1960s, first as an assistant United States attorney on the prosecutor's side of the table and later as defense counsel on the defense side of the table. If I have any special claim to competence in the matter, it is this. Mine are the skills and the interests and the experiences of a trial lawyer. And so far as I know, no one with the skills and the interests and the experiences of an American trial lawyer, apart from those who prosecuted and defended Alger Hiss, has ever publicly examined the evidence. It is an extraordinary thing. Books and articles have been written about this case by journalists, by psychiatrists. As a matter of fact, there is one book by a lawyer, but he's an English lawyer, as a matter of fact, an English judge named Lord Jowitt. His book is of limited utility because Lord Jowitt tells the story very well indeed, but when he comes to a high point he always says, "And then they did something inexplicable. But they do things inexplicably in the United States," and then he proceeds to the next chapter. And that wants a certain something in satisfying one's appetite for information about the case. Well, so much by way of bibliographic preface, ladies and gentlemen, let's get down to that story.

It begins on September 3, 1939, which was just a couple of days after the public announcement of the Hitler/Stalin pact, the agreement between Nazi Germany and the Soviet Union sometimes called the Molotov-Ribbentrop Pact. On that day a man named Whittaker Chambers visited Assistant Secretary of State, A.A. Burley. Now, Burley has long since died. What we have are the notes that Burley took as he talked with Chambers on that day. The notes were taken with a number-two pencil on a standard lawyer's yellow pad of the kind that we're all familiar with. With my own eyes I have seen those notes and insofar as they are relevant, ladies and gentlemen, this is what the notes say. There are five lines that deal with Alger Hiss:

The first line says, "assistant to Sayre—CP," which I assume means Communist party—1937.

The next line, "member of the Underground COM.—active."

Third line, "Baltimore Boys."

Fourth line, "wife, Priscilla Hiss, socialist."

And then the fifth line, "early days of New Deal."

That, as I say, was in early September 1939. What happened? Nothing.

Nothing happened until March 20, 1945, when the man in charge of security for the State Department, a man named Raymond Murphy, so far as I know unrelated to the prosecutor and later the federal judge whom I mentioned a couple of minutes ago. This Raymond Murphy, chief of security for the State Department, sat down and interviewed Whittaker Chambers. Why he conducted this interview I have been unable to determine. At the end of the interview, apparently after Chambers left the office, Murphy dictated to his secretary a memorandum of the nature of the interview, what had been discussed, what it is that Chambers had said to Murphy. Insofar as relevant for our purposes, this is what that memorandum says. I'm now quoting Raymond Murphy.

"It seems that in 1934 with the establishment of the Agricultural Adjustment Administration and the introduction of much reform legislation in Washington, the Communist party decided its influence could be felt more strongly by enlisting the active support of Underground

workers not openly identified with the party and never previously affiliated with the party, but whose background and training would make them possible prospects as affiliates under the guise of advancing reform legislation. A Hungarian whose party name was J. Peters, was selected by the Central Committee to supervise the work from New York. Peters's Washington representative and contact man was Whittaker Chambers. The opportunity presented itself for the formation of an Underground group with the appointment to a leading position in the Agricultural Adjustment Administration in 1934 of one Harold Ware. Ware had worked for years in collectivization projects in Russia. He was a son of Ella Reeves Bluer, a veteran American Communist, by one of her numerous marriages. On being assigned to this agency, Ware found a group of very promising, ambitious young men with advanced social and political ideas. Among them were Lee Pressman, Alger Hiss, Henry Collins, and Charles Kramer. They all joined the Communist party and became leaders of cells. No cell had over 10 members. This was the nucleus of the Communist Underground in Washington. The purpose was for each member to advance as high as possible in the government to shape legislation favorable to the program of the Communist party. The top leaders of the Underground were, one, Harold Ware, two, Lee Pressman, three, Alger Hiss, in the order of their importance."

Murphy spoke with Chambers once more. The second conversation took place in August 1946 and, again, when the conversation was over, Murphy dictated a memorandum recounting the conversation. Insofar as relevant for our purposes, this is what Murphy's memorandum says.

"The Communist Underground in Washington is believed to have been set up some time in 1933 after the inauguration of President Roosevelt. Chambers does not know how or when it was set up, but he believes that Harold Ware played a prominent part in creating the Underground and in enlisting key members. Ware, of course, would have acted pursuant to orders from the Central Committee of the Communist party of the United States. There were meetings in Washington chaired by the Hungarian, J. Peters, who would give pep talks on Communist theory. Peters would then talk to each leader separately. Peters

often discussed morale with Chambers. Peters praised the Hiss boys to Chambers very highly. Peters asked Alger Hiss personally to break with the party in early 1938, but Hiss refused with tears in his eyes and said he would remain loyal to the party. After Chambers's break with the party, a woman named Grace Hutchins."

And I now speak in my own voice—I have been unable to ascertain the identity of Grace Hutchins.

"After Chambers's break with the party, Grace Hutchins telephoned Chambers's mother on Long Island one night and said that if he, Chambers, did not return to the party by the following Thursday, it was a question of his death."

Well, who is the man, Whittaker Chambers, telling this lurid tale? Here is a concise biography of Whittaker Chambers, essentially as testified to by Chambers himself from the witness stand at the trial. So there's no real controversy as to the truth or accuracy of any of these facts.

Chambers was born in 1901 in Philadelphia and spent his boyhood years on Long Island. He attended the Rockville Center High School, a public high school, where he was selected to write the class prophecy. He did write it. As required by the school rules, he submitted the text of the prophecy to the principal so that the principal could read it. The principal read it and ordered Chambers not to say it at the commencement. So Chambers sat down and wrote a second prophecy, the text of which he submitted to the high school principal. The high school principal said, "This one is satisfactory. This one you may say at the commencement." When called upon to speak at the commencement, Chambers said not the second, but the first. The consequence was that he did not receive his high school diploma. Instead, he ran away from home.

He was now 18 years old and he supported himself by working as a day laborer on various street corners and railways in Washington, in Baltimore, and in New Orleans, always using a false name. He returned home from time to time and worked at various jobs in advertising agencies and the like in New York City, again, always using false names. He enrolled at Williams College, where he stayed just a couple of days and then left. In 1920 Chambers enrolled at Columbia College. He very quickly became rather a character on the Morningside Heights campus. He was the editor of the student magazine called "Morningside" and in that magazine Chambers published a play of his own authorship titled, "A Play for Puppets." The play is about various characters, included among them being Jesus himself. And Chambers represents Jesus as dressed in a gray kimono with long red hair, obstinate, proud, distrustful of women. And this caused talk at Columbia, the consequence of which was that Chambers withdrew from Columbia College in January 1923.

In February 1925 Chambers joined the Communist party. He was working at the time in the New York Public Library. In April 1927 his employers at the library accused him of theft. They went to his locker and discovered eight library books and a quantity of Communist pamphlets of one sort or another. Chambers took the officials to his home where the officials found 56 copies of books, apparently stolen from the Columbia University library. The consequence of this was that Chambers was fired from his job at the public library.

Now, Chambers had a brother named Richard born in 1904, curiously, the very year of Alger Hiss's birth. In September 1926 Richard had committed suicide by putting his head inside of an oven and inhaling the fumes. Before doing this, Richard had asked Whittaker to enter into a suicide pact with him. Whittaker had refused and now Richard's suicide had a psychologically devastating effect on Chambers. He was apparently paralyzed. He remained in bed, substantially immobile, for three months. He attributed his brother Richard's inability to cope with an irrational world to his failure to find any kind of strength or support in the Communist movement. So Chambers decided that, for himself, he would reach out to that movement for the necessary support. He now became a fanatical Communist. He was involved in some internecine disputes within the Communist party, but essentially he worked continuously for the Communist party through those years in the 1920s, always using false names, giving false information on applications for passports and the like and, ultimately, in 1937 or 1938, he broke with the Communist party.

Now, of course, Chambers had been a professed atheist until that point. In 1940 he was baptized an Episcopalian and about a year later, he and his wife and children became practicing Quakers. In April 1939 Chambers went to work for *Time* magazine as a kind of almost freelance book reviewer. He turned out to have fabulous journalistic gifts and in very quick order Chambers moved through the hierarchy at *Time* magazine. Beginning, as I say, as virtually a freelance book reviewer, he wrote foreign news, he wrote art criticism, he wrote movie reviews and, in due course, he became senior editor of *Time* magazine with principal responsibility for all of *Time* magazine's cover stories. And if there's anyone in the audience who was reading *Time* magazine's cover stories in those years, you will recall some of the cover stories that Whittaker Chambers personally wrote. *Time*'s cover story on Pope Pius XII, for example, on Arnold Toynbee, on Marian Anderson, on Reinhold Niebuhr, on Albert Einstein—all were written by Whittaker Chambers. His salary in 1939 was $30,000 a year, which works out to many times that in 1988 dollars. And finally, on December 10, 1948, Chambers resigned from *Time*. Well, that was Whittaker Chambers.

Now, who is Alger Hiss, the man of whom Chambers was making these lurid accusations, the man Chambers said was a member of the Communist Underground in Washington? Once again, this is a condensed biography of Alger Hiss as recounted by Hiss on the witness stand. There is no real controversy as to the truth or accuracy of any of these facts.

Alger Hiss was born in 1904. He went to Johns Hopkins where, upon graduation, he was elected to Phi Beta Kappa. He then attended the Harvard Law School where he was an editor of the *Law Review*. He received his degree in the class of 1929, not an auspicious year for any law school graduate, but it had no particular problems for Alger Hiss because his first job was assured. His first job, secured for him by Professor Felix Frankfurter, was that of law clerk to Justice Oliver Wendell Holmes. After serving his year's clerkship with Justice Holmes, Hiss began as an associate at the firm of Choate, Hall and Stewart in Boston. By mutual agreement among that firm, a New York firm I'll mention in a moment and Hiss, Hiss moved from Boston to New York in the course of 1932 and became an associate at the firm of Cotton, Franklin, Wright and Gordon, today known as Cahill Gordon. [Cahill, Gordon and Reindell LLP in 2009]

In 1933, Hiss decided that he would prefer the public practice of law to the private practice of law and so he entered government service as assistant general counsel of the Agricultural Adjustment Administration. Two years later he became legal assistant to the Special Committee of the United States Senate investigating the munitions industry, commonly known as the Nye Committee after Senator [Gerald] Nye, the Committee's chairman. After a year he entered the Justice Department, where he served as special attorney in the Office of the Solicitor General. In 1936 he transferred to the State Department as personal assistant to Francis Sayre, then Assistant Secretary of State. When Sayre left to take on other duties, Hiss joined the staff of Stanley Hornbeck, who was the State Department's principal advisor on political affairs.

In 1944 Hiss served as secretary to the American delegation to the Dunbarton Oaks Conference which began to work out the international economic regime that would fall into place upon the conclusion of hostilities at the end of World War II. In 1945 Hiss was appointed director of the Office of Special Political Affairs and accompanied President Franklin Roosevelt to the meeting of the Big Three that took place that year in Yalta. When the organizing conference to set up the United Nations was held in San Francisco in 1945, it was Alger Hiss who was elected to serve, and did serve, as Secretary General. And there is a marvelous trivia question for you. Who was the first Secretary General of the United Nations? Those of us who have any idea of the answer would probably say Trygve Lie. The answer really is Alger Hiss because it was Hiss who served as Secretary General of the San Francisco meeting. It was Alger Hiss who personally carried the executed original copy of the Charter of the United Nations from San Francisco to Washington, where Hiss presented it to President Truman, and by President Truman it was transferred to the archives of the United States in which the document now reposes. At the end of 1945 with the title of pincipal advisor, Hiss accompanied the United States delegation to the first meeting of the United Nations General Assembly held in London.

In February 1947 Hiss left government service to become president of the Carnegie Endowment for International Peace, the chairman of the board of the Carnegie Endowment in those years being John Foster Dulles.

Well, given each man's record and asked to choose between the two, I should think that any fair-minded person would have taken the word of Alger Hiss. But as of August 3, 1948, there was no need for anyone to make the choice, for Chambers's allegations about Alger Hiss were unknown to Hiss. Things soon changed.

I have to pause to sketch in, in very broad strokes indeed, a bit of the political background that's necessary to an understanding of what occurred. As of August 1948, the House of Representatives was controlled by the Republican party. Among the standing committees of the House of Representatives was the Committee on Un-American Activities, commonly called the House Un-American Activities Committee, or its acronym, HUAC. The chairman of the Un-American Activities Committee was a congressman from New Jersey named J. Parnell Thomas, who later served a two-year federal prison sentence for demanding and accepting kickbacks from the office staff. Simply because his name will be mentioned once or twice, the committee's principal investigator and chief administrator was a man named Robert Stripling. And the junior Republican member of the committee was the brand-newly elected congressman from Southern California, Richard Nixon.

Now, in the spring of 1948, for reasons that I really have not been able to determine (and the reasons are unimportant), Stripling sent two investigators to New York City to speak with Chambers, who, remember, was a senior editor of *Time* magazine. Chambers said to these two investigators in effect, "Now, look, I was a member of the Communist party. I have broken with the Communist party. I have put my life together again. I do not wish to relive that episode in my life. Therefore, leave me alone. I don't want to appear before the committee. I don't want to talk about either my experiences as a member of the Communist party and I don't want to name anybody else who had been a member of the Communist party. I repeat, leave me alone."

And the committee left him alone. Stripling paid no further attention to Chambers until July or so 1948 when, for political reasons, Chambers began to be a man of considerable potential importance to the committee. And painting in very broad strokes indeed, here is why. The committee had conducted a series of public hearings at which the committee had heard the testimony of a woman named Elizabeth Bentley. And Elizabeth Bentley was Warner Brothers' idea of a femme fatale—a Soviet female spy with long blonde hair and very attractive and very well spoken. And Elizabeth Bentley had taken the witness stand before the nation under the auspices of HUAC and had said that she, Elizabeth Bentley, was a courier for Communist spies operating throughout the United States. And it began to appear after a while that Elizabeth Bentley was some kind of psychotic liar and HUAC was concerned that it was made to look the fool, that HUAC had supplied a forum to a woman of no credibility whatsoever.

And so, for reasons that will be obvious, HUAC was desperate to find a witness of some modest degree of credibility who could testify in such a manner as in some respect or another to back up or corroborate the testimony that had been given by Elizabeth Bentley. Stripling thought of the senior editor of *Time* magazine. And as senior editor of *Time* magazine, Whittaker Chambers did possess a certain residual credibility. A subpoena was served on Chambers. He responded to the subpoena, coming to Washington and testifying in executive session, that is to say the public was not present, newspaper reporters were not present. He testified before HUAC on the morning of August 3, 1948. After listening to him for a couple of hours, the committee said, "We will now go into public session." They threw the doors open, the news media were allowed into the room, and Chambers now repeated in public what earlier in the morning he had said in private. And what is it that he repeated? What is it that he had said? That he, Whittaker Chambers, had worked for a group that was part of the Communist Underground in Washington in those early years of the New Deal and that attached to the group was Alger Hiss.

The very next morning the committee received a telegram from Alger Hiss and this is what the telegram said in relevant part. This is Hiss speaking. He said,

"My attention had been called by representatives of the press to statements made about me before your committee this morning by one Whittaker Chambers. I do not know Mr. Chambers and insofar as I am aware, have never laid eyes on him. There is no basis for the statements made about me to your committee. I would appreciate it if you would make this telegram a part of your committee's record and I would further appreciate the opportunity to appear before your committee to make these statements formally and under oath."

And now, reading a little bit between the lines, I tell you that I don't have any doubt whatsoever that every member of HUAC, at least every Republican member of HUAC, broke into a cold sweat at this point, assuming that somehow they had managed to find a second Elizabeth Bentley, that Whittaker Chambers was telling a tale about Alger Hiss that had no basis in fact whatsoever and, if it did have a basis in fact, he was talking about somebody else. It wasn't the Alger Hiss who was the President of the Carnegie Endowment for International Peace, and the committee was about to suffer a second public black eye.

In any event, Hiss asked for an opportunity to appear publicly. The committee hastened to grant him that opportunity. Hiss said, "I want to appear forthwith." The next morning Hiss testified before the committee. He testified in public and he began by saying that he had a prepared statement that he wished to read. The committee treated him with exquisite courtesy and said, "Please, Mr. Hiss, read whatever statement you care to make." And insofar as we need be concerned with it, this is the statement that he read. This is Alger Hiss speaking to the committee. He said,

"I am here at my own request to deny unqualified various statements about me which were made before this committee by one Whittaker Chambers the day before yesterday. I am not and never have been a member of the Communist party. I do not and never have adhered to the tenets of the Communist party. I am not and never have been a member of any Communist front organization. I have never followed the Communist party line directly or indirectly. To the best of my knowledge, none of my friends is a Communist."

There then followed several paragraphs that really do not bear directly upon what is our concern this evening, but I do not have the strength of will to resist the temptation, ladies and gentlemen, to tell you what's in those paragraphs, so let me tell you. Remember, he says, "To the best of my knowledge, none of my friends is a Communist," and he then proceeds to say, "However, in the interest of full disclosure, I remind you that I attended the Yalta Conference as a principal political advisor to President Roosevelt and at the Yalta Conference, I met and, in a sense, became friendly with Josef Stalin. And to the best of my knowledge, Josef Stalin is a Communist." In any event, having recounted what I've summarized to you, Hiss winds up as follows:

"Except as I have indicated, the statements made about me by Mr. Chambers are complete fabrications. I think my record in government service speaks for itself."

The committee was desperate to bring it about that the explanation would be the relatively innocent one of mistaken identity, that Chambers was, in fact, talking about someone other than the Alger Hiss who was now known to the public as the president of the Carnegie Endowment. So Stripling at this point produces an Associated Press photograph that had been taken of Whittaker Chambers just several days earlier when Chambers had appeared before the committee. And he shows the photograph to Hiss and he says, "Do you recognize this man? Whatever name you may have known him by and in whatever connection you may have come to know him, do you know him?" Well, Hiss looked at the photograph and I think I'd better give you Hiss's exact words. And while I'll do my best to refrain from undue editorial comment, I can't refrain from it entirely. We remind ourselves that Hiss is a very able lawyer and an extremely intelligent man and, of course, would be aware of exactly what was happening and he would know that there are times when it's necessary to be something less than absolutely straightforward when responding to these questions. What was the question again? Do you know this man under whatever name or in any connection? These are the exact words of Hiss's answer.

"I've never seen that man, but I would like to see him. Then I think I would be better able to tell whether I had ever seen him."

There was some additional testimony of no great consequence and Hiss was excused with the committee's thanks and I take these thanks as expressed sincerely and meaning what the words say.

They thanked Hiss for his cooperation and for his candor and now they called Chambers back, hoping, I suppose, that they could establish through Chambers's testimony that the whole thing was some kind of ghastly mistake. Chambers appeared in Executive Session, so the press is not there, on August 7. They showed Chambers a newspaper photograph of Alger Hiss that had been taken just a couple of days before and they said, in effect, "Is this the man you are speaking of? Is this the man you know as the member of the Communist Underground?" Well, Chambers took a look at the photograph and he said,

"Absolutely. This is the Alger Hiss I knew as a member of the Communist Underground. But more than that, to prove to you that I know the man, let me tell you things about him that could not be known by anyone who was not personally acquainted."

And he now proceeded to run through various minutiae of the Hiss household, the kind of thing you wouldn't know unless you were a close friend. We needn't detain ourselves unduly over this, but for example, Chambers mentioned the nickname by which Hiss referred to his wife Priscilla and the nickname that Priscilla used when she referred to Alger. The nickname that they both used when they referred to their children. He referred to Hiss's hobby. He said, "It is not widely known that Hiss has a hobby. He can't devote much time to it, he's very busy, of course, but he's wildly enthusiastic about it." And what is the hobby? The hobby is ornithology, bird watching. And where do you watch birds in Washington but up and down the Barge Canal. "And one day," said Chambers, "I vividly recall that Hiss was just overflowing with excitement because while out walking on the C&O Barge Canal, he had seen a bird that is very rare in the Washington area and it was a great day in his life as an ornithologist that he had seen this bird. And what kind of bird was it? It was a prothonotary warbler." Well, the committee said, "Well and good," and they now excused Chambers and sent him back and asked Hiss to return once more in Executive Session. And it took a couple of days to get everybody pointed in the same direction, so we're now up to August 16. On August 16, Stripling had found some photographs of Chambers taken not by newspaper people a couple of days before, but taken back in the 1930s, back in the times of which Chambers was speaking when he described the Underground at work in Washington. They had two different sets of pictures of Whittaker Chambers taken in the 1930s. They showed these sets of pictures to Hiss in that Executive Session and, once again, I think we should stick with Hiss's exact words. Hiss looked at the photographs and this is what he said. He said,

"I cannot recall any person with distinctness and definiteness whose picture this is, but it's not completely unfamiliar."

Hiss then said, "I'd feel a lot better about it if I could see the man face-to-face."

Do you realize to this point they had not confronted each other? Each had been testifying, as it were, tête-à-tête to HUAC, but they had never been in the same room together. There had never been the kind of confrontation that presumably would nail the identification down one way or another. Hiss said, "I'd like to see the man," and he then said, and remember, Hiss does have an extraordinary intelligence, he said, "You know, I protest the testimony I give about my personal life." The committee had asked him some questions about nicknames, hobbies, and the like because he said, "I can give you this information about nicknames and hobbies and the like and for reasons that I can't even guess at, this information may, in some fashion, be leaked by HUAC to Whittaker Chambers so that Chambers has the information and then Chambers then uses the information, pretending to have had it all along, so as to make it seem that he, Chambers, is virtually a life-long friend of mine and there's nothing that I can do to counteract this kind of thing. And I protest it and I don't want to give this kind of information if there's the possibility that it's going to be used in that way against me."

It was Nixon who stepped in. Now, remember, he was the junior Republican congressman on the committee. It was Nixon who stepped in and tried to reassure Hiss that there would be no leaks from the committee, that the information would not be misused, that he need not concern himself about any such corruption of the process as Hiss apparently had in mind.

And then a strange thing happens. All I can do is recount to you what you see on the record. This conversation essentially between Nixon and Hiss is going on when suddenly Hiss kind of breaks in and changes the key in the musical sense, suddenly raises a new subject and he says, lawyer that he is, he says, "May I say something for the record?" And Nixon says, "Certainly." And Hiss says, "I have written a name on this pad that I have in front of me. This is the name of a person I knew in 1933 or 1934 who spent some time in my house. And he not only spent some time in my house, but he sublet an apartment from me. And I'd like to see Chambers face-to-face because it's always conceivable that Whittaker Chambers is this man whose name has just popped into my mind and whose name I have written down on the yellow pad in front of me. I cannot imagine why this man would be making statements of this kind about me, but it's always a possibility."

Nixon picks up the questioning and he says, "Is this man who spent time with you in 1933 or 1934 a man with whom you are still acquainted?" And Hiss said, "No, he's not." And then Hiss said, "And he wasn't named Carl." You see, Chambers had testified that in the Underground nobody used his real name and that Chambers's Underground name was Carl. So Hiss said, "The man I knew did not use the name Carl and he certainly did not use the name Whittaker Chambers." And then Hiss says, "Now the name of the man I brought in, and he may have no relation to this whole nightmare, but the name of the man I brought in is a man named George Crosley. I met him when I [Hiss] was working for the Nye Committee. He, Crosley, was a writer. He hoped to sell articles to magazines about the munitions industry."

"Very well," said the committee, "It's obvious that we're going to need to arrange some kind of face-to-face confrontation to bring this matter to a head." "Meanwhile, Mr. Hiss," said one or another member of the committee, "there are some questions of a more or less personal nature I'd like to ask." The questions are asked and, despite his protest of just 10 minutes earlier, Hiss answers the questions readily and without any further protest. And the questions were, "What is the nickname by which you refer to your wife? What is the nickname by which your wife refers to you? What nickname do you and your wife use for your children?" And his answers coincided precisely with the information that had been testified to by Whittaker Chambers. And then they said to him, "And by the way, do you have a hobby?" "Yes." "And what is that hobby?" "Bird watching. I'm an amateur ornithologist. I like to watch birds." "Where do you watch birds?" He said, "In Washington it's a little bit difficult, but the best place is the Chesapeake and Ohio Barge Canal." And then they said to him, "Did you ever see an unusual bird on the Barge Canal?" And he said, "Yes, I did." And they said, "What kind of bird was it?" And he said, "It was a prothonotary warbler."

Well, at that point, I suppose that you could have cut it with a knife in the room, as the saying goes. The one thing on which everybody was perfectly agreed was that there had to be a confrontation. Now, there was a lot of colloquy on this. Let me reduce it to the minimum that you need to understand what then happened and what you are now going to see, ladies and gentlemen. Because it was the summertime and people were at vacation homes and the like, Washington was not a convenient place to have this confrontation meeting. New York City was much less inconvenient to everybody than Washington or any other city that one might think of.

So it was agreed that the confrontation would take place in New York. That meant that a subcommittee had to be appointed to preside over the confrontation. The subcommittee was appointed and that raised the further question, who should preside over this subcommittee? And you might think—indeed, the years since have led us all to believe that the politicians wanted this job because they saw it as the making of a career. The sense I get from reading the statements that were coming out at the time was that no politician wanted this job. HUAC had had the embarrassing experience of sponsoring to the American nation this apparent mad woman Elizabeth Bentley. And here was a good chance that they were sponsoring a second mad person to the American nation, namely Whittaker Chambers. The chairman said, in effect, "I don't want it." Since he was the chairman, he was in position to do this. He said, "I don't want it, you take it," referring to the next most senior Republican. The next most senior Republican said, "I don't want it, you take it," referring to the next. "I don't want it, you take it," and so on down the line until we got to the last, who said, in effect, "I don't want it, you . . ." but there was nobody there because he was the junior member. And that is how Richard Nixon came to be chairman of that subcommittee. He got the job because there was no one to whom he could buck it. The buck stopped there because of his lack of seniority.

Well, there was where? Where were they going to have the confrontation? And no government building was readily available, so what they decided to do was take a suite in a hotel and have the hearings in the hotel suite. For those of you with a limitless appetite for this stuff, you can't see the suite or the hotel anymore, but you can see the place when you next go to New York City, if you stand at the corner 42nd Street and Lexington Avenue, you will see on one of the intersections—it's the northwest intersection—the Grand Hyatt Hotel. Those of you of an age to remember will recall that the Grand Hyatt Hotel used to be the Commodore Hotel and some 10 years ago or whenever it was, it was stripped down to the steel structure and the new hotel was built over that preexisting steel structure. That was the Commodore Hotel, which was the site of the meeting. The meeting that is the confrontational meeting, took place in room 1400. And, ladies and gentlemen, if I can have your attention over there, stage left, your right, let me explain what you're looking at. That is a rough representation of the living room in that hotel suite. There was a sofa and that's represented by the two chairs next to each other, looking out at you. In front of the sofa was a coffee table and at the head of the coffee table and at the foot of the coffee table were the two chairs more or less facing each other. Now, ladies and gentlemen, I have to tell you that even my powers of eloquence fail at the prospect of conveying to you the bizarre and even incredible nature of what took place when that subcommittee hearing occurred finally in Suite 400 of the Commodore Hotel. I am, therefore, not going to try to do it. I'm not going to undertake an enterprise doomed to failure.

I have called upon some of my friends to help me and they're going to help me in this sense. I'm going to ask them to come up and they will take a place consistent with the place occupied by the actual person when the subcommittee hearings occurred. And they will read to you from the stenographic transcript. Please understand that none of this is invented, nothing has been left out. We've corrected a couple of grammatical errors but, beyond that, no changes have been made. And, remember, this is exactly and absolutely and actually how it occurred. Now, who will be playing the various parts? And we understand that their real personalities have nothing to do with the assumed personalities that they will have for the next 10 or 15 minutes. Playing Whittaker Chambers we've got Jamie Palmquist at that end of the coffee table. Playing his antagonist, if you will, playing Alger Hiss will be James Trost. Playing the congressman presiding over the hearings, the junior Republican from Southern California, Richard Nixon, we've got Steven Bujasi, Steve. And Steve will be seated on the sofa, as was the real Congressman Nixon. Now, in order to keep production costs to a minimum, ladies and gentlemen, we have taken all of the other characters and melded them into one. And you might call this character miscellaneous or everybody else or any such title that you please and miscellaneous or anybody else will be read for us or played for us by Sarah Polskey. And now, ladies and gentlemen, when our technical people are finished, we'll just take it from the top, as they say in show biz.

RICHARD NIXON: Mr. Hiss, the man sitting here is Mr. Whittaker Chambers. I ask you now if you have ever known that man before?

ALGER HISS: Will you ask him to say something? Can I ask him something?

RICHARD NIXON: Yes. Mr. Chambers, will you tell us your name and your business?

WHITTAKER CHAMBERS: My name is Whittaker Chambers.

ALGER HISS: Would you mind opening your mouth wider?

WHITTAKER CHAMBERS: My name is Whittaker Chambers.

ALGER HISS: I said, would you open your mouth? You know what I'm referring to, Mr. Nixon, will you go on talking.

WHITTAKER CHAMBERS: I am Senior Editor of *Time magazine*.

ALGER HISS: May I ask whether his voice, when he testified before, was comparable to this?

RICHARD NIXON: His voice?

ALGER HISS: Or did he talk a little more in a lower key?

MISCELLANEOUS CHARACTER: I would say it is about the same now as we have heard.

ALGER HISS: Would you ask him to talk a little more?

RICHARD NIXON: Read something, Mr. Chambers.

WHITTAKER CHAMBERS: I would like to read from . . .

ALGER HISS: I think he is George Crosley, but I would like to hear him talk a little longer. Are you George Crosley?

WHITTAKER CHAMBERS: Not to my knowledge.

RICHARD NIXON: You are Alger Hiss, I believe.

ALGER HISS: I certainly am. That was my recollection.

WHITTAKER CHAMBERS: I quote, "Since June . . ."

RICHARD NIXON: Just a moment. Since some repartee goes on between these two people, I think Mr. Chambers should be sworn.

ALGER HISS: That is a good idea.

MISCELLANEOUS CHARACTER: You do solemnly swear, sir, that the testimony that you shall give to this committee will be the truth, the whole truth, and nothing but the truth, so help you God?

WHITTAKER CHAMBERS: I do.

RICHARD NIXON: Mr. Hiss, may I say something? I suggested that he be sworn and when I say something like that, I want no interruption from you.

ALGER HISS: Mr. Nixon, I think there is no occasion for you to use that tone of voice with me and I hope the record will show what I have just said.

RICHARD NIXON: The record shows everything that is being said here today.

MISCELLANEOUS CHARACTER: You were going to read . . .

WHITTAKER CHAMBERS: I am reading from *Newsweek* magazine. Tobin for labor. Since June, Harry S. Truman had been peddling the labor secretaryship left vacated by Louis B. Schellenbach's staff in hope of gaining the maximum political advantage from the appointments.

ALGER HISS: May I interrupt?

MISCELLANEOUS CHARACTER: Yes.

ALGER HISS: The voice sounds a little less resonant than the voice that I recall of the man I knew as George Crosley. The teeth look to me as though either they have been improved upon or that there has been considerable dental work done since I knew George Crosley, which was some years ago. I believe I am not prepared without further checking to take an absolute oath that he must be George Crosley.

RICHARD NIXON: May I ask a question, Mr. Chambers?

ALGER HISS: I would like to ask Mr. Chambers, if I may . . .

RICHARD NIXON: I will ask the questions at this time. Mr. Chambers, have you had any dental work since 1934 of substantial nature?

WHITTAKER CHAMBERS: Yes, I have.

RICHARD NIXON: What type of dental work?

WHITTAKER CHAMBERS: I have had some extractions and a plate.

RICHARD NIXON: Have you had any dental work done in the front of your teeth?

WHITTAKER CHAMBERS: Yes.

RICHARD NIXON: And what was the nature of that work?

WHITTAKER CHAMBERS: That is a plate in place of some of the upper dentures.

RICHARD NIXON: I see.

ALGER HISS: Could you ask him the name of the dentist that performed these things? Is that appropriate?

RICHARD NIXON: Yes. What is the name?

WHITTAKER CHAMBERS: Dr. Hitchcock of Westminster, Maryland.

ALGER HISS: That testimony of Mr. Chambers, if it can be believed, would tend to substantiate my feeling that he represented himself to me in 1934 or 1935 or thereabouts as George Crosley, a freelance writer of articles for magazines. I would like to find out from Dr. Hitchcock if what he has just said is true because I am relying partly . . . one of my main recollections of Crosley was the poor condition of his teeth.

RICHARD NIXON: Can you describe the condition of your teeth in 1934?

WHITTAKER CHAMBERS: Yes. They were in very bad shape.

RICHARD NIXON: The front teeth were?

WHITTAKER CHAMBERS: Yes, I think so.

ALGER HISS: Mr. Chairman . . .

RICHARD NIXON: Excuse me. Before we leave the teeth, Mr. Hiss, do you feel that you would have to have the dentist tell you what he did to the teeth before you can tell us anything about this man.

ALGER HISS: I would like a few more questions asked. I didn't intend to say anything about this because I feel very strongly that he is Crosley, but he looks very different in girth and in other appearances—hair, forehead, and so on. Particularly the jowls. Did you ever go under the name of George Crosley?

WHITTAKER CHAMBERS: Not to my knowledge.

ALGER HISS: Did you ever sublet an apartment on 29th Street from me?

WHITTAKER CHAMBERS: No, I did not.

ALGER HISS: You did not?

WHITTAKER CHAMBERS: No.

ALGER HISS: Did you ever spend any time with your wife and child in an apartment on 29th Street in Washington when I was not there because I and my family were living on P Street?

WHITTAKER CHAMBERS: I most certainly did.

ALGER HISS: You did or did not?

WHITTAKER CHAMBERS: I did.

ALGER HISS: Would you tell me how you reconcile your negative answers with your affirmative answer?

WHITTAKER CHAMBERS: Very easily, Alger. I was a Communist and you were a Communist.

ALGER HISS: Would you be responsive and continue with your answer?

WHITTAKER CHAMBERS: I do not think it is needed.

ALGER HISS: Then that is the answer?

RICHARD NIXON: I will help you with the answer, Mr. Hiss. The question, Mr. Chambers, is, as I understand it, that Mr. Hiss cannot understand how you would deny that you were George Crosley and, yet, admit that you spent time in his apartment. Now, would you explain the circumstances. I don't want to quit that until Mr. Hiss agrees that that is one of his questions.

ALGER HISS: You have the privilege of asking any questions you want. I think that is an accurate phrasing.

RICHARD NIXON: Go ahead.

WHITTAKER CHAMBERS: As I have testified before, I came to Washington as a Communist functionary, a functionary of the American Communist party. I was connected with the Underground group, of which Mr. Hiss was a member. Mr. Hiss and I became friends. To the best of my knowledge, Mr. Hiss himself suggested that I go there and I accepted gratefully.

ALGER HISS: Mr. Chairman . . .

RICHARD NIXON: Just a moment. How long did you stay there?

WHITTAKER CHAMBERS: My recollection was about three weeks. It may have been longer. I brought no furniture, I might add.

ALGER HISS: Mr. Chairman, I don't need to ask Mr. Whittaker Chambers any more questions. I am now perfectly prepared to identify this man as George Crosley.

RICHARD NIXON: Would you spell that name?

ALGER HISS: C-r-o-s-l-e-y.

RICHARD NIXON: You're sure? One "s"?

ALGER HISS: That is my recollection. I have a rather good visual memory and my recollection of his spelling of his name is C-r-o-s-l-e-y. I don't think that would change as much as his appearance.

MISCELLANEOUS CHARACTER: You will identify him positively now?

ALGER HISS: I will on the basis of what he has just said positively identify him without further questioning as George Crosley.

That testimony, of course, was given in private in the hotel suite. Some 10 days later on August 25, Hiss and Chambers testified in public. Hiss now identified Chambers as George Crosley, the writer he had met in 1933 or 1934 and Chambers identified Hiss as a member of the Communist Underground in Washington and that, ladies and gentlemen, would have been that—one of the two obviously a liar, but no corroboration of either and, thus, no possible conviction for perjury—when on August 27, just two days after the public testimony, Chambers appeared on a radio program called *Meet The Press*. The first question asked was, "Are you willing to say now, when your statements are not privileged, that Alger Hiss is or ever was a Communist?" And Chambers replied, "Alger Hiss was a Communist and he may be one now." And one month later to the day, Alger Hiss sued Whittaker Chambers for libel.

Now, as is customary in civil actions, Hiss's attorney in the libel suit took Chambers's deposition and on the possibility that there are some members of the audience and some people who may look at this tape in the future who are not lawyers or at least who do not engage in litigation practice, let me pause for just a moment to tell you briefly what a deposition is. It is a session conducted, usually in the conference room of a lawyer's office. There is no judge, no jury, the public is not present. The purpose of the deposition is to permit each side to ask the other side whatever questions it wishes to the end that each side become knowledgeable about the case, that each side knows all the information that is available to the other side about the issues presented in this case so that each side is adequately prepared and when tried to a jury, the case unfolds smoothly and completely and in accordance with modern conceptions of procedure and the arts of the courtroom and matters of that kind. Well, on November 5, 1948, ladies and gentlemen, a session took place at the office of Alger Hiss's lawyer in Baltimore and one of the questions asked at that session was as follows. "Mr. Chambers, did you ever obtain documents from Alger Hiss for transmittal to the Communist party?" And once again, let me drop a kind of extemporized footnote here to explain what I have no doubt was going on. You see, at this point or to this point in the proceedings, whatever the extraordinary nature of the events to which Whittaker Chambers had been testifying, he had said nothing to indicate that espionage had been committed. He had talked about an underground group, he had talked about advancing Communist causes and the like, but he had said nothing about stealing information or otherwise obtaining documents from the federal government for transmittal to the Soviet Union. In a word, he had said nothing about espionage. Since he had said nothing about it, I assume that Hiss's lawyer, a man named Marbury, by the way, William Marbury, who is still alive and somewhat active in practice in Baltimore—I assume that Mr. Marbury wanted to be sure that when the libel case finally was tried, there would be no suggestion of espionage. In short, there had been no suggestion of espionage when Chambers testified before HUAC and there was going to be no suggestion of espionage when Chambers testified before the jury that would ultimately decide the libel case. A lawyer sometimes called this closing doors or freezing the testimony so that, even though it may not be so good for you, that's it and it's not going to get any worse and it's not going to change between now and the time of trial.

So, again, what was the question? "Mr. Chambers, did you ever receive from Alger Hiss documents or other governmental information for transmittal to the Communist party?" And Chambers's response was a forthright, "No," perfectly consistent with the testimony he had given at HUAC. No, there was no espionage. Well, that was on November 5.

At the end of the day the deposition had not been completed. It was necessary to continue it on another day and the date that was selected, simply having in mind the lawyers' other commitments and so forth, was November 16. Well, had we been in that lawyer's conference room on November 16, we would have seen Mr. Marbury, Hiss's lawyer, we would have seen Mr. Cleveland, that's Chambers's lawyer, we would have seen Mrs. Chambers, but we would not have seen Mr. Chambers. Instead, Chambers's lawyer said words to this effect. "Chambers got tied up. He can't be here today. But, Mr. Marbury, you mentioned to me that you had some questions that you wanted to put to Mrs. Chambers, Esther Chambers, Chambers's wife. Here she is. Why don't we use the day putting questions to her, take her deposition, and Chambers will be here tomorrow." Well, that was agreeable to Mr. Marbury and so that's what was done. The questions that were put to Mrs. Chambers on that day were of no great consequence. At the end of the day, Mrs. Chambers's deposition was concluded and on the next day, there was Whittaker Chambers, ready to continue his deposition. Now, what had happened in that intervening time and, more specifically, why did Chambers not appear to continue his deposition on the date that originally had been set, November 16th? Well, the best explanation that's available to us is the explanation that Chambers himself gave at the trial. At the trial of the criminal case, a good deal in the future, Chambers testified as to what it was that occupied him and that brought it about that he needed that extra day. Let me give you the story as Chambers told it. These are Chambers's words, elicited by questions from the lawyers. I am leaving out the questions, but they really don't add anything, they amount to "and what happened next" and "what did you do then" and the like. So here is Whittaker Chambers telling us what he did over that intervening time. Chambers said:

"I went to New York and I went to Brooklyn, where I saw Nathan Levine, my wife's nephew, to get an envelope in which as I recalled it, were some handwritten specimens from Mr. Hiss. I remembered having given Levine the envelope. I remembered that there were some typewritten notes. I believe I gave Levine that envelope in May or June 1938.

We went to Levine's apartment on Sterling Place, then we walked over to his mother's house. We went upstairs. Levine stood on the bathtub in an old back bathroom. He reached into an old, unused dumbwaiter shaft and brought out this envelope that I had given him in 1938. It was very dusty. I took the envelope into the kitchen at the end of the hall and opened it. Levine came in for a moment to get a broom or a dustpan or something to clean up the mess we were making. He came back in five or so minutes, I'm not quite sure. I, meanwhile, opened the envelope and in the envelope I found three or four handwritten notes in Mr. Hiss's handwriting and some 45 pages of typed documents which Mrs. Hiss typed and three cans of film, 35mm film."

Most of us are familiar with how those cameras work. The film ends up in a little can and he says that in the envelope he found three cans of that 35mm film, all of it, by the way, exposed. This is Chambers speaking again. He said:

"I did not appear the following day to continue my deposition. I told my lawyer, Mr. Cleveland, that I would like another day to consider the question of whether I should introduce these documents into the pretrial examination, into the deposition. Mr. Cleveland therefore arranged with Mr. Marbury, Hiss's lawyer, for my wife to be deposed on the day when I would otherwise have been deposed. On November 17 I continued my deposition and gave my lawyer the notes in Hiss's handwriting and the documents typed by Mrs. Hiss."

Now, observe that what Chambers gave his lawyer was not the complete contents of that envelope. What Chambers gave his lawyer was roughly two-thirds of the content of that envelope. You had the handwritten notes, notes apparently in Hiss's handwriting, you had these documents, according to Chambers, documents typed by Mrs. Hiss. But, for whatever reason, Chambers did not give the 35mm film to his own lawyer. Now, what happened at that deposition on November 17 is now before us insofar as we need it to understand the events of the trial of Alger Hiss. But I do not have the strength to resist the temptation, ladies and gentlemen, to tell you in somewhat greater detail what occurred. Because, after all, as I mentioned at the outset, I think of myself as a trial lawyer. I know that a good many of you in the room or otherwise watching this tape are trial lawyers. We've all had this experience and you can't help but experience a kind of sympathy for a fellow lawyer going through it yet again. In this instance, the fellow lawyer is Mr. Marbury, Hiss's lawyer, and what he was going through was, I am sure, something as follows.

They resume on November 17. Here is Whittaker Chambers and here is Mr. Marbury. And Mr. Marbury is a very proper, dignified gentlemen, and after assembling his vest and the other things that go into the making of a lawyer's uniform, Mr. Marbury said, "Are you ready to proceed, Mr. Chambers?" And Chambers replied, "Well, yes, I am, Mr. Marbury. But before doing so, can we return to something that came up the other day?" And at that point, I tell you, those of you who are not lawyers or not trial lawyers, your heart stops. You say to yourself, though, control, at all times, control. And so with aplomb, with savoir faire, with a polish that would do credit to the court of Louis XIV, Mr. Marbury said, "Well, of course we can return to what we discussed the other day. What is it you wish to return to?" And Chambers said, "Well, do you remember you asked me the question did I ever receive documents or other information from Alger Hiss for transmittal to the Soviet Union? Do you remember you asked me that question?" And at that point I am sure that Mr. Marbury stopped breathing. But, still, you must at all costs continue. He said, "Yes, yes, I remember." And Chambers said, "Well, remember the answer I gave you? The answer was no, I never received such documents." "Yes," said Mr. Marbury, "I remember that answer." "Well," said Mr. Chambers, "I want to change my answer." "What do you want to change your answer to?" And his reply was, "I want to change my answer to yes. I did receive documents and other information from Alger Hiss for transmittal to the Soviet Union." Translating that into plain English, what Chambers was now saying for the first time in this series of events was that there had been espionage. This was not simply a mere set of young lawyers engaged in some kind of covert study group activity, this was spy stuff. This was espionage and Chambers was saying, yes, it had happened.

I can't begin to describe what Mr. Marbury must have felt at that moment, but every trial lawyer has experienced moments of that kind. Well, you take a deep breath and you say, "Do you have any proof of that?" And he said, "Yes, I do, I have written corroboration of it," referring to the handwritten notes and the typed documents that he had given to his own lawyer, Mr. Cleveland. And Marbury said, "Well, what is the corroboration?" And Chambers said, "Well, there are these handwritten notes in the typed documents." "Where are they?" said Mr. Marbury. "I gave them to Mr. Cleveland." And Marbury turned to Mr. Cleveland and said, "Do you have them?" "Yes." "Where do you have them?" "Right here," pointing to his briefcase, leaning against the leg of the table. "May I have them?" said Mr. Marbury. "Of course," and out they came on to the table. Two-thirds of the contents of that envelope that Chambers had left with his wife's relative, Nathan Levine—the handwritten notes and the typed documents. We'll be hearing more about those documents, so let's pause for a moment and ask ourselves, what about the film? Why wasn't the film produced? Well, of course, the simple answer to that simple question is that the film wasn't produced at the deposition simply because Chambers had not given the film to his lawyer. If he had given the film to the lawyer, the lawyer would have produced it. But the lawyer had no way of knowing that the film existed because Chambers had said nothing of it. Why didn't Chambers give the film to his lawyer? There I have no answer for you. And Chambers published an autobiography some years later. He talked about this episode, but he never came forward with what I would call a satisfactory explanation of why he never gave the film to his lawyer.

In any event, there now occurred an episode too exquisite to omit. Having said which, I must ask you please to understand that I cannot prove, in the lawyer's sense, anything that I will be explaining to you for the next 5 or 10 minutes at most. I can put it together, I can read between the lines, I can do my best to be a kind of historical Sherlock Holmes, piecing the evidence together as best we can, but by way of citation, by way of textual authority, no, I cannot prove it. But something akin to the following seems to have taken place.

After the public testimony at which each man, in effect, accused the other of being a liar, but since there was no corroboration there could be no successful prosecution for perjury, Richard Nixon went into one of those depressions of his. He decided that his political career was over, that HUAC had been made to look a fool and that he, in this instance, stood for HUAC. And if the nation was laughing at the Un-American Activities Committee, they were, in fact, laughing at Richard Nixon, who had provided the platform upon which Whittaker Chambers could sit or stand when he made these accusations about Alger Hiss. And Mrs. Nixon, anxious to pull her husband out of this blue funk, apparently said to him, "Let's take a vacation." And he said, "I'm not cut out for vacations." And she said, "Yes, let's go on vacation," and she finally got him to agree to go on vacation. And the vacation that they agreed to go on was, believe it or not, a Caribbean cruise. And you'll forgive the unduly personal note. It's wonderful to think of the Love Boat down there on the Caribbean and who is it, the heart and soul of social activities on the Love Boat, the leader of the conga line, the man you go to when you need jokes to be told, when you need the tone of the occasion to be lightened—there he is, Richard Nixon, wondering what was going to happen to him now that his career had been cut short before it ever had a chance to get started. Well, back in Washington, it was assumed that Nixon's career was indeed over and that HUAC had been caught a second time and it was Nixon who was going to take the brunt of it. Everybody understood that there could be no prosecution for anything because of the lack of corroboration. And then occurred the session at the deposition in Mr. Marbury's office, when the two-thirds of the contents of that envelope were produced. Not the photographs, remember, but rather the handwritten notes and the typed documents. The legal grapevine is always very much alive and before too many hours had gone by, even though that deposition session was closed to the public, the word was all over the street in Washington and Baltimore and New York that corroboration had finally been produced. It had been produced at that deposition session in Mr. Marbury's office in Baltimore.

Now, Nixon didn't know this. He was on the cruise ship. The committee was more or less nonfunctional except for Stripling, the administrative head of the committee, who was keeping things together as best he could in the old House office building. A man named Bert Andrews, who was then the head of the New York Bureau of the New York *Herald Tribune,* a newspaper that is no longer being published, heard on the grapevine about the production of these documents at the deposition in Washington and he took a walk one afternoon to HUAC's offices in the House office building and who was there but Stripling. And he said to Stripling, "Have you heard?" And Stripling said, "No, heard what?" "There's been a deposition session," said Andrews, "and at the deposition session, they have produced corroboration. Documents. I hear," said Andrews, "some of them are in Hiss's handwriting. Documents to suggest that there's all kinds of communication going on back and forth between Hiss and Chambers. Heaven only knows what they add up to, but there is now something upon which the committee can proceed, something to suggest that this is not some psychotic's dream, that there's some truth and reality to the allegations that Whittaker Chambers has been making about Alger Hiss." "Oh, my God," said Stripling, "we'd better tell the boss." And the boss in this instance was Richard Nixon because he was in charge of that subcommittee.

Well, Andrews agreed that you'd really better tell the boss and so they sent a radiogram to the Love Boat and what they said in the radiogram, because they didn't want to get into all kinds of detail, was simply to the effect of, "Amazing revelations at deposition in libel case. Suggest strongest you return to Washington at once." Well, Nixon being the man that we've come to know, this was mother's milk to him. It was a chance to do something. It was a chance to break out of this depressive pattern and somehow restore himself to overcome this first of the so many crises that ultimately he would overcome. And so he wired back that, yes, he would return, but the question was how do you return when you're in the middle of the Caribbean on a cruise ship? And what they did, as I gather from the newspapers of the time, was send a destroyer to meet the cruise ship and where they met was the open ocean. And the cruise ship was floating along and the destroyer pulled up alongside of it and what they did was sling a breeches buoy. The mariners in the room will know what that is. I really am not quite sure what it is, but it's some arrangement for getting someone from one ship to another. They slung the breeches buoy from the destroyer to the cruise ship and they put Nixon in the seat and they hauled him over from the Love Boat to the destroyer. And I have not been able to find it, but somewhere, somewhere, somewhere, there must be a photograph of Richard Nixon being hauled over from the Love Boat to the destroyer. Just has to be.

They get him on to the destroyer, they take him to Miami or whatever the nearest big city was, they put him on a plane, and they take him back to Washington on a direct line from the airport to HUAC's offices. He comes huffing and puffing into the office and he says to Stripling, "What's going on? Why did you get me back in such emergency circumstances?" And Stripling now tells Nixon what has happened, at least according to the grapevine. And Nixon, who, after all, is no fool and is a lawyer and understands the significance of these things . . . Nixon says, "Oh my God, that's right, there is now corroboration and who knows what else? But now wait a minute. If they produced the handwritten notes and the typewritten documents down in Baltimore, maybe there's something else. And, in any event, why didn't we get it? Why was it for the deposition session that we had to wait before these documents could be produced? Stripling, didn't you ever serve that guy," referring to Whittaker Chambers. "Didn't you ever serve him with a subpoena duces tecum?" That's the piece of paper that says produce the documents upon pain of being held in contempt of court. "Stripling, didn't you ever serve him with a subpoena duces tecum?" And, again, I can't demonstrate it by way of authority or documentation, but I'm sure it happened. I'm sure that Nixon looked at Stripling and said, "Subpoena? I thought you had served him with a subpoena." And Stripling must have looked right back at him and said, "No, I thought you served him with a subpoena." And they looked at each other and they agreed that there was no point in mutual recriminations, the thing had been done. But let's serve him with a subpoena now because, who knows, he may have more. Little did they know that he had more and what he had were the photographs that were in the envelope and which, for reasons to this day unexplained, he had not turned over to his lawyer.

And so a subpoena was prepared and what next happens is best told from the viewpoint of Whittaker Chambers. And here is that viewpoint as articulated from the witness stand in the course of Chambers's testimony at the trial. Chambers said, and once again I'm simply omitting the lawyer's connecting questions. He said:

"The film," (and, by the film, I mean these are photographs of State Department documents, I assume that you've realized by now, but we'll be talking about them in somewhat greater detail later on). "The film," said Chambers, "I kept in my house for a few days. I had to go to Washington to testify before a Loyalty Board in the State Department, a matter that has nothing to do with this case. I had to go to Washington to testify and that morning, as I was about to leave the house, actually I had my overcoat already on, the telephone rang and it was Mr. Stripling of HUAC. And Stripling said when I got finished with my business, would I please step into his office? I did so and as I did so, he served me with the subpoena duces tecum ordering me to produce to the committee all materials of any kind in my possession connected with various people among whom was Alger Hiss." (And, of course, we know that the film was there.)

Chambers continues, "When I finished in the State Department that day—this is the matter unrelated to this case—I, Chambers, was accompanied home by the two investigators from HUAC, Mr. Wheeler and Mr. Apel. At the farm . . ." (Chambers lived in a little suburb of Baltimore called Westminster, Maryland. His house was surrounded by five acres used primarily for gardening purposes and it was Chambers's habit to call this "the farm." So that's the reference to the farm.)

"At the farm," says Chambers, "I took the investigators into the kitchen and I went out into the backyard to get the film. Before I had gone to Washington that day, I had put the film inside a pumpkin."

And there's always that reaction because people who may know nothing at all about the Alger Hiss case somehow connect it with a pumpkin and with Pumpkin Papers. This case goes by the name of the Pumpkin Papers. And, as you see, they really were pumpkin films, but they were in a pumpkin, there's no doubt about that.

And said Chambers, "I simply went to the pumpkin and I reached into the one into which I had put the film that morning and I took out the film and I wiped it off because it was a little bit sticky, and I gave it to the committee investigators and they took the film back to Washington and, at least for those purposes, that was the last I knew about it."

Well, what was Hiss's response to the production of these films, which, as I've said, are simply photographs of State Department documents? We'll be going into them in somewhat greater detail at a later point and I think in the long run it will be more efficient if we wait until later. For present purposes why don't we just leave it that what Hiss said to the FBI when they came around and asked for his reaction to Chambers's production of these papers was the following. This is Hiss talking to us through the FBI. He says:

"I've learned from talking with Mr. Marbury, my lawyer, and from reading the depositions that Mr. Chambers claims these documents and others like them were obtained by me from the State Department, that I took them to my home where typewritten copies of the larger documents were made on a typewriter in my home by either my wife or me. Chambers claimed that I then returned the documents to State Department files. The FBI agents have told me that Mr. Chambers claims that on some occasions I turned over the actual State Department documents to him, upon which he would have photographic copies made in a manner unknown to me and then would return the originals to me for replacement in the files of the State Department. I deny that any of the above claims with Mr. Chambers is true. I also deny that I ever gave the originals of these documents to Mr. Chambers at any time for any purpose whatsoever."

Well, now, ladies and gentlemen, though these documents may have done something and perhaps even have gone far, to permit a claim of espionage to be advanced in a rational and lawyer-like way, you must understand that the statute of limitations had long since run on espionage. It was no longer any legal possibility of a prosecution for espionage, but maybe there were other possibilities and the government was anxious to pursue those other possibilities.

On December 15, 1948, Hiss was called before a grand jury sitting in the United States Courthouse in Lower Manhattan, Foley Square—that's the Southern District of New York. And he was simply asked whether he had ever given government documents to Chambers. And he replied, "No." He was then asked, "Have you ever seen Chambers since the winter 1936?" And, again, Hiss's reply was, "No." And that afternoon the grand jury handed up an indictment charging Alger Hiss with two counts of perjury. Each of his denials, the grand jury alleged, was false.

Now, ladies and gentlemen, the rest of our time together will be spent talking about the trial, telling the story of the trial, analyzing the evidence at the trial, and trying to come up with an answer to the question with which we started, you recall, does the evidence support or justify the jury's verdict of guilt?

The case of Alger Hiss went to trial on May 31, 1949, in the United States District Court for the Southern District of New York before Judge Samuel H. Kaufman and a jury. As I've mentioned a couple of times, Thomas F. Murphy was the prosecutor. He represented the government. And representing the defense was Lloyd Paul Stryker. The trial lasted until July 8, 1949, when the jury reported itself deadlocked and was discharged. It turns out, we know from what the jurors told the newspaper reporters afterwards, that the final vote had been eight to four in favor of conviction. Now, since it was the second trial that produced the guilty verdict, it is the second trial that should engage the bulk of our attentions and energies. Still, there are a couple of aspects of the first trial that I should talk about if only because they did not repeat themselves at the second trial. They were unique to the first trial and so, unless we talk about them in connection with the first trial, we will never talk about them.

First, Judge Samuel Kaufman. I mention it only lest there be any misunderstandings. There is a federal judge, Irving Kaufman, who is very well known, who served as a chief judge of the Court of Appeals for the Second Circuit, as well as a district judge himself, many years before that. This is a different Judge Kaufman, there is no relation between them. The Judge Samuel Kaufman, who presided over the first Alger Hiss case has been dead for many years now and I speak as a kind of ward of the Southern District of New York, as a lawyer who served as an assistant U.S. attorney in that courthouse and regards himself as one who grew up as a lawyer in that ambiance with those judges and with those lawyers. Let me report that in the corridors of the Southern District of New York it is commonly said that Judge Kaufman was heavily predisposed in favor of the defense. Whether that is true or not I have no idea. I simply pass it on to you as what the gossip is.

The defense was handled by Lloyd Paul Stryker. Those of you of a certain age will, of course, recognize Stryker's name. Those of you who are students of trial advocacy in the United States will also recognize his name. Lloyd Paul Stryker was regarded as the preeminent criminal lawyer of his generation. There was virtually no major criminal case in the United States that was not offered to Stryker in the days of his prime. Among many extraordinary things about the man is the fact that, in addition to running a phenomenally successful and, of course, extremely demanding law practice as a criminal defense lawyer, Stryker was a very able writer. His work on the art of advocacy has, I think, never been surpassed and rarely been equaled. As a matter of fact, if anyone wished to undertake a course of reading on the art of advocacy, one could do much worse than recommend that he or she start with Stryker's book.

If one is interested in the traditions of the English Trial Bar, one will, of course, know about and want to know even more about Thomas Erskine, the greatest of all barristers. The standard biography of Thomas

Erskine is by Lloyd Paul Stryker. Where he got the time to do it, heaven only knows. Stryker, because he was a mature man in full possession of the techniques of the courtroom, was able to do things that those of us less spectacularly gifted cannot do and others of us will not be able to do for some time simply because the patina of the years must be acquired. With some trepidation, because I do not wish to be accused of misleading any young lawyer, one of the things that Stryker was able to do exquisitely and which has to be handled with a great deal of caution because it can so easily go wrong—one of the things that Stryker can do is defend a criminal case by turning it into comedy. Now, every criminal lawyer knows that once a jury starts to laugh, chances are there will not be a conviction. Now, you may not get an acquittal, but you're probably going to get a hung jury because a laughing jury is not a convicting jury. They just can't bring themselves to convict. It is, however, very difficult to get a jury to laugh. Juries understand that trials are serious business indeed and that the affairs of the courtroom are not trifling affairs. And so you have to be as good as Stryker was and as laden with years as Stryker was and as ingratiating as Stryker was to be able to handle this kind of defense. Now, we do not have the time to go into the way in which Stryker turned the first trial into comedy. I ask you simply to accept it from me as one who has read and reread and re-reread the transcript of the first trial that that is precisely what he did. And it may well be the only thing that could have been done against Thomas Murphy, the prosecutor. I remind you that I tried several cases before Judge Murphy when he was a judge years later, and I should tell you, and it will be quite clear in what I say, that I am just filled with admiration for Judge Murphy. He is one of the very best judges I have ever been before. If I had to pick one judge before whom I could try a case, it would be Judge Murphy, and every lawyer I know who came out of that courthouse at about that time would agree with me that Judge Murphy was really the best of a very able group of judges. As an opponent in the courtroom, Judge Murphy must have been formidable in the extreme and I speak there just as softly as I know how. For those of you who have never seen Judge Murphy, let me describe him to you. And, ladies and gentlemen, I am exaggerating not by one-eighth of an inch. Judge Murphy, who, by the way, is with us still—he lives in retirement in Arizona where occasionally he tries a case and where lawyers regard him the way I've told you I regard him—Judge Murphy is approximately 6'4" tall. He weighs at least 300 pounds and, as the saying goes, it's all whip cord and leather. In addition, Judge Murphy has all of his hair, which is a wonderful gift for nature to give you. Judge Murphy has all of his hair and he wears it in "Gay 90s" bartender style. That is to say, in the morning, he combs it straight forward, then parts it in the middle and at 90 degrees out to the right and left. It makes for a certain *je ne sais quoi*. But you don't run into that kind of appearance very often. Now, to match the "Gay 90s" bartender hairdo, there is Judge Murphy's mustache. Judge Murphy wears a "Gay 90s" bartender mustache and it goes out at least 18 inches or so it seems to the spectator, at least 18 inches on either side and turns in a wonderful curlicue. And from underneath that magnificent mustache, there comes a voice, the voice of Judge Murphy, a voice so low that were it two tones lower, only dogs could hear him. Judge Murphy is a past master of the law of evidence and the law of procedure. There is nothing that can happen in a courtroom that he hasn't seen before and that he is not fully the master of. He is very widely read in the English and the French classics and has a lightning sense of humor, which he pretty much keeps to himself on the bench, but if ever it's necessary, there it is. I repeat, he would be a formidable antagonist indeed. And if ever a lawyer were equipped to deal with Judge Murphy, it was Lloyd Paul Stryker, who dealt with him by turning the entire case into an occasion for comedy. He had that jury laughing and, sure enough, the result, as we know, is a hung jury and ultimately not an acquittal, but a discharge of the jury on the grounds of an inability to agree upon a verdict in the face of evidence . . . well, you'll judge for yourself what the evidence was because we'll begin to hear about it in just a moment.

It is the practice in the Southern District of New York that when a case needs to be retried because of a reversal on appeal or, as in this instance, because of a jury disagreement, it is assigned to a different judge. That is simply custom. It's unwritten local law in the Southern District of New York. Pursuant to that custom, the Hiss case was reassigned for trial to Judge Henry W. Goddard, who was then the senior judge in point of service in the Southern District of New York. With Judge Goddard presiding, the case began its retrial on November 17, 1949. Once again, the government was represented by Thomas Murphy. But now the defense was headed not by Lloyd Paul Stryker, but by a distinguished Boston lawyer, a Harvard Law School classmate of Alger Hiss's named Claude Cross. Mr. Cross, as I understand it, was a senior litigation partner and, as a matter of fact, was in charge of the litigation department at one of the major Boston law firms and was as able as big firm litigators get. But to be that able is not to say that you are equipped to handle the likes of Thomas Murphy. Mr. Cross, as I understand it, is no longer with us; he died some years ago. But were he here, I have no doubt that he would be the first to associate himself with the statement I now make, that Mr. Cross was simply overmatched. He was unable to cope with Murphy because virtually every lawyer in the United States would have been unable to cope with Murphy.

Just to give you some idea, the first book written about the Alger Hiss case was by Alistair Cooke, whom we all know as the host of *Masterpiece Theatre*. Cooke was then a young journalist covering American affairs for the *Manchester Guardian,* a very well-respected English paper. Cooke turned his dispatches back to the *Guardian* into a book-length account of both trials. He called the book *Generation on Trial,* and in many ways it is, to this very day, the single best book ever written about the Hiss cases. At one point Cooke describes sitting in the rows reserved for journalists watching Murphy cross-examine a witness. Now, Murphy had his back to the audience and so sitting in the journalists' reserved section, Cooke could see only Murphy's back. And as he looked at Murphy's back, according to Cooke in the book, Cooke was able to say to himself only, "Heavens, that man's tailor must measure out the cloth for his suits not by the yard, but by the acre." Well, that gives you some idea of what you're dealing with.

From here on in we're talking only about the second trial. Both sides, ladies and gentlemen, seemed to me to have adopted the same theory of the trial and the theory of the trial was that nothing was to be held back. Each side wanted to appear to that jury as presenting every person who could be found, whose life had touched the life of either Whittaker Chambers or Alger Hiss, no matter how tangentially. Now this may be a difficult case to decide. I don't think it's a difficult case to understand and, in any event, you begin with a two-count perjury indictment. That's all you have. The indictment is a half a page of typewriting. And in this two-count perjury case, do you know how many witnesses were called in total by both sides? One hundred and twelve witnesses. Which leads me to say that this case was probably overtried. One hundred and twelve is a lot for a two-count conspiracy case, especially when you have it in mind that the story, whether you take the prosecution's side of it or the defense's side of it is essentially simple. And the verdict, no matter how you dress it up, really turns upon one thing—the jury's assessment of the credibility of the two protagonists, Chambers and Hiss. Yes, among those 112 witnesses there were lots of so-called corroborating witnesses, but as we shall see, the corroborating witnesses, in fact, ended up corroborating virtually nothing, though the documentation was a different story entirely.

I say that the story, whichever side you accept, the government or the defense, was essentially simple. And it was. And here it is. Whittaker Chambers testified, and this is the government's story, that in 1934 while he was in Washington as a member of the Communist Underground, Chambers had been introduced to Alger Hiss at a downtown restaurant. The man making the introduction was Harold Ware, the organizer of a Communist apparatus in Washington, and also part of the introductions was one J. Peters, whom Chambers described as the head of the whole Underground of the American Communist party. Peters said that Hiss was to be disconnected from Ware's apparatus and was to become a member of a parallel organization under Chambers. At that time, Hiss was counsel to the Nye Committee and his first assignment in the new organization was to obtain official documents dealing with the munitions traffic and this he did.

In 1936 Hiss entered the State Department. In January 1937, under instructions from his superiors in the Communist party, Whittaker Chambers arranged a meeting, a clandestine, secret meeting among three men—himself (Whittaker Chambers), Alger Hiss and one Colonel Bykov, a colonel and a real honest-to-God military official who held the rank of colonel in the NKVD, the Soviet Secret Police apparatus. The meeting took place at a movie theater in downtown Brooklyn. Colonel Bykov spoke Russian and German. Alger Hiss spoke only English. Whittaker Chambers spoke English and German, so it was Chambers's German that provided the common language that permitted the three of them to communicate. He acted as informal interpreter and, hence, was in a position to tell what the conversation was. And the conversation, according to Chambers, was as follows. Bykov said that the Soviet Union was endangered—remember this is 1936—the Soviet Union was endangered by the fascist powers—Nazi Germany, Mussolini's Italy, and, I suppose, Franco's Spain—and that Hiss could greatly help if he would procure documents from the State Department. Hiss said that he would and a few days later the following arrangement was put into being.

Hiss would bring documents home from the State Department every week or 10 days. He would just bring home the documents that were on his desk at closing time that afternoon. By prearrangement, Chambers would come to Hiss's house and pick up those documents. Remember, it's before the era of the Xerox machine or the like. Chambers would drive to Baltimore, where he delivered the documents to a professional photographer who was part of the Underground. The photographer photographed the documents and returned to Chambers the original documents plus the exposed film. Chambers now drove back to Washington. It might have been 2 or 3 o'clock in the morning, but he rang the doorbell in the Hiss household. When somebody answered the door, he gave the original documents back to Hiss so that Hiss could return them to the files first thing the following morning, hence minimizing the risk of detection. The film would be sent by Whittaker Chambers to the appropriate intelligence people in the Kremlin, presumably by diplomatic pouch.

Let me interrupt myself. You will observe that under this process all that was received was the set of documents that happened to be on Hiss's desk that evening every week or every 10 days. And, obviously, this was unsatisfactory because you were missing the documents of the intervening days. So in the middle of 1937 Chambers was instructed by his superiors to tell Hiss to change the mode of procedure. Hiss brought documents home every night, or as nearly as they could manage it, given the security considerations. Some of the documents were typed verbatim in the Hiss household. Other documents were typed in summary form. On the day every week or 10 days when Chambers came to call, Chambers would be given the original documents of that day, plus the typed copy documents of the intervening eight or nine or 10 days. The whole shebang would be taken to Baltimore, everything would be photographed by the photographer. The originals of that day would be returned to Hiss so that they could be put back in the files of the State Department the following morning. The film would be sent by Chambers to the Kremlin, presumably through diplomatic pouch. And every once in a while when there was a document that Hiss thought was particularly important but which, for some reason, he could not bring home, Hiss would make a handwritten summary of the document and that document was photographed and otherwise treated in the manner in which they were treating original documents.

On April 15, 1938, according to Chambers, Chambers broke with the Communist party and altogether ceased his espionage activities. He retained some of the papers and exposed film which Hiss had given him earlier that year. He put them in an envelope and delivered them to his wife's relative, Nathan Levine, for safekeeping. In addition to their relationship in these covert activities, according to Chambers, the two families were fairly close, they saw each other with some frequency, they spent holidays and vacations together, they stayed in each other's homes, they occasionally took vacation trips together, and that was it.

On the other side you have the defense story and what that is, is Alger Hiss's testimony which, boiled down to its essentials, really comes to nothing more than the following. In December 1934 or maybe January 1935, Hiss was counsel to the Nye Committee. Chambers came to see Hiss, introducing himself as George Crosley, a freelance writer of articles on the munitions investigation that the Nye Committee was conducting. They had various luncheon meetings because one of Hiss's responsibilities as counsel to the Nye Committee was to supervise relations with the press, to see to it that the newspaper people were content.

At a later meeting between Chambers and Hiss, Chambers mentioned that he was planning to come to Washington with his wife and his infant child and he needed a place to live, and he wanted to come to Washington to be able to work full-time on these articles. The Hisses had just recently purchased a house on P Street in Washington. They had been living in a rented apartment on 28th Street and there was a certain period of time left to run on the lease on the 28th Street apartment. Hiss offered to sublet the 28th Street apartment to Chambers for the period of time remaining on that lease and Chambers, as George Crosley, agreed to the sublet arrangement. When the time came for Chambers, as Crosley, to move in, he had some story about the furniture van having been delayed. So Hiss allowed the Chamberses to live in the P Street place for a couple of days without any rent at all. In due course, the Chamberses moved in. He never paid the rent, however, and he and the Hisses met only a few more times. None of them could ever quite put his finger on the exact number of meetings. In any event, the last meeting between the two men occurred in the spring of 1936 when Hiss refused Chambers's request for a small loan and Hiss said something like, "I've been making you these loans from time to time. You've always promised to repay, but you never have repaid. It's perfectly obvious I am never going to be repaid. Let us agree to disagree. We are no longer friends. I don't want to have anything further to do with you. You don't have to repay me anything, you don't have to pay me anything on the sublet apartment. Quit, over, end of relationship." As to the Hisses visiting the Chamberses, never happened. As to the Chamberses visiting the Hisses, never happened except for that time when there was the overlap on the house and the apartment that I've mentioned. There were no vacation trips that the families took together, there were no holidays spent together, there were no terms of intimacy upon which the two families lived.

"Moreover," said Hiss, "I have never been a Communist, I've never given State Department documents to Chambers and my loyalty and devotion to the interests of the United States are known to a large number of persons of unquestionable integrity."

There is the defense case. Well, the jury has to choose between the two and in choosing between the two I guess you come up with a verdict.

It seems to me that in studying the evidence—remember, at the second trial that's all we're concerned with—a reasonable juror trying to make sense of this welter of materials would boil it all down to 10 points or categories. And what I would like to propose to you is the following. Let us by understood resolution turn ourselves into the jury. We are the jury that heard the evidence adduced at that second trial. We are the jury whose responsibility it is to resolve that evidence in the form of a verdict one way or the other. Now, we need a foreman to preside over the deliberations. I have the floor and I will not yield it. And so, for better or for worse, ladies and gentlemen, I am your foreman, and with all the fairness that I can manage, I will do my best to lead us through what I think your average reasonable juror would regard as an average reasonable way of analyzing the 10 points or categories into which all of the evidence somehow, with a certain naturalness, seems to fall in no particular order.

First, Chambers's familiarity with Hiss's personal life. Now, this has loomed large in all later writing about the case. How could Chambers know, for example, that Hiss once saw a prothonotary warbler unless Chambers's story were true? And the answer, I think, is that Chambers's knowledge of Hiss's personal life is absolutely irrelevant. Chambers's ability to recount the homely details of daily existence in the Hiss household does nothing to prove the grand jury's charge, which one must always remind oneself was perjury, that Hiss had lied about delivering official documents to Chambers. Since by Hiss's own testimony, he and Chambers had been acquainted, with the Chambers family once spending a few days as house guests of the Hisses, Chambers's knowledge of personal details was understandable and perfectly consistent with Hiss's innocence. And if simply for ease of bookkeeping you want to think of a kind of scale that I have up here on the table—one side for the prosecution, the other side for the defense and we'll put each item of evidence into one side or the other—this item of evidence, I should think, goes nowhere. It counts neither for the defense, nor for the prosecution, and we recall always that this is a criminal case in which the government's responsibility is to prove the truth of the charge beyond a reasonable doubt. So we're up to the second category of evidence and there is nothing to go on either side of our pair of balances.

Next, I referred to it a little while ago, I promised that we'd deal with it in a modest amount of detail, let us now turn to it—the testimony of the so-called corroborating witnesses. As I said earlier, each side seems to have called every possible witness who might have buttressed or contradicted one story or the other and that evidence really amounts to very little, if anything. Since we don't have unlimited time, let me give you, fellow jurors, just three examples. And I represent to you that these are representative examples. This is typical of the whole.

First, Whittaker Chambers testified that in 1934 or 1935, while having lunch with Alger Hiss at a Georgetown restaurant, Hiss had introduced Chambers to a woman named Plum Fountain. Hiss said it never happened and, speaking for myself, of what earthly relevance is that? Why should that have been put before the jury? You begin to get a sense of what I mean when I say that each side seems to have wanted to present absolutely everything that touched upon the life of either Hiss or Chambers, no matter how tangentially. Believe it or not, they found Plum Fountain. Her name as of the time of the trial was Olivia Fountain Tassoni. And Mrs. Tassoni testified that when she was a young woman her nickname was Plum. And, "Yes," she said, "I do know Alger Hiss. But I have no memory of ever meeting or seeing Whittaker Chambers." And the only intelligent response you can make to that is, so what? If Chambers were telling the truth, it is hardly remarkable that Mrs. Tassoni would fail to remember a passing introduction some 10 years after it occurred. And if Chambers were lying, he might have heard Hiss once mention his friend, Plum Fountain. The name is impossible to forget once you hear it and Chambers might have simply retained the name for some future use. In short, the evidence amounts to nothing on either side of the scales.

Second, Chambers testified that on August 10, 1937, he and the Hisses took an automobile trip, a kind of weekend holiday, to Peterborough, New Hampshire, where they saw an amateur production of Oliver Goldsmith's comedy, *She Stoops to Conquer* and stayed overnight at an inn called Bleak House. Sort of English literature relived. The Hisses denied it all. Well, the prosecution proved beyond peradventure of doubt that *She Stoops to Conquer* had been performed by a local amateur company in Peterborough, New Hampshire on the day in question, August 10, and that Hiss's employment records showed him on annual leave from August 2 to August 14. The defense proved, also beyond peradventure of doubt, that the Bleak House guest book contains no registration for Chambers or the Hisses under their own name or under any other name whatsoever. So the evidence is kind of equal. It corroborates each man in part and positively proves the truthfulness of neither.

And now third. Remember, Hiss said that the Hisses never visited the Chamberses, that there was no social relationship whatsoever. Forgive me, fellow jurors, but if we were sitting in the jury room, at this point I would say, "Did you catch this? Could you believe it when you heard it?" Just listen. In 1936 the Chamberses were living in Baltimore in a dingy apartment, in a down-at-heels apartment building on a street called Utah Place. And because, by his own admission, Whittaker Chambers was supporting himself and his family at the time by working as a spy for the Soviet Union, he was, of course, using a false name and the name happened to be Cantwell. Now, here's a man who is a self-admitted spy for the Soviet Union living in circumstances that come right out of a Graham Greene novel. And you know what? In that dingy apartment, in that run-down apartment building, on that depressing street called Utah Place, the Cantwells, our Russian spies, had a maid. Only in America do Russian spies have maids, but they had a maid, a Mrs. Edith Murray. And the government found Mrs. Murray and she was called as a government witness and she said that Mrs. Hiss was a frequent visitor to the Cantwell home. And she recalled that on one occasion Mrs. Hiss came with Mr. Hiss. On another occasion, she recalled, Mrs. Hiss stayed the night in order to care for the Chambers child while Mrs. Chambers went to New York the next morning for a doctor's appointment. Now, that seems pretty powerful, especially since the Hisses denied any such events. But what I have just summarized to you, fellow jurors, is what Mrs. Murray testified to on direct examination.

And as every trial lawyer knows and as the rest of you should keep in mind, after direct examination, you know what comes? That's right, cross-examination. And things frequently look different on cross when you compare them with the way they looked on direct. For example, Mrs. Murray testified that before coming to the courthouse and identifying Mr. and Mrs. Hiss in roughly the manner that I have described to you, she, Mrs. Murray, had been shown photographs of the Hisses by the FBI. And when the FBI first showed her Mrs. Hiss's photograph, Mrs. Murray's first response was, "It looked like I thought maybe it was an actress or something. I said to myself, 'Maybe it was someone I saw in the movies.'" And according to Mrs. Murray when they brought her to the courthouse and showed her Alger Hiss's photograph, Mrs. Murray's first response had been, "Well, it looked like I'd seen him, but I told the FBI I wasn't sure. I told the FBI I didn't know." Further, it developed that Mrs. Murray had suffered a severe nervous breakdown in 1942 requiring hospitalization and that before testifying the FBI had driven her down to Chambers's farm in Westminster, Maryland, for a three-hour face-to-face private conversation with Mr. Cantwell, as she knew him. (With Mr. Chambers, as we know him.) Well, I don't know whether Mrs. Murray's testimony was false, but I certainly doubt that any juror would be persuaded by it beyond a reasonable doubt.

Which brings us to the third category of testimony, which is something I've mentioned in passing, but which we certainly have not gone into in any kind of detail. And this is Chambers's testimony about other people. Chambers named Alger Hiss in the manner that I have been discussing for a couple of hours now, but he also named other names. For example, he mentioned Julian Wadley, Donald Hiss, Lee Pressman, Nathan Witt, John Apt and various others.

Now, one of these men, Julian Wadley, took the stand at the second trial and he admitted it all. What he said was that he, Wadley, was an economist; he was on the professional staff at the Treasury Department; he was part of an underground group that was headed by Whittaker Chambers; and what he did was bring documents home and give them to Chambers and they had that arrangement with the documents that we've heard about in connection with Alger Hiss. What did Julian Wadley know about Alger Hiss? Absolutely nothing, because the first rule of spying, of course, is that no spy should know what any other spy is doing. You compartmentalize their activities to the extent possible.

Donald Hiss also testified—that's Alger Hiss's younger brother. He denied the whole thing. And the others simply did not testify. As students of the historical record, we know that they did not testify, because their lawyers told counsel that if called to the stand they would simply take their privilege against self-incrimination, so they were not called to the stand. We, as jurors in the second trial, would know only that Wadley admitted it. We know that Donald Hiss denied it. And we know that neither of them really had any light to shed on the relations that may or may not have existed between Whittaker Chambers and Alger Hiss. So you kind of cancel everything out. In any event, the crux of what was before us, the jury, for determination at the second trial is whether Chambers told the truth about Alger Hiss. We are not concerned with whether he told the truth about Julian Wadley or Donald Hiss or the others, so that this category of evidence, I should think, amounts really to nothing or next to nothing.

Which brings us, fellow jurors, to the fourth category and do you realize if you look at this imaginary balance that I have up here with me, there is nothing on the prosecution's side of it. But let's see. There is the next category of evidence and the next category of evidence consists of proof of Hiss's character.

Let me sketch in very broad strokes a bit of the background you need to understand the importance of the proof on character. Criminal lawyers know that acquittals have been obtained on character, and character means the kind of evidence that says to a jury essentially, "The defendant is a good man and because he is a good man, it is not likely that he did what this indictment charges him with doing and, therefore, he should be acquitted." Now, the technical nature of the testimony, what it is that the character witness actually says when he takes the stand is unimportant. What is important is the identity of the character witness. When you call a good, solid citizen as a character witness, the jury tends to be impressed by the caliber of the person who is prepared to come to court and stand up for the defendant.

Well, Lloyd Paul Stryker knew this very well, indeed, and called many character witnesses at the first trial. This is not the occasion and we don't have the time to go into it, but just to whet your appetite and perhaps we can reserve it for some other time—among the character witnesses called at the first trial was Felix Frankfurter, no longer a professor at the Harvard Law School selecting Alger Hiss to be Oliver Wendell Holmes's law clerk, but rather associate justice of the United States Supreme Court Felix Frankfurter. He testified as a defense witness, a character witness to be sure, and if you're not satisfied with one Supreme Court justice, how about a second one? Stanley Reed also testified as a character witness at the first trial, so you have two knights of the Supreme Court testifying on the defense side of the case. The professional outcry was sufficient so that this was not repeated at the second trial and you did not have any justices of the Supreme Court on the stand. But you did have justices, for example, of the United States Court of Appeals for the First Circuit. You had district court judges—John Foster Dulles testified as a character witness. And so on and so on and so on. At the first trial, Lloyd Paul Stryker made much of the character witnesses and I'm sure that he was wise in doing so because I'm sure that the character witnesses played a considerable part in bringing about that hung jury.

At the second trial, Claude Cross tried to cover the same terrain. He didn't call Frankfurter, he didn't call Reed, he didn't call any other justices of the Supreme Court, but he called 19 character witnesses. And when Murphy stood up to deliver his final speech, his summation to the jury, I have no doubt that he regarded the character witnesses as the single most important evidence that he had to deal with, as the single strongest item of evidence that the defense had come up with. And the reason I say that is I'm not privy to Judge Murphy's strategic thinking about the case, but if you look at the transcript of his summation, you will see that after beginning with the standard, "Thank you for your consideration," et cetera, et cetera, Murphy turns immediately to the character witnesses and he spends the first three or four pages of transcript of his summation dealing with the character witnesses. He wants the jurors while they're fresh and he knows that he's got to dispel the aura that has been created by these character witnesses right at the start.

Now, how does he do it? He does it as follows and this comes right from the transcript and that's why I'm more comfortable standing up, because that's how I like to try cases. Please understand, since I now can see many of you and I couldn't see you when I was sitting over there under the spotlight, many of you are fairly young, which remember is a description, not a criticism. We all envy you your youth and we who are older must be at some pains not to mislead you in any way. So please understand that the argument that you're about to hear me make and, in fact, it is Judge Murphy's argument verbatim at the second trial, that argument might not go down well today. We have a kind of different view of the ethical responsibilities of counsel, of the things that can be said, that should be said, that ought not to be said, and you guide yourself accordingly. But still . . . Murphy uses as his transition the word extraordinary. He says something to the jury about this being an extraordinary case in so many ways, the extent to which the world is paying attention to it, the extent to which there's media coverage, the enormous importance of the issues involved, so many ways, and then the rest is Judge Murphy. So please understand that you have before you not puny yours truly, but all 300 pounds of Judge Murphy with the mustache 18 inches out on either side. He said:

"So much about this case is extraordinary. Well, what's another one of the extraordinary things beyond what I've already mentioned? The defendant has called 19 character witnesses, more than one-third the number of his total witnesses. And they have testified to Hiss's reputation for integrity, for loyalty, for honesty and veracity. They've told you what the gossip is that they've heard, the accumulation of gossip over the years that they've heard about him and what that is. And all of them said that his reputation is good. Well the charge in this case is technically perjury. But underlining the charge of perjury is the government's claim that Alger Hiss participated in the commission of espionage; that he was a spy for the Soviet Union. And I ask you, what kind of reputation does a good spy have? Of course, it must be good. The fox barks not when he goes to steal the lamb. No, the spy's reputation must be good. We're here on a search for truth, we're not concerned with reputations. Reputation poppycock. Just think how many people could call good reputation witnesses, just think. Benedict Arnold, a major general in our army. He sold out West Point to the enemy and before they caught Major Andre right up there in Tarrytown, don't you believe that Major General Benedict Arnold could have called George Washington as a character witness? And Brutus before he stabbed Caesar, don't you think he could have stood in front of the Roman senate and called upon the great Augustus and said, 'Tell them what kind of a man I am'? And lastly, the devil himself. You remember that play that Mr. Chambers wrote. The devil was a fallen angel and before he was thrown out of heaven, he was in the sight of God. He could have called upon the Almighty himself as a character witness. Well character witnesses belong to another era. This is the age of reason. This is the age of common people. And what we want are facts. We're here, you are here, Judge Goddard is here to ascertain the facts. We don't want gossip."

I should think that as we sat and discussed the case in our role as jurors in the second trial, we would have agreed that there really was no answer to it; that the evidence of Hiss's reputation came to nothing one way or the other and we would have proceeded to the fifth point or category. And this is the evidence with respect to Chambers's mental state.

Now, the defense proposed to call a psychiatrist who was going to give his professional opinion of Chambers's mental state. There was technical argument from Murphy and from Claude Cross as to whether this was proper. Judge Kaufman at the first trial, by the way, held it not to be proper and had not allowed the psychiatrist to testify. Judge Goddard saw it differently. He said that he would allow the psychiatrist to testify. The psychiatrist was Dr. Carl Binger, an alumnus of Harvard College and of the Harvard Medical School. He had studied psychiatry at Heidelberg and Zurich. He was then associate professor of Clinical Psychiatry at the Cornell Medical School. In due course, he became professor of medicine at the Harvard Medical School and chief of psychiatry at Massachusetts General. And he was probably one of America's preeminent psychiatrists, if not, indeed, America's single preeminent psychiatrist. Now, Dr. Binger had never met Whittaker Chambers and, of course, he had never conducted a clinical examination, but he had observed Whittaker Chambers on the witness stand, he had read many of Whittaker Chambers's writings, and he had been given the facts of Whittaker Chambers's life. Upon the basis of all of which Dr. Binger had an opinion. And what was his opinion with respect to Whittaker Chambers's mental state? This was it, and these are the exact words. And if you have a taste for this stuff, you will relish it. It feels so wonderful when you say it.

Dr. Binger said, "I think Mr. Chambers is suffering from a condition known as psychopathic personality, which is a disorder of character of which the outstanding features are behavior of what we call an amoral or asocial or delinquent nature. And among the symptoms of this condition are chronic, persistent, and repetitive lying and a tendency to make false accusations."

And that's it. Chronic, persistent, and repetitive lying and a tendency to make false accusations.

Well, I have great faith in juries generally. I'm inclined to think that juries know what to do with testimony of that kind. But still, sometimes a lawyer has to work at it and in this case Murphy decided to work at it. You may know that my own view of cross-examination is that cross-examination should almost always be very short. Murphy's cross-examination of Dr. Binger runs in printed form to 190 pages. It extended over five or six days. And you will well want to ask me the question, why did Murphy cross-examine Dr. Binger for five or six days? And I think I have an answer for you. Murphy cross-examined Dr. Binger for five or six days because he was having too much fun to stop. That is why. It is the single most devastating cross-examination of a psychiatrist that has ever taken place, I believe, in any American or English courtroom. It is essential reading for any lawyer who is preparing to cross-examine a psychiatrist, and it is enormously entertaining.

Now, obviously, for 190 pages, we can't sit here and read it back and forth to each other. So let me take just one example. Now, remember, Dr. Binger had never met and had never examined Whittaker Chambers, but one of the things he relied upon in coming to this diagnosis of his was that he had observed Whittaker Chambers on the witness stand and he said that one of the things that he had observed when Chambers was on the witness stand was that Chambers had no relationship with the lawyer asking the questions. Instead of looking at the lawyer, Chambers would look at the ceiling, demonstrating what I think psychiatrists like to call lack of affect. And, said Dr. Binger, "This is a major symptom of a psychopathic personality."

Murphy, on cross-examination, asked him whether he still believed that and Dr. Binger said, "Oh, yes, yes, I certainly do. He," referring to Chambers, "sat in this very chair," referring to the witness chair, "and he had very little relationship with the inquirer, he frequently looked up at the ceiling as if trying to recall something that he had previously said." And at that point Murphy came in with the question.

He said, "Now, Doctor, we made a count this morning of the number of times that you looked at the ceiling. And during the first 10 minutes you looked at the ceiling 19 times. The next 15 minutes, 20 times. The next 15 minutes, 10 times, and the following 10 minutes 10 times, making a total in 50 minutes 59 times that you looked at the ceiling, Doctor. And I was just wondering, Doctor, whether that is a symptom of psychopathic personality." I can imagine that there was a long pause and the doctor then said, "Not alone." Murphy said, "Not alone?" "No." And that was it, he moved to something else. And we, as jurors, can take it as good sport. As I say, it's quite entertaining. It brings a smile to the face. It sweetens one's dreams, generally cheers one up, but when you retired to deliberate if you are the jury, as we are, I think that Dr. Binger's testimony will play no part whatsoever. So be it. Except we've now covered 5 out of the 10 points of evidence that are there to be covered and there is nothing on the prosecution side of it.

So let's turn to the sixth point. This is one that's before us, but up until now I have not emphasized it or underlined it or drawn your attention to it in any special way. And this sixth point, fellow jurors, is the time of Chambers's break with the Community party. Do you remember Raymond Murphy, the chief security man of the State Department, with whom we began way, way back? In his [Chambers's] conversation with Raymond Murphy at the State Department held on August 28, 1946, a memorandum of which we read aloud, you will recall, and again in his testimony before HUAC, Chambers fixed the time of his break with the Communist party as the end 1937. At the trial, however, Chambers said that he broke with the Communist party on April 15, 1938. So it's the end of '37 or mid-April of '38. And the difference, while seemingly unimportant and for most of us kind of boring—this is the kind of tedious detail that we don't like to get into, but the difference, fellow jurors, is absolutely crucial. Because, you see, most of the government documents which Chambers produced at the Baltimore deposition or turned over to HUAC in the form of the film that was left in the pumpkin, most of those documents are dated in 1938. None of them later than April 1, 1938. If Chambers, then, had left the

Communist party in the latter part 1937, as he first said, he could not have obtained the documents from Hiss in the manner he described. But if he had left the party on April 15, 1938, it was at least physically possible for him to have obtained the documents in that manner. Now, the only explanation of the difference ever offered by Chambers was that his earlier statements had simply been mistaken and that when he came to testify at the trial, his memory was more accurate because he'd had time to think about it, he'd reviewed it with the FBI, et cetera, et cetera, et cetera. Now, doing our best to be jurors at the second trial, I think we would agree without undue discussion that for a man like Whittaker Chambers, his break with the Communist party was probably the single most important event of his life. And I would say further that the time of that break would be just as important an event in his life. Chambers's fuzziness of recollection as to when the break occurred I find very difficult to accept and I think the jury would, too. As a matter of fact, I'd go so far as to say that were there nothing else to support Whittaker Chambers's testimony, the verdict at this point would have to be for the defense, for Hiss, not guilty, because the government must prove the charge beyond a reasonable doubt.

I say were there nothing else. Well, there is a great deal, a great deal else. And to that great deal else, let us now turn. And we're up to item or category number seven, the rug. And who at this late date thinks of this case in connection with a rug? We know about the pumpkin and Pumpkin Papers. We may have a vague recollection that a typewriter will figure in the case and we'll be hearing about the typewriter pretty soon. But what about a rug? Well, let me just remind you of the fact. I lay the facts before you, fellow jurors, and in a way I throw up my hands and I say that if you can do anything with this, more power to you, but I can't do much with it at all. Chambers testified that at some point in their relationship, Colonel Bykov, the NKVD agent with whom they had had the meeting at the movie theater in Brooklyn, Colonel Bykov announced to Chambers that the Soviet people wished to make a palpable gesture of appreciation to Hiss and others of Chambers's colleagues who were helping the Soviet Union by bringing information home from the government. In short, he wanted to give a gift to Alger Hiss, a gift from the Soviet people in recognition of the work of the American Communists. Those are the words of Whittaker Chambers and I must say that the words are kind of serious and this is serious business. You're talking about spies giving each other gifts as a kind of memorial of the work that they are doing on behalf of the nation for whom they are engaged in spying activities. And now it may be that I am simply revealing my low and essentially trivial nature here, but when one spy gives a gift to another spy, what is the gift? A cyanide capsule? A silver bullet? A dagger that you can conceal in the heel of your shoe? We've all seen the 007 movies and we know how these things are done. But in this case, they weren't done that way. The gift to memorialize the work that Alger Hiss was doing on behalf of the Soviet people was to be a rug, believe it or not, a rug. And how is it all done?

According to Chambers, who knew nothing about rugs or the like, an amount of money, a fairly large amount of money, considering the time and the Great Depression that was in its depths at that point, a large amount of money was sent to a Columbia art historian named Meyer Shapiro, and Professor Shapiro was asked to take that money and go buy four rugs. One was for Alger Hiss and of the other three, one was for each of the other three people working for Whittaker Chambers. Who those people are, who will ever know? In any event, Shapiro was to buy the rugs and send them to a member of the group named George Silverman. And according to Chambers, in January 1937 the rugs appeared in the back of George Silverman's car, which was parked in the parking lot of a restaurant on the Washington Baltimore Highway. By prearrangement Chambers appeared. He carried one of the rugs from Silverman's car to his own car, then found Hiss parked at a nearby parking lot, delivered the rug from his, Chambers's car, to Hiss's car and at that point Hiss drove away with the rug. And that's how the transfer of the rug was arranged. Now, Professor Shapiro, who is a man of unquestioned integrity and extraordinary reputation as a professor of art history at Columbia, testified pretty much in accordance with what Chambers had said. According to Shapiro's testimony, at the end of 1936 he received a sum just a little bit less than $900 with instructions from Chambers to use that money to buy four oriental rugs—one for Alger Hiss and the other three for whoever it was who was working with Whittaker Chambers in other parts of the government. Shapiro's testimony was confirmed by the invoices of the Massachusetts importing company from whom the rugs were purchased. According to Shapiro, he purchased the rugs and sent them in accordance with Chambers's instructions to a man named Silverman in Washington. And, of course, it was through Silverman that the rug ultimately was transferred to Alger Hiss. There was no cross-examination of Professor Shapiro and to this day nobody questions the veracity of what Professor Shapiro described on the witness stand. And what he described on the witness stand, you see, is a process by which the rugs were acquired.

Now, Chambers's account of how the rugs were acquired has to be true because it is confirmed in every important respect by the testimony of Professor Shapiro, which, as we've said, nobody quarrels with to this day. Where would Chambers have obtained almost $900 to send to Shapiro back in 1936? These were the depths of the Great Depression. The $900 represented an enormous sum of money and Chambers, remember, didn't really work for a living, he performed, speaking loosely, odd jobs for the Communist party and for the NKVD. That was what he did. He could have obtained $900 from only one source and that source was Colonel Bykov. Now, at the other end of the transaction, it is equally clear that Hiss did receive a rug from Chambers. He admitted receiving it. He told the judge that the rug was on the floor of his son's bedroom at their house in New York and, indeed, he volunteered to produce the rug in court the next morning, though the judge reassured him that there was no need for that to be done. If the circumstances of the obtaining of the rug, then, are beyond question, and at the other end the circumstance that the rug is presently or was presently in the possession of Alger Hiss was beyond question, all that remains is a disagreement as to the circumstances under which the rug was transferred to Alger Hiss. According to Hiss, it was the midnight knock on the door and Whittaker Chambers dumping the rug into

Hiss's arms saying, "Here, a wealthy patron wants me to give this to you," and Hiss accepting it as a kind of part payment on the rent that was due on the apartment that had been sublet to him in Washington. On the other hand, you've got Chambers's testimony that, in fact, the transfer was made on the parking lot on the road between Baltimore and Washington and it did, indeed, represent the presentation of a gift on behalf of the Soviet people to those who are helping the Soviet people in their crusade against international fascism. Which would a jury accept? It seems to me that it would take a very gullible jury indeed to accept Hiss's version of these events.

And so we pass to the eighth point of evidence and, remember, to this moment there is nothing to go on the prosecution's side of the scales. The Hisses asked Chambers how much it would cost to get a new automobile that was in working condition. Chambers replied that it would take approximately $400 and the Hisses gave him the $400 a day or two later. Now, if that's true, if the Hisses gave Chambers $400 in November 1937, then Hiss's assertion that he last saw Chambers in the spring 1936 is false. And a jury might rationally go on to conclude that the rest of Hiss's testimony is also false. Now, Mr. and Mrs. Hiss had a joint savings account at the Riggs National Bank in Washington and the bank's records show a withdrawal of $400 on November 19, 1937, four days before Chambers bought the car in question. The Hisses shrugged it off as a coincidence. They had withdrawn the $400 to buy furniture for their new house. But the government proved that the lease on the new house was not signed until December 2 at the earliest and that the Hisses had charge accounts at various department stores as well as a checking account, thereby making cash purchases unnecessary. If that $400 was a coincidence, it goes beyond any coincidence I would ever expect a jury to believe.

Which brings us, fellow jurors, to the next to last point in the evidence and there is still nothing on either side of the scales except possibly the date of Chambers's break with the Communist party and that, of course, figures on the defense side not the prosecution side. Well, what is this ninth category of proof? It deals with the Hisses' transfer of a car. In 1935, maybe early 1936, the Hisses owned a 1929 Ford. The car was in good working order, but it was kind of old and ratty looking, and Hiss was rising in the federal government and he decided that his position required a somewhat more presentable automobile, so he was going to buy a new car. The old car would produce virtually nothing by way of trade-in. There was little purpose served in throwing the car away; that was disgracefully wasteful. And so what Hiss wanted to do was take the old car, which, remember, was still in working order, and give it to the Communist party so that it could be delivered, finally, to some Communist party worker who would be able to make use of the car. Chambers was opposed to this arrangement, but he dutifully reported it to J. Peters, the Hungarian in New York who ran the entire operation, and all Chambers knew from that point on is that somehow the car had been transferred to the Communist party. Now, here is what the documents show and in a prodigy of investigation, the FBI did find the documents of title on this car. The certificate of title on the reverse bears an assignment filled out in Hiss's handwriting. Remember, the front part says this car belongs to Alger Hiss, in effect. You turn it over, "I, Alger Hiss, assign title in this car to the Cherner Motor Company," which is a large Ford agency in Washington. And Hiss's signature is admitted by Hiss to be genuine and, in any event, it's notarized by a notary public in the Justice Department and everybody agrees that that is Hiss's signature. The dealer's reassignment then says, in effect, "I, the Cherner Motor Company, further assign this car to one William Rosen." And the next document is an application for a new certificate of title signed by William Rosen. Now, all of the Cherner Motor Company's invoices for those days are machine numbered and the numbers run consecutively and no number is missing. Nor is there an invoice for this transaction. Presented with these documents, I don't see how a jury could disbelieve Chambers. As Chambers said, Hiss arranged to give the car to a Communist party worker and someone who wanted to be helpful to the Communist party at the Cherner Motor Company, who knew how to work such arrangements, simply handled it off the books. Now, what about William Rosen, the fellow who ends up owning the car? He was found and called to the stand. He was asked, I think, two questions. We, as jurors at the second trial, will remember the two questions. First, were you ever a member of the Communist party or, rather, had you been a member of the Communist party in 1936? And second, what's your connection with this car? How did you come to have this car? To both questions he replied privilege against self-incrimination and was immediately excused. We, as the jury in the second trial, would not know, but it's too good not to mention, that Rosen appeared with counsel before us at the second trial and his counsel was Emanuel Bloch, who served also as counsel for Julius and Ethel Rosenberg, as many of you may recall. In any event, this evidence of the automobile certainly comes down on the government side of the case, not on the defense side of the case. Whether it amounts to proof beyond a reasonable doubt, who knows? But we still have a final category of evidence to analyze and review and to that category let us turn.

This is the tenth category involving the documents—the papers. And what were they again? Remember that they are the photographs Chambers had concealed in the pumpkin, the celebrated Pumpkin Papers, the handwritten notes, concededly in Hiss's handwriting and, finally, typewritten copies of State Department documents. These had been turned over at the Baltimore deposition, remember, as having been prepared on a day when Chambers could not get to his household and it was necessary to make copies of these documents. Now, let's talk first about the photographs, the celebrated Pumpkin Papers. They are two rolls of developed microfilm containing a total 58 frames. In all, they constitute eight documents, five of them concerning negotiations for a trade agreement with Germany and three are miscellaneous incoming cables. All of them show on their face that they were received in Francis Sayre's office. Remember, he is the Assistant Secretary of State. And many of them bear Hiss's initials, showing that he had read these documents. The government proved through technical evidence that the 58 frames had been exposed at the same time through a camera owned by one Felix Inslerman, who was Chambers's chief photographer in this Underground, operating out of a photography store that he had in Baltimore. And the Kodak technical people could testify that the film had been manufactured in 1937, the photographs being photographs of documents dated in early '38, remember . . . late '37 and very early '38. So the physical dates all match.

Now, Chambers said that the source of these documents was Hiss. Hiss denied it and there is no independent evidence pointing either way. It was at least possible that Chambers had a source other than Hiss, for Wadley, remember, admitted turning over government papers to Chambers. And Chambers, without mentioning names, had made it abundantly clear to Wadley, according to Wadley, that Chambers had other sources inside the State Department. And, thus, the jury—that's us—might well have found itself unable to conclude beyond a reasonable doubt that Hiss rather than Wadley or another was the source of the microfilm documents. To my own considerable surprise then, fellow jurors, I conclude that the so-called Pumpkin Papers figure neither way in this case. They don't go on the defense side of it and they don't go on the prosecution side of it.

Which brings us to the penciled memoranda, memoranda in Hiss's handwriting. They all summarize State Department documents. The earliest is dated in January 1938, the latest in March 1938. Two of them are on stationery bearing Office of the Assistant Secretary of State letterhead and the other two are on common scratch paper. All of them are creased as if they had been folded carefully in half. None of them is crumbled. Chambers testified that these notes were made by Hiss when he was unable to bring documents out of his office overnight and Hiss, remember, testified that they were made for his own use. One of his responsibilities was to review the incoming cable traffic every morning. And as soon as Francis Sayre, the Assistant Secretary of State, arrived, Hiss would sit down and brief Sayre on what that traffic was. In order to assist him in that briefing, Hiss would make notes for his own use and these were some of those notes. Chambers testified that the notes were made by Hiss when he couldn't bring the documents home for photographing. Hiss said, "No, they were made for my own use to help me when I briefed Sayre in the morning on the overnight cable traffic." And, again, there is no independent evidence to show one way or another that Hiss gave the memoranda to Chambers. Maybe Chambers found them in a wastepaper basket. Maybe somebody stole them and gave them to Chambers. Maybe Hiss prepared them for use in briefing Sayre, as he said, but then passed them on to Chambers as Chambers said. On balance, I think a reasonable jury would decide that Chambers's story, at least to this point, had not been proved beyond a reasonable doubt.

Which brings us to the final item of evidence, one which I tell you, fellow jurors, I find inescapably damning. And this really is the heart, the crux, the soul of the case. These are the typewritten copies of documents turned over by Mr. Marbury to Mr. Cleveland at the Baltimore deposition. They are 43 pieces of paper. Each of them is a copy or a summary of a State Department document dated between January 5 and April 1, 1938. Chambers testified that they had been typed by the Hisses and given to him, Chambers, for transmittal to Colonel Bykov. The Hisses denied it. And do you see why I tell you as your foreman, as your colleague, as your fellow juror, that these are the documents at the heart of the case? Were these typed on behalf of the Hisses or on a typewriter owned by the Hisses, owned or controlled by the Hisses? Because, you see, if they were typed on behalf of the Hisses or on a typewriter owned by the Hisses, the only purpose of the preparation of these documents was espionage. There can be no innocent explanation. And that's why, once you've resolved the significance of these typed documents, you've really resolved the case.

Now, everybody saw this from the start and the first thing the FBI did was to go out and try to find the typewriters. Hiss, on December 4, 1938, gave a fairly lengthy statement to the FBI. He was unclear about what typewriters he had at home. I must say that even in my most prosecutorial moods, I would not tax him with that uncertainty because who really remembers what kind of typewriter you had in your house five, six, or seven years ago? In any event, when you got finished with all of the confusion and the thrashing about, it became clear that the typewriter that was in the Hiss household in late '37 and early '38 was a Woodstock typewriter that had belonged to Mrs. Hiss's father, who ran an insurance agency. And when the father retired from the insurance business, he had given the typewriter to his daughter, Priscilla Hiss, and she kept it around the house. In due course, later on, they had given the typewriter away to a friend of their housemaid and the typewriter had disappeared into the community. Actually, Mrs. Hiss's first thought was that she had given the typewriter to a junkman. Well, it turned out to the contrary. It turned out that what she had done is give the typewriter to her housemaid, a Mrs. Catlett, who wanted the typewriter for use by her two sons.

And I've got to take a moment to talk about these sons and I want to do so calling things by their right name and mincing no words about it and I'm confident that in doing so I will not be misunderstood, fellow jurors. Mrs. Catlett's two boys lived in a basement apartment around the corner from where the Hisses lived and where Mrs. Catlett, their mother, worked. And in that basement apartment, for reasons that are their own business, not ours and not mine, they had a kind of nonstop party. At any time of the day or night there were drinks available, there were things to smoke available, music played, there was dancing going on, and so forth. What these boys did to support themselves, well, one can only speculate. For whatever reason, Mrs. Catlett wanted the typewriter for her boys to have. Now, what in heaven's name were they going to do with that typewriter? And the answer seems to be that they thought that the typewriter was a very pleasant curio to have around the apartment and in the living room, which was the central focus of the nonstop party, there was a kind of mantelpiece. And on the mantelpiece was the typewriter. And it stood there as a sort of totem object, a work of sculpture—call it what you will, but it functioned more nearly as a work of art than as a device for producing typewriting. In any event, J. Edgar Hoover said to the FBI, "I want that Woodstock typewriter found. You've got Mrs. Catlett, you've got her two boys to whom she says she gave the typewriter," and they agree that they got the typewriter from her, but they couldn't remember what happened to it. "I want you to find the typewriter." And the entire resources of the federal government were turned to that task. Find the typewriter. The word went out. Elliott Ness himself, I suppose, led a contingent of untouchables to find that typewriter. Every pawn shop in the District of Columbia, every curio shop, every Salvation Army secondhand store, every typewriter shop, every office equipment shop—each one was scoured by FBI agents looking for this crucial Woodstock.

And the fact is that it came time for the first trial and they didn't have it. And the reason they needed it, of course, was to do something to prove on what typewriter were these documents typed? Because if they were typed on the Woodstock typewriter that the Hisses owned, that closed the circle; that made the government's case for the reasons that we've sketched out. And if it's otherwise, then it's otherwise. But you have to find the typewriter, don't you, to know whether the typewriter typed these documents? And the reason you need the typewriter is, and just a bit of technical stuff here, which is of no great difficulty, the face of every typewriter is unique, as is a human fingerprint. You look at the face of this Woodstock, if only you can find the Woodstock, and you see the little imperfections and the like which inevitably creep in over the years of use. You compare the typeface with the typeface that you see in the copies of the State Department documents that were turned over at the deposition session and when you blow up the photographs so that it's easy to examine, really, anybody can see the similarities. You don't have to be a great expert. A 12-year-old would be able to say, well, it's perfectly obvious that this document was typed on this typewriter. But if you don't have the typewriter, how can you do it? Well, the FBI figured out a way of doing it. And this is not widely known. It may have been widely known at some time, but it has long since been forgotten and it may well be that if there's a single key to understanding the Hiss trial, this is it. You can go through the same intellectual process if you have a document that you know was typed on that Woodstock, even though you don't have the Woodstock. Do you see what you would do? Here is document A, which we all know was typed on the Woodstock. Photograph and blow up the typeface that you see in that document A and compare it with the typeface that you see in the State Department documents that were turned over at the deposition session, for example. And if they are identical, they are identical. It shows that the Woodstock typed these documents. And if they're not identical, then, of course, different consequences flow. By finding the common ancestor, if you will, you can prove whether or not the State Department documents were typed on the Woodstock.

Well, what they did now was ask Mrs. Hiss whether she could remember doing anything on that Woodstock typewriter in late '37 or early '38 and, yes, she could. She was an alumna of Bryn Mawr College and, as such, she was secretary of her class and one of her responsibilities was to prepare an Annual Report to the dean's office as to what the class was doing and who was accomplishing what and so forth. "Those reports," said Mrs. Hiss, "were typed by me on the Woodstock." The FBI simply went to the dean's office at Bryn Mawr and asked if they had the reports. They did have the reports. The reports were simply blown up on ordinary photograph paper and you compared the typeface that you see on those Bryn Mawr alumni reports with the typeface that you see on the State Department documents turned over at the deposition session and it is instantly obvious, fellow jurors, and it would be to us because we would have had the photographs here in the jury room with us. It is instantly obvious that they were typed on the same typewriter. And lest there be any needless controversy about it, all of this material was turned over to the defense before the first trial. The defense retained a typewriter expert of its own and the defense typewriter expert said, "That's my conclusion." The Woodstock typewriter that typed the Bryn Mawr alumni report typed these State Department documents that were produced at the deposition session. The defense then went to a second typewriter expert and he came up with the same opinion and in his opening statement at the first trial, Lloyd Paul Stryker formally conceded to the jury that the typewriter that typed the Bryn Mawr alumni reports was the typewriter that typed those State Department documents that had been turned over at the deposition session and that that typewriter was the Woodstock in question.

Now, just as a footnote, obviously the jurors wouldn't know any of this, but we know it and it's worth keeping in mind. At some point along the way there was a break in the trial and Edward McLean, another one of Hiss's law school classmates assisting on the defense and later a federal judge of great ability himself, decided to see whether he could find the typewriter. And he went out, as I understand it, into the black community in the District of Columbia, and within two hours had the typewriter. The entire FBI had expended hundreds of thousands of dollars of taxpayer money trying, without success, to find that typewriter. Ed McLean found it and I believe it cost him, in total, $25, and that includes some carfare and I think he paid $20 to the man who ultimately was found to be in possession of the typewriter.

Well, that meant that it was for the defense to explain how in heaven's name the State Department documents had come to be typed on the Woodstock. There is the damning fact that somehow must be explained. Now, how do you explain it? We don't have the time to go into it and so I won't go into it. I will simply tell you that it was here, as well as at other points, that Stryker was at his best and he had the jury rolling on the floor with laughter at the thought of the Catlett boys and their nonstop party and somehow people getting in and there's the typewriter up on the mantelpiece and somehow unauthorized use of the typewriter was made and conceivably people who were conspirators with Whittaker Chambers, who were anxious to frame Alger Hiss, got to the typewriter through the party at the Catlett boys' basement apartment and that's how the State Department documents came to be made.

And Claude Cross, I suppose one might say, made a mistake, but I really don't want to say that because I'm not sure of that, speaking as a trial lawyer myself, I could have done any better. He used the same explanation. And I don't think he should have done it because it was Thomas Murphy that he had to deal with. Lloyd Paul Stryker had done it in such a way as substantially to take the wind out of Murphy's sails so that Murphy just wasn't able to hit it out of the ballpark automatically. But when Cross did it, suggesting, remember, that people got in and typed this stuff, Murphy was able to hit it out of the ballpark.

With the same caution that these days, perhaps, this would be regarded as just a little bit intemperate, let me give you some idea of what Murphy did in his summation with respect to this problem the defense had. How do you explain the fact that the typewriter that typed the Bryn Mawr alumni reports also typed the State Department documents that were produced at the deposition by Chambers's lawyer?

And what Murphy does is go through various theories—I'm not going to go through them all—and he gives them numbers and the numbers mount up very quickly. And he does it deliberately so that before you know it we're at theory number 103. And he said, "Well, now, let's talk about this theory 103. How is it proved? Well, you start off with the fact that the Catletts had the typewriter and there's the picture of their hall. You see how these two things follow? The Catletts had it and there's the hall where they used to keep it. And there's the back entrance. And you see all that space back there? People come in and out there all the time. There's the den and there are the dancers. And now what probably happened, " Mr. Cross testified, "is that somebody, not Chambers, Chambers is too smart, but one of Chambers's conspirators, one of his confederates—uh huh, those are good names, aren't they? Conspirators, confederates, yeah one of those people went up to the Volta Place House and asked innocent Mrs. Catlett, the mother of the Catlett boys, he said, 'I'm the repairman, where's the machine?' Oh, I can see it now. It's terrific. You have this guy coming with a Woodstock hat on and it says Woodstock Repair and maybe he's got a jumper and it also says Woodstock. And he rings the bell. No, no, no, it's not a bell, you have to pull that one, remember she said. And he says to Mrs. Catlett, 'I'm the repairman, I've come to the fix the typewriter." And then witty Mrs. Catlett says, 'Well, which one do you want? The Remington, the Royal, the L.C. Smith, which one?' 'No, we want the Woodstock.' 'Ah, the Woodstock. That's over at my boys' house on P Street.' And then the next scene, it's the middle of one of these dances and you see Chambers sneaking in at night and he mingles, mingles, mingles. He mingles with the dancers and then he types, he types, he types this stuff holding the State Department documents in one hand while he types with the other. Oh, Mr. Cross, you've got to do better than that."

The conviction was returned on January 21, 1950. Judge Goddard sentenced Hiss to five years imprisonment. The Court of Appeals for the Second Circuit affirmed and the Supreme Court declined to review the case. In March 1951, Hiss went to jail. A year later, Judge Goddard denied Hiss's motion for a new trial on the ground of newly discovered evidence. The newly discovered evidence was the claim of forgery by typewriter, which I trust you would see absolutely holds no water. It's totally incoherent because nobody forged anything on any typewriter. The typewriter identification was done by comparison with the Bryn Mawr alumni reports, not by comparison with the Woodstock typewriter. The fact that Ed McLean found the typewriter was a mere accident; it didn't affect the case one bit. The case would have been tried exactly the same way had the typewriter never been found.

In any event, fellow jurors, this was no mere contest of oaths. Three things: the evidence of the rug, of Hiss's $400 loan to Chambers, and of the transfer of Hiss's car to William Rosen prove, at least to my mind, beyond any reasonable doubt that Chambers's account of their relationship, not Hiss's, was true. And one thing—the evidence of the typed State Department papers proves beyond any reasonable doubt that when Hiss denied to the grand jury that he had ever given official documents to Chambers, he was lying. Twenty out of 24 jurors had been sure of his guilt and they were right. Thank you.

Chapter 9

What Happened in Erie?

A Probing Examination of *Erie v. Tompkins*

IRVING YOUNGER: April 25, 1938, ladies and gentlemen, was a Monday. And in those years, Monday was decision day in the Supreme Court. At noon the justices took their places; godlike in the center was Charles Evans Hughes, and ranged alternately on his right and his left, in order of their seniority, the associates: James Clark McReynolds, Louis Brandeis, Pierce Butler, Harlan Fiske Stone, Owen Roberts, Hugo Black and Stanley Reed. For those of you who have been counting, you're up to eight and you wonder where is the ninth? The ninth was Benjamin Cardozo, who is home sick that day, the sickness which turned out some two months later to be his final illness.

The first item of business was the calendar of motions for admission to the Bar of the Supreme Court. Twenty-eight motions were made and 28 were granted. Now came the announcement of written opinions. There were 12 that day of which the seventh was in Case No. 367, *Erie Railroad Company v. Tompkins.* The question for decision, it began, is whether the oft-challenged doctrine of *Swift v. Tyson* shall now be disapproved. Those words announced to the world a decision that all lawyers acknowledge to be one of the most remarkable in the Supreme Court's history. It is the keystone of the procedure course taught at every American law school today. In the eight months following the decision, no fewer than 15 articles in legal periodicals took the case as their subject. The case has been referred to, as of this date, 2,785 times by the United States District Courts, 2,117 times by the courts of appeals, and 181 times by the Supreme Court itself for a total of 5,083; or, a steady one-and-a-half citations per week from the date of the decision down to this very moment. The case has been examined, dissected, buried, exhumed, and redissected until it seems that nothing more can possibly be found in it.

Yet all of this teaching, exploitation, and citation treats the case as a sort of sport of nature, a spontaneous manifestation on the Supreme Court's docket, sprung full-blown from Justice Brandeis's formidable brow. But, of course, *Erie v. Tompkins* was no such thing. It had an origin and a history. The plaintiff sued the defendant. There were pleadings. The case was tried before a judge and a jury. Neither side knew or could have known at the beginning that theirs was to be the celebrated case that overruled *Swift v. Tyson*, for neither side was aware of events behind the curtain in the Supreme Court. To the litigants it was a lawsuit and, like every lawsuit, a story. Now, the story in *Erie v. Tompkins* is better than most and what I propose, ladies and gentlemen, is to embellish the occasion this afternoon with the story of *Erie v. Tompkins*.

Now, I know my audience. I know better than to bandy footnotes with any of you. And so I shall not pause for citation of authority. Let me just tell you now, once and for all at the beginning, that had you this talk in printed as opposed to oral form, there is no sentence that would not have appended to it at least one footnote. Many would have two and some would have three. In short, ladies and gentlemen, I have invented nothing. It took place exactly as you will hear it from me. And it all begins in Hughestown, Pennsylvania, traversed by the tracks of the Erie Railroad, which in 1934 was a village of some 2,800 souls. At the corner of Hughes Street and the tracks of the Erie Railroad stood the house of one William Colwell. Now, Colwell was awakened sometime after 2 o'clock that morning—that was the morning of Friday, July 27—by a tapping at his front door. Someone was running up and down the street, shouting that there had been an accident. William Colwell got out of bed and he began to put on his trousers. "Don't go," said his wife. "Them fellows out there are crazy." But William Colwell went. He found a man, crumpled against the outside rail. Between the rails lay the man's severed right arm. The man was his neighbor, Harry James Tompkins.

Now, Tompkins was then 27 years old. He'd been born in the neighborhood. He'd left school at the age of 14 and gone to work in a factory. In due course, he had acquired the craft of metal molding at the Pittston Steel Works and he had become a member of the union, a fact of which he was very proud. But in 1934, which I remind you is the depths of the Great Depression, he had been laid off and he was supporting himself, his wife, and his then-infant daughter by doing odd jobs around the community. After supper on July 26 he had walked to his mother-in-law's house several miles away and had stayed there until 12:30 or 1 o'clock the following morning. Some friends had given him a lift in an automobile and let him out at a footpath that had been worn down over the years by people acting as pedestrians, moving along the pathway parallel to the tracks of the railroad. Apparently, in railroad parlance, that would be called a parallel footpath. In due course, I say, Tompkins would have been led by that parallel footpath back to his own home. Instead, he was hit by a train. The ambulance had been called; he was taken to the hospital. The stump of his right arm was removed, after which he made a swift recovery. Upon leaving the hospital, he went in search of a lawyer.

Now, in that summer, the summer of 1934, a visitor to the office building at 11 Broadway in lower Manhattan of New York City might have observed on the directory in the lobby downstairs the name of Bernard G. Nemeroff, a lawyer then 27 years old. Nemeroff practiced in partnership with Bernard Kaufman, also 27. The two of them rented space in the somewhat larger suite of an older lawyer, one of whose associates was Aaron Danzig, all of 21 years old. Now, Bernard Nemeroff's parents, as you will instantly have recognized from his surname, were of Eastern European extraction. But Nemeroff had grown up in quaint, easy circumstances in New York City. He had attended Erasmus Hall High School, a public high school which was then one of the best in New York City. He had gone to Pennsylvania State for his undergraduate work. He remained at Penn State for two years and, were Nemeroff here speaking for himself, he would tell you for himself that he was never much of a student. He stayed at Penn State for two years when he decided that the smarter thing to do was to return to New York, work during the day for various law firms, go to law school at night and, as soon as he finished law school, become a lawyer, because in those days you did not need an undergraduate degree to be eligible to take the bar examination. Well, that's what Nemeroff did. He left Penn State, he came back to New York City, he worked as a clerk for various law firms, and in the evenings he took courses in the part-time division of the New York University Law School. He spent two hours an evening in the classroom. The rest of his working time was devoted to the law firms who paid him his weekly salary. His academic record he, himself, would say was not distinguished. But in his own defense he would also say, "I had only one F." And for those of you who are curious about such things, it was an F in the Corporations course taught in those years by, of all people, Judge Crater, for whom they are still looking.

Now, Nemeroff graduated in 1929 and I need not remind you of what 1929 represents in American history. It was not an auspicious year in which to be graduated from a not very good law school, the part-time division, moreover, and to have an academic record that would not attract anybody's attention. There were no jobs available to Nemeroff. There were no associateships at Cravath, Swain and Moore, paying with bonuses in the first year $100,000. There were no clerkships with federal or state judges. What there was for Nemeroff was nothing, which meant that he simply hung out his shingle. He opened that office in that office building on 11 Broadway. And, having hung out his shingle, Nemeroff waited. And he waited and he waited. And I think it is fair to say that after five years, how to put it delicately, his practice had not bloomed.

Now, Nemeroff had gotten married and begun to raise a family in this time and the reason he had the wherewithal to do so is that his father was a quite successful businessman. His father was in the shirt manufacturing line. He made men's shirts and what he did was have small plants in various small towns up and down the eastern seaboard, staying away from New York City essentially so as to avoid problems with the unions. One of the elder Nemeroff's plants was in Hughestown, Pennsylvania. And, as a matter of fact, that was the largest employer in the town of Hughestown. So Nemeroff, as a successful businessman, was well known, at least by reputation, to everybody in Hughestown, including, of course, Harry James Tompkins, who needed a lawyer. Now, there were no lawyers practicing in that community with a population of 2,800, so Tompkins went to see the elder Nemeroff. And I cannot represent to you, ladies and gentlemen, that I have documentation that a conversation as follows took place, but I am morally certain that a conversation very close to this must have taken place. In my mind's eye I see Tompkins sitting down with Mr. Nemeroff and saying, "Look, Mr. Nemeroff, at what the railroad did to me. They took away my right arm. They left me with nothing and I'm a working man. I work with my hands; without my right arm, I'm good for nothing. I've got to sue the railroad." And in my mind's eye, I see Mr. Nemeroff saying, "Yes, Harry, I understand that you must sue the railroad." And Tompkins said, "And Mr. Nemeroff, I need a lawyer to sue the railroad for me. Can you recommend me to a lawyer?" And Mr. Nemeroff, doubtless thinking of young Bernard sitting there at 11 Broadway, waiting for the clients, must have looked Tompkins in the eye and said, "Do I have a lawyer for you!"

And so it came about that Harry James Tompkins was represented in his claim against the Erie Railroad by Bernard Nemeroff, also 27 years old, then representing essentially his first client. Because Nemeroff was understandably nervous—this was a heavy case, this was an arm-off case—for those of you in the audience who may not be familiar with the working jargon of lawyers, lawyers who do this kind of practice tend not to categorize their cases by legal concept, but rather by the injury claimed, so that you will have soft tissue cases, suture cases, broken bone cases, leg-off and arm-off cases, and then finally you have death cases and you understand where each case will fit in on this scale.

Nemeroff took Tompkins's arm off case and he brought in Kaufman and Danzig to help with the research. And research those three young men did in plenty. According to Tompkins, he had been on that parallel footpath, which ran along the Erie Railroad tracks, when a freight train came moving in the opposite direction. Now, this was how Tompkins described it at the trial. These are Tompkins's own words taken from the trial transcript. He said:

"I heard the whistle and I seen the headlight of the train, but I kept right on walking. I'd walked it plenty of times and I wasn't a bit afraid. And when I got to a certain point all but a few steps away, the engine passed me. But I kept moving right along and suddenly something came up in front of me, a black object that looked like a . . . like a door. And I went to put my hands up and I guess before I got them up, I was hit. I woke up in the receiving room of the hospital."

Well, now, Nemeroff and his young colleagues reasoned that it was not enough to prove that the railroad carelessly had permitted a door to swing loose on a moving freight car. The real question was whether the railroad owed a duty to Tompkins to guard against that specific kind of carelessness. Now, Nemeroff's research disclosed that under the Pennsylvania cases, uniquely among the states, a traveler like Tompkins on a parallel footpath is regarded as a trespasser to whom the railroad owes a duty merely to avoid wanton negligence. And for those of you who are not familiar with the concept of wanton negligence, it means essentially that you can't do it on purpose. If you're the Erie Railroad under these cases, you can't deliberately kill someone who is walking on a parallel footpath. But so long as you haven't done it deliberately, then you are free of liability. And, of course, Tompkins could not prove any such wanton negligence with respect to the Erie Railroad, so that to sue in the Pennsylvania courts was to invite disaster; the case would be dismissed.

Happily, there was an alternative. Tompkins was a citizen of Pennsylvania. The Erie Railroad was a New York corporation and the matter in controversy, damages for a lost right arm, certainly exceeded what was then the jurisdictional amount of $3,000. So, as every lawyer will instantly recognize, you had diversity jurisdiction and the case would lie in the United States District Court. But might it be, Nemeroff and his colleagues wondered, that the United States District Court would apply the Pennsylvania cases, holding that travelers on a parallel footpath are trespassers to whom the railroad owes merely a duty to avoid wanton negligence? If so, the result was foregone. Again, unable to prove the railroad guilty of such wanton negligence, Tompkins would never get to the jury. So more research, more time in the library, more number-two pencils worn to a stub. And those young men found what they needed. It was Section 34 of the Judiciary Act of 1789, enacted by the very first Congress. And in that section the first Congress said, "The laws of the several states, except where the Constitution treaties or statutes of the United States shall otherwise require or provide, shall be regarded as rules of decision in trials at common law in the courts of the United States in cases where they apply." And, having read that, the only possible question you can have is what does it mean? It seems to say that the laws of the several states shall apply in cases where they apply. Yes, yes, to be sure. But have we baked any loaves here? Has that moved anything forward? Obviously, you need a case in which a court tells you what Congress intended by this rather strange language of Section 34 and, lo and behold, they found their case.

In 1842 Justice Story for a unanimous Supreme Court in a case called *Swift v. Tyson* had glossed Section 34 as follows. The key language of Justice Story's opinion is as follows, just to give you the flavor of it. He said, "We have not now the slightest difficulty in holding that this section, upon its true intendment and construction . . . does not extend to contracts and other instruments of a commercial nature, the true interpretation and effect whereof are to be sought, not in the decisions of the local tribunals, but in the general principles and doctrines of commercial jurisprudence." Now, that is the language of 1842 and it is language adapted to the facts of *Swift v. Tyson*. Restating that language in terms more useful to us, it says that with exceptions not here relevant, general law—not state law, but general law—supplies the rule of decision in a federal diversity case.

And I pause to note, ladies and gentlemen, that underlying Justice Story's opinion is an idea, an interesting idea about the nature of law, that law is clear, definite, unchanging and certain, capable of ascertainment by any intelligent and well-trained judge, whether that judge be state or federal. As James Wilson, one of the lesser-known founding fathers, said in his lectures on law first published in 1804, "Order, proportion, and fitness pervade the universe. Around us we see, within us we feel, above us we admire a rule from which a deviation cannot or should not or will not be made." Obviously, then, every judge will come up with answers to legal questions identical with those arrived at by every other judge, no matter the jurisdiction the judge serves. It signifies nothing. Justice Story might have been heard to say that a federal judge will determine the law for himself in a diversity case rather than look to the decisions of state judges, for the law does not vary with the judge. In James Wilson's word, the law is beyond deviation.

Now there were other reasons for *Swift v. Tyson*, of course. For one, federal judges tried primarily diversity cases. Congress withheld until 1875 the power to try federal question cases generally. Were federal judges automatically to accept the rulings of state courts, it would mean a subordination of their status inconsistent with the prestige of a national judiciary. For another thing, the structure of doctrine in the states was undeveloped and full of gaps. And there were few volumes of reports or treatises embodying that ideal common law that existed no one knew where, but which every judge truly spoke. So to Nemeroff and his colleagues the point was simple. In a diversity case, the federal court applied general law, not the law of the state. And general law, they found, in the sense of the majority rule, the rule applied in every state except Pennsylvania. Well, the general rule was contrary to the Pennsylvania rule. A railroad, held all states outside Pennsylvania, owed a duty of ordinary care to a pedestrian like Tompkins, walking on a footpath that ran parallel to the railroad tracks.

So into a federal court, but which one? The district court in Pennsylvania or the district court in New York? Not Pennsylvania. No. For

Nemeroff and his friends were not licensed in Pennsylvania. The preferred court, plainly and obviously, was the United States District Court for the Southern District of New York. And in that court, on August 29, 1934, the case of *Tompkins v. the Erie Railroad* was begun.

Now, the Erie Railroad was hardly helpless. It had been represented for many years by the New York City firm of Stetson, Jennings and Russell. In 1920, John W. Davis had completed his ambassadorship to Great Britain and joined the firm as senior partner. By 1934, the name of the firm was Davis, Polk, Wardwell, Gardner and Reed, with offices at 15 Broad Street in the Wall Street area of Manhattan. The firm's chief trial lawyer was Theodore Kiendl and sometime during the summer of 1934, Kiendl went to work on the case. He was then 44 years old. He was a graduate of Columbia College and the Columbia Law School. He'd been a partner in Stetson, Jennings and Russell since 1923 and he remained a member of the firm and its successors until his retirement in 1965. And, of course, the firm continues in practice to this very day. We know it as simply Davis Polk.

The first thing Kiendl did was to call in a young man who was working for Davis Polk as a summer clerk that summer. He was a student at the Yale Law School. His name was S. Hazard Gillespie. And what Kiendl said to Gillespie was, "Gillespie, go to the library and find out whether it would help the railroad if the law of Pennsylvania were to be applied. Never mind whether we can figure out an argument to persuade a judge to apply the law of Pennsylvania. Assuming that we had such an argument, would it be helpful to our client?" I pause to tell you, because I, at least, find it interesting, that Gillespie returned to the law school, finished his work there, in due course became a member of the New York Bar, returned to Davis Polk as a full-time associate. He later was a partner of the firm. Indeed, he later occupied Kiendl's position as the senior partner in charge of the Litigation Department of the firm. He served as president of the New York State Bar Association and as United States attorney for the Southern District of New York, in which position in April 1960, he had the limitless wisdom to appoint me one of his assistants.

Now, of course, as I've said, Kiendl told Gillespie that he should assume that there was an argument that might persuade a judge to apply the Pennsylvania cases. All he wanted Gillespie to find out was whether the Pennsylvania cases, if applied, would help the Erie Railroad. Gillespie replied that, yes, it would help the Erie Railroad, but it's going to be very difficult to come up with an argument as to why the Pennsylvania cases should be applied here in view of the general law doctrine of *Swift v. Tyson*. "Well," said Kiendl, "we'll worry about that when the time comes." After all, the prevalent view of the nature of law is changing. It's no longer regarded as a brooding, but definite presence in the courtroom. It's come to be seen as an expression of social utility, a set of rules designed to accomplish desirable goals as perceived by the judge. And so an ingenious lawyer, and Kiendl was certainly an ingenious lawyer, might well be able to shape an argument for overruling *Swift v. Tyson* or for limiting the reach of the holding of *Swift v. Tyson*, but that was the stuff of appeal. First, it was necessary to try the case.

Now, the complaint was straightforward. Tompkins had been on that parallel footpath, when, through the Erie Railroad's negligence, he was struck by a projection from a moving freight train all to his damage in the sum of $100,000. And the answer was equally concise. Erie denied the essential allegations of the complaint and asserted the affirmative defense of contributory negligence. By the summer of 1936, all discovery had been completed and the case was ready for trial. It was assigned to United States District Judge Samuel Mandelbaum.

And, ladies and gentlemen, it is not possible for me to resist saying a word, and yet another word, about Judge Samuel Mandelbaum. Samuel Mandelbaum was born in Poland. He was born in Poland in 1884. He came to the United States as a youth, not as an infant. He was 12 or 13 years old when his parents came here. And his parents and Mandelbaum and his many brothers and sisters settled on the Lower East Side, the 4th Assembly District. And I've got to tell you just a little bit about the politics of that Lower East Side and, in doing so, I know that I will not be misunderstood in any way. But I want to see things as they are and call things by their right name. The reigning politician on the Lower East Side in those days was a Tammany hack, people would have said, named John F. Ahearn. And he had seen his constituency change from overwhelmingly Irish to overwhelmingly Jewish and that was as the great wave of immigration changed from Irish to Jewish. Those Jews, of course, came, almost all of them, from Eastern Europe, not from Germany and, of course, not from Spain and Portugal. They came from Russia and Poland. Ahearn wanted to retain his position of power and he understood as a practical politician that the way to retain his position of power was to remain popular with the new settlers—the Jews—who were coming to live on the Lower East Side. And the way to remain popular with them was to give them the feeling that he represented them just as loyally as he had represented the Irish people who had lived there in the generation before. In short, largesse had to be distributed to the Jews just as generously as it had been distributed to the Irishmen. And that is what Ahearn did. He spotted bright and promising young Jews, he insisted that they get an education and he moved them forward in public life just as quickly as he could. Ahearn spotted Mandelbaum as bright, energetic, imaginative, compassionate. He insisted that Mandelbaum get an education. Principally, Ahearn meant, learn English. And that Mandelbaum did by going to night school and ultimately he got a high school equivalency diploma. And then Ahearn insisted that Mandelbaum go to law school and become a lawyer. You could do so, as I said before, without having gone to college.

And so from a high school equivalency diploma, Mandelbaum went directly to evening law school and, in due course, he had his law degree and he had become a lawyer. And he had clients that came to him through the political process and those clients lived on streets with names like Delancey and Hester and Rivington, having come to New York from places with names like Warsaw and Minsk and Lodz. Mandelbaum's accent remained to the day of his death, the accent of his clients. Not for Samuel Mandelbaum the plummy cadences of Harvard and Yale, of Minnesota and Hamline. No. Mandelbaum's diction was perfect Yiddish. His consonants hard, his Ws more V than W, his lilt liturgical.

Well, in 1923 Tammany's elders rewarded Mandelbaum's faithful services to the Lower East Side by bringing about his nomination and election to the State Assembly, the lower House of the state legislature, which sits, of course, in the state capital, which is Albany, a city 150 miles or so up the Hudson River. In the state legislature, Mandelbaum worked diligently for slum clearance and low-cost public housing. His devotion, his humility, and his self-effacing kindness endeared him to all his colleagues, urban and upstate, Republican and Democrat. When Franklin Roosevelt was elected governor, Mandelbaum became a member of what the newspapers liked to call the Turkey Cabinet. And let me tell you what the Turkey Cabinet was, and here I depart from the printed record as it were, but I'm telling you what you could read if you were looking at editions of *The New York Times* from those days.

Franklin Roosevelt was governor and, as we all know, Franklin Roosevelt was a master politician and a polio victim. He was confined to a wheelchair for all of his mature life. Franklin Roosevelt wanted to know what was happening in the state of New York. He wanted ears and eyes out there and he didn't want to rely for those ears and eyes upon the bureaucrats because he just couldn't trust them to be bright enough for his purposes. And so Roosevelt had a set of friends, lawyers, politicians, policemen, whoever, from various parts of New York State who came together at the executive mansion in Albany once a week to have lunch. They always met on Monday. And over the lunch table they would talk about what was happening in the state, what concerned people, what were the issues of the day, not as the newspaper saw those issues, but as the people of the state of New York saw those issues. And Mandelbaum was a member of that cabinet. Now, why was it called the Turkey Cabinet? There was no provision in the state budget to pay for these informal political luncheons and so the governor paid for them himself. And that meant that Mrs. Madame the governor cooked the lunch herself. And that was Eleanor Roosevelt, and she was a great woman in many respects, but the kitchen was not one of the places in which she was great. Eleanor's repertoire apparently was very limited. She could cook only one thing that she could rely upon with respect to edibility and which would also be sufficient in quantity for the 25 or so people who met every Monday and that one thing was turkey. In addition, kosher turkey, in view of Mandelbaum, was readily available even in Albany. And so it was turkey every Monday. Turkey, turkey, turkey and, naturally, the newspapers came to call this the Turkey Cabinet.

Now in 1932, Governor Roosevelt, of course, became President Roosevelt. And in that same year the leaders of Tammany Hall brought about the nomination of Samuel Mandelbaum to be a state senator, a member of the Upper House of the state legislature. And in the same election that elected Franklin Roosevelt President of the United States, Sam Mandelbaum was elected a state senator. By 1936, two or three years later, he had become a considerable power in the New York Democratic organization. Now, remember, the legislature met in Albany, which is 150 miles or so up the Hudson River from New York. These days you can take a comfortable bus or fly. In those days you took a train. For most people it wasn't much to talk about, but one of the reasons that Franklin Roosevelt and Sam Mandelbaum got along so well is that Franklin Roosevelt was a polio victim confined to a wheelchair and Sam Mandelbaum had a congenital birth defect involving a malformed hip of some kind. He walked with a pronounced limp. He needed to use a cane all of his life. And there were lengthy periods when he was in absolute agony and there was no way to treat the pain, he just had to bear it. And so they had a kind of common ground between them as sufferers in a roughly parallel way. Now, once again, I have to tell you, ladies and gentlemen, that I cannot document the following conversation. I have no piece of paper to prove to you that it took place, but I am morally certain that it did take place. And when it did take place, it was a tête-à-tête conversation between Sam Mandelbaum on the one hand and Eleanor Roosevelt on the other. They had become fairly close. As a matter of fact, it is quite likely that Eleanor Roosevelt's first view of a slum neighborhood came when Sam Mandelbaum gave her a kind of guided tour of his Assembly District down on the Lower East Side. Her eyes were opened to the issues which thereafter made her a world figure by Sam Mandelbaum. And, once again, I've got to say that in my mind's eye, I see it happening. I can see Mandelbaum, sitting down, perhaps, over a cup of coffee at Katz's Delicatessen on Delancey Street and Broadway in New York and saying to her, "Eleanor, I'm tired, Eleanor." And she said, "Why are you tired, Sam?" He said, "I schlepped up to Albany. I can't sleep. It hurts. Eleanor, I can't do it anymore." "Well, so what do you want to do, Sam?" "Eleanor, I want to be a judge." And she said, "You want to be a judge, Sam?" "Yeah, I want to be a judge." And she said, "But Sam, you aren't much of a lawyer." And I can imagine, he said, "I'm not asking to be a lawyer, I'm asking to be a judge." And she said, "Well, now, Sam, what kind of judge can you be?" And he must have replied, "I want to be a magistrate." A magistrate, the kind of judge he'd seen in action, the kind of judge who deals with poor people, who handles the problems that poor people get into.

Sam must have said, "I want to be a magistrate." And Eleanor must have said, "Sam, two, three, four years ago maybe Franklin could have done something for you because he was governor and he had a hand in appointing magistrates. But, Sam, he's not governor anymore. He has nothing to do with appointing magistrates. He's President of the United States now and the only kinds of judges he appoints are federal judges." And Mandelbaum must have said, "So all right, so I'll be a federal judge." That conversation, I repeat, must have taken place because just four working days later, the Justice Department submitted to Congress a bill adding three seats to the Southern District of New York, three brand new seats. The Congress enacted the bill like that, the President signed it like that, and the first name that went in as a judge to be appointed to fill one of those new seats was the name of Samuel Mandelbaum.

Now that appointment, ladies and gentlemen, evoked unprecedented opposition from the press and the organized bar. *The New York Times* denounced judicial spoils. Word spread that Mandelbaum was the choice of Eleanor Roosevelt, as he may have been, that he had never tried a case, as he never had, and that Mandelbaum had set foot in the federal courthouse only once and then out of curiosity to see what it was like.

The chairman of the American Bar Association's Judiciary Committee castigated Mandelbaum as a mere politician, deficient in the specialized knowledge and experience required of a federal judge. The president of the New York County Lawyer's Association called Mandelbaum unqualified by learning and experience for the performance of the duties of this great office. The Association of the Bar of the City of New York added its voice to the opposition. But when a senate subcommittee began its hearings on Mandelbaum's nomination, it was deluged with letters and telegrams in support, all of them praising the nobility of Mandelbaum's character and his devotion to public service. None of those letters or telegrams said anything of his skills and experience as a lawyer, perhaps because there was nothing to say.

On June 21, 1936, Mandelbaum was confirmed. On July 10, he was sworn in as a judge of the United States District Court for the Southern District of New York. His first assignment was the criminal calendar, essentially sitting on the bench with a senior colleague and simply watching the process and getting a sense of how it is done. And then, once again, I've got to assure you that the following conversation had to have taken place, though I can't document it. The chief judge said, "Sam, you've been sitting here on the criminal calendar seeing how it's done, you've seen how it's done, I think it's time for you to solo. I think the best calendar for you to take, since really you're doing all this stuff for the first time, is the civil jury calendar. They are civil cases rather than criminal, so the pressure is a little bit less. And since it's a jury case, just do whatever seems sensible and the jury is going to decide the case. You don't have to worry about anything." Mandelbaum said, "So, all right, I'll take the civil jury calendar," and his first case in every possible sense of the word was *Erie v. Tompkins*. The trial started on October 5, 1936, and continued through the 6th, the 7th and the 13th.

Now, unwilling to trust himself with so serious a case, Nemeroff, recognizing that this, too, was his first case, had brought in trial counsel, a very experienced lawyer who specialized in presenting the plaintiff's side of various tort cases. His name was Everett Hunt. And because Everett was a stockily built man, everybody called him Stubby. And his associate was a fellow named Bill Walsh. Now, Stubby Hunt, interestingly, was an accomplished bridge player. Apart from the law, his only real interest in life was playing bridge. And the same statement could be made about Theodore Kiendl. Each of them played bridge at the tournament level and they knew each other as opponents at the bridge table as well as occasionally opponents in the courtroom. They were contrasts in courtroom style. In court, Kiendl was cold and brilliant. He liked to work from one of those huge accountant's ledgers in which he wrote out in his own handwriting every question for every witness and every detail of his plan for the trial. Hunt was seemingly disorganized, yet he was quick and infallible in finding holes in the opposition's case to exploit. Hunt was warm and he was funny and, of course, he was a gifted actor.

The plaintiff's proof went in smoothly. Tompkins had been struck by something protruding from that train while walking on the pathway. His hospital bill—remember, this was the Great Depression—his hospital bill, believe it or not, 30 some odd days in the hospital, was $89. His doctor's bill was $350. He had been earning between $21 and $28 a week for the five years before the accident. Without his right arm, he could no longer work. And that was it; the plaintiff rested.

The defendant now moved to dismiss. And I just thought you'd be as entertained as I was. I read the transcript looking for Judge Mandelbaum's first statement of any kind on any subject in the course of this trial and this is where it came. The defendant made his motion to dismiss after the plaintiff rested and Kiendl said something to the effect of, "We have given Your Honor our brief in which we set forth the cases upon which we rely." And Mandelbaum said, "I have read them and I shall continue reading them." That was it. Well, now, Kiendl came to the point and here for the first time the theme of *Erie v. Tompkins* finds a voice. Kiendl said, "I want to call to Your Honor's attention the fact that this permissive pathway doctrine is not applicable in this case under the decisions of the highest court of Pennsylvania." And all Mandelbaum said was, "Motion denied." The defendant's case consisted chiefly of attempts to prove that the train had been inspected and its doors found to be secure. Nor should Tompkins have been on that path in the middle of the night only inches from the track. Perhaps he lost his footing and he slipped under the wheels. That's how the accident came to happen and at least he was partially responsible for the tragedy. At that point, both sides rested and, after summation, Kiendl asked the judge to charge that the plaintiff had not pleaded nor proved wanton negligence as required by the cases in Pennsylvania. Judge Mandelbaum simply said, "Refused." That was that.

On October 13, 1936, Judge Mandelbaum charged the jury, in essence, that the plaintiff was obliged to prove the railroad's negligence. The railroad had a duty to use reasonable care with regard to people like Tompkins walking on that parallel footpath. The jury, which consisted of 12 men, retired to deliberate and, after two-and-a-half or three hours of deliberation there was a verdict for Tompkins in the amount of $30,000. Now, Kiendl moved to set the verdict aside. A few days later, Judge Mandelbaum denied the motion and one week later the clerk entered judgment. With interest of $165 and statutory costs of $95, the total came to $30,260.

Now, not long after this, Nemeroff received a telephone call from Tompkins. And I think it's worth talking about this telephone call lest it disappear altogether from the pages of history. According to Tompkins, the owner of the gas station in Hughestown had come to him, to Tompkins, and said that a friend who worked for the railroad wanted Tompkins to know that the railroad was prepared to settle the case for $7,500. The sum was enormous to Tompkins and he was very tempted to take the appropriate steps to settle the case for that amount. "No, no, no," said Nemeroff. "Don't you realize that the sum is paltry? It is 25 percent of the jury's verdict. It is insufficient compensation for a lost right arm and, as a matter of fact, the railroad has no right trying to settle with you without talking to me first." In any event, Tompkins seemed unpersuaded and uncomfortable about the whole thing. So Nemeroff, really desperate on the point, said, "Where are you now?" And he replied, "I'm speaking to you from the pay phone in Hughestown." And Nemeroff said, "Get on a bus and come to New York. I'll meet the next bus from Hughestown." And Nemeroff did meet him.

He physically took possession of Tompkins. He took him to his house on Long Island. He brought him to the guest room upstairs where he locked him in and kept him there for five days, allowing him out only for food, water, and use of the bathroom.

After five days, Nemeroff figured that the risk of a precipitate settlement had passed and it was safe to let Tompkins out of the guest room and permit him to go back to Pennsylvania, which is what he did. Erie, meanwhile, was appealing to the Second Circuit. In those days, the appellant prepared assignments of error, a listing of the things that you claim need to be rectified by the appellate court. There were 18 assignments of error of which the 10th—remember, it's now no longer the tail at the end of the dog, it's now right in the middle—the 10th assignment of error read as follows. "The court," referring to Judge Mandelbaum, "The court below erred failing to hold at the conclusion of the plaintiff's case that the permissive pathway doctrine did not apply under the decisions of the highest court of Pennsylvania."

Now, Erie's brief supporting its assignments of error set forth three points. The first argued that Judge Mandelbaum's rulings on certain evidentiary matters were incorrect. Second, they argued that Tompkins should not have been on that footpath in the middle of the night, that this was contributory negligence as a matter of law.

Let me just pause with a kind of personal footnote there. From the beginning of the trial through the argument in the Supreme Court, the railroad insinuated that Tompkins had been drinking at his mother-in-law's house all through the preceding night and he'd really had a lot to drink by the time those people in the car let him out at the parallel footpath. And when the train came by, Tompkins somehow got dizzy and he lost his footing and fell under the wheel and that's how the accident happened. But they had no proof of this. Tompkins, of course, denied it and nobody at the mother-in-law's house confirmed it and nobody who was in the car confirmed it. So it was wholly a matter of insinuation and that, I think, is what the second point in the Second Circuit brief was all about. That it was contributory negligence as a matter of law for Tompkins to have been on that footpath in the middle of the night and really they want to get the judges thinking about what was going on in the mother-in-law's house all through the night before. The third point argued that the only duty the railroad owed to Tompkins was the duty to refrain from wanton negligence of which there was no proof whatsoever. Now, curiously, although Kiendl's discussion of that third point included the statement that Federal Courts must apply state common law where the highest courts of the state have completely established a settled policy regarding local matters, Kiendl omitted reference of any sort to *Swift v. Tyson*. He didn't cite it, he didn't refer to it. And my personal guess as to why he didn't cite it or refer to it is that he didn't know what to say about it. After all, the case had been around for a hundred years. It may have been incorrectly decided at the outset, but after 100 years, people get used to it, people know what it means. Why bother to change it after you've developed all of that experience with a particular precedent? So he figured the best thing to do was make no mention of the case at all and that's the way he handled it.

The plaintiff's brief was signed by Nemeroff, by Stubby Hunt, and by Bill Walsh and it simply responded in lawyer-like fashion to the points raised by the Erie Railroad. "As to the key point," said the plaintiff's brief, "Federal courts may exercise independent judgment whenever the law of the place of the injury is contrary to a general common law as decided by the federal and other state courts." In short, they argue for general law rather than application of the law of the state.

The appeal was heard and on June 7, 1937, decided by a panel of three judges and the three judges were Judge Learned Hand, Judge Thomas Swan, who had come to the Second Circuit from the Deanship of the Yale Law School, and Judge Martin Manton, later to be chief judge of the Second Circuit and, in due course, to serve a prison term of two years after being convicted of accepting bribes in connection with his judicial work. The opinion was by Thomas Swan, who said, "Since the general rule contrary to Pennsylvania's is that a traveler on a common pathway that runs parallel to a railroad track is owed a duty of ordinary care by the railroad, the case had been submitted to the jury with proper instructions." The jury having rendered its verdict, there was nothing left to discuss, not even *Swift v. Tyson*, which Judge Swan did not so much as cite. I suppose because he, too, thought it unnecessary on the grounds that it was so well known that there was no reason to put another citation in Shepard's.

Well, Kiendl now had no choice but to petition the Supreme Court for certiorari. But he was faced with a tactical problem of some difficulty. As I understand the practice that prevailed in those days, the taking of the appeal by the railroad to the Second Circuit acted as an automatic stay on the judgment. Once the Second Circuit had affirmed the judgment as the Second Circuit had done, there was no automatic stay provision. The plaintiff was entitled to proceed to enforce the judgment unless the defendant got a stay of execution from the Supreme Court or from a justice of the Supreme Court. Now, the way you get a stay from the Supreme Court is to make a motion for a stay. But it was pointless to make a motion because it was summertime—as a matter of fact, it was July—and the Supreme Court was deep in its summer recess. As I'm sure everybody in the audience is aware, though, the justices split up the circuits so that each of them is responsible for one or more identified circuits and you call that justice the Circuit Justice for this circuit. And where lawyers must make an application, but for one reason or another, cannot make the application to the entire Supreme Court, they will make the application to that individual justice. And you make the application in whatever way is reasonable. Such applications have been made over the telephone. Sometimes you go to the justice's office in his home town. Occasionally you will go to the justice's home. It has happened that the Justice asks the lawyers to meet at the library of the law school in the city. Whatever it may be and whatever the Justice wants, why that's the way you do it.

Well, Kiendl needed to make an application for a stay. Obviously, he couldn't make a motion to the Supreme Court itself because the court was in recess. He telephoned the Clerk of the Supreme Court and the Clerk of the Supreme Court informed Kiendl that, as, of course, Kiendl knew, the Circuit Justice for New York and the Second Circuit was Benjamin Cardozo and Cardozo was available at his home in Mamaroneck,

New York, which is an upper-class residential suburb on Long Island Sound, just to the north of the Bronx, if you're familiar with the geography of New York City. Cardozo was a lifelong bachelor and he lived in this house with butlers and housekeepers and the like, but he was essentially the complete household and he had inherited the house from his family, which had considerable wealth. Kiendl arranged with Cardozo's secretary to appear at Cardozo's home in Mamaroneck on a certain date, at a certain hour, for the purpose of making the application for a stay.

Now, Stubby Hunt was going to be there to oppose the application and Nemeroff has told me that he remembers Hunt informing him, Nemeroff, that the application for a stay would be made and argued to Justice Cardozo at Cardozo's home. And Hunt asked Nemeroff if he would like to attend and Nemeroff said, "You can't keep me away." Said Nemeroff, "First, I have never in my life seen a justice of the United States Supreme Court. Second, here's a chance to see one at home." I can imagine that Nemeroff might have thought to himself, do they really have homes? Third, this is Benjamin Cardozo. Imagine being in Cardozo's presence. And fourth, Nemeroff said to Hunt, "Is there any chance of the application being granted?" And Nemeroff remembers that Hunt replied, "There's no chance whatsoever because the standard for determining the application for a stay is whether or not the individual justice thinks it likely that the full Court will grant certiorari." And said Hunt to Nemeroff, "How can Cardozo think the full Court is likely to grant certiorari in this case, which is a garden variety tort case? The last time the Supreme Court granted certiorari in a plain old tort case was decades and decades ago." And remember what I said at the start, to the lawyers in this case, it was just another case. They were unaware of events going on behind the curtain in the Supreme Court. To them it was a tort case and the Supreme Court is not likely to grant certiorari in a plain old tort case, which has nothing to make it distinctive or especially important to the Supreme Court. Nemeroff remembers that he responded, "Oh, am I relieved. All right. There's no chance of the stay being granted, but I want to be there."

And on the date in question, at the hour in question, Nemeroff and Stubby Hunt were there and there was Kiendl to make the application on behalf of the railroad. And Nemeroff says that to his dying day he will not forget it. The butler received them and ushered them into the living room. At the other end of the living room there was a flight of stairs running up to the second floor where, obviously, the living quarters, the bedrooms and the like, were located. And it was the kind of flight of stairs only Scarlett O'Hara really knows how to walk down. And at the appointed hour, as if by magic, there appeared at the top of the flight of stairs the vision of Justice Benjamin Nathan Cardozo, wearing . . . Nemeroff recalls every detail . . . beige trousers, a black velvet smoking jacket, and black bedroom slippers. His left hand the Justice kept in the pocket of his smoking jacket. In his right he held a perfectly folded white handkerchief, which from time to time he dabbed to his lips in that manner. Huh. It's beyond description. Kiendl made his application for the stay and he made the kinds of arguments that you would expect him to make—essentially the arguments that he would have been making to the Second Circuit. But then he said something and here I speak as a sometime student of and commentator upon the craft of the courtroom. Then Kiendl said something which marks him as a virtuoso. At the end of his application, having made the standard arguments with nothing especially memorable about it, Kiendl said, "Mr. Justice, I want to be frank with you." He said, "If Your Honor grants the application for a stay, we will move expeditiously to perfect our petition for certiorari and, if the petition is granted, we will comply with whatever time requirements are set down as to filing the brief on the merits. But if Your Honor denies the application for a stay, there will be no petition for certiorari. Obviously the Erie Railroad can pay this judgment; we will simply pay it tomorrow if Your Honor denies the stay today." Do you hear the melody behind those notes? Do you realize what he's saying to Cardozo? What he's saying to Cardozo is that, "If you don't give me a stay, you don't get this case in the Supreme Court. No stay, no case." And he knew his audience the way every trial lawyer needs to know his audience. Cardozo had been appointed in 1932, not that many years before, to fill the vacancy created by Holmes's resignation. As all of you know, he was a man of enormous subtlety and learning, having served for many years on New York's highest court, the Court of Appeals, having served with extraordinary distinction. Disregard of state court decisions under the rubric of general law authorized by *Swift v. Tyson* was hardly to be expected of Cardozo. Surely Cardozo was no believer in the unlimited sway of *Swift v. Tyson*. Surely Cardozo would have been pleased to have the issue of general law considered once again by all of the justices. And here was Kiendl saying that without a stay there would be no petition for certiorari and no chance for the nine once again to consider *Swift v. Tyson*. After listening to the opposition to the application for a stay, Cardozo, on the spot, granted it. There was a stay in place at once and the case now moved to the United States Supreme Court.

The petition for certiorari was filed on August 30, 1937. The practice in those days required the petitioner to list the assignments of error that he asked the Supreme Court to correct and, now, remember, this assignment of error was 10 out of 16 in the Second Circuit. Now, in connection with the petition for certiorari in the Supreme Court, this assignment for error has become the first. And what does it say? It says, "The trial court refused to apply the established Pennsylvania rule to the effect that the doctrine of permissive pathways along a railroad's right of way is not recognized in Pennsylvania and that, in consequence, the only obligation of the railroad is to refrain from willful or wanton negligence." Now, shorn of the circumstances peculiar to this particular plaintiff and this particular accident, the issue stood out—what was to become of *Swift v. Tyson*? As the biographer of Charles Evans Hughes tells us, "*Erie v. Tompkins* came to the court after years of brooding by several of its members over the inconsistent practice of applying different versions of the common law in the federal and in the state courts."

The petition for certiorari was granted on October 11, 1937. And Kiendl's brief for the appellant followed on January 3, 1938. And it is an exercise in how a brief should be written. First it was necessary to persuade the court that the failure to apply Pennsylvania law made a difference in that if Pennsylvania law had been applied, the outcome might well have been different and that is what point 1 argues. Second, you've got to show the court that Pennsylvania law is, indeed, favorable to the railroad. And that's what point 2 argues. It sets forth the Pennsylvania cases establishing the requirement that the railroad merely avoid wanton negligence with respect to a pedestrian on a parallel footpath. And now, third, it becomes necessary for the railroad, for Kiendl, to face up to *Swift v. Tyson*. How do you make an argument to the court to the effect that the Southern District of New York should have applied the Pennsylvania rule in this case, given *Swift v. Tyson*? Well, one possibility is simply to ask the court to overrule *Swift v. Tyson*. But, as we said before, it's been around for almost 100 years, everybody is familiar with it. Why overrule it after we've all gotten used to it? Now, Kiendl has been dead for many years; there was no way for me to interview him. The only, as it were, record that he leaves behind as to his strategic thinking was a memorandum that he dictated some years later as to how he formulated the railroad's position in this case. With respect to this point, what are you going to do with *Swift v. Tyson*? This is what Kiendl says in the memorandum: "After the granting of the petition for certiorari, we were faced with the dilemma of attacking the doctrine of *Swift v. Tyson* directly or endeavoring to suggest that this doctrine was inapplicable in the instant case. Convinced that a head-on attack might be fatal, we decided to present the case based on the argument that we had come up with."

Now, what was that argument? It was a tour de force. Now, remember, all subsequent courts had assumed that the holding, the teaching of *Swift v. Tyson* was that when a federal judge sits in a diversity case, the rule of decision is general law, whatever the federal judge thinks makes sense is the rule and state law really has nothing much to do with it. What Kiendl did to begin with was go back and carefully read Story's opinion. It's a rather useful piece of advice generally. Always begin by reading the opinions. They are not the end of wisdom, but frequently they are the beginning, at least of being better informed about the case. He read the opinion carefully and he realized that what Story actually said was that with respect to a good many matters, the federal judge sitting in a diversity case is to apply general law. "But," said Story, "where there is a matter of peculiar local concern. . . ." " and what would such a matter be? Real property within the state is a peculiar local concern. And with respect to such a matter of peculiar local concern, the highest courts of the state have enunciated a rule clearly and unequivocally, then the federal court in a diversity case should follow the rule enunciated by the courts of that state. Well, that's a kind of exception to the general law doctrine of *Swift v. Tyson*. And what Kiendl did was rely upon it. He didn't ask the court to overrule *Swift v. Tyson*. He didn't ask the court to ignore it, he asked the court to apply it. He said, "This is a matter that involves real estate. That pathway that is worn out by people walking along the tracks over the years is real property belonging to the railroad. With respect to that real property, the Supreme Court of Pennsylvania has over the years enunciated a rule that has become absolutely clear to everybody concerned with such matters. Story himself says that that rule then becomes the rule of decision for a federal judge to apply in a federal diversity case." And do you see what it does? It avoids the problem of arguing to overrule a decision that has been with us for 100 years and that all of us have become comfortable with. That really is an extraordinary piece of lawyering.

And finally, in the appellant's brief, it was necessary to try to overcome any sympathy that the justices might feel for Tompkins, who, after all, had lost a right arm. And Kiendl did it by arguing that Tompkins had been guilty of contributory negligence as a matter of law in walking along that pathway in the middle of the night. Now, that's nothing to argue in the Supreme Court, that's doomed to failure. And Kiendl would know that—of course he would know that. He made that argument on the off-chance that he could get a justice or two thinking about the possibility that as Tompkins walked on that footpath at 2 o'clock in the morning, he was drunk, and when he slipped under the wheels he was at least partially responsible for what happened to him.

Now, Tompkins's brief was written by the three-man team of Nemeroff, Kaufman and Danzig, our friends from the beginning, with help from their colleagues from Stubby Hunt's office. Stubby Hunt had passed away at about this time and so his office associates helped with the writing of the brief. Sharply and forcefully, the brief argued that general law applied, that general law imposed a duty of reasonable care on the railroad. Since the jury had been charged on that theory, there was no error below. And, as to Kiendl's suggestion that *Swift v. Tyson* be read in the way that Kiendl suggested, they simply said, "There is no authority whatsoever to support that view of *Swift v. Tyson*." There is a reply brief, but it simply replied. There's no need to talk about it separately.

On Monday, January 31, 1938, the court convened, as usual, at noon. Chief Justice Hughes and Justices McReynolds, Brandeis, Butler, Stone, Roberts and Black were present. As soon as they had seated themselves, the chief called upon Stanley Reed to step forward and be inducted as an associate justice. And because of the special nature of the occasion, the courtroom was unusually crowded with guests. The spouses of the justices were there. Reed's successor as solicitor general, Robert Jackson, later to become a Supreme Court justice himself, was there. Attorney General Homer Cummings, was there. Labor Leader John Lewis was there. The ritual of inducting the new justice took about a minute. The marshall escorted the new justice to his chair on the extreme right of the bench. Next to him was the chair in which normally Cardozo would be sitting, but that chair was empty because Cardozo was home ill of the sickness of which he would die in a couple of months. Ironically, the man who granted the stay, making it possible for the whole case to be in the Supreme Court, was not there to participate in the decision on the merits. The chief announced the reading of opinions—there were 15. The clerk noted various orders and then the chief justice said, "Arguments." The first argument on the calendar that afternoon was *Erie v. Tompkins*. Kiendl argued for Erie and an office associate of Stubby Hunt named Reese argued for Tompkins.

Now, there is no transcript of the argument. All we have is Kiendl's recollection of what occurred. And this is what he said, dictating to his secretary many years later.

"At the time of the oral argument, I had not proceeded very far before Mr. Justice Brandeis pointedly inquired about our views with regard to the *Swift v. Tyson* case. In the ensuing discussion, I could not refrain from expressing my view that the doctrine of that case was unfortunate in its consequences, but that, nevertheless, its acceptance by so many courts for so many years precluded me from suggesting that the doctrine be overruled. Practically all the members of the court then participated in a discussion of *Swift v. Tyson* and a large part of my argument revolved about it."

On the next Saturday, February 5, 1938, the justices met to confer about the cases that had been argued during the preceding week. *Erie v. Tompkins* was among them. Chief Justice Hughes opened discussion with this comment. He said, "If we wish to overrule *Swift v. Tyson*, here is our opportunity." And it quickly appeared that all but Butler and McReynolds agreed that the time had come. Hughes assigned the opinion to Brandeis and it was filed with the assent of Hughes, Stone, Roberts and Black. Cardozo's illness, as we've already pointed out, prevented him from participating. Butler wrote a dissenting opinion in which McReynolds joined and Reed—and remember, it had been Reed's first day on the court and *Erie v. Tompkins* was the first case argued that day—Reed concurred in the result only, disavowing *Swift v. Tyson* on nonconstitutional grounds exclusively, and a personal point. This is Stanley Reed, the juniorest justice, talking about a case which was his first case as a Supreme Court justice, and he writes an opinion saying not, "I disagree with you, Louie," talking about Louis D. Brandeis, but rather, "Louie, you have made a mistake in your legal analysis." Now that takes guts. That's takes real guts. And Stanley Reed had them and I applaud him for it. Well, the Supreme Court remanded the case for further proceedings, because technically the record was silent as to what the Pennsylvania rule was and so forth. On July 12, 1938, in another opinion by Judge Swan joined by Judges Manton and Learned Hand, the Second Circuit held that under Pennsylvania law, the railroad owes a pedestrian like Tompkins only a duty to refrain from wanton negligence. And since Tompkins was able neither to plead nor to prove that high degree of culpability, it was pointless to try the case a second time. Accordingly, the Second Circuit itself directed judgment for Erie.

Now it was Tompkins's turn to petition for certiorari. He did so and on October 24, 1938, his petition was denied. And so, ladies and gentlemen, ended the litigation between Harry James Tompkins and the Erie Railroad. Its fame, I suppose, will be everlasting. But for a time immediately after the Supreme Court's decision on April 25, it seemed that no one outside the profession would ever hear of it. *Law Week* had treated the case prominently on the front page of its issue of April 26, but no general newspaper mentioned it. On Wednesday, April 27, Professor, as he then was, Felix Frankfurter, wrote his friend, President Franklin D. Roosevelt, as follows. He said, "I certainly didn't expect to live to see the day when the court would announce, as they did on Monday, that it itself has usurped power for nearly 100 years. And think of not a single New York paper, at least none that I saw, having a nose for the significance of such a decision." But the silence persisted. On May 2, 1938, Justice Stone wrote privately to Arthur Krock, who was then the editor of the editorial page of *The New York Times,* in order to bring to Krock's attention to this case which Stone said was "The most important opinion since I have been on the court." Well, that note certainly brought the case to Krock's attention. On May 3, Krock devoted his Editorial Page column to *Erie v. Tompkins*, heading it, "A Momentous Decision of the Supreme Court." And the next day's column was also devoted to *Erie v. Tompkins*. And on May 6, two or three days later, Krock reported that the two columns had produced a shower of approving letters from lawyers. On July 25, Solicitor General Robert Jackson, as he then was, addressed the Section on Real Property, Probate and Trust Law of the American Bar Association at its annual meeting. His subject was, "The Rise and Fall of *Swift v. Tyson*."

The dam, you see, had broken. And as this afternoon, I trust proves, the flood has yet to recede. But it was a lawsuit like any other. Tompkins had sued, Tompkins had lost. After the Circuit Court's decision on remand, Tompkins went home to Pennsylvania. He had no money. He was unable to work. Without a right arm, there was really nothing that he could do. Nemeroff recalls that he, Nemeroff, sent Tompkins small sums from time to time, but Nemeroff eventually lost touch with him. And, as a matter of fact, today Nemeroff does not know what happened to Tompkins. I can report to you, and this is the first audience who is receiving such a report, that just four or five days ago I got some further information about Tompkins. I got it by having an item put in the Hughestown, Pennsylvania newspaper. There is, and has been since 1948, a weekly newspaper in Hughestown, Pennsylvania, and the item simply was that a fellow named Harry James Tompkins, who used to live in this town, had a great case in the Supreme Court. Does anybody know anything about Tompkins and his family? And a couple of people wrote in with information. It appears that Tompkins returned to Pennsylvania, did his best to earn a living, and apparently managed to earn a living. He raised that infant daughter of his. She ultimately married and had two children of her own so that Tompkins was a grandparent. Tompkins was apparently an affable fellow and he was liked by everybody in the community. He apparently enjoyed a drink every once in a while. He tended to a certain verbosity when he drank and when he did drink, people recalled, inevitably he got to talking about his great case in the Supreme Court. And everybody in the town assumed that he was fantasizing. He never had a great case. He knew nothing about the Supreme Court. It was just a simple soul trying to demonstrate that he, too, was worth considering.

Well, on the day the Circuit Court announced its judgment ultimately in favor of the Erie Railroad, Nemeroff, who had gone to the courthouse that day wearing what he thought was his lucky blue suit, remembers that he came out of the courthouse and he stood on the steps and he raised his fists to the skies and he swore an oath to himself that never again would he permit himself to be involved in litigation. He went on, as a matter of fact, to become a specialist in foreign commercial transactions, international commercial transactions, I guess we law professors would say. He founded a prosperous law firm specializing in that field of practice. He, himself, is now pretty much retired. He spends just a couple of months in New York City supervising the law firm and the rest of the time he lives on a lavish houseboat moored in the canal off Collins Avenue in Miami Beach. Some time after the Circuit Court's decision in favor of the railroad, Theodore Kiendl, in keeping with his lifelong custom in concluded cases, simply burnt his entire file on *Erie v. Tompkins*. And, best of all, on some unknown day, ladies and gentlemen, between 1938 and 1946, District Judge Samuel Mandelbaum, for whatever reason—obviously, we cannot reconstruct the reason—thought that he would like to take a look at Justice Brandeis's opinion in *Erie v. Tompkins*. As you know, every federal judge has a kind of life tenancy on a fairly complete law library and it is substantially complete with respect to federal matters and certainly will include a complete run of the United States Reports. Judge Mandelbaum reached up to the shelf and took down his copy of Volume 304 of the United States Reports. And that, ladies and gentlemen, is the book I am holding in my hand. If you were able to look at it with me, you would see stamped on the inside front covers, "Judge Mandelbaum, Property of U.S." If you were to turn to page 70, you would have not the first page of the case report—that's page 64—but at page 70 you have that early point in the opinion in which Justice Brandeis refers for the first and only time to "the trial judge" who refused to rule that the applicable law precluded recovery. Well, what Judge Mandelbaum did was to take a pencil and, again, for reasons on which we can only speculate, he wrote in the margin. There is Judge Mandelbaum's writing running along the margin of that page. And, by the way, we have ascertained that it is his writing. Now, I cannot reproduce the accent or the tone of voice, but the inimitable syntax of Judge Mandelbaum is right there in what he wrote in the margin. And this is what he wrote: He said, "Because of the *Swift v. Tyson* case, although before this case I never knew of its existence, to be truthful. And for the confusion this decision brought about, it might have been better to leave it alone and stand by good old Swifty."

Thank you.

Chapter 10

In Praise of Simplicity

IRVING YOUNGER: If at this moment, ladies and gentlemen, I had three wishes, I would use the first of them to acquire the gift of tongues so that I might better be able to express the honor it is to have been asked to speak to you today. But, of course, with honor goes obligation. And my first obligation was to select a topic. Your president was no help. When I asked him for a suggestion, his response was, "Whatever you want." And when I asked your program chairman, she said, "Who listens?" And, so you see, it was left to me, alone and unaided, to find a subject. What topic is correct, I asked myself, for some 300 men and women, perhaps one-half of you judges or lawyers or law professors, the rest highly intelligent.

And then it came to me, the right, the perfect, the inevitable topic sprang to my mind. I name it, however, with diffidence, aware that on this occasion and before this audience, its suitability will by no means be obvious. Some of you may regard it as a subject too unaccustomed to be entirely appropriate. It may be said that in talking about it I have been excessively ingenious, going beyond the merely unusual and touching the strange.

My topic, ladies and gentlemen, is virtue. Not moral virtue, of course not. For with respect to moral virtue, reverence, temperance, chastity—each one of you is beyond improvement. Rather, I shall talk about intellectual virtue, a quality of thought that distinguishes mind from merely caprice or appetite. With an eye on the clock, I shall talk about only one aspect of intellectual virtue, but an aspect particularly in want of a champion among lawyers and judges and law professors. That one aspect of intellectual virtue is simplicity. And if you must have a title for this talk, call it "In Praise of Simplicity."

Now, it has long been understood by practitioners of disciplines other than the law that simplicity marks the master. Simplicity walks together with high seriousness, the hallmark of large intention and great accomplishment. Some citations to support my text:

First, from literature, here are three of the most celebrated passages from the most celebrated writer who has ever lived. First, the beginning of the 18th Sonnet:

> Shall I compare thee to a summer's day?
> Thou art more lovely and more temperate.
> Rough winds do shake the darling buds of May,
> And summer's lease hath all too short a date.

Next the beginning of Hamlet's celebrated soliloquy on death:

> To be, or not to be—that is the question:
> Whether 'tis nobler in the mind to suffer
> The slings and arrows of outrageous fortune
> Or to take arms against a sea of troubles
> And by opposing, end them. . . .

And finally, Prospero's farewell from the Tempest:

> Our revels now are ended: these, our actors,
> As I foretold you, were all spirits and
> Are melted into air, into thin air;
> And, like the baseless fabric of this vision,
> The cloud-capped tow'rs, the gorgeous palaces,
> The solemn temples, the great globe itself,

Yea, all which it inherit, shall dissolve,
And like this insubstantial pageant faded,
Leave not a rack behind. We are such stuff
As dreams are made on, and our little life
Is rounded with a sleep. . . .

Well, I don't suppose that there's anything finer in all of English and perhaps in all of the world's literature. And those three passages, ladies and gentlemen, use a total of 153 words, not one of which might not be spoken in ordinary conversation. One word of the 153 contains four syllables, five contain three syllables, 35 contain two syllables, and 112—almost three-fourths of the whole—are words of one syllable. Simplicity indeed.

My second example comes from pictorial art. On the ceiling of the Sistine Chapel, Michelangelo paints a picture of God transmitting the spark of life to Adam and fashions an image of awesome power, and many of you have been to Rome and have seen it with your own eyes. All of us have seen it in reproduction. And what is that image? Simply God's finger touches Adam's. A 12-year-old can understand it. Only a Michelangelo can create it.

And, third, from music, some of you will know Beethoven's Opus 111, the 32nd or last piano sonata. Remember the second movement? It is a theme in variations. It is one of the most profound things music has to offer, and Beethoven made it of a theme consisting of the simple interval of a fourth and variations woven largely of trills, simple trills.

Ah, but enough of other disciplines. Let me turn now to that curious mixture of many arts and exemplar of none—our infinitely demanding and infinitely fascinating master/mistress, the law. How stands simplicity with the law? Not well, I fear. Walk through the library. Observe the shelves. They bulge with treatises, statutes, law reviews, regulations, digests, and case reports. No, whatever its other charms, the law is hardly simple. But worse, we lawyers have made of simplicity a vice, the shameful badge of a mind too lazy or too weak to be suitably complicated. Now, who doesn't recall a professor at law school saying, "Really, that won't do. It's just too simple," or an appellate court saying, "The judge below failed to grasp the complexity of the problem," or a trial judge saying to some poor working lawyer, "Counselor, isn't your argument far too simple?" Well, ladies and gentlemen, I am here to speak up for simplicity. I lament the law's lack of it. I condemn the perversion that turns it into a sin. I preach the faith that simplicity is good in itself and I assert that were lawyers, judges, legislators, and law professors only brave enough to be simple, the law would be improved in four different ways.

First, lucidity. Much of what lawyers and judges and law professors say is incomprehensible. Here is an example drawn from a recent issue of a leading law review. Now, tact forbids me to name it, but lest there be any awkward misunderstandings, I'll give you a hint. The name of this law review contains four letters, of which the first comes very near the end of the alphabet. One of our best-known professors writes an article about entrapment, a doctrine familiar to all students of the criminal law. From that article, I quote a footnote: "However, entrapment is examined primarily to demonstrate the need for a rule shift in overseer focus from citizen to authority and not to detail what might constitute appropriate police conduct." What does that mean? Nothing, I suspect, absolutely nothing. And if it does mean something, observe that you can discover the author's thought only by shoveling away the rubbish of complexity and that, I say, is an undesirable state of affairs. A legal system, like any system of thought, should be clear. We lawyers or judges or law professors have an obligation to those we serve, the public at large, to speak lucidly about the law. We owe it to the public to practice simplicity of language.

Second, candor. Lawyers and judges should call things by their right name and state the real reasons for what they do. Only then will it be possible to engage in intelligent analysis and criticism, resulting in the exposure and correction of error, the elimination of irrationality, and the transmission to our successors of a body of law better and more coherent than the one we received from our predecessors. Yet, many of us have fallen into a habit which dishonors candor. We do not call things by their right name, but by elaborate wrong names. We explain our decisions not as what they are, but as something else—easier and always more complicated than the truth. I draw my example here from the Supreme Court's decisions of a dozen years or so ago. In a case called *Warth v. Seldin*, which you will find at 422 *U.S. Reports* 490, various petitioners had sued the town of Penfield, a suburb of Rochester, New York, claiming that Penfield's zoning ordinance unlawfully operated to exclude persons of low and moderate income from living in the town. The Supreme Court dismissed that case for lack of standing. Well, go and read or reread the majority opinion and when you're done with it, ask yourself whether standing was really the problem. I think you'll say, no, the real problem is that the petitioners were raising enormously sensitive issues of race and economic class, which the court was unwilling to face. The court chose to avoid those issues by adding some very complicated wrinkles to the already much-vexed law of standing. But would it not have been better for the court to say straight out that some issues can be decided only when the time is right and the time is not right for the issues in this case? The simple approach, you see, serves where the disingenuous fails. Candor would be appreciated in judicial opinions as much as elsewhere.

And now, third, aesthetics. Yes, aesthetics. Beauty. Beauty may exist in a legal system as well as in a salt cellar if the salt cellar is by Cellini. Now, I make no utilitarian argument for it. I say only that we should seek beauty everywhere and take pleasure in it wherever we find it, even in a statute. Now, here is my idea of a statute which is a thing of beauty. It's Section 2302 of the Uniform Commercial Code. It says simply, "If the court as a matter of law finds the contract or any clause of the contract to have been unconscionable at the time it was made, the court may refuse to enforce the contract, or it may enforce the remainder of the contract without the unconscionable clause, or it may so limit the application of the unconscionable clause as to avoid an unconscionable result." Doesn't that bring a tear to the eye?

Contrast it now with the Internal Revenue Code. The aesthetic pleasure we take in our profession would be vastly increased were some United States District Judge one fine morning to file the following, which I have written and freely give to any judge who cares to use it. It goes as follows. "This is a class action in which the plaintiff taxpayer on behalf of himself and all others similarly situated, sues for a judgment declaring the Internal Revenue Code unconstitutional. His argument is, 1) he does not understand it; 2) no one understands it; and 3) it is therefore invalid. Well, the theory is novel to be sure, but not for that reason necessarily wrong.

Let us examine the code.

"Item: I doubt that the ordinary citizen of average education and normal mental endowment can grasp the meaning of a sentence more than 50 words long. The Code contains sentences of 379 words, of 385 words, and the longest single sentence I have been able to find in the Code is 506 words long. For those of you taking notes, that sentence will be found in Section 7701A-19.

"Item: Apart from mere length, I doubt that the ordinary citizen can grasp the meaning of a sentence which does not run more or less in a straight line from beginning through middle to end. What then is the ordinary citizen to make of this, the last sentence of Section 509A? And I should be at some pains to note that I am speaking of the Internal Revenue Code as of today. That is to say, following the so-called reforms and simplifications of 1986. Well, it's Section 509A of the Code and it reads as follows. 'For purposes of Paragraph 3, an organization described in Paragraph 2 shall be deemed to include an organization described in Section 501C, 4, 5 or 6, which would be described in Paragraph 2 if it were an organization described in Section 501C(3).'

"Now, I do not wish to expand this opinion unduly and so for additional illustrations, I refer interested persons to any page of the Internal Revenue Code selected at random. Now, the due process clause means many things, but one of them, assuredly, is that the enactments of Congress, whatever their subject matter, be understandable to an ordinary citizen upon the application of ordinary diligence. This may be the first case holding a statute void for undue complexity, but I trust it will not be the last. The Internal Revenue Code is declared unconstitutional." Well, there you have my opinion.

But now the fourth reason I advance in support of simplicity—elegance, elegance. Six-and-a-half centuries ago, ladies and gentlemen, William Ockham wrote, "Pluralitas non est ponenda sine neccesitate." Well, of course, of course, you remember that. That's Ockham's Razor. Given two ways of saying or doing or explaining something, one simpler than the other, always prefer the simpler. You might put it this way: don't make it more complicated than it has to be. That is an axiom of all intellectual work. Philosophers, mathematicians, scientists, use it to this very day. The simple is more likely than the complex to be true. And if truth is itself too complex a measure, then put it that the simple is more elegant than the complex.

I draw my example here from the field in which as a sometime teacher of law I specialize—evidence. Now, the keystone rule in the law of evidence is the rule against hearsay. Hearsay is not admissible, with exceptions, of course. Now, in the Federal Rules of Evidence there are 27 specific exceptions and a cancel essentially for any other hearsay as good as that which the rules specifically make admissible. Now that's complicated. And because it's complicated, it's inelegant. I would reformulate the rule to say that hearsay is admissible unless a trial judge in his or her sound discretion thinks it fair to exclude it. That's the rule every judge applies anyway. It's about as much as any appellate court can do with hearsay and observe that it takes a clumsy contraption of exception piled upon exception piled upon exception and turns it into an object of plain and simple elegance.

Well, there, ladies and gentlemen, you have my praise of simplicity. It is a virtue good in itself as artists and scientists have long known. It would make our craft and mystery more lucid, candid, beautiful, and elegant. I want simplicity for the law because I love the law. And if this, my praise, has seemed to you fond and foolish, call it lover's folly, please, and forgive me for my love's sake.

Curriculum Vitae

Irving Younger

Date of Birth	November 30, 1932, New York, NY
Date of Death	March 13, 1988, Minneapolis, MN
Marital-Family Status	Married Judith T. Younger (Professor of Law, University of Minnesota Law School); two children
Education	Public schools in New York City Bronx High School of Science (Science Valedictorian) Harvard College, A.B., Magna Cum Laude, 1953; Field of concentration: English literature. Phi Beta Kappa. At Harvard, served as President of Harvard Theatre Group and of Lowell House Music Society. In summer of 1952, awarded fellowship to attend Salzburg Seminar in American Studies, Salzburg, Austria, as assistant to Robert Lowell in course in American poetry. New York University School of Law, LL.B. 1958. Editor-in-Chief, New York University Law Review, 1957–58. Order of the Coif. LL.D. Lewis and Clark, 1981, Honorary Degree
Military Service	United States Army, 1953–55. Honorable discharge in rank of Private First Class.
Bar Memberships	New York United States Supreme Court United States Court of Appeals for the Second Circuit United States District Court for the Southern District of New York United States District Court for the Eastern District of New York

Professional History, 1958–65

Associated with Paul, Weiss, Rifkind, Wharton & Garrison, New York City, 1958–60.

Assistant United States Attorney for the Southern District of New York, 1960–62.

Visiting Lecturer, Cornell Law School, 1961.

Partner in Younger & Younger (and successor firms), New York City, 1962–65.

Counsel (part-time), Special Committee on Ethics, New York State Legislature, 1963.

Adjunct Assistant Professor of Law, New York University School of Law, 1962–65.

Professional History, 1965–68

Professor of Law, New York University School of Law;
appointed as Associate Professor on September 1, 1965, promoted to Professor on September 1, 1967; resigned December 31, 1968, after election to judgeship. In these three years, served as Chairman of Curriculum Committee, Chairman of Faculty-Student Committee, and member of Faculty Recruitment Committee

Professional History, 1965–68, continued

Visiting Professor of Law, University of Naples, Italy, summer 1968.

Member, Mayor's Committee on Court Delay and Sentencing.

Member, Criminal Courts Committee of The Legal Aid Society.

Member of Executive Committee, Society for the Libraries of New York University.

President, New York University Law Review Alumni Association.

Consultant, Sub-Committee on Improvements in Judicial Machinery of the Committee on the Judiciary, United States Senate, 1966.

Consultant, National Advisory Commission on Civil Disorders (Kerner Commission) 1967–68.

Professional History, 1968–74

Elected Judge of the Civil Court of the City of New York, January 1, 1969. Resigned July 1, 1974 to accept appointment to professorship at Cornell. In addition to sitting in Civil Court, served by designation as Acting Justice of Supreme Court.

Adjunct Professor of Law, New York University School of Law, January 1, 1969–74.

Adjunct Professor of Law, Columbia Law School, January 1, 1971–74. Teacher of the Year, 1973–74, by vote of the Columbia Law School Student Senate.

Lecturer, National College of the State Judiciary, 1972–74.

Lecturer, Appellate Judges' Seminar, 1969–73.

Member, State-Federal Judicial Council for the State of New York (by appointment of Chief Judge Fuld).

Member, Committee on Modernization of Court Processing of Cases (by appointment of Presiding Justice Stevens).

Chairman, Education Committee of National Conference of Special Court Judges, American Bar Association.

Association of the Bar of the City of New York ~ Chairman of Special Committee on Penology; Member of Committee on Federal Courts; Member of Committee on Federal Legislation; Member of Committee on Criminal Courts; Member of Entertainment Committee; Member of Committee on Memorials.

New York County Lawyers' Association ~ Member of New York County Lawyers' Foundation, Inc.

Institute for Trial Judges (Hunter College) ~ Member of Board of Sponsors.

On July 1, 1974, appointed Samuel S. Leibowitz Professor of Trial Techniques, Cornell Law School. Member of Curriculum Committee and of Committee on Faculty Appointments. Resigned effective December 31, 1980.

Professional History, 1974–80

Samuel S. Leibowitz Professor of Trial Techniques, Cornell Law School (1974–80).
In addition to teaching courses at the law school, taught undergraduate courses at the College of Arts & Sciences at Cornell University.

Member of faculty, National Institute for Trial Advocacy, Boulder, CO 1974–80.

Northeast Regional Director, National Institute for Trial Advocacy, 1975–79.

Chairman, Section on Trial Advocacy, Association of American Law Schools, 1975–77.

Chairman, Committee on Teaching of Trial Advocacy, Section of Litigation, American Bar Association, 1975–78.

Special Counsel, New York State Commission of Correction, 1976–77.

Visiting Professor of Law, Harvard Law School, 1978–79.

Consultant, United States Attorney General's Advocacy Institute.

Member of Advisory Board, The Review of Litigation.

Member of faculty, Advanced Trial Advocacy Workshop, 1979–80.

Member, Implementation Committee of the Judicial Conference of the United States on Admission of Attorneys to Federal Practice.

Professional History, 1981–88

January 1, 1981–84, member of Williams & Connolly, Washington, D.C.

Adjunct Professor of Law, Georgetown University Law Center, 1981–84.

Principal faculty member for The Professional Education Group, Minnetonka, Minnesota, 1981–88 [continuing legal education seminars, speeches and recordings ~ www.proedgroup.com ~ 800.229.CLE1 (2531)].

Visiting Professor, University of Minnesota Law School, 1984–85.

Marvin J. Sonosky Professor of Law, University of Minnesota Law School, 1985–88.

Professional Associations

American Law Institute

American Bar Association

New York State Bar Association

Association of the Bar of the City of New York

American Historical Association

Organization of American Historians

Lectures & Papers Delivered*—a sampling …*

1979 William O. Douglas Lecture, Gonzaga University School of Law. "The Idea of Sanctuary."

1979 John R. Coen Memorial Lecture, University of Colorado School of Law. "On Judicial Opinions Considered as One of the Fine Arts."

1979 Ben J. Altheimer Lecture, University of Arkansas School of Law. "The Facts of a Case."

1980 Society for the Humanities, Cornell University. "Ulysses in Court."

1980 Charles Evans Hughes Lecture, New York County Lawyers' Association. "Law, Liberty, and the Congress of the United States."

1980 Association of the Bar of the City of New York. "Expert Witnesses."

17 Articles for General Readership

(Excluding book reviews, newspaper articles, music criticism, and other ephemera)

"A Machine is Not Enough," *Saturday Review*, December 31, 1966, p. 20.

"Laying Down the Law to Number-One Lawman," *The New Republic*, March 14, 1967, p. 11.

"The Perjury Routine," *The Nation*, May 8, 1967, p. 596.

"Pornography and Violence," *The Nation*, August 14, 1967, p. 120.

"The Perjury Routine—Joinder and Rejoinder," 3 *Criminal Law Bulletin* 615 (1967).

"Judicial Opinions as Literature: Wishful Thinking by a Reader of Both," 22 *Record of the Association of the Bar of the City of New York* 706 (1967).

"Milking the Pension Funds," (with Judith T. Younger as co-author), *The Nation*, May 20, 1968, p. 662.

"From Here to Obscenity," *The Nation*, September 2, 1968, p. 184.

"The Judge," *Case & Comment*, May/June 1969 p. 41.

"Was Alger Hiss Guilty?" 60 *Commentary* 23 (August 1975).

"In Praise of Simplicity," 62 *American Bar Association Journal* 632 (1976).

"Memoir of a Prosecutor," 62 *Commentary* 66 (October 1976).

"L'Eminence Plat," *National Review*, October 28, 1977, p. 1245.

"Writers in the Law," *Cornell Law Forum*, June 1978, p. 2.

"Taking Watergate Seriously," *National Review*, July 7, 1978, p. 849.

Articles for General Readership, continued

"In Defense of the 'Litmus Test,'" *National Review*, November 14, 1980, p. 1393.

"Socrates and Us," 66 *Commentary* 46, December 1980.

35 Technical Articles

"Evidence (N.Y. Survey)," 33 *N.Y.U. L. Rev.* 1288 (1958).

"Evidence (N.Y. Survey)," *34 N.Y.U. L. Rev.* 1594 (1959).

"Congressional Investigations and Executive Secrecy: A Study in the Separation of Powers," 20 *U. Pitt. L. Rev.* 755 (1959).

"Priority of Pretrial Examination in the Federal Courts—A Comment," 34 *N.Y.U. L. Rev.* 1271 (1959).

"Citizens Who Publish Abroad: A Study in the Pathology of American Copyright Law," 44 *Cornell L. Q.* 215 (1959).

Preliminary Hearings in Federal Criminal Procedure, prepared for the Sub-Committee on Improvements in Judicial Machinery of the Committee on the Judiciary, United States Senate and printed in the Sub-Committee's Hearings on the United States Commissioner System (1966).

"Wiretapping, Electronic Eavesdropping, and the Police," 42 *N.Y.U. L. Rev.* 83 (1967).

"Sovereign Admissions," 43 *N.Y.U. L. Rev.* 108 (1968).

"The Requirement of Corroboration in Prosecutions for Sex Offenses in New York," 40 *Fordham Law Review* 263 (1971).

"A Judge's View of Unconscionability," *Uniform Commercial Code Law Journal* (Spring, 1973).

"Confrontation and Hearsay," 1 *Hofstra Law Review* 32 (1973).

"Statements of Past Physical Condition as an Exception to the Rule against Hearsay," 19 *N.Y. Law Forum* 777 (1974).

"Some Additional Observations on the Competence of Trial Counsel," 47 *N.Y. State Bar Journal* 284 (1975).

"Evidence, in 'The Second Circuit Review, 1973–74 Term,'" 41 *Brooklyn Law Review* 1183 (1975).

"Computers and the Law of Evidence," 10 *International Society of Barristers Quarterly* 150 (1975).

"Computer Print-outs in Evidence," 2 *Litigation* 28 (1975), reprinted in *Use of Computers in Litigation* (ABA 1979).

"Hearsay and Confrontation," 2 *National Journal of Criminal Defense* 65 (1976).

Technical Articles, continued ...

"Impeachment with Prior Bad Acts under the Federal Rules of Evidence," 11 *International Society of Barristers Quarterly* 171 (1976), reprinted in 20 *Trial Lawyers Guide* 121 (1976).

"Three Essays on Character and Credibility under the Federal Rules of Evidence," 5 *Hofstra Law Review* 7 (1976).

"Cicero on Cross-Examination," 3 *Litigation* 18 (1977).

"Professional Responsibility," 43 *Brooklyn L. Rev.* 863 (1977).

"Persuading to Acquit," 3 *Litigation* 28 (1977).

"On Technology and the Law of Evidence," 49 *Colo. L. Rev.* 1 (1977), reprinted 12 *International Society of Barristers Quarterly* 239 (1977).

"What Happened in Erie," 56 *Texas L. Rev.* 1010 (August 1978).

"Evidence Commentary, in the Second Circuit Review 1976–77 Term," 44 *Brooklyn L. Rev.* 111 (1978).

"Pride and Perjury," 31 *Stanford L. Rev.* 313 (1979).

"The Idea of Sanctuary," 14 *Gonzaga L. Rev.* 761 (1979).

"Quasi in Rem Defaults after *Shaffer v. Heitner*: Some Unanswered Questions," 45 *Brooklyn L. Rev.* 675 (1979).

"Unlawful Peremptory Challenges," 7 *Litigation* 23 (1980).

"In Search of Premises," 34 *Miami L. Rev.* 807 (1980).

"Reflections on the Rule Against Hearsay," 32 *S. Car. L. Rev.* 281 (1980).

"The Facts of a Case," 3 *UALR L.J.* 345 (1980).

"Three Footnotes to Legal History," 7 *Cornell Law Forum.* 15 (1980).

"On Judicial Opinions Considered as One of the Fine Arts," 51 *Colo. L. Rev.* 341 (1980).

"Admissibility of Statements on Past Physical Condition," 184 *N.Y. L. J.* 1 (1980).

14 Books and Monographs

The Art of Cross-Examination (Chicago 1976).

Article VII of the Federal Rules of Evidence, in The Liability of Professionals: Malpractice (Ann Arbor 1976).

An Irreverent Introduction to Hearsay (Chicago 1977).

Examinations, in Looking at Law School (New York 1977).

Credibility and Cross-Examination (Florida 1977).

Books and Monographs, continued

The Rules of Evidence: Do They Affect Persuasion?, in Persuasion: The Key to Success in Trial (Ann Arbor 1978).

The Lawyer's Relation with Non-Clients and The Lawyer's Responsibilities to the Public, in Professional Responsibility (American Bar Association 1978).

Psychological Testing that Might Invade the Province of the Jury, in New Frontiers in Litigation (Ann Arbor 1979), reprinted in *The Best of ICLE 1978–79.*

Materials for the Basic Course in Evidence (1980) ... republished as *Principles of Evidence*, now in its 5th Ed (2007—with Michael Goldsmith, David A. Sonenshein).

The Art of Advocacy, in Advocacy in the 80's (Ann Arbor 1980), reprinted in 15 *International Society of Barristers Quarterly* 291 (1980).

Imaginary Judicial Opinions, 1989, The Professional Education Group, Minnetonka, MN.

Persuasive Writing, 1990, The Professional Education Group, Minnetonka, MN.

Some of My Life [autobiography] 1991, The Professional Education Group, Minnetonka, MN.

13 Continuing Legal Education — Attorney Professional Development recordings

NOTE: All of the following are available exclusively from The Professional Education Group, 12401 Minnetonka Boulevard, Minnetonka, Minnesota 55305-3994—www.proedgroup.com

Evidence for Trial Lawyers (Original recording 1987)—Updated with commentary by Professor Stephen D. Easton in 2008 (6 hours—DVD and audio CD)

Credibility & Cross-Examination (3 hours, DVD, audio CD and MP3)
Includes "The 10 Commandments of Cross-Examination"

Expert Witnesses (3 hours, DVD, audio CD and MP3)

Jury Selection (3 hours, DVD, audio CD)

Hearsay (3 hours, DVD, audio CD)

Discovery (4 hours, DVD, audio CD)

Scientific Evidence (3 hours, DVD, audio CD)

Confrontation (3 hours, DVD, audio CD)

Classic Speeches on Law and Life ... (DVD or audio CD)

In Praise of Simplicity

On Judicial Opinions Considered as one of the Fine Arts

What Happened in Erie? [Erie Railroad Co. v. Tompkins], 304 U.S. 64 (1938)]

The Trial of Socrates, the Congress of the United States, and Us

The Trial of Alger Hiss

41 Judicial Opinions

Battani, Ltd. v. Bar-Car, Ltd., 59 Misc.2d 530, 299 N.Y.S.2d 629 (1969)

Bierman v. City of New York, 60 Misc.2d 497, 302 N.Y.S.2d 696 (1969)

Central Budget Corp. v. Knox, 62 Misc.2d 66, 307 N.Y.S.2d 936 (1969)

Jobse v. Connolly, 60 Misc.2d 69, 302 N.Y.S.2d 35 (1969)

Lewis v. Lewis, 59 M.2d 525, 299 N.Y.S.2d 755 (1969)

McConaghley v. City of New York, 60 Misc.2d 825, 304 N.Y.S.2d 136 (1969)

People v. Autorino, 61 Misc.2d 217, 305 N.Y.S.2d 124 (1969)

Robinson v. Merlite Land Sea & Sky, Inc., 60 Misc.2d 462, 305 N.Y.S.2d 289 (1969)

Sears Roebuck & Co. v. Austin, 60 Misc.2d 908, 304 N.Y.S.2d 131 (1969)

Star Credit Corp. v. Molina, 59 Misc.2d 290, 298 N.Y.S.2d 570 (1969)

Tilbern Realty, Inc. v. Lax Drug Co., Inc., 59 Misc.2d 515, 299 N.Y.S.2d 758 (1969)

White v. Empire Mutual Insurance Co., 59 Misc.2d 527, 299 N.Y.S.2d 998 (1969)

Alibrandi v. Helmsley, 63 Misc.2d 997, 314 N.Y.S.2d 95 (1970)

DuBose v. Velez, 63 Misc.2d 956, 313 N.Y.S.2d 881 (1970)

Gimbel Bros., Inc. v. Swift, 62 Misc.2d 156, 307 N.Y.S.2d 952 (1970)

Hirent Realty Corp. v. Mosley, 64 Misc.2d 1011, 317 N.Y.S.2d 592 (1970)

Johnson v. Block, 62 Misc.2d 126, 306 N.Y.S.2d 698 (1969)

Mondella v. Erie Lackawanna R. Co., 62 Misc.2d 989, 310 N.Y.S.2d 237(1970)

People v. McMurty, 64 Misc.2d 63, 314 N.Y.S.2d 194 (1970)

Weg v. Lippman, 63 Misc.2d 352, 312 N.Y.S.2d 862 (1970)

Abbett Realty Corp. v. Osnowicz, 65 Misc.2d 927, 319 N.Y.S.2d 213 (1971)

Davis v. John Hancock Mutual Life Insurance Co., 64 Misc.2d 791, 316 N.Y.S.2d 722 (1970)

Devon Service Inc. v. Ashreh Supply Corp., 68 Misc.2d 15, 324 N.Y.S.2d 802 (1971)

Dorrell Associates v. Urb Products Corp., 67 Misc.2d 716, 324 N.Y.S.2d 507 (1971)

Edwards v. Roe, 68 Misc. 2d 278, 327 N.Y.S.2d 307 (1971)

500 West 174 Street v. Vasquez, 67 Misc. 2d 993, 325 N.Y.S.2d 256 (1971)

Herman v. Branch Motor Express Co., 67 Misc. 2d 444, 323 N.Y.S.2d 794 (1971)

Jiang v. First National City Bank, 65 Misc. 2d 150, 317 N.Y.S.2d 635 (1971)

Margolies v. Lawrence, 67 Misc. 2d 468, 324 N.Y.S.2d 418 (1971)

People v. Kern, 67 Misc.2d 495, 324 N.Y.S.2d 442 (1971)

Judicial Opinions, continued ...

Sirico v. Cotto, 67 Misc. 2d 636, 324 N.Y.S.2d 483 N.Y. City Civ. Ct. (1971)

Teachers College of Columbia University v. Claussell, 67 Misc .2d 826, 325 N.Y.S.2d 50 N.Y. City Civ. Ct. (1971)

34 & 7 Realopp Corp. v. Seafood City, Inc., 67 Misc. 2d 625, 324 N.Y.S.2d 768 N.Y. City Civ. Ct. (1971)

Harlem River Consumers Cooperative, Inc. v. Manufacturers Hanover Trust Co., 68 Misc. 2d 608, 327 N.Y.S.2d 903 N.Y. City Civ. Ct. (1972)

150 East 58th St. Associates v. Birnbaum, 68 Misc. 2d 756, 327 N.Y.S.2d 878 N.Y. City Civ. Ct. (1972)

Haberman v. Wager, 73 Misc. 2d 732, 342 N.Y.S.2d 405 N.Y. City Civ. Ct. (1973)

Ellis v. Tower Health Club, Inc., 73 Misc .2d 319, 342 N.Y.S.2d 135 N.Y. City Civ. Ct. (1973)

Gramford Realty Corp. v. Valentin, 71 Misc. 2d 784, 337 N.Y.S.2d 160 N.Y. City Civ. Ct. (1972)

Yates v. Kaplan, 75 Misc. 2d 259, 347 N.Y.S.2d 543 N.Y. City Civ. Ct. (1973)

Raab v. Bowery Sav. Bank, 77 Misc. 2d 1054, 355 N.Y.S.2d 748 N.Y. City Civ. Ct. (1974)

Federal Ins. Co. v. Fries, 78 Misc. 2d 805, 355 N.Y.S.2d 741 N.Y. City Civ. Ct. (1974)

Index

A

ABA Journal, 103
Accrediting, 397–401, 468–470
A Distant Mirror (Tuchman), 346
Adoption of Harvey case, 304
The Adventure of the Greek Interpreter, 344
Advocacy, craft of, 115, 312–313
Ahearn, John F., 589
American Bar Association, 92, 593, 606
American Export case, 212–214
American Psychiatric Association, 100
Anderson, Margaret, 479–481, 483–487, 490
Anderson, Marian, 517
Andrews, Bert, 540
Apt, John, 557
Arnold, Benedict, 560
Assertive conduct, 268–271
Atlas, Nicholas, 498
Attlee, Clement, 461

B

Bailey, Lee, 189–191, 195–201
Batson v. Kentucky, 311
Battle of Britain, 163–164
Beach, Sylvia, 477, 491, 496, 498, 508
Bean v. the United States, 135, 218, 222–223, 225
Bennett, John Wheeler, 461
Bentley, Elizabeth, 520, 521, 527
Berle, Milton, 362
Binger, Carl, 101–102, 418, 447, 561–563
Black, Hugo, 579
Body language, in jury selection, 382
Borden, Lizzie, 452–453
Brandeis, Louis, 579–580, 604–605, 608
Brennan, William, 149
Bujasi, Steven, 528
Burley, A. A., 513
Butler, Pierce, 579, 604–605
Byrne, Matthew, 40

C

Califano, Joe, 135
Camus, Albert, 428
Cardozo, Benjamin Nathan, 295, 297, 307, 579, 598–601, 604
Carsons, Edward, 442
CDC. *See* Center for Disease Control
Celotex case, 74
Center for Disease Control (CDC), 214, 229
Cerf, Bennett, 490–491, 493, 494–495, 501, 505
Chambers, Richard, 516
Chambers, Whitaker, 101–102, 418, 513–517, 519–544, 549–557, 560–571, 575–577
Chesterton, G.K., 471
Christie, Agatha, 346
Churchill, Winston, 164
Code of Professional Responsibility, 97, 106
Collins, Henry, 514
Colwell, William, 580–581
Commins, Dorothy, 510
Commins, Saxe, 510
Common Law of Evidence, 131, 214
Commonwealth v. Soares, 385, 387
Communication, in cross-examination, 422

Competence, in cross-examination, 417–420
Conboy, Martin, 506–508
Conduct, 281
Contradiction, 403
Cooke, Alistair, 548
Coppolino v. State, 183–187, 189–191, 193–196, 199–202, 204–206, 219–220, 224
Corboy, Phil, 341
Costello, Frank, 402
Crawford v. Washington, 232
Credibility, in cross-examination, 395–474
Credit reports, in discovery, 26
Crosley, George, 525
Cross, Claude, 548, 559, 561, 575
Cross-examination, 395–474
Cummings, Homer, 604

D

Danzig, Aaron, 581, 584, 603
Darrow, Clarence, 257, 338, 414, 417, 442, 446–447
Databases, in discovery, 24
Daubert v. Merrel Dow Pharmaceuticals, 95, 159–160
Davis, John W., 587
Dean, John, 337
Dewey, Thomas, 511
Dickey, Bill, 367
DiMaggio, Joe, 367, 368–369, 393
Discovery, 3–93
Dowd v. Calabrese, 181
Drake, Paul, 146
Dubliners (Joyce), 480
Dulles, John Foster, 519, 558
Duncan v. Louisiana, 486

E

Edmonson v. Leesville Concrete Company, 311
Eliot, T.S., 480, 498
Ellis v. International Playtex Co., 213–215
Equal Protection Clause, 107
Erie Railroad Company v. Tompkins, 579–608
Ernst, Morris, 492–494, 496, 499–504, 506–510
Erskine, Thomas, 545
Escalating, in cross-examination, 451–453
Expert witnesses, 95–158

F

Fair Credit Reporting Act, 26
Farber, Marge, 185
Federal Rules of Civil Procedure, 3–4, 5, 11–14, 35, 48, 50, 59, 61, 63, 66, 72, 74, 77–78, 80, 87, 314
Federal Rules of Evidence, 56, 84, 95–96, 98–99, 122, 125, 130–131, 133, 139, 142, 149, 159–160, 203, 211–214, 216, 220, 222, 231–233, 241, 246–247, 249, 253, 260, 262, 263, 268, 273, 274, 276, 286, 290, 292, 294, 295, 308, 309, 396, 398, 401, 416, 431, 432, 435, 441, 615
Federal Tort Claims Act, 222–223
Federal Trade Commission, 215
Federal Ultimate Issue Rule, 125
Finesilver, Sherman, 135–136, 223–224, 225
Fleming, Peter, 337
Fletcher v. Rylands, 292
FOIA. *See* Freedom of Information Act
Fountain, Olivia, 554
Frankfurter, Felix, 511, 517, 558, 606
Freedom of Information Act (FOIA), 25–26
Friendly, Henry, 113–114, 254, 260
Frye test, 159, 160, 170–177, 179–181, 183, 198–199, 201–202, 204–206, 216, 228
Frye v. United States, 159

G

General Electric Company v. Joiner, 160
Georgia v. McCollum, 311
Gerling, Enid, 316–317
Gillespie, S. Hazard, 587–588
Goddard, Henry W., 101, 548, 561, 577

Goering, Hermann, 163–165,460–463
Goldsmith, Oliver, 555
Gordon, Cahill, 518
Grant, Cary, 362
Gray's Anatomy, 143–144
Greene, Graham, 556
Greene, Harold, 182
Grimes v. Employers Mutual Liability Insurance Company, 268
Guillain-Barré Syndrome, 135

H

Hamilton, Alexander, 123
Hand, Augustus, 506, 509, 560
Hand, Learned, 506–509, 543, 597, 605
Hassett, Buddy, 367
Heap, Jane, 479–481, 483, 484–487, 490
Hearsay, 231–310
Helpern, Milton, 188–196, 199
Henry, Tommy, 367
Henry VI (Shakespeare), 361
Hepburn, Katherine, 362
Herbert v. Lando, 90
Hickman v. Taylor, 79–80
Hiss, Alger, 102, 418, 511–577
Hiss, Donald, 557
Hiss, Priscilla, 513, 523, 572
Hitchcock, Alfred, 511
Holmes, Oliver Wendell, 495, 517, 558
Hoover, Edgar J., 572
Hope, Bob, 176
Hornbeck, Stanley, 518
Houghton v. New Jersey Manufacturers Insurance Co., 26
House Un-American Activities Committee (HUAC), 519–521, 524, 527, 534, 539–542, 563
HUAC. *See* House Un-American Activities Committee
Hughes, Charles Evans, 579, 601
Hunt, Stubby, 593–594, 599–600, 603–604
Hutchins, Grace, 515

I

Inslerman, Felix, 569
Internal Revenue Code, 613–614
Internal Revenue Service, 89
Interrogatories, 61–66
Investigation, in discovery, 14, 18–19

J

Jackson, Robert, 462, 604, 606
J.E.B. v. Alabama, 312
Jewelry, importance of, 347–348
Johnson v. Lutz, 294–295, 297–300, 302
Johnson v. Minihan, 469
Joking, in courtroom and, 392
Joyce, James, 477, 479–487, 489–491, 494, 496–498, 505, 506, 508, 510
Joyce, Nora, 510
Jurors, information about, 315–316
Jury selection, 311–393

K

Kaufman v. Edelstein, 109, 113–114
Kaufman, Samuel, 544–545
Kaye, Danny, 176
Keller, Charlie, 367
Kelly v. Wasserman, 295, 298–300
Kiendl, Theodore, 587–588, 594–595, 597–604, 608
Klopfer, Donald, 501
Knopf, Alfred, 491
Kramer, Charles, 514
Ku Klux Klan, 425, 433–434, 436–438
Kumho Tire Company v. Carmichael, 95, 160

L

Language precision, in cross-examination, 403
Leading questions, in cross-examination, 404, 407, 409, 449–450, 455
Leon, Paul, 496–497, 506
L'Étranger (Camus), 428
Levine, Nathan, 535–536, 538, 551
Lewis, Jerome B., 257
Lewis, John, 604
Lewis, Wyndham, 480
Lincoln, Abraham, 413

Lindey, Alexander, 492
Little Review (magazine), 479, 480, 481, 483, 484, 485, 488, 498
Local custom, in jury selection, 314–315, 317

M

MacDowell, Gerty, 478, 482
Mandelbaum, Samuel, 588, 589, 591, 592, 608
Mann Act, 247–248
Manton, Martin, 506, 509–510, 597
Marbury, William, 534–539, 543
Marsden, Warren, 265, 267–268
Marshall, John, 237–240, 242, 251
Matter of Shore case, 108–109
Mays, Willie, 367–368
McCrea v. Adams, 386
MCI v. AT&T, 354
McLean, Edward, 575, 577
McReynolds, James Clark, 579, 604, 605
Mima Queen and Child v. Hepburn, 235–238
Mishler, Jacob, 259
Mitchell, John, 337, 467–468
MLI v. Hillman, 305
Model Code of Evidence, 241
Moeller, Philip, 487
Molotov-Ribbentrop Pact, 513
Moses, Robert, 255
Motion for summary judgment, 73–74
Murphy, Raymond, 513–514, 563
Murphy, Thomas, 102, 447, 512, 544, 546–548, 559, 575
Murphy v. the National Railroad Passenger Corporation, 119–120
Murray, Edith, 556

N

National Railroad Passenger Corporation, 119
Nemeroff, Bernard G., 581–587, 593, 595–597, 599–600, 603, 607
Niebuhr, Reinhold, 517
Nixon, Richard, 459, 519, 525, 528–533, 539–541
Nizer, Louie, 407
North, Oliver, 42
Note-taking, 328–331

O

Occupational groups, in jury selection, 390
Ochoa, Severo, 106, 117–119, 121, 137–138, 150
Odyssey (Homer), 478, 480–482
Ollert v. Ziebell, 281
Oral depositions, 29–31
Ouija Board Association, 168, 181
Out-of-court statement, 241–246, 251–252, 259, 261, 263, 267, 273

P

Palmquist, Jamie, 528
Patent application, 21
Person v. Association of the Bar of the City of New York, 107
Pegler, Westbrook, 407
People v. Centolella, 271
People v. Singer, 470
People v. Wheeler, 384–385
Peters, J., 524–525, 549, 568
Polskey, Sarah, 528
Portrait of the Artist as a Young Man (Joyce), 480, 498
Pound, Ezra, 480–481, 483, 485–486, 489
Powers v. Ohio, 311
Pressman, Lee, 514, 557
Previous litigation experience, in jury selection, 389

Q

Quinn, John, 479–481, 483–490

R

Race, question of, 380
Redirect examination, 258–259
Reed, Stanley, 558, 579, 604–605
Regina v. Hicklin, 506
Reynolds, Quentin, 406–407
Reynolds v. Pegler, 407
Rizzuto, Phil, 367
Roberts, Owen, 579, 604

Roosevelt, Eleanor, 590–592
Roosevelt, Franklin Delano, 503, 506, 514, 518, 522, 590–591, 606
Rosen, William, 568
Rosenberg, Ethel, 569
Rosenberg, Julius, 569
Ruffing, Red, 367
Ruth v. Fenchel, 149

S

Sandburg, Carl, 361
Santiago case, 430
Saypol, Irving, 317
Sayre, Francis, 518, 569–571
Scientific evidence, 159–229
Securities and Exchange Commission, 23
Shakespeare, William, 339, 361
Shapiro, Meyer, 565–566
Shepard v. United States, 306
She Stoops to Conquer (Goldsmith), 555
Silverman, George, 565–566
Sirico v. Cotto, 131
SJC. *See* Supreme Judicial Court
S.S. Brennan, 497
Stalin, Josef, 522
State v. Brown, 228
State v. Dowling, 228
State v. Graham, 175
State v. Santiago, 430
State v. Walsted, 228
Stirnweiss, George, 367
Stone, Harlan Fiske, 579
Stripling, Robert, 519–520, 522, 524, 540–542
Stryker, Lloyd Paul, 418, 544–548, 558, 559, 574–575
Sullivan, Brendan, 42
Sumner, John, 483–484, 486, 490
Supreme Judicial Court (SJC), 385
Swain v. Alabama, 311, 384–385, 387
Swan, Thomas, 597–598
Swift v. Tyson, 579, 580, 585–586, 588, 597–598, 601–606, 608

T

Tariff Act, 499
Thomas, J. Parnell, 519
Tla-Koo-Yel-Lee v. United States, 424, 426
Tompkins, Harry James, 581, 583–588, 594–597, 603–606
Toynbee, Arnold, 517
Tracy, Spencer, 141–142
Trollope, Anthony, 499
Trost, James, 528
Truman, Harry, 518
Tuchman, Barbara, 346
Twain, Mark, 445

U

Ulysses (Joyce), 477–510
Umberger, Joseph, 194–199, 201, 219
Uniform Rules of Evidence, 241
United States v. Biener, 246–251, 259, 263
United States v. DeSisto, 253
United States v. Kilbourne, 282
United States v. Lopez, 203
United States v. Masson, 123–125
United States v. Palacios, 262
United States v. Riccardi, 406
United States Supreme Court, 90

V

Vesco, Robert, 337

W

Wadley, Julian, 557, 570
Wall Street Journal, 275, 346
Walsh, Bill, 594, 597
Ward, Artemus, 480
Ward v. Kovacs, 126, 129, 227
Ware, Harold, 514, 549
Warth v. Seldin, 613
Washington, George, 504, 560
Watt, Robert Watson, 163, 176–177
Wigmore, John Henry, 286
Williams, Edward Bennett, 375–377, 464
Wilson, James, 586
Witt, Nathan, 557
Wright v. Tatham, 264–268

Z

Zippo Manufacturing v. Rogers Manufacturing, 303